# Reconsidering Funds of Hedge Funds

# Reconsidering Funds of Hedge Funds

## THE FINANCIAL CRISIS AND BEST PRACTICES IN UCITS, TAIL RISK, PERFORMANCE, AND DUE DILIGENCE

Edited By

## Greg N. Gregoriou

**SUNY Plattsburgh, School of Business
and Economics, Plattsburgh, NY**

AMSTERDAM • BOSTON • HEIDELBERG • LONDON • NEW YORK • OXFORD
PARIS • SAN DIEGO • SAN FRANCISCO • SYDNEY • TOKYO
Academic Press is an imprint of Elsevier

Academic Press is an imprint of Elsevier
The Boulevard, Langford Lane, Kidlington, Oxford, OX5 1GB, UK
225 Wyman Street, Waltham, MA 02451, USA

First published 2013

**British Library Cataloguing in Publication Data**
A catalogue record for this book is available from the British Library

**Library of Congress Cataloguing in Publication Data**
A catalog record for this book is available from the Library of Congress

ISBN: 978-0-12-401699-6

For information on all Academic Press publications
visit our website at **store.elsevier.com**

Printed and bound in the United States of America

13 14 15 16 10 9 8 7 6 5 4 3 2 1

# Contents

# Foreword

The passage of the Uniform Prudent Investor Act of 1994 (UPIA) created an opportunity for the growth and development of Funds of Hedge Funds (FoHFs) providing institutional investors access to the high return of hedge funds by allowing them to diversify their risk exposure and to delegate their due diligence responsibilities to these FoHFs. However, the global financial crisis in 2008 was a major challenge to FoHFs. Poor returns and the flight of institutional capital during the financial crisis have led to a major reduction of assets under management by FoHFs. Recovery has been slow despite improved returns subsequent to the crisis. The economic environment remains a challenge for small FoHFs, but large FoHFs see opportunities and are attracting new capital. This book is a collection of studies that for the first time analyses in some depth the impact of the crisis on the FoHFs industry and the risks and opportunities that lie ahead.

The financial crisis in 2008 and the unfortunate coincidence of the Madoff scandal at the end of the year drew attention to the risks associated with hedge fund investing. A number of chapters in this volume address the need to develop new tools to calibrate — and control — these sources of risk.

Institutional clients demand increased attention to operational due diligence. Improved transparency and oversight are essential. This has led to the development of Undertakings for Collective Investment in Transferable Securities (UCITS) FoHFs. This institutional framework, originally created to standardize mutual fund structures in Europe, has come to be employed by FoHFs mainly in Europe but increasingly in USD accounts. Because these were originally designed for mutual funds, the improved transparency and oversight comes at the cost of severe restrictions on the strategies and instruments available to the funds. Among other things the investments are limited to relatively liquid securities. This provides operational flexibility but at the same time limits the investible universe of securities. This book examines carefully the nature of this tradeoff and the costs that it imposes, not only in terms of operational complexity but also in terms of potential reduction in returns. Since organizational frameworks of this nature can increase the comfort level of institutional clients, there may be opportunities for large FoHFs who can manage the cost and complexity of these arrangements.

The financial crisis also drew attention to the financial risks associated with hedge fund investments. It was thought that diversification alone would suffice to control and even eliminate financial risk. Indeed, this was perceived to be a major advantage of FoHFs in the period leading up to the crisis. However, the crisis revealed that many hedge funds were not immune to the economy-wide credit and liquidity risk that characterized that period. This exposure gave rise to excessive tail risk at many FoHFs. A number of chapters in this book address the need to develop new ways to measure this risk exposure and to develop performance measures that appropriately account for it. The consensus appears to be that there is good news. A variety of data sources suggests that FoHFs had favorable returns even after accounting appropriately for this risk, with evidence that large FoHFs had disproportionately higher returns.

The last section of the book addresses in some detail the legal and regulatory risks facing the FoHFs industry both in the United States and around the world. The UPIA, which applies to United States fiduciary investors, provides the clearest statement of what constitutes prudent investing in English law-based systems: a fiduciary investor must, in investing and managing fund assets, consider the purposes, terms, distribution requirements and other material circumstances of the fund. In the past FoHFs have relied on the somewhat illusory benefits of diversification. Overdiversification not only leads to diminished returns; it also increases legal risk to the extent that it renders more difficult their necessary due diligence responsibilities. At the same time there are significant opportunities for those FoHFs large enough to absorb the expenditures associated with appropriate due diligence and the increased costs of compliance that have arisen as a result of the financial crisis.

While the financial crisis had a significant and negative impact on most FoHFs, the bottom line is that the industry can meet the challenges it faces and that there are significant opportunities available for those FoHFs able and willing to take advantage of them.

**Stephen J. Brown**
David S. Loeb Professor of Finance, NYU Stern School of Business

A native of Montreal, Professor Gregoriou obtained his joint PhD at the University of Quebec at Montreal in Finance which merges the resources of Montreal's four major universities UQAM, McGill, Concordia, and HEC. Professor Gregoriou has published 45 books, 60 refereed publications in peer-reviewed journals and 22 book chapters since his arrival at SUNY (Plattsburgh) in August 2003. Professor Gregoriou's books have been published by McGraw-Hill, John Wiley & Sons, Elsevier-Butterworth/Heinemann, Taylor and Francis/ CRC Press, Palgrave-MacMillan and Risk Books. His articles have appeared in the Review of Asset Pricing Studies, Journal of Portfolio Management, Journal of Futures Markets, European Journal of Operational Research, Annals of Operations Research, Computers and Operations Research, etc. He has also been quoted several times in the New York Times and the Financial Times of London. Professor Gregoriou is hedge fund editor and editorial board member for the *Journal of Derivatives and Hedge Funds*, as well as editorial board member for the *Journal of Wealth Management*, the *Journal of Risk Management in Financial Institutions*, *Market Integrity*, *IEB International Journal of Finance*, *The Journal of Quantitative Methods for Social Sciences*, and the *Brazilian Business Review*. Professor Gregoriou's interests focus on hedge funds, funds of funds, and CTAs. He is EDHEC Research Associate in Nice, France, Research Associate at the Caisse de dépôtet placement du Québec (CDPQ) Chair in Portfolio Management at the University of Quebec at Montreal and is lecturer at the School of Continuing Studies at McGill University in Montreal.

# Contributors

**Paul U. Ali** is an Associate Professor at Melbourne Law School. He has published widely on banking and finance law, in particular on the legal design and regulation of structured financial products. Paul has worked in the banking & finance and corporate groups of two leading Australian law firms. He has also worked in the securitization team of a major bank and has been a principal of a private capital firm. Paul holds an SJD from the University of Sydney.

**David Edmund Allen** is Professor of Finance at Edith Cowan University, Perth, Western Australia. He is the author of three monographs and over 80 refereed publications on a diverse range of topics covering corporate financial policy decisions, asset pricing, business economics, funds management and performance bench-marking, volatility modeling and hedging, and market microstructure and liquidity.

**David Ardia** is Assistant Professor of Finance at University Laval (Québec City) and conducts research on financial econometrics. Previously he was Head of Research at Tolomeo Capital AG, a Swiss-based hedge fund. In 2008, he received the Chorafas prize for his book "Financial Risk Management with Bayesian Estimation of GARCH Models" published by Springer. He is the author of several scientific articles and statistical packages. He holds an MSc in applied mathematics, an MAS in finance and a PhD in Bayesian econometrics.

**Yigit Atilgan** is an Assistant Professor of Finance at the School of Management in Sabanci University, Istanbul. His doctoral dissertation is on the information flow from option markets to stock markets. His research interests include empirical asset pricing and international finance. His teaching interests include portfolio theory, fixed income theory, and valuation. Professor Atilgan received an MS in Finance from the University of Rochester, and a PhD from Baruch College, City University of New York.

**Turan G. Bali** is the Dean's Research Professor of Finance at Georgetown University. Turan G. Bali specializes in asset pricing, risk management, fixed income securities, and financial derivatives. A founding member of the Society for Financial Econometrics, he has worked on consulting projects sponsored by major financial institutions and government organizations in the US and other countries. In addition, he currently serves as an associate editor for the *Journal of Banking and Finance*, the *Journal of Futures Markets*, the *Journal of Portfolio Management*, the *Review of Financial Economics*, and the *Journal of Risk*. Prior to joining the faculty at Georgetown University, Bali was the David Krell Chair Professor of Finance at the City University of New York's Baruch College and Graduate School and University Center. He also has held visiting faculty positions at New York University and Princeton University, reviewed books for several publishers, and served on the review committees of the National Science Foundation, Research Grants Council of Hong Kong, Scientific and Technological Research Council of Turkey, and Social Sciences and Humanities Research Council of Canada. With more than 50 published articles in economics and finance journals, Bali's work has appeared in *The Journal of Finance, Journal of Financial Economics, Management Science, Journal of Monetary Economics, Journal of Financial and Quantitative Analysis*, and many others. He also serves as an ad-hoc reviewer for more than 50 journals in economics, finance, statistics, and operations research. Bali holds a PhD and an MPhil in financial economics from the Graduate School and University Center of the City University of New York and a BA in economics from Bogazici University in Istanbul, Turkey.

**Wolfgang Bessler** is Professor of Finance and Banking at Justus-Liebig-University in Giessen. Previously, he was a faculty member at Syracuse University, at Rensselaer Polytechnic Institute, and at Hamburg University. He has published widely in the leading finance journals. His research interests concentrate on corporate finance and asset management, in particular hedge funds and mutual funds. He serves on the editorial board of various international finance journals.

**Monica Billio** is Full Professor of Econometrics at the University Ca' Foscari of Venice, where she teaches Econometrics and Financial Econometrics. She graduated in Economics from the University Ca' Foscari of Venice and holds a Doctorate in Applied Mathematics obtained at the University Paris IX Dauphine in 1999. Her main research interests include financial econometrics, with applications to risk measurement and management, volatility modeling, hedge funds, financial crises, and systemic risk; business cycle analysis; dynamic latent factor models; and simulation based inference techniques. She participates in many research projects financed by the European Commission, Eurostat, and the Italian Ministry of Education, Universities, and Research (MIUR). The results of these and other research projects have appeared in peer-refereed journals including *Journal of Econometrics, Journal of Financial Economics, Journal of Statistical Planning and Inference, Journal of Empirical Finance, Journal of Financial Econometrics, Computational Statistics and Data Analysis, Journal of Forecasting* and *European Journal of Operational Research*. Moreover, she is head of the School of Global Development, Treviso branch of the University Ca' Foscari of Venice, Deputy Head of the Department of Economics, President of the Teaching Committee of the Masters Degree in Economics and Finance, and member of the Teaching Committee of the PhD in Quantitative Economics at the same University.

**Szabolcs Blazsek** has a PhD in Economics from Universidad Carlos III de Madrid, Spain. He is a Professor of Finance in the School of Business in Universidad Francisco Marroquín, Guatemala. He teaches several courses at both undergraduate and graduate levels. His articles have appeared in the following publications: *Journal of Econometrics, European Journal of Finance, Applied Financial Economics, Applied Economics,* and *Applied Economics Letters.*

**Laurent Bodson** is KBL Affiliate Professor of Financial Management at HEC Management School — University of Liège. Laurent is also co-founder and Head of Asset Management Solutions of Gambit Financial Solutions S.A., a spin-off company of HEC Management School — University of Liège that produces sophisticated software solutions for investor profiling, portfolio optimization, and risk management. His areas of expertise include portfolio and risk management, as both a practitioner and researcher. He is also specialized in investment analysis, style analysis, and market price behavior. Laurent has published in leading international scientific journals.

**Raymond Robert Boffey** has an extensive academic career in Australia, beginning with Curtin University of Technology and then moving to Edith Cowan University. Throughout his career, Ray has taken study leave to accept positions in industry, mainly with the Reserve Bank of Australia and BankWest. Ray has also been a board member of the University Credit Society Ltd. He specializes in Capital Markets, Investment Finance, and Banking.

**Kris Boudt** is Assistant Professor of Finance at KU Leuven and a research partner at FINVEX. In 2009—2011 he was a visiting scholar at the University of Illinois at Chicago. His main research interests focus on computational finance, financial econometrics, and portfolio and risk management. He is coauthor of the PortfolioAnalytics and RTAQ econometric software packages. His research has been published in *Computational Statistics and Data Analysis, Journal of Empirical Finance, Journal of Financial Econometrics,* and *Journal of Risk* and RISK magazine, among others. He holds an MSc in economics and a PhD in applied econometrics.

**Alessandro Carretta** is Full Professor in Financial Markets and Institutions and Director of the PhD Program in Banking and Finance at University of Rome 'Tor Vergata,' Italy. He has been teaching banking and finance for more than 25 years, formerly at the Universities of Urbino, Lecce, and Milan Bocconi and he is currently the President of the Italian Academy of Management. His main research interest relates to banking management, focusing on banking groups and diversification; regulation and control; and corporate governance, culture, and organizational change in banks. He has widely published in this area, more than 100 books and articles in academic journals. Professor Carretta is a member of committees and boards of several journals, research bodies, and financial institutions.

**Laurent Cavenaile** is a PhD candidate at the Stern School of Business, New York University. Before joining NYU he was assistant lecturer working within the KBL chair of HEC — University of Liège. He holds a Masters degree in economic sciences from University of Liège (2008) and an MSc in financial economics at the University of Maastricht (Netherlands). His main research areas are the investment funds industry, financial economy, and macroeconomics. His publications include articles on hedge funds, on several measures of performance and risk assessment, and on economic growth.

**Raphaële Chappe** practiced as an attorney for eight years in the financial services industry. In her last position, she worked as a Vice President with Goldman Sachs in the Tax Department, where her principal responsibilities consisted in providing tax and legal advice with respect to the firm's proprietary and balance sheet investments, as well as long-term strategic initiatives. She has extensive teaching experience in business, economics, and finance, both at the graduate and undergraduate level, in a variety of universities, including NYU Polytechnic University, Long Island University, Parsons The New School for Design, and John Jay College of Criminal Justice. Her current research interests include finance and risk management, law, and economics, as well as the political, economic, and social implications of the evolution of the financial sector in the aftermath of the financial crisis. Raphaële holds a Master of Laws (LLM) in International Tax from New York University (School of Law) and a Masters degree in Comparative Business Law from the University of Pantheon-Sorbonne in Paris. She is currently pursuing her Ph.D. in economics at the New School for Social Research in New York City.

**Alain Coën** is Full Professor of Finance at the Graduate School of Business (ESG) of the University of Quebec in Montreal (UQAM). Before joining ESG-UQÀM, he was Associate Professor of Finance at EDHEC School of Management. He obtained his PhD in Finance from the University of Grenoble, and his PhD in Economics from the University of Paris 1 Panthéon-Sorbonne. He holds a Master of Arts in Economics with major in Macroeconomics from Laval University and an Accreditation to supervise research (HDR) from Paris Dauphine University. He has been visiting professor at Paris-Dauphine University, University of Paris-Ouest-Nanterre, Laval University, HEC — University of Liège, and University of Sherbrooke. His research interests focus on asset pricing, international finance, hedge funds, business cycles, and financial econometrics. He has published in several international leading journals and has written a book in financial management.

**Philippe Cogneau** is a PhD candidate in finance at the HEC Management School of the University of Liege (Belgium). He holds degrees in mathematics, computer science, and financial risk management. Philippe has experience of more than twenty years in the banking sector in the following areas: information technology, ALM, accounting, finance, legal & internal reporting, credit risk, and market risk.

**Na Dai** obtained her PhD at the University of Kansas and is an Assistant Professor of Finance at the school of business at the University of Albany (SUNY). Her research is primarily focused on venture capital, private equity, hedge funds, private investment in public equity (PIPE), and small business financing. Her scholarly works have appeared in finance journals such as *Financial Management, Journal of Banking and Finance, Journal of Corporate Finance, Journal of Empirical Finance, European Financial Management*, and entrepreneurship journals such as *Journal of Business Venturing* and *Entrepreneurship Theory and Practice*. She has contributed scholarly book chapters to *Companion to Private Equity, Oxford Handbook of Venture Capital, Oxford Handbook of Private Equity, Institutional Money Management: An Inside look at Strategies, Players, and Practices*, and *Oxford Handbook of Corporate Governance*. Much of Na Dai's work is online at SSRN: http://ssrn.com/author=332421.

**Justina Dambrauskaite**, CFA, joined IAM in October 2011 as a quantitative analyst. She has over five years of investment experience in the hedge fund industry, and has worked as a quantitative analyst for Pamplona Capital Management, and as a translator for Tilde IT. She holds a Bachelor of Statistics degree from Vilnius University and an MSc in Investments from the University of Birmingham.

**Jeannine Daniel** is a Senior Investment Analyst at Kedge Capital (UK) in London. Jeannine joined Kedge from Ivy Asset Management, where she was charged with coordinating the firm's European research efforts, which included the sourcing and investment due diligence of managers across various hedge fund strategies. Prior to Ivy, Jeannine worked as an analyst for Barclays Global Investors and JP Morgan Chase. She holds a BSc (Hons) in Business Management & Economics from the University of London.

**Serge Darolles** joined Lyxor as a Research Analyst in 2000 and develops mathematical models for various investment strategies. Prior to joining Lyxor, Serge held consultant roles at Caisse des Dépôts & Consignations, Banque Paribas and the French Atomic Energy Agency. He specializes in econometrics and has written numerous articles which have been published in several academic journals. He is an Adjunct Professor of Finance at Paris Dauphine University where he teaches financial econometrics. Serge holds a PhD in Applied Mathematics from Toulouse University and a postgraduate degree in Economics and Statistics at Ecole Nationale de la Statistique et de l'Administration Economique, Paris.

**Philippe Debatty** is 'Partner-Manager' in Fuchs & Associés Finance in Luxembourg and is specialized in dynamic asset allocation processes. He holds a degree in Economics and is also a Chartered Alternative Investment Analyst (CAIA). He has over 25 years of experience in banking and finance, mostly in Luxembourg, where he held different high level responsibilities in Asset Management and Capital Markets. He is a member of different associations in Luxembourg and is a lecturer at the Institut de Formation Bancaire Luxembourgeois and IFE.

**K. Ozgur Demirtas** is an Associate Professor of Finance at Baruch College City University of New York and Sabanci University. His primary research interests are in the area of empirical asset pricing, time-series and cross-sectional variation in stock returns, investments, risk management, portfolio theory, and stock market anomalies. His work has been published in top academic journals including the *Journal of Monetary Economics, Journal of Financial and Quantitative Analysis, Journal of Banking and Finance, Review of Finance, Journal of Futures Markets,* and *Journal of Portfolio Management,* among others. He has been elected the best teacher within the finance department of Zicklin School of Business and of Baruch College. In 2010, he was listed among the top 20 professors out of more than a million professors in the United States, Canada, Scotland, and the United Kingdom by ratemyprofessor LLC. Professor Demirtas received his PhD in Finance from Boston College.

**Daniel Dietrich** studied economic science at the Technische Universität Chemnitz, Germany with an emphasis on finance. In his final paper, he analyzed the pros and cons of a hedge fund investment via managed accounts and managed account platforms. Daniel works at an Austrian financial services company in the field of research and development.

**Martin Eling** is professor in insurance management and director of the Institute of Insurance Economics at the University of St. Gallen (Switzerland). From 2009 to October 2011 he was Professor in Insurance and Director of the Institute of Insurance Science at the University of Ulm (Germany). He received his doctoral degree from the University of Münster (Germany) and his habilitation from the University of St. Gallen (Switzerland). In 2008 he was visiting professor at the University of Wisconsin-Madison (USA). He has published articles in leading international journals such as the *Journal of Risk and Insurance,* the *Journal of Banking and Finance,* and *Insurance: Mathematics and Economics.* Since November 2009 he has been research fellow at the Independent Institute in Washington, DC. Furthermore, he has served as Erasmus visiting professor at the University of Torino and the University of Urbino.

**Florian Haberfelner** is Senior Investment Manager, Hedge Funds for Feri Institutional Advisors GmbH in Frankfurt. Feri is a privately owned investment manager. Florian's responsibilities include the quantitative and qualitative analysis of single hedge funds. Florian has been working for Feri since September 2009. Before joining Feri, Florian worked for several years at an asset management boutique specializing in Alternative Investments. He was a voting member of the Asset Allocation Committee, conducted due diligence on hedge funds, and held the position of Head of Quantitative Research. Florian studied International Business Administration at the University of Vienna. He is a CFA charterholder.

**Haidar Haidar** is currently a PhD candidate at Sussex University, Brighton, UK. He has extensive experience in industrial collaborations with companies such as International Asset Management (FoHF in London) in asset management, and with the Shoreham, UK research branch of Ricardo Plc (a worldwide Engineering Consultancy company) on engine performance testing algorithm.

**Ying-Lin Hsu** is an associate professor with the Department of Applied Mathematics and the Institute of Statistics at National Chung Hsing University, Taiwan. His major research interests include statistical applications in industrial engineering, finance, and bioinformatics.

**Georges Hübner** (PhD, INSEAD) is Full Professor of Finance and the *Deloitte Chair of Portfolio Management and Performance* at HEC — Management School of the University of Liège (Belgium). He is also Associate Professor of Finance at Maastricht University (the Netherlands) and Affiliate Professor at EDHEC (France — Singapore). Georges regularly delivers executive teaching in various European institutions including INSEAD, and delivers, among other activities, preparation seminars for the GARP (Global Association of Risk Professionals) certification. He has published numerous books and research articles about credit risk, and on hedge funds and portfolio performance in internationally renowned scientific outlets such as *Journal of Banking and Finance*, *Journal of Empirical Finance*, *Review of Finance*, *Financial Management*, and *Journal of Portfolio Management*. He obtained the best paper award 2002 of the *Journal of Banking and Finance*, and the Operational Risk & Compliance Achievement Award 2006 for the best academic paper. He is the inventor of the Generalized Treynor Ratio, a popular portfolio performance measure. He is also co-founder and scientific director of Gambit Financial Solutions, a spin-off company of HEC Liège that produces sophisticated software solutions for investor profiling, portfolio optimization, and risk management.

**Dieter Kaiser** is Managing Director at Robus Capital Management Limited in London, an asset management firm focusing on credit opportunity and credit special situations investing in Europe. From 2007 to 2011 Dieter was Director at Feri Trust GmbH in Bad Homburg, Germany where he was responsible for hedge fund selection and the management of hedge fund portfolios. From 2003 to 2007 he was responsible for institutional research at Benchmark Alternative Strategies GmbH in Frankfurt, Germany. He has written numerous articles on alternative investments that have been published in both leading academic and professional journals and is the author and editor of nine books. Dieter Kaiser holds a Bachelor of Arts in Business Administration from the University of Applied Sciences Offenburg, a Master of Arts in Banking and Finance from the Frankfurt School of Finance and Management, and a PhD in Finance from the Chemnitz University of Technology. On the academic side, he is a research fellow at the Centre for Practical Quantitative Finance of the Frankfurt School of Finance and Management.

**Akhmad Kramadibrata** holds a Post graduate diploma in Finance from Edith Cowan University and a Bachelor of Commerce in Accounting from Curtin University of Technology, Perth, Australia. He currently works as a Research Assistant in the School of Accounting, Finance and Economics at Edith Cowan University.

**Chung-Ming Kuan** is an Academician, Academia Sinica (elected 2002) and also a chair professor with the Department of Finance at National Taiwan University.

His research fields span econometric theory, financial econometrics, and macroeconomic forecasting.

**Philipp Kurmann** is a research assistant and PhD student at the Center for Finance and Banking, Justus-Liebig-University in Giessen. He graduated in business administration and received an M.A. in economics from the University of Wisconsin-Milwaukee. His main research interests concentrate on empirical asset-pricing and asset management.

**Iliya Kutsarov** is Senior Investment Manager, Hedge Funds for Feri Institutional Advisors GmbH in Frankfurt. Iliya's responsibilities include quantitative and qualitative analysis of single hedge funds focusing on Equity Hedge strategies. In addition to that, he maintains the firm's proprietary systems that support the hedge fund selection and risk management process. Iliya has been with Feri since 2004. He joined the firm as a student assistant and after finishing his studies in 2007 was employed as a full time investment analyst. Prior to Feri Iliya worked for a start-up online shop where he was responsible for sales completion and accounting. Iliya studied Finance and Quantitative Methods in Economics at J.W. Goethe University Frankfurt am Main and holds a Diploma in Business Administration. He is a CFA charterholder.

**R. McFall Lamm Jr.** is the chief investment officer at Stelac Advisory Services LLC, an investment management and consulting boutique in New York City. He was formerly the Chief Investment Officer of Deutsche Bank's Global Hedge Fund Group in London. Prior to that he was Chief Investment Strategist and headed the Global Portfolio Management business at Bankers Trust Company. Dr. Lamm has managed hedge fund portfolios for more than a decade and written extensively on various topics including the role of hedge funds in asset allocation. He is well known for publishing 'Why Not 100% Hedge Funds' in 1999, which helped spark growth in the industry beginning at the turn of the millennium.

**François-Serge Lhabitant**, PhD is currently the Chief Executive Officer and Chief Investment Officer of Kedge Capital. He was formerly a Member of Senior Management at Union Bancaire Privée, where he was in charge of quantitative risk management and subsequently, of the quantitative research for alternative portfolios. Prior to this, François-Serge was a Director at UBS/Global Asset Management, in charge of building quantitative models for portfolio management and hedge funds. On the academic side, François-Serge is currently a Professor of Finance at the EDHEC Business School (France), and a visiting professor at the Hong Kong University of Science and Technology. He is the author of several books and has published numerous research and scientific articles in the areas of quantitative portfolio management, alternative investments (hedge funds) and emerging markets.

**Thomas Maier** is Senior Investment Manager, Hedge Funds for Feri Institutional Advisors GmbH in Frankfurt. Thomas' responsibilities include the quantitative and qualitative analysis of single hedge funds, specializing in the Event Driven strategy. Additional screening and monitoring as well as the ongoing and continuous search for new investment opportunities are part of his responsibilities. Before joining Feri in 2007 Thomas worked as a researcher at the University of Munich, Department of Economics. He studied Mathematics and Economics at the LMU Munich and at the University of Cambridge, U.K., and holds a Diploma in Mathematics and a PhD in Economics. In his PhD thesis he examined the dynamics of real estate prices. His teaching focuses on financial markets and real estate markets. Thomas also gathered experience in the software and consulting industry and is a CFA charterholder.

**Kaleab Y. Mamo** is currently a Masters student in Economics at University of Toronto. He graduated from University of Venice and University of Paris 1 with a Masters degree in quantitative economics. He worked as a research assistant at the University of Venice from 2008 to 2009. His research interests include financial econometrics, risk measurement and management, hedge funds, securities valuation, capital markets, cost of capital, and behavioral finance.

**Gianluca Mattarocci** has a Master of Arts in Asset Management and a PhD in Banking and Finance both from the University of Rome Tor Vergata. He is lecturer of Economics and Management of Financial Intermediaries and Faculty member of the PhD in Banking and Finance at the University of Rome Tor Vergata. He has been teaching Corporate Finance at the University of Rome Tor Vergata since 2007 and during the academic year 2011−2012 he was visiting scholar at Old Dominion University. His main research interest relates to risk management and real estate. In addition, he has published widely in these areas and is member of board of numerous academic journals.

**Bernard Minsky** joined IAM in March 2004 as Head of Portfolio Analysis and Risk Management. Prior to joining IAM, he spent ten years at Goldman Sachs International as co-head of the Firm wide Risk Team in Europe and then as risk manager for the Prime Brokerage in Europe. Qualified in accounting and finance and a Chartered Statistician, he spent 20 years as a consultant in econometric and statistical applications for a number of leading management consultancy firms before entering the financial services industry. Bernard has a BSc in Mathematics & Statistics from the University of Sussex, an MSc in Mathematics from the University of London, and is a Visiting Fellow in Mathematics at the University of Sussex.

**Marcus Müller** graduated from Technische Universität Chemnitz, Germany (diploma in Economics), and studied at the University of Salamanca, Spain. Marcus started his career with Benchmark Financial Solution in Frankfurt and Société Générale in Paris. Later he had worked as hedge fund analyst and in product development for Benchmark Capital Management and as an analyst and project manager for Asset Allocation Alpha. In the last years he conducted due diligence on various managed account platforms, fund of hedge funds and single hedge funds. Since 2012 Marcus works in Market Risk Controlling at Österreichische Volksbanken AG. Since 2011 Marcus is a holder of the right to use the Chartered Alternative Investment Analyst designation (CAIA).

**Staley Roy Alford Pearce** came from a background in commercial and merchant banking in South Africa. He has since worked at Edith Cowan University, Australia, for an extensive period during which he taught in the areas of derivatives, investments, and banking. His recent interests have been in the fields of personal finance and superannuation.

**Razvan Pascalau** is an Associate Professor of Economics within the School of Business and Economics at SUNY Plattsburgh. He holds a PhD in Economics and MSc degree in Finance from the University of Alabama. His past work experience includes a short stint at the Ministry of Finance in Romania as Counselor of European Integration and hedge fund consulting. His research interests include areas such as Empirical Asset Pricing, Applied Time Series Econometrics and Microeconometrics. He has published articles in journals such as the Review of Asset Pricing Studies, Geneva Risk and Insurance Review, and the International Journal of the Economics and Business among others and co-edited 4 books on Financial Econometrics.

**Loriana Pelizzon** is Associate Professor of Economics at the University of Venice. She graduated from the London Business School with a doctorate in Finance. She was Assistant Professor in Economics at the University of Padova from 2000 till 2004 and recently Visiting Associate Professor at MIT Sloan. Her research interests are in risk measurement and management, asset allocation and household portfolios, hedge funds, financial institutions, systemic risk, and financial crisis. Her work includes papers published in the *Journal of Financial Econmics, Journal of Financial and Quantitative Analysis, Journal of Financial Intermediation, Journal of Empirical Finance, Journal of Banking and Finance,* and *Computational Statistics and Data Analysis.* Pelizzon has received the EFA 2005 — Barclays Global Investor Award for the Best Symposium paper, FMA European Conference 2005 best conference paper award, and the Award for the Most Significant Paper published in the *Journal of Financial Intermediation* 2008. She teaches Financial Economics and Investments within the International Master in Economics and Finance program and Economics and Financial Economics within the undergraduate program. She received the Best Teacher award in 2007 and 2008 at the Ca' Foscari University of Venice. She is one of the coordinators of the European Finance Association (EFA) Doctoral Tutorial, a member of the EFA Executive Committee, and a member of the BSI GAMMA Foundation Board. She has been involved in NBER and FDIC projects as well as EU and Inquire Europe projects. She frequently advises banks, pension funds, and government agencies on risk measurement and risk management strategies.

**Robert John Powell** has 20 years' banking experience in South Africa, New Zealand, and Australia. He has been involved in the development and implementation of several credit and financial analysis models in banks. He has a PhD from Edith Cowan University, where he currently works as an Associate Professor, teaching and researching in banking and finance.

**Christian Proaño** is an Assistant Professor of Economics at the New School for Social Research. He received a doctorate in economics from Bielefeld University

(Germany) in 2008, and a diploma in economics in 2004. His research areas include international finance, monetary policy, expectations formation and behavioral macroeconomics, income distribution, and nonlinear macro-econometrics, fields in which he has published numerous articles. Previously, he worked at the German Institute for Economic Research (DIW Berlin) and at the Macroeconomic Policy Institute (IMK) in the Hans-Böckler-Foundation (in Düsseldorf, Germany) in the departments of Macroeconometric Modeling and Forecasting. He is co-author (with Peter Flaschel and Gangolf Groh) of *Keynesian Macroeconomics* (in German) and *Topics in Applied Macrodynamic Theory* (with Peter Flaschel, Gangolf Groh, and Willi Semmler).

**Jason Scharfman**, Esq., CFE, CRISC is the Managing Partner of Corgentum Consulting, LLC (www.Corgentum.com), a provider of comprehensive operational due diligence reviews of traditional and alternative investments including hedge funds, private equity, real estate, and funds of hedge funds. He is recognized as one of the leading experts in the field of hedge fund operational due diligence and is the author of *Hedge Fund Operational Due Diligence: Understanding the Risks* (John Wiley & Sons, 2008) and *Private Equity Operational Due Diligence: Tools to Evaluate Liquidity, Valuation and Documentation* (John Wiley & Sons, 2012). He has written extensively on the subject of operational due diligence and travels and speaks worldwide on hedge fund operational risks.

**Oliver A. Schwindler** is currently portfolio manager of a volatility arbitrage UCITS hedge fund, managed by KSW Vermögensverwaltung AG. He founded HF-Analytics GmbH in 2009 and still acts as Managing Partner of the firm. He developed HF-Analytics quantitative performance rating for funds of hedge funds. Prior to founding HF-Analytics he worked as Senior Investment Manager at Feri Institutional Advisors, where he analyzed hedge funds and co-managed hedge fund portfolios. Previously, he was a research and teaching assistant at the Chair of Finance of Bamberg University, where he wrote his PhD thesis on Value Added of Funds of Hedge Fund Managers. Dr. Schwindler earned a Masters Degree with honors at University of Regensburg and received his PhD Summa Cum Laude from Bamberg University. In addition, he holds the Chartered Alternative Investment Analyst designation and is a visiting lecturer at the University of Bamberg. He is also research associate at EDHEC-Risk Institute.

**Willi Semmler** is Professor of Economics at New School University, at the Center for Empirical Macroeconomics at Bielefeld University, and Research Fellow at the Bernard Schwartz Center for Economic Policy Analysis. He also evaluates research projects for the European Union, serves as a consultant for the World Bank, and regularly writes columns for the German *Spiegel*. He is author or co-author of more than 85 refereed articles in international journals and is author or co-author of 11 books. His recent publications include the second edition of his book *Asset prices, Booms and Recessions* (Springer Publishing House, 2006) and a co-edited book *Foundations of Credit Risk Analysis* (Elgar, 2007). He is a member of the New York Academy of Sciences and has been a visitor of Columbia University, Stanford University and the Cepremap in Paris. He was

Fortis-Bank Visiting Professor of the University of Antwerp, Visiting Professor at the University of Marseilles/Aix-en-Provence and has taught financial economics for the European Quantitative Economics Doctorate (QED) Program at universities in Italy, Spain, Portugal, and Germany. He has served to evaluate research projects for the National Science Foundations of Austria, Germany, Belgium, and the U.K. He has also taught at Bielefeld University and serves on the Board of Directors for the Center for Empirical Macroeconomics, Bielefeld University. He is on the scientific committee of the Society for Nonlinear Dynamics and Econometrics, the Society for Computation in Economics and Finance, and the Workshop on Computational and Financial Econometrics.

**Samuel Sender** holds the position of Applied Research Manager at EDHEC-Risk Institute. He has conducted research on the organization and regulation of pension funds, on ALM and capital management, on portfolio construction, on econometrics of the financial markets and business cycle indicators, and on the costs and impacts of financial regulation within the industry. Samuel has served as a consultant for numerous organizations. He holds a degree in statistics and economics from ENSAE (Ecole Nationale de la Statistique et de l'Administration Economique) in Paris.

**Hany A. Shawky** is Professor of Finance and Economics at the University at Albany, State University of New York. He received his PhD degree in Finance from the Ohio State University. Dr. Shawky is the founder of the Center for Institutional Investment Management at the University at Albany and served as its director from September 2002 through December 2007. Professor Shawky specializes in investment management and portfolio performance evaluation and is widely published in academic and applied journals on issues dealing with asset pricing, stock market behavior, international financial markets, and electricity markets. He has published over 50 refereed scholarly articles in finance and economics journals, and was the recipient of the School of Business Research Award in 1996, 2001, and 2004. Professor Shawky teaches investments and corporate finance and has regularly participated in executive training programs for bankers and corporate executives. He serves on a number of advisory boards and is a director on the board of trustees of a small cap equity mutual fund. He has served as a consultant to many private and public organizations. Professor Shawky was recently listed among the 'Most Prolific Authors in the Finance Literature: 1959–2008' with a percentile ranking in the top 2% of finance faculties worldwide (Heck and Cooley, 2009). He ranked #550 among the 17 601 finance faculties that has published at least one article in the top 26 core finance journals.

**Abhay Kumar Singh** is a Btech graduate and holds an MBA in Finance from the Indian Institute of Information Technology in Gwalior, India and has a PhD in Finance from Edith Cowan University in Western Australia. He currently works as a Post-Doctoral Fellow in the School of Accounting, Finance and Economics at Edith Cowan University.

**Simone Siragusa** obtained his Bachelors degree from the University of Brescia in 2002 and his Masters in Finance from the University of Lugano, Switzerland in 2005. Simone is a PhD student at the University of Lugano (2006–present), where his supervisor is Professor Barone Adesi Giovanni. His interests include clustered covariance and copulae, hedge fund replication models, stochastic volatility models, and numerical methods. His professional experience is in Risk management (market and credit risk). He currently works as Head of Risk Management at Dinamis Advisors (Switzerland). Dinamis Advisors is an advisory company managing private and institutional money.

**Marcus Storr** is Head of Hedge Funds for Feri Institutional Advisors GmbH in Frankfurt. Marcus is responsible for the entire hedge fund allocation for institutional clients and high net worth individuals, and for general strategy allocation as well as manager selection/due diligence. In addition he is responsible for Hedge Fund Operations. Before joining Feri in 2005 Marcus was Head of the Strategic Advisory Team at Sachsen LB in Leipzig, Germany reporting directly to the CEO. Prior to this he had senior responsibility in the Investment Banking Industry in London. From 1999 to 2003 he was a Director of the Global Equities department of Dresdner Kleinwort Wasserstein and was responsible for European equity research within the Capital Goods sector as well as being the lead analyst on several successful IPOs/Corporate Finance transactions. His research team was consistently rated at top levels in annual research surveys. Prior to this he worked for Robert Flemings (JPMorgan Chase) as an equity analyst. Marcus holds a Masters degree in Finance/Capital markets and International Management/Economics from Humboldt University of Berlin. In addition, he had a two-year apprenticeship as a bank manager. He has been a speaker at numerous hedge fund conferences/seminars worldwide and is a sought after interview partner.

**Qi Tang** is Reader of Mathematics at Sussex University, in charge of the quantitative finance programs. He gained his PhD from Universite Paris Sud, and has worked as consultant for various management consultancy firms, investment funds, and FoHF and engineering firms on computation and modeling projects.

**Mathieu Vaissié** is a Senior Portfolio Manager at Lyxor Asset Management, and a Research Associate with the EDHEC Risk Institute. Prior to joining Lyxor, he took part in the creation and the development of the EDHEC Risk Institute, where he was Senior Research Engineer, and Co-head of the Indexes and Benchmarking research program. His research focus is on the benchmarking of hedge fund returns and optimal allocation decisions involving alternative investment strategies. Mathieu has published over 50 articles in academic and practitioner journals. He holds a Masters degree in management from EDHEC Business School and a PhD in Finance from Paris Dauphine University. Mathieu is a CAIA (Chartered Alternative Investment Analyst) charter holder.

**Stéphane M. F. Yen** is an associate professor with the Department of Accounting and the Institute of Finance at National Cheng Kung University, Taiwan. His research interests involve financial econometrics, alternative investments, and socially responsible investing.

**Louis Zanolin** is CEO and Co-Founder of Alix Capital, a pioneer research firm specializing in UCITS hedge funds based in Switzerland. Alix Capital is the Index Provider to the UCITS Alternative Index, the leading benchmark for UCITS hedge funds. Louis has over 12 years of experience in the alternative investment industry. Prior to founding Alix Capital in 2010, Louis was the founder and CEO of NARA Capital, a specialized fund of hedge funds based in Switzerland. Louis holds a Bachelors degree in Architecture from the Engineering School of Geneva and has a Certificate in Quantitative Portfolio Management from the University of Geneva. Louis also holds the Chartered Alternative Investments Analyst (CAIA) designation.

# Acknowledgments

I thank the handful of anonymous referees for their selection of articles. In addition, I also thank J. Scott Bentley, Ph.D., executive finance editor at Elsevier, for his helpful suggestions in ameliorating this book, as well as Lisa Jones, senior project manager and Kathleen Paoni, editorial project manager. In addition, I thank Pertrac for the use of PerTrac Analytics which enabled critical parts of our analysis in Chapter 9. Many thanks also go to Louis Zanolin CEO of Alix Capital.

I also thank Sol Waksman President at BarclayHedge and Beto Carminhato for supplying the UCITS funds of hedge funds data for Chapter 9. Each contributor is responsible for his or her own chapter. Neither the editor nor the publisher is responsible for chapter content. Finally, I thank Richard Oberuc Sr., President of LaPorte Asset Allocation and Dynaporte for reviewing and making suggestions to numerous chapters.

## Chapter 1  After the Crisis: The Withering of the Funds of Hedge Funds Business?

*R. McFall Lamm, Jr.*

### Abstract

The funds of hedge funds (FoFHs) business was robust and growing very rapidly prior to the financial market crisis in 2008, driven largely by the exceptional returns offered by hedge fund investing. However, the crisis had a profound impact on FoHFs as redemption suspensions by hedge fund managers essentially caused the industry to grind to a halt. Even after hedge funds began to return capital in 2009, FoHFs were overly cautious and carried too much cash exposure. Performance suffered accordingly and assets under management shrank precipitously. FoHFs did not share in the hedge fund industry rebound experienced post crisis — while hedge fund assets are back to near 2007 peak levels, FoHFs assets are only half as great as they were. Does this mean that the FoHFs business is in permanent decline? The answer appears to be no because the underperformance gap versus the broad-based hedge fund industry appears to have been only temporary. Even so, FoHFs face major challenges. These include pressure on fees in a new low return world and stiff competition where due diligence and other FoHFs services have become commoditized.

## SECTION 1  DUE DILIGENCE AND RISK MANAGEMENT
### Chapter 2  Evaluating Trends in Funds of Hedge Funds Operational Due Diligence

*Jason Scharfman*

### Abstract

This chapter provides an overview of trends in the fund of hedge funds approach to operational due diligence. In particular the chapter analyzes pre-2008 and post-2008 trends in operational due diligence design and resource allocation. Post-2008 funds of hedge funds have also broadened the scope of their operational due diligence reviews. This chapter also analyzes the reasons for these increases as well as discussing the increase in the use of third-party consultants to assist in the due diligence process.

## Chapter 3   The Limits of UCITS for Funds of Hedge Funds

*Jeannine Daniel and François-Serge Lhabitant*

### Abstract

'Undertakings for Collective Investments in Transferable Securities' (UCITS) is a European regulatory regime originally created to standardize mutual fund structures in Europe and facilitate their cross-border distribution once they have been authorized in one member state of the European Union. Several funds of hedge funds have rolled out investment vehicles under the UCITS framework — the so-called Newcits — and now openly market them to retail investors. In this chapter, we review the various challenges and restrictions faced by funds of hedge funds (FoHFs) operating under the UCITS framework. We show that UCITS restrictions and additional compliance costs are expected to have a large impact on performance and restrict the ability to exploit longer-dated market dislocations. This might explain the relatively low number of UCITS FoHFs and their difficulties in attracting sizeable investor capital.

## Chapter 4   Due Diligence: Lessons from the Global Financial Crisis for Funds of Hedge Funds with Particular Emphasis on the Asia—Pacific Region

*David Edmund Allen, Staley Roy Alford Pearce, and Robert John Powell*

### Abstract

Undertaking due diligence on funds of hedge funds (FoHFs) is critical to prospective investors in understanding the performance and strategy of any fund of funds. This article examines the experience of the FoHFs Sector in key Asia—Pacific markets prior to, during, and after the global financial crisis (GFC) including an analysis of the inflow and outflow of money from the funds, and the implications for due diligence. Drawing on the experience gained in these markets, recommendations are made on key factors that should be included in the due diligence process.

## Chapter 5   The Use of Managed Accounts by Funds of Hedge Funds

*Marcus Müller and Daniel Dietrich*

### Abstract

The financial crisis highlighted some of the drawbacks funds of hedge funds (FoHFs) can experience when investing in traditional onshore/offshore hedge funds. Many single hedge funds suspended redemptions, activated gate provisions, or created side pockets. Opaque investment risk and counterparty risk was another drawback and fraud cases came to light as well. One possible solution against such adversities seemed to be making investments via managed accounts (MACs). This chapter discusses possible structures, and the advantages and limitations of three types of MACs for FoHFs. Furthermore, we have formulated several hypotheses concerning the use of MACs and reasons for or against this type of hedge fund investment. These hypotheses are tested in a survey under FoHFs companies.

## Chapter 6  Choice of Risk Measure in Evaluating UCITS Funds of Hedge Funds

*Alessandro Carretta and Gianluca Mattarocci*

### Abstract

Undertakings for Collective Investment in Transferable Securities (UCITS) funds of hedge funds (FoHFs) are a fast-growing investment opportunity because of their distinctive characteristics with respect to other financial instruments. Constraints applied on UCITS FoHFs investment selection can affect performance and risk and make these instruments different in relation to other FoHFs. The hedge fund literature has thoroughly analyzed risk-adjusted performance (RAP) measures to determine the limits of the assumption of normality in evaluating such investment opportunities. While new RAP measures have been proposed to overcome these limits, no such empirical evidence exists for UCITS FoHFs. This chapter evaluates the relevance of the choice of risk measure in selecting the best investment opportunities among a set of UCITS FoHFs for the period 2003—2011. The results demonstrate that, even if the rankings according to different RAP measures are correlated, RAP measures that remove the assumption of a normal return distribution may increase the persistence of the results, and an investments selection process based on such measures may lead to better performance, even during the global financial crisis.

## SECTION 2  UCITS PERFORMANCE
### Chapter 7  UCITS Funds of Hedge funds — The New Panacea?

*Louis Zanolin*

### Abstract

This chapter examines the universe and characteristics of UCITS funds of hedge funds (FoHFs). We first provide an overview of the market in terms of size and number of funds. We look at the attributes of UCITS FoHFs in terms of liquidity and fees. We then review the various legal structures allowing the implementation of multi-manager portfolios in the UCITS framework. We also present the main characteristics of the different types of investment managers. The following sections of the chapter focus on the performance of UCITS FoHFs against the performance of single UCITS hedge funds. We find that UCITS FoHFs performed worse than single UCITS hedge funds adjusted for funds of funds fees but with a slightly lower volatility and smaller maximum drawdowns.

## Chapter 8  The Return Potential of UCITS Funds of Hedge Funds: An Analysis of their Investment Universe

*Marcus Storr, Thomas Maier, Florian Haberfelner, and Iliya Kutsarov*

### Abstract

Since the financial crisis in 2008 the growth of the UCITS hedge fund universe has been tremendous. Regulatory oversight, better liquidity, and transparency are the characteristics perceived by investors as the main benefits. However, these benefits come at a cost, in the form of investment restrictions, elevated costs levels, or counterparty risk. This chapter provides a comparison of the structure and descriptive characteristics of the 'offshore' and the 'onshore-UCITS' hedge fund world. The study focuses on a comparison of portfolios constructed out of UCITS hedge funds with those built out of offshore hedge funds. Selected risk and performance measures are analyzed for different types of fund of hedge fund portfolios. The temporary evolvement of those parameters over time is evaluated. Finally, we provide an assessment of the attractiveness of the 'onshore' and 'offshore' hedge fund universe.

## Chapter 9  How Geography, Flows, and Size Affect the Risk-Adjusted Performance of UCITS III Funds of Hedge Funds

*Greg N. Gregoriou, Dieter Kaiser, and Razvan Pascalau*

### Abstract

This chapter investigates (i) the relationship between flows and performance and (ii) how the geographical location, currency trading, strategy, and geographical focus affect the risk-adjusted performance of funds of hedge funds (FoHFs) that are structured in accordance with the Undertaking in Collective Investment in Transferable Securities (UCITS). We use UCITS compliant FoHFs from the BarclayHedge database from March 2006 to December 2011 and investigate the pre and post crisis, as well as the crisis periods. We use the Fung and Hsieh (2004) return decomposition model to adjust the returns for several risk factors. We find that over the sample period the correlation between flows and returns is generally weak ($-0.02$), but becomes stronger during extreme market movements like the one occurring between September 2008 and March 2009 (i.e., 0.48). More recently, the worsening of the European Sovereign debt crisis in the second half of 2011 and the geographical proximity of UCITS FoHFs to those risks has led to stalled growth and even decreases of UCITS FOHFs assets under management (AUM) even as their performance has increased.

## Chapter 10 Funds of Hedge Funds versus Do-It-Yourself Funds of UCITS

*Samuel Sender*

### Abstract

Funds of hedge funds (FoHFs) are often thought to have excess skewness relative to the S&P 500. We illustrate, by means of novel econometric methods, that this arises because of a buy-and-hold strategy with respect to underlying hedge funds, which exhibit excess skewness with respect to the S&P 500. FoHFs also inherit the complexities and reporting biases of hedge fund investing. UCITS-compliant hedge funds, by contrast, are free of these biases, thus allowing investors to access alternative payoffs in a transparent way. Tailored, do-it-yourself UCITS FoHFs can be created without hedge fund managers and associated fees and biases, if they are based on an index.

## SECTION 3 PERFORMANCE

## Chapter 11 Predicting Funds of Hedge Funds Attrition Through Performance Diagnostics

*Philippe Cogneau, Philippe Debatty, and Georges Hübner*

### Abstract

The analysis of individual mutual funds survivorship reveals that a model based on the consideration of a wide class of performance measures can be a solid predictor of their disappearance. Given the importance of performance fees, this phenomenon is likely to be all the more relevant for funds of hedge funds (FoHFs). In this analysis, we apply a diagnostics methodology to predict the disappearance of FoHFs from databases, which we consider a sign of their attrition. Our research shows that prediction is also possible for these types of hedge funds, and even that the predictive ability of the model is stronger than for mutual funds.

## Chapter 12 Does Fund of Hedge Fund Size Matter? Size versus Performance Before, During, and After the Crisis

*Jeannine Daniel and François-Serge Lhabitant*

### Abstract

Over the past few years, the funds of hedge funds (FoHFs) landscape has changed considerably, with an increase in concentration among the larger players. Many institutional investors have supported this trend by allocating primarily to the larger FoHFs, as they place more importance on operational infrastructure. By contrast, many private investors continue to affirm that smaller FoHFs perform better than larger ones. In this chapter, we discuss the relationship between asset size and performance in the FoHFs world, and assess it both qualitatively and empirically.

## Chapter 13 Normalized Risk-Adjusted Performance Measures Revisited: The Performance of Funds of Hedge Funds Before and After the Crisis

*Laurent Bodson, Laurent Cavenaile and Alain Coën*

### Abstract

This chapter revisits the performance of funds of hedge funds (FoHFs) after the 2008 global financial crisis using normalized risk-adjusted performance measures based on multi-factor models. (i) We develop performance measures able to capture the variety of systematic risk sources. (ii) We deal with the impact of smoothing on the risk return properties of FoHFs using an adjustment technique for illiquidity. (iii) We implement unbiased estimators to correct for the econometric bias induced by errors-in-variables (EIV) in asset pricing models. With these different adjustments, we analyze the persistence and stability of performance measures before and after the crisis for a data base of funds of hedge funds. Our results clearly show that the normalized risk-adjusted performance measures corrected for smoothing effect and EIV outperform the alternative measures before and after the crisis.

## Chapter 14 The Impact of the 2008 Financial Crisis on Funds of Hedge Funds

*Na Dai and Hany A. Shawky*

### Abstract

This chapter examines the performance of funds of hedge funds (FoHFs) before and after the 2008 financial crisis. We investigate the impact this crisis had on the level and the distribution of assets under management within the industry and further explore if asset diversification among individual FoHFs had any significant effect on performance during the crisis. Using data from The Lipper TASS hedge fund database, we employ both a quintile ranking methodology and regression analysis to examine our research questions. Our main findings show that FoHFs performance was severely impacted by the crisis and that in general large funds suffered less than small funds. Diversification as measured by the number of focuses was not a major factor in preventing poor performance. The poor performance and the high attrition rates during the crisis suggest that FoHFs were not sufficiently agile to be able to effectively respond to the severe liquidity shortages that were characteristic of the 2008 financial crisis.

## Chapter 15 Forecasting Funds of Hedge Funds Performance: A Markov Regime-Switching Approach

*Szabolcs Blazsek*

### Abstract

We compare the predictive accuracy of out-of-sample and multi-step ahead forecasts of the performance of five funds of hedge funds (FoHFs). Index performance is measured by the excess rate of return above the Morgan Stanley Capital International Global Equity market index. Data are obtained from Hedge Fund Research (HFR) for the period January 1990 to January 2012. We employ a large number of autoregressive (AR) and Markov-switching (MS) AR specifications for the conditional mean of excess returns. We use generalized autoregressive conditional heteroscedasticity (GARCH) and MS-GARCH specifications for the conditional volatility of excess returns. Forecasting precision of competing models is compared in sub-periods before, during, and after the financial crisis. Determinants of FoHFs regimes are investigated by an endogenous switching AR model, where a probit specification identifies the determinants of regime-switching dynamics.

## Chapter 16 A Panel Based Quantile Regression Analysis of Funds of Hedge Funds

*David Edmund Allen, Akhmad Kramadibrata, Robert John Powell, and Abhay Kumar Singh*

### Abstract

This chapter analyzes the aggregate performance of a series of funds of hedge funds (FoHFs) as captured by BarclayHedge fund data in a panel context. The analysis features a study of the sensitivity of the quantiles of the hedge fund return distributions to a set of factors chosen to capture the size of the FoHFs, movements of global stock markets, interest rates, and currencies. This study analyzes 152 FoHFs drawn from the Barclays FoHFs database for the time period of January 2002 to December 2011, covering 10 years. The comparative analysis between a linear regression panel model and a panel quantile regression model shows that the effect of the factors (or explanatory variables) changes across quantiles of the FoHFs return distribution.

## SECTION 4 FUND OF HEDGE FUND ALPHA
### Chapter 17 Reward-to-Risk Ratios of Funds of Hedge Funds

*Yigit Atilgan, Turan G. Bali, and K. Ozgur Demirtas*

### Abstract

This chapter examines if the fund of hedge fund portfolios dominate the US equity and bond markets based on alternative measures of reward-to-risk ratios. Standard deviation is used to measure total risk, and both nonparametric and parametric measures of value-at-risk are used to measure downside risk when the reward-to-risk ratios are computed. We find that the fund of funds index has higher reward-to-risk ratios compared to several stock and bond market indices. This result is particularly strong when the risk measures are calculated from the most recent year's data and is robust as the measurement window is extended to four years.

## Chapter 18 The Short-Run Performance Persistence in Funds of Hedge Funds

*David Ardia and Kris Boudt*

### Abstract

There is extensive empirical evidence that funds of hedge funds (FoHFs) quickly change their investment bets in function of the changing market conditions. In this chapter, we first analyze the stability of risk exposure and performance of FoHFs during the period January 2005 to June 2011. We then study the short-run persistence of performance in the FoHFs industry. Past performance is measured using the one-year trailing return as well as risk-adjusted measures such as the Sharpe ratio and the fund's alpha based on the Carhart (1997) or Fung and Hsieh (2004) factor models. Over the examined time-frame, we consistently find that using risk-adjusted return measures improves the risk-adjusted performance of the moment investment strategy. This finding holds for the financial crisis period as well as the pre- and post-crisis periods.

## Chapter 19 'Seeking Alpha': The Performance of Funds of Hedge Funds

*Willi Semmler, Christian Proaño, and Raphaële Chappe*

### Abstract

As for other active investment portfolios, hedge fund performance is typically measured by alpha and beta coefficients. Roughly, the beta and alpha terms measure the passive and active components of the return, respectively. Presumably, it is the ability to deliver high alphas that is responsible for the rise of the hedge fund industry. Our goal is to test this hypothesis for funds of hedge funds (FoHFs) and determine whether we can confirm statistically significant positive alphas. By using monthly returns from November 2002 to February 2012 for a sample of 5509 FoHFs combining both active and inactive (defunct) funds in the Bloomberg database, we estimate a linear 'risk' multi-factor model to provide a decomposition of fund return between a passive portfolio of indices, and manager-specific alpha. We perform a time-series regression by ordinary least square (OLS) for each fund in our sample, regressing monthly returns against eight indices. We can confirm statistically significant positive alphas for only 506 out of 5509 funds in our sample, which is not even 10% of them. This would suggest that investors should not automatically assume that all FoHFs are able to select the best-performing hedge funds, but instead should carefully pick those funds that will create manager-specific alpha.

## Chapter 20　Quantitative Insight into Management of Funds of Hedge Funds and Consequences on Fund Alpha Performance

*Justina Dambrauskaite, Haidar Haidar, Bernard Minsky, and Qi Tang*

### Abstract

In this chapter, we study the performance behavior of classified funds of hedge funds (FoHFs) according to certain risk criteria before, during, and after the recent financial crisis of 2008–2009. Our methodology uses nine well-known risk measures to rank FoHFs, in order to calculate the first two corresponding principal components, PC1 and PC2, of these rank vectors. The factor loadings of these principal components are reviewed and interpreted as styles (PC1 as consistency and PC2 as aggression). The universe of FoHFs is classified according to these styles as BL = (low consistency, low aggression), BR = (high consistency, low aggression), TL = (low consistency, high aggression), TR = (high consistency, high aggression), and the remainder (scores moderate in either of the principal components). We examine the performance behavior of the four classes BL, BR, TL, and TR whereby this classification method provides an indication as to returns and management styles of FoHFs.

## Chapter 21　Selecting Top Funds of Hedge Funds Based on Alpha and Other Performance Measures

*Ying-Lin Hsu , Chung-Ming Kuan, and Stéphane M. F. Yen*

### Abstract

We evaluate the performance of funds of hedge funds (FoHFs) in the Hedge Fund Research (HFR) dataset using the stepwise SPA testing procedure of Hsu *et al.* (2010). We find that the subprime crisis affected the performance of FoHFs, yet well-selected 'elite' FoHFs are still able to outperform model-free and model-dependent benchmarks post crisis. The hot-hand effect among 'elite' FoHFs is not eliminated by the crisis. These elites consistently deliver good performance such as a larger alpha than do their followers in the aftermath of the crisis.

## Chapter 22　Funds of Hedge Funds Strategies and Implications for Asset Management: Is Diversification Enough?

*Simone Siragusa*

### Abstract

The global financial crisis of 2008–2009 has attracted a great deal of attention with regard to funds of hedge funds (FoHFs). Over the last 20 years institutional investors, pension funds, insurance companies, and endowment funds have allocated capital to alternative assets for downside equity risk management as well as offering investors broader diversification. As reported by Brown *et al.*

(2004) FoHFs offer poor value to investors. However, Ang *et al.* (2005) use the Certainty Equivalence Principle and find that FoHFs add value for risk averse investors. We use various Hedge Fund Research (HFR) FoHF indexes to determine whether that add value to a portfolio as well as examine the implication of higher moments, co-moments, and market neutrality. We employ Certainty Equivalence Return Maximization in our analysis to construct portfolios by taking into account different utility functions, different levels of risk aversion and higher moments.

# SECTION 5  TAIL RISK

## Chapter 23  The Intertemporal Relation between Tail Risk and Fund of Hedge Fund Returns

*Yigit Atilgan, Turan G. Bali, and K. Ozgur Demirtas*

### Abstract

This chapter investigates the predictive relation between funds of hedge funds (FoHFs) returns and tail risk. We find that tail risk as measured by both nonparametric and parametric value-at-risk positively predicts future fund of funds returns. We investigate the source of this finding by focusing on the individual moments of the empirical FoHFs return distribution. We find that variance and skewness do not have any significant predictive power, whereas kurtosis positively predicts future returns on funds of funds. The positive relation between kurtosis and future FoHFs returns is robust after controlling for past FoHFs returns and a large set of macroeconomic variables associated with business cycle fluctuations.

## Chapter 24  Tail Risk Protection for Funds of Hedge Funds

*Oliver A. Schwindler*

### Abstract

The financial crisis of 2008 clearly showed that funds of hedge funds (FoHFs) can exhibit tail risks most investors had not been aware of. Several studies have discussed the type of tail risks FoHFs can be exposed to as well as how tail risk can be measured. However, almost none of these studies provides suggestions and methods for mitigating these tail risks. This chapter provides a dynamic hedging strategy for equity tail risks to which fund of hedge funds are normally exposed. Given the well documented negative correlation between equity returns and volatility indices, on option implied volatility levels, one of the simplest way to hedge against equity tail risk is to buy an out-of-the money call option on the VIX Index. However, the rolling costs for buying every month a call option on the VIX are quite high. This chapter discusses a dynamic hedging strategy that minimizes the rolling costs while being able to provide tail risk protection during the equity drawdown phases occurring during the time elapsing since VIX options trading started on the CBOE in February 2006.

## Chapter 25  Autocorrelation, Bias, and Fat Tails: An Analysis of Funds of Hedge Funds

*Martin Eling*

### Abstract

In this chapter we apply the performance evaluation framework introduced in Eling (2006) to funds of hedge funds (FoHFs). The performance evaluation takes into account autocorrelation, bias, and fat tails in returns and is an adjusted version of the modified Sharpe ratio presented by Gregoriou and Gueyie (2003). Under this performance measure we analyze FoHF performance over the period 1994 to 2011 and in different subperiods (pre-crisis and post-crisis). We find that FoHFs lose some of their attractiveness when autocorrelation, bias, and fat tails in returns are taken into account. Moreover, we document the substantially lower performance of FoHFs following the financial crisis. It thus seems that some FoHFs are still recovering from losses incurred during the financial crisis.

## Chapter 26  Crisis and Funds of Hedge Funds Tail Risk

*Monica Billio, Kaleab Y. Mamo, and Loriana Pelizzon*

### Abstract

Hedge funds sold the dream to investors of being able to easily hedge risk. However, long-term capital management (LTCM) and the recent crisis show that this is not the case. The new frontier in this field is the construction of portfolios of hedge funds, the so-called funds of hedge funds (FoHFs). The aim is to eliminate risk through diversification. This chapter investigates data on FoHF indexes provided by Barclay Hedge and Hedge Fund Research (HFR). Our research shows that during this recent crisis, FoHFs presented large and fat left-hand tails. Using our decomposition procedure based on a multifactor switching regime model we found that credit risk was by far the most important factor for tail risk of FoHFs during the crisis. Other important factors include term spread and momentum.

## Chapter 27  Funds of Hedge Funds, Efficient Portfolios, and Investor Clientele: Empirical Evidence from Growth and Financial Crisis Periods

*Wolfgang Bessler and Philipp Kurmann*

### Abstract

This chapter analyzes whether funds of hedge funds (FoHFs) significantly contribute to portfolio efficiency and whether similar efficiency gains can be accomplished with single-strategy hedge funds. We explicitly differentiate between the periods before and during the recent financial crisis and investigate the benefits of FoHFs from the perspective of heterogeneous investor clienteles such as conservative and aggressive investors. In our empirical analysis we employ mean-variance spanning tests and control for the well known non-normality of FoHFs returns by taking excess kurtosis and tail risk into account. The results suggest that FoHFs are an attractive asset class for conservative investors in all market environments as indicated by significant improvements of the global minimum variance (GMV) portfolio. However, the tangency portfolio representing the optimal investment for aggressive investors is more sensitive to the economic conditions and distributional assumptions. After controlling for kurtosis and tail risk, efficiency gains are consistently reduced, though still highly significant for the GMV portfolio. Our empirical results are robust to de-smoothing FoHFs returns. As these findings hold irrespective of the particular FoHFs strategy, we conclude that it may be beneficial for investors to consider sub-indices for portfolio construction instead of diversifying across the entire FoHFs universe. Our results add to the recent literature on portfolio optimization suggesting that over-diversification in the FoHFs industry may be hardly beneficial from an investor's perspective.

## SECTION 6   REGULATION

### Chapter 28   Regulation: Threat or Opportunity for the Funds of Hedge Funds Industry?

*Serge Darolles and Mathieu Vaissie*

**Abstract**

A tidal wave of regulation is hitting financial markets world wide as a result of the credit crisis of 2008–2009 and this time around the hedge fund world will not be immune. We argue in this chapter that, unlike conventional wisdom, regulation could be an opportunity for the funds of hedge funds (FoHFs) industry. The only necessary condition is fair treatment of hedge fund investments. We take the Solvency II framework as an example and show how the implementation of the granularity adjustment, first introduced for implementation in the Basel framework, makes it possible to take into account the diversification potential of FoHFs and in turn reconcile the outcome of the standard formula with empirical evidence.

### Chapter 29   Funds of Hedge Funds and the Principles of Fiduciary Investing Following the Global Financial Crisis

*Paul U. Ali*

**Abstract**

Funds of hedge funds (FOHFs) are an increasingly common way for institutional investors as well as high-net-worth individuals to access the hedge fund sector. Unsurprisingly, there have been renewed calls in the wake of the global financial crisis to subject the hedge fund sector to greater regulatory scrutiny but this has not undermined the role played by FoHFs in intermediating between investors and hedge funds. A FoHF is, in essence, a 'feeder' structure which aggregates the contributions of the investors in the FoHFs and allocates that capital across a broad pool of hedge funds. In this manner, an investor can efficiently obtain exposure to a diversified portfolio of hedge fund managers and hedge fund investment styles. This chapter examines the impact of the global financial crisis on the fiduciary principles that apply to many of these investors (such as pension funds, family offices, endowments) when selecting FoHFs and also on the actual design of FoHFs.

## Chapter 30  Understanding the Regulation Impact: US Funds of Hedge Funds after the Crisis

*David Edmund Allen, Robert John Powell, and Abhay Kumar Singh*

### Abstract

The aftermath of the Global Financial Crisis has heralded substantially increased regulation in the United States which impacts on funds of hedge funds (FoHFs). This chapter weighs up the pros and cons of this shifting regulation landscape and examines the impact of key regulation such as the Dodd−Frank Act on funds and fund volumes. We also discuss potential flow-on effects of the European AIFM directive on the US FoHFs industry.

## Chapter 31  Canada and Australia: Do They Provide a Regulatory Model for Funds of Hedge Funds?

*David Edmund Allen, Raymond Robert Boffey, and Robert John Powell*

### Abstract

Australia and Canada have both been applauded by many commentators as having weathered the global financial crisis (GFC) far better than most of their global counterparts. In large part, this is due to the financial services regulatory framework in these countries which encourages and ensures prudent investment practices. Australia and Canada were not immune to global events during the crisis, but showed strong resilience in weathering their impact. This chapter compares the pre- and post-GFC regulations and regulatory framework similarities and differences between these two countries in the context of funds of hedge funds (FoHFs) and attempts to isolate those features which contribute to a sound investment climate.

## Chapter 32  South African Regulatory Reforms of Funds of Hedge Funds

*David Edmund Allen, Akhmad Kramadibrata, Robert John Powell, and Abhay Kumar Singh*

### Abstract

The financial services industry in South Africa is subject to strong regulation. Investments in funds of hedge funds (FoHFs) have been impacted by regulations such as limitations on pension fund investments and exchange controls which restrict flows of funds overseas and encourage local investment. Nonetheless, South Africa has experienced strong FoHFs growth and changing regulation is opening up investment opportunities in these products. This chapter examines FoHFs in South Africa, with particular emphasis on the changing regulatory climate in South Africa before, during, and after the global financial crisis.

# CHAPTER 1

# After the Crisis: The Withering of the Funds of Hedge Funds Business?

R. McFall Lamm, Jr.

Stelac Advisory Services LLC, New York, NY, USA

## 1.1. INTRODUCTION

From the early 2000s up to the financial crisis, the funds of hedge funds (FoHFs) business was one of the most rapidly growing sectors of the financial products world. Indeed, FoHFs assets under management (AUM) multiplied 10-fold from the turn of the century to a peak at well over US$2 trillion at the beginning of 2008. Growth in FoHFs assets even exceeded the pace of expansion in the underlying hedge fund industry with the FoHFs market share rising from around a third of total hedge fund assets in 1999 to half at the market crescendo (Figure 1.1).

The feeding frenzy driving asset flows into FoHFs was in large part due to the stellar performance record of the 1990s, when returns significantly exceeded those of plain-vanilla stock and bond portfolios. This point was made by Edwards and Liew (1999), Lamm (1999), Swensen (2000), and others who increased awareness of the advantages of hedge fund investing. However, the key event sparking industry expansion was the bursting of the technology bubble from 2000 to 2002. As investors watched the NASDAQ and S&P 500 fall 78% and 49% from peak to trough, hedge funds and FoHFs collectively delivered positive returns. Very soon afterward, institutional consultants began to bless

Reconsidering Funds of Hedge Funds. http://dx.doi.org/10.1016/B978-0-12-401699-6.00001-0

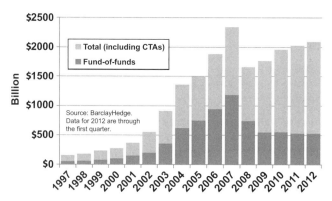

**FIGURE 1.1**
Hedge fund industry AUM.

allocations to hedge funds as suitable investments. This unleashed a massive flood of inflows from pension funds, endowments, and foundations that continued unabated until the financial crisis.

The original business proposition put forward by FoHFs was very enticing and offered extraordinary value for investors. FoHFs provided hedge fund due diligence, manager selection, and portfolio management in one convenient package. Costs were reasonable with most FoHFs charging a 1.5% management fee, which was about the same as that of active equity managers.

Less popular were FoHFs incentive fees of as much as 10–15%. However, incentive fees were typically applied only when a cash hurdle rate was exceeded, making the charges more palatable especially when investors believed they would receive a superior return stream with downside protection during adverse market developments. Furthermore, because it was costly and time-consuming for investors to build their own hedge fund portfolios in what was an opaque and highly specialized field, FoHFs offered institutions an easy first step and immediate exposure. FoHFs also provided a doorway for private investors – many of whom lacked sufficient scale and expertise to construct adequately diversified portfolios – into hedge fund nirvana.

Another competitive advantage often promoted by FoHFs was that they had access to the best hedge fund managers who often would not accept money from new investors. FoHFs could easily meet the larger minimum investments often required by very successful hedge funds and often qualified for better terms – 'most favored nation' status – because they brought large amounts of assets to eager recipients. Investors could not hope to receive the equivalent treatment on their own.

## 1.2. INSTITUTIONAL VERSUS PRIVATE INVESTOR FoHFs

The surge in institutional investments after the 2000–2002 market crash led to a sharp polarization of the FoHFs industry. Some firms such as Grosvenor,

Blackstone, Blackrock, Lyxor, Mesirow, and Pacific Alternative Asset Management concentrated on serving the nascent institutional market. Others such as Permal and GAM, as well as banks such as Credit Suisse and JP Morgan, specialized in satisfying private investor demand.

The institutional and private investor segments of the FoHFs industry operate quite differently. Institutionally oriented FoHFs tend to have lower fees due to economies of scale and intense competition for the large pools of money typically available. Furthermore, because US institutions traditionally made larger allocations to hedge funds than their counterparts in Europe and elsewhere, the institutional FoHFs business became very US-centric.

In contrast, FoHFs focusing on the private investor market segment needed large distribution networks, which required higher fees to compensate sales staff. In addition, because US private investors are subject to substantial taxes on FoHFs returns, they tended to limit hedge fund allocations in preference to tax-advantaged assets.[1] This was not the case for investors with money stashed in the European tax havens. As a result, FoHFs based in Europe came to control a disproportionately large share of private investor assets.

The US institution-dominated FoHFs segment evolved into a fairly sophisticated and professional enterprise. However, less regulation in Europe gradually led to an erosion of standards in private investor FoHFs. Naïve high-net-worth individuals in European tax havens were a particularly inviting target since they were largely captive, not well-informed, and could not loudly protest mismanagement in public. Fees escalated as some private banks even began to apply sales charges to initial FoHFs investments. Some FoHFs managers became overly aggressive and began to charge costs to the fund that should have been absorbed in management fees. A few FoHFs began to employ leverage to amplify performance (and help offset high fees) while others took to investing directly in other assets such as stocks using investor funds supposedly earmarked for hedge funds. Perhaps most egregious was the emergence of fund-of-fund-of-funds (i.e., fund managers created portfolios of FoHFs while extracting yet another layer of fees).

For sure, such shenanigans were atypical in the private investor segment — adverse publicity could potentially damage reputations and ultimately harm business. Nonetheless, there was a dark tint around the edges of the European FoHFs business. The problem was compounded by woefully inadequate transparency. For example, many FoHFs did not disclose the names of the hedge funds held in the portfolio, much less the rationale behind manager engagements or terminations. In many cases, investors received no more than a monthly statement accompanied by a one-page

---

[1] A common rule-of-thumb is that approximately 80% of FoHFs returns are short-term capital gains, which are taxed at ordinary income rates that approach 50% in high-tax states.

newsletter that contained little except vague jargon describing why industry returns were up or down. Imagine investing in a hedge fund portfolio and knowing virtually nothing about how your money was invested, but this was commonplace.

If that is not enough, FoHFs marketing was often less than candid. Sales personnel often touted hedge fund exposure via FoHFs as offering good returns, low volatility, no or little downside risk, and zero correlation with stocks. Left unsaid was the fact that hedge funds could deliver substantially negative returns or even 'blowup' and that correlation with equity markets had reached uncomfortably high levels.

## 1.3. THE BUBBLE BURSTS

As everyone is aware, the collapse of Lehman in 2008 precipitated a sharp drop in financial asset prices that proved the most extreme since the Great Depression. Hedge funds were caught up in the maelstrom and the majority experienced unprecedented drawdowns with even some icons such as Citadel and Farallon faltering. FoHFs passed through the sharp losses on their underlying hedge fund portfolios directly to investors.

The reactions to large FoHFs losses by institutions and private investors were quite different. For example, Williamson (2010, p. 1) reported that the assets of the top 25 FoHFs declined 37% from mid 2008 to the end of 2009 while FoHFs managers with a majority of assets owned by institutions experienced a decline of only 23%. In this regard, 'institutions were a life raft for FoHFs managers' except for a few firms 'like Union Bancaire Privee and Man Group, which had exposure to the Madoff Ponzi scheme.' For institutions, there was no rush to redeem.

In stark contrast, private investors were shocked by the sharp losses sustained by FoHFs — losses that many had been led to believe could never occur. Panic ensued and private investors began to redeem in droves. As the rush to exit intensified, FoHFs managers were ensnared in a situation where numerous hedge funds in their portfolios had suspended redemptions and their capital was locked up indefinitely. This in turn made it impossible for FoHFs to honor redemption requests from their investors.

Of course, most FoHFs did their best to meet redemption demand by exiting from hedge funds that were not locked up. However, this approach left FoHFs holding the worst-wounded managers, and their portfolios soon became top-heavy with near dead and dying hedge funds burdened with illiquid assets where no one knew how long the work-out process would take. Furthermore, in cases where exit was possible, FoHFs often had to pay pejorative early redemption charges, thus reducing liquidation proceeds and exacerbating losses. The only option available for most FoHFs managers was to exit when they could and wait for struggling hedge funds in their portfolios to begin to return capital.

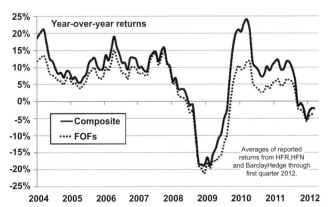

**FIGURE 1.2**
Composite hedge fund industry return versus FoHFs.

As a result, FoHFs performance dipped substantially below that of the hedge fund industry during the redemption hiatus in 2009.[2] For example, FoHFs losses were more or less in line with the hedge fund industry in 2008 — a negative 21.4% for FoHFs versus losses of 19.0% for the hedge fund industry according to Hedge Fund Research (HFR). However, in 2009 — a strong performance rebound year — HFR reports that hedge funds gained 20.0% while FoHFs returned only 11.5%. The 8.5% underperformance gap was unprecedented. Hedge Fund Net (HFN) and BarclayHedge report even larger differentials of 9.9% and 13.5%, respectively (Figure 1.2).

By 2010 most hedge funds were again making redemptions and FoHFs were gradually able to unwind frozen positions and rebalance their portfolios. Nonetheless, an unusually wide underperformance gap persisted with the hedge fund industry returning 10.6% in 2010 while FoHFs delivered only 5.2% based on an average of returns reported by HFR, HFN, and BarclayHedge.[3]

## 1.4. THE AFTERMATH OF CRISIS

The mass exodus by private investors caused the share of hedge fund industry assets held by FoHFs to decline during and after the crisis. BarclayHedge data show that FoHFs assets peaked at 51% of hedge fund industry assets in 2007, but fell to 26% by the end of 2011. HFR data show a lower peak — at 45% of assets in 2006 — and a milder decline to 34% of assets at the end of 2010. Regardless of the exact amount, it is clear that the FoHFs industry shrank drastically more than the broad hedge fund industry.

---

[2]While many FoHFs permit quarterly redemption with 45 days' notice, others require longer. Most investors did not become aware of the carnage in FoHFs performance until after the September stock market collapse. This meant that the peak in redemption demand did not come until the end of the year and in the first quarter of 2009.
[3]HFR, HFN, and BarclayHedge data are used because these sources report performance for both hedge fund industry composite and FoHFs, have the longest track records, and also make their data publicly available via website.

What accounts for the extreme shrinkage of the FoHFs industry? First, as already discussed, much of the decline in FoHFs assets was clearly due to the departure of private investors who were not prepared by their brokers and bankers for the significant losses experienced in 2008. These investors learned the truth the hard way and voted with their feet. Most will likely never return to FoHFs investing.

Second, while institutions were not in the vanguard of FoHFs investment liquidations, they nonetheless suffered from the significant underperformance of FoHFs versus the hedge fund industry. To avoid a repeat of this in the future, institutions that invested in FoHFs in anticipation of eventually managing their own hedge fund portfolios were no doubt spurred to expedite the process. For example, Williamson (2011) reports numerous examples of institutions shifting from FoHFs to direct hedge fund investing. In addition, Jacobius (2012) shows that for the top 200 defined benefit plans, FoHFs investment fell sharply from nearly 50% of institutional hedge fund holdings in 2006 to approximately 25% in 2011 (Figure 1.3).

An added motivation for direct investing in hedge funds by institutions *in lieu* of using FoHFs was that doing it yourself became significantly easier after the financial crisis. Hedge funds made a concerted effort to improve transparency and communication — important institutional requirements — in a conscious effort to acquire stickier pension fund money to rebuild their asset base. Moreover, the available talent pool of professionals knowledgeable about direct hedge fund investing swelled after many FoHFs reduced staff. This allowed institutions to recruit their own in-house experts or hire consultants at more reasonable fees. Why settle for potential FoHFs illiquidity and underperformance when you can eliminate the intermediary through direct investment?

Paradoxically, it now appears that the FoHFs underperformance gap was largely a temporary phenomenon arising from the severe conditions experienced during the crisis. Indeed, HFR reports that the hedge fund industry lost 5.3% in 2011 while FoHFs posted a negative 5.5% — the wide underperformance differential of 2009 and 2010 had shriveled to almost nothing.

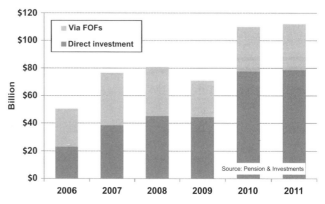

**FIGURE 1.3**
Top 200 pension FoHFs assets.

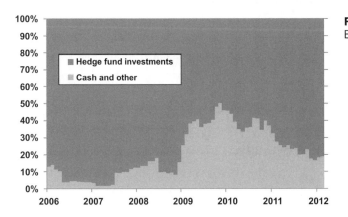

**FIGURE 1.4**
Estimates of FoHFs hedge fund exposure.

## 1.5. THE EXCESS CASH PROBLEM

While the redemption mismatch between FoHFs and hedge funds initially played a role in causing the underperformance gap, FoHFs were also at fault in 2009 and 2010 by allowing cash holdings to accumulate to inordinately high levels. Ostensibly, the rationale behind cash accumulation was to meet future redemption obligations and to provide a safety net to protect against ongoing duress in the global financial system. This miscalculation proved costly. My estimates indicate that FoHFs investments in hedge funds may have fallen to almost half of total assets at the nadir in December 2009. Cash holdings, the monetization of early redemption fees, and other factors account for the remaining exposure based on a sample of 42 prominent FoHFs (Figure 1.4).[4] These high cash holdings and the payment of early redemption fees clearly represented a drag on performance at the time and were major contributors to the performance gap. Now, with the investment environment stabilized and redemption stress ended, FoHFs have redeployed liquidity into hedge funds and reverted to more normal cash levels.

## 1.6. COULD FoHFs PROBLEMS HAVE BEEN PREVENTED?

To some analysts, it is not surprising that hedge fund and FoHFs performance deteriorated significantly in 2008. The reason is that the hedge fund world changed dramatically during its evolution from the small cottage industry of the

---

[4]The estimates of FoHFs hedge fund exposure are derived using an algorithm that produces the best fit between average reported returns for 42 FoHFs presuming that each held an underlying portfolio that delivered the average of HFR, HFN, and Barclay composite hedge fund returns. The algorithm used is: $r_t^{FOF} = w_t(1 - d_t f^I)r_t^{HF} + (1 - w_t)r_t^C - f^F + \varepsilon_t$, where $r_t^{FOF}$ is the average 42-FoHFs return, $r_t^{HF}$ is the hedge fund composite return, $r_t^C$ is the cash return (3-month Treasuries), $w_t$ is the portion of FoHFs assets invested in hedge funds, $f^I$ is the incentive fee, $f^F$ is the fixed FoHFs fee, and $\varepsilon_t$ is measurement error. The binary performance fee variable $d_t$ equals zero if the underlying hedge fund portfolio's return is negative and unity if the underlying hedge fund return is positive year-to-date. The relationship is estimated via restricted least squares subject to $0 \leq w_t < 1$.

**FIGURE 1.5**
FoHFs return correlations with equities.

1990s to the behemoth it became in the new millennium. For example, global macro funds dominated the hedge fund world in the 1990s and accounted for nearly half of industry assets — as underscored by Morley (2001) and Lamm (2002). By 2008, global macro funds represented less than 20% of assets. In their place were cohorts of equity long/short managers and other equity-related strategies, which comprised as much as two-thirds of industry assets when the financial crisis ensued. As the transition to dominance by equity-linked strategies unfolded, the correlation between FoHFs returns and equities rose significantly, reaching 0.9 by 2006 (Figure 1.5).

The steady rise of hedge fund and FoHFs correlation with equities did not go unnoticed among industry practitioners. Lamm (2004) described the situation as one where hedge fund industry performance was morphing into little more than camouflaged equity beta. The obvious solution promoted by Lamm (2003, 2005) was greater diffusion in FoHFs hedge fund portfolios — away from correlated strategies such as equity long/short and towards global macro managers — in order to improve portfolio diversification characteristics. Nonetheless, the vast majority of FoHFs continued to invest in a mix of hedge funds that essentially mirrored the industry's composition and its growing dependence on equity-linked strategies.

The equity correlation reality struck full force with the financial crisis as the precipitous decline in stock prices was transmitted directly through as large losses for FoHFs investors. In this regard, the FoHFs industry could have done better in 2008 if portfolios were more diversified and firmly tilted to global macro strategies, which did in fact produce positive returns during the period. That said, if one was investing in FoHFs to mimic hedge fund industry returns, the performance slump of the FoHFs industry was unavoidable.[5]

---

[5]There were actually a few well-known FoHFs that specialized in macro strategies that performed fairly well in 2008, such as Permal Macro Holdings. Such funds represented only a small portion of industry assets, however.

As for the deleterious effect of redemption suspensions, such conditions had not occurred previously and would have required planning for a contingency never before experienced. Of course, in theory one might imagine that redemption suspensions might happen under certain circumstances and there were a few FoHFs that had a policy of restricting their exposure to hedge funds that only offered monthly liquidity. This approach paid off well during the crisis because the underlying hedge funds traded assets in liquid markets and did not suspend redemptions. However, the longer-term performance of such FoHFs usually is worse than average since the best managers normally require at least quarterly notice and some form of lock-up or early withdrawal penalty. As a result, to provide competitive performance the vast majority of FoHFs did not limit themselves to funds with monthly liquidity and it is difficult to see how the FoHFs industry could have escaped the redemption problem.

## 1.7. THE ROLE OF PERFORMANCE DECAY

One other factor that may explain the rise of direct hedge fund investing and tempered the rebound in FoHFs assets is the ongoing decline in hedge fund performance compared with other assets. That is, even before the financial crisis, the return stream delivered by hedge funds (and FoHFs) was significantly deteriorating versus plain-vanilla stock and bond portfolios. This is illustrated in Figure 1.6, which shows running 10-year Sharpe ratios using FoHFs returns reported by HFR, HFN, and BarclayHedge versus the performance of a 60% stock/40% bond portfolio as represented by S&P 500 and Barclay Aggregate returns.

Figure 1.6 clearly shows that FoHFs (and, by default, hedge funds) provided superior risk-adjusted returns for trailing 10-year periods through 2010, though the difference was narrowing. However, by 2011 the Sharpe ratios for FoHFs had converged with those of the plain-vanilla stock and bond portfolio for the first time. Now, for almost a year the trailing 10-year Sharpe ratio for FoHFs has fallen

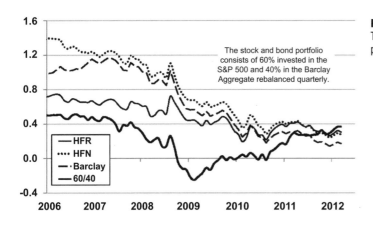

**FIGURE 1.6**
Ten-year Sharpe ratios: FoHFs versus plain-vanilla stock and bond portfolio.

below that of the 60% stock/40% bond portfolio. This suggests that at least for the past decade, holding FoHFs in lieu of a plain-vanilla stock and bond port-folio has not enhanced investment performance.[6]

Astute asset allocators may have noticed the downward trend in FoHFs perfor-mance and taken this into account in making decisions about how much hedge fund exposure is desirable. If one expected the Sharpe ratio decay to continue, then this may have tempered allocations to FoHFs and reduced inflows. Furthermore, the relatively greater decline in FoHFs performance *vis-à-vis* the hedge fund industry may have encouraged more direct investment in hedge funds than would otherwise be the case since a reasonable expectation is that one should be able to realize better performance by eliminating FoHFs fees.

Note that this conclusion — that the returns of FoHFs are no better than a plain-vanilla stock and bond portfolio over the past decade, takes reported perfor-mance at face value. As is well known, hedge fund and FoHFs performance is overstated due to survivor bias as described by Fung and Hsieh (2000, 2009), Liang (2000), and others. Recently, Xu *et al.* (2011) found that survivor bias in FoHFs returns over the 1994–2009 period averaged from 0.2% to 3.9% annu-ally using various measures of bias. In addition, Dichev and Yu (2011) argue that the return investors actually receive — the dollar-weighted return — averaged 6.1% for FoHFs versus a buy-and-hold return of 13.8% over the 1980–2008 period. For this reason, the actual performance of FoHFs may be a bit worse than indicated.

## 1.8. OUTLOOK

AUM for FoHFs have remained stagnant at around US$0.5 trillion dollars for the past 4 years. This contrasts with the overall hedge fund industry, which has experienced a rebound back to near the peak reached at the beginning of 2008. Whether the FoHFs industry starts to grow again remains to be seen. Never-theless, it is clear that FoHFs face a quite challenging future.

I believe there are three major developments that will shape the evolution of the industry. First, many analysts expect investment returns to be subdued in the coming years due to demographics, the paying down of unprecedented sovereign debt accumulated since the crisis, and the imposition of new austerity measures such as higher taxes. In such an environment, it will become increasingly difficult to justify FoHFs fees. For example, a 1.5% FoHFs management fee plus incentive appreciably reduces investors' returns if financial assets are delivering only low single-digit performance. This was less of an issue in the double-digit returning world of the past. However, if low

---

[6]The results are even more significant if one examines the past half-decade — FoHFs returns are much lower than for a 60% stock/40% bond portfolio on a risk-adjusted basis. As for total returns, a 60% stock/40% bond portfolio has performed substantially better than FoHFs over the past 10 years.

returns become reality, FoHFs will likely find themselves facing fee reduction pressure in order to deliver meaningful performance for investors and retain assets. Otherwise, disintermediation via direct hedge fund investing is poised to continue.

Fees for institutional investors have probably declined in recent years due to heightened competition. This does not appear to be the case for private investors, although it is difficult to know precisely because of privately negotiated rates and the proliferation of multiple share classes. In a sample of 118 FoHFs, Ineichen (2002) found the most common fee structure was a flat management fee of 1% and an incentive fee of 10%. The second most common structure was a 1% management fee and 15% incentive with all funds in this category having hurdle rates approximating T-bills. The median manager had a flat fee of 1.2%; however, the range was from 0% to 3%. My own non-scientific sample of 42 large and well-known FoHFs shows an average management fee of 1.2% and an incentive fee of 5% in 2011. This is not very different from Ineichen's findings of a decade ago.

Incentive fees for FoHFs appear to make little sense. After all, the investor is paying for a basket of services: due diligence, portfolio management, and manager selection. These are similar to the services provided by active equity and fixed-income managers who do not charge incentive fees. While some FoHFs have eliminated incentive fees, others have not. I suspect that any FoHF that flourishes in the future will likely be forced to eliminate incentive fees to be competitive. This may encourage consolidation as profitability declines for smaller market participants whose survival is now dependent on incentives.

A second major change likely in the FoHFs business is the evolution of more specialist funds. For example, more FoHFs will concentrate in equity long/short managers (as proxy equity exposure) or global macro (to offer true zero correlation with other assets). Certainly, a considerable number of FoHFs already specialize. For example, of the 1300 FoHFs that self-listed on Bloomberg in April 2012, more than 20% report that they specialize by strategy (Table 1.1). At a minimum, FoHFs that do not differentiate themselves in this way are likely to provide more clearly articulated investment strategies rather than the obfuscation that often prevails today.

Third, it remains likely that at some point a successful investment vehicle will emerge that allows one to effectively index hedge fund exposure — either synthetically via clone or directly by investing in a basket of hedge funds. Numerous firms have made efforts to do this in recent years via exchange-traded funds (ETFs), exchange-traded notes (ETNs), mutual funds, or other structures. However, virtually all the efforts are seriously flawed in one way or the other: fees are too onerous, the investment strategies naïve, or the underlying hedge funds subpar. When a successful index product eventually arrives, FoHFs will be forced to demonstrate that they add relative value or risk a loss of assets.

| Table 1.1 | FoHFs Classifications by Style | | |
|---|---|---|---|
| **FoHFs Strategy** | **Assets (US$ billion)** | **Share (%)** | **Equity Correlation** |
| Multistyle | 188.6 | 77.8 | 0.71 |
| Long/short equity | 13.5 | 5.6 | 0.87 |
| Commodity trading advisor/ managed futures | 9.6 | 4.0 | −0.02 |
| Macro | 9.7 | 4.0 | 0.29 |
| Equity market neutral | 5.9 | 2.4 | 0.48 |
| Fixed income | 5.9 | 2.4 | NA |
| Fixed income arbitrage | 2.1 | 0.9 | 0.60 |
| Convertible arbitrage | 2.0 | 0.8 | 0.68 |
| Distressed debt | 1.7 | 0.7 | 0.74 |
| Emerging market equity | 1.4 | 0.6 | 0.78 |
| Long-biased equity | 0.5 | 0.2 | 0.90 |
| Merger arbitrage | 0.4 | 0.2 | 0.78 |
| Statistical arbitrage | 0.3 | 0.1 | 0.49 |
| Other | 0.8 | 0.3 | NA |
| *Total* | *242.5* | *100.0* | |

Classifications for approximately 1300 FoHFs from Bloomberg as of 10 April 2012. Equity correlations are over the past 5 years between S&P 500 returns and HFR hedge fund strategies except macro (from Credit Suisse First Boston) and fixed-income arbitrage (from HFN).

## CONCLUSION

The original value proposition of FoHFs remains largely intact — an investor receives a diversified hedge fund portfolio in one fell swoop. Unfortunately, FoHFs are no longer *avant garde*, and their returns are increasingly no better than those attainable from stock and bond investing. While some of the problems experienced by FoHFs during and after the financial crisis were one-time events and unlikely to be repeated — such as redemption suspensions and the underperformance gap versus the broad hedge fund industry in 2009 and 2010 — the road back to growth will likely be difficult. The new-found ease of direct hedge fund investing represents a particularly tough challenge since such disintermediation improves market efficiency.

In the institutional market segment, the FoHFs that flourish in the future are likely to be those that serve institutions especially well by providing a competitive alternative to direct hedge fund investing. Already, the distinction between recommending a portfolio of hedge funds and actually managing it through a FoHFs structure is blurring. Even so, small- and even medium-sized institutions will continue to represent a viable market suitable for FoHFs.

In the private investor world, successful FoHFs will need to provide much more transparency than they do today with a clearly articulated investment strategy. They also will need to specialize more by offering exposure to hedge fund portfolios that exhibit fundamentally differentiated characteristics that complement broad-based investment programs. Offering camouflaged equity beta is no longer adequate. Last but not least, any FoHF that wants to grow and still charges incentive fees needs to drop them fast.

## References

Dichev, I. D., & Yu, G. (2011). Higher Risk, Lower Returns: What Hedge Fund Investors Really Earn. *Journal of Financial Economics, 100*(2), 248−263.

Edwards, F., & Liew, J. (1999). Hedge Funds versus Managed Futures as Asset Classes. *Journal of Derivatives, 6*(3), 475−517.

Fung, W., & Hsieh, D. (2000). Performance Characteristics of Hedge Funds and Commodity Funds: Natural vs. Spurious Biases. *Journal of Financial and Quantitative Analysis, 35*(3), 291−307.

Fung, W., & Hsieh, D. (2009). Measuring Biases in Hedge Fund Performance Data: An Update. *Financial Analysts Journal, 65*(3), 1−3.

Ineichen, A. (2002). Advantages and Disadvantages of Investing in Fund of Hedge Funds. *Journal of Wealth Management, 4*(4), 47−62.

Jacobius, A. (2012). Top 200 Pension Funds Still Carrying Torch for Alternatives. *Pensions and Investments*. Special Report, February 6.

Lamm, R. M. (1999). Why Not 100% Hedge Funds? *The Journal of Investing, 8*(4), 87−97.

Lamm, R. M. (2002). How Good are Equity Long/Short Managers? *Alternative Investments Quarterly.* January (2), 17−25.

Lamm, R. M. (2003). Asymmetric Returns and Optimal Hedge Fund Portfolios. *The Journal of Alternative Investments, 6*(2), 9−21.

Lamm, R. M. (2004). Hedge Funds: Alpha Deliverers or Providers of Camouflaged Beta? *Alternative Investment Management Association Journal, 61*(April), 14−16.

Lamm, R. M. (2005). The Answer to your Dreams? Investment Implications of Positive Asymmetry in CTA Returns. *The Journal of Alternative Investments, 7*(4), 22−32.

Liang, B. (2000). Hedge Funds: The Living and the Dead. *The Journal of Financial and Quantitative Analysis, 35*(3), 309−326.

Morley, I. (2001). Alternative Investments: Perceptions and Reality. *The Journal of Alternative Investments, 3*(4), 62−67.

Swensen, D. (2000). *Pioneering Portfolio Management: An Unconventional Approach to Institutional Investing*. New York: The Free Press.

Xu, E. X., Liu, J., & Loviscek, A. L. (2011). An Examination of Hedge Fund Survivor Bias and Attrition Before and During the Global Financial Crisis. *Journal of Alternative Investments, 13*(4), 40−52.

Williamson, C. (2010). Institutions Were a Life Raft for Fund-of-Funds Managers. *Pensions and Investments*. Special Report, April 5.

Williamson, C. (2011). Institutions Drop Funds of Funds for Direct Hedge Fund Investments. *Pensions and Investments*. Special Report, September 19.

# SECTION 1
# Due Diligence and Risk Management

# CHAPTER 2

# Evaluating Trends in Funds of Hedge Funds Operational Due Diligence

Jason Scharfman
Corgentum Consulting, LLC, Jersey City, NJ, USA

**Chapter Outline**

2.1. Introduction  17
2.2. Increased Focus on Operational Due Diligence  18
2.3. Chapter Goals  18
2.4. What is Operational Risk?  19
2.5. The Different Types of Operational Risk  19
2.6. Operational Risk in a FoHFs Context  19
2.7. FoHFs Operational Due Diligence Frameworks  20
2.8. The Madoff Effect  21
2.9. Deep-Dive Operational Due Diligence  23
2.10. Broadening Scope Reviews and Declining Checklist Approaches  24
2.11. The Increasing Role of Operational Due Diligence Consultants  25
Conclusion  26
References  27

## 2.1. INTRODUCTION

Due diligence is a core component of the overall funds of hedge funds (FoHFs) investing process.

While asset allocation may set the tone for the types and percentages of different hedge fund strategies that a FoHFs portfolio should contain, due diligence performs the heavy lifting of actually locating and vetting managers that will be allocated capital. Without the due diligence function, FoHFs managers would have no mechanism by which to whittle down the universe of investable hedge funds. In this way, it is due diligence that drives the asset allocation process and not the other way around.

The types of due diligence performed by FoHFs can be generally classified into two broad categories: *investment due diligence* and *operational due diligence*.

Reconsidering Funds of Hedge Funds. http://dx.doi.org/10.1016/B978-0-12-401699-6.00002-2
Copyright © 2013 by Elsevier Inc. All rights reserved.

Investment due diligence, as its name implies, focuses on evaluating primarily the investment-related merits of a hedge fund manager. Framed in this context, operational due diligence, on the other hand, effectively functions as gap-filler due diligence. It can be thought of as focusing on evaluating the other types of risks associated with hedge fund management. Stated plainly, operational due diligence can be thought of as seeking to answer everything but, 'Will this hedge fund manager make money?'

## 2.2. INCREASED FOCUS ON OPERATIONAL DUE DILIGENCE

The operational risks associated with hedge fund investing have received much attention in recent years. Among the FoHFs community in particular, this increased attention has been focused around instances of actual hedge fund fraud. Such concerns have been heightened by the unfortunate revelations of actual frauds and Ponzi schemes orchestrated by individuals such as Bernard Madoff and Samuel Israel to name but two. Hedge fund operational risk has also received renewed attention over the past few years for reasons outside of fraud as well. FoHFs and their investors have increasingly realized that even honest hedge fund managers, with less than 'best practice' operational infrastructures, can also suffer substantial losses that can result in hedge fund failures. As a result, there has been a shifting paradigm with regard to the attention paid towards operational due diligence in the FoHFs industry.

## 2.3. CHAPTER GOALS

Before outlining the goals of this chapter, it is worth pausing for a moment to note two points related to hedge fund operational risk and due diligence that are not covered in this chapter, but are still pertinent to our discussion. (i) This chapter does not provide a detailed description of each different type of hedge fund operational risk. For example, there is no explanation of how a hedge fund back office may conduct a triangular reconciliation with brokers and an administrator. (ii) This chapter also does not provide a detailed description of techniques that may be employed to perform operational due diligence reviews. Examples of these types of techniques would be approaches to reviewing audited financial statements or guidance on conducting on-site hedge fund manager visits. Such tasks are better accomplished by other books dedicated to those subjects (Scharfman, 2008).

Instead, the goals of this chapter are to provide an overview of recent developments with regard to FoHFs approaches towards detecting, analyzing, evaluating, and monitoring operational risk in hedge funds. This analysis will include a discussion of trends in approaches taken by FoHFs in designing operational due diligence functions, as well as recent increases in the depth and scope of operational due diligence. In order to analyze trends, it is first useful to take a step back and briefly introduce the concept of operational risk and how its definition has evolved in a hedge fund context.

## 2.4. WHAT IS OPERATIONAL RISK?

If you ask different people in the hedge fund and FoHFs industry to define operational risk, you will likely receive a myriad of different responses. These responses would likely vary by each individual's role. For example, the Chief Financial Officer of a hedge fund may focus their description of operational risk around cash management and oversight. A Chief Operating Officer of a hedge fund may describe operational risk as being grounded in the traditional back office processes such as trade settlement and reconciliation. A FoHFs portfolio manager may consider operational risk to be a hedge fund manager being convicted of a crime. So who is correct? Well, each of these answers is correct; however, none of them is complete. In a hedge fund context, the term *operational risk* is typically utilized as an umbrella term that encompasses all of the types of risks referenced in our example above and much more. This is both the opportunity and challenge presented by those seeking to define operational risk in a hedge fund context.

## 2.5. THE DIFFERENT TYPES OF OPERATIONAL RISK

To start off a discussion of operational risk, we first have to determine what type of operational risk we are talking about. The concept of operational risk is not unique to investing. Indeed, outside of the investment industry, other fields ranging from manufacturing to medicine have their own definitions and approaches towards evaluating risk. Even within the field of investing, operational risk is thought of in different ways. For example, certain investment organizations such as banks may consider operational risk to be the risk of employees walking out of the office with company property or a water pipe bursting and damaging company property. In the banking industry, the concept of operational risk also plays a key role in the Basel Accords that seek to supervise and measure operational risk. While there may be some commonalities in the rudimentary elements of each of these kinds of operational risk across different disciplines, in the hedge fund context, operational risk takes on its own unique characteristics.

## 2.6. OPERATIONAL RISK IN A FoHFs CONTEXT

Several years ago in the FoHFs arena, if you mentioned the term operational risk, most people probably assumed you were just talking about a traditional firm's back office operations. This was likely due to the fact that the word *operational* in 'operational risk' comes from the concept of operations. This does not mean that FoHFs investors performing operational due diligence a few years ago were only limiting their operational due diligence reviews solely to hedge fund back office reviews, but this was the logical starting point of such reviews. This affiliation with the back office has been a historical stumbling block within the FoHFs industry for raising awareness of all of the different types of risks operational due diligence actually encompasses. As operational due diligence has become a topic of greater interest among investors, FoHFs have increasingly broadened their

| Table 2.1 | Common Major Hedge Fund Operational Risk Categories (Scharfman, 2012) | |
| --- | --- | --- |
| Trade flow analysis | Valuation policies and procedures | Business continuity and disaster recovery |
| Cash oversight, management and transfer controls | Quality and appropriateness of fund service providers | Information security |
| Compliance infrastructure | Custody procedures | Insurance coverage |
| Human capital | Regulatory risk | Tax practices |
| Documentation risk (i.e., legal documents, audited financial statements, International Swaps and Derivatives Association, etc.) | Counterparty risk | Board of directors |

scope of what they consider to be operational risk. Table 2.1 outlines some of the more common major categories of hedge fund operational risk which a FoHF would typically review.

As the reader can see by reviewing the items in Table 2.1, operational risk in a hedge fund context cuts a broad swath across the spectrum of what are sometimes referred to as purely non-investment related risks. Now that we have a basic understanding of the types of hedge fund operational risk, we can next provide an overview of common structures employed by FoHFs to detect and analyze these risks.

## 2.7. FoHFs OPERATIONAL DUE DILIGENCE FRAMEWORKS

Studies have shown that in recent years the FoHF industry has taken four primary approaches towards designing an operational due diligence function (Scharfman, 2009). These four frameworks are *dedicated, shared, modular,* and *hybrid* approaches. A key differentiator among each of these frameworks is who is actually performing the operational due diligence work.

For example, under a *dedicated framework*, a FoHF employs at least one employee whose full-time job is evaluating operational risk at hedge funds. This can be contrasted with a *shared framework* where fund of hedge fund employees, whose primary responsibilities are reviewing investment related risks, also take responsibility for evaluating operational risk. Under both the dedicated and shared frameworks, a FoHFs manager is still conducting some level of review of underlying hedge fund operational risk. The difference is that, as the name implies, under the dedicated review, there is an employee focused on performing due diligence on these risks, whereas under a shared framework no such dedicated resource exists.

One of the more interesting approaches FoHFs have taken in designing operational due diligence functions is the *modular approach*, which could be considered as an offshoot of the shared approach. A modular setup involves the use of so-called domain experts that are already employed in other functions at FoHFs. For example, a FoHF may employ individuals in the roles of General Counsel and Chief Financial Officer. A General Counsel and a Chief Financial Officer likely have an educational background or training in the areas of law and accounting, respectively. These are two very important skill sets for performing an operational due diligence review. As such, under a modular approach a FoHF may opt to leverage off of its existing employees' skill sets and involve them in the operational due diligence process. The reason that this can be considered as an offshoot of the shared module is because these so-called domain experts' primary job is not to perform operational due diligence, which is also one of the potential drawbacks of this approach. Another unique aspect of the modular approach is that in some instances these domain experts may be corralled by an operational generalist, who does not possess domain expertise in any one area, but, rather, coordinates the work of the domain experts.

Finally, under the final *hybrid approach,* a FoHFs organization designs an operational due diligence function that either encompasses or differs from any of the above approaches. A common example of the use of a hybrid approach would be a FoHF that employs a shared model, but also works with a third-party operational due diligence consultant to perform hedge fund operational risk reviews. Table 2.2 provides a summary of the four different commonly employed FoHFs operational due diligence frameworks.

## 2.8. THE MADOFF EFFECT

Now that we have provided an introduction to the concept of operational risk, as well as common frameworks employed by FoHFs during the operational due diligence process, we can next examine developing trends in the industry. First, we can analyze trends with regard to the actual operational risks reviewed by FoHFs.

Both in the pre-Madoff and post-Madoff era, there were certain operational risks that were considered best practice for a FoHF to include in its operational due diligence reviews. These core risks are risks that all FoHFs should review at a minimum when evaluating an underlying hedge fund. Without a review that touches on these minimum core areas, a FoHF is leaving itself, and its investors, uninformed and potentially exposed to major risk areas. Examples of these core minimum factors reviewed should include those outlined in Table 2.1 including audited financial statement risk, hedge fund service provider risk, and valuation risk.

That is not to say that FoHFs approaches towards operational due diligence have not changed over time. In particular, studies have shown the development of a so-called *Madoff Effect* that has influenced investors, including FoHFs approaches towards operational due diligence (Scharfman, 2010). This Madoff Effect effectively describes the phenomenon that occurs after a hedge fund fraud

**Table 2.2**   Common FoHFs Operational Due Diligence Frameworks

| Operational Due Diligence Framework | Framework Summary | Potential Drawbacks | Potential Advantages |
|---|---|---|---|
| Dedicated | At least one employee solely focused on operational due diligence. | Operational due diligence reviews may be limited by skill sets of dedicated operational analysts. An example of this would be a dedicated analyst who has an accounting background, but has no experience or training in reviewing fund legal documentation or compliance risks. | Dedicated focus of at least one individual on operational due diligence. |
| Shared | Employees focused on investment due diligence and also have responsibility for operational due diligence. | ■ No employees dedicated to focusing on operational risk.<br>■ Potential for conflict of interest among investment and operational concerns. | Analysts with investment backgrounds on managers may be keyed into certain risks that may require an operational analyst time to get up to speed on. |
| Modular | Use of already-employed domain experts (who have other jobs at FoHFs such as General Counsel or Chief Financial Officer) to assist with limited review of certain hedge fund operational risks within their areas of expertise. Modular approaches may also employ the use of an operational generalist. | ■ Domain experts are not dedicated to focusing on operational risk.<br>■ Domain experts are conducting limited-scope reviews (i.e., the General Counsel is only reviewing fund legal documentation). When this occurs risks that may only be uncovered by connecting the dots across multiple areas of a hedge fund's operational risk landscape may be lost.<br>■ If an operational generalist is utilized, they may not have enough expertise to oversee the work of domain experts. | Domain expertise may facilitate more comprehensive topic-focused reviews in certain risk areas. |
| Hybrid | Combination of any of the above three approaches or completely different approach. This approach typically employs the use of a third-party operational due diligence consultant. | Drawbacks noted in the above frameworks may be present in this case depending on the approach employed. | ■ Advantages noted above may be present depending on framework.<br>■ The use of a third-party operational due diligence consultant can provide additional expertise including more multidisciplinary operational due diligence reviews and enhanced familiarity with common hedge fund operational practices. |

is uncovered. Studies have shown that when a fraud such as the Bernard Madoff case is revealed, investors tend to focus their due diligence efforts on other funds around the causes of the most recent fraud. In particular, a study by Corgentum Consulting, an operational due diligence consulting firm and your author's employer, showed that, in the post-Madoff era, FoHFs substantially refocused their operational due diligence efforts in three of the key red flag areas prevalent in the Madoff fraud (Scharfman, 2010). Specifically, these increases came in the areas of cash controls and management, quality and length of relationship with service providers, and transparency and reporting.

## 2.9. DEEP-DIVE OPERATIONAL DUE DILIGENCE

One of the largest trends in operational due diligence in recent years has been an increase in the *depth* of reviews within each core operational risk category. To clarify what is meant by depth, let us consider the example of a review of a hedge fund's service provider.

A common hedge fund service provider is a fund administrator. Fund administrators can perform a number of functions including net asset value calculation and processing subscriptions and redemptions. Even several years ago, in the pre-Madoff era, it would be considered standard for a FoHF to contact a fund administrator to first confirm a hedge fund's ongoing relationship with the firm. Additionally, several years ago it would be standard to inquire what percentage of a hedge fund the administrator was to value independently of the hedge fund. Beyond this there were a number of other areas, including inquiries into the administrator's approaches for processing subscription and redemptions that a FoHF would likely go into.

Over the past few years, with regard to administrator reviews in particular, the number of questions asked during the operational due diligence process by FoHFs about different processes has significantly increased. This is what is meant by increasing depth and has resulted in what is commonly termed today to be the new standard: *deep-dive operational due diligence.*

For example, focusing on the area of administrator valuation, a deep-dive operational due diligence review would likely go into additional areas that may have only been covered tangentially before. Examples of the types of questions that may be asked during a deep-dive review include:

- What are the valuation sources employed by the fund administrator?
- What does the administrator view as acceptable discrepancies in valuation differences between itself and a hedge fund?
- Does the administrator receive copies of any internal valuation memoranda produced by the hedge fund? If yes, what does it do with this information?
- Is the administrator conducting any review of the models or inputs utilized for illiquid or hard to value positions?
- Have there been cases where the administrator has overruled a hedge fund's provided price? If so, when?

Under this deep-dive trend, over the past several years, more FoHFs have been delving into greater detail in operational risk areas they were already covering. This is not to say that in the pre-Madoff era certain FoHFs or other institutional investors were not already going to this increased level of detail. On the contrary, many large FoHFs shops were covering a lot of operational ground. Rather, the acknowledgement of this trend is to highlight the increase in deep-dive operational due diligence reviews throughout the funds of hedge funds industry.

## 2.10. BROADENING SCOPE REVIEWS AND DECLINING CHECKLIST APPROACHES

Truth be told, deep-dive operational due diligence reviews also encompass a related trend of not only increasing the depth of operational due diligence reviews, but increasing the scope of such reviews as well. To be clear, whereas the depth involves going deeper into certain hedge fund risk areas that are already being covered, the concept of *broadening scope reviews* refers to the concept of covering new operational risk areas that may have been previously neglected. This trend of expanding the types of operational risk covered by FoHFs is grounded in part in a shifting attitude towards modeling hedge fund failures due to operational risk-related reasons.

As suggested above, the modern incarnation of funds of hedge funds operational due diligence has its roots in evaluating traditional hedge fund back office procedures. The thinking went that if fraud or other operational problems were to occur, this would be the most convenient and potentially damaging area for it to occur in. This belief may still ring true today. For example, the ability of a hedge fund manager to falsely book trades or manipulate cash movements could be disastrous for investors. Piggybacking off of this focus around traditional back office procedures, certain FoHFs may have developed checklist-type approaches towards operational due diligence. The motivation behind such checklists was in part perhaps for FoHFs to avoid exposure to the exact reasons that led to certain historical hedge fund failures or frauds for operational reasons. In recent years, there has been a trend to move away from such checklist-type approaches.

FoHFs have increasingly acknowledged that checklist approaches to operational due diligence are generally self-limiting in nature. That is to say if something is not on the checklist it may not be covered. In addition to their scope-limiting nature, checklists are often targeting backward-looking risks. Increasingly, the FoHFs community is acknowledging that fraudulent activity cannot be predicted solely by utilizing models.

This is not to say that models and analysis of historical frauds cannot be useful to FoHFs. On the contrary, by analyzing historical fraud and using the results of this analysis to improve their operational due diligence process, a FoHF can reduce the likelihood of being exposed to the same type of fraud as previously occurred. Recent academic research in this regard has focused in part around analyzing historical data such as regulatory filings to provide indications of operational weaknesses (Brown *et al.*, 2009). The point is, however, that the facts and circumstances of each fraud are unique. While models may be predictive in nature they are not foolproof enough to be relied on with absolute certainty in this regard. As such, there has been an increasing trend of FoHFs broadening the scope of hedge fund operational risk reviews.

Returning to our example of FoHFs many years ago focusing primarily on back office-related risks, there are a myriad of other operational risk areas which could prove equally deadly for hedge fund investors outside of the back office. Consider, for example, the area of compliance. With new Securities and Exchange Commission registration requirements a hedge fund that does not have its act together can face serious fines or even fund closure if a fund is not in compliance. However, compliance is not an area that may have traditionally been considered in a back-office-focused review. Therefore, the FoHFs industry has broadened the scope of hedge fund operational risk reviews over time to include areas such as compliance. Other hedge fund risk areas that are today more commonly reviewed by FoHFs include information security risk and *meta risk*. *Meta risk* includes risk that may not fit nicely into a predefined hedge fund risk area, such as risks related to a hedge funds organizational culture (Scharfman, 2008). This trend of FoHFs increasingly covering a wider and wider area during operational due diligence has served to foster enhanced collaboration between the investment and operational due diligence processes as well.

## 2.11. THE INCREASING ROLE OF OPERATIONAL DUE DILIGENCE CONSULTANTS

Another trend in the evolution of FoHFs operational due diligence has been the increasing role of operational due diligence consulting firms. Operational due diligence specialist consulting firms are being used more frequently, to solely focus on performing operational due diligence reviews of fund managers including hedge funds. Due to the increasingly specialized and complex nature of hedge fund operational risks, more FoHFs have begun working with these specialized consultants. Another key factor driving this increased use of consultants is their independence. Leading operational due diligence consultants, such as Corgentum Consulting, are not compensated in any way by the hedge funds they review. Additionally, unlike traditional investment consultants, in order to maintain their independence operational due diligence consultants should not be compensated based on whether or not a FoHF invests with a manager.

The ways in which FoHFs have utilized operational due diligence consulting firms has changed over time. Today, operational due diligence consultants can work with a FoHFs manager in a number of different capacities. For newer FoHFs or managers that are re-evaluating their operational due diligence function, a consultant can assist in developing an operational due diligence program. Once a program has been established some FoHFs outsource the entire operational due diligence function to a consultant. Others may perform some operational due diligence work internally and outsource certain aspects of reviews to a consultant. Still other FoHFs may have an operational due diligence consultant perform deep-dive reviews on select hedge funds on a case-by-case basis. An example of this would be a FoHFs manager who does not maintain internal valuation expertise. This FoHFs manager may feel equipped to review the valuation policies of a highly liquid long–short hedge fund, but may feel less confident with more illiquid strategies, such as distressed funds. In this case, the FoHFs manager may engage a consultant to help perform a comprehensive review with respect to valuation for these more illiquid strategies.

Even FoHFs that follow a dedicated operational due diligence framework, and employ staff focused solely on conducting operational risk reviews, work with third-party operational due diligence consultants. In these cases, a consultant can serve as another pair of hands should there be too many hedge funds for the internal team to review. Additionally, internal operational due diligence employees at a FoHF may want a third-party opinion with regard to the operational risks of a particular hedge fund. Furthermore, as outlined above in certain cases, internal operational due diligence teams may have expertise in certain areas, but feel they could benefit from utilizing a consultant to bolster due diligence reviews in areas outside of their expertise.

When evaluating an operational due diligence consultant, FoHFs have become increasingly focused around the independence of the firm, experience in conducting reviews of different hedge fund strategies on a global basis, and most importantly the multidisciplinary nature of the consultants' operational due diligence methodology. Similar to the deficiencies of certain operational due diligence frameworks, certain operational risk consultants may attempt to overly focus on certain areas that they are comfortable reviewing, while ignoring other important risks. Increasingly, as FoHFs become more educated about the use of operational due diligence, consulting firms have embraced multidisciplinary reviews over limited scope reviews. This trend towards the increased use of consultants that use multidisciplinary reviews seems to mirror the above-referenced trends of deep-dive due diligence and broadening scope reviews.

## CONCLUSION

Operational due diligence is an evolving field. FoHFs have increasingly devoted more resources and time towards performing deep-dive operational due diligence reviews of hedge funds. These reviews have increased not only in the depth of items covered during the operational due diligence review process, but the scope of non-investment-related risks covered as well. Motivations for the increased attention paid to operational due diligence have included hedge fund frauds, as well as a growing acknowledgment that honest hedge funds can fail for operational reasons. To facilitate the growing interest in this area, FoHFs are increasingly utilizing operational due diligence firms to assist with the operational due diligence process. As operational due diligence reviews become increasingly more comprehensive, FoHFs must ensure that they have the appropriate level of resources and diversity of skills to conduct detail oriented, mutlidisciplinary operational risk reviews.

## References

Brown, S. J., Goetzmann, W. N., Liang, B., & Schwarz, C. (2009). Estimating Operational Risk for Hedge Funds: The ω-Score. *Financial Analysts Journal, 5*(1), 43–53.

Scharfman, J. (2008). *Hedge Fund Operational Due Diligence: Understanding the Risks.* Hoboken, NJ: Wiley Finance.

Scharfman, J. (2009). *Analyzing Operational Due Diligence Frameworks In Fund of Hedge Funds.* Jersey City, NJ: Corgentum Consulting.

Scharfman, J. (2010). *The Madoff Effect — An Analysis of Operational Due Diligence Trends.* Jersey City, NJ: Corgentum Consulting.

Scharfman, J. (2012). *Private Equity Operational Due Diligence: Tools to Evaluate Liquidity, Valuation and Documentation.* Hoboken, NJ: Wiley Finance.

CHAPTER 3

# The Limits of UCITS for Funds of Hedge Funds



**Jeannine Daniel*** **and François-Serge Lhabitant**†
*Kedge Capital (UK) Ltd, London, UK
†Kedge Capital Fund Management, St Helier, Jersey

**Chapter Outline**

**3.1. Introduction 29**
**3.2. The UCITS Industry 30**
**3.3. Challenges for a UCITS FoHFs Manager 31**
3.3.1. Gaining Exposure 31
3.3.2. Lack of Depth of the Investment Universe 33
3.3.3. Geographic Bias 36
3.3.4. Manager Self-Selection Bias 36
3.3.5. Size and Operational Efficiency 37
**3.4. Performances 38**
**Conclusion 39**
**Acknowledgments 40**
**References 40**
**Recommended Reading 40**

## 3.1. INTRODUCTION

'Undertakings for Collective Investments in Transferable Securities' (UCITS) are a set of European Directives targeting pooled investment schemes – otherwise known as investment funds. Their primary goals are: (i) to develop a single funds market across the European Union, (ii) to create a harmonized legal framework that facilitates the cross-border offering of UCITS funds across the European Union once they have been authorized in *one* member state, and (iii) to establish a minimum level of investor protection through strict investment limits and disclosure requirements for all UCITS funds.

Adopted in 1985, the original UCITS Directive has been implemented into national legislation in the various EU countries, but many considered it imperfect due to several investment limitations. As a result, it only enjoyed moderate success until its third revision in 2001. One of the key developments introduced by UCITS III was to broaden significantly the range of available financial

Reconsidering Funds of Hedge Funds. http://dx.doi.org/10.1016/B978-0-12-401699-6.00003-4

instruments. This allowed the creation of far more dynamic funds than was previously the case and immediately increased the appeal of UCITS funds. As a result, the UCITS label became a recognized brand in Europe for retail investors and the ideal vehicle for promoters wishing to distribute their funds widely.

An unintended consequence of this success was the sudden interest by alternative asset managers in UCITS structures — the so-called 'Newcits' products. Several hedge fund managers created a UCITS version of their flagship offshore fund. For them, UCITS represented an answer to investor demands for enhanced liquidity and transparency, and more importantly a potential avenue to aggressively market to a new type of untapped clientele, namely retail investors. Not surprisingly, UCITS FoHFs (Funds of Hedge Funds) followed, officially to 'add value' through diversification, manager selection, portfolio construction, better liquidity, and/or lower minimum investments.

The reality is that post-2008 many European and to a much lesser extent US and Asian FoHFs firms were faced with challenged business models on the heels of poor performances, unexpected liquidity restrictions (gates, side pockets), and questionable Madoff exposure. The UCITS solution was therefore seen as a lifeline, a possible way for them to reinvent themselves, and rebuild investor confidence via new regulated alternative investment vehicles, as well as being an avenue to increase scale into their typically heavy fixed cost business.

The fifth revision of the UCITS Directives is now under way but the general consensus is that UCITS have been so far a relative success story (e.g., see Cumming *et al.*, 2012). However, in this chapter, we evidence that this success primarily happened in the traditional long-only space. The development of a diversified and performing UCITS *alternative investment* offering has been seriously lagging, particularly at the FoHFs level, which is usually the entry point for less-sophisticated investors. We discuss the major reasons behind this phenomenon and, in particular, the limits facing a FoHFs manager in order to operate under the UCITS framework, the possible workaround solutions, and their potential issues. We also compare UCITS and non-UCITS FoHFs returns in order to quantify the performance gap resulting from the UCITS constraints. Our conclusion is that UCITS FoHFs have a long way to go before becoming attractive investments for unrestricted and sophisticated investors.

## 3.2. THE UCITS INDUSTRY

According to the European Fund and Asset Management Association (EFAMA), at the end of March 2012, there were 36 106 funds operating under the UCITS format and managing EUR 5961 billion (i.e., 71% of the total European investment fund market). However, most of these UCITS funds invest exclusively in *long-only* traditional asset classes such as equity (39%), bonds (20%), and money market investments (4%), or run *long-only* balanced mandates (26%) (see Figure 3.1). Within the 'Others' category, UCITS hedge funds regroup close to 1000 players managing approximately EUR180 billion. This is relatively small

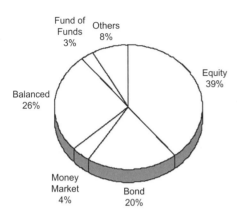
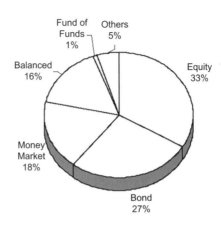

**FIGURE 3.1**
Breakdown of the UCITS industry by number of funds (left) and AUM (right).
*(Delbecque, 2012)*

by any standard — it only represents 3% of the UCITS universe and less than 2.5% of the total offshore hedge funds assets, according to UBS (2012).

The UCITS Fund of Mutual Funds plus FoHFs category counts 923 players managing approximately EUR59 billion of assets (i.e., approximately 1% of the total UCITS assets). This group is in severe contraction, with a 29.7% decline of the number of FoHFs and a 41% decline of their assets under management (AUM) compared to December 2010. However, we need to keep in mind that the label includes funds of long-only funds as well as FoHFs, the topic of interest in this chapter.

The UCITS FoHFs subcategory counts 100 vehicles managing approximately EUR4 billion (US$5 billion) of assets at the end of Q1 2012. This represents merely 0.1% of the entire UCITS universe and only a few percent of the overall FoHFs business mix measured by assets. More importantly, the majority of the players in this category have less than US$100 million of AUM, which means their long-term viability is questionable if they cannot grow. In fact, 11 UCITS FoHFs had to shut down in 2011, some within only 1 year of launch, due to a lack of investor interest and poor performance. It therefore seems that the UCITS success so far has mostly been achieved in the traditional asset space, but not really in the alternative investment universe.

## 3.3. CHALLENGES FOR A UCITS FoHFs MANAGER

Establishing a FoHF under the UCITS format is feasible, but as difficult as hammering square pegs into round holes. In particular, all UCITS funds are subject to mandatory eligible asset rules, investment restrictions, and concentration limits. Not surprisingly, these will considerably limit the ability to create a robust FoHFs portfolio.

### 3.3.1. Gaining Exposure

It is essential to remember that the UCITS framework was originally created to host long-only retail mutual funds following relatively straightforward investment strategies. As a result, it considerably restricts the nature of the assets that are eligible for investment by UCITS funds. The initial UCITS Directive only allowed investments in *transferable securities* listed on a stock exchange, but failed to provide a clear definition. The UCITS III Directive broadened the investment universe to include money market instruments, cash deposits with credit institutions, financial derivatives that meet certain criteria, and shares of other UCITS funds. Not surprisingly, shares of unregulated offshore hedge funds are not considered as eligible assets and UCITS FoHFs can only invest up to a maximum of 10% of their total net assets in such unregulated investments.[1] UCITS FoHFs managers must therefore gain most of their hedge fund exposure through alternative ways. In the following, we will detail some of the most common approaches.

*UCITS-square.* A first plain-vanilla solution consists in limiting the investment universe to UCITS hedge funds, as they are considered as eligible assets and therefore not subject to any aggregate cap. While relatively straightforward, this solution will essentially introduce some limits in terms of available strategies, as discussed hereafter.

*Managed account platforms.* Recently, a number of sell-side intermediaries have launched managed account platforms and are trying to convince hedge fund managers to open an account with them. Some of their key marketing arguments to investors are the increased transparency through mandated reporting and risk measurement processes. A second plain-vanilla solution for creating a UCITS FoHF consists in investing exclusively through managed accounts, which themselves invest exclusively in eligible assets. In such a case, it is possible to consolidate all the positions at the UCITS FoHFs level (full transparency) and ensure compliance with all the UCITS regulatory requirements such as diversification, no excessive leverage, and no physical short positions. While theoretically appealing, this solution is in practice much more restrictive than UCITS-square as the number of hedge fund managers operating on managed account platforms is extremely limited.

*Exposure through structured products.* Structured products that meet the 'transferable securities' criteria are eligible assets, even if they are linked to assets that are themselves ineligible under the UCITS Directive. UCITS FoHFs may therefore use structured products such as a series of delta one notes or structured swaps to gain *indirect* exposure to a portfolio of offshore hedge funds. However, note that the UCITS diversification guidelines require a minimum of 16 different issuers under the 5/10/40 rule and a UCITS FoHF cannot hold more than 10% of the total debt issued by any single issuer. This therefore rules out the solution of having all delta notes issued from a single segregated entity.

*Exposure through index derivatives.* Under certain conditions, index derivatives may be considered as eligible assets, even if the assets underlying the index are

---

[1] This 10% ratio has since been renamed the 'trash ratio,' as it allows UCITS FoHFs to invest in nearly anything.

themselves non-eligible under the UCITS Directive. As a result, it is possible for a FoHF to gain *indirect exposure* to offshore hedge funds by sponsoring the creation of a hedge fund index and then buying a derivative contract — typically a total return swap — on that index.

It is now well known that most hedge fund indices are of poor quality and subject to several biases (e.g., see Lhabitant, 2008). Regulators have therefore imposed a series of minimum requirements for financial indices underlying a financial derivative instrument to be acceptable. In particular, the index:

- Must represent an adequate benchmark for the market to which it refers.
- Must be published in an appropriate manner, for instance on the Internet. The index construction rules should also be adequately described and easily available.
- Must be independently managed from the management of the UCITS.
- Needs to be sufficiently diversified, with no index constituent representing more than 20% of the NAV.
- Cannot be backfilled.

Not surprisingly, a survey conducted by KdK Asset Management in 2009 (Keime and de Koning, 2009) evidenced that most investors preferred UCITS FoHFs with direct investments in eligible assets rather than structured product solutions. The latter were perceived as generating additional structuring costs and increasing counterparty risk. Their future regulatory treatment was also questionable, as one could argue that some of them essentially circumvented the spirit of the UCITS Directive.

## 3.3.2. Lack of Depth of the Investment Universe

One of the often-quoted advantages of pooled investment vehicles over direct allocations is their superior diversification potential. In theory, the same logic applies to FoHFs: their larger size should allow them to gain exposure to more funds and strategies than smaller investors would normally be able to achieve, therefore resulting in a better diversification. Unfortunately, in practice, this principle is severely challenged in the UCITS space due to some stringent investment restrictions that ultimately limit the set of available hedge fund strategies. As a practical matter, the most problematic ones are centered on liquidity requirements, minimum diversification rules, and leverage limits.

*Liquidity.* A key principle of the UCITS Directive is to ensure high levels of liquidity, even during periods of market stress. UCITS hedge funds must therefore provide a net asset value (NAV) as well as the possibility to redeem at this NAV at least twice a month. Redemption proceeds must be paid in full within 14 days — a sharp contrast versus the offshore hedge fund practice of holding off a certain percentage of redemption proceeds until the audit is completed. Gates can only be applied under exceptional circumstances and must be limited to 10% per redemption date, thus a maximum 20% gate per month. Moreover, the marginal ability for UCITS funds to invest in OTC derivatives is limited as such instruments must be valued at short notice in order to provide a NAV.

*Minimum diversification.* UCITS funds must be properly diversified and are therefore subject to a series of diversification limits, but the most famous one is the 5/10/40 rule, which can be summarized as follows: no single holding can represent over 10% of the UCITS NAV and the total number of holdings exceeding 5% cannot add up to more than 40%.

*Leverage.* This hallmark of traditional offshore hedge funds is severely limited in the UCITS world. In practice, UCITS hedge funds must limit their leverage to 100% of NAV (i.e., their maximum gross exposure can be 200%) and short-term borrowings are limited to 10% of NAV.[2] Moreover, the maximum over-the-counter derivative counterparty exposure is limited to 10% of NAV and the assumption of leverage through financial derivatives is strictly controlled.

For some hedge fund strategies, these rules should not be a matter of concern. For instance, providing their gross exposure does not exceed 200%, most long/short equity strategies can easily be migrated from an offshore fund to a UCITS format with little change in investment practices apart from taking short exposures through equity swaps rather than cash equities. The use of synthetic short selling entails additional operational and control activities such as active collateral management and counterparty risk monitoring, but should not dramatically affect the investment strategy. Similarly, managed futures and global macro can also be migrated from an offshore fund to a UCITS format as they are highly liquid and involve primarily trading listed derivatives, which are eligible assets. A few adjustments are needed, such as replacing commodity derivatives with physical delivery by derivatives on commodity indices or structured products, but here again the investment strategy may remain the same. As a result, it is therefore not surprising to observe that the primary strategies in the UCITS hedge fund universe are long/short equity (25.79%), managed futures (11.65%), and global macro (11.65%) (see Figure 3.2) (Per-Trac, 2012).

The situation is quite different for other hedge fund strategies, which often must be severely adapted in order to fit into a UCITS format. Let us mention a few examples:

- Equity strategies targeting less liquid equities such as micro caps or that need a longer time horizon to realize their profits such as deep-value investing will have a difficult time complying with the liquidity requirements.
- Equity market neutral strategies such as statistical arbitrage do require higher levels of leverage than permitted under the UCITS framework to deliver a sufficient alpha.

---

[2]Note that a UCITS hedge fund may ask to be considered as 'sophisticated.' This attribute will allow for more latitude in definition of leverage within a value at risk framework.

**FIGURE 3.2**
Split of the UCITS hedge fund universe by investment strategy.
*(PerTrac, 2012)*

- Event-driven strategies deal with eligible assets, but their relatively high concentration in, for example, merger arbitrage positions will often violate the UCITS diversification requirements.
- Distressed securities strategies will not be eligible due to the illiquid nature of their underlying securities.
- Credit strategies will be unable to trade assets such as mortgages (residential mortgage-backed securities, commercial mortgage-backed securities) and bank loans, which are not securities.
- Convertible arbitrage strategies will usually have to focus on the most liquid part of the convertible market, where there are fewer opportunities and must avoid venturing into inefficiently priced convertibles due to market illiquidity.
- Fixed-income arbitrage strategies often run a very high level of leverage, which can often result in their positions representing a significant percentage of their NAV. In addition, it is difficult for them to build synthetic short exposure to non equity instruments.
- Emerging market debt and equity securities may not be liquid enough to be eligible, which might explain why they appear to be the least-represented strategy in Figure 3.2 despite strong investor demand.

UCITS FoHFs managers trying to build a diversified portfolio in terms of strategies are directly affected by these observations. (i) They do not have access to the full array of offshore hedge fund strategies. They must concentrate on long/short equity and possibly scaled-down versions of a few other strategies. (ii) It is not possible for them to be a liquidity provider. In a traditional FoHF, the Portfolio Manager of a fund will occasionally move down the liquidity spectrum (by allocating to a less liquid hedge fund) to capture excess returns that would compensate the investor for the temporary lack of liquidity in their positions. (iii) It is difficult for them to build and adapt their strategy allocation over time, as there is not much flexibility to increase the risk of the fund of fund at certain junctures, e.g., to participate in more leveraged strategies in a boom when credit is tightening, and equities are in a upward trajectory. As a result, a UCITS FoHF can easily end up as a 'diluted' product, with significant negative tracking error versus the performances of the original strategies, and expenses per unit of active risk are generally higher than in a non-UCITS FoHF.

### 3.3.3. Geographic Bias

The European origin of the UCITS concept has led to a regional bias on a look-through basis. Simply stated, UCITS hedge funds and as a result UCITS FoHFs are very European-centric. For instance, 70% of UCITS hedge funds use the EUR as their base currency, which does not help in the current European confidence crisis. The majority of their investments are biased towards European stocks and bonds, and even the teams are local, with France, the United Kingdom, Germany, Switzerland, and Luxembourg accounting for 78% of all management companies' location and 88% of assets. This bias will naturally extend to UCITS FoHFs and likely dramatically reduce their investment universe outside of the Euro zone.

### 3.3.4. Manager Self-Selection Bias

Another important bias for FoHFs managers is the self-selection bias (i.e., the distortion caused when the set of potential investments chooses itself). Simply stated, offshore hedge funds are private structures. There is no legal requirement for their managers to create a UCITS version of their fund for the general public and comply with all the associated restrictions. If they do, it is on a completely voluntary basis, which will be primarily driven by incentives.

For younger and less experienced managers, becoming UCITS-compliant might sound like an attractive proposition — they essentially give away some portfolio management flexibility in exchange for potentially more AUM. However, for established and successful offshore hedge fund managers with a solid long-term track record, the incentives are quite different. (i) They typically already have a stable long-term and loyal investor base willing to pay the traditional 2% and 20% fees, and these fees do not need to be shared with platforms and distributors. (ii) For the latter there is a preconceived notion or preference towards 'quality clients' rather than potentially retail orientated and hot money assets associated with UCITS, which have a reputation of being potentially more short term in nature.[3] (iii) Many managers are not even considering establishing a UCITS version of their fund simply because part of their strategy may not be replicable under the UCITS format.

---

[3]Note that the same argument could also apply at the FoHFs level and the 'quality' of companies looking to set up a UCITS multimanager product in the first place.

This inevitably leads to a situation whereby potentially only the younger and/or poorer quality hedge funds are incentivized to set up UCITS vehicles. The 'quality' of UCITS funds therefore available for a UCITS FoHF is suboptimal. There are in fact a number of practical examples whereby well-established, performing hedge fund managers have cloned their flagship product to one in a UCITS format (setting aside a limited amount of capacity), only to later close it — upon the realization that capacity was more constrained and that they could redeploy the assets to more attractive non-UCITS-compliant investors paying full fees.

### 3.3.5. Size and Operational Efficiency

UCITS hedge funds are characterized by a high number of small- or medium-sized structures. As an illustration, the average UCITS hedge fund size in 2012 is only EUR167 million (US$200 million), down from EUR300 million (US$400 million) in 2008. Moreover, this number is skewed by the asset base of a few large established players. In practice, 75% of UCITS hedge funds are still managing less than US$100 million — not much when one considers the swath of onerous additional compliance requirements required by UCITS. FoHFs managers allocating to such small hedge funds are likely to be exposed to some serious business risk and susceptible to a misallocation of resources. For example, the validating of the investment and operational due diligence thesis of a UCITS HF by a FoHFs manager requires time and resources. This may be ill spent if a manager closes a few months later in a case whereby an insufficient asset level relative to setup costs, make a product untenable.

A similar observation applies to a UCITS FoHF. According to UBS (2012), the median UCITS FoHF size was only EUR28 million. For sophisticated investors, this is often a deal breaker. They typically have investment policies that limit their allocation to a fund to a certain percentage of its assets, generally 5% or 10%. Smaller UCITS FoHFs will therefore not attract large investments, and they will remain small (Figure 3.3).

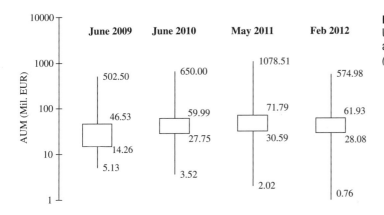

**FIGURE 3.3**
UCITS FoHFs — fund size statistics (largest, average, median, and smallest).
*(Data from UBS AG).*

## 3.4. PERFORMANCES

To date, UCITS FoHF performance appears to have been a scenario of 'over promised, under delivered.' As an illustration, Figure 3.4 shows the evolution of a US$100 investment in the UCITS Alternative Index Fund of Funds, which tracks the performance of UCITS FoHFs on a broad basis, versus the UCITS Alternative Index Global, which tracks the performance of UCITS hedge funds also on a broad basis. In both cases, constituents are equally weighted in the index and the starting date is January 2008.

The performance of both indices is clearly disappointing. Since inception, the UCITS FoHF index has achieved a total performance of −16.9% or, equivalently, an average annualized performance of −4.1% and an annualized volatility of 3.80%. As a reminder, the stated investment objectives of UCITS FoHFs generally include performance targets of 5−7% *per annum* with limited volatility (i.e., less than 5%). Since inception, the UCITS hedge fund index has achieved a total performance of −0.72% or, equivalently, an average annualized performance of −0.16% and an annualized volatility of 4.0%.

Historically, UCITS FoHFs have therefore underperformed UCITS hedge funds every single year since 2008 and almost 64% of the time on a month-by-month basis. Of course, one could argue UCITS FoHFs are adding an extra layer of fees, but the size of the gap between them and the UCITS hedge fund performances seems to suggest that there is consistent value destruction. On the volatility side, there seems to be no reduction of the volatility when moving from the average UCITS hedge fund to the average UCITS FoHF. This may be due to the relatively limited set of investment strategies we discussed previously.

Note that UCITS FoHFs have also underperformed offshore hedge fund indices (Table 3.1 and Figure 3.5).

**FIGURE 3.4**
Evolution of a US$100 investment in the UCITS Alternative Index Fund of Funds versus the UCITS Alternative Index Global.
(*Data from www.ucits-alternative. com*).

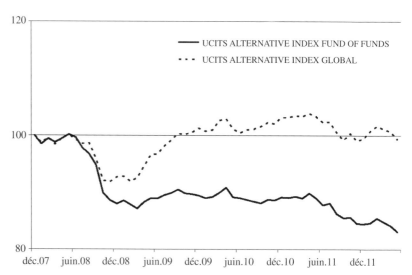

| Table 3.1 | | Table of Monthly Returns (%) and Key Statistics (%) of the UCITS Alternative Index Fund of Funds versus the UCITS Alternative Index Global | | | | | | | | | | |
|---|---|---|---|---|---|---|---|---|---|---|---|---|

| | Jan | Feb | Mar | Apr | May | Jun | Jul | Aug | Sep | Oct | Nov | Dec | Year-to-Date |
|---|---|---|---|---|---|---|---|---|---|---|---|---|---|
| *UCITS Alternative Index Fund of Funds* | | | | | | | | | | | | | |
| 2012 | 0.18 | 0.99 | −0.80 | −0.75 | −1.25 | | | | | | | | −1.64 |
| 2011 | −0.10 | 0.26 | −0.36 | 1.00 | −0.96 | −1.35 | 0.37 | −2.14 | −0.84 | 0.10 | −1.27 | −0.05 | −5.25 |
| 2010 | −0.50 | 0.25 | 0.80 | 1.02 | −1.87 | −0.16 | −0.35 | −0.35 | −0.31 | 0.71 | −0.14 | 0.60 | −0.33 |
| 2009 | 0.63 | −0.79 | −0.80 | 1.31 | 0.77 | −0.04 | 0.66 | 0.41 | 0.68 | −0.73 | −0.16 | −0.28 | 1.64 |
| 2008 | −1.52 | 0.98 | −0.66 | 0.66 | 0.73 | −0.52 | −1.87 | −1.08 | −1.98 | −5.16 | −1.46 | −0.69 | −12.01 |
| *UCITS Alternative Index Global* | | | | | | | | | | | | | |
| 2012 | 1.37 | 0.87 | −0.49 | −0.47 | −1.36 | | | | | | | | −0.10 |
| 2011 | 0.01 | 0.31 | −0.18 | 0.53 | −0.50 | −1.00 | 0.08 | −1.81 | −1.33 | 1.18 | −1.30 | 0.35 | −3.64 |
| 2010 | −0.52 | 0.24 | 1.64 | 0.27 | −1.71 | −0.69 | 0.53 | 0.14 | 0.42 | 0.71 | −0.21 | 1.07 | 1.86 |
| 2009 | 0.11 | −0.92 | 0.66 | 2.14 | 2.19 | 0.17 | 1.45 | 1.02 | 1.19 | −0.14 | 0.32 | 0.75 | 9.27 |
| 2008 | −1.35 | 0.93 | −1.14 | 1.06 | 0.66 | −0.88 | −0.71 | 0.11 | −2.81 | −3.96 | −0.28 | 0.91 | −7.35 |

Data from www.ucits-alternative.com.

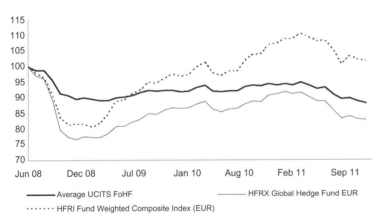

**FIGURE 3.5**
Average UCITS FoHFs compared to HFRI and HFRX hedge funds.
*(UBS, 2012)*

Legend: —— Average UCITS FoHF   —— HFRX Global Hedge Fund EUR   ······ HFRI Fund Weighted Composite Index (EUR)

## CONCLUSION

UCITS FoHFs have proliferated in the past few years, despite the lack of diversity and underlying funds. However, at a time when capital raising is proving tough, they still have to prove they are truly attractive *for investors*. Better liquidity terms, tougher investment restrictions, more regulation, and additional transparency may come at a cost − and this cost is ultimately paid in forgone performance by investors. They may also incur additional risks, such as reduced diversification, the complexity of structured solutions, and additional counterparty risks. As a result, critics have long held that UCITS FoHFs were not always suitable for retail investors and they might be proven right. So far, the growth of assets invested in UCITS FoHFs has been relatively limited, and most of the new products are still working hard to grow and reach their critical mass. Investors seem to remain skeptical about the ability of these new products to deliver the same old level of 'alpha.' All that glitters is not gold.

## Acknowledgments

The views expressed in this chapter are exclusively those of the authors and do not necessarily represent the views of, and should not be attributed to, the various entities they are or have been affiliated with.

## References

Cumming, D., Imad Eddine, G., & Schwienbacher, A. (2012). Harmonized Regulatory Standards, International Distribution of Investment Funds and the Recent Financial Crisis. *European Journal of Finance, 18*(3-4), 261–292.

Delbecque, B. (2012). Trends in the European Investment Fund Industry in the First Quarter of 2012. *EFAMA Quarterly Statistical Release, 49*.

Keime, P. & de Koning, H. (2009). *UCITS FoHFs Survey*. KdK Asset Management, London.

Lhabitant, F. (2008). Hedge Fund Indices for European Retail Investors: An Oxymoron. *The Journal of Financial Transformation, 23*(10), 145–153.

PerTrac (2012). *The Coming of Age of Alternative UCITS Funds*. New York: Working Paper, PerTrac.

UBS (2012). *UCITS Funds of Hedge Funds — Current State of Affairs and Near Term Outlook*. London: UBS.

## Recommended Reading

Advent Software (2010). *UCITS Come to the Fore: Opportunities and Challenges for the Funds Industry*. London: Working Paper.

De Koning, H. (2010). *UCITS: Latest Hype or Investor Panacea? The Hedge Fund Journal, Commentary Section*. June Edition. Available at http://www.thehedgefundjournal.com/node/6555.

Hedge Fund Intelligence (2012). *Global Hedge Fund Assets Edge Up Slightly*. London: Working Paper.

Hedge Fund Research (2012). *Global Hedge Fund Industry Report Asian Hedge Fund Industry Report — First Quarter 2012* (pp. 11–20). Available at www.HedgeFundResearch.com.

# CHAPTER 4

# Due Diligence: Lessons from the Global Financial Crisis for Funds of Hedge Funds with Particular Emphasis on the Asia–Pacific Region

**David Edmund Allen, Staley Roy Alford Pearce, and Robert John Powell**
Edith Cowan University, School of Accounting, Finance and Economics,
Joondalup, Western Australia, Australia

## 4.1. INTRODUCTION

It was the US Securities Act of 1933 that brought the term due diligence into popular usage, with its recognition therein as an effective defense by a broker-dealer accused of inadequate disclosure when shares in a company were being offered for sale. If the broker could show that it had exercised due diligence in investigating the company, it would not be liable for non-disclosure. 'Diligence' connotes industriousness, conscientiousness, honesty, and hard work, and the thinking appears to be that at least some quantum (the 'due' level) of these must be in evidence if the duty is to be discharged. If one is held not to have displayed due diligence, the implication is that the investigation has been less than thorough.

From these beginnings the term has spread to many and varied contexts, one of which remains any setting in which an investment manager, charged with the responsibility of investing other people's money, is required to investigate and then select amongst a number of alternative investments — with ongoing

Reconsidering Funds of Hedge Funds. http://dx.doi.org/10.1016/B978-0-12-401699-6.00004-6

monitoring and re-evaluation to follow. Exactly how the due diligence responsibility is to be discharged depends upon the context: often a regulatory regime will be in effect that prescribes the very practices and procedures that ensure satisfaction of the responsibility or they may be dictated by an industry code of practice. The observation of due diligence principles should result in mitigation of avoidable investment risk.

This chapter examines due diligence in a funds of hedge funds (FoHFs) context. Particular emphasis is placed on the Asia–Pacific region. This region is home to approximately 60% of the world's population. Key FoHFs markets include China, Japan, Australia, Hong, and Singapore. While the Asia–Pacific hedge fund industry is small by global standards, it has experienced substantial growth as well as a stronger and more rapid recovery from Global Financial Crisis (GFC) events than most leading hedge fund markets. We commence by discussing hedge fund due diligence generally, followed by general due diligence of FoHFs. Thereafter, we turn to an examination of performance and due diligence before, during, and after the GFC. We make recommendations on due diligence in a post-GFC environment, followed by conclusions.

## 4.2. DUE DILIGENCE WHEN INVESTING IN A HEDGE FUND

The investment manager who contemplates investing in a hedge fund may face a more demanding due diligence requirement than one who considers only more orthodox investments. What complicates the task is the very wide variety of investment strategies in which hedge funds may be engaged. Famously, they are portrayed as 'absolute return' entities, which, if the aspiration is realized, will produce positive returns in all market conditions. They are not confined to 'long' positions in any asset market, but may take 'short' positions as well; they may use leverage to boost asset holdings; derivatives may be bought or sold; the number of individual assets held may be large; and they may be invested in any of a wide range of asset types, from subprime mortgages to toll roads; many assets may be hard to value, since they are not traded and so have no market price. In general, there is a lack of clarity about just what an individual hedge fund is doing. Brown and Goetzmann (1997) maintain that hedge funds, like mutual funds, can often 'game' their strategy by choosing a classification popular at the time, making it essential for due diligence and analysis to be performed prior to investment.

What is at once evident is the potential for a hedge fund to construct a strategy that aggregates numerous different risks and thereby produces an investment vehicle laden with risk. For an investment manager considering exposing their flock of investors to such a vehicle, due diligence becomes supremely important. It is difficult to lay down a set of principles and procedures that will cover all these multifarious activities and that, if followed, will ensure discharge of the due diligence responsibility. Nonetheless, some have tried to enumerate the matters that should be investigated. AIMA (Alternative Investment Management

Association, 2009; Roodt, 2010) has listed, *inter alia*, the following factors for consideration in assessing and selecting among hedge funds: understanding the strategy/strategies followed by the fund, understanding the risks inherent in the strategies, identifying markets covered and instruments used recognizing and recording the use of leverage, and tracking the record of key investment staff.

## 4.3. INVESTMENT IN A FoHF and Due Diligence

A FoHF invests in a number of hedge funds — anywhere from 10—100, with the average number of underlying hedge funds being 30—40. Obviously a major attraction of such a ready-made portfolio of hedge funds is the diversification that it brings among different multistrategy funds. The question may arise, why an investment manager would choose to invest in a FoHF rather than creating their own hedge funds portfolio. To this there are two answers. (i) Those who construct FoHFs would claim to have a level of expertise that others lack. This point is particularly persuasive if it is borne in mind that the sheer number of hedge funds available for investment is in excess of 7 500 (see Section 4.4). FoHFs managers may cut through a good deal of the complexity facing investors by selecting among this vast number. These attractions may well count most with first-time hedge fund investors. (ii) The minimum possible size of investment in an individual hedge fund may put construction of one's own hedge fund portfolio beyond the means of many an investor/investment entity, whereas the minimum investment in FoHFs may be more affordable. Moreover, sometimes the only way to access a particular hedge fund is via a FoHF. These possible benefits of investment in FoHFs come at a significant cost, however: as well as the fees levied by the managers of the individual constituent hedge funds, there are those of the FoHFs managers to be paid.

We have seen that the very nature of a hedge fund makes due diligence on the part of an investment manager peculiarly important. How much more important, then, is due diligence when investment in a FoHF is contemplated! Each and every constituent fund has the potential to pursue a number of inherently risky strategies, so that the total risk of the FoHF may assume massive proportions. How much correlation there is between different constituent funds or between the investments held by those funds is probably impossible to estimate, but the fact that the whole hedge fund sector has usually risen or fallen in unison must cast doubt on claims of a lack of correlation.

We have seen that a wide variety and large number of assets and strategies may be encompassed in a single hedge fund. Both of these will mushroom in a FoHF and anybody contemplating investing in a FoHFs must recognize that the number of underlying or ultimate investments is likely to be huge. The major difficulty that confronts an investor in a FoHF, then, is that the sheer number of investments to be analyzed and monitored may well be daunting. There is the same need as in the case of investment in a single hedge fund to understand the fund's strategy/strategies and the attendant risks, the markets and instruments in which it invests, and its use of leverage, but this is multiplied by the number of hedge funds in FoHFs. These features of FoHFs imply that the due diligence process simply cannot be at the same level of detail as is possible with more orthodox investments. After all, even in the case of an investment manager who purchases a position in a conventional equity mutual fund, for example, it is questionable whether due diligence should extend to including examination of each underlying equity investment (such as capital structure, earnings and dividend history, ownership structure, and liquidity). After all, the share-selection expertise of the management of the mutual fund has implicitly been recognized already.

The important point here, however, is that in the case of a FoHF, there are so many underlying individual investments that detailed tracking of each is extremely complex, but nonetheless, extremely important. Stulz (2007) found investing in FoHFs is a way of sharing due diligence costs with other investors. Brown *et al.* (2008) found effective due diligence is a source of hedge fund alpha and that large FoHFs can absorb the fixed costs associated with due diligence. Gregoriou and Rouah (2003) found that emphasis of larger funds on due diligence and regular monitoring of their managers has allowed them to survive much longer than smaller ones.

## 4.4. ASIA–PACIFIC HEDGE FUND AND FoHFs GROWTH AND PERFORMANCE

The figures in this section are obtained from HFR (Hedge Fund Research, 2012). The worldwide hedge fund industry consists of more than 7 500 funds with US$2.1 trillion in assets. Asia's share of this is approximately 4% by value and 14% by number, having smaller size funds than the United States and Europe. Management firm location for Asian hedge funds is predominantly China (53%), which includes Hong Kong, followed by Singapore (17%), Australia (9%), Japan (7%), and India (2%), with the rest spread among other Asian countries. Over the period from the start of 2003 to end 2011, Asian hedge funds grew 210% by number and 163% by value. Year-by-year growth for Asian hedge funds as compared to the total global industry is shown in Table 4.1. It can be seen that the growth in the number of Asian funds has outpaced the global industry, whereas the opposite is true of fund values.

Figure 4.1 summarizes the performance in the Asia–Pacific region from the start of 2005 to the end of 2011.

Table 4.1 and Figure 4.1 show total hedge funds, while Table 4.2 and Figure 4.2 display FoHFs only. The total hedge fund figures are obtained from the HFRX Asia with Japan index from Datastream. The FoHFs figures are obtained from our own index constructed using figures obtained from the individual performance reports on the websites of 16 of the largest FoHFs in the Asia–Pacific region.

In line with global equity and hedge fund markets, the pre-GFC period was one of strong growth in the Asia–Pacific region, followed by a sharp fall during the

| Table 4.1 | Hedge Fund Growth | | | |
|---|---|---|---|---|
| | Hedge Fund Asset Growth (%) | | Hedge Funds Number Growth (%) | |
| | Asia | Global | Asia | Global |
| 2003 | 31.08 | 31.09 | 23.28 | 10.16 |
| 2004 | 23.92 | 18.61 | 24.01 | 14.16 |
| 2005 | 19.66 | 13.65 | 31.20 | 15.31 |
| 2006 | 32.97 | 32.49 | 16.19 | 8.61 |
| 2007 | 37.77 | 27.58 | 36.50 | 5.43 |
| 2008 | −35.89 | −24.69 | −7.23 | −10.34 |
| 2009 | 6.90 | 13.72 | 1.17 | 0.56 |
| 2010 | 9.30 | 19.82 | 0.77 | 4.61 |
| 2011 | −1.56 | 4.73 | 3.34 | 4.47 |
| Total | 162.60 | 221.01 | 210.92 | 63.59 |

Data from Hedge Fund Research (2012).

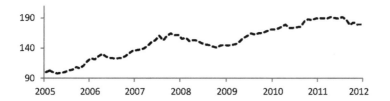

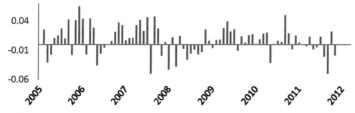

**FIGURE 4.1**
Asia–Pacific hedge fund performance January 2005–December 2011: (top) index and (bottom) returns.

| Table 4.2 | Asia–Pacific FoHFs Performance | |
|---|---|---|
| **Year Ended** | **FoHF Index** | **FoHFs Returns (%)** |
| 2005 | 111 | 16.1 |
| 2006 | 120 | 19.0 |
| 2007 | 127 | −0.8 |
| 2008 | 104 | −34.1 |
| 2009 | 114 | 28.8 |
| 2010 | 121 | 6.4 |
| 2011 | 116 | −0.8 |

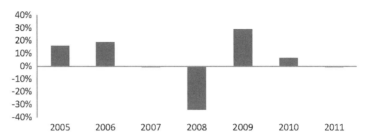

**FIGURE 4.2**
Asia–Pacific FoHFs returns.

GFC. Of note is the strong recovery post-GFC, with both hedge funds and FoHFs recovering their GFC return losses. Global hedge funds showed total returns growth for the 7-year period to 2011 of close to 40% (Asia–Pacific 90%). As a benchmark, the S&P 500 (per figures on Datastream) only achieved a total 7-year return of approximately 20%. These trends are elaborated on in the ensuing sections.

## 4.5. BEFORE THE GFC

During the early and mid 2000s hedge funds were finding a strong following among institutions as well as wealthy individuals. Growth in FoHFs was greatly surpassing that of single hedge funds. Global FoHFs as a percentage of total funds grew from 17% in 2002 to 36% in 2008 (Hedge Fund Research, 2011). This large growth coupled with the highly leveraged structure of hedge funds begged the question as to how the risk in these funds was being managed and whether adequate due diligence was being undertaken, and spawned much debate about the need for increased regulation (e.g., see Oesterle, 2006).

While New York and London have always been the centers of the global hedge fund industry, the decade before the GFC saw considerable growth in the number of hedge funds in the Asia–Pacific region, as elsewhere. Table 4.1 shows an annual average growth rate of 26% in the number of Asia–Pacific hedge funds for the 5 years to 2007. While in the early 2000s Japan accounted for the largest share of hedge fund assets of any Asian center, Hong Kong and Singapore offered particular advantages that led to rapid growth in the hedge fund industry in these two market places. Both centers could boast a series of drawcards, including well-established capital markets, low taxes, vast pools of money for investment, an English-speaking workforce, and broadly benign regulatory regimes; and a particular drawcard in the case of Singapore was substantial government investment in hedge funds.

Hong Kong was traditionally the gateway to financial investments in greater China. In the early 2000s, China was not a very popular hedge fund investment location due to stringent regulation, but this was changing rapidly. The opening of financial markets and economic growth in China led to high growth of hedge fund investments in mainland China. The greater China region has subsequently become, by far, the greatest hedge fund powerhouse in Asia (as noted earlier, in 2011, China, including Hong Kong, accounted for more than half of the hedge fund management firm locations in Asia). Australia was also attracting hedge fund investors to the Asia—Pacific region during the pre-GFC period, with Australian FoHFs returns outperforming global markets.

## 4.6. COLLAPSE: 2008

Until 2007 it appeared that hedge funds could do no wrong and were set to take an ever-more dominant position in securities markets. Between 1990 and 2008 their assets under management grew nearly 50-fold from US$39 billion to US$1.9 trillion (Hedge Fund Research, 2012). However, in 2008 the world changed almost overnight and in that calendar year global hedge fund assets dropped 25% (Table 4.1).

Many funds closed their doors. Notably, assets of Asia—Pacific hedge funds fell at a faster rate than global funds in 2008: 36% per Table 4.1. These declines were the combined result of negative performance (Asian FoHFs fell 34% per Figure 4.2) and net redemptions by investors. While the collapse of equity markets was obviously the key background event, the specific underlying diffi-culties included a number of factors. (i) Bans on short selling in some markets ruled out some accustomed strategies. (ii) There were unduly high holdings of illiquid assets. (iii) Heavy leverage prompted forced sales of assets when share prices declined and consequently added downward pressure on (for example) equity prices; sometimes this was to the accompaniment of margin calls and further forced sales, while withdrawal of credit could produce similar results. (iv) There was the jittery state of mind of many hedge fund clients. While these may have originally comprised a core of wealthy individuals, there were by now numbers of institutions, some of which (e.g., pension funds) had ongoing cash needs and so wished to sell out of hedge funds. (v) It was said that FoHFs managers were particularly hasty in exiting the hedge funds in which they were invested at the first sign of trouble. (vi) There was the unstable capital structure of hedge funds, typically encompassing few long-term liabilities and with quarterly redemptions by investors allowed; for FoHFs the position was even worse, as most marketed themselves as providing monthly liquidity. In turn, fear of redemptions produced a wish to build cash in anticipation and a consequent wave of asset sales at falling prices. Many funds reacted by suspending redemptions.

The same factors as obliterated hedge funds generally of course hit the FoHFs that invested in them, but the devastation was even greater. FoHFs as a percentage of the total number of hedge funds fell from their peak of 36% in 2008 to 28% in 2010 (Hedge Fund Research, 2011). For this greater deci-mation there was an added and specific reason: Bernie Madoff. Some large FoHFs had invested with Madoff and, not surprisingly, their investors felt such a disaster was just what they paid FoHFs to avoid. Gregoriou and

Lhabitant (2009) found a long list of red flags for the Madoff saga that should have been identified by due diligence.

## 4.7. AFTER THE STORM

With the recovery in share prices from early 2009, hedge funds and FoHFs also emerged from the gloom. In 2009 and 2010, we witnessed somewhat of a revival of the industry and a renewed confidence. Global hedge fund assets resumed their growth (36% over the 2 years to 2010 per Table 4.1). Figure 4.1 shows how Asian hedge funds accelerated well past their 2007 pre-GFC peak by 2011 and Asian FoHFs regained all their GFC losses. In the industry generally, greater concentration was evident: the largest firms grew more rapidly than the rest. In part, this recovery resulted from many managers offering an improved service. Some offered investors greater transparency, with investors able to track the whereabouts of their assets on a daily basis. Many introduced the offer of 'separate' or 'managed' accounts and cut performance fees.

The hedge fund and FoHFs regulatory environment, both outside and within Asia, changed after the GFC, with a greater focus on consumer protection, reporting, disclosure, and registration. In the United States, where previously hedge funds escaped registration requirements, the Dodd—Frank Act now requires hedge fund advisors exceeding a specified threshold to register with the Securities and Exchange Commission, subjecting them to regulations which apply to all investment advisors. In the European Union, the Alternative Investment Fund Managers (AIFM) Directive subjects hedge funds to increased compliance, disclosure, and monitoring requirements. South Africa, which has historically had very stringent investment controls, has gone the other way, relaxing a number of controls over the past decade, including post-GFC. These changes, including reduction in exchange controls and reduced restrictions on pension fund investments in hedge funds and FoHFs, considerably opened up the hedge funds markets in South Africa as well as allowing greater off shore investments by South African investors.

In the Asia—Pacific region, hedge fund and FoHFs investments in Hong Kong have always had the same registration requirements as all mutual funds, whereas Singapore had more relaxed registration requirements. The tighter controls in Hong Kong prior to the GFC have meant that there has not been a need for any significant changes in a post-GFC environment. Singapore, on the other hand, is in the process of tightening registration and licensing requirements. China has traditionally had stringent regulations relating to foreign investment in mainland China, but the market has been opening up with relaxations in controls. Australia has had the same licensing requirements for hedge funds and FoHFs as for all other investments, but is in the process of introducing stronger disclosure requirements for hedge funds and FoHFs. The strong financial services regulation in Australia is seen as one of the key contributors to that economy having fared far better during the GFC than many of its global counterparts.

## 4.8. THE REQUIREMENTS OF DUE DILIGENCE IN A POST-GFC ENVIRONMENT

Due diligence has to be practiced and evidenced at two stages in the process of investment in a FoHF: in the initial selection of a fund and in the subsequent ongoing monitoring of that fund. Compliance with sound principles in the first should assist with the second. At both stages the most practical means of ensuring compliance with the canons of due diligence is likely to be via a checklist of questions or list of principles such as provided by AIMA (Alternative Investment Management Association, 2005, 2009) which covers aspects such as the manager and organization, strategies and risks, performance, liquidity, fees and commissions, taxes, and offering documents. An Australian Prudential Regulation Authority post-GFC article (Roodt, 2010) builds on these elements, maintaining that one of the key lessons from the GFC for FoHFs investment due diligence is the assessment of the investment manager's ability to evaluate and monitor constituent hedge funds, and to construct portfolios of hedge funds by considering multifactor exposure and complementarity analysis. FoHFs also need the systems and processes to be able to combine positions from hedge funds, with ongoing monitoring and the ability to take corrective action being essential elements.

Based on our analysis in this chapter, we propose that there are two critical elements that are essential to FoHFs due diligence in a post-GFC environment, and which should complement traditional due diligence: the market in which the fund invests and the performance of the funds under extreme conditions such as those seen in the GFC. First, with regard to the markets in which the funds are invested, our study has highlighted the differences in regulations and in returns performance that exist between Asia and other global markets, and how these regulations are changing. A market's regulations impact not only on registration and compliance, but can also impact on returns. In addition, countries such as Canada, Australia, Asia, and South Africa show how strong regulation can contribute to economic stability and investment performance. FoHFs in these regulated nations generally had a much swifter and stronger recovery from the GFC than in other global nations. Thus it is essential to the investor and fund manager to understand the markets, from a regulatory, economic, risk, and past hedge funds returns perspective.

Second, the substantial downturns during the GFC shown in Table 4.1 and Figure 4.1 highlighted the need to understand extreme risk — losses that can occur in the most extreme tail of the distribution. Prior to the GFC, it was popular to use value at risk (VaR) as a measure of potential losses in a portfolio of assets. The problem with VaR is that it measures losses up to a specified threshold and says nothing of losses beyond that threshold. Since the GFC, there has been increased recognition of the need to use measures which do capture extreme risk. For example, Gregoriou and Pascalau (2011) use copulas to capture fully the joint distribution of hedge funds and FoHFs returns and survival under extreme left-tail events; other studies (Allen and Powell, 2011; Allen et al., 2011) show how quantile regression and conditional value at risk (CVaR) can capture tail events and be used as tools in investment decisions; Simonian (2011) contends that focusing on tail risk is becoming a necessity in preventing irrecoverable losses and demonstrates how to incorporate the measurement of tail risk into multifactor models. All of these studies support the view that simple linear approaches do not accurately capture risk in dynamic economic circumstances and more focus needs to be placed on extreme losses. That has implications for due diligence in that managers or investors need to undertake some form of extreme tail risk modeling or stress testing to capture extreme losses.

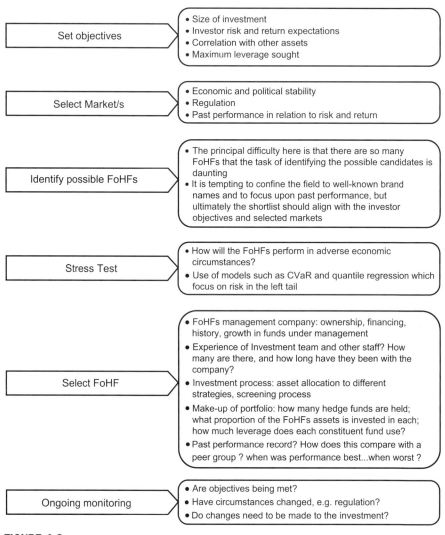

**FIGURE 4.3**
Six-step FoHFs due diligence model.

We propose the six-step FoHFs due diligence model in Figure 4.3. The steps include setting objectives that meet the investor's needs, identifying markets and then FoHFs that align with these objectives, stress testing to understand performance in adverse circumstances, selecting the most appropriate fund based on a combination of management and performance factors, and then closely monitoring whether the funds are on track to meet the objectives (making changes as necessary). This model is not intended as an exhaustive set of due diligence principles, but, rather, a broad framework under which due diligence should be undertaken, and it should be supplemented with detailed specific questions and principles such as those proposed by AIMA, mentioned above.

## CONCLUSION

The GFC changed the landscape for hedge funds and FoHFs. Investors have become more acutely aware of extreme risk and most geographical global markets have seen rapid regulatory change in the aftermath of the crisis. These events have significant implications for due diligence with greater emphasis, in particular, needing to be placed on aspects such as identifying potential extreme risk, on understanding the impact of country specific regulation changes when selecting markets and funds, and on ongoing close monitoring of the funds.

## Acknowledgments

We thank the Australian Research Council for funding support.

## References

Allen, D. E., & Powell, R. J. (2011). Measuring and Optimising Extreme Sectoral Risk in Australia. *Asia—Pacific Journal of Economics and Business, 15*(1), 1—14.

Allen, D. E., Singh, A. K., & Powell, R. J. (2011). Minimising Loss at Times of Financial Crisis. Quantile Regression as a Tool for Portfolio Investment Decisions. *Annals in Financial Economics, 6*(1), 63—85.

Alternative Investment Management Association (2005). *AIMA Canada's Hedge Fund Investor Checklist.* Available at http://aima-canada.org/aima_can_publications.html.

Alternative Investment Management Association (2009). *Guide to Sound Practices by Funds of Hedge Funds Managers.* Available at www.aima.org.

Brown, S. J., & Goetzmann, W. N. (1997). Mutual Fund Styles. *Journal of Financial Economics, 43,* 373—399.

Brown, S. J., Fraser, T. L., & Liang, B. (2008). Hedge Fund Due Diligence: A Source of Alpha in a Hedge Fund Portfolio Strategy. *Journal of Investment Management, 6*(4), 23—33.

Gregoriou, G. N., & Lhabitant, F. S. (2009). Madoff: A Flock of Red Flags. *Journal of Wealth Management, 12*(1), 89—97.

Gregoriou, G. N., & Pascalau, R. (2011). A Joint Survival Analysis of Hedge Funds and Funds of Funds Using Copulas. *Managerial Finance, 38*(1), 82—100.

Gregoriou, G. N., & Rouah, F. (2003). Selecting Funds of Hedge Funds: A Survey of the 20 Largest Funds. *Pensions: An International Journal, 8*(3), 217—221.

Hedge Fund Research (2011). *Global Hedge Fund Industry Report — Year End 2011.* Available at www.HedgeFundResearch.com.

Hedge Fund Research (2012). *Asian Hedge Fund Industry Report — First Quarter 2012.* Available at www.HedgeFundResearch.com.

Oesterle, D. A. (2006). Regulating Hedge Funds. *Entrepreneurial Business Law Journal, 1,* 1–42.

Roodt, C. (2010). *Hedge Fund Investment by Superannuation Funds.* Available at www.apra.gov.au.

Simonian, J. (2011). Mind the Tails! Anticipatory Risk Management for Target-Date Strategies. *The Journal of Risk, 3,* 45–54.

Stulz, R. M. (2007). Hedge Funds Past, Present, and Future. *Journal of Economic Perspectives, 21*(2), 175–194.

CHAPTER 5

# The Use of Managed Accounts by Funds of Hedge Funds

Marcus Müller* and Daniel Dietrich[†]
*Österreichische Volksbanken AG, Vienna, Austria
[†]Triple Alpha Beteiligung GmbH, Vienna, Austria

## 5.1. ADVERSITIES OF FUNDS OF HEDGE FUNDS IN 2008

The financial crisis reached its peak in 2008. As well as losing capital with their various strategies, hedge fund investors faced additional problems such as the suspension of redemptions, the activation of gate provisions, the creation of

Reconsidering Funds of Hedge Funds. http://dx.doi.org/10.1016/B978-0-12-401699-6.00005-8
Text copyright © 2013 by Elsevier Inc. All rights reserved.
Survey Figures and Data © Marcus Miller and Daniel Dietrich

side pockets/illiquid share classes, or increased counterparty risk emanating from (prime) brokers and custodians. In some cases the real dimensions of investment risk and style drifts only came to light when fund managers had to explain losses and when the number of investors committed to redeem their fund shares grew significantly. Furthermore, cases of fraud caused losses and added worries in a time of unprecedented uncertainty, with funds of hedge funds (FoHFs) being one of the most affected asset classes. FoHFs faced redemptions from their own clients and had to explain the performance or counterparty risk in an industry that was defined by its private character and lack of public information.

One of the reasons for this lack of transparency is the classical onshore/offshore fund structure, which does not include many publication requirements and which allows arbitrary liquidity terms. There were numerous single hedge funds where managers and certain strategies performed well during the crisis, but this may have been due to the use of managed accounts (MACs).

The remainder of the chapter is organized as follows. Stylized structures of MACs for FoHFs will be introduced in Section 5.2. Section 5.3 discusses advantages and disadvantages that may accompany MACs, and hypotheses about the use of MACs by FoHFs are formulated. These hypotheses are tested in Section 5.4 with the survey results from FoHFs. Sections 5.5 and 5.6 present the summary and conclusions.

## 5.2. MAC STRUCTURES FOR FoHFs

Cao *et al.* (2010) discuss several stylized operational structures in the hedge fund industry. They argue that in an 'outside "feeder" FoHFs model' (a FoHF that invests in independent single hedge funds with different brokers) provides the advantages of intermediation functions such as 'monitoring, diversification, risk management, due diligence efficacy, and investment-and-withdrawal allocation.' Conversely, they find certain drawbacks to this structure, such as the absence of a stable internal investor base and the risk of redemptions, and consequently poor liquidity terms. Additionally, Cao *et al.* (2010) claim that low internal investments can lead to negative selection and using different brokers instead of one large broker leads to inferior (broker) services. One could argue that diversification across several brokers and fund managers by successful FoHFs paid off during the financial crisis, and reduced risk. Despite these different views, the current study extends the basic (outside feeder FoHFs) model from Cao *et al.* (2010) by three different types of MACs. It should be noted that these are stylized structures that include basic counterparties and functions. In reality more details can be added and variations might exist. Nonetheless, this distinction might help to distinguish between several concepts often referred to as 'managed accounts (MACs)' or 'managed account platforms (MAPs).'

## 5.2.1. Separately Managed Accounts

A separately managed account (SMAC) constitutes a brokerage account in the name of the investor and is monitored by one or more hedge fund manager(s). The advisor/hedge fund manager can trade his/her investment strategy but cannot transfer cash in or out of the account. Hence, the FoHF (investor) has direct ownership of assets and liabilities.

The idea behind this legal entity is that hedge fund managers run these accounts *pari passu* to their benchmark fund or by following special investment guidelines. Usually such accounts are opened at prime brokers and with an administrator calculating the net asset value (NAV) of the account for the FoHF (see Figure 5.1). The FoHF and the hedge fund manager negotiate all terms of the investment management agreement, such as investment amount or investment guidelines, and select the preferred counterparties. In the trading process the manager is subject to the agreed investment guidelines and the agreed trading procedures with all counterparties. Furthermore, the investor has the right to close the account and withdraw his/her funds without notice. The performance of such a SMAC should track the performance of the benchmark fund as the same positions are traded on the account as on the benchmark fund. In addition, the investor has the opportunity to insert investment guidelines in the mandate prohibiting, for example, the trading of illiquid securities. The maximum leverage or exposure to an investment region or asset classes can also be fixed in the contract. However, such restrictions may have an impact on the investment strategy of the hedge fund manager, which in turn can cause a tracking error to the benchmark fund.

The FoHF has ownership of the SMAC and therefore not only the direct control of the underlying assets, but also the responsibilities of implementing and

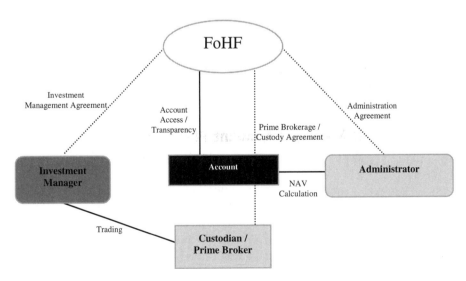

**FIGURE 5.1**
Possible simplified structure of a SMAC.

maintaining the legal and business infrastructure with all requisite counterparties. It remains up to the FoHF to ensure that the terms of each agreement meet the needs.

## 5.2.2. External Managed Account Platform

External Managed Account Platforms (EMAPs) bundle the principles of SMACs for several hedge fund programs and offer them to external investors, like FoHFs. EMAPs provide the entire range of infrastructure required for the inception and ongoing monitoring of MACs. This service includes all middle and back office functions, risk monitoring, and the reconciliation of the portfolio valuation. As a result, according to Giraud (2005) this allows the platform to strictly monitor the hedge fund manager. Such platforms are often owned by investment banks, which enables the hedge fund manager to replicate the trading strategy and offer the opportunity to issue fund derivatives based on the platform programs. Nonetheless, there are also EMAPs without a direct (investment) bank affiliation. In most cases, due diligence by the platform provider or a third party precedes the launch of new programs on the platform. Additionally, the hedge fund manager has to negotiate the terms and conditions with the platform provider. During this process, all relevant counterparties are defined (e.g., the prime broker of the hedge fund on the platform and the administrator).

In order to use economies of scale and lower the minimum investment amount for all users of EMAPs, there is often one MAC per program owned by a commingled fund vehicle (see Figure 5.2). This vehicle is usually managed by the platform provider and advised by the hedge fund manager. The ultimate decision-making power (e.g., for closing an account) is with the directors of the fund, who include members of the platform provider. In the case that one program is negatively affected by huge losses, there will normally be some type of ring fence between the different MACs/fund vehicles of one platform.

The assets are owned by the fund vehicle and the FoHFs investors own shares of this fund. As with other fund vehicles, the assets are held by prime brokers/custodians and the value is calculated by an administrator. Unlike with typical onshore/offshore funds, the EMAP is the manager of the fund, and controls all counterparty agreements, has full portfolio transparency, and monitors the negotiated investment guidelines.

## 5.2.3. Internal Managed Account Platform

An Internal Managed Account Platform (IMAP) is an attempt to combine the approach of SMACs and EMAPs for large institutional investors, such as FoHFs. Like an external platform, IMAPs run a number of MACs with various hedge fund managers. Figure 5.3 denotes this by shadowing all vehicles and entities that appear more than once. However, the sole/main investors of the accounts are the internal FoHFs vehicles of the FoHFs company running the platform. Therefore, it could also be defined as a structured effort by a FoHF to combine a number of SMACs: the FoHF selects the hedge fund managers on the platform

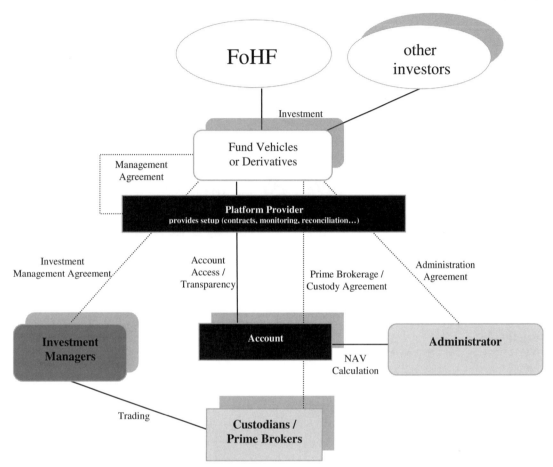

**FIGURE 5.2**
Possible simplified structure of an EMAP.

(due diligence), sets up all contracts with counterparties (e.g., trading advisor, prime brokers, and administrators), executes middle and back office functions, monitors the investment guidelines (risk management), and changes the allocation in the portfolio. Compared to SMACs and EMAPs, the operational setup of IMAPs is probably the most complex; however, the control and transparency on a portfolio level is probably the largest.

## 5.3. HYPOTHESES, ADVANTAGES, AND DISADVANTAGES OF MACS

As many FoHFs struggled to perform and to explain losses and/or had to impose liquidity restrictions on their investors, the FoHFs industry lost the credibility essential for fulfilling their main functions: the selection of single managers (due diligence), portfolio construction, and/or the monitoring of the investments

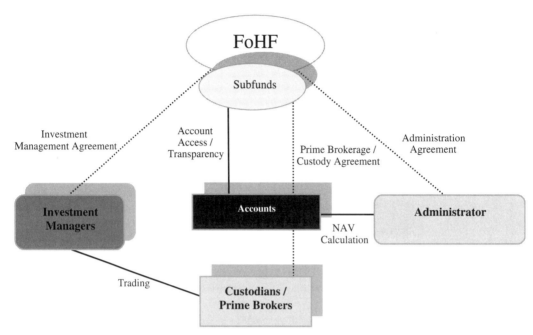

**FIGURE 5.3**
Possible simplified structure of an IMAP.

(risk management). Hence, hedge fund investments with a lower fee structure than for FoHFs, such as investable indices or replication products, gained attention and FoHFs felt compelled to improve their setup to fulfill their clients' new investment requirements (which are also influenced by new regulation).

- *Hypothesis 1: The use of MACs by FoHFs increased after the financial crisis.*

### 5.3.1. Advantages

*LIQUIDITY*

Lockup periods, gate provisions, the right to suspend the redemption of fund shares (refusal to calculate the net asset value), or the right to create side pockets are common attributes of onshore/offshore hedge funds' private placement memoranda. Depending on the strategy, the age of the fund, and assets under management (AUM), the liquidity terms can vary. If predominantly distressed or not publicly traded instruments are used, the liquidity of an onshore/offshore fund should reflect these markets in order to avoid the use of gates, the creation of side pockets, or the suspension of redemptions in the case many investors want to redeem.

The users of SMACs and IMAPs negotiate the duration of the contract and the timing of subscriptions and redemptions with the hedge fund manager on an individual basis. Owning all assets in the dedicated account allows them to sell the entire portfolio at their own discretion as the ultimate influence on the account's liquidity. On the contrary, EMAPs are mainly structured as fund vehicles or fund derivatives with a third counterparty like an investment bank. Therefore, gating clauses, the right to suspend redemptions, or even lockup and side pocket provisions might exist, but their activation is controlled by the EMAP or their independent counterparties and not influenced by the hedge fund manager. The provider of the EMAP negotiates the liquidity terms with the fund manager in an investment management agreement and usually all investors have the same liquidity terms. EMAP providers offering fund derivatives reserve the right to offer better liquidity terms to internal rather than to external clients. Nonetheless, EMAPs generally tend to offer better liquidity terms than the comparable benchmark funds of the same manager. For hedge fund managers this can be problematic as they have to explain to their onshore/offshore investors the preferential liquidity terms of their programs based on EMAPs.

In general, it should be pointed out that MACs do not improve the liquidity of the underlying securities, but they avoid the discretionary activation of unfavorable liquidity terms by hedge fund managers. One important distinction between SMACs/IMAPs and EMAPs is that the latter usually offer commingled investment structures that do not solve the problem of the influence other investors' investment decisions have on the investment vehicle. In particular, if other investors want to redeem fund shares (e.g., in times of stress) the remaining investors might have to cope with imbalanced portfolios or with the costs of closing the investment vehicle. FoHFs have to balance the subscriptions and redemptions from their clients and steer the portfolio towards the wanted weightings. Due to the avoidance of gates, suspension of redemptions, side pockets, or lockup periods, SMAC or IMAP solutions seem better able to cope with the liquidity management on a portfolio level. EMAPs normally have the advantage of similar liquidity terms on the given platform, in contrast to very different terms on the benchmark fund (or MAC) level.

Several papers (e.g., Agarwal *et al.*, 2009; Haberfelner *et al.*, 2006) have shown that more illiquid funds can use their additional degrees of freedom and they can earn a liquidity premium. Nonetheless, Boyle *et al.* (2008) found that during the financial crisis less liquid funds generated larger losses and higher volatility. Furthermore, Ang and Bollen (2008) showed that for investors there are costs associated with the illiquidity that are not included in the performance returns reported by less liquid funds.

Bollinger *et al.* (2011) analyzed the change of investor preferences after the financial crisis. They came to the conclusion that FoHFs investors significantly prefer those vehicles with lower lockup periods and single hedge fund investors significantly prefer lower total redemption terms. This implies that FoHFs have to avoid lockups when investing in single funds, which recognize in their inflows that more liquidity is preferred by investors.

- *Hypothesis 2: MACs help FoHFs to avoid liquidity problems like suspension of redemptions, gates, or lockups.*

*CONTROL OF ASSETS AND FEE PAYMENTS*

In contrast to classical onshore/offshore hedge funds, SMAC- or IMAP-based solutions have the assets directly assigned to the account(s) of the investors/ FoHF (prime) broker/custodian. In EMAPs the accounts are assigned to the commingled fund structures and set up by the platform provider. These structures offer the opportunity to control all securities and cash flows by the investor/FoHF or the platform provider. Therefore, the fraud risk can be minimized, but cannot be totally eliminated. If investors had chosen to invest in a MAC with Madoff Securities LLC, money would have been lost because brokerage and auditing reports had been fabricated. In addition, Gurnani and Vogt (2010) point out that the selection of independent and top-tier counterparties is critical for the successful implementation of MACs.

In classical onshore/offshore funds there are often distinctions in the segregation of assets, as well as collateral (rehypothecation) and cash positions. Using MACs provides the opportunity to negotiate these terms with the brokers. Hence, it should be better to assess the exact counterparty risk and make clear decisions regarding cash management. During the financial crisis FoHFs that invested in classical onshore/offshore funds often had no direct information about where assets and cash were deposited, and needed to base their decisions on information from single hedge funds.

- *Hypothesis 3a: MACs help FoHFs in order to manage counterparty risk.*
- *Hypothesis 3b: MACs help FoHFs in order to manage cash positions.*

Classical onshore/offshore funds deliver annual audited reports and semiannual non-audited reports to their shareholders. These rare reports are the main source for analyzing the fee payments and expenses paid by investors.

- *Hypothesis 3c: MACs help FoHFs in order to control fee payments.*

*TRANSPARENCY AND RISK MANAGEMENT*

According to a study by Golitz and Schröder (2010), investors are dissatisfied with the quality of hedge fund reporting. In particular, the information policy on liquidity and operational risk is regarded as inadequate by investors.

As the accounts of SMACs and IMAPs are directly assigned to the investor/FoHF, there is almost complete portfolio transparency due to electronic access to the (prime) broker(s)/custodians. EMAP providers have the same transparency, but non-disclosure agreements with the hedge fund managers limit the degree of details they are allowed to provide their investors. Often gross and net exposures regarding asset classes, sectors, regions, liquidity, or credit risk are available for investors, but the single-line positions remain secret. The full data is available for users of SMACs and IMAPs, and EMAP providers. Therefore, they can monitor the investment guidelines and risk limits set up in the investment management agreement. Depending on the strategy and the resources of the user, analyses about the strategy, the style drifts and the investment risks can be made. These risks range from market exposures, over liquidity, and credit data to the counterparty risk.

When IMAPs are used, this information is available for all or most of the funds within a FoHF. If the data from different accounts, managers, and counterparties can be combined, the detailed risk analysis can be extended to entire FoHFs portfolios. Additional risks like unwanted exposures, concentrations, and crowded trades might be identified, and hedges or effective portfolio insurance can be added as an overlay.

As Gurnani and Vogt (2010) point out, risk management can be improved through more transparency, but the effect on the industry cannot be assessed because the use of the additional information depends on the investors and their risk management systems.

- *Hypothesis 4a: MACs help FoHFs in order to understand the investment risk associated with a single manager.*
- *Hypothesis 4b: MACs help FoHFs in order to understand the overall portfolio risk over several managers.*

### TAX EFFICIENCY

Users of SMACs and IMAPs might be able to choose the preferred domicile of their accounts from a tax perspective. The full account/portfolio transparency of SMACs and IMAPs is also beneficial for tax purposes. EMAPs often provide tax-transparent reporting for a lot of domiciles of their investors. Classical onshore/offshore funds are often not tax transparent and subject to penalty taxation. Additionally, Doline *et al.* (2009) point out that for SMACs or IMAPs there might be the possibility to generate losses from certain securities in order to neutralize gains from similar trades from another account.

## 5.3.2. Disadvantages

### COSTS

FoHFs investors who decide to invest via SMACs and IMAPs have to bear the costs themselves. This includes the costs for the opening of the account, and all legal costs for negotiations and required agreements. Moreover, there are additional costs for the administering and monitoring of the account. With the investment through an EMAP an additional fee level emerges (often called risk monitoring fee) for the investor.

- *Hypothesis 5: MACs are problematic for FoHFs due to the associated fee structure.*

### TRACKING ERROR

Bollinger *et al.* (2009) compared 143 MAC funds (from EMAPs) with their benchmark funds during the December 1999–May 2009 period. Their results illustrate that MACs underperformed their underlying offshore funds regardless of the strategy pursued. On average, there was an underperformance of 1.8% *per annum* during the observation period. Only 4% of the considered MACs outperformed their benchmark funds. In the period between January 2006 and December 2008, the tracking error was even more significant. The managers most affected by this fact were those pursuing relative value strategies. Hence, it can be concluded that these strategies are most vulnerable to limitations related to maintaining MACs.

In their paper, Gurnani and Vogt (2010) described how they used MACs and how their companies were able to generate a positive tracking error over their hedge fund portfolio compared to the benchmark funds. They analyzed data of SMACs from Investcorp Investment Advisory LLC and Allstate Investments LLC, and found a statistically highly significant monthly outperformance of 66 basis points (7.9% *per annum*) compared to the benchmark funds. As the observation period was rather short (May 2006–December 2009) and the number of distinct accounts ranged from five to 42 over that period, the results are probably not representative for the entire sphere of MAC investors and in all investment horizons. Nonetheless, their study provides a rare insight into the experience of users of SMACs.

- *Hypothesis 6: MACs are problematic for FoHFs due to the tracking error risk.*

### OPERATIONAL COMPLEXITY

For investors and for hedge fund managers MACs are more complex in their operational structure due to the involvement of additional counterparties and/ or the individual setup of systems; in particular, an investment realized through a SMAC and an IMAP results in greater effort for investors. Due to the status of being the owner of the account, the investor is responsible for all the middle and back office functions, for the active monitoring, and also for the legal and business infrastructure. All these tasks can be outsourced to third parties, yet this involves extra costs. With an investment through an EMAP all these tasks are the responsibility of the platform provider and investors get access via a fund (derivative).

- *Hypothesis 7: MACs are problematic for FoHFs due to the complex operational setup.*

### DIRECT OWNERSHIP OF ASSETS

Due to this legal ownership, the FoHF is fully responsible and liable in the event of regulatory breaches in SMACs and IMAPs. This applies for both fiduciary aspects and the implementation of the investment strategy (e.g., insider trading or trading of prohibited securities). With fund investments into EMAPs this responsibility is not with the investor.

### INVESTMENT UNIVERSE

While users of SMACs and IMAPs negotiate their investment terms with the hedge fund managers themselves, EMAPs have to negotiate in a way to offer an attractive vehicle for their clients. EMAPs promise liquidity and transparency, and therefore often focus on highly liquid strategies. For this reason, Gagnon (2009) argues that illiquid strategies or the trading of hard-to-value securities are not suitable for their purpose. Consequently, there is a limited access to such strategies (e.g., distressed securities) in the investment universe of EMAPs. Kaiser and Müller (2009) add that strategies that are subject to capacity limitations and therefore do not meet the minimum investment requirements of an EMAP provider are a constraint on the investment universe as well.

One reason for a hedge fund manager not to offer a MAC is the fear of jeopardizing his/her strategy by disclosing the financial positions of his/her portfolio. In particular, managers exploiting inefficiencies of niche markets can be affected by such disclosure, if competitors use this information to replicate the investment strategy or to bet against it. Such imitators may increase the trend and profit, but according to Weber (2006) they also increase the risk of short squeezes that could cause higher potential losses. Allowing SMACs and IMAPs might also be problematic for hedge fund managers as they cannot be sure that their portfolio is not replicated by investors without paying management and performance fees.

Gagnon (2009) points out that the higher effort related to a MAC mainly prevents established hedge fund managers, who can refer to a long and strong track record, from replicating their strategy on a separate account, since they do not rely on new investors. In contrast, start up managers or managers with a weak performance accept this additional effort to raise their AUM.

- *Hypothesis 8: MACs are problematic for FoHFs due to the limited universe of investable hedge fund managers.*

## 5.4. SURVEY

### 5.4.1. Questionnaire and Data

In order to analyze the use of the various kinds of MACs a survey of FoHFs management companies was conducted. Based on data from the *Hedge Fund Journal* using the largest FoHFs management firms from 2008 to 2010 and Bloomberg data covering smaller companies, the survey was conducted with 21 firms participating.

As shown in Figure 5.4 the participant companies had different origins, ages, and sizes. It should be pointed out that the entire FoHFs market cannot be represented in such a survey. According to the indication by the participants their AUM had been between US$73 and US$158 billion as of December 2011.[1] As the survey is biased towards large FoHFs from Switzerland and the United Kingdom, it should be viewed as the first empirical study to distinguish between several concepts of MACs.

---

[1]In this survey the participants were asked about their AUM in ranges (e.g., US$5–10 billion. For details see the last graph in Figure 5.4). Realistically, their total AUM was approximately US$100 billion. According to BarclayHedge the total AUM of the FoHFs industry was US$532.4 billion in Q4 2011.

Where is your principal office location for fund of fund activities?

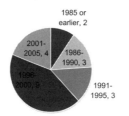

When did your company start the Fund of Hedge Fund activities?

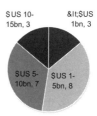

What are the total AUM of your Fund of Hedge Fund business (as of December 2011)?

**FIGURE 5.4**
Overview of the survey participants.

## 5.4.2. Results

*THE USE OF MACS BY FoHFs*

The survey shows that the use of all three types of MACs has increased after the financial crisis and the outlook remains positive. In particular, SMACs and IMAPs gained a lot of attention after 2008 (see Figure 5.5).

In the survey, the three types of MACs were compared to the classical onshore/offshore fund vehicles that might have caused problems for FoHFs during the crisis. As shown in Figure 5.6 the clear preference for onshore/offshore funds compared to SMACs has diminished and the importance of SMACs has increased. This trend can be confirmed as FoHFs started to target higher allocations for investments via SMACs. In comparison to the time before 2008, EMAPs − in contrast to onshore/offshore funds − show no real increase in their importance, but the outlook is slightly positive. This obser-vation is supported by the increase of target allocations by some survey participants. After 2008, IMAPs have been gaining the most popularity compared to classical onshore/offshore funds and according to this survey

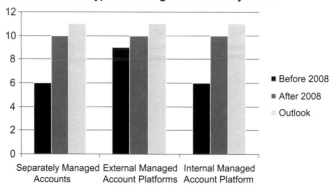

**FIGURE 5.5**
The use of MACs before and after the financial crisis by FoHFs.

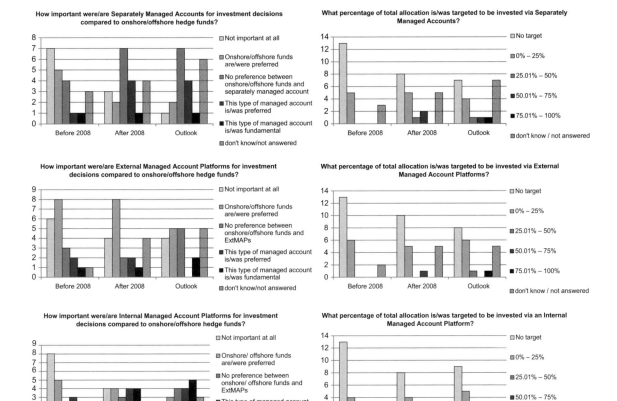

**FIGURE 5.6**
The preference of different MACs compared to onshore/offshore funds and target allocations.

this trend will continue. It should be pointed out that some FoHFs had already used IMAPs before the crisis, and that more companies seem to follow and target allocations of a number of participants are already above 75% (see last graph in Figure 5.6).

## THE ADVANTAGES OF MACS

Not all participants in the survey have experience with all three types of MACs. This is reflected by unanswered questions or selecting 'don't know' in the survey. The detailed answers for the expected advantages of MACs can be found in Figure 5.7. According to the literature, one of the major advantages of MACs is the avoidance of liquidity problems, such as suspension of redemptions, gates, or lockups. Overall, the survey participants agreed with this argument for all three types of MACs. Regarding the full transparency that MACs are supposed to deliver, there is agreement for IMAPs and SMACs, but also some disagreement for EMAPs.

You had the experience that these kinds of managed account are beneficial for your fund of funds business by avoiding liquidity problems (lock-ups, gates, suspension of redemptions).

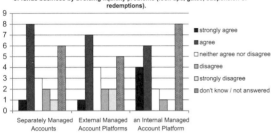

You had the experience that these kinds of managed account are beneficial for your fund of funds business by allowing the understanding of the total investment risk of a single manager.

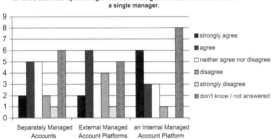

You had the experience that these kinds of managed account are beneficial for your fund of funds business by improving cash management.

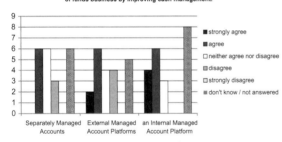

You had the experience that these kinds of managed account are beneficial for your fund of funds business by offering full transparency.

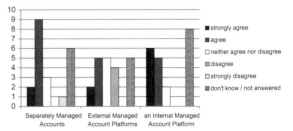

You had the experience that these kinds of managed account are beneficial for your fund of funds business by the ability to consolidate risk management on a fund of funds level.

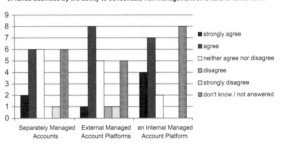

You had the experience that these kinds of managed account are beneficial for your fund of funds business by managing counterparty risk effectively.

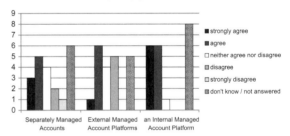

You had the experience that these kinds of managed account are beneficial for your fund of funds business by the control of fee payments.

**FIGURE 5.7**
Survey results of the advantages of MACs.

All three MAC types seem to enhance the ability to consolidate risk management on a FoHFs level with a more positive opinion about IMAPs and SMACs. Overall, MACs seem to be beneficial to the cash management of FoHFs, but SMACs and EMAPs also face criticism in this survey. IMAPs are regarded as very capable of managing counterparty risk. Yet, a good deal of the respondents doubt that this also applies for SMACs and EMAPs. Similar to the previous arguments, the control of fee payments is seen most positively when using IMAPs, and is also true for EMAPs and SMACs.

## THE DRAWBACKS OF MACS

The detailed answers for the expected drawbacks of MACs can be found in Figure 5.8. According to this study FoHFs mainly agree with the thesis that the number of single fund managers available for the three kinds of MACs is rather

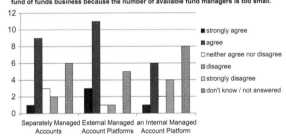
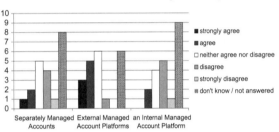
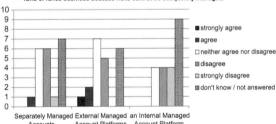
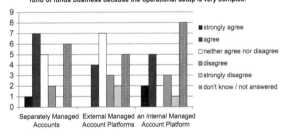
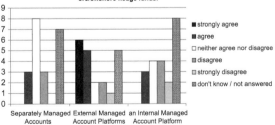

**FIGURE 5.8**
Survey results of the drawbacks of MACs.

small. Only some users of IMAPs disagree. With regard to EMAPs, there are more respondents agreeing that the tracking error can cause problems. For SMACs the answers are biased towards a disagreement with this statement and this bias is even larger for IMAPs. Nonetheless, most participants neither agree nor disagree or did not answer the question/did not know.

To test the opinion about the overall risk management it was asked if MACs are not sufficient. There is a clear disagreement that IMAPs and SMACs would lead to insufficient risk management. FoHFs have a different opinion for EMAPs, as some survey participants can agree with this statement. The hypothesis of problems caused by a highly complex setup is supported for SMACs and IMAPs. On the contrary, EMAPs are viewed as less complex in the operational setup. Survey participants clearly agree that higher EMAP fees are problematic compared to onshore/offshore funds. Contrarily, for SMACs this statement is equally agreed and disagreed, and participants slightly disagree with this statement when it comes to IMAPs.

## 5.5. SUMMARY

The survey shows that the three different types of MACs described in this paper are also used and viewed differently by FoHFs. The use of all types of MAC by FoHFs has increased after the financial crisis. As summarized in Table 5.1, in

| Table 5.1 | Hypotheses and Survey Results from FoHFs for the Three Types of MACs | | |
|---|---|---|---|
| | **Agreement for the Argument** | | |
| **Argument** | **SMACs** | **EMAPs** | **IMAPs** |
| *Use of MACs* | | | |
| The use increased after 2008 | yes | yes | yes |
| *Advantages* | | | |
| Avoiding liquidity problems (lockups, gates, suspension of redemptions) | yes (strong) | yes | yes (strong) |
| Getting full transparency | yes | not clear | yes |
| Understanding the total investment risk of a single manager | yes | not clear | yes (strong) |
| Ability to consolidate risk management on a fund-of-funds level | yes (strong) | yes | yes (strong) |
| Improving cash management | yes (strong) | yes | yes (strong) |
| Managing counterparty risk | yes | not clear | yes (strong) |
| Control of fee payments | yes | not clear | yes (strong) |
| *Drawbacks* | | | |
| Number of available fund managers is too small | yes | yes (strong) | yes |
| Tracking error is too large | not clear | yes | not clear |
| Operational setup is very complex | yes | not clear | not clear |
| Total fees are higher compared to onshore/offshore hedge funds | not clear | yes | not clear |

several of the points survey participants generally go along with the answers regarding SMACs and IMAPs that could be explained by a similar operational setup, which is extended on the entire FoHFs level in the case of IMAPs. Contrarily, EMAPs that often offer commingled investment vehicles differ from the other two types of MACs. Many of the advantages of MACs, such as better liquidity, more transparency, and better risk management possibilities, can be found in IMAPs and SMACs. These advantages seem to go hand in hand with an increasingly complex operational setup. Contrarily, EMAPs are less complex, but seem to have fewer advantages and a higher fee load. Therefore, FoHFs investors should analyze as part of their due diligence whether MACs are used and which types are preferred.

As well as the use of MACs, FoHFs started to use other investment vehicles after the financial crisis to avoid the problems of classic onshore/offshore funds. The most famous example is 'Undertakings for Collective Investments in Transferable Securities' (UCITS) funds, which can also be based on the infrastructure of MACs. Other investment vehicles like single-investor funds have gained attraction as well and limit some of the drawbacks of MACs. In particular, single hedge fund managers are more comfortable with a fund vehicle instead of a MAC structure with its huge potential for influence by the investor.

## CONCLUSION

Setting up an IMAP and using SMACs extensively is associated with the costs of setting up the operational infrastructure. Probably large FoHFs companies have the necessary economies of scale to grow in this direction. Nonetheless, EMAPs and specialized companies offering SMACs can provide smaller FoHFs investment possibilities and tools to use MACs in an efficient way as well.

It is not clear whether other hedge fund investors increasingly use MAC solutions; however, all these investors faced the same environment during the financial crisis. Through regulations such as Basel III or Solvency II, transparent investments via MACs can accelerate the momentum for MACs. New providers of MAC solutions and platforms will increase the competition, lower the costs, and enhance the available services.

## Acknowledgments

We gratefully acknowledge the participation of all survey participants, and important feedback from Michael Kreusslein and Florian Haberfelner.

## References

Agarwal, V., Daniel, N. D., & Naik, N. Y. (2009). Role of Managerial Incentives and Discretion in Hedge Fund Performance. *Journal of Finance, 64*(5), 2221–2256.

Ang, A., & Bollen, N. P. B. (2008). *Locked Up by a Lockup: Valuing Liquidity as a Real Option, Working Paper, Centre for Hedge Fund Research*. London: Risk Management Laboratory, Imperial College Business School.

Bollinger, G., Guidotti, I., & Pochon, F. (2009). *Managed Accounts and Tracking Error Risk*. Paris: Working Paper, Olympia Research.

Bollinger, G., Guidotti, I., & Pochon, F. (2011). Hedge Fund Investing in the Aftermath of the Crisis: Where did the Money Go? *Journal of Alternative Investments, 14*(2), 8–17.

Boyle, P., Li, S., & Zhu, Y. (2008). *Hedge Fund Redemption Restrictions, Financial Crisis, and Fund Performance*. Waterloo, Ontario: Working Paper, School of Business and Economics, Wilfrid Laurier University.

Cao, Y., Ogden, J. P., & Tiu, C. I. (2010). Who Benefits From Funds Of Hedge Funds? A Critique Of Alternative Operational Structures. In *The Hedge Fund Industry*. NY: Working Paper, School of Management, University at Buffalo-SUNY.

Doline, B. H., Geller, J., & Zimmermann, V. L. (2009). An Investment Decision for the New Economic Reality: Hedge Funds or Discretionary Managed Accounts? *Alternative Intelligence Quotient, 30*(2), 27.

Gagnon, M. (2009). *Realignment of Interest in Hedge Fund Investing Using a Managed Account Platform*. Montreal: White Paper, Innocap.

Giraud, G.-R. (2005). *Mitigating Hedge Funds' Operational Risk: Benefits and Limitations Of Managed Account Platforms*. Nice: Working Paper, EDHEC Business School.

Golitz, F., & Schröder, D. (2010). Hedge Fund Transparency: Where Do We Stand? *Journal of Alternative Investments, 12*(4), 20–35.

Gurnani, D., & Vogt, C. (2010). *Separate Accounts as a Source of Hedge Fund Alpha*. NY/Northbrook, IL: Working Paper, Investcorp Investment Advisory LLC and Allstate Investments LLC.

Haberfelner, F., Kaiser, D. G., & Kisling, K. (2006). Vor- und Nachteile der Investition in Hedgefonds über Managed-Account-Plattformen. *Absolutreport, 35*(12), 32–43.

Kaiser, D. G., & Müller, M. (2009). Alternative Investments. In D. Farkas-Richling, T. R. Fischer, & A. Richter (Eds.), *Private Banking und Family Office*. Stuttgart: Schaeffer-Poeschel.

Weber, T. (2006). Positions- und Risikotransparenz von Hedgefonds. In M. Busack, & D. G. Kaiser (Eds.), *Handbuch Alternative Investments, Band 1*. Wiesbaden: Gabler.

# CHAPTER 6

# Choice of Risk Measure in Evaluating UCITS Funds of Hedge Funds

**Alessandro Carretta and Gianluca Mattarocci**

University of Rome Tor Vergata, School of Economics, Department of
Economics and Finance, Rome, Italy

## Chapter Outline

## 6.1. INTRODUCTION

Funds of hedge funds (FoHFs) are funds that invest in hedge funds with various styles while constantly monitoring their performance and assessing portfolio-rebalancing opportunities as a result of adverse market environments (Gregoriou, 2003). The main advantage of a FoHF over a direct investment in hedge funds is that investors have access to a diversified basket of hedge funds with reasonable liquidity (Amenc and Vaissié, 2006). Empirical analyses demonstrate that about only 10–20 hedge funds are sufficient to maximize the return–risk profile of a FoHF (i.e., Brown *et al.*, 2012) and the efficacy of the diversification strategy varies according to differences between the funds included in the portfolio (Shawky *et al.*, 2012). The difference between FoHFs and multistrategy hedge funds is that FoHFs can pick the best managers and thus more than offset any fee advantage offered by multistrategy managers (Reedy *et al.*, 2007).

Retail investors' demand for alternative products has grown in the last decade (Pascual and Cuellar, 2007) and regulators are currently defining a new framework to protect their interests when investing in the hedge fund industry (Hauser and Petit, 2008). The 'Undertakings for Collective Investment in Transferable Securities' (UCITS) structure represents an opportunity offered by regulators to the hedge fund industry to solicit both retail and institutional investors on a cross-border basis, thus broadening investor bases and asset availability (Johannsen, 2011).

The literature on UCITS FoHFs focuses on their investment constraints and points out their implications for fund managers' investment strategies (i.e., Anderberg and Bolton, 2006). Performance analyses of this type of FoHF are still limited and currently no evidence is available of the impact of the assumption of normal returns on the ranking of investment opportunities.

Performance analyses of FoHFs demonstrate that the assumption of normality significantly affects evaluation of the investment's risk-to-return profile depending on the risk measure selected (Gregoriou and Gueyie, 2003). This chapter studies the impact of the choice of risk measure on a ranking of UCITS FoHFs and provides empirical evidence of the usefulness of more complex risk measurements in selecting the best investments. The results demonstrate that even if the rankings constructed using different risk-adjusted performance (RAP) measures are correlated, removing the normality assumption may positively affect their persistence and thus impact the investment strategy's performance. Regarding the global financial crisis period, an investment selection process based on past RAP measures may prevent losses and certain RAP measures that do not assume normality may allow for a better performance than that measured according to the Sharpe ratio.

The remainder of this chapter is organized as follows. Section 6.2 gives a detailed literature review of FoHFs performance measurements, and presents a standard mean—variance framework and the main limits of the normality assumption. Section 6.3 discusses the empirical analysis of a sample of UCITS FoHFs for the period 2003—2011, and evaluates the impact of the risk measure choice on investment strategies for the previous year's best and worst performers. Subsection 6.3.3 summarizes our work and its implications, followed by our conclusions.

## 6.2. LITERATURE REVIEW

Performance analyses of FoHFs normally demonstrate a positive relation between fund size and fund manager experience due to the higher managerial capabilities required for managing any unexpected distress scenario and the greater amount of money available to construct a diversification strategy (Fuss *et al.*, 2009). The relationship between performance and fund flow is negative because above-average fund flows usually adversely affect the future performance of top-performing funds and the largest funds due to the capacity constraints of FoHFs (Xiong *et al.*, 2009).

In a mean—variance framework, the Sharpe ratio is also proposed as a simple approach to evaluate hedge funds (Gulko, 2003). This measure represents excess return with respect to a risk-free investment for each unit of risk assumed and a risk-averse investor will select investment opportunities with a higher Sharpe ratio (Sharpe, 1994). Empirical analyses demonstrate that the Sharpe ratio for

FoHFs is normally lower than for the average hedge fund industry but, due to their lower correlation with the performance of other asset classes, FoHFs may be useful in a diversification strategy (e.g., Denvir and Hutson, 2006). The RAP measure is also positively related with fund size and, unlike hedge funds, larger FoHFs normally show a better risk-to-return tradeoff and a higher survival probability (Ammann and Moerth, 2008).

An alternative RAP measure frequently used in the hedge fund industry is Jensen's alpha — an index of extra return related to a manager's active management strategy (Alexander and Dimitriu, 2005). Even if there is no consensus on the risk-to-return model adopted, the alpha measure can be used to identify the value created at different stages of the investment selection process. Empirical analyses demonstrate that, for other FoHFs, the main source of value is always related to strategic asset allocation (e.g., Reedy *et al.*, 2007).

The extra return obtained with respect to a benchmark can also be standardized by considering the ratio between alpha and a standard measure of the error represented by the residuals of the linear regression between the multifactor model and historical performance (normally the standard deviation of the error term). This measure, defined as the information ratio, penalizes FoHFs whose performance is less predictable with the multifactor model selected to compute alpha (Gregoriou *et al.*, 2007).

The RAPs normally adopted to evaluate FoHFs frequently assume the normality of the returns, even if the underlying assets are characterized by non-normal behavior (i.e., Amo *et al.*, 2007). This assumption can be theoretically justified by the central limit theorem but is not supported by the data (Beckers *et al.*, 2007). Only a few studies on FoHFs compare RAP measures that assume a normal distribution with those that remove this simplified assumption and they demonstrate a lack of coherence between rankings defined using different types of risk measures (e.g., Gregoriou and Gueyie, 2003). There is no evidence, however, that the results for UCITS FoHFs can be generalized to the FoHFs market.

## 6.3. EMPIRICAL ANALYSIS

### 6.3.1. Sample

We obtain a sample of FoHFs for the period 2003–2011 from the Bloomberg database. We consider all FoHFs classified by both Bloomberg and Morningstar databases as UCITS-compliant, and collect all information available from 1 January 2003 (or the starting date of the fund if the fund is born later) to 31 December 2011. The final database includes 106 funds, but the sample composition is not stable over time due to the increase in the number of new funds launched in more recent years (see Figure 6.1).

Only around the 17% of funds were started before 2003 and more than 61% were born during the global financial crisis (2007–2011). The database provides only weekly data and we are therefore unable to consider any survivorship bias

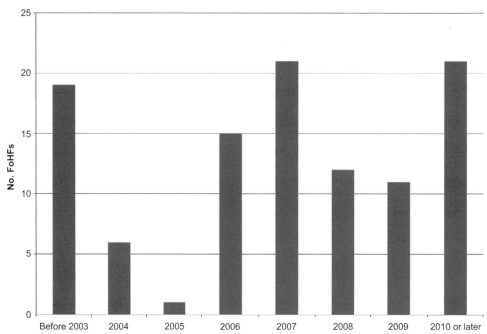

**FIGURE 6.1**
Sample breakdown by year.

affecting the data. In accordance with the literature (i.e., Laube *et al.*, 2011), we measure the performance of the FoHFs, considering fund appreciation in the time horizon $t_1 - t_2$:

$$_{t_1}Return_{t_2} = \ln\left(\frac{Price_{t_2}}{Price_{t_1}}\right), \qquad (6.1)$$

where, due to the characteristics of the database, a weekly lag exists between the two prices observed $(t_2 - t_1)$.

We perform a preliminary Shapiro–Wilk test on the returns to determine whether the returns of the FoHFs can be approximated using the normal distribution assumption (see Table 6.1).

Given a threshold of 90%, more than 92% of the FoHFs in each year exhibit performance behavior that is not coherent with the assumption of normality. If we consider a more selective threshold ($\alpha = 99\%$), the percentage of FoHFs that reject the hypothesis of normality is lower but, excluding 2005, still higher than 52%. The lack of normality affects a higher number of funds during the crisis period with respect to the rest of the time period analyzed. To construct the RAP measures, we also collect data from the Bloomberg database on the risk-free rate for a 3-month horizon for the reference country of each FoHF.

| Table 6.1 | Test for the Normality of the Return Distribution |

| | | Shapiro–Wilk test | | | | |
| | | α = 99% | | α = 95% | | α = 90% | |
| Year | No. of funds | No. of FoHFs | % FoHFs | No. of FoHFs | % FoHFs | No. of FoHFs | % FoHFs |
|---|---|---|---|---|---|---|---|
| 2003 | 19 | 10 | 52.63 | 10 | 52.63 | 18 | 94.74 |
| 2004 | 25 | 15 | 60.00 | 17 | 68.00 | 24 | 96.00 |
| 2005 | 26 | 12 | 46.15 | 18 | 69.23 | 24 | 92.31 |
| 2006 | 41 | 26 | 63.41 | 28 | 68.29 | 41 | 100.00 |
| 2007 | 62 | 34 | 54.84 | 47 | 75.81 | 62 | 100.00 |
| 2008 | 74 | 68 | 91.89 | 72 | 97.30 | 76 | 100.00 |
| 2009 | 85 | 70 | 82.35 | 72 | 84.71 | 85 | 100.00 |
| 2010 | 106 | 86 | 81.13 | 89 | 83.96 | 106 | 100.00 |
| 2011 | 106 | 92 | 86.79 | 99 | 93.40 | 106 | 100.00 |

$H_0$: Non-normality of the return distribution.

## 6.3.2. Methodology

We select the most widespread RAP scale-independent used in asset management (Sharpe index) and we test the effect of possible changes on the investment's risk profile. On the basis of the available literature (i.e., Eling, 2008), we identify 12 RAP measures that are constructed based on the excess return with respect to the risk-free rate (as in the Sharpe ratio). The RAPs considered are the following:

$$_{t_1}Sharpe_{t_2} = \frac{_{t_1}R_{t_2} - _{t_1}R_{t_2}^{Rf}}{\sigma(R_t)} \tag{6.2}$$

$$_{t_1}ROPS_{t_2} = \frac{_{t_1}R_{t_2} - _{t_1}R_{t_2}^{Rf}}{\frac{1}{t_2 - t_1}\sum_{t=t_1}^{t_2} \max\left|R_t^{Rf} - R_t, 0\right|^0} \tag{6.3}$$

$$_{t_1}ROAS_{t_2} = \frac{_{t_1}R_{t_2} - _{t_1}R_{t_2}^{Rf}}{\frac{1}{t_2 - t_1}\sum_{t=t_1}^{t_2} \max\left(R_t^{Rf} - R_t, 0\right)^1} \tag{6.4}$$

$$_{t_1}Sortino_{t_2} = \frac{_{t_1}R_{t_2} - _{t_1}R_{t_2}^{Rf}}{\sqrt[2]{\frac{1}{t_2 - t_1}\sum_{t=t_1}^{t_2} \max\left(R_t^{Rf} - R_t, 0\right)^2}} \tag{6.5}$$

$$_{t_1} Kappa_{t_2}^{n=3} = \frac{_{t_1}R_{t_2} - _{t_1}R_{t_2}^{\mathrm{Rf}}}{\sqrt[3]{\dfrac{1}{t_2 - t_1} \displaystyle\sum_{t=t_1}^{t_2} \max\left(R_t^{\mathrm{Rf}} - R_t, 0\right)^3}} \tag{6.6}$$

$$_{t_1} Kappa_{t_2}^{n=4} = \frac{_{t_1}R_{t_2} - _{t_1}R_{t_2}^{\mathrm{Rf}}}{\sqrt[4]{\dfrac{1}{t_2 - t_1} \displaystyle\sum_{t=t_1}^{t_2} \max\left(R_t^{\mathrm{Rf}} - R_t, 0\right)^4}} \tag{6.7}$$

$$_{t_1} Calmar_{t_2} = \frac{_{t_1}R_{t_2} - _{t_1}R_{t_2}^{\mathrm{Rf}}}{\left|_{t_1}MDD_{t_2}\right|} \tag{6.8}$$

$$_{t_1} Sterling_{t_2} = \frac{_{t_1}R_{t_2} - _{t_1}R_{t_2}^{\mathrm{Rf}}}{\displaystyle\sum_{i=1}^{n} \frac{1}{n}\left|_{t_1}MDD_{t_2}^{i}\right|} \tag{6.9}$$

$$_{t_1} Burke_{t_2} = \frac{_{t_1}R_{t_2} - _{t_1}R_{t_2}^{\mathrm{Rf}}}{\sqrt{\displaystyle\sum_{i=1}^{n} \frac{1}{n}\left(_{t_1}MDD_{t_2}^{i}\right)^2}} \tag{6.10}$$

$$_{t_1} VaR\ Ratio_{t_2} = \frac{R_t - R_{\mathrm{rf}}}{_{t_1}VaR_{t_2}} \tag{6.11}$$

$$_{t_1} CVaR\ Ratio_{t_2} = \frac{_{t_1}R_{t_2} - _{t_1}R_{t_2}^{\mathrm{Rf}}}{_{t_1}CVaR_{t_2}} \tag{6.12}$$

$$_{t_1} MVaR\ Ratio_{t_2} = \frac{_{t_1}R_{t_2} - _{t_1}R_{t_2}^{\mathrm{Rf}}}{_{t_1}MVaR_{t_2}} \tag{6.13}$$

$$_{t_1} Sharpe\ Omega_{t_2} = \frac{_{t_1}R_{t_2} - _{t_1}R_{t_2}^{\mathrm{Rf}}}{e^{-rf}{}_{t_1}E[\max(_tR_t - _tR_t^{\mathrm{Rf}}, 0]_{t_2}} . \tag{6.14}$$

In all the equations the numerator $({}_{t_1}R_{t_2} - {}_{t_1}R_{t_2}^{\mathrm{Rf}})$ represents the extra return of the FoHFs with respect to the risk-free rate, while the denominator changes with each measure. In accordance with the literature and the sample's characteristics, the risk-free rate is the yearly equivalent of a 3-month Treasury bill issued by the FoHFs reference country.

Equation (6.2) represents the Sharpe index — a measure of excess return with respect to the risk-free rate for each unit of risk assumed (Sharpe, 1994). This measure takes into account the overall distribution of results and assumes the normality of returns to summarize the investment's risk profile, considering only the first and second moments of the return distribution.

Equations (6.3)–(6.7) are constructed using the lower partial moments of the performance distribution, thus considering only the distribution of results lower than a given threshold (the risk-free rate). Equation (6.3) defines the Return on Probability of Shortfall (ROPS) constructed using the lower partial moment of order zero that represents the excess return with respect to the probability of losses (Pedersen and Rudholm-Alfvin, 2003). Equation (6.4) defines the Return on Absolute Shortfall (ROAS) using the lower partial moment of order one that measures the excess return with respect to the mean expected loss (Pedersen and Rudholm-Alfvin, 2003). Equation (6.5) proposes the Sortino measure that uses the lower partial moment of order two that measures the excess return with respect to downside risk (Sortino and Forsey, 1996). Equations (6.6) and (6.7) consider the lower partial moments, respectively, of orders three and four to define the investment's return—risk profile (kappa), considering, respectively, the distribution's skewness and kurtosis (Kaplan and Knowles, 2004).[1]

Equations (6.8)–(6.10) are constructed considering only the maximum amount of losses (maximum drawdown) on the yearly time horizon. Equation (6.8) considers only maximum losses and defines a measure (*Calmar ratio*) that computes the excess return with respect to the worst performance achieved (Young, 1991). Equation (6.9) takes into account the fund's $n$ worst performances and defines an index (*Sterling ratio*) equal to the ratio of the excess return to the arithmetic mean of these $n$ losses (Kestner, 1996).[2] Equation (6.10) considers the square root of the sum of the squares of $n$ drawdowns and defines a measure (*Burke ratio*) as the ratio between the excess return with respect to a risk-free rate and this average of maximum drawdowns (Burke, 1994).[3]

Equations (6.11)–(6.13) use the value at risk (VaR) as a proxy of risk exposure for the yearly time horizon, using a confidence level of $\alpha$ percent.[4] Equation (6.11) computes the ratio between the VaR and the investment at time zero, and defines a measure (*VaR ratio*) of the ratio of excess return to this risk exposure (Dowd, 2000). Equation (6.12) considers the average loss for a given threshold — the so-called conditional variable (CVaR) — and computes an index (*CVaR ratio*) as the ratio between excess return and the mean VaR (Agarwal and Naik, 2004).

---

[1]The kappa measure could be constructed by also considering higher orders but, for the purpose of the analysis, we set an upper limit of four for the order.

[2]On the basis of the literature, only the five highest losses are normally considered (Eling and Schuhmacher, 2007).

[3]On the basis of the literature, only the five highest losses are normally considered (Eling and Schuhmacher, 2007).

[4]All measures constructed based on the VaR consider the minimum threshold of 95% normally used in the evaluation of hedge funds (Guizot, 2007).

Equation (6.13) takes into account the non-normality of the distribution for extreme losses as well, using the Cornish–Fisher expansion to modify the VaR estimates, and defines a measure (*MVaR ratio*) as the ratio between excess return and the maximum corrected exposure (Gregoriou and Gueyie, 2003).

Equation (6.14) is derived from the omega measure – the ratio between the area of returns and losses related to the investment (Shadwick and Keating, 2002). It is possible to rewrite the omega using the put–call parity rule proposed by Black and Scholes (Kazemi *et al.*, 2004). A Sharpe–omega measure could thus be written as the ratio between excess return and the value of a put option with strike price equal to $R_f$ and a time horizon coherent with the evaluation period (1 year).

Following approaches presented in the literature to test the relevance of choices in the construction of a RAP measure (i.e. Eling and Schuhmacher, 2007), we perform a year-by-year correlation between rankings based on different performance measures, using Spearman's rank correlation coefficient. The analysis of the correlation considers all funds listed at time $t$ independently from the starting list date. To check the robustness of the relation identified by the Spearman correlation measure, we also perform a non-parametric test ($\chi^2$) of the degree of independence between rankings.

The literature shows that, using standard RAP measures, the performance of FoHFs is much more persistent than that of individual hedge funds (Beckers *et al.*, 2007). Following other studies (e.g., Carhart, 1997), we construct a 1-year contingency table to compare the ranks at time $t-1$ and $t$ of all funds listed at time $t-1$, and we present for each year and for each RAP measure the percentage of persistence of funds in the same decile or quartile ranking.

To evaluate the usefulness of the different RAP measures in selecting the best investments in a 1-year time horizon, we use an investment strategy simulation approach. Following other studies (e.g., Gregoriou and Pascalau, 2010), we analyze the performance of investing in the top one, five, and 10 funds – identified by different RAP measures – with respect to that achievable by replicating the overall market index or using a naïve diversification strategy.

1. *Benchmark.* We consider all the funds available at time $t-1$ and invest the same amount of money ($i_t = j_t = 1/N_t$) in each of them. We update the portfolio composition every year and compute the yearly performance.
2. *Naïve strategy: one FoHF.* We randomly select one FoHF from all the funds available at time $t-1$ and invest all the money in it. We update the portfolio composition every year and compute the yearly performance.
3. *Naïve strategy: five FoHFs.* We randomly select five FoHFs from all the funds available at time $t-1$ and invest the same amount of money in each of them. We update the portfolio composition every year and compute the yearly performance.
4. *Naïve strategy: 10 FoHFs.* We randomly select 10 FoHFs from all the funds available at time $t-1$ and invest the same amount of money in each of

them. We update the portfolio composition every year and compute the yearly performance.

5. *Top-performing FoHFs at time* t − 1. We consider the ranking defined for each RAP at time $t-1$ and select only FoHFs ranked first in year $t$. We update the portfolio composition every year and compute the yearly performance.

6. *Top five performing FoHFs at time* t − 1. We consider the ranking defined for each RAP at time $t-1$ and select only the top 10 FoHFs in year $t$, investing the same amount of money in each of them. We update the portfolio composition every year and compute the yearly performance.

7. *Top 10 performing FoHFs at time* t − 1. We consider the ranking defined for each RAP at time $t-1$ and select only the top 10 FoHFs in year $t$, investing the same amount of money in each of them. We update the portfolio composition every year and compute the yearly performance.

To evaluate the effect of the global financial crisis on the investment selection, we compute the compound performance achieved for the full time horizon (2004−2011), and for subperiods 2004−2007 and 2008−2011, respectively, before and during the financial crisis.

## 6.3.3. Results

A preliminary analysis evaluates whether the change in risk measure significantly affects the results obtained for the investment selection process for different RAPs. We construct rankings of the investment FoHFs available at time $t$ for each year on the basis of the 12 RAP measures mentioned earlier. We perform a standard Pearson correlation analysis between the different rankings for the overall time horizon and for the two subperiods 2003−2007 and 2008−2011 (see Table 6.2).

Looking at the overall time horizon, results demonstrate that correlations between the rankings constructed using different RAP measures are quite high but never statistically significantly on the basis of a $\chi^2$-test. For the overall time horizon (2003−2011), the Sharpe ratio shows a higher correlation with omega and the Burke and Calmar ratios, while the lower-correlated RAPs are the ROPS, the VaR, and the CVaR. Comparing the pre-crisis period (2003−2007) with the crisis period (2007−2011), we frequently find the correlation between rankings to be decreased and the significance of the correlation measures disappear; therefore during the crisis the probability of misalignments is increased.

Comparing rankings constructed using the same RAP measure for the same set of funds in two subsequent years, we note some interesting results (see Table 6.3). If we consider the persistence of funds in the same decile for two subsequent years, only around 10%, on average, maintain the same percentile over a 1-year time horizon. As expected, when the quartile distribution is taken into account, the average persistence increases over time and the value is at least doubled.

**Table 6.2**  Correlation Matrix of Rankings Constructed for the Overall Period and Before and After the Global Crisis

| Measure | Period | Sharpe | ROPS | ROAS | Sortino | Kappa (n=3) | Kappa (n=4) | Burke | Calmar | Sterling | VaR | CVaR | MVaR | Omega |
|---|---|---|---|---|---|---|---|---|---|---|---|---|---|---|
| Sharpe | 2003–2007 | 1 | | | | | | | | | | | | |
| | 2008–2011 | | | | | | | | | | | | | |
| | 2003–2011 | | | | | | | | | | | | | |
| ROPS | 2003–2007 | 0.67 | 1 | | | | | | | | | | | |
| | 2008–2011 | 0.15 | | | | | | | | | | | | |
| | 2003–2011 | 0.37 | | | | | | | | | | | | |
| ROAS | 2003–2007 | 0.71 | 0.95** | 1 | | | | | | | | | | |
| | 2008–2011 | 0.38 | 0.79 | | | | | | | | | | | |
| | 2003–2011 | 0.53 | 0.85 | | | | | | | | | | | |
| Sortino | 2003–2007 | 0.85** | 0.90** | 0.91** | 1 | | | | | | | | | |
| | 2008–2011 | 0.61 | 0.74 | 0.83 | | | | | | | | | | |
| | 2003–2011 | 0.71 | 0.81 | 0.87 | | | | | | | | | | |
| Kappa (n=3) | 2003–2007 | 0.25 | 0.42 | 0.42 | 0.32 | 1 | | | | | | | | |
| | 2008–2011 | 0.32 | 0.72 | 0.45 | 0.62 | | | | | | | | | |
| | 2003–2011 | 0.45 | 0.75 | 0.56 | 0.67 | | | | | | | | | |
| Kappa (n=4) | 2003–2007 | 0.72 | 0.84 | 0.79 | 0.82 | 0.35 | 1 | | | | | | | |
| | 2008–2011 | 0.31 | 0.55 | 0.37 | 0.50 | 0.62 | | | | | | | | |
| | 2003–2011 | 0.48 | 0.67 | 0.53 | 0.63 | 0.68 | | | | | | | | |
| Burke | 2003–2007 | 0.92** | 0.80 | 0.80** | 0.93 | 0.27 | 0.82 | 1 | | | | | | |
| | 2008–2011 | 0.71 | 0.60 | 0.61 | 0.88 | 0.72 | 0.56 | | | | | | | |
| | 2003–2011 | 0.79 | 0.69 | 0.71 | 0.91 | 0.75 | 0.67 | | | | | | | |
| Calmar | 2003–2007 | 0.87** | 0.76 | 0.72** | 0.86 | 0.21 | 0.83 | 0.91** | 1 | | | | | |
| | 2008–2011 | 0.74 | 0.60 | 0.67 | 0.91 | 0.62 | 0.47 | 0.91* | | | | | | |
| | 2003–2011 | 0.81 | 0.70 | 0.74 | 0.92 | 0.67 | 0.60 | 0.93 | | | | | | |
| Sterling | 2003–2007 | 0.87 | 0.81 | 0.77 | 0.92 | 0.62 | 0.80 | 0.96 | 0.94 | 1 | | | | |
| | 2008–2011 | 0.62 | 0.46 | 0.59 | 0.75 | 0.42 | 0.33 | 0.69 | 0.83 | | | | | |
| | 2003–2011 | 0.69 | 0.57 | 0.68 | 0.80 | 0.55 | 0.46 | 0.75 | 0.86 | | | | | |
| VaR | 2003–2007 | 0.24 | 0.43 | 0.37 | 0.34 | 0.24 | 0.40 | 0.34 | 0.49 | 0.26** | 1 | | | |
| | 2008–2011 | 0.26 | 0.29 | 0.25 | 0.31 | 0.31 | 0.29 | 0.35 | 0.34 | 0.26 | | | | |
| | 2003–2011 | 0.41 | 0.44 | 0.41 | 0.45 | 0.46 | 0.43 | 0.48 | 0.47 | 0.42 | | | | |
| CVaR | 2003–2007 | 0.42 | 0.48 | 0.43 | 0.46 | 0.33 | 0.50 | 0.51 | 0.54 | 0.35** | 0.82 | 1 | | |
| | 2008–2011 | 0.26 | 0.30 | 0.26 | 0.31 | 0.30 | 0.30 | 0.35 | 0.34 | 0.27 | 0.98 | | | |
| | 2003–2011 | 0.42 | 0.45 | 0.42 | 0.46 | 0.46 | 0.44 | 0.48 | 0.48 | 0.43 | 0.98 | | | |
| MVaR | 2003–2007 | 0.84** | 0.70 | 0.66 | 0.78 | 0.26 | 0.76 | 0.86 | 0.87 | 0.89** | 0.45 | 0.58 | 1 | |
| | 2008–2011 | 0.66 | 0.21 | 0.30 | 0.45 | 0.32 | 0.27 | 0.54** | 0.55** | 0.36 | 0.73 | 0.74 | | |
| | 2003–2011 | 0.74 | 0.41 | 0.47 | 0.59 | 0.46 | 0.46 | 0.66 | 0.66 | 0.50 | 0.77 | 0.78 | | |
| Omega | 2003–2007 | 0.78 | 0.58 | 0.57 | 0.73 | 0.09 | 0.69 | 0.78 | 0.83 | 0.85** | 0.27** | 0.40** | 0.75 | 1 |
| | 2008–2011 | 0.81 | 0.25 | 0.30 | 0.54 | 0.42 | 0.32 | 0.60 | 0.70 | 0.54 | 0.37 | 0.41 | 0.65 | |
| | 2003–2011 | 0.84 | 0.44 | 0.48 | 0.66 | 0.54 | 0.49 | 0.69 | 0.77 | 0.64 | 0.51 | 0.51 | 0.73 | |

This table shows the pairwise linear correlation and $\chi^2$-test results between rankings based on different RAP measures for both the overall time horizon and the two subperiods before and after the global financial crisis.
$\chi^2$-tests significant at the *95% and **99% levels.

| | Table 6.3 | Persistence in the Rankings (%) for each RAP Measure on a Yearly Time Horizon | | | | | | |
|---|---|---|---|---|---|---|---|---|
| | 2004 | 2005 | 2006 | 2007 | 2008 | 2009 | 2010 | 2011 |
| *Decile persistence between rankings at time* t $-$ 1 *and* t | | | | | | | | |
| Sharpe | 15.79 | 12.00 | 11.54 | 12.50 | 4.92 | 1.37 | 14.12 | 5.66 |
| ROPS | 21.05 | 16.00 | 14.29 | 5.00 | 8.06 | 4.11 | 19.54 | 7.48 |
| ROAS | 15.79 | 12.00 | 14.29 | 7.50 | 12.90 | 12.33 | 21.84 | 6.54 |
| Sortino | 26.32 | 16.00 | 7.14 | 2.50 | 4.92 | 4.11 | 6.90 | 6.54 |
| Kappa ($n = 3$) | 21.05 | 4.00 | 10.71 | 15.00 | 1.64 | 2.74 | 16.09 | 9.43 |
| Kappa ($n = 4$) | 21.05 | 4.00 | 7.69 | 2.50 | 1.64 | 4.11 | 9.30 | 13.21 |
| Calmar | 11.11 | 0.00 | 15.38 | 12.50 | 3.33 | 10.96 | 6.02 | 8.57 |
| Sterling | 22.22 | 4.35 | 11.54 | 12.50 | 8.33 | 6.85 | 7.23 | 12.50 |
| Burke | 0.00 | 11.11 | 0.00 | 15.38 | 3.85 | 3.57 | 7.14 | 4.05 |
| VaR | 0.00 | 6.67 | 0.00 | 10.53 | 5.88 | 13.04 | 20.75 | 4.17 |
| CVaR | 0.00 | 0.00 | 15.38 | 18.75 | 2.94 | 8.70 | 18.87 | 3.16 |
| MVaR | 15.79 | 8.00 | 7.69 | 17.50 | 1.64 | 1.37 | 11.76 | 3.77 |
| Omega | 31.25 | 17.65 | 18.75 | 5.00 | 4.17 | 6.67 | 5.88 | 8.65 |
| *Quartile persistence between rankings at time* t $-$ 1 *and* t | | | | | | | | |
| Sharpe | 47.37 | 16.00 | 30.77 | 32.50 | 13.11 | 10.96 | 32.94 | 9.43 |
| ROPS | 26.32 | 32.00 | 21.43 | 10.00 | 20.97 | 10.96 | 41.38 | 15.89 |
| ROAS | 36.84 | 32.00 | 25.00 | 22.50 | 19.35 | 16.44 | 32.18 | 12.15 |
| Sortino | 42.11 | 28.00 | 28.57 | 25.00 | 13.11 | 17.81 | 19.54 | 11.21 |
| Kappa ($n = 3$) | 57.89 | 16.00 | 21.43 | 30.00 | 16.39 | 12.33 | 32.18 | 16.98 |
| Kappa ($n = 4$) | 21.05 | 16.00 | 23.08 | 12.50 | 31.15 | 19.18 | 27.91 | 24.53 |
| Calmar | 27.78 | 17.39 | 42.31 | 20.00 | 25.00 | 20.55 | 16.87 | 15.24 |
| Sterling | 44.44 | 21.74 | 26.92 | 30.00 | 18.33 | 23.29 | 22.89 | 15.38 |
| Burke | 20.00 | 11.11 | 8.33 | 30.77 | 15.38 | 10.71 | 28.57 | 6.76 |
| VaR | 9.09 | 20.00 | 23.08 | 21.05 | 14.71 | 19.57 | 28.30 | 5.21 |
| CVaR | 18.18 | 20.00 | 23.08 | 31.25 | 8.82 | 15.22 | 26.42 | 6.32 |
| MVaR | 57.89 | 12.00 | 42.31 | 32.50 | 4.92 | 9.59 | 37.65 | 5.66 |
| Omega | 56.25 | 23.53 | 25.00 | 25.00 | 8.33 | 13.33 | 15.29 | 21.15 |

The persistence of rankings is measured by comparing the ranking positions at time $t - 1$ and $t$ for all FoHFs available at time $t$, and computing the number of funds ranked in the same quartile or decile in two subsequent years.

The choice of the quartile distribution instead of the decile distribution affects not only average persistence, but also the highest and lowest persistent RAP measures. For decile persistence, more stable rankings are constructed using the ROPS (average persistence 11.94%) and more unstable rankings are constructed using Burke (average persistence 5.64%), while for the quartile analysis the more stable RAP is Kappa corrected for asymmetry (average persistence 22.43%) and the more unstable RAP is defined by the VaR ratio (average persistence 16.46%).

Excluding the Kappa corrected for skewness, during the financial crisis the time persistence of rankings is, on average, lower and the RAP that is more affected by the crisis is MVaR; in the period 2008−2010 this finding indicates a mean persistence that is lower than 40% of the mean computed in the pre-crisis period.

Once the differences in the persistence of rankings over time are determined, we study the performance of an investment strategy at time $t$ focused on the top performers at time $t-1$ identified on the basis of different RAP measures (see Table 6.4). Investment strategies based on selecting only top performers identified on the basis of past values of RAP measures frequently beat the market and normally outperform a naïve investment selection process. Considering the Sharpe ratio, investment in last year's top performer yields, on average, earnings of more than 3% with respect to the market, while investments in the top five and 10 performers negatively impact performance, decreasing the average extra return with respect to the market to 3.11% and 1.03%, respectively.

When we consider investment strategies focusing on only one FoHF, the best selection criteria are those based on ROPS, which yield, on average, an extra return with respect to the market higher than 5.8%. The choice of only one FoHF is a risky strategy because the excess return can vary from 39.30% (2008) to $-46.2\%$ (2011), and there is no clear relation between market trend and the difference between the performance achieved with the strategy selected and the benchmark.

Regarding strategies that construct a more diversified portfolio (top five or 10 funds), the number of years in which each strategy outperforms the market increases (66% of cases for the top five strategies and 69% of cases for the top 10 strategies) even if the average extra return is lower. The CVaR value at time $t-1$ represents the best criterion for selecting both a portfolio of five FoHFs that outperform the market (on average, by 3.70%) and a portfolio of 10 FoHFs on the basis of past performance (on average, outperforming the market by 3.24%). Strategies constructed for higher numbers of FoHFs (five or 10) are frequently characterized by a smaller range of variation of the extra returns achieved with respect to the strategy of investing in only the top performer.

On a multiyear time horizon, the analysis of the overall performance is affected not only by the return achieved by the investment strategy each year but also by the sequence of results obtained in the time horizon. We compute the compound performance achieved for the full time horizon (2004–2011), and for the subperiods 2004–2007 and 2008–2011 (see Table 6.5). Even a naïve diversification strategy not focused on only one FoHF outperforms the market for the overall time horizon and the pre-crisis period. This finding demonstrates that market replication is not an efficient solution for investors interested in maximizing performance in a growing market scenario.

The Sharpe ratio allows one to construct an investment portfolio that outperforms the market for the overall time horizon considered because it can obtain extra yields during the crisis that overcomes the underperformance of the pre-crisis period. Examining strategies based on other RAP measures, choosing to invest in only the top-performing FoHFs on the basis of past ROAS, Kappa corrected for asymmetry, VaR, or CVaR values allows maximization of overall performance and beats the market in both the pre-crisis and crisis periods. For all the other RAP measures, the top-performing fund strategy works only in the

| Table 6.4 | Investment Strategy Performance (%) with Respect to the Market Benchmark |

| | | 2004 | 2005 | 2006 | 2007 | 2008 | 2009 | 2010 | 2011 |
|---|---|---|---|---|---|---|---|---|---|
| Benchmark | | 6.14 | 5.86 | 7.14 | 7.50 | −19.39 | 7.66 | 3.22 | −6.42 |
| *Investment strategy/FoHFs selection criteria [extra performance (%) with respect to the benchmark]* | | | | | | | | | |
| Naïve diversification | 1 fund | 1.62 | 2.62 | 0.55 | −0.63 | −1.51 | 3.50 | 1.61 | 4.54 |
| | 5 funds | 6.19 | 7.69 | 10.36 | 8.54 | −2.94 | 9.47 | 5.09 | −3.74 |
| | 10 funds | 4.89 | 5.75 | 9.72 | 9.52 | −8.57 | 10.52 | 2.82 | −8.72 |
| Sharpe$_{t-1}$ | Top 1 | −1.53 | −0.38 | 2.83 | 4.25 | 1.79 | 11.50 | 0.58 | 5.85 |
| | Top 5 | −0.48 | −2.33 | 4.48 | 1.73 | 2.15 | 2.74 | −0.87 | 0.85 |
| | Top 10 | −0.69 | −0.84 | 4.13 | 3.63 | 2.32 | 10.16 | −2.24 | 1.41 |
| ROPS$_{t-1}$ | Top 1 | 4.34 | 28.26 | 9.44 | 10.95 | 39.30 | −14.91 | 16.22 | −46.62 |
| | Top 5 | 2.89 | 12.64 | 6.28 | 1.61 | 13.13 | −6.94 | 15.79 | −34.97 |
| | Top 10 | 1.38 | 8.80 | 4.91 | 0.83 | 3.59 | −5.03 | 10.18 | −18.85 |
| ROAS$_{t-1}$ | Top 1 | 4.34 | 13.61 | 9.44 | 10.95 | 39.30 | −14.91 | −8.83 | 4.67 |
| | Top 5 | 1.55 | 10.02 | 5.28 | 3.97 | 11.35 | −6.94 | 1.19 | 1.16 |
| | Top 10 | 0.84 | 6.33 | 4.77 | 4.04 | 7.48 | −4.61 | 2.92 | −0.88 |
| Sortino$_{t-1}$ | Top 1 | −1.53 | −7.57 | 9.44 | 10.95 | 1.79 | −14.91 | −8.83 | 0.07 |
| | Top 5 | 1.32 | −0.25 | 4.83 | 2.37 | −0.56 | −6.94 | 1.18 | −2.83 |
| | Top 10 | 0.53 | 1.99 | 3.76 | 4.15 | −5.79 | −3.96 | 1.03 | −0.42 |
| Kappa $(n=3)_{t-1}$ | Top 1 | 4.34 | 6.15 | −6.50 | −0.57 | 1.79 | −4.75 | −8.83 | −46.62 |
| | Top 5 | 1.38 | 6.72 | 4.06 | −1.47 | −4.60 | −2.27 | 4.35 | −28.42 |
| | Top 10 | 0.15 | 9.00 | 3.84 | 0.52 | −3.69 | −2.43 | 6.72 | −19.60 |
| Kappa $(n=4)_{t-1}$ | Top 1 | 3.47 | 7.10 | −3.49 | −2.64 | 1.79 | 2.88 | 1.52 | 0.55 |
| | Top 5 | 3.47 | −0.18 | 4.13 | 0.22 | 5.11 | 0.40 | 9.51 | −18.64 |
| | Top 10 | 1.54 | −0.39 | 3.42 | 1.28 | 4.92 | −4.89 | 6.89 | −15.04 |
| Calmar$_{t-1}$ | Top 1 | 1.70 | −0.38 | 9.44 | 4.77 | −1.76 | −14.91 | 3.84 | 0.07 |
| | Top 5 | 1.00 | −1.74 | 4.48 | 1.85 | −2.57 | −6.94 | 0.16 | 1.28 |
| | Top 10 | 0.25 | −0.06 | 4.22 | 3.70 | −3.38 | −3.56 | 0.80 | −0.71 |
| Sterling$_{t-1}$ | Top 1 | 1.70 | −7.57 | 9.44 | 4.86 | −4.29 | −14.91 | 3.84 | 0.07 |
| | Top 5 | −0.65 | −3.75 | 3.10 | 3.44 | −1.45 | −6.94 | 0.16 | 2.59 |
| | Top 10 | −0.57 | −0.06 | 4.22 | 4.73 | −3.36 | 0.45 | 0.11 | 2.66 |
| Burke$_{t-1}$ | Top 1 | −2.47 | −0.38 | 1.39 | 0.06 | 1.79 | −14.91 | 0.24 | −1.38 |
| | Top 5 | 2.71 | 12.20 | 5.15 | 3.07 | −0.91 | −7.81 | −2.27 | −0.60 |
| | Top 10 | 2.39 | 9.16 | 4.22 | 0.77 | 0.19 | 4.35 | −0.19 | −0.02 |
| VaR$_{t-1}$ | Top 1 | −3.10 | 10.30 | 0.64 | −6.61 | 2.59 | 7.86 | 4.62 | 0.07 |
| | Top 5 | 0.31 | 3.95 | 2.24 | 2.08 | 15.27 | 3.27 | 2.42 | −0.51 |
| | Top 10 | 0.98 | 5.96 | 2.69 | 3.45 | 6.13 | 2.82 | 2.13 | −0.62 |
| CVaR$_{t-1}$ | Top 1 | −3.10 | 10.30 | 0.64 | −2.64 | 1.52 | 7.86 | 4.62 | 0.07 |
| | Top 5 | 1.72 | 3.95 | 1.90 | 2.63 | 14.82 | 3.27 | 2.42 | −1.11 |
| | Top 10 | 0.98 | 5.96 | 3.00 | 1.44 | 10.44 | 2.82 | 2.13 | −0.83 |
| MVaR$_{t-1}$ | Top 1 | −1.19 | 11.46 | 0.64 | 7.99 | 19.29 | −15.07 | −1.15 | 4.67 |
| | Top 5 | −0.01 | 5.05 | 2.89 | 4.97 | −3.43 | −3.40 | −1.56 | 1.95 |
| | Top 10 | 0.51 | 2.01 | 3.50 | 3.17 | −0.71 | −0.95 | −1.19 | 1.79 |
| Omega$_{t-1}$ | Top 1 | 2.47 | 1.71 | 7.21 | 4.24 | −13.49 | −6.37 | 0.58 | 0.91 |
| | Top 5 | 1.59 | 3.01 | 4.06 | 2.02 | −0.25 | 9.46 | −0.87 | 1.88 |
| | Top 10 | 0.85 | 2.97 | 1.54 | 1.53 | −4.07 | 13.22 | −1.04 | 1.52 |

The performance of investment strategies based on different RAP measures at time $t-1$ is computed on a yearly time horizon. We identify the top-performing FoHFs at time $t-1$ for each year and measure the performance achieved by an investment strategy focused only on these funds. We consider different portfolio sizes (one, five, and 10 FoHFs) and compare their results against the overall market and a naïve diversification strategy.

**Table 6.5** Yield of Investment Strategies (%) Before and During the Financial Crisis

| | | Pre-Crisis (2004–2007) | Crisis (2008–2011) | Overall Time Horizon |
|---|---|---|---|---|
| Benchmark | | 29.39 | −16.16 | 8.48 |
| *Investment selection criteria* | | | | |
| Naïve diversification | 1 fund | 3.48 | 7.46 | 11.19 |
| | 5 funds | 37.41 | −9.07 | 24.94 |
| | 10 funds | 29.78 | −20.90 | 2.66 |
| $Sharpe_{t-1}$ | Top 1 | 5.16 | 20.83 | 27.06 |
| | Top 5 | 3.32 | 4.92 | 8.40 |
| | Top 10 | 6.27 | 11.75 | 18.75 |
| $ROPS_{t-1}$ | Top 1 | 62.50 | −26.46 | 19.51 |
| | Top 5 | 25.16 | −20.72 | −0.78 |
| | Top 10 | 16.68 | −12.04 | 2.63 |
| $ROAS_{t-1}$ | Top 1 | 43.94 | 13.12 | 62.81 |
| | Top 5 | 22.30 | 6.07 | 29.72 |
| | Top 10 | 16.87 | 4.60 | 22.25 |
| $Sortino_{t-1}$ | Top 1 | 10.51 | −20.98 | −12.67 |
| | Top 5 | 8.47 | −9.01 | −1.31 |
| | Top 10 | 10.79 | −8.98 | 0.85 |
| $Kappa\ (n=3)_{t-1}$ | Top 1 | 2.97 | −52.82 | −51.42 |
| | Top 5 | 10.93 | −30.35 | −22.74 |
| | Top 10 | 13.95 | −19.37 | −8.12 |
| $Kappa\ (n=4)_{t-1}$ | Top 1 | 4.13 | 6.89 | 11.31 |
| | Top 5 | 7.78 | −5.97 | 1.35 |
| | Top 10 | 5.94 | −9.38 | −3.99 |
| $Calmar_{t-1}$ | Top 1 | 16.16 | −13.13 | 0.91 |
| | Top 5 | 5.62 | −8.02 | −2.85 |
| | Top 10 | 8.28 | −6.74 | 0.98 |
| $Sterling_{t-1}$ | Top 1 | 7.87 | −15.36 | −8.71 |
| | Top 5 | 1.98 | −5.76 | −3.89 |
| | Top 10 | 8.46 | −0.24 | 8.20 |
| $Burke_{t-1}$ | Top 1 | −1.43 | −14.37 | −15.60 |
| | Top 5 | 24.89 | −11.26 | 10.83 |
| | Top 10 | 17.39 | 4.34 | 22.48 |
| $VaR_{t-1}$ | Top 1 | 0.45 | 15.84 | 16.36 |
| | Top 5 | 8.83 | 21.29 | 32.00 |
| | Top 10 | 13.68 | 10.76 | 25.91 |
| $CVaR_{t-1}$ | Top 1 | 4.73 | 14.63 | 20.05 |
| | Top 5 | 10.58 | 20.09 | 32.80 |
| | Top 10 | 11.80 | 15.02 | 28.59 |
| $MVaR_{t-1}$ | Top 1 | 19.68 | 4.84 | 25.48 |
| | Top 5 | 13.45 | −6.38 | 6.21 |
| | Top 10 | 9.47 | −1.08 | 8.29 |
| $Omega_{t-1}$ | Top 1 | 16.47 | −17.80 | −4.26 |
| | Top 5 | 11.10 | 10.27 | 22.50 |
| | Top 10 | 7.07 | 9.12 | 16.83 |

The performance of investment strategies based on different RAP measures at time $t-1$ is computed for the overall time horizon and the pre-crisis and crisis periods. We identify the top-performing FoHFs at time $t-1$ for each year and measure the performance achieved by an investment strategy focused only on these funds. We consider different portfolio sizes (one, five, and 10 FoHFs) and compare their results against the overall market and a naïve diversification strategy.

pre-crisis or crisis period. In addition, during the crisis period, even if the performance achieved is better than the benchmark, the overall performance is negative.

When more diversified portfolios are taken into account, the maximum extra performance decreases but it is still possible to identify an investment strategy that can maximize the extra return for the overall time horizon and for both subperiods: the best selection criteria for a portfolio of five or 10 FoHFs are based on past values of the CVaR.

## CONCLUSION

The analysis of performance achieved by UCITS FoHFs demonstrates that these investments also suffer from a lack of normality of returns, as for all other hedge funds (e.g., Carretta and Mattarocci, 2008). Analysis of the ranking constructed using different RAP measures reveals that the choice of risk measures significantly affects the ranks defined and their persistence over time.

Moreover, the choice of RAP measures impacts on the ability of an investment strategy based on past RAP values to beat the market. Past performance information normally leads to higher performance with respect to a naïve diversification strategy and the usefulness of this information is greater when the investment strategy is diversified among different FoHFs than when all the resources are concentrated on only the top performer. Determining the best RAP measure to evaluate the FoHFs industry is difficult because it is impossible to identify a measure that maximizes the difference between the investment strategy and the market benchmark for all the years considered.

Considering the periods before and after the global financial crisis separately, the choice of RAP measures impacts investment returns differently, with more significant differences during the crisis period. In the pre-crisis period the assumption of normality could imply lower performance with respect to the other investment strategies. During the crisis period only a few RAP measures allow one to construct investment strategies not based on the assumption of a normal distribution that beat the market.

A more detailed dataset of the characteristics of the UCITS FoHFs considered may provide further insight into the relation between fund characteristics and rank on the basis of different RAP measures and allow one to test whether certain features (e.g., leverage) affect the ranking constructed using various RAPs more than others. More information about the funds considered may also allow the definition of more complex investment strategies based on past RAP values that identify different weights for each FoHF on the basis of specific characteristics (e.g., size).

## Acknowledgments

This chapter is the result of the authors' combined efforts and continuous exchange of ideas. The introduction of the paper is ascribed to A. C. and the other sections to G. M. The authors wish to thank Dr Riccardo Mariano for his valuable research advice.

## References

Agarwal, V., & Naik, N. Y. (2004). Risk and Portfolio Decisions Involving Hedge Funds. *Review of Financial Studies, 17*(1), 63–98.

Alexander, C., & Dimitriu, A. (2005). Rank Alpha Funds of Hedge Funds. *Journal of Alternative Investments, 8*(2), 48–61.

Amenc, N., & Vaissié, M. (2006). Determinants of Funds of Hedge Funds' Performance. *Journal of Investing, 15*(4), 46–62.

Ammann, M., & Moerth, P. (2008). Performance of Funds of Hedge Funds. *Journal of Wealth Management, 11*(1), 46–63.

Amo, A. V., Harasty, H., & Hillion, P. (2007). Diversification Benefits of Funds of Hedge Funds: Identifying the Optimal Number of Hedge Funds. *Journal of Alternative Investments, 10*(2), 10–21.

Anderberg, K., & Bolton, L. (2006). UCITS: A Developing Model for the Future of the European Investment Fund Marketplace. In Euromoney (Ed.), *International Investment & Securities Review.* Colchester: Euromoney Yearbooks.

Beckers, S. E., Curds, R., & Weinberger, S. (2007). Funds of Hedge Funds Take the Wrong Risks. *Journal of Portfolio Management, 33*(3), 108–121.

Brown, S. J., Gregoriou, G. N., & Pascalau, R. (2012). Diversification in Funds of Hedge Funds: Is it Possible to Overdiversify? *Review of Asset Pricing Studies, 2*(1), 89–110.

Burke, G. (1994). A Sharper Sharpe Ratio. *Futures, 23*(3), 56.

Carhart, M. M. (1997). On Persistence in Mutual Fund Performance. *Journal of Finance, 52*(1), 57–82.

Carretta, A., & Mattarocci, G. (2008). Performance Evaluation of Hedge Funds: A Comparison of Different Approaches. In A. Carretta, F. Fiordelisi, & G. Mattarocci (Eds.), *New Drivers of Performance in a Changing Financial World.* Basingstoke: Palgrave Macmillan.

Denvir, E., & Hutson, E. (2006). The Performance and Diversification Benefits of Funds of Hedge Funds. *Journal of International Financial Markets, Institutions and Money, 16*(1), 4–22.

Dowd, K. (2000). Adjusting for Risk: An Improved Sharpe Ratio. *International Review of Economics and Finance, 9*(3), 209–222.

Eling, M. (2008). Does the Measure Matter in the Mutual Fund Industry? *Financial Analysts Journal, 64*(3), 54–66.

Eling, M., & Schuhmacher, F. (2007). Does the Choice of Performance Measure Influence the Evaluation of Hedge Funds? *Journal of Banking and Finance, 31*(9), 2632–2647.

Fuss, R., Kaiser, D. G., & Strittmatter, A. (2009). Measuring Funds of Hedge Funds Performance Using Quantile Regressions: Do Experience and Size Matter? *Journal of Alternative Investments, 12*(2), 41–53.

Gregoriou, G. N. (2003). Performance Evaluation of Funds of Hedge Funds Using Conditional Alphas and Betas. *Derivatives Use, Trading & Regulation, 8*(4), 324–344.

Gregoriou, G. N., & Gueyie, J. P. (2003). Risk-adjusted Performance of Funds of Hedge Funds Using a Modified Sharpe Ratio. *Journal of Wealth Management, 6*(3), 77–83.

Gregoriou, G. N., & Pascalau, R. (2010). Selecting Prior Year's Top Fund of Hedge Funds as This Year's Choice. *Journal of Wealth Management, 13*(2), 61–68.

Gregoriou, G. N., Hubner, G., Papageorgiou, N., & Rouah, F. D. (2007). Funds of Funds versus Simple Portfolios of Hedge Funds: A Comparative Study of Persistence in Performance. *Journal of Derivatives & Hedge Funds, 13*(2), 88–106.

Guizot, A. (2007). *The Hedge Fund Compliance and Risk Management Guide.* Chichester: Wiley.

Gulko, L. (2003). Performance Metrics for Hedge Funds. *Journal of Alternative Investments, 5*(4), 88–95.

Hauser, J., & Petit, M. (2008). Examining Alternative Strategies within the Context of UCITS III Regulations. *Journal of Securities Law, Regulation & Compliance, 2*(1), 19–28.

Johannsen, K. R. (2011). Jumping the Gun: Hedge Funds in Search of Capital Under UCITS IV. *Brooklyn Journal of Corporate, Financial & Commercial Law, 5*(2), 473–501.

Kaplan, P. D., & Knowles, J. A. (2004). Kappa: A Generalized Down-side Risk-adjusted Performance Measure. *Journal of Performance Measurement, 8*(1), 42–54.

Kazemi, H., Schneeweis, T., & Gupta, B. (2004). Omega as a Performance Measure. *Journal of Performance Measurement, 8*(3), 16—25.

Kestner, L. N. (1996). Getting a Handle on True Performance. *Futures, 25*(1), 44—46.

Laube, F., Schiltz, J., & Terraza, V. (2011). On the Efficiency of Risk Measures for Funds of Hedge Funds. *Journal of Derivatives & Hedge Funds, 17*(1), 63—84.

Pascual, J. L., & Cuellar, R. C. (2007). The Challenges of Launching, Rating and Regulating Funds of Hedge Funds. *Journal of Derivatives & Hedge Funds, 13*(3), 247—262.

Pedersen, C. S., & Rudholm-Alfvin, T. (2003). Selecting a Risk-Adjusted Shareholder Performance Measure. *Journal of Asset Management, 4*(3), 152—172.

Reedy, G., Brady, P., & Patel, K. (2007). Are Funds of Funds Simply Multi-Strategy Managers with Extra Fees? *Journal of Alternative Investment, 10*(3), 49—61.

Shadwick, W., & Keating, C. (2002). A Universal Performance Measure. *Journal of Performance Measurement, 6*(3), 59—84.

Sharpe, W. F. (1994). The Sharpe Ratio. *Journal of Portfolio Management, 21*(1), 49—58.

Shawky, H. A., Dai, N., & Cumming, D. (2012). Diversification in the Hedge Fund Industry. *Journal of Corporate Finance, 18*(1), 166—178.

Sortino, F. A., & Forsey, H. J. (1996). On the Use and Misuse of Downside Risk. *Journal of Portfolio Management, 22*(2), 35—42.

Xiong, J., Idzorek, T., Chen, P., & Ibbotson, R. (2009). Impact of Size and Flows on Performance for Funds of Hedge Funds. *Journal of Portfolio Management, 35*(2), 118—130.

Young, T. (1991). Calmar Ratio: A Smoother Tool. *Futures, 20*(1), 40.

# SECTION 2
# UCITS Performance

# CHAPTER 7

# UCITS Funds of Hedge Funds — The New Panacea?

**Louis Zanolin**
Alix Capital SA, Geneva, Switzerland

**Chapter Outline**

## 7.1. INTRODUCTION

In 2002, when the European Commission introduced Directive 2001/108/EC,[1] the hedge fund industry paid little if no attention at all to it. However, the new Directive, whose purpose was to extend the range of assets eligible for investment by 'Undertakings for Collective Investment in Transferable Securities' (UCITS) and commonly known as the UCITS III Directive, was going to be the foundation of an important evolution of the alternative industry for the upcoming years.

During the first years following its entry into force, only few investment managers realized the new investment and distribution opportunities introduced by this Directive. One had to wait until 2008 with the financial crisis to see an increase of interest in UCITS structures from hedge fund markets participants. As many investors were impacted by the loose regulation and supervisory oversight of the offshore hedge fund industry, a number of issues were raised that would lead to irreversible changes in investor concerns and needs. Requests for stricter regulation, greater transparency, and enhanced liquidity often came as the most important characteristics put forward by investors after the 2008 crisis. Simultaneously, a number of industry players realized that the UCITS framework covered most of these points while being flexible enough to accommodate the majority of liquid hedge funds strategies.

At the same time a number of exogenous factors, such as the uncertainties surrounding the introduction of the AIFM (Alternative Investment Fund Managers) directives[2] and its potential consequences for the distribution of offshore hedge funds to the European investor community compelled a number of hedge fund investment managers to look at UCITS if not as a substitute, then surely as an alternative to their offshore offering. For all these various reasons, the number of single UCITS hedge funds grew from less than 200 funds after 2008 to more than 750 funds at the end of March 2012. The total assets managed in single UCITS hedge funds met the same level of progression, growing from EUR30 billion assets under management (AUM) to EUR123 billion within the same period. The growth of the number of single UCITS hedge funds led to the development of the UCITS funds of hedge funds (FoHFs) market.

---

[1]Council Directive 2001/108/EC amending Council Directive 85/611/ECC on the coordination of laws, regulations, and administrative provisions relating to undertakings for collective investment in transferable securities (UCITS), with regard to investments of UCITS, available at: http://www.esma. europa.eu/system/files/Dir_01_108.PDF. Council Directive 85/611/ECC had been amended six times between 1988 and 2008.

[2]Proposal for a Directive on Alternative Investment Fund Managers, available at http://ec.europa. eu/internal_market/investment/alternative_investments_en.htm#directive.

## 7.1.1. Market Size

According to Alix Capital's UCITS Alternative Index database,[3] there were about 114 UCITS FoHFs at the end of March 2012 (or 8.29% of UCITS hedge funds and FoHFs combined) compared to 32 in January 2008 (or 5.31% of UCITS hedge funds and FoHFs combined). This represents an average annual growth of 64% since 2008.

With EUR4.6 billion, UCITS FoHFs represent 3.62% of the global AUM (UCITS hedge funds and FoHFs combined). The percentage of UCITS FoHFs versus single UCITS hedge funds has remained constant over the last year. The average level of assets managed by UCITS FoHFs — established at EUR41.8 million — is still rather small. As illustrated in Figure 7.1, as of March 2012, 41.7% of UCITS FoHFs had less than EUR20 million AUM. Only 14.7% of these funds (or 11 funds) managed over EUR100 million.

The average small size of UCITS FoHFs in terms of AUM has to be put into perspective with the average size managed by the UCITS single hedge funds, 48% of which manage less than EUR50 million. The continuous flow of new fund launches weighs on the shape of the assets distribution curve. With the exception of a few funds launched by large investments banks or investment managers, most new funds begin with less than EUR50 million AUM. Some specific issues also account for the average small size of UCITS FoHFs. The first is the general lack of

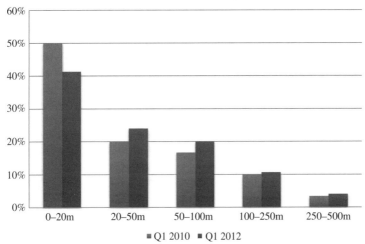

**FIGURE 7.1**
UCITS FoHFs classified by size (million EUR): Evolution from March 2010 to March 2012.

---

[3]Alix Capital is the official Index Provider to the UCITS Alternative Index. Alix Capital is also the publisher of the *UCITS Alternative Index Quarterly Industry Report* — a research support dedicated to the UCITS hedge funds industry published 4 times a year, available at: http://www.ucits-alternative.com/page-report.html. Most of the charts and data in this chapter are taken from the Q1 2012 Report or from the UCITS Alternative Index website (http://www.ucits-alternative.com).

appetite for FoHFs products since the 2008 crisis. No matter the type of structure, either UCITS or offshore, FoHFs have generally been losing assets since 2008. The second aspect is performance. As developed in Section 7.5, UCITS FoHFs have suffered negative performance on average since 2008. This has obviously limited the interest in and collection of new assets for this type of product.

### 7.1.2. Launches and Closures

On average, two new UCITS FoHFs were launched each month between 2008 and 2011. However, the bulk of new launches occurred in the year 2010 during which 53 new UCITS FoHFs were launched. The pace of new launches then declined in 2011 with only 15 new launches. During the same time frame, 13 UCITS FoHFs have closed.[4] Figure 7.2 illustrates these data.

The main reason that funds promoters usually put forward for closing their funds is related to the lower than expected inflows. The level of AUM required for a fund to operate in a viable manner depends on the size and the type of investment manager. Investment managers with a large product offering and significant AUM base are generally swift to close a fund that has not reached the expected level of AUM after a certain delay. Smaller or specialized investment managers are generally more inclined to continue to operate a fund despite smaller AUM or to wait a longer period of time before deciding to wind it down. The high attrition rate between 2008 and end 2011 needs also to be put in the context of a difficult period for the overall asset management industry. Numerous players have witnessed their AUM diminish no matter the type of legal structure or investment style.

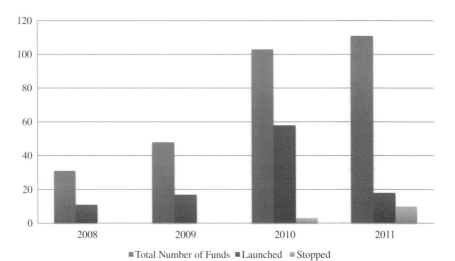

**FIGURE 7.2**
UCITS FoHFs launches and liquidations 2008–2012.

[4]As of December 2011.

Lastly, it is important to mention that the attrition rate for UCITS hedge funds products is more 'visible' than for offshore hedge funds products. Due to the reporting obligations of UCITS any fund closing is made public and monitored, whereas only the handful of related parties are generally aware of the wind down of a particular offshore fund. This difference in reporting obligation makes it difficult to draw any exact comparison.

## 7.1.3. Jurisdiction

UCITS FoHFs can be based in any country of the European Community. However, the location of UCITS FoHFs is in reality concentrated in a small number of member states. These are either the ones with the largest financial centers, such as the United Kingdom, France, and Germany, or the ones with important and recognized experience in international fund management administration, such as Luxembourg and Ireland. Figure 7.3 presents the main locations as of March 2012.

At the end of March 2012, 57% of all UCITS FoHFs were registered in Luxembourg. Ireland and France were the second and third largest places of incorporation with, respectively, 17.6% and 11.8%. The geographical distribution of assets indicates that Luxembourg was not only attracting the largest number of funds but also the most important ones in terms of AUM. If we focus on the evolution of domicile over recent years, we can observe that the proportion of funds choosing Luxembourg, and to a lesser extent Ireland, was increasing in both relative and absolute terms compared to all other jurisdictions.

There are several reasons for the success of Luxembourg and Ireland versus the other jurisdictions. The first is their long-term and in-depth experience in the field of investment funds. Luxembourg and Ireland have over the last two decades built a unique knowhow in the creation and administration of both long-only and alternative funds. They are therefore a natural choice for promoters looking for competences in the field of UCITS hedge funds.

The second one is market recognition. Over the last years, Luxembourg and Ireland have developed a reputation for quality and experience within the

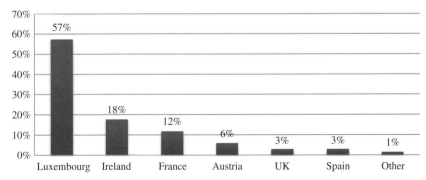

**FIGURE 7.3**
Location of FoHFs by country Q1 2012.

European market place and beyond. They are perceived as market standards for many funds promoters and investors. A majority of investment managers targeting international investors for their UCITS funds consequently tend to base their funds within one of these two countries.

Finally, UCITS are European directives that need to be transposed into national laws by each member state. In the past this process has led to some divergent interpretations of the directives and therefore to differences in their application between countries. This has generated some form of regulatory arbitrage between various jurisdictions. In addition, some member states are reputed to be more punctilious with the interpretation of the certain aspects of law. Some are also less reactive to authorization processes. All these differences explain why certain jurisdictions attract more funds than others.

## 7.2. FUND STRUCTURES

The UCITS III Directive, as may be amended from time to time, allows various forms of UCITS FoHFs. While there is a specific text describing the rules for funds of funds, a number of additional routes have been developed over the years to offer investor allocation to various hedge funds strategies within the UCITS framework. While these alternative routes were generally not designed to accommodate a portfolio of hedge funds, they have been adapted and clarified over the years by the Commission of European Securities Regulators (CESR) and later on by the European Securities and Markets Authority (ESMA).

The two most frequent structures in terms of number of funds and AUM are the funds of funds structure and the index funds structure. More recently, alternative constructions such as funds of managed accounts or exchange-traded funds (ETFs) have appeared. Below we provide a description of these various approaches.

### 7.2.1. Type of Structures

*FUND OF FUNDS*

UCITS fund of funds is the most commonly used structure for UCITS FoHFs. It takes its source directly from the UCITS III Directive.

This Directive says that UCITS funds are allowed to invest in units of other investments funds provided that:

- The investment in one single other fund does not exceed 20%.
- The investment in UCI[5] funds does not exceed 30% of its assets and the UCI must offer equivalent investor protection rules as UCITS regulations.

---

[5]An Undertaking for Collective Investment (UCI) is an investment fund that does not meet the criteria set by the EU Directives to render it eligible for distribution in more than one EU member state.

- The underlying investment fund has not invested more than 10% of its assets in units of another investment fund.
- Investment in another investment fund may not exceed 25% of the fund's units.

As far as the second criterion is concerned, it is the responsibility of each national regulator to provide guidance as to which UCI could be considered as offering equivalent investor protection rules as UCITS regulations. This might lead to some different interpretations depending on the country of incorporation. This structure can be considered as the purest UCITS FoHFs structure among all the different options. This is confirmed by the high proportion of new funds launched favoring this legal framework. In 2011, more than 80% of the new funds of funds launched used this FoHFs structure.

### HEDGE FUND INDEX FUNDS

The hedge fund index fund is the second most preferred approach. The approach follows the rules of the Index chapter of the UCITS III Directive. This Directive led to divergent interpretations notably regarding hedge funds indices. The CESR issued a guideline in July 2007[6] that set out the criteria with which a hedge funds index must comply in order to be eligible under the UCITS index regulation. To be considered eligible, a hedge funds index must:

- Be sufficiently diversified.
- Be considered as an adequate benchmark for the market it refers to.
- Be published in an appropriate manner.
- Follow pre-determined rules and objective criteria for selection and rebalancing of the components.
- Not accept any payment from potential index components.
- Not recalculate previously published index values (no backfilling).

The index performance is then replicated in the UCITS fund through the use of a total return swap. The exposure to hedge funds returns is usually gained via investment in liquid non-UCITS hedge funds or shares of hedge fund managed accounts. In essence, the use of the index structure allows getting exposure to instruments or investment funds that would normally not be eligible under the UCITS Directives.

The portion of funds that have selected the index structure represents only 12% of the total number of UCITS FoHFs. Historically, a number of funds promoters chose this option given the limited number of underlying UCITS hedge funds available. Following the growth of the number of single UCITS hedge funds since 2008 and by consequence the enlargement of the investment universe, this argument has become less relevant. While the index structure presents the possibility for a fund of funds to access funds that are non-UCITS and therefore a larger universe of components, it also involves additional costs and risks. For example, the use of swap introduces an additional counterparty — the swap provider. Although the

---

[6]CESR/07-434 CESR's guidelines concerning the classification of hedge fund indices as financial indices. Available at: http://www.esma.europa.eu/system/files/07_434.pdf.

counterparty risk can be partly mitigated via various over-collateralization techniques, it remains nevertheless an extra source of risk. Furthermore, the use of a total return swap adds an extra level of costs to the fund structure.

*FUNDS OF MANAGED ACCOUNTS*

In the fund of managed account structure the investment manager allocates the capital to several different subadvisors. Each advisor is responsible for trading the allocated capital following defined guidelines and risk limits. The relationship and asset segregation are governed by a contract between the fund and each subadvisor. From a regulatory perspective, the various subadvisor pools are not seen as individual trading pools, but as one global pool. UCITS limits and guidelines such as leverage or asset diversification are monitored at the aggregate level by the investment manager or the managed account platform provider. As a consequence, the fund is not considered technically as a fund of funds, but as a multiadvisor fund.[7] The main drawbacks of this structure are the lack of statutory segregation of liability between the various subadvisors and the fact that the contractual segregation may not be enforceable in the event of insolvency of one of the various involved parties. In other words, the assets of one or more sub-portfolios may be used to compensate liabilities of another subportfolio — a situation that would not be possible in the FoHFs or index models.

*ETFs*

A UCITS ETF is a UCITS fund of which at least one unit is continually tradable on at least one regulated market. The first UCITS ETFs tracking the performance of hedge funds indices were launched in 2010 and have rapidly grown substantial AUM. Many investors have been attracted by the possibility to obtain exposure to hedge funds returns via a liquid and highly regulated vehicle.

The liquidity is provided by one or more market makers offering prices at which the shares can be purchased and sold by investors. Investors have also the possibility to trade at net asset value (NAV) under certain circumstances. The official NAV of the UCITS funds being only available with a few days lag, the price at which investors can then trade on the secondary market may differ from the official NAV. Investors willing to trade on the secondary market may therefore trade at a discount or a premium to NAV.

Technically, UCITS ETFs are structured as index funds. The underlying index performance is usually based on the performance of a basket of managed accounts that meet the UCITS constraints. The exposure to the relevant hedge fund portfolio is gained via a total return swap, also called synthetic exposure in the ETF language.

Figure 7.4 summarizes the four main structures available for UCITS FoHFs, with the respective number of funds and AUM for each category.

---

[7]The fund can therefore be considered for inclusion by UCITS funds of funds.

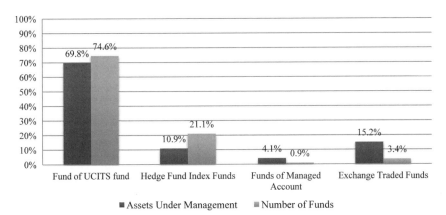

**FIGURE 7.4**
Assets and number of funds by fund type Q1 2012.

## 7.2.2. Multi- versus Single-Strategy FoHFs

Similar to the offshore FoHFs industry, the first UCITS FoHFs were mostly multistrategy. With the growth in the universe, a number of single-strategy UCITS FoHFs have been launched since 2010. In terms of number of funds, 77% of all UCITS FoHFs are multistrategy, while 23% focus on one strategy. Single-strategy funds also represent 17.42% of the total assets managed in UCITS FoHFs. About 70.4% of all single-strategy UCITS FoHFs are index funds based on managed accounts (or 68.5% of all assets). Figure 7.5 illustrates the allocation of number of funds between the various single strategy UCITS FoHFs. The largest portion of them focuses on Equity Long/Short followed by Commodity Trading Advisors (CTAs) and Systematic Macro. These two strategies represent more than half of all the strategy specific UCITS FoHFs.

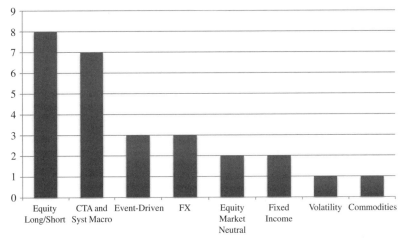

**FIGURE 7.5**
Breakdown of single-strategy FoHFs by number of funds per strategy Q1 2012.

## 7.3. INVESTMENT MANAGERS

### 7.3.1. Investment Manager Groups

UCITS FoHFs investment managers can be divided into three distinct groups. Each of these groups has launched UCITS FoHFs to answer specific needs or regulatory evolutions. Below we describe the main characteristics of the various categories.

*OFFSHORE-AND-ONSHORE INVESTMENT MANAGERS*

The category of Offshore-and-Onshore Investment Managers is composed of investment managers who have traditionally proposed offshore products then launched UCITS vehicles. In 2012, this group had 20 constituent funds, most of which started after the 2008 crisis. Investment managers from this category have generally launched their UCITS FoHFs to access a new type of client as well as to compensate for the market shares they were losing with their offshore vehicles. In practice, none of them has really been successful in raising substantial AUM to this date. The only exceptions are investment managers who have been awarded mandates by institutional clients or banks with no in-house expertise to manage a portfolio of UCITS funds by themselves.

*ONSHORE-ONLY INVESTMENT MANAGERS*

The category of Onshore-Only Investment Managers is composed of those who are mainly active in offering onshore products within their geographic area. Onshore-Only Investment Managers were the first to exploit the emergence of onshore hedge funds and to create funds of funds with an absolute return mandate, even prior to the entry into force of the UCITS III Directive. In some cases the products were launched as onshore country specific funds of funds that later become UCITS-compliant with the evolution of the UCITS Directive. These players usually have a strong focus on their own onshore market and little cross-border presence. They are also characterized by their predisposition to mix hedge and long-only funds.[8]

*GLOBAL AND PRIVATE BANKS*

This group of Global and Private Banks accounts for the largest AUM (60% of the total assets managed in UCITS FoHFs). This comes as little surprise given the size of its constituents and their distribution capabilities. The banks' two main reasons for launching UCITS FoHFs are the need to compensate for the diminishing interest of their main client base for offshore structures as well as to take advantage of the simplified and unified cross-border distribution possibilities. Until recently, Global and Private Banks needed to have one specific product for each different country in which they were selling their products. With UCITS they now have one single product that can be distributed

---

[8]In order to be part of the Alix Capital UCITS FoHFs database, funds needs to have a long-term exposure to UCITS hedge funds higher than 50%.

| Table 7.1 | UCITS FoHFs AUM Distribution by Type of Investment Manager Q1 2012 | | | |
|---|---|---|---|---|
| | Number of Funds | Total AUM (EUR million) | Average AUM (EUR million) | Median AUM (EUR million) |
| Offshore-and-Onshore Investment Managers | 20 | 833 | 42 | 22 |
| Onshore-Only Investment Managers | 34 | 1039 | 31 | 14 |
| Global and Private Banks | 60 | 2833 | 47 | 18 |
| *Total* | *114* | *4705* | *41* | *19* |

throughout Europe and beyond, and to all their clients. This group is also characterized by its inclination to use more complex fund structures such as index-based funds or ETFs, given their in-house capabilities.

Table 7.1 illustrates that UCITS FoHFs offered by Global and Private Banks are the larger group both in terms of number of funds and total AUM. Table 7.1 also shows that none of the three investment managers groups has more than EUR50 million AUM on average, with a median around EUR20 million.

## 7.3.2. Location of Investment Managers

At the end of Q1 2012, 38% of all UCITS hedge funds managers were located in the United Kingdom, while France, Switzerland, and Germany were home to, respectively, 15%, 14%, and 13% of UCITS FoHFs investment managers. The importance of the United Kingdom comes as little surprise given the weight of London in the European asset management industry. However, the significance

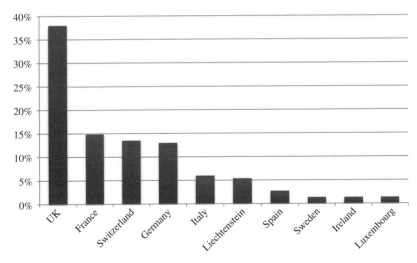

**FIGURE 7.6**
Location of FoHFs investment advisors by country Q1 2012.

of the other main European financial centers such as France, Germany, and Switzerland has been increasing over recent years, passing from a total of 6% at the end of 2009 to 27% in March 2012, as illustrated in Figure 7.6.

US-based UCITS FoHFs managers represent only 1% of all managers. This clearly results from the European-centric nature of the UCITS framework. Even if the trend witnessed in the single UCITS hedge funds space seems to suggest an increasing presence of US managers,[9] it is difficult to say at this stage if something similar will happen in the UCITS FoHFs industry.

## 7.4. FUNDS LIQUIDITY AND FEES

### 7.4.1. Liquidity

Liquidity is one of the most important characteristics of UCITS FoHFs. Similarly to the regulations governing single funds, UCITS FoHFs are compelled to offer liquidity at least as frequently as twice a month. In practice, less than 2% of UCITS FoHFs are offering fortnightly liquidity. The vast majority of UCITS funds have either daily (54.2%) or weekly (44.1%) liquidity. The liquidity profile of UCITS FoHFs has remained constant since the first observations in 2008.

Table 7.2 illustrates that funds launched by Onshore-Only Investment Managers tend to be more liquid than funds launched by Offshore-and-Onshore Investment Managers or Global and Private Banks. The higher liquidity is also reflected with the lower average notice period for redemption (2.9 versus 3.5 days for the entire sample).

Table 7.3 presents the liquidity profile of the various vehicles. It is no surprise that ETFs offer the best liquidity profile as they can be bought and sold on the secondary market on a continuous basis. Table 7.3 also illustrates that, on average, UCITS FoHFs using the index structure tend to be slightly more liquid and have a shorter notice period than those using the funds of funds

| Table 7.2 | Liquidity of Funds by Type of Investment Manager Q1 2012 | | | |
|---|---|---|---|---|
| | **Daily Liquidity (%)** | **Weekly Liquidity (%)** | **Bimonthly Liquidity (%)** | **Average Notice Period (days)** |
| Offshore-and-Onshore Investment Managers | 12 | 82 | 6 | 4.06 |
| Onshore-Only Investment Managers | 46 | 50 | 4 | 2.9 |
| Global and Private Banks | 23 | 77 | 0 | 4.0 |
| *Total* | *28* | *70* | *3* | *3.5* |

---

[9]*UCITS Alternative Index Quarterly Industry Report* Q1 2012, Alix Capital, Available at: http://www.alternativeucits.com/page-report.html.

| Table 7.3 | Liquidity of Funds by Type of Fund Structure Q1 2012 | | | |
|---|---|---|---|---|
| | **Daily Liquidity (%)** | **Weekly Liquidity (%)** | **Bimonthly Liquidity (%)** | **Average Notice Period (days)** |
| FoHFs | 23 | 74 | 2 | 4 |
| Index funds | 38 | 63 | 0 | 2.5 |
| ETFs | 100 | 0 | 0 | 0 |
| *Total* | 28 | 70 | 3 | 3.5 |

methodology. The Funds of Managed Accounts category is not presented since it is composed of only one fund and therefore can not be deemed representative of a category.

One aspect that is generally less well known by the public is the fact that UCITS FoHFs can implement redemption gates or suspensions. The UCITS III Directive indeed authorizes a fund to limit its redemptions up to 10% per any dealing date under certain circumstances (gate). This means that investors in a fund with weekly liquidity might have to wait up to 10 weeks to be fully paid back if the funds implement a gate on its redemptions.

The other possibility is the suspension of NAV and of redemptions. Conditions describing when such a suspension can be realized are specifically described in the Directive.

The main difference with the offshore hedge funds in the use of gates or suspensions lies in the responsibility of the various funds' counterparties as well as the stricter oversight of the local financial authorities. With the UCITS regulations, the reason behind a gate or a suspension must be based on rational and indisputable facts, and be well documented. An investment manager who implements a gate or a suspension for reasons that are not deemed valid by the financial authorities exposes itself to severe sanctions that could ultimately lead to the forced liquidation of the fund.

The liquidity offered by UCITS hedge funds allows FoHFs managers to implement active portfolio and risk management techniques. In contrast, the possibility to adjust the allocation of the portfolio in most offshore FoHFs is often highly restricted given the low liquidity of the underlying funds. In addition, their inflows and outflows usually happen on a monthly or even quarterly basis only. As a result, effective portfolio and consequently risk management implementation for offshore FoHFs is more limited. UCITS FoHFs are not facing the same issues given the liquidity of its authorized underlying investments.[10]

---

[10]At the end of Q1 2012, 51.3% of the underlying eligible single UCITS hedge funds offered daily liquidity and 47.4% weekly liquidity (source: *UCITS Alternative Index Quarterly Industry Report Q1 2012*).

While the investment managers of UCITS FoHFs benefit from improved reba-lancing opportunities with regard to their investments, they are also subject to more frequent subscription and redemption activities. Consequently and despite the important liquidity of its underlying investments, these investment managers have to make sure that their portfolio is always in a position to satisfy the redemption requests. Being able to quickly adjust the portfolio to meet more frequent trading activities while maintaining the target portfolio allocation is one of the greatest challenges of UCITS FoHFs managers.

### 7.4.2. Fees

Most UCITS FoHFs charge both management and performance fees. Out of the 114 funds taken into account in this chapter, 10 UCITS FoHFs (or 8.8 % of all funds) charge only management fees, while only one fund charges exclusively performance fees. The rest of the sample charges both management and performance fees.

On average UCITS FoHFs charge 1.14% for management fees and 8.77% for performance fees *per annum*.[11] By means of comparison, Dewaele *et al.* (2011b) found that the average level of fees for the funds of funds sample analyzed in their paper (UCITS and non-UCITS combined) stands at 1.45% for manage-ment fees and 9.26% for performance fees *per annum*.[12] Table 7.4 illustrates that there are no major differences between the various types of funds providers with regard to the level of fees.

Table 7.5 presents the average level of fees with respect to the type of fund structure. With an average of 0.79% of management fees and no performance fees, ETFs demonstrate clearly the lowest fee levels.

However, this basic observation limited to fees only does not provide any information about the total costs or expense ratio of the various structures. Most of them have additional costs impacting the performance. For example, ETFs

| **Table 7.4** | Average Level of Management and Performance Fees by Type of Investment Advisors Q1 2012 | | |
|---|---|---|---|
| | **Number of funds** | **Average Management Fees (%)** | **Average Performance Fees (%)** |
| Offshore-and-Onshore Investment Managers | 20 | 1.17 | 8.38 |
| Onshore-Only Investment Managers | 34 | 1.15 | 8.86 |
| Global and Private Banks | 60 | 1.12 | 8.85 |
| *Total* | *114* | *1.14* | *8.77* |

[11]The share class with the lowest fee schedule is taken into account in this calculation.
[12]Average based on 4571 globally based offshore and onshore FoHFs.

| Table 7.5 | Average Level of Management and Performance Fees by Type of Fund Structure Q1 2012 | | |
|---|---|---|---|
| | **Number of funds** | **Average Management Fees (%)** | **Average Performance Fees (%)** |
| FoHFs | 86 | 1.17 | 8.85 |
| Index funds | 24 | 1.14 | 8.86 |
| ETF | 4 | 0.79 | 0.00 |
| *All funds* | *114* | *1.14* | *8.77* |

performance might be impacted by the bid and ask spread cost, while index funds bear the cost of total return swap.

This will be developed in Section 7.5.

## 7.5. RETURN AND RISK ANALYSIS

The existing research papers on UCITS hedge funds performance, such as Tuchschmid *et al.* (2010), Dewaele *et al.* (2011a), Darolles (2011), and Pascalau (2011), focus on the performance of single UCITS hedge funds, and on the difference of returns between UCITS hedge funds and their equivalent offshore pairs or indices. The authors verified whether there was a significant regulatory cost of implementing certain strategies in a UCITS format.

Comparisons between offshore and UCITS FoHFs are more difficult given the different sets of constraints of UCITS FoHFs (liquidity, leverage, etc.) as well as the size of the investable universe and the number of available strategies.

It is important to note that the limited amount of data makes the exercise of performance analysis for UCITS hedge funds difficult and maybe not really relevant. Furthermore, the market conditions during the period for which data are available (January 2008–March 2012) were extreme and probably do not reflect long-term market conditions. In order to perform the analysis of the return, funds belonging to the same category have been aggregated in a synthetic average, and statistics were used to calculate each average. The number of constituents of the various indices is not equal and can be rather small in some cases (i.e., the ETFs average is made of only four constituents). This could lead to some extreme values and increased volatility measures.

### 7.5.1. Analysis of UCITS FoHFs versus UCITS Single Hedge Funds

In this section we compare the performance of single UCITS hedge funds versus the performance of FoHFs. To this end, we use three datasets:

- The performance of single UCITS hedge funds.
- The performance of single UCITS hedge funds, adjusted to the average management and performance fees of UCITS FoHFs (as defined above in

Section 7.42); this data corresponds to the performance of a random UCITS FoHF, which also bears the additional costs of its own management and performance fees.

■ The performance of UCITS FoHFs.

For single UCITS hedge fund performance, we use the UCITS Alternative Index Global (UAI Global) benchmark from Alix Capital. This benchmark tracks the performance of all single UCITS hedge funds included in Alix Capital's database (764 funds as of March 2012), and is equally weighted and rebalanced on a monthly basis.[13] The second value, as explained above, is computed using the performance of the UAI Global adjusted to the average management and performance fees of UCITS FoHFs as calculated in Section 7.42, yielding management fees of 1.14% and performance fees of 8.77%. Lastly, the performance of UCITS FoHFs is calculated using the equally weighted monthly rebalanced performance of all UCITS FoHFs used in the chapter. Figure 7.7 summarizes the results.

It can be seen from Figure 7.7 that from January 2008 to March 2012 UCITS FoHFs have, on average, returned lower performance than both single UCITS hedge funds and adjusted UCITS FoHFs. In other words, a theoretical UCITS FoHF investing in all single UCITS hedge funds from the UAI Global, and charging the average management and performance fees of a UCITS FoHF,

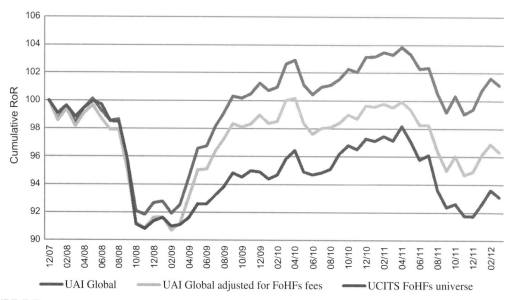

**FIGURE 7.7**
Cumulative performance of UCITS FoHFs versus single UCITS hedge funds and single UCITS hedge funds adjusted for average FoHFs fees, March 2012.

---

[13]UCITS Alternative Index official website www.ucits-alternative.com.

| Table 7.6 | Performance and Risk Table of UCITS FoHFs versus Single UCITS Hedge Funds and Single UCITS Hedge Funds Adjusted for Average FoHFs Fees | | | |
|---|---|---|---|---|
| | Annualized (*M*) Compound Return (%) | Annualized (*M*) Standard Deviation (%) | Annualized (*M*) Sharpe Ratio | Maximum Drawdown (%) |
| UAI Global | 0.26 | 4.060 | −0.40 | −8.29 |
| UAI Global adjusted for FoHFs fees | −0.88 | 4.059 | −0.69 | −9.31 |
| UCITS FoHFs universe | −1.67 | 3.88 | −0.92 | −9.19 |

From January 2008 to March 2012.

would have performed better than the average UCITS FoHFs covered in this chapter. Table 7.6 presents the annualized return, volatility, and maximum drawdown for the three groups.

UCITS FoHFs have achieved their performance with slightly lower volatility than the two other groups and lower maximum drawdowns than the UAI Global adjusted for FoHFs fees.

## 7.5.2. Analysis of Investment Managers

Figure 7.8 shows that the cumulative performance has been negative since 2008 for all types of investment managers.

The performance of the various providers clearly displays a higher dispersion of return during the first 18 months of analysis (January 2008–June 2009) than during the second part of the study. The higher volatility is not only explained by the extreme market conditions witnessed during this period, but also by the smaller size of the universe during this time. The total number of funds of the sample was 31 at the end of 2008 against 48 at the end of 2009.

Table 7.7 illustrates that the first two groups produced similar annualized returns over the period ranging from January 2008 to March 2012. However, the volatility for the Onshore-Only Investment Managers is half that of the Offshore-and-Onshore Investment Managers. Offshore-and-Onshore Investment Managers present a higher maximum drawdown.

In terms of correlation, the Offshore-and-Onshore Investment Managers group displays slightly lower correlation to the equity market than the other type of investment managers as indicated in Table 7.8. This group also indicated a zero correlation to the bond market while the other groups tend to be negatively correlated to bonds.

## 7.5.3. Analysis of Fund Structure

In this section we observe the return-to-risk profile of the various types of UCITS FoHFs structures. As for previous analyses, the results of the Fund of Managed

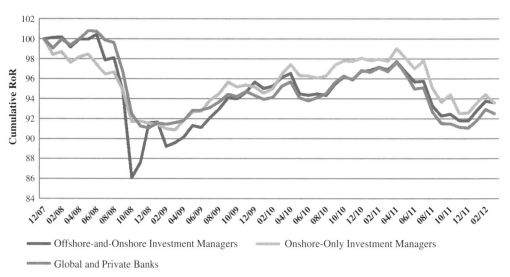

**FIGURE 7.8**
Cumulative return of UCITS FoHFs by type of investment manager from January 2008 to March 2012.

| Table 7.7 | Performance and Risk Table of UCITS FoHFs by Type of Investment Manager | | | |
|---|---|---|---|---|
| | Annualized (*M*) Compound Return (%) | Annualized (*M*) Standard Deviation (%) | Annualized (*M*) Sharpe Ratio | Maximum Drawdown (%) |
| Offshore-and-Onshore Investment Managers | −1.54 | 6.28 | −0.53 | −14.29 |
| Onshore-Only Investment Managers | −1.54 | 3.63 | −0.96 | −9.11 |
| Global and Private Banks | −1.81 | 3.77 | −0.99 | −9.64 |
| *All Funds* | *−1.67* | *3.88* | *−0.92* | *−9.19* |

From January 2008 to March 2012.

| Table 7.8 | Correlation to Bonds and Equities of the Various Types of Investment Managers | |
|---|---|---|
| | Correlation to MSCI World LC | Correlation to Citi WGBI LC |
| Offshore-and-Onshore Investment Managers | 0.65 | −0.01 |
| Onshore-Only Investment Managers | 0.76 | −0.20 |
| Global and Private Banks | 0.73 | −0.30 |
| *All Funds* | *0.74* | *−0.21* |

From January 2008 to March 2012.

Accounts structure is not displayed as it is made of only one component. The statistics for the various groups as displayed in Table 7.9 indicate that, on average, ETFs performed worse than the other structures. Table 7.9 also confirms a higher volatility and larger maximum drawdown for that category. The higher volatility of this group is essentially due to the mark to market impact of the secondary market trading activities. The smaller number of constituents of this group also explains part of its higher volatility.

Table 7.9 also indicates that index funds returned lower return with higher volatility and larger drawdowns than FoHFs. There are several reasons that support this finding. The first is the cost linked to the use of total return swap needed to replicate the index strategy into the UCITS funds. We estimate that the cost of the swap to be between 40 and 50 basis points *per annum*. The other reason is that investment managers tend to use the index structure to access funds or strategies, such as commodities hedge funds or hedge funds based on managed accounts platforms that are not available or not allowed in the UCITS format and which might present a higher volatility.

The analysis by instruments as presented in Table 7.10 indicates that index funds present a lower correlation to equity and a smaller negative correlation to bonds than the other instruments. As expected, ETFs present a higher correlation to equity than the other groups. However, none of these variations is significant in terms of absolute numbers.

| Table 7.9 | Performance and Risk Table of UCITS FoHFs by Type of Fund Structure | | | |
|---|---|---|---|---|
| | Annualized (*M*) Compound Return (%) | Annualized (*M*) Standard Deviation (%) | Annualized (*M*) Sharpe Ratio | Maximum Drawdown (%) |
| FoHFs | −1.86 | 3.44 | −1.10 | −9.69 |
| Index funds | −2.69 | 4.44 | −1.04 | −12.38 |
| ETF | −3.40 | 8.41 | −0.60 | −23.88 |
| *All funds* | −1.67 | 3.88 | −0.92 | −9.19 |

From January 2008 to March 2012.

| Table 7.10 | Correlation to Bonds and Equities of the Various Types of the Various Fund Structures | |
|---|---|---|
| | Correlation to MSCI World LC | Correlation to Citi WGBI LC |
| FoHFs | 0.72 | −0.29 |
| Index funds | 0.55 | −0.16 |
| ETF | 0.78 | −0.34 |
| *All funds* | 0.74 | −0.21 |

From January 2008 to March 2012.

## CONCLUSION

Despite significant growth since 2008, the UCITS FoHFs universe is still relatively small in terms of AUM. The study period is relatively short and is characterized by unusually high volatility, and might therefore not be representative of long-term market conditions. For all these reasons it is difficult to draw any final conclusion about the status and the possible added value offered by UCITS FoHFs. One can, however, observe the following trends.

On average and for the time period analyzed, UCITS FoHFs have returned lower performance than the performance of single UCITS hedge funds adjusted for FoHFs fees. The performance differences between the various funds structures are not significant. ETF is the only structure that indicates results notably different from those of the other groups. ETFs display higher volatility and larger drawdowns. The various groups show similar levels of correlation to bonds and equities. With 86 out of 114 funds, the FoHFs structure is currently the most used format in the UCITS FoHFs industry.

In terms of fees, ETFs present the lower fee structure. However, the results of the performance analysis shows that despite the low fee, ETFs performed the worst during the sample period. This confirms that in addition to management fees, other costs such as bid and ask spreads impact the performance of this type of fund. Despite displaying better performance than ETFs, index funds present lower return and greater volatility than UCITS FoHFs due to the higher implied structure costs and different investment universe.

The study of the various types of investment managers indicates that funds managed by Onshore-Only Investment Managers tend to have better liquidity than the other groups. In terms of performance and risk, Offshore-and-Onshore Investment Managers display more important drawdowns and higher volatility than the other groups. All investment managers groups display similar levels of correlation to bonds and equities. It will be interesting to see how the UCITS FoHFs universe will evolve in the next few years. Upcoming regulatory changes might impact the use of certain instruments and structures. At the same time UCITS FoHFs investment managers will gain experience in managing the opportunities and threats offered by the greater liquidity and stricter regulation. This will probably create a distinctive group of FoHFs with different characteristics than the existing offshore ones.

### Acknowledgments

I would like to thank Dravasp Jhabvala of Alix Capital for his research assistance, and my dear wife Caroline Linh for her patience during the writing of the paper and her kind help proofreading my texts.

### References

Darolles, S. (2011). *Quantifying Alternative UCITS, Lyxor Asset Management MAP Studies: Empirical Research on Hedge Funds, Oct 2001*. Available at http://www.lyxor.com/fileadmin/_fileup/lyxor_wp/document/710935_MapStudies_Oct_2011_01.pdf.

Dewaele, B., Markov, I., Pirotte, H., & Tuchschmid, N. (2011a). *Does Manager Offshore Experience Count in the Alternative UCITS Universe.* Available at http://papers.ssrn.com/sol3/papers.cfm?abstract_id=1966520.

Dewaele, B., Pirotte, H., Tuchschmid, N., & Wallerstein, E. (2011b). *Assessing the Performance of Funds of Hedge Funds, CEB Working Paper 11/041.* Available at http://papers.ssrn.com/sol3/papers.cfm?abstract_id=1929097.

Pascalau, R. (2011). *An Empirical Analysis of US Dollar Trading Newcits.* Available at http://papers.ssrn.com/sol3/papers.cfm?abstract_id=1910658.

Tuchschmid, N., Wallerstein, E., & Zanolin, L. (2010). *Will Alternative UCITS Ever Be Loved Enough To Replace Hedge Funds?* Available at http://papers.ssrn.com/sol3/papers.cfm?abstract_id=1686055.

# CHAPTER 8

# The Return Potential of UCITS Funds of Hedge Funds: An Analysis of their Investment Universe

**Florian Haberfelner** [*], **Iliya Kutsarov** [*], **Thomas Maier** [*], **and Marcus Storr** [†]

[*]Senior Investment Manager, Feri Trust GmbH Haus am Park,
Bad Homburg, Germany

[†]Head of Hedge Funds, Feri Trust GmbH Haus am Park,
Bad Homburg, Germany

## 8.1. INTRODUCTION

Over the last 20 years the offshore hedge fund industry has evolved into a major player within the financial markets. The number of offshore hedge funds grew tremendously before the latest financial crisis with total assets under management (AUM) approaching close to US$2 trillion. Since the financial crisis in 2007 and 2008, the growth of the 'Undertakings for Collective Investment in Transferable Securities' (UCITS) hedge fund universe has accelerated in particular in Europe, to some extent in Asia, and to a lesser extent in the Americas. Based on Directive 2001/107/EC and 2001/108/EC and registered based on it, UCITS funds can be easily launched in one member state of the European Union and then be distributed into other member states within the European Union. Some interesting aspects regarding passporting and regulatory oversight are discussed by Dickinson, C. (2011). Offshore hedge funds, on the other hand, are not regulated. The substantial increase in the availability of UCITS hedge funds can be seen as a response to investor demand and is certainly a function of the disappointing behavior of several offshore hedge funds during the financial crisis. In that period numerous hedge fund managers caused frustration among investors when they introduced redemption suspensions, implemented gates, and created side pockets. In addition, the investment community was confronted with several fraud cases among hedge funds. Regulatory oversight, better liquidity, and transparency are the characteristics perceived by investors as the main benefits provided by UCITS hedge funds. However, those benefits come at a cost, in the form of investment restrictions, potentially elevated costs levels, counterparty risk, etc.

This chapter aims to compare the offshore and UCITS hedge fund universe, thereby assessing the return potential for investors investing in either of those universes. As two 'worlds' of offshore and onshore (UCITS) hedge fund investments are now available we intend to provide a quantitative comparison of the two. We focus the analysis on the TASS offshore hedge fund database and the Eurekahedge UCITS hedge fund database. This analysis is structured into three sections, starting with a descriptive comparison of the two universes. Subsequently we will compare the return potential of the onshore and offshore hedge fund universe by comparing the expected returns of randomly built funds of hedge funds (FoHF) portfolios. Additionally, several risk factors are analyzed and compared for those portfolios. The performance and risk for the pre-crisis (January 2005−March 2007) and post-crisis (April 2007−December 2011) environment are evaluated. These results lead to an assessment of the attractiveness of the onshore and offshore hedge fund universe. Finally, we will summarize our findings and arrive at conclusions for all results.

## 8.2. DESCRIPTIVE COMPARISON OF THE UCITS VERSUS THE OFFSHORE HEDGE FUND UNIVERSE

In this section we provide a descriptive analysis of both hedge fund universes — offshore and UCITS — with regard to number of funds, AUM, strategy distribution, and fees. In the offshore space the analyzed universe is based on data provided by TASS, while the universe in the UCITS space is based on the dedicated UCITS database provided by Eurekahedge.

The analyzed TASS offshore hedge fund universe was fine-tuned and manually adjusted in several ways. First, our adjusted database includes also all funds that stopped reporting ('dead funds') during the last 10 years.

However, biases like backfill bias (hedge funds choose to report only with a time lag of several months, often conditionally on their performance) or liquidation bias (liquidating hedge funds may choose to no longer report after the decision to liquidate is taken) are still present in the data material. Given that the Eurekahedge UCITS database was set up in 2010, we have to suspect that it is subject to significant selection biases for the period predating its launch.

Each hedge fund — both in the UCITS and the offshore space — was then classified manually according to its strategy description into the four main hedge fund styles: Equity Hedge, Event Driven, Relative Value, and Tactical Trading. This classification was necessary in order to have comparable results in both universes (UCITS and offshore) and to exclude erroneous or inconsistent datasets, typically present when comparing and analyzing data from different data base providers.

Figure 8.1 shows that the number of funds pertaining to the offshore universe (containing all alive and dead funds until the end of 2011) is significantly higher than in the UCITS space. The hedge fund style with the lowest prevalence in the offshore universe is Event Driven with 817 funds, still outnumbering the total UCITS universe (482 funds) almost by a factor of 2.

In addition there has been a classification into a scheme of major hedge fund strategies: Convertible Arbitrage, Commodity Trading Advisors (CTAs), Equity Market Neutral, Event Driven, Fixed Income, Long/Short Equity, Macro, etc. Figure 8.2 shows that the strategy distribution in the UCITS universe differs significantly from that in the offshore universe (again the universes contain all live and dead funds until the end of 2011). While in the offshore space the number of Fixed Income strategy hedge funds and the number of hedge funds following a CTA strategy are larger than the number of Macro hedge funds, in the UCITS universe the Macro strategy is the second most often implemented strategy. In both universes the number of Long/Short Equity funds outweighs all other strategies by far and contributes almost 50% of the number of total funds.

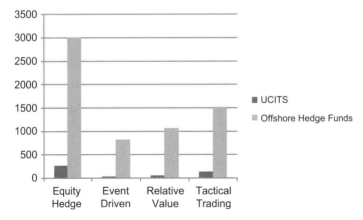

**FIGURE 8.1**
Number of hedge funds per hedge fund style: data as of December 2011. Dark bars, UCITS; light bars, offshore.

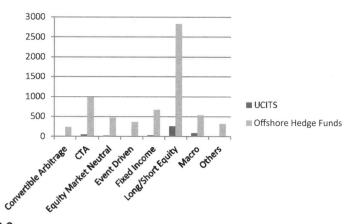

**FIGURE 8.2**
Distribution of UCITS hedge funds and offshore hedge funds among strategies. Dark bars, UCITS; light bars, offshore.

## 8.2.1. Number of Funds Over Time

Since 2005, in particular the number of UCITS hedge funds has increased considerably. However, especially after the financial crisis of 2007 and 2008 the number of UCITS-based products has risen almost exponentially. In contrast to the offshore universe, the financial crisis neither stopped nor slowed the further increase in the number of UCITS hedge fund launches. In fact, directly after the acceleration of the crisis in late 2008 the limit of 200 reporting UCITS funds has been consistently broken, as can be seen in Figure 8.3. However, the number of UCITS funds peaked in August/September 2011 at 417 in a period of stress caused by the European sovereign debt crisis. Ever since then the number of reporting UCITS funds has been slowly but steadily decreasing.

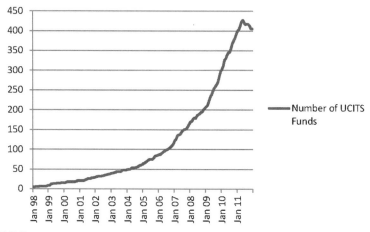

**FIGURE 8.3**
Number of UCITS funds available (Eurekahedge).

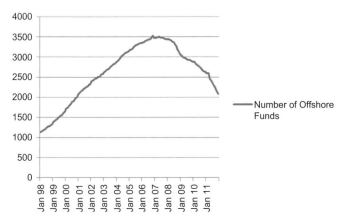

**FIGURE 8.4**
Number of offshore funds available (TASS).

A different picture can be drawn about the offshore universe: the number of offshore funds had reached its peak already in November 2006 (Figure 8.4).

This top level of around 3500 offshore hedge funds alive was relatively steady until the real breakout of the financial crisis in mid 2008. Since then the number of offshore funds has been ever-decreasing to an approximated level of 2000 at the end of 2011. One interesting observation can be gained by considering the total number of hedge funds (offshore and UCITS): the decrease in the number of offshore hedge funds is more than three times as large as the increase in number in UCITS funds, showing that the decline in the number of offshore funds seems to have occurred for a very different reason than just the increasing popularity of UCITS funds. On the other hand, it is also clear that the shift towards UCITS funds caused by the financial crisis is not the only trigger for a shrinking hedge fund universe as the number of offshore funds had reached its peak already in 2006, way before the breakout of the financial crisis. At this point in time the number of total hedge funds seemed to have reached a certain level of saturation, independently of any UCITS consideration. Possible explanations might include the increasing competition to raise assets for emerging funds in an environment where the existing amount of market inefficiencies (commonly referred to as 'alpha') is eaten up by too many competitors. Obviously the financial crisis in 2007 and 2008 then tremendously enforced this shrinking process in the offshore hedge funds universe.

Eurekahedge provides similar results regarding the number of hedge funds alive (here based on both offshore and UCITS hedge funds) during the peak period in 2006 and 2007 (see Figure 8.5). However, their estimates state a lower number of funds at all times before the financial crisis and a higher number of funds after the financial crisis.[1]

---

[1]According to HFR's estimate the total number of hedge funds shrank slightly after the crisis of 2008 and 2009, but then fully recovered to the 2007 level by the end of 2011.

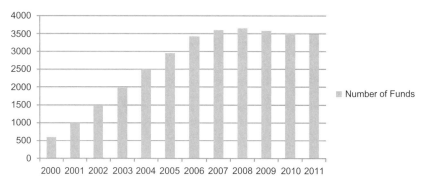

**FIGURE 8.5**
Number of total hedge funds (offshore and UCITS) (Eurekahedge, 2012).

The fraction of dead funds in the UCITS universe is very different to the offshore universe. While in the UCITS space 405 funds out of 482 ever-existing UCITS hedge funds were still alive at the end of 2011, the offshore universe of alive funds makes up less than one-third (2087 live offshore hedge funds and a total of 6412 funds in the universe).

The main findings of this section can be summarized as follows. Neither the launch of UCITS funds nor the financial crisis itself is likely to be the main trigger of the beginning of the decline in the number of offshore hedge funds. Nonetheless, the financial crisis of 2007 and 2008 and the corresponding shift in terms of risk consideration in general — and liquidity considerations in particular — did foster the ascent of UCITS funds and the decline in the number of offshore hedge funds.

## 8.2.2. Comparison Strategy

Taking the universe of offshore hedge funds as a benchmark, a slight shift in the hedge fund style distribution can be recognized. In 2005, funds managed in the Equity Hedge strategy made up 42% of the total universe (Figure 8.6). At the end

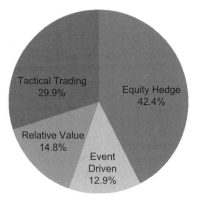

**FIGURE 8.6**
Major hedge fund strategies in the offshore space in 2005.

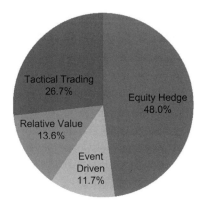

**FIGURE 8.7**
Major hedge fund styles in the offshore space at the end of 2011.

of 2011 they made up more than 48%, at the cost of all other major hedge fund strategies (Figure 8.7).

A few years ago only a few hedge funds were existent and the only relevant hedge fund strategies were Equity Hedge and Relative Value. Equity Hedge was by far the dominating hedge fund strategy in the whole universe. Up to 2006, Equity Hedge represented consistently approximately two-thirds or more of all hedge funds in the UCITS wrapper.

To analyze the evolvement of hedge fund strategies in the UCITS universe we focus on the period beginning in August 2006 — the first time when more than 100 UCITS hedge funds were reported — in order to have a minimum of statistical reliability in our numbers. In August 2006, the analyzed UCITS universe shows the distribution of hedge fund styles as shown in Figure 8.8.

As compared to the offshore universe it can be seen that in the UCITS universe for 2006 the Equity Hedge strategy is clearly over-represented at the cost of mainly the

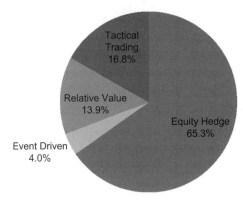

**FIGURE 8.8**
Major hedge fund styles in the UCITS space in August 2006.

Event Driven and Relative Value strategy. Since then the distribution of hedge fund strategies in the UCITS universe has slightly converged towards the distribution in the offshore space. Equity Hedge is still the dominant style in the UCITS universe; however, at the end of 2011 Equity Hedge made up only 56% of all funds in the UCITS universe (Figure 8.9). Also, the percentage of Relative Value strategies has decreased since 2006. Event Driven and, in particular, Tactical Trading strategies did not just gain in absolute number of UCITS hedge funds pursuing these styles, but also in percentage terms. To a large extent this increase — especially in the Tactical Trading space — may be attributed to the effects of the financial crisis when substrategies like CTAs (at the end of 2011 representing roughly 10% of the UCITS universe) did well and therefore incited further investor demand.

In the UCITS universe the Event Driven strategy is almost only represented by the substrategy Merger Arbitrage, which is easily implementable in the UCITS format and does not build on any illiquid assets. Other Event Driven strategies where the exposure to illiquid assets is a crucial part of the investment strategy, like Distressed Debt or Special Situations, are completely missing in the UCITS universe at the end of 2011. A further extensive overview of the strategy distribution of UCITS funds — although based on a slightly different universe than ours — is provided at a report by Naisscent Capital (2012).

The same applies to the Relative Value strategy. Almost all UCITS funds within this hedge fund strategy apply an arbitrage strategy in the fixed income market and/or convertible bond markets. More sophisticated substrategies requiring the use of illiquid underlying assets are either strongly under-represented (e.g. Structured Credit with only two reporting funds) or missing (e.g. Trade finance/ Asset-based lending funds and closed-end-fund-arbitrage strategies).

Consequently, FoHFs investing solely into the UCITS universe have only limited ability to create a diversified portfolio in terms of strategies compared to the way a fund of fund investing offshore has.

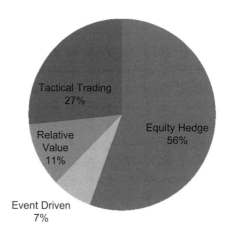

**FIGURE 8.9**
Major hedge fund styles in the UCITS space at the end of 2011.

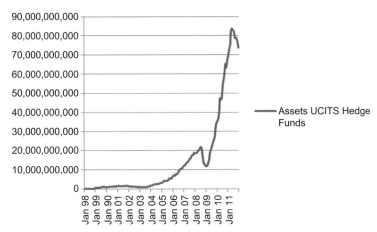

**FIGURE 8.10**
AUM (in US$) of UCITS hedge funds.

### 8.2.3. UCITS AUM Over Time

Similarly to the analysis of the development of the number of UCITS funds over time, that there was a large increase in AUM of UCITS hedge funds can be stated, as can be seen in Figure 8.10.

A strong decrease has taken place during economic and financial downturns. The latest trough in assets coincides with the financial crisis of 2007 and 2008 when the reported AUM in the analyzed UCITS Hedge funds universe fell from US$22 billion in July 2008 to US$12 billion in January 2009. AUM at the end of 2011 were approximately US$74 billion. Unlike in past crises, the European sovereign debt crises brought UCITS assets down by only 12% until the end of 2011 (from a level of US$84 billion). However, the nuance is that in late 2011 a decrease in assets also coincides with a decrease in the number of UCITS hedge funds (compare Figure 8.3).

Looking at the development of AUM reported for the total hedge fund space, AUM reached its peak in 2007 (still before the real breakout of the financial crisis, although later than the peak in the number of funds, which was in 2006). This might indicate that the number of funds in the offshore space could be a better and earlier indicator for future financial trouble than the actual AUM.

### 8.2.4. Fee Structures

It is often assumed that it is more costly to invest into UCITS hedge funds than into offshore hedge funds due to more complex structures, etc. However, our data shows that this is not generally true if we only consider the explicit fee levels. Looking at the cost structures of the live funds (at the end of 2011) it can be seen clearly that on average both management fees and performance fees are lower in the UCITS universe than in the offshore universe. Similar results, especially regarding management fees, are derived in a study of Barclays Capital, 2011. One reason for this is the ability to charge a relatively high level of '2 + 20' in the offshore universe regardless of the strategy. Any fee reduction in the offshore world might be interpreted as sending out low-quality signals of investment expertise.

Almost three-quarters of the funds in the offshore universe still charge the classical 20% performance fee or more, whereas in the UCITS universe this level of incentive fee is only charged by roughly 50% of all managers (see Figure 8.11).

A similar distribution can be observed regarding management fees (see Figure 8.12). Although not as pronounced as in the case of performance fees, still the most often charged management fee by offshore hedge funds is 2%. In contrast, the most often charged management fee by a UCITS manager is 1.5%, followed by 1%.

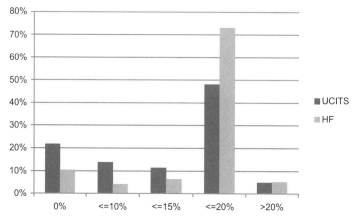

**FIGURE 8.11**
Distribution of incentive fees in the offshore and in the UCITS universe. Dark bars, UCITS; light bars, offshore.

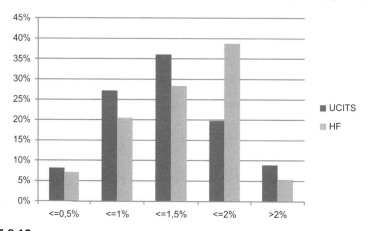

**FIGURE 8.12**
Distribution of management fees in the offshore and in the UCITS universe. Dark bars, UCITS; light bars, offshore.

These management fee and performance fee distributions are pretty robust regarding the inclusion of dead funds in the universe as well. However, it must be noted that the fact that the UCITS universe comprises a slightly different strategy distribution might have consequences for the fee distribution as well. It is possible that the relatively high portion of Relative Value and Event Driven funds in the offshore universe as compared to the UCITS universe also leads to a slight increase of average fees in the UCITS universe. This is affirmed by the fact that most traditional asset managers who wrap their classical absolute return vehicle in the UCITS format are typically following Equity Hedge or Tactical Trading strategies. As those absolute return vehicles traditionally bear lower fees than classical offshore hedge funds — especially lower incentive fees — they bring down the average fee level of UCITS funds.

However, several hedge fund managers are offering the same or similar investment strategies both in offshore format and in a UCITS wrapper. In these cases many examples can be shown where the UCITS structure bears higher fees than its offshore counterpart. Further, it must be noted that the level of explicit fees might not be a good indicator of the total cost level investors have to bear when investing into a hedge fund strategy via a UCITS wrapper. In fact, several usually non-transparent cost layers (swap fee, index fee, etc.) typically render UCITS funds more expensive than their offshore counterparts. Also, implicit costs (higher opportunity costs due to higher cash allocations and certain risk exposure limits as well as high tracking errors to their offshore counterparts due to the lack of access to certain asset classes like loans, trade claims, etc.) have to be considered while comparing total effective costs. See Ralston, G. & Butler, D. (2011) for a smart discussion on that topic.

## 8.3. PERFORMANCE COMPARISON OF SIMULATED UCITS FoHFs VERSUS OFFSHORE FoHFs PORTFOLIOS

### 8.3.1. Methodology: Construction of Randomly Simulated FoHFs Portfolios

In this section we construct simulated offshore and UCITS funds of hedge funds (FoHFs) portfolios from the available sets of offshore and UCITS single hedge funds, and examine their characteristics. We choose a simulation methodology versus direct comparison of the existing single UCITS and offshore FoHFs mainly for two reasons. (i) The depth of the UCITS FoHFs universe as well as its track record is insufficient. Moreover, single-strategy dedicated UCITS FoHFs barely exist. (ii) The simulation methodology allows us to control for the number of funds in each portfolio, the allocation to each hedge fund strategy, and the rebalancing time frame. In this way it is ensured that offshore and UCITS portfolios both follow exactly the same construction process. As a result it is ensured that the potential difference between offshore and UCITS portfolios can be attributed only to the underlying sets of single funds. The goal is to obtain results that allow us to compare the return potential of both universes and to compare the risk characteristics at the same time.

We compare six sets of synthetic FoHFs portfolios: two multistrategy (each containing 12 funds chosen randomly) and four single-strategy FoHFs portfolios (each containing six funds chosen randomly). All portfolios have an equal fund weighting and are rebalanced monthly. Each portfolio is reconstructed every 6 months by random selection from the relevant population of funds that have at least a 12-month track record at the date of selection. The first set of multistrategy FoHFs portfolios, here called *unconstrained multistrategy portfolios*, follows an unconstrained selection process, i.e., there are no restrictions with regard to the weighting of the underlying hedge fund strategy allocation due to a randomly chosen number of funds for each strategy. Hence, each strategy weighting within each of the simulated FoHFs portfolios could differ significantly, with each single fund weighting, however, being equal. The multistrategy FoHFs portfolios in the second set, here called *constrained multistrategy portfolios*, are equally weighted (each of 25% weight) with regard to each of the four hedge fund strategies, which further implies that there are always three funds from each strategy in the portfolio due to the general equal weight of each single fund. The four sets of *single-strategy portfolios* for all major hedge fund styles, i.e., Relative Values, Event Driven, Equity Hedge, and Tactical Trading, are selected exclusively from the relevant underlying strategy hedge fund universe. Within each universe (offshore and UCITS) we simulate 10 000 FoHFs portfolios over a 7-year time frame between January 2005 and December 2011. Hence, the result of this methodology provides us with a randomly generated performance distribution and additional risk characteristics.

### 8.3.2. Returns, Risk, and Diversification Characteristics of Simulated FoHFs Portfolios

Tables 8.1–8.3 summarize the simulation results and present descriptive statistics for the distribution of the annualized return, the volatility, the Sharpe ratios, and the correlation to the MSCI World Index ('Corr. MSCI') for each set of portfolios.

| Table 8.1 | Unconstrained Multistrategy Portfolios | | | | | | |
|---|---|---|---|---|---|---|---|
| | **Offshore** | | | | **UCITS** | | |
| | Return *per annum* (%) | Volatility (%) | Sharpe (2%) | Corr. MSCI | Return *per annum* (%) | Volatility (%) | Sharpe (2%) | Corr. MSCI |
| Maximum | 13.9 | 13.68 | 1.59 | 0.872 | 13.4 | 14.20 | 1.24 | 0.908 |
| 75% percentile | 6.8 | 8.67 | 0.61 | 0.752 | 6.9 | 10.73 | 0.51 | 0.836 |
| *Median* | *5.4* | *8.00* | *0.43* | *0.712* | *5.6* | *9.99* | *0.36* | *0.816* |
| 25% percentile | 3.9 | 7.41 | 0.23 | 0.664 | 4.2 | 9.30 | 0.21 | 0.793 |
| Minimum | −4.2 | 5.35 | −0.52 | 0.233 | −2.0 | 6.41 | −0.33 | 0.600 |
| *Mean* | *5.5* | *8.08* | *0.43* | *0.703* | *5.7* | *10.04* | *0.36* | *0.813* |

| Table 8.2 | Constrained Multistrategy Portfolios | | | | | | | |
|---|---|---|---|---|---|---|---|---|
| | **Offshore** | | | | **UCITS** | | | |
| | Return per annum (%) | Volatility (%) | Sharpe (2%) | Corr. MSCI | Return per annum (%) | Volatility (%) | Sharpe (2%) | Corr. MSCI |
| Maximum | 14.5 | 13.00 | 1.78 | 0.872 | 9.7 | 10.28 | 1.35 | 0.894 |
| 75% percentile | 6.9 | 7.46 | 0.74 | 0.717 | 5.1 | 7.22 | 0.48 | 0.831 |
| Median | 5.6 | 6.85 | 0.52 | 0.672 | 4.1 | 6.67 | 0.32 | 0.810 |
| 25% percentile | 4.2 | 6.29 | 0.31 | 0.617 | 3.2 | 6.17 | 0.17 | 0.786 |
| Minimum | −3.3 | 4.51 | −0.46 | 0.141 | −1.3 | 4.26 | −0.44 | 0.603 |
| Mean | 5.6 | 6.94 | 0.52 | 0.662 | 4.2 | 6.72 | 0.33 | 0.807 |

A descriptive comparison between unconstrained offshore and unconstrained UCITS multistrategy portfolios in Table 8.1 reveals similar mean (5.5% for offshore versus 5.7% for UCITS) and similar medians, at 5.4% and 5.6%, respectively. At the same time the return dispersion as measured through the difference between the maximum and the minimum return portfolios is higher for offshore than for UCITS (18.1% versus 15.5%). The mean volatility of offshore portfolios (8%) is significantly lower than the UCITS mean volatility (10%). Additionally, offshore portfolios exhibit higher average Sharpe ratios.

Comparing the results of the constrained portfolio simulations it is seen that the set of offshore portfolios displays a higher mean return with similar mean volatility. Like in the case of unconstrained portfolios, the dispersion of offshore returns is greater. It is to be noted though that the bigger dispersion is to the upside of the median. Similar to the results from the unrestricted simulations the average Sharpe ratio of offshore portfolios is higher than the average Sharpe ratio of UCITS portfolios.

The results for the single-strategy portfolios resemble the results for the constrained multistrategy portfolios, with some noticeable exceptions. The mean and the median offshore Relative Value, Event Driven, and Tactical Trading portfolios perform better than the mean and the median of portfolios for the corresponding UCITS portfolios. In particular, the mean and the median Event Driven offshore portfolios exhibit considerably higher rates of returns than the mean and the median UCITS portfolios. Conversely, the set of simulated offshore Equity Hedge portfolios exhibit a mean and a median that are both lower than the mean and the median of the set of simulated UCITS Equity Hedge portfolios. The return dispersion within the offshore single-strategy portfolios is greater than the dispersion within UCITS returns. The biggest difference in return dispersion of UCITS versus offshore is observed among Event Driven portfolios.

| Table 8.3 | Single-Strategy Portfolios | | | | | | | |
|---|---|---|---|---|---|---|---|---|
| | Offshore | | | | UCITS | | | |
| | Return per annum (%) | Volatility (%) | Sharpe (2%) | Corr. MSCI | Return per annum (%) | Volatility (%) | Sharpe (2%) | Corr. MSCI |
| Equity Hedge | | | | | | | | |
| Maximum | 19.4 | 19.23 | 1.48 | 0.883 | 17.0 | 21.94 | 1.21 | 0.910 |
| 75% percentile | 7.3 | 12.55 | 0.48 | 0.785 | 7.9 | 15.51 | 0.42 | 0.846 |
| Median | 5.1 | 11.46 | 0.28 | 0.746 | 5.8 | 14.47 | 0.26 | 0.826 |
| 25% percentile | 3.0 | 10.49 | 0.08 | 0.704 | 3.7 | 13.47 | 0.11 | 0.804 |
| Minimum | −6.6 | 7.51 | −0.65 | 0.355 | −5.9 | 9.63 | −0.46 | 0.664 |
| Mean | 5.4 | 11.59 | 0.28 | 0.739 | 6.0 | 14.52 | 0.27 | 0.823 |
| Event Driven | | | | | | | | |
| Maximum | 18.8 | 16.07 | 1.76 | 0.839 | 5.9 | 9.65 | 0.80 | 0.845 |
| 75% percentile | 6.7 | 8.94 | 0.61 | 0.727 | 2.5 | 6.65 | 0.08 | 0.755 |
| Median | 5.1 | 7.96 | 0.39 | 0.688 | 1.7 | 5.99 | −0.06 | 0.727 |
| 25% percentile | 3.4 | 7.13 | 0.17 | 0.641 | 0.9 | 5.39 | −0.18 | 0.694 |
| Minimum | −7.4 | 4.57 | −0.64 | 0.241 | −2.5 | 3.43 | −0.56 | 0.423 |
| Mean | 5.2 | 8.12 | 0.41 | 0.680 | 1.7 | 6.05 | −0.04 | 0.721 |
| Relative Value | | | | | | | | |
| Maximum | 16.7 | 18.08 | 2.29 | 0.769 | 8.7 | 9.21 | 1.51 | 0.838 |
| 75% percentile | 6.8 | 7.51 | 0.81 | 0.550 | 4.8 | 5.87 | 0.55 | 0.723 |
| Median | 5.1 | 6.40 | 0.49 | 0.469 | 3.8 | 5.25 | 0.35 | 0.681 |
| 25% percentile | 3.3 | 5.53 | 0.19 | 0.368 | 2.9 | 4.75 | 0.16 | 0.627 |
| Minimum | −9.8 | 3.04 | −0.88 | −0.206 | −1.6 | 3.06 | −0.52 | 0.204 |
| Mean | 5.2 | 6.67 | 0.51 | 0.450 | 3.9 | 5.35 | 0.36 | 0.666 |
| Tactical Trading | | | | | | | | |
| Maximum | 16.8 | 18.14 | 1.75 | 0.616 | 13.3 | 8.98 | 2.08 | 0.745 |
| 75% percentile | 7.9 | 9.77 | 0.66 | 0.243 | 6.1 | 5.36 | 0.88 | 0.451 |
| Median | 6.1 | 8.96 | 0.45 | 0.145 | 4.9 | 4.82 | 0.60 | 0.357 |
| 25% percentile | 4.2 | 8.23 | 0.24 | 0.051 | 3.6 | 4.37 | 0.32 | 0.248 |
| Minimum | −5.4 | 5.59 | −0.80 | −0.324 | −2.4 | 2.80 | −0.63 | −0.255 |
| Mean | 6.3 | 9.06 | 0.46 | 0.146 | 4.9 | 4.91 | 0.60 | 0.344 |

The sets of volatilities for offshore Event Driven, Relative Value, and Tactical Trading portfolios display higher means than the sets of the corresponding UCITS single-strategy portfolios. The opposite volatility pattern is observed for the Equity Hedge portfolios where the UCITS portfolios exhibit on average higher volatility than the offshore ones. With regard to Sharpe ratios, Equity Hedge offshore and UCITS portfolios are similar on average, while offshore Event Driven portfolios are notably better than UCITS Event Driven portfolios. The set of Relative Value offshore portfolios exhibits a higher mean Sharpe ratio than the set of UCITS Relative Value portfolios. In contrast, offshore Tactical Trading portfolios display a lower mean Sharpe ratio than UCITS Tactical Trading portfolios.

The correlations with MSCI World are used as a proxy for the diversification characteristics of the simulated portfolios. A comparison between offshore and UCITS simulated portfolios reveals the same pattern across all portfolio types. The average MSCI World correlation of offshore portfolios is always lower than the average correlation of corresponding UCITS portfolios. This observation is basically in line with the results of McKenzie, F. (2012) who compared the beta of UCITS and offshore hedge funds. The biggest relative difference is observed at the Tactical Trading strategy where the average correlations of portfolios constructed from offshore funds is about 60% lower than the average correlation of portfolios of UCITS funds (0.146 average offshore correlation versus 0.344 average UCITS correlation). Similarly, the median MSCI World correlation of simulated offshore portfolios within a given strategy is always lower than the median correlation of UCITS portfolios within the same strategy. Moreover, the minimum and the maximum correlations exhibited by offshore simulated portfolios are also lower than the minimum and the maximum correlations exhibited by corresponding UCITS portfolios. In particular, the difference between the minimum correlation portfolios is considerable (e.g. the portfolio with the minimum correlation within the set of the relative value offshore simulated portfolios exhibits a negative correlation of −0.206, while the correlation of the minimum correlation UCITS portfolio within relative value is a positive value of 0.204). Assuming that lower MSCI correlations are an indication for better diversifying characteristics it could be concluded that portfolios of offshore funds dominate UCITS portfolios in terms of diversification benefits.

### 8.3.3. Return Distributions of Simulated FoHFs Portfolios: A Statistical Comparison

The descriptive comparison of the randomly simulated FoHFs portfolios revealed that there are noticeable differences between the performance of offshore FoHFs portfolios and that of simulated UCITS FoHFs portfolios. Nevertheless, the observed differences might not be statistically significant. Moreover, offshore and UCITS annualized returns might follow the same probability distribution. We therefore test for distribution equality with the Kolmogorov–Smirnov test. Additionally, we employ the Welch $t$-test to check if the mean annualized return for the simulated offshore portfolios is significantly different from the mean annualized return for the corresponding UCITS portfolios. The distribution functions are graphically depicted in Figure 8.13. The test results are presented in Table 8.4.

As Table 8.4 reveals, the results from both tests are unambiguous. For each of the six sets of simulated FoHFs portfolios the null hypothesis of equal distribution is rejected. Similarly, the null hypothesis of equal means is also rejected. The results show that the return distributions of the portfolios constructed from offshore single hedge fund strategies differ significantly from the return distributions of portfolios constructed from UCITS hedge funds. Moreover, the offshore portfolios exhibit significantly higher means across portfolio types except for portfolios within the equity hedge strategy.

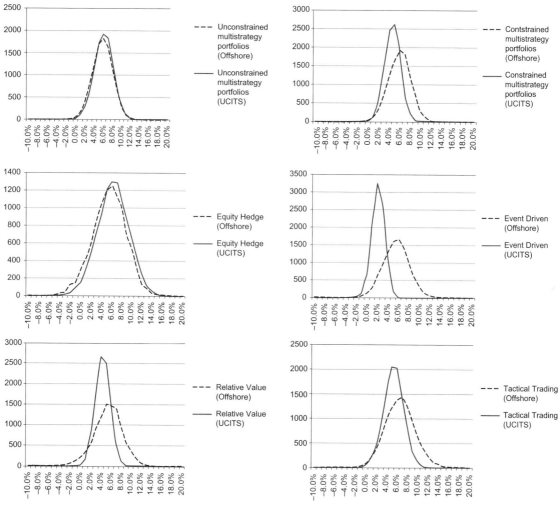

**FIGURE 8.13**
Distribution functions of FoHFs portfolios.

| Table 8.4 | Probability Distribution: Entire Period: January 2005–December 2011 | |
| --- | --- | --- |
| | Welch *t*-Test[1] | Kolmogorov–Smirnov Test[2] |
| Unconstrained multistrategy portfolios | 5.7150 | 0.0405 |
| Constrained multistrategy portfolios | 55.0744 | 0.3310 |
| Equity Hedge | 14.9373 | 0.0814 |
| Event Driven | 125.0119 | 0.6768 |
| Relative Value | 37.3465 | 0.3115 |
| Tactical Trading | 36.6552 | 0.2399 |

[1]Null hypothesis: same mean; rejection at 99% confidence level for t-values greater than 2.58.
[2]Null hypothesis: same distribution; rejection at 99% confidence level for Kolmogorov–Smirnov test values greater than 0.0163.

## 8.3.4. The Crisis and the Aftermath: A Time-Dependent Comparison of FoHFs Portfolios

Evaluating the results of the FoHFs simulation for two individual time windows – pre-crisis (from January 2005 to March 2007) and crisis/post-crisis (from April 2007 to December 2011) – provides a surprisingly different picture for the multistrategy portfolios as well as for the single-strategy portfolios. The performance and the risk characteristics for the constrained and unconstrained multistrategy portfolios for both periods are shown in Tables 8.5 (unconstrained portfolios) and 8.6 (constrained portfolios).

Pre-financial crisis, the simulated unconstrained multistrategy FoHFs portfolios within the UCITS universe show a significantly higher performance and Sharpe ratio than the FoHFs constructed out of offshore hedge funds, with an average performance of 17.4% for the UCITS FoHFs portfolios and 10.9% for the offshore FoHFs portfolios, and an average Sharpe ratio of 2.02 and 1.63, respectively. Subsequent to the crisis this picture turns upside down with the performance as well as the risk-adjusted performance (Sharpe ratio) being better for the offshore simulated FoHFs portfolios, showing an average performance of 0.4% for the UCITS fund of funds portfolios and 2.9% for the offshore FoHFs portfolios.

The result for the constrained multistrategy portfolios with four equally weighted strategies are different compared with the unconstrained portfolios. Pre-crisis the performance is only slightly better for the constrained UCITS FoHFs portfolios with an average performance of 10.9%, 9.9% for the offshore FoHFs portfolios. However, after the crisis the average offshore FoHF portfolio

| Table 8.5 | Unconstrained Multistrategy Portfolios | | | | | | |
|---|---|---|---|---|---|---|---|
| | **UCITS** | | | | **Offshore** | | |
| | Return per annum (%) | Volatility (%) | Sharpe (2%) | Corr. MSCI | Return per annum (%) | Volatility (%) | Sharpe (2%) | Corr. MSCI |
| *Pre-Crisis: January 2005–March 2007* | | | | | | | | |
| Maximum | 30.5 | 12.04 | 3.31 | 0.952 | 28.3 | 13.33 | 4.21 | 0.935 |
| 75% percentile | 19.1 | 8.30 | 2.23 | 0.846 | 12.6 | 6.11 | 1.94 | 0.790 |
| *Median* | 17.3 | 7.60 | 2.01 | 0.818 | 10.8 | 5.46 | 1.61 | 0.742 |
| 25% percentile | 15.4 | 6.93 | 1.80 | 0.786 | 9.0 | 4.88 | 1.29 | 0.683 |
| Minimum | 8.3 | 4.14 | 0.90 | 0.575 | 2.7 | 2.94 | 0.11 | 0.123 |
| *Mean* | 17.4 | 7.64 | 2.02 | 0.814 | 10.9 | 5.54 | 1.63 | 0.729 |
| *Crisis: April 2007–December 2011* | | | | | | | | |
| Maximum | 9.9 | 16.32 | 0.91 | 0.925 | 16.4 | 16.04 | 1.55 | 0.897 |
| 75% percentile | 2.1 | 11.62 | 0.01 | 0.858 | 4.8 | 9.69 | 0.32 | 0.762 |
| *Median* | 0.4 | 10.66 | −0.15 | 0.839 | 2.9 | 8.85 | 0.10 | 0.719 |
| 25% percentile | −1.4 | 9.75 | −0.31 | 0.817 | 0.9 | 8.09 | −0.12 | 0.667 |
| Minimum | −9.9 | 6.24 | −0.90 | 0.635 | −9.5 | 5.61 | −0.94 | 0.203 |
| *Mean* | 0.4 | 10.71 | −0.14 | 0.835 | 2.9 | 8.95 | 0.11 | 0.709 |

shows stronger performance than the average UCITS portfolio (3.5% versus 1.1%). The Sharpe ratios for the average offshore portfolio is also higher than for the average UCITS FoHFs portfolio. Similarly to the results for the entire period (January 2005–December 2011), Tables 8.5 and 8.6 show that the correlation towards the MSCI World Index is consistently higher for the UCITS-based FoHFs portfolios for both periods. This implies that the UCITS world inherits a higher long bias character than the offshore hedge fund world and is more influenced by the equity market performance.

For the single-strategy FoHFs portfolio the picture differs significantly for the pre-crisis period. UCITS FoHFs portfolios for liquid strategies like Equity Hedge (performance mean 22.0% *per annum* for UCITS FoHFs and 14.2% *per annum* for offshore FoHFs, see Table 8.7) and Tactical Trading (performance mean 8.8% *per annum* for UCITS FoHFs and 5.6% *per annum* for offshore FoHFs, see Table 8.10) show not only higher performances, but also much better risk-adjusted returns with means of the Sharpe ratios of 2.01 for Equity Hedge and 1.59 for Tactical Trading (see Tables 8.7 and 8.10). The Sharpe ratios for the offshore FoHFs portfolios for these strategies are only 1.64 for Equity Hedge and 0.46 for Tactical Trading (see Tables 8.7 and 8.10). For the Event Driven strategy offshore FoHFs portfolios have a higher performance and higher Sharpe ratio pre-crisis, implying that the available Event Driven UCITS universe has a significant lower quality compared to the offshore world (see Table 8.8). The Relative Value portfolio simulation for the pre-crisis data shows that the UCITS world again appears to be superior with performances of 4.96% *per annum* for the UCITS FoHFs and 3.47% for the offshore FoHFs with the Sharpe ratio also being higher (see Table 8.9).

| Table 8.6 | Constrained Multistrategy Portfolios |

| | UCITS | | | | Offshore | | | |
|---|---|---|---|---|---|---|---|---|
| | Return per annum (%) | Volatility (%) | Sharpe (2%) | Corr. MSCI | Return per annum (%) | Volatility (%) | Sharpe (2%) | Corr. MSCI |
| *Pre-Crisis: January 2005–March 2007* | | | | | | | | |
| Maximum | 18.6 | 7.04 | 3.28 | 0.940 | 19.9 | 9.80 | 3.73 | 0.929 |
| 75% percentile | 12.1 | 4.97 | 2.18 | 0.824 | 11.4 | 5.36 | 1.99 | 0.764 |
| *Median* | *10.8* | *4.56* | *1.94* | *0.791* | *9.8* | *4.73* | *1.65* | *0.710* |
| 25% percentile | 9.6 | 4.16 | 1.71 | 0.753 | 8.2 | 4.20 | 1.31 | 0.639 |
| Minimum | 5.5 | 2.69 | 0.68 | 0.479 | 1.7 | 2.31 | −0.07 | 0.079 |
| *Mean* | *10.9* | *4.58* | *1.95* | *0.786* | *9.9* | *4.83* | *1.66* | *0.693* |
| *Crisis: April 2007–December 2011* | | | | | | | | |
| Maximum | 9.1 | 11.96 | 1.13 | 0.931 | 12.8 | 15.06 | 1.57 | 0.881 |
| 75% percentile | 2.4 | 8.03 | 0.06 | 0.846 | 5.4 | 8.33 | 0.46 | 0.730 |
| *Median* | *1.1* | *7.33* | *−0.12* | *0.824* | *3.6* | *7.54* | *0.21* | *0.680* |
| 25% percentile | −0.2 | 6.68 | −0.29 | 0.800 | 1.7 | 6.84 | −0.04 | 0.620 |
| Minimum | −6.1 | 4.31 | −0.90 | 0.599 | −10.0 | 4.33 | −1.02 | 0.071 |
| *Mean* | *1.1* | *7.38* | *−0.11* | *0.821* | *3.5* | *7.66* | *0.22* | *0.668* |

**Table 8.7**   Equity Hedge: Single-Strategy FoHFs Portfolios: Pre-Crisis versus Crisis

| | UCITS | | | | Offshore | | | |
|---|---|---|---|---|---|---|---|---|
| | Return per annum (%) | Volatility (%) | Sharpe (2%) | Corr. MSCI | Return per annum (%) | Volatility (%) | Sharpe (2%) | Corr. MSCI |
| Pre-Crisis: January 2005–March 2007 | | | | | | | | |
| Maximum | 43.3 | 16.17 | 3.45 | 0.944 | 33.9 | 16.20 | 4.08 | 0.949 |
| 75% percentile | 24.8 | 10.96 | 2.26 | 0.835 | 16.8 | 8.43 | 1.97 | 0.790 |
| Median | 21.7 | 9.94 | 1.99 | 0.802 | 13.9 | 7.35 | 1.62 | 0.742 |
| 25% percentile | 19.0 | 9.01 | 1.75 | 0.763 | 11.3 | 6.44 | 1.29 | 0.679 |
| Minimum | 7.7 | 5.55 | 0.64 | 0.545 | −6.0 | 4.02 | −0.98 | 0.089 |
| Mean | 22.0 | 10.03 | 2.01 | 0.796 | 14.2 | 7.57 | 1.64 | 0.726 |
| Crisis: April 2007–December 2011 | | | | | | | | |
| Maximum | 12.6 | 24.99 | 0.86 | 0.931 | 17.7 | 22.81 | 1.26 | 0.896 |
| 75% percentile | 1.5 | 17.18 | −0.03 | 0.863 | 4.1 | 14.15 | 0.16 | 0.798 |
| Median | −1.1 | 15.81 | −0.19 | 0.843 | 1.1 | 12.72 | −0.07 | 0.758 |
| 25% percentile | −3.8 | 14.56 | −0.35 | 0.821 | −1.8 | 11.50 | −0.30 | 0.711 |
| Minimum | −15.4 | 9.70 | −0.91 | 0.670 | −14.2 | 7.93 | −1.08 | 0.293 |
| Mean | −1.1 | 15.88 | −0.19 | 0.840 | 1.1 | 12.90 | −0.06 | 0.749 |

**Table 8.8**   Event Driven: Single-Strategy FoHFs Portfolios: Pre-Crisis versus Crisis

| | UCITS | | | | Offshore | | | |
|---|---|---|---|---|---|---|---|---|
| | Return per annum (%) | Volatility (%) | Sharpe (2%) | Corr. MSCI | Return per annum (%) | Volatility (%) | Sharpe (2%) | Corr. MSCI |
| Pre-Crisis: January 2005–March 2007 | | | | | | | | |
| Maximum | 6.8 | 3.26 | 2.33 | 0.599 | 44.4 | 20.15 | 6.61 | 0.889 |
| 75% percentile | 5.0 | 2.71 | 1.26 | 0.483 | 13.0 | 4.97 | 2.72 | 0.682 |
| Median | 4.5 | 2.45 | 1.02 | 0.438 | 11.2 | 4.15 | 2.23 | 0.599 |
| 25% percentile | 4.1 | 2.22 | 0.81 | 0.387 | 9.6 | 3.54 | 1.77 | 0.496 |
| Minimum | 2.2 | 1.75 | 0.06 | 0.031 | 0.0 | 1.79 | −0.35 | −0.256 |
| Mean | 4.5 | 2.47 | 1.04 | 0.431 | 11.5 | 4.44 | 2.26 | 0.575 |
| Crisis: April 2007–December 2011 | | | | | | | | |
| Maximum | 6.6 | 11.55 | 0.75 | 0.864 | 14.3 | 19.10 | 1.52 | 0.867 |
| 75% percentile | 1.5 | 7.88 | −0.08 | 0.772 | 4.4 | 10.22 | 0.27 | 0.740 |
| Median | 0.3 | 7.06 | −0.24 | 0.743 | 2.2 | 9.04 | 0.02 | 0.698 |
| 25% percentile | −0.8 | 6.32 | −0.38 | 0.708 | 0.0 | 8.01 | −0.21 | 0.651 |
| Minimum | −5.5 | 3.88 | −0.90 | 0.424 | −15.1 | 4.93 | −1.08 | 0.213 |
| Mean | 0.3 | 7.13 | −0.22 | 0.736 | 2.1 | 9.23 | 0.04 | 0.691 |

In the crisis period the picture is turned upside down. For all four single strategies we get better performance and risk-adjusted returns for the offshore FoHFs portfolios simulated from the offshore hedge fund universe compared to the UCITS universe. So what is the explanation for such a sharp deterioration of 'quality' of the UCITS universe compared to the offshore universe? We believe that survivorship bias in the pre-crisis data, higher fees, a limited 'tool box' for the UCITS manager, and a lack of talent could explain the differences between the UCITS and the offshore universes.

The available UCITS database was only launched in 2010. The UCITS hedge fund universe has only taken off with regard to the number of funds and their AUM since the financial crisis. With hedge funds usually providing historic performance numbers to databases only subsequent to 'good' performance we believe that this element of survivorship bias within the UCITS hedge fund universe pre-crisis should not be underestimated. Hence, the pre-crisis performance of the simulated UCITS FoHFs portfolios has been *ex post* increased as managers launching UCITS hedge funds included their good pre-crisis performance in the available databases only subsequent to the crisis.

Secondly, we believe that implicit fees within UCITS hedge funds, such as swap trading fees or bid/ask spreads are generally reducing the expected return of UCITS hedge funds. Additionally, we view the tool box for managers within the UCITS hedge fund universe as limited compared to the offshore world. Due to liquidity provisions potentially attractive illiquid assets offering additional risk premia cannot be accessed through UCITS funds. Furthermore, the need to hold higher levels of cash in UCITS hedge funds due to regulatory liquidity

**Table 8.9**   Relative Value: Single-Strategy FoHFs Portfolios: Pre-Crisis versus Crisis

| | UCITS | | | | Offshore | | | |
|---|---|---|---|---|---|---|---|---|
| | Return per annum (%) | Volatility (%) | Sharpe (2%) | Corr. MSCI | Return per annum (%) | Volatility (%) | Sharpe (2%) | Corr. MSCI |
| Pre-Crisis: January 2005–March 2007 | | | | | | | | |
| Maximum | 17.1 | 8.83 | 2.72 | 0.883 | 19.2 | 12.96 | 6.12 | 0.883 |
| 75% percentile | 10.0 | 5.54 | 1.58 | 0.748 | 9.7 | 3.92 | 2.43 | 0.572 |
| Median | 8.5 | 4.92 | 1.34 | 0.700 | 8.1 | 3.22 | 1.88 | 0.469 |
| 25% percentile | 7.1 | 4.35 | 1.09 | 0.645 | 6.7 | 2.69 | 1.35 | 0.346 |
| Minimum | 2.3 | 1.94 | 0.07 | 0.331 | 0.4 | 1.29 | −0.34 | −0.398 |
| Mean | 8.6 | 4.96 | 1.34 | 0.693 | 8.2 | 3.47 | 1.92 | 0.451 |
| Crisis: April 2007–December 2011 | | | | | | | | |
| Maximum | 8.3 | 10.41 | 1.66 | 0.873 | 19.2 | 21.61 | 2.32 | 0.781 |
| 75% percentile | 2.8 | 6.08 | 0.17 | 0.762 | 6.1 | 8.70 | 0.60 | 0.558 |
| Median | 1.6 | 5.25 | −0.07 | 0.721 | 3.7 | 7.32 | 0.23 | 0.470 |
| 25% percentile | 0.4 | 4.58 | −0.28 | 0.667 | 1.2 | 6.21 | −0.11 | 0.363 |
| Minimum | −5.2 | 2.50 | −1.11 | 0.137 | −16.7 | 3.26 | −1.35 | −0.241 |
| Mean | 1.6 | 5.39 | −0.04 | 0.704 | 3.5 | 7.65 | 0.26 | 0.450 |

| Table 8.10 | Tactical Trading: Single-Strategy FoHFs Portfolios: Pre-Crisis versus Crisis |
|---|---|

| | **UCITS** | | | | **Offshore** | | | |
|---|---|---|---|---|---|---|---|---|
| | **Return per annum (%)** | **Volatility (%)** | **Sharpe (2%)** | **Corr. MSCI** | **Return per annum (%)** | **Volatility (%)** | **Sharpe (2%)** | **Corr. MSCI** |
| *Pre-Crisis: January 2005–March 2007* | | | | | | | | |
| Maximum | 17.6 | 9.90 | 3.60 | 0.773 | 34.1 | 20.08 | 2.82 | 0.905 |
| 75% percentile | 10.2 | 4.69 | 1.89 | 0.544 | 8.1 | 8.80 | 0.79 | 0.585 |
| *Median* | *8.7* | *4.21* | *1.58* | *0.465* | *5.4* | *7.65* | *0.44* | *0.503* |
| 25% percentile | 7.3 | 3.79 | 1.29 | 0.374 | 2.8 | 6.67 | 0.10 | 0.405 |
| Minimum | 1.7 | 2.12 | −0.10 | −0.163 | −7.7 | 2.91 | −1.25 | −0.195 |
| *Mean* | *8.8* | *4.27* | *1.59* | *0.452* | *5.6* | *7.83* | *0.46* | *0.487* |
| *Crisis: April 2007–December 2011* | | | | | | | | |
| Maximum | 14.5 | 10.22 | 2.17 | 0.760 | 22.7 | 21.75 | 1.99 | 0.653 |
| 75% percentile | 4.8 | 5.69 | 0.58 | 0.460 | 8.9 | 10.40 | 0.73 | 0.225 |
| *Median* | *3.1* | *4.97* | *0.22* | *0.351* | *6.4* | *9.43* | *0.47* | *0.110* |
| 25% percentile | 1.4 | 4.35 | −0.13 | 0.220 | 3.8 | 8.51 | 0.20 | −0.001 |
| Minimum | −6.9 | 2.31 | −1.44 | −0.348 | −9.0 | 5.45 | −1.00 | −0.406 |
| *Mean* | *3.0* | *5.08* | *0.23* | *0.332* | *6.4* | *9.53* | *0.47* | *0.112* |

requirements should also be seen as a characteristic, being a drag on performance. A smart discussion on the restrictions of UCITS Funds and their failure to produce low tracking errors to their offshore counterparts is provided by Hirst, T. (2011). Finally, although not quantifiable and probably unfair for some UCITS hedge fund managers, we believe that the most talented offshore hedge fund manager are not in need of raising AUM through the launch of UCITS funds, hence implicitly reducing the manager quality within the UCITS hedge fund universe.

## CONCLUSION

In this chapter we provided a detailed descriptive comparison of the onshore (UCITS) and offshore hedge fund universes with regard to strategy distribution, number of funds, AUM, and fees. We observed that the number of UCITS hedge funds has been increasing while the number of offshore funds has already peaked and has been declining subsequently. Similarly, the UCITS AUM have grown rapidly, especially since the aftermath of the financial crisis, while the AUM in offshore funds have dropped significantly. On the other hand, we noted that Event Driven and Relative Value strategies are still under-represented in the UCITS universe as most of the UCITS managers follow Equity Hedge and Tactical Trading investment styles. This fact might limit the proper implementation of a Tactical Strategy Allocation (TSA) as described by Anand, G., Maier, T., Kutsarov, I. & Storr, M. (2011). The comparison of the *explicit* offshore and UCITS fees did not reveal any major differences. We would assume, though, that the *implicit* UCITS costs are higher.

We analyzed the performance of the offshore and the UCITS hedge fund universes in the FoHFs context by constructing FoHFs portfolios. We used a simulation methodology to construct random FoHFs from the offshore and from the UCITS universe, respectively. Based on the above analysis we drew the following conclusions that have significant relevance for how hedge fund allocation might be pursued by investors, in particular in Europe. Our results indicate that over a longer-term period FoHFs portfolios constructed with offshore funds provide higher absolute returns, higher risk-adjusted returns, and better diversifying characteristics than UCITS portfolios. Additionally, the return distributions of the set of offshore FoHFs and the set of UCITS FoHFs are significantly different. Splitting the time period into the pre-crisis period and crisis period, we observed that UCITS FoHFs portfolios were superior in terms of return potential and Sharpe ratios in the pre-crisis window, while in the crisis window offshore FoHFs portfolios exhibited significantly higher absolute and risk-adjusted returns. The divergence between the results in the two time periods is explainable with the potentially stronger survivorship bias of the UCITS database as it was launched in 2010, much later than the start of the offshore database and much later than the end of the pre-crisis period. The better absolute and risk-adjusted performance of offshore portfolios versus UCITS portfolios in the crisis period and overall, we believe, comes from the higher implicit fees of UCITS single funds, the smaller tool box available for UCITS managers due to regulatory oversight, and the regulatory restrictions in terms of liquidity, leverage, and concentration.

This chapter suggests that constructing FoHFs through offshore funds provides on average a better way to invest into hedge funds than constructing FoHFs through UCITS hedge funds. Our conclusion, though, is certainly not denying any single manager excellence within the UCITS hedge fund universe. With more data becoming available for the UCITS hedge fund space over the next couple of years, it might be reasonable to analyze both hedge fund worlds — onshore versus offshore universe — again to see if the two universes will continue to diverge or eventually start to converge.

# References

Anand, G., Maier, T., Kutsarov, I., & Storr, M. (2011). Importance of Tactical Strategy Allocation on Fund-of-Hedge-Funds Allocations. *Journal of Wealth Management, 14*(2), 49−58.

Barclays Capital (2011). *Hedge Fund Pulse, UCITS: To Be or Not to Be.* London: Working Paper, Barclays Capital.

The Eurekahedge Report, New York and Singapore, Eurekahedge, April 2012.

Dickinson, C. (2011). The Uses and Abuses of UCITS. *Structured Products, 7*(5), 12−15.

Hirst, T. (2011). UCITS: Wrapped up. *Fund Strategy.* February, 27.

McKenzie, F. (2012). Alpha UCITS: An Oxymoron? *InvestmentEurope, 19*(1), 23−25.

Naisscent Capital, A. G. (2012). *Alternative UCITS Performance Guide.* Winterthur: Working Paper, Naisscent Capital AG.

Ralston, G., & Butler, D. (2011). Market Monitor: The Great Debate − Is UCITS Suitable for Hedge Funds? *Professional Wealth Management, 95.*

# CHAPTER 9

# How Geography, Flows, and Size Affect the Risk-Adjusted Performance of UCITS III Funds of Hedge Funds

**Greg N. Gregoriou**[*], **Dieter Kaiser**[†], **and Razvan Pascalau**[*]

[*]SUNY Plattsburgh, School of Business and Economics,
Plattsburgh, NY, USA

[†]Managing Director, Robus Capital Management Limited,
Bad Homburg, Germany

## 9.1. INTRODUCTION

The 'Undertaking in Collective Investment in Transferable Securities' (UCITS) Directives were originally created in 1985 and over the years have expanded to include broader concepts, such as alternative investment techniques in 2001. Traditionally, even though mutual funds that are structured according to the UCITS Directive (UCITS funds) have been considered as European-based investment vehicles with EUR as the base currency, numerous funds are now also based in US$. The latest UCITS IV Directive implemented in July 2011 will no doubt provide new regulations and/or amendments to the current UCITS III structure.

Despite the poor performance of small and large single-manager hedge funds and funds of hedge funds (FoHFs), respectively, during the 2008–2009 crisis, institutional investors are now looking for alternative types of 'alternatives.' With 22% of FoHFs dying during the crisis, a number significantly higher than the number of single-manager hedge fund deaths, this poses a serious threat to the FoHFs industry (Brown *et al.*, 2012b). One avenue for investors is the twist on UCITS-compliant hedge funds and FoHFs because of the more stringent

Reconsidering Funds of Hedge Funds. http://dx.doi.org/10.1016/B978-0-12-401699-6.00009-5

directives such as higher transparency, increased regulation and limitation of leverage, restrictions on concentration of assets, increased liquidity, and maximum redemption period being semi-monthly. UCITS FoHFs offer daily or weekly redemptions typically not available in the still mostly 'offshore' hedge fund industry, and provide an advantage over traditional FoHFs by offering investors greater safety and an attempt at solving the liquidity issue. The UCITS liquidity directive obliges hedge funds to hold few positions in assets that are illiquid, which are known to restrict the investment managers' strategy and thereby affect the performance of UCITS FoHFs (Keime and de Koning, 2009). Certain conventional hedge fund strategies typically applying leverage, trading less liquid instruments, and using short sales may find, under the new UCITS regime, they may experience subpar performance (and/or tracking error to the Offshore Flagship fund) and, coupled with the more frequent withdrawals may result in a bubble that may likely burst in the next crisis.

One drawback of traditional FoHFs is the added layer of management and performance fees.[1] The added security features such as regulation or higher operational costs due to more frequent net asset value calculation of the UCITS structure will certainly come at a higher cost than for non-UCITS funds and fund performance may suffer as a result. In addition, since the crisis institutional investors have sought shelter in UCITS-compliant hedge funds and UCITS FoHFs for this reason. Industry numbers nearing US$200 billion of capital under management in UCITS funds as at December 2011 (Alix Capital Database, www.alixcapital.com), well up from the US$121 billion in the first quarter of 2010 (Tuchschmid *et al.*, 2011), may signal a potential bubble in the UCITS universe. With higher fees, UCITS structures command the clawbacks and, in the case of a black swan event, may be far worse than offshore single-manager hedge funds and FoHFs.

With the tide quickly turning, the number of FoHFs currently being set up is beginning to mirror the traditional growth of FoHFs since the mid 1990s (Tuchschmid *et al.*, 2011). Investors are paying more attention to UCITS FoHFs due to their low volatility, higher risk-adjusted performance, lower drawdowns, and limited leverage.[2] The new Directives only allow an upper limit of 20% in underlying hedge funds that are not UCITS-compliant or other types of investments. One misconception is that in the UCITS III and IV structures investors believe they can withdraw their entire investment at any time; however, there are 'gates' that still remain unknown to many investors. In essence, investors are pouring money into UCITS-compliant FoHFs that must invest in other UCITS-compliant hedge funds. However, both UCITS hedge funds and FoHFs have gate provisions that allow them to limit the withdrawal at 10% per trading date. Therefore, in extreme market conditions, UCITS investors might face similar issues as with offshore hedge fund investments. The reasoning for

---

[1]Some FoHFs only charge a management fee of 1–3%.
[2]The leverage an underlying UCITS fund can use is strictly from its derivatives positions.

this growth is that in the next crisis UCITS FoHFs are expected to provide better returns than their counterparts; however, some investors are skeptical and believe there could be a mass exodus of UCITS hedge funds, thereby affecting the returns of UCITS FoHFs.

In addition, a number of market participants have addressed their concerns with respect to value at risk issues, more specifically regarding the parameters imposed by the regulator. With a maximum loss of 20% at 1 month with a 95% confidence level the regulators have actually been quite generous in terms of risk limits. The risk of strategies with short-volatility-type payoff profiles may not be well controlled with these types of measures.

With respect to the number of UCITS FoHFs being created, a 2009 survey concluded that 80% of the largest 30 FoHFs managers plan to create a UCITS FoHFs (Keime and de Koning, 2009). Finally, according to a recent survey by PerTrac (2012), Europe has 94.30% of all UCITS funds with very little dispersion outside continental Europe. In the same report as of October 2011, 69.83% of UCITS funds were denominated in EUR, while 15.21% were in US$ and 10.83% were in GBP. However, there has been discussion regarding the performance of small or large UCITS FoHFs during the crisis and post-crisis.

## 9.2. LITERATURE REVIEW

The main emphasis in the hedge fund industry and more particularly with FoHFs is that due diligence conducted after the financial crisis is now more rigorous. The reason small FoHFs died during the crisis was the lack and cost of due diligence reports. According to Brown *et al.* (2012a), the average cost of a due diligence report circulated in the industry is approximately US$12 500 and can run as high as US$50 000 for tailormade reports requested by clients. For small FoHFs with US$25–200 million the due diligence reports dig into the management fees; however, for large FoHFs this is not the issue (Brown *et al.*, 2012b). The FoHFs manager job of selection is now limited to the pool of UCITS III-compliant hedge funds as their underlying managers. Although the universe for UCITS hedge funds is far smaller than the entire industry,[3] Pascalau (2011) puts the level at 311. The most popular domicile attracting UCITS FoHFs is Luxembourg because of its recognized infrastructure and added knowledge they provide (e.g., see PerTrac, 2012; Meakin, 2010). In addition, during the 2009–2011 period seven out of 51 UCITS FoHFs were set up outside Luxembourg or Ireland; since June 2009, Luxembourg has managed to receive 65.7% of money flows with Ireland coming in second place with 26% (UBS, 2011). The UBS report also states that the number of UCITS FoHFs is outpacing their traditional

---

[3]The numbers of live UCITS-compliant hedge funds and FoHFs were 585 and 48, respectively, in the BarclayHedge database as of 31 December 2011. As of May 2012 UCITS FoHFs had EUR3.07 billion under management and in UCITS single-manager hedge funds had EUR129 billion (www.alixcapital.com). In the Alix Capital database there were 78 live UCITS FoHFs and 689 live UCITS single-manager hedge funds as of 31 May 2012.

FoHFs counterparts with live UCITS FoHFs growing in size. Could this imply that more capital will flow towards UCITS FoHFs? What about the 2008–2009 financial crisis as well as future crises – will investors favor UCITS FoHFs?

Meakin (2010) suggests that UCITS FoHFs attract predominantly institutional investors and high-net-worth individuals with retail clients following closely. Additionally, it seems that investors that are used to investing in hedge funds via offshore structures continue to do so while new investors prefer the easier-to-settle UCITS way. However, all the constraints and regulations set forth by the UCITS directives in terms of leverage and liquidity may turn out to be counterproductive, since some hedge fund strategies require leverage to produce above-average returns (Stefanini *et al.*, 2010). As a result the increased transparency will likely produce subpar performance in the UCITS FoHFs industry since the underlying single-manager funds have to be disclosed at 100%, giving FoHFs no advantage in their manager selection process.

According to Fieldhouse (2010), UCITS funds launched today are to a large extent from well-known and respected investment firms in the industry, and are recognized to be providers of superior risk management abilities and additional transparency. FoHFs managers have embraced the UCITS structure along with its regulatory framework since directives have changed the landscape and mind set of hedge fund investing, thereby directly affecting FoHFs.

Using the seven-risk-factor model developed by Fung and Hsieh (2004), Tuchschmid *et al.* (2011) find that there is a lack of strong evidence that UCITS hedge funds outperform traditional single-manager hedge funds on a risk-adjusted basis. One must be careful here when interpreting the results since the period under investigation is short. Furthermore, the authors also find lower risk associated with UCITS funds than with traditional hedge funds – a finding confirmed by Darolles (2011). In addition, Darolles (2011) concludes that for a UCITS fund to be successful the manager must have a lengthy track record managing a hedge fund. In a more recent study using the BarclayHedge database, Pascalau (2011) investigates UCITS funds and concludes that UCITS FoHFs[4] provided better risk-adjusted performance than traditional FoHFs during the January 2006–March 2010 period. Pascalau (2011) also finds that UCITS FoHFs have a minimum requirement of US$46 040 as an initial investment and in terms of performance UCITS funds denominated in GBP are at the top of the list. Finally, Teo (2009a) uses geography to assess the performance of Asian hedge funds via an augmented four-factor model of Fung and Hsieh (2004).

Traditionally, hedge fund studies have concluded an inverse relation exists between assets under management (AUM) and fund performance (e.g., see Teo, 2009b; Shawky and Wang, 2011). One must also consider that the data period under investigation can play a major role in the size issue; however, no studies

---

[4]The sample used by Pascalau (2011) consists of 24 active UCITS FoHFs and in 2006 only two live UCITS FoHFs existed in the BarclayHedge database.

have investigated if size matters in terms of performance for UCITS FoHFs. In addition, Dewaele *et al.* (2011) using cross-sectional analysis conclude that offshore hedge fund manager experience can increase the performance of UCITS funds, but the authors fail to investigate the size issue.

There is no doubt that there are many inquisitive investors wondering what will happen to both UCITS hedge funds and UCITS FoHFs in the next crisis. Will history repeat itself and will 22% or more of UCITS FoHFs die, similarly to their FoHFs counterparts during the 2008–2009 crisis? Should investors invest in large or small UCITS FoHFs? What about UCITS FoHFs inflows and outflows during the past crisis and during negative S&P 500 months? Does the geographical location and focus of the UCITS FoHFs manager matter? Does the jurisdiction of the UCITS FoHFs custodian matter? What about the optimal number of underlying single-manager hedge funds in a UCITS FoHF? Is the added cost of UCITS hedge funds and FoHFs worth it to achieve stable returns? How do UCITS FoHFs in the Barclay database fare against other FoHFs benchmarks? These and other questions need to be answered so the industry, can obtain a clearer picture of what in lies ahead for this new structure.

## 9.3. DATA

We use monthly performance data net of all fees of live and dead funds that reported to the BarclayHedge database. The data spans from January 2000 to December 2011, and UCITS FoHFs data consist of 50 live and five dead funds. We acknowledge the presence of survivorship bias and a negligible backfill bias in the data since BarclayHedge only started collecting data on dead funds in January 2011. In addition, we recognize that due to the small number of UCITS FoHFs in the database the statistical analysis may suffer from the small-sample issue.

## 9.4. PERFORMANCE OF AND FLOWS INTO UCITS FoHFs

Beginning March 2006, BarclayHedge started collecting monthly information on the AUM managed by UCITS FoHFs. Figure 9.1 shows the total AUM managed by UCITS FoHFs from March 2006 to January 2012. Thus, at the start of the sample in April 2006 the total amount of AUM was only about US$350 million. Thereafter the total AUM grew steadily until it peaked at US$1.4 billion in June 2008. That period marked the worsening of the financial crisis and as a result investors began to withdraw money from alternative investments vehicles, including UCITS FoHFs. The pullout continued until February 2009 when the total AUM reached a low of about US$678 million, by which time UCITS FoHFs had lost about 52% of the AUM they managed at the peak in the summer of 2008. However, beginning with spring 2009 UCITS FoHFs started to recover and grow at an impressive rate until the AUM peaked at US$5.2 billion in April 2011.

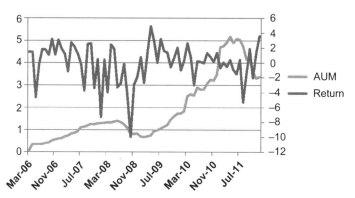

**FIGURE 9.1**
Relationship between total UCITS FoHFs AUM (left-hand axis; US$ billion) and cross-average raw returns (right-hand axis; %) on a monthly basis.

The worsening of the European sovereign debt crisis in 2011 led investors to again pull out, such that at the start of 2012 UCITS FoHFs were managing approximately only US$3.4 billion. Therefore, over an 8-month period UCITS FoHFs lost about 35% of their AUM.

Figure 9.1 also shows the average monthly raw performance of the 55 funds over the sample period (i.e., March 2006–January 2012). Until June 2008, their performance had been relatively stable with an excellent performance in the second part of 2006. However, beginning with June 2008 their performance deteriorated considerably following the general downward trend in the market. In October 2008 alone UCITS FoHFs lost 9.94%. The funds bounced back only in spring 2009 when performance spiked to 4.88%. Still, since that peak UCITS FoHFs returns have been on a slightly downward trend that was only reversed in early Fall 2011.

To get a better understanding of the pattern of flows in and out of those funds, Figure 9.2 shows the monthly flows into UCITS FoHFs and their rolling 6-month correlation, where the flows are computed by:

$$Flow_t = \frac{AUM_t - AUM_{t-1}(1 + r_t)}{AUM_{t-1}}, \tag{9.1}$$

where $r_t$ denotes the current month's performance.

Figure 9.2 confirms the evidence in Figure 9.1, whereby there were significant inflows until Spring 2008 when Bear Stearns collapsed. The low performances afterwards led to a significant trend reversal that averaged 5.15% outflows from April 2008 to February 2009. Figure 9.2 also shows that in the crisis period from September 2008 to March 2009, the rolling 6-month correlation between returns and flows averaged 0.3, whereby until Spring 2009 the correlation coefficient averaged −0.04. Over all the sample, the average correlation between returns and flows has generally been very weak at −0.02 but increased during extreme market movements, being either positive (February 2010–February

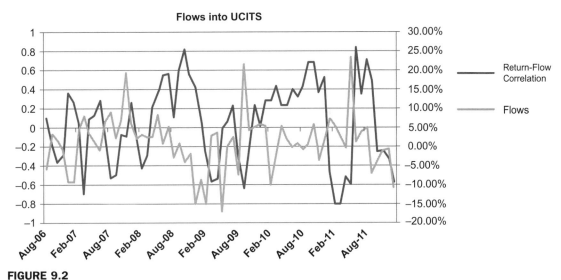

**Flows into UCITS**

**FIGURE 9.2**
Average monthly flows into UCITS FoHFs (right-hand axis; %) and the rolling 6-month correlation between flows and returns (left-hand axis). Flows are computed using equation (9.1).

2011) or negative (September 2008–March 2009). One may also note a significant decrease in funds inflow beginning with the summer of 2011 following the spread of the budget deficit crisis to several European countries.

## 9.5. RISK ANALYSIS

The previous section has shown that UCITS FoHFs performance has been mixed and that especially throughout the financial crisis of 2008 they tanked along with the market. The question then remains whether those investment vehicles are able to generate alpha or whether their performance is simply due to following the general trend in the market. In order to answer this question we follow Fung and Hsieh (2004) to adjust the raw returns for risk and estimate the managerial alpha. Specifically, we employ the seven-factor risk model that has been used extensively in the hedge fund literature and that is acknowledged to do a good job to account for the risk dynamics. In addition, we acknowledge that all UCITS funds are located in Europe, trade in currencies other than the US Dollar and hence are exposed to significant exchange rate risk when converting and reporting returns in US Dollars. In order to control for this particular type of risk we also employ a US$ index. The risk-adjustment equation (9.2) writes in the following way:

$$
\begin{aligned}
r_{it} = {}& \alpha + \beta_1 PTFSBD_t + \beta_2 PTFSFX_t + \beta_3 PTFSCOM_t + \beta_4 Bond\ Factor_t \\
& + \beta_5 Equity\ Factor_t + \beta_6 Credit\ Spread_t + \beta_7 Size\ Spread_t \\
& + \beta_8 US\ Dollar\ Index_t + \varepsilon_t
\end{aligned}
\tag{9.2}
$$

where $i = 1, \ldots, 55$ funds, $t = 1, \ldots, T$ months, $\alpha_{it}$ is the manager's contribution (Fung–Hsieh alpha) of fund $i$ for month $t$, $r_{it}$ is the fund return in excess of the risk-free rate (e.g., 1-month US$ Libor rate), *PTFSBD* is the excess return of the PTFS bond lookback straddle, *PTFSFX* is the excess return of the PTFS currency lookback straddle, *PTFSCOM* is the excess return of the commodity lookback straddle, *Bond Factor* is the change in the monthly market yield of the 10-year treasury constant maturity yield, *Equity Factor* is the S&P 500 Index monthly total excess return, *Credit Spread* is the monthly change in the Moody's Baa yield minus 10-year treasury constant maturity yield, and *Size Spread* is the Wilshire 5000 Market Index return less S&P 500 total return. In all cases, excess returns are computed by subtracting the monthly US$ Libor rate. The appraisal ratios are obtained by dividing the fund alphas over the residual standard deviation.

To compare the performance of UCITS FoHFs, Table 9.1 employs a relatively broad set of FoHFs benchmarks. Those benchmarks are the BarclayHedge FoHF

| Table 9.1 | | Descriptive Statistics on UCITS FoHFs | | | | | |
|---|---|---|---|---|---|---|---|
| | N | Number of Hedge Funds | AUM (US$) | Manager AUM (US$) | Alpha | Volatility | Appraisal Ratio |
| *Currency* | | | | | | | |
| CHF | 5 | 14.67 | 29491500 | 4946262750 | 1.94 | 1.14 | −0.63 |
| EUR | 23 | 15.75 | 99689333 | 34046937769 | −0.49 | 1.89 | −0.33 |
| GBP | 3 | 13.67 | 350878333 | 2965000000 | −0.33 | 0.48 | −1.29 |
| US$ | 8 | 11.50 | 18231571 | 3702510200 | −1.08 | 1.65 | −1.28 |
| *Domicile* | | | | | | | |
| Austria | 3 | 21.67 | 101006333 | 283250000 | 0.04 | 1.99 | 0.04 |
| France | 8 | 14.5 | 205017750 | 3800000000 | −1.93 | 2.37 | −0.96 |
| Ireland | 8 | 5.00 | 41438000 | 11200000000 | −0.90 | 0.98 | −1.18 |
| Luxembourg | 16 | 18.08 | 34578625 | 2898599481 | 0.40 | 1.51 | −0.24 |
| UK | 2 | 18.00 | 499480500 | 205000000 | 0.29 | NA | NA |
| *Strategy* | | | | | | | |
| Unspecified | 23 | 13.95 | 136017304 | 2786931941 | −0.06 | 2.10 | −0.36 |
| Diversified | 19 | 14.35 | 38352579 | 5545871368 | −0.70 | 0.97 | −1.04 |
| *Geographical focus* | | | | | | | |
| Eastern and Western Europe | 2 | 17.00 | 34246000 | 3900000000 | −1.86 | 2.39 | −0.78 |
| Global markets | 31 | 14.55 | 103965686 | 3824631652 | −0.49 | 1.54 | −0.67 |
| North America−Europe | 2 | 4.00 | 405000 | 2500000 | −0.25 | 2.65 | 0.02 |
| Western Europe | 2 | 15.00 | 34813000 | 7000000000 | 5.07 | 1.36 | −2.76 |
| *Benchmark FoHFs* | | | | | | | |
| BarclayHedge | | | | | 1.93 | 1.25 | 1.54 |
| Eurekahedge | | | | | −3.14 | 1.55 | −2.02 |
| Greenwich | | | | | −3.47 | 1.75 | −1.98 |
| HFR Multi-Strategy | | | | | −3.60 | 1.57 | −2.29 |
| HFR Composite | | | | | −3.75 | 1.71 | −2.19 |
| HFR Offshore | | | | | −3.85 | 1.79 | −2.14 |
| HFR Onshore | | | | | −3.60 | 1.66 | −2.17 |

Returns are expressed on a monthly basis.

Index, the Eureka FoHF Index, the Greenwich FoHF Index, and the HFR Multi-Strategy, HFR Composite, HFR Offshore, and HFR Onshore FoHF Indexes provided by the Hedge Fund Research database. Table 9.1 shows the respective alpha, volatility, and appraisal ratios for each one of those indexes.

In addition to the risk-adjusted performance measures, Table 9.1 shows the number of underlying hedge fund managers and the respective AUM. First, Table 9.1 shows the descriptive statistics based on the trading currency. Most (51%) FoHFs use the EUR as the trading unit, while about 15% of them trade in the US$. Irrespective of the trading currency, all FoHFs have less than 20 managers in the portfolio with the US$-based funds having the smallest number at 12 on average. The funds trading in GBP are the largest with approximately US$351 million under management. Not surprisingly, the US$ trading funds have the lowest number of managers because they have the lowest number of AUM, even though the corresponding FoHF managers manage the most AUM among their peers. This evidence indicates that the average US$ trading FoHFs manager appears more 'diversified' than the other FoHF managers. As a result of exchange rate differences, a direct comparison across currencies may not accurately reflect the funds' performance. We nevertheless attempt to do so as a crude way to assess performance given the small sample available. The Swiss trading funds appear to be the only ones with a positive alpha, while the US$ trading UCITS have the lowest risk-adjusted performance. This result is confirmed by a comparison of the appraisal ratios where the US$ and GBP UCITS have the lowest risk-adjusted return per unit of risk. The EUR trading UCITS show on average the highest alpha volatility.

Most UCITS FoHFs are located in Luxembourg, with Ireland and France also being popular locations. Even though the Luxembourg-based funds have the second largest number of single-manager funds in the portfolio at 18, they have the smallest AUM. At first this combination might lead one to expect a lower performance given the (un)affordability of due diligence costs required with the proper selection of managers. Nevertheless, those UCITS FoHFs display the largest monthly alpha and the smallest alpha volatility, respectively. One may also notice that UCITS FoHFs based in France have the lowest alpha and the highest alpha volatility, deeming them the worst performers. For the rest, UCITS FoHFs based in the United Kingdom have the largest AUM on average at US$500 million. Even though UCITS FoHF managers based in Ireland manage the most AUM, their funds have the smallest AUM.

While roughly one half of UCITS FoHFs do not have a stated strategy, the other half simply pursue a diversified strategy. Among UCITS FoHFs with a stated strategy, on average they have around 20 underlying hedge fund managers in the portfolio. UCITS following a diversified strategy are much smaller in size, by more than three times that of those without a specified strategy, and as a result their smaller size may translate into a lower alpha and appraisal ratio, respectively.

Depending on the geographical focus, most (56%) UCITS FoHFs have a global focus. Those funds are also the largest. The other UCITS with a narrower geographical focus are not as well represented in the sample and as a result, the conclusions need to be interpreted with care. For instance, the two UCITS FoHFs focused on Western Europe display an unusually large monthly alpha at 5.07%. However, this appears to be the case only because those two funds have a very short track record that starts in April and November 2010, respectively.

Relative to the usual FoHFs benchmarks, UCITS FoHFs generally perform better across the classifications listed with the exception of the Barclay FoHF index relative to which they generally underperform. For comparability purposes, we focus on the US$ trading UCITS FoHFs. Thus, the latter outperform all indexes with the exception of the Barclay FoHF Index, and have lower volatility than the Greenwich and HFR FoHF indexes, respectively. Based on the appraisal ratio comparison, again US$ UCITS FoHFs outperform all indexes with the exception of the Barclay FoHF Index.

## CONCLUSION

This chapter investigates, on the one hand, the relationship between performance and flows into UCITS FoHFs, and, on the other hand, provides a detailed analysis across several dimensions of UCITS FoHFs risk-adjusted performance. The chapter finds first that while over the entire sample period the correlation between flows into UCITS FoHFs and their performance has been relatively weak at −0.03, as expected performance and flows into UCITS FoHFs are closely connected during extreme market movements like that between September 2008 and March 2009. In addition, correlation has increased during prolonged market-wide increases from February 2010 until February 2011. As a consequence, following the recovery in early 2009 the flow−return correlation was quite high and the growth in average monthly AUM was vigorous until summer 2011. Indeed, it appears that since the UCITS investment vehicle is mostly a European concept, UCITS FoHFs flows have suffered from the worsening of the European sovereign debt crisis in the second half of 2011 even though their performance has improved in that period. Hence, investors in UCITS FoHFs seem to make use of the high liquidity they provide to investors by increasing their exposure to them in bull markets and decreasing their exposure in bear markets. Particularly the latter can increase liquidity problems in a time of crisis, which could even lead to contagion with offshore fund structures of the same manager if positions between the vehicles overlap.

In addition, the study finds that over the sample period UCITS FoHFs risk-adjusted performance was generally superior to that of the typical FoHF index. Thus, at least for the US$ trading funds, UCITS FoHFs have outperformed all major indexes with the exception of the BarclayHedge FoHF Index. In addition, their alpha volatility is comparable to or even lower than that of the benchmarks. Overall, UCITS FoHFs appear to be solid alternatives to the traditional FoHFs even though their geographical proximity to the European debt situation and risks appears to have recently (i.e., after the summer of 2011) stalled their growth.

## Acknowledgments

We thank the President of BarclayHedge (www.barclayhedge.com) Sol Waksman for use of the live and dead UCITS data, as well as Beto Carminhato and Alicia Miller. In addition, we thank Joe Campbell and Francine English at PerTrac for use of the PerTrac (www.pertrac.com) software and indexes. We thank the President of Alix Capital (www.alixcapital.com) Louis Zanolin for making several comments and suggestions. Alix is the largest index provider of UCITS hedge funds and UCITS Commodity Trading Advisors (CTA) strategies.

## References

Brown, S. J., Goetzmann, W. N., Liang, B., & Schwarz, C. (2012a). Trust and Delegation. *Journal of Financial Economics, 103*(3), 221–234.

Brown, S. J., Gregoriou, G. N., & Pascalau, R. (2012b). Diversification in Funds of Hedge Funds: Is It Possible to Overdiversify? *Review of Asset Pricing Studies, 2*(1), 89–110.

Darolles, S. (2011). *Quantifying Alternative UCITS.* Available at SSRN: http://ssrn.com/abstract=1945798.

Dewaele, B., Markov, I., Pirotte, H., & Tuchschmid, N. S. (2011). *Does Manager Offshore Experience Count in the Alternative UCITS Universe?* Available at SSRN: http://ssrn.com/abstract=1966520.

Fieldhouse, S. (2010). Harnessing the Potential of UCITS Hedge Funds. *The Hedge Fund Journal.* July–August, 2.

Fung, W., & Hsieh, D. A. (2004). Hedge Fund Benchmarks: A Risk-based Approach. *Financial Analysts Journal, 60*(5), 65–80.

Keime, P., & de Koning, H. (2009). *UCITS FoHFs Survey.* London: KdK Asset Management.

Meakin, T. (2010). *Outlook Bright for UCITS Fund of Hedge Funds.* Hedge Funds Review, August. New York: Incisive Media.

Pascalau, R. (2011). An Empirical Analysis of US$ Trading Newcits. *Journal of Wealth Management, 14*(3), 84–94.

PerTrac (2012). *The Coming of Age of Alternative UCITS Funds.* New York: Working Paper, PerTrac.

Shawky, H. A., & Wang, Y. (2011). *Liquidity Risk and the Size–Performance Relationship in the Hedge Fund Industry.* NY: Working Paper, SUNY (Albany).

Stefanini, F., Derossi, T., Meoli, M., & Vismara, S. (2010). *Newcits – Investing in UCITS Compliant Hedge Funds.* Hoboken, NJ: Wiley.

Teo, M. (2009a). Geography of Hedge Funds. *Review of Financial Studies, 22*(9), 3531–3561.

Teo, M. (2009b). *Does Size Matter in the Hedge Fund Industry?* Working Paper, Singapore Management University School of Business.

Tuchschmid, N. S., Wallerstein, E., & Zanolin, L. (2011). *Will Alternative UCITS Ever be Loved Enough to Replace Hedge Funds?* Available at SSRN: http://ssrn.com/abstract=1686055.

UBS (2011). *UCITS Funds of Hedge Funds: An Appraisal of the Current State of the Industry.* New York: UBS.

# CHAPTER 10

# Funds of Hedge Funds versus Do-It-Yourself Funds of UCITS

**Samuel Sender**
EDHEC-Risk Institute, Nice, France

## 10.1. INTRODUCTION

There are at least three possible reasons to invest in hedge funds: accessing outperformance, alternative risk factors (alternative betas), or risk management. As investing in hedge funds is truly complex, requiring costly supervision, due diligence, and manager selection, traditionally most investors prefer to choose funds of hedge funds (FoHFs). The supervision from FoHFs managers is costly with an added layer of management and in some cases performance fees. We revisit the concept of risk management (defined here as the aim to protect investors against large losses, in the spirit of portfolio insurance) by assessing and testing the non-linearity of FoHFs at the relevant investment horizon by means of non-parametric regressions of cumulative returns. This technique is robust regarding the short-term issue of return smoothing or manipulation and allows testing for risk management (i.e., the fact that a fund manager reacts differently to a long than to a short series of negative returns). We show that the average FoHF does not perform risk

Reconsidering Funds of Hedge Funds. http://dx.doi.org/10.1016/B978-0-12-401699-6.00010-1

management, but has a linear exposure to hedge fund indices and thus inherits the average excess skewness of underlying hedge funds. This explains and confirms the (average) negative skewness of Brown *et al.* (2012). We argue that FoHFs inherit many of the hedge fund reporting biases such as backfilling, survivorship, and self-selection biases, but also to a certain extent return smoothing or manipulation, which make the selection process of a good FoHF particularly difficult.

'Undertaking in Collective Investment in Transferable Securities' (UCITS)-compliant hedge funds are hedge fund strategies packaged as UCITS. They are thus supervised like retail funds, and forced liquidation is rare. Funds are liquid and reporting is subject to strict standards. Reporting is not voluntary as in hedge funds; however, UCITS-compliant hedge funds must report and therefore much of the hedge fund database biases are not present with UCITS.[1] Some database providers now categorize these funds as a style and calculate strategy indices just like traditional hedge funds databases do. It is thus feasible to invest in representative strategies of UCITS-compliant hedge funds by means of investable indices. It is best to select strategies that are proven to keep their diversification benefits with regard to standard asset classes by providing protection against extreme conditions or tail returns.

UCITS-compliant hedge funds bring a sophistication into a regulated framework that benefits typical FoHFs investors as it can avoid much of the complexity associated with hedge fund strategies, with associated direct costs much lower than management fees: the direct cost of structuring hedge fund strategies as UCITS (administrative, depositary, valuation, reporting, and other organizational costs) is much lower[2] than FoHFs fees. However, there are also indirect costs to such transformations, and it is now important to properly document both direct (structuring and compliance) and indirect (those resulting from a transformation of the original strategies) costs.

This chapter is organized as follows. Section 10.2 addresses the complexities in hedge fund investing. Section 10.3 introduces long-term non-parametric regressions as a means to visualize and test in a robust manner non-linearities of hedge fund returns. A regression of Barclay and UCITS-compliant FoHFs indices on their underlying hedge fund index and a linear model test show that the average excess negative skewness in FoHFs can be attributed to linear (buy-and-hold-like) exposure of FoHFs to their underlying hedge fund indices. This also

---

[1]There is no survivorship bias as funds need to report as long as they exist up to the point of liquidation. A depositary must assess the valuation process and in many instances there is an independent valuator; returns cannot be revised in the future. This, in addition to the use of liquid and predominantly listed instruments, strongly limits return manipulation. Databases can choose the funds they include, so backfilling can be avoided very easily (especially in any index).

[2]Depositary costs depend on the nature of the fund and can be in the 5–20 basis points range. Many hedge funds usually have valuation and risk management systems and expenses, and thus compliance costs would be fractional. In a UCITS some functions such as risk management and compliance must be independent, which may represent some fixed (salary) costs.

shows that FoHFs (either UCITS or unregulated) have severely underperformed their reference indices in recent years. Section 10.4 illustrates that UCITS-compliant hedge funds facilitate the creation of FoHFs and the access to alternative risk premia with the incorporation in classical long-only portfolios of strategies that are proven to diversify and to provide protection against extreme conditions. Section 10.5 addresses the regulatory challenge facing UCITS-compliant hedge funds and we hope this current chapter clarifies the debate, notably by distinguishing sophistication from complexity. There is a final section on the conclusions arrived at.

## 10.2. ISSUES WITH HEDGE FUND INVESTING — THE CASE OF FoHFs

Faced with a great complexity and a lack of transparency, most investors delegate the tasks of investing, with the necessary fund selection and due diligence processes, to FoHFs managers.[3] However, FoHFs have been shown to have drawbacks, as excess diversification can penalize risk-adjusted returns. Lhabitant and Learned (2002) demonstrate that diversification empirically decreases volatility yet leads to penalizing skewness and kurtosis, and Brown *et al.* (2012) show that only a quarter of FoHFs can afford to perform the due diligence they are supposed to do, thus adding operational issues as resulting in greater tail risk.

In addition, since FoHFs are hedge funds, they inherit the biases of this asset class. The academic literature had praised hedge funds for their superior returns and their ability to diversify away from traditional risk factors. Agarwal *et al.* (2009) demonstrate that incentives and regulation lead to superior returns in hedge funds compared to regulated alternatives.[4] Note that incentives in UCITS are compatible with those of hedge funds since performance fees are allowed in UCITS, but not in the case of American mutual funds.[5]

Following the 2008 crisis, the performance of hedge funds and FoHFs has deteriorated. Fung and Hsieh (2004) and more recently Garcia and Almeida

---

[3]Another attraction of delegation is that in practice it relieves institutional investors from their own responsibility and risk with regard to the underlying funds. Only very large pension funds with large investments in hedge funds can afford to perform due diligence.

[4]Agarwal *et al.* (2009) compare the difference in means and other descriptive statistics — volatility, Sharpe ratio, or alpha with respect to factor models, and the factors used here and for the panel regression are past returns plus the Carhart (1997) four-factor model extended from Fama and French (1993), or the Fung and Hsieh (2004) seven-factor model. Agarwal *et al.* (2009) also show that the manager's offshore experience is statistically significant.

[5]In American mutual funds, fulcrum fees (i.e., variable fees) are allowed provided they are symmetric (so that the manager's remuneration is lowered in the case of underperformance). These fees are never used, and thus there is no regulatory-driven incentive to risk-shifting in European Alternative UCITS, contrary to what is possible in side-by-side management (for contradictory analysis of this phenomenon in the United States, see Cessi *et al.*, 2006; Nohel *et al.*, 2010).

(2012) explain the sources of performance of hedge fund strategies as arising from identified 'alternative betas' such as lookback straddle options and better assess hedge fund reporting biases. In addition, the literature has been far more critical of the sources of alpha in hedge funds and FoHFs alike.[6]

Overall, reporting biases lead to an overestimation of hedge fund performance. Patton *et al.* (2012) analyze revisions to past hedge fund performance, unveiling a new layer of complexity and biases in hedge funds (downwards revisions arise more from poor fund managers).[7] Aiken *et al.* (2012, p. 2) using recent FoHFs data confirm the unproven common view that 'performance in commercial hedge fund databases suffers from a positive selection bias which exaggerates the true average skill of hedge fund managers. Additionally, […] the performance of funds even after they exit the databases – the so-called "dead" funds. After delisting, funds have worse performance than funds that continue reporting.'

## 10.3. TESTING FOR NON-LINEARITIES IN HEDGE FUND RETURNS – A NEW APPROACH

The recent literature is critical of FoHFs managers, but does not explicitly test whether they perform risk management with respect to their reference hedge fund indices. Yet, without transparency of the underlying hedge fund holdings, one cannot directly test whether FoHFs managers are performing risk management. Any non-linear payoff (e.g., with respect to the benchmark S&P 500) may just as well come directly from holding hedge funds with non-linear payoffs.

This chapter introduces long-term non-parametric regressions – a conceptual innovation that has the following benefits:

- They allow an immediate visualization of the conditional properties of a given asset class, thus a direct assessment of the benefits of such an asset class over time.
- They also allow visualizing and testing for risk management, i.e. a non-linear dependency of one asset class on its underlying components (Figure 10.1 shows that the average FoHF has an excess negative skewness relative to the S&P 500, but Figure 10.2 shows the average FoHF has a linear exposure to hedge fund indices, which means that any excess skewness is due to the underlying hedge funds).
- This technique is robust to return manipulation.

The main objective of risk management usually is to protect against large cumulative losses. Thus, the dependency on stock returns may not only be non-linear; it may also be non-Markov, depending on the full history of past returns,

---

[6]It could be argued that the replication of such exotic betas would be costly in practice and dependent on the ability to benefit from fair pricing in the over-the-counter (OTC) market; thus the value-added of a fund from an investor can differ from the alpha generally used by academics.
[7]Note that possible future revisions should in theory pose great problems for regulators, because they undermine the principle of fair treatment of investors or unit holders.

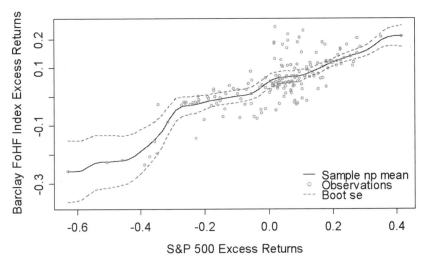

**FIGURE 10.1**

BarclayHedge FoHFs Index versus S&P 500 total return. Excess returns, December 1996–March 2012. The figure exhibits a long-term (9-month) non-parametric regression, using the Barclay FoHFs Index excess returns over T-bills as a regressand and the S&P 500 total return excess returns over T-Bills as a regressor, and displays stationary bootstrapped standard errors. All returns are logarithmic returns. The sensitivity of FoHFs to the S&P increases during large (cumulative) market falls, hence the term 'di-worsify' (Lhabitant and Learned, 2002). After very significant market falls have been experienced, the sensitivity to market indices appears to be greatly diminished — this is a sign of effective risk management. However, since there is a limited number of observations around this range, stationary-bootstrapped standard errors illustrate that what happens at this end of the range is subject to significant uncertainty from a statistical standpoint.

not simply on the current return. In a universe where FoHFs invest in hedge funds, their overall exposure to underlying hedge funds would depend on the past history of returns. A linear regression of monthly FoHFs returns on underlying hedge fund index returns would be of poor quality and fundamentally means nothing, just as a regression is not the adequate way to estimate the exposure of a Constant Proportion Portfolio Insurance (CPPI) fund to the market.

In addition, the traditional monthly regressions are undermined by the ability to manipulate reported returns. Patton *et al.* (2012) show that return manipulation takes place (hedge fund reporting is not just about smoothing). As one cannot assume a process for the short-term smoothing process, the quarterly unsmoothing technique[8] used in much of the literature may be insufficient to uncover the actual true dependency: if the hedge fund manager manipulates returns to exhibit low correlation with its reference index (S&P 500 or a generic hedge fund index such as the BarclayHedge FoHF Index used

---

[8]Brown *et al.* (2012), follow the path of Evans and Archer (1968) to unsmooth quarterly returns using an autoregressive process.

**(a)**

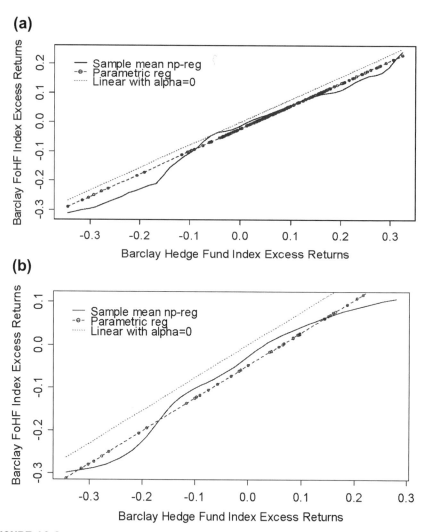

**FIGURE 10.2**

(a) Linear versus non-parametric model, excess returns, Barclay FoHFs Index versus Barclay Hedge Fund Index, December 1996—March 2012. The figure exhibits long-term regressions, using the Barclay FoHFs Index excess returns over T-bills as a regressand and the Barclay Hedge Fund Index excess returns over T-Bills as a regressor. Non-parametric and linear (parametric) regressions are shown. The dotted line represents the parametric regression without trend (alpha). Returns are log-returns, annualized. The Barclay FoHFs Index has a linear relationship with the Barclay Hedge Fund Index (the linear specification cannot be rejected). When using long-term performance measure with hedge fund performance as the sole driver, the underperformance of FoHFs is explained by its lower risk exposure (it has a beta of 0.77 and a negative alpha of 2% annualized). (b) Linear versus parametric model, excess returns, Barclay FoHFs Index versus Barclay Hedge Fund Index, December 2007—March 2012. Panel (b) is the same as (a), but with data starting in December 2007 (Figure 10.4 below analyzes UCITS FoHFs over the same time frame). Since 2007, FoHFs have had a negative yearly alpha or drift of 4.8% annualized, comparable in magnitude to that of UCITS FoHFs (Figure 10.4) — even if the bias in hedge fund indices may explain part of the underperformance in FoHFs.

in this paper), traditional regressions may provide a biased or at least a partial measure of tail risk. Return manipulation could contribute[9] to explaining the so-called tail risk of hedge funds where the actual correlation with the risk factors, often greater that than reported, is revealed during large market drops or increases.[10]

The strategy we propose is a non-parametric analysis of the dependency of cumulative hedge fund returns on those of the S&P 500,[11] which counters these possible biases by filtering out market noise of both the regressor and the regressand. In addition, the strategy allows for directly testing risk management in FoHFs by capturing non-linearities or conditional fund exposure due to risk management over the life of the hedge fund. To remain consistent, we rely on non-parametric estimates of the standard error, based on (stationary) bootstrap (Box 10.1).

Figure 10.1 shows that FoHFs on average, based on the BarclayHedge FoHFs Index, have non-linearities with respect to the S&P 500 index, which in a parametric setup would be interpreted as negative excess skewness — a skewness that is greater than that of the S&P 500. More precisely, in normal circumstances, beyond the smoothing period and at the holding horizon considered (9 months) the aggregate FoHFs has a stable and positive relationship with the S&P 500, but during large drops in the S&P 500, tail risk materializes, which is the opposite of risk management (the purpose of portfolio insurance is to protect against large losses, not to reinforce them), and the 2008 crisis had a major effect on hedge funds and FoHFs. These non-linearities are statistically significant with our model test rejecting the linear specification for a regression model.

As both hedge funds and FoHFs have similar non-linear exposures with respect to the S&P 500, and as FoHFs aim broadly at provide investors with an exposure to hedge funds, it is interesting to assess whether the relationship between the BarclayHedge FoHFs Index and the main Barclay Hedge Fund Index is linear. Figure 10.2a and b illustrates that this relationship is indeed quasi-linear. And Figure 10.4 shows that UCITS FoHFs similarly have a quasi-linear exposure with respect to the UCITS hedge fund index (Global Index from the Geneva-based firm, Alternative-UCITS). In all cases, FoHFs, UCITS-compliant or not, have a significant negative drift (the dotted curve, which represents the linear model with a zero-drift assumption, is over recent years much more above the dashed curves for underlying fund indices).

---

[9]We can also guess a more fundamental driver of such tail risk that is present in a diversified portfolio. Diversification fails during crisis periods and hedge funds tend to correlate to 1.
[10]Hedge fund managers do report returns with a lag that makes filtering possible. Filtering out noise involves reporting 0% returns 2 months in a row when the market gains then loses 5% leading to low volatility and correlation to market returns. However, a 20% market fall will reveal the true market exposure. Cumulative returns would do the same in all circumstances.
[11]The use of non-parametric regressions makes it hard to use more than one explanatory factor on such a dataset (low frequency and limited number of points).

## BOX 10.1. BOOTSTRAP FOR NON-PARAMETRIC REGRESSIONS

Politis and Romano (1994) introduced the stationary bootstrap, which conceptually is a circular block-bootstrap with random block size, as a means of calculating standard errors of estimators and constructing confidence regions for parameters based on weakly dependent stationary observation, and show that this procedure has adequate consistency and convergence properties.

Politis (2003) shows the variations that can be applied on time-series analysis. Depending on the nature of the problem, the idea of residual-based bootstrapping typically is used for non-linear autoregressive or linear autoregressive heteroscedastic processes.

Few papers are focused on the use of bootstrap (as non-parametric statistics) for non-parametric regressions.

McMurry and Politis (2008) show that residual-based bootstrap involves the following steps: computation of a pilot non-parametric regression $Y = r(X) + \varepsilon$, bootstrap of residuals to generate new series $Y^* = r(X) + \varepsilon^*$, and estimate again the functional $r$. Technically, residuals at the extreme values of the $X$ sample are discarded. This technique applies straightforwardly to period return regressions, but not to cumulative regressions.[12]

With non-parametric regressions, which involve *a priori* unknown dependence structure, the most consistent way forward is to have a non-parametric estimate of the standard error (i.e., a bootstrap estimate). As we do not estimate a model for monthly returns, but rather for cumulative returns, we cannot naturally rely on residual-based bootstrap (Politis, 2003; McMurry and Politis, 2008). Correcting residuals from cumulative returns would require a much larger sample size than we have; therefore, we stationary-bootstrap monthly log-returns and assess the variation from the set of non-parametric regression obtained. We do not use the bootstrapped sample to estimate the mean slope/regression form, since this would involve relying on an artificial sample.

---

[12]As for parametric regression, standard errors of a regression on cumulative returns are underestimated because of the overlap and autocorrelation induced by such a cumulation.

Over the recent period, FoHFs managers have underperformed their respective benchmarks by more than 4% yearly (Barclay FoHFs Index and Alternative-UCITS Global Index for UCITS FoHFs). In addition, FoHFs managers do not perform risk management (if anything, the non-linear relationship with FoHFs indicates otherwise).

Many investors do not possess the expertise to identify the appropriate FoHF. As individual FoHFs show a wide dispersion of the risk exposures and performance, the selection of a FoHFs is a difficult task (see Figure 10.3 for an illustration). Unless thinking that building 'funds of FoHFs' with yet another layer of fees is an appropriate way to get over this complexity, investors might

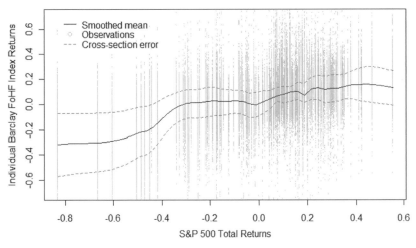

**FIGURE 10.3**

Individual Barclay FoHFs Index cumulated returns versus S&P 500 total returns, January 1994–March 2012. This graph plots 9-month annualized cumulative returns for each individual fund as a function of the S&P 500 total returns. We include both the live and graveyard Barclay FoHFs databases. The smoothed means ±1 standard deviation of the cross-section of cumulated returns are reported. During periods of low market returns, individual hedge funds have cross-sectional volatility of almost 25%, which results in widely different outcomes depending on the type of FoHFs selected.

be interested in more transparent ways of investing in alternative investment strategies. Section 10.4 illustrates how UCITS-compliant hedge funds can help in this regard.

## 10.4. UCITS-COMPLIANT HEDGE FUNDS AS A FIT FOR FoHFs Construction

UCITS-compliant hedge funds have attracted a lot of attention in Europe in the wake of the recent crisis (Box 10.2). The UCITS class is one of the only asset classes that have witnessed constant net inflows throughout the recent crisis and beyond. With assets under management in the EUR125 billion range in early 2012, UCITS-compliant hedge funds have experienced a growth of more than 300% in the last 3 years.

Contrary to the opaqueness of hedge funds and their high costs as well as the temptation to stop reporting returns if the fund experiences poor performance, regulated UCITS-based compliant hedge funds offer unbiased reporting and investable reference indices, making their constituents very enticing to potential investors.

UCITS-compliant hedge funds offer an advantage of high-quality reporting, making the creation of representative unbiased investable indices feasible. In

## Box 10.2. UCITS

UCITS is a regulatory framework with detailed reporting and valuation obligations. UCITS greatly facilitates the distribution of funds to any investor in Europe and beyond: UCITS products are widely recognized in Latin America, Asia, and the Middle-East, where they are sometimes also recognized as retail products.

- A strategy packaged as UCITS will be able to sell to any investor (retail or professional) in Europe and to many investors beyond the borders of Europe.
- UCITS is an internationally recognized label and European statistics show that UCITS products are sold worldwide with 40% being sold outside of Europe.
- The UCITS framework has likewise enriched the list of eligible assets (CESR 2007 advice on eligible assets) and expanded the possibilities for leverage (recommendation EC/2004/383); so-called sophisticated UCITS, sometimes more vaguely called UCITS III funds, allow a large number of alternative strategies to be packaged as UCITS.
- Swaps to access commodities are a debated issue, but allowed at least in some jurisdictions.
- UCITS must invest in liquid financial securities, must be able to value their units at least twice a month, and investments must allow at least 20% of the assets to be redeemed.
- UCITS face a number of quantitative restrictions that limit concentration risk (5% per issuer, 25% for a credit institution), counterparty risk (10%), investments in other funds (20% for a single fund, 30% in other funds overall), and naked short sales are forbidden.
- In UCITS V, it is likely that depositaries will face close to unconditional restitution obligation.
- Many restrictions (concentration, investments in target funds, restitution) can be circumvented by means of derivatives. Derivatives also make the limited transparency requirements of UCITS (an annual report with a balance sheet and a description of transaction) useless.
- ESMA (2012) focuses on transparency in UCITS, notably on the use of indices. HF UCITS that replicated hedge fund performance by so-called strategy indices, which are proprietary and opaque, are likely to be particularly affected by these developments.

addition, UCITS allows incentives similar to those in unregulated hedge funds.[13] Conversely, the requirement to invest in illiquid assets is a restriction faced by UCITS-compliant hedge funds.[14]

---

[13]Opacity is sometimes valued as a way to protect proprietary strategies and we could go as far as to say that UCITS also offers opacity to those searching for it. The balance sheet of a UCITS-compliant hedge fund or FoHF only needs to be made available on a quarterly or yearly basis. For active strategies this may have few implications in terms of information protection. Furthermore, a fund that uses OTC derivatives to access market exposure is almost opaque to its investors, because the content of such derivatives remains unknown to the reader of a balance sheet.

[14]A vague definition of the concept of liquidity in UCITS regulation made it possible for UCITS, from hedge funds to money market funds, to invest in illiquid strategies, just as had been the case for American mutual funds (see Amenc and Sender, 2010). The use of strategy swaps, when they were opaque, also made it possible to escape UCITS restrictions.

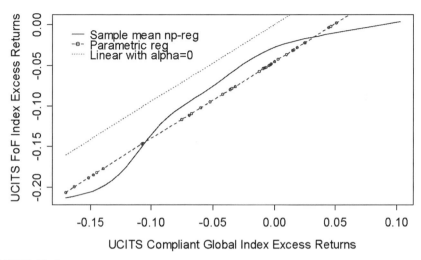

**FIGURE 10.4**

Linear versus non-parametric model, Alternative-UCITS FoHFs Index versus Alternative-UCITS Global Index, December 2007–March 2012. This figure reads as Figure 10.2b, but the regressand is the UCITS FoHFs Index excess returns over the JPM EUR 3-month cash returns and the regressor the UCITS-compliant Global Index excess return. The linear model, based on 9-month cumulative log-returns, illustrated on annualized data, shows a 9-month beta of UCITS FoHFs of 86% on the UCITS-compliant Global Index, but a negative drift of 4.5%. This index is present on a much more reduced time frame than its Barclay Hedge Fund counterpart, and thus the figure must indeed be compared to Figure 10.2b.

FoHFs managers can implement risk management or dynamic strategies more easily when choosing UCITS rather than hedge funds as underlying funds, because UCITS are more liquid — they usually provide daily liquidity or on a biweekly basis at worst.[15] Of course, some UCITS strategies are themselves based on risk management (commodity trading advisors, etc.). A Geneva-based firm, Alternative-UCITS, provides strategy indices that simply group available UCITS-compliant hedge funds into their main strategy type.

UCITS products also benefit from regulatory dictated supervision (with reporting to the regulator, compliance checks made internally as well as by a depositary, etc.), which implies that one can invest in them with minimal due diligence costs. They were designed to provide retail investors with worry-free investing.

Figure 10.4 shows that the average FoHFs manager in the UCITS space does not do a better job than the average FoHFs manager per se. They both seem at best to exhibit a buy-and-hold scheme, with a severe negative drift in recent years.

However, if one seeks to diversify away from traditional equity investments by means of hedge fund investments, one may seek exposure to the diversifiers with

---

[15]Managed account platforms usually maximize liquidity, but remain less transparent than UCITS and more prone to reporting biases. Investable hedge fund indices usually select hedge funds based on managed platforms.

low or non-linear exposure to market indices. Our methodology makes it easy to assess the characteristics of each type of strategy, but this is beyond the scope of this chapter.

## 10.5. REGULATORY RISKS AROUND UCITS HEDGE FUNDS

The expansion of the UCITS boundaries was initially allowed to provide better opportunities such as diversification, risk management, and sophistication to retail investors. These concepts are at the core of the expansion of eligible assets and of the notion of sophisticated UCITS (often called UCITS III) that made possible so-called UCITS-compliant hedge funds. Moreover, because alternative strategies have traditionally been accessed via funds of funds, UCITS-compliant FoHFs have also been created (although these represent a small share of the total assets under management of UCITS-compliant hedge funds).

The supply and demand for UCITS-compliant hedge funds (Sender, 2012) is exacerbated by an inconsistent patchwork of regulations that artificially drive the demand towards UCITS by giving insufficient incentives for the supply of Alternative Investment Fund Managers Directive (AIFMD) funds.[16] Regulators have become wary of the rise of UCITS-compliant hedge funds if they feel AIFMD is the natural regulation for alternative strategies and that the rise of UCITS is a form of regulatory arbitrage.

Regulators now focus on the definition and identification of complex products with the idea of restricting their distribution. The 2008 crisis has underlined the dangers of hidden risks and fees as well as asymmetries of information and conflicts of interest in product distribution. These features justify the introduction of regulations such as the Markets in Financial Instruments Directive (MIFID) regulation. However, the over-ambitious goal that products should be well-understood by (retail)[17] investors has become inconsistent with most of the current approach to regulations, which are usually based on the assumption that retail investors have a very poor understanding of financial markets.[18] 'Understanding' is not a well-defined concept in practice, and could lead to risky outcomes for the fund investors and the European fund industry as a whole (e.g.,

---

[16]Sender (2012) points out that AIFMD does not provide good distribution opportunities, because the purchase of AIFMD funds will still be constrained by national regulations and institutional investors such as insurance companies.

[17]By definition, retail investors know little about financial markets — even about the simple asset classes such as bonds.

[18]The imprecise synthetic risk indicator in the Key Investor Information Document (KIID) was agreed precisely because regulators assumed that investors could not agree on anything more accurate and rooted in financial theory. The reluctance to give accurate indications of non-financial risks in the KIID can be explained by the same attitude. The EC and UK regulators believe that financial advice is generally of poor quality.

by a *de facto* product fragmentation where UCITS-compliant hedge funds are pushed outside the boundaries of UCITS).

It is the duty of regulators to favor better diversification opportunities in the fund management industry. Its *raison d'être* is precisely to provide the diversification and professional management that retail investors cannot afford at a reasonable cost, and both the available techniques such as risk management and investment opportunities have evolved in scope since the first UCITS directive in 1986.[19] Yet, by definition, sophisticated products that provide greater diversification and better risk management for retail and regulated investors,[20] as was the original intention behind the expansion of the UCITS boundaries, are more difficult to 'understand.'

We hope that the comparison of the complexities of accessing hedge-fund strategies, by expertise for investors, by means of FoHFs or UCITS-compliant hedge funds, will give insight on the current debate.

## CONCLUSION

There are several reasons to invest in hedge funds and FoHFs. The first would be to access the most talented managers, who would be attracted by compensation packages typical of hedge funds, with option-like remuneration (Agarwal *et al.*, 2009). Another possible motivation is to externalize risk management, thus achieving non-linear payoffs compared to traditional management (or the S&P 500). Non-parametric regressions illustrate that the average FoHFs does not perform risk management, but rather exhibits buy-and-hold-like features with respect to underlying hedge fund indices, thus exhibiting excess skewness relative to the S&P 500. In addition, the complexity in hedge fund investing leads most investors to rely on FoHFs. However, FoHFs inherit many of the complexities in hedge fund investing and choosing an adequate manager remains a highly complex task. If the same holds true for UCITS-compliant FoHFs, UCITS-compliant hedge funds allow hedge fund expertise to be delivered in a transparent and regulated framework that makes investing decisions simple.

---

[19]Of course, the expansion of the UCITS boundaries must be controlled and one should distinguish between instruments made to diversify from those aims to get around UCITS restrictions. Swaps and derivatives are needed to access commodities markets without the fuss of delivery, yet ESMA (2012) is correct to limit the use of swaps to access strategy-based indices when they are in effect strategies structured and operated by the index provider and not by the UCITS, usually derived from proprietary applications that cannot be controlled.

[20]The notion of sophisticated investor is now taken with a grain of salt and by default they will be assumed less knowledgeable than before.

## Acknowledgments

I thank Stéphane Grégoir for his very useful comments; I thank Louis Zanolin and Dravasp Jhabvala from Alix Capital for making available their quality alternative UCITS indices.

## References

Agarwal, V., Daniel, N., & Naik, N. (2009). Role of Managerial Incentives and Discretion in Hedge Fund Performance. *The Journal of Finance, 64*(5), 2221−2256.

Aiken, A., Clifford, C., & Ellis, J. (2012). *Out of the Dark: Hedge Fund Reporting Biases and Commercial Databases.* Available at SSRN. http://ssrn.com/abstract=1519914.

Amenc, N., & Sender, S. (2010). *Are hedge-fund UCITS the cure-all?* EDHEC-Risk Publication.

Brown, S., Gregoriou, G., & Pascalau, R. (2012). Is It Possible to Overdiversify? The Case of Funds of Hedge Funds. *Review of Asset Pricing Studies, 2*(1), 89−110.

Carhart, M. (1997). On Persistence in Mutual Fund Performance. *The Journal of Finance, 52*(1), 57−82.

Cessi, C., Gibson, S., & Moussawi, R. (2006). *For Better or Worse? Mutual Funds in Side-by-Side Management Relationships with Hedge Funds.* Working Paper. http://papers.ssrn.com/sol3/papers.cfm?abstract_id=905600.

ESMA. (2012). Guidelines on ETFs and other UCITS issues. July.

Evans, J., & Archer, S. (1968). Diversification and the Reduction of Dispersion: An Empirical Analysis. *Journal of Finance, 3*(1), 761−767.

Fama, E., & French, K. (1993). Common Risk Factors in the Returns on Stocks and Bonds. *Journal of Financial Economics, 33*(1), 3−56.

Fung, W., & Hsieh, D. (2004). Hedge Fund Benchmarks: A Risk-based Approach. *Financial Analysts Journal, 60*(5), 65−80.

Garcia, G., & Almeida, C. (2012). Robust Assessment of Hedge Fund Performance through Nonparametric Risk Adjustment. *EDHEC Business School and EDHEC Risk Institute Working Paper.*

Lhabitant, F., & Learned, M. (2002). *Hedge Fund Diversification: How Much is Enough? FAME Research Working Paper 52.* Available at SSRN. http://ssrn.com/abstract=322400.

McMurry, T., & Politis, D. (2008). Bootstrap Confidence Intervals in Nonparametric Regression With Built-in Bias Correction. *Statistics & Probability Letters, 78*(15), 2463−2469.

Nohel, T., Wang, Z., & Zheng, L. (2010). Side-by-side Management of Hedge Funds and Mutual Funds. *Review of Financial Studies, 23*(6), 2342−2373.

Patton, A., Ramadorai, T., & Streatfield, M. (2012). *Change You Can Believe In? Hedge Fund Data Revisions.* Available at SSRN. http://ssrn.com/abstract=1934543.

Politis, D. (2003). The Impact of Bootstrap Methods on Time Series Analysis. *Statistical Science, 18*(2), 219−230.

Politis, D., & Romano, J. (1994). The Stationary Bootstrap. *Journal of the American Statistical Association, 89*(428), 1303−1313.

Politis, D., & Romano, J. (2003). The Stationary Bootstrap. *Journal of the American Statistical Association, 89*, 1303−1313.

Sender, S. (2012). The Impact of European Product Regulations on Global Product Structuring. *Journal of Alternative Investments, 15*(2), 98−117.

# SECTION 3
# Performance

# CHAPTER 11

# Predicting Funds of Hedge Funds Attrition Through Performance Diagnostics

**Philippe Cogneau**[*], **Philippe Debatty**[†], **and Georges Hübner**[**]
*HEC Management School, University of Liège, Liège, Belgium
†Fuchs & Associés Finance S.A, Luxembourg
**Deloitte Chair of Portfolio Management and Performance, HEC Management School, University of Liège, Liège, Belgium

## 11.1. INTRODUCTION

In a recent paper, Cogneau and Hübner (2012) analyze the predictability of disappearances of mutual funds through the use of their past performance metrics. They build a model that predicts reasonably well the attrition of mutual funds. Many other researchers have in the past performed similar research, but the originality of their work is the systematic use of a large panel of measures proposed in the economic literature. Indeed, since the seminal papers on portfolio management, in the 1950s and 1960s, more than 100 different

Reconsidering Funds of Hedge Funds. http://dx.doi.org/10.1016/B978-0-12-401699-6.00011-3

measures[1] have been introduced in the literature. Cogneau and Hübner show that building a model restricted to classical measures underperforms a more comprehensive set of performance measures in predicting a fund's disappearance (e.g., Somers' $D$, an indicator of predictive ability of the model, falling from 0.404 to 0.321).

In the context of hedge funds, this type of research is very recent. Many studies of this kind focus on the use of classical measures, such as Chapman *et al.* (2008), Ng (2008), Chan *et al.* (2006), Baquero *et al.* (2005), and Malkiel and Saha (2005). Most often, researchers prefer to integrate specific characteristics of the hedge funds, such as watermark, lockup period, or incentive fees (e.g., see Lee, 2011). In a recent analysis, Liang and Park (2010) consider different risk measures to adjust performance. They show that semi-deviation, value at risk (VaR), conditional VaR (CVaR), expected shortfall, and tail risk are better predictors than standard deviation — especially the latter two.

In this chapter, we follow the vein of Cogneau and Hübner (2012) and integrate a wide panel of performance measures. The context is very specific and potentially very insightful; however, given the very high attrition of funds of hedge funds (FoHFs) consecutive to the financial crisis of 2008, it is of critical importance to be able to determine whether their disappearance from databases — presumably resulting from a freeze and/or liquidation — could have been reasonably foreseen. If one were to find a way to exploit past information about their behavior to indicate their likelihood of attrition, this could provide a useful toolkit in the context of a potential next crisis. We show that, with proper use, information contained in reported risk-adjusted performance provides a useful basis for the detection of funds that will cease publishing their prices — this event being an indication of a fund's distress. We consider the logit model in this study.

Our results show that FoHFs are particularly prone to this type of analysis regarding their attrition behavior during or after the 2008 financial crisis. A proper treatment of performance metrics in a retrospective analysis of 3 years induces a prediction of an individual fund's attrition from the database that reveals to be particularly accurate: by considering the third of the funds with the worst score on the logistic function, we can detect *ex ante* 90% of the subsequent failing funds. The consequences of such findings for portfolio construction are likely to be of great interest for portfolio construction and rebalancing decisions, and can even have a strong impact on liquidity risk and total returns when one considers the penalties associated with a failing fund.

Section 11.2 discusses the data and sample construction. In Section 11.3, we explain how the performance measures are computed and treated to reach the desired array of usable metrics. Section 11.4 discusses the results, followed by our conclusions.

---

[1]An extensive review can be found in Cogneau and Hübner (2009a, 2009b).

## 11.2. DATA AND VARIABLE CONSTRUCTION

### 11.2.1. Fund Database

We use a database of 2926 FoHFs from the BarclayHedge hedge fund database with monthly returns, starting in January 1995 and ending in November 2011. However, most of the funds had no returns after April 2010, so we do not consider values posterior from that date. The database contains no information on the closing of the funds; furthermore, the interruption of data publication does not imply that a fund has closed. However, this information is very relevant for the investor. Therefore, we decided to consider the last month of publication of the prices as our target variable.

To avoid the complexities of managing the currencies, we restrain the set to the funds issued in US$. Finally, in the presence of 'cousin' funds,[2] presenting similar series of returns, we keep only one member of the family.

### 11.2.2. Market Data

For the risk-free rate, we take the 13-week US Treasury bill (T-bill) rate. We consider the S&P 500 as a proxy for the equity market. We get the inflation rate from the US Federal Reserve website. Data on the 13 hedge fund indexes are retrieved from the EDHEC-Risk website, as a basis for benchmarking all funds in the database.

For the computation of performance measures based on multifactor models, we downloaded from K. French's website the premia for the Fama–French and Carhart risk factors. Finally, we used the following market data in the computation of the conditional alphas: spread between 10 years BAA and AAA corporate bonds (given by Moody's), spread between 10-year government bond and 13-weeks US T-bill rates, the inflation in the United States, and the VIX (volatility) index.

### 11.2.3. Descriptive analysis of the funds

As the series of EDHEC benchmarks begins in January 1997, the sample of returns of the hedge funds is censored for the period before 1997 and we remain with 160 months of data, from January 1997 to April 2010. We drop off all funds either with less than 36 consecutive values of the returns, or having at least five pairs of consecutive identical returns, or with at least three triples of consecutive identical returns. The final sample contains 1350 funds. The majority of those funds report between 3 and 8 full years of returns, as shown in Table 11.1.

About half of the funds have published prices till the end of the considered period. For the 586 funds that ceased publishing, the interruption always happened during or after the financial crisis: 180 in 2008, 314 in 2009, and 92 in 2010. We report descriptive statistics in Table 11.2.

---

[2]It happens often that an issuer company presents different variations, addressed to different classes of investors, but which are in reality the same fund.

**Table 11.1** Number of Funds per Complete Year of Returns

| | No. of years | | | | | | | | | | | Total |
|---|---|---|---|---|---|---|---|---|---|---|---|---|
| | 3 | 4 | 5 | 6 | 7 | 8 | 9 | 10 | 11 | 12 | 13 | |
| Count | 153 | 187 | 165 | 178 | 127 | 132 | 67 | 64 | 74 | 72 | 131 | 1350 |
| Percentage | 11.3 | 13.9 | 12.2 | 13.2 | 9.4 | 9.8 | 5.0 | 4.7 | 5.5 | 5.3 | 9.7 | 100.0 |

**Table 11.2** Summary Statistics of the Fund Returns

| | N | Mean (%) | Standard Deviation (%) | Skewness | Kurtosis | Minimum (%) | Maximum (%) |
|---|---|---|---|---|---|---|---|
| Min | 36 | −2.93 | 0.17 | −9.81 | −0.96 | −53.23 | 1.00 |
| Max | 160 | 3.56 | 13.01 | 6.15 | 109.23 | 0.24 | 56.76 |
| Mean | 90 | 0.37 | 2.43 | −1.21 | 5.51 | −9.02 | 6.07 |
| S.D. | 38 | 0.42 | 1.29 | 1.29 | 7.62 | 5.64 | 4.72 |

The average monthly return is 0.4% and is slightly positive, but with high variations from −53.2% to +56.8%. On average, the distributions of returns are left skewed and present a positive excess kurtosis: this characteristic of leptokurtic distribution is common in finance and especially for hedge funds. Furthermore, a Jarque–Bera test rejects the normality at a threshold of 95% for 1172 funds of the sample (i.e., 86.8% of the total). This encourages us to consider modern performance measures, instead of more classical measures that were introduced in the context of normal distribution of the returns.

## 11.3. THE TREATMENT OF PERFORMANCE MEASURES

### 11.3.1. Performance Computation

As in Cogneau and Hübner (2012), we compute 147 series of different performance measures[3] for each fund. These are computed on 125 sliding periods of 36 months, starting in January 1997 and ending in April 2010. In total, we get all performances for 75 165 pairs (fund, period).

Some measures, like the Information Ratio (IR), require the availability of a benchmark: we determine it through a Sharpe-style analysis (Sharpe, 1992), refined thanks to the algorithmic procedure of Lobosco and DiBartolomeo (1997), with the hedge fund indexes. We consider the 13 indexes published on

---

[3]The complete list of computed performances is given in Table 11.A1 in the Appendix.

| Table 11.3 | Repartition of the Benchmark Indexes According to Style Analysis |
| --- | --- |
| Convertible Arbitrage | 3.63% |
| CTA Global | 4.63% |
| Distressed Securities | 2.77% |
| Emerging Markets | 11.12% |
| Equity Market Neutral | 6.43% |
| Event Driven | 2.28% |
| Fixed Income Arbitrage | 3.17% |
| Global Macro | 3.61% |
| Long/Short Equity | 6.95% |
| Merger Arbitrage | 5.65% |
| Relative Value | 0.81% |
| Short Selling | 1.95% |
| Funds of Hedge Funds | 39.08% |
| Risk Free | 7.87% |

the website of EDHEC and the 13-week T-bill rate. Table 11.3 gives the proportion obtained for each index in the whole panel of retained funds.

We see that the index 'Funds of Hedge Funds' represents more than a third of all the returns. The index 'Emerging Markets' represents more than 11%. The importance of other indexes is lower; in particular the index 'Relative Value' is the benchmark for less than 1% of the total.

## 11.3.2. Elimination of Redundant Measures

It is expected that some redundancy is present between the 147 measures. While Eling and Schuhmacher (2007) and Eling (2008) estimate that the redundancy is strong between performance measures, other studies (Plantinga and de Groot, 2001; Zakamouline, 2011; Haas Ornelas *et al.*, 2012) show that the measures can encompass significantly different dimensions.

To eliminate the potential redundancy in the measures, we normalize their values by a linear transformation to center them on 0 and to give them a standard deviation equal to 1. Then, we build the matrix with Kendall correlations between the 75 165 computed values and systematically we eliminate all measures that present a correlation higher than 85% with another measure on the residual set. We remain with a set of 58 measures,[4] listed in Table 11.A2 in the Appendix.

These results present great similarities with the analysis in Cogneau and Hübner (2012) on mutual funds and with a weekly frequency of returns, as the main

---

[4]The correlation matrix of the remaining 58 measures is too wide to be published here, but we can supply it upon any request. It displays some very low and even negative correlations. This confirms the results of Plantinga and de Groot (2001), Zakamouline (2011), and Haas Ornelas *et al.* (2012).

aspects of performance (market timing, preference based, return-based ratios, gain-based ratios, return-based differences, and gain-based differences) are clearly represented. As a proof of coherency between these two studies, we notice that 43 from those 58 measures were already selected in the analysis of mutual funds. Conversely, the very classical measures, i.e. Sharpe ratio and Treynor ratio, are excluded. The analysis of mutual funds reached a similar conclusion.

## 11.4. LINKING FUND PERFORMANCE TO SUBSEQUENT ATTRITION

We first discuss the results of the logistic regression analysis, then present the implications for portfolio construction and persistence in performance.

### 11.4.1. Logistic Regression Analysis

We apply our approach on the global sample of 1350 funds. We proceed to a logistic regression, where the independent variables are the 58 performance measures computed on 36 months, selected through the correlation threshold mentioned above, and the dependent variable is the interruption of publication of prices in the next 3 months. This information is clearly distinctive from the question of the likelihood of a fund's disappearance within a given time interval, but it presents specific interest. Indeed, as summarized by Grecu *et al.* (2006), the literature presents two explanations for which funds do not report their performance any more: funds that cease to report when they perform poorly relative to other funds and they will finally fail, or funds that have no incentive to continue reporting their performance, because they do not need to attract additional capital. In both cases, the information is relevant to the investor and consequently our analysis is of practical interest.

To check the significance of the results, we consider Somers' $D$ as a synthetic indicator of the ability of the performance measures to predict the disappearance time of the fund (Somers, 1962). We build the model of the logistic regression with the following algorithm. We start by computing Somers' $D$ for each measure considered individually in a logistic regression and we rank them. We build a first model with only one measure – the measure with the highest individual Somers' $D$ – and we compute the Schwarz Criterion of this model. Then, we loop on the 57 remaining measures, by decreasing[5] individual Somers' $D$. At each step, a new measure is added in the model and a new logistic regression is executed:

- If the Schwarz criterion increases, the variable is rejected;
- If the Schwarz criterion decreases but the weight of the measure is not significant enough,[6] we check the evolution of the Somers' $D$: if it does not increase, the variable is also rejected.

---

[5]For the first four iterations, we add a condition on the selected measure: its correlation with the measures already in the model must be lower than a predefined threshold – this is to ensure a sufficient diversity of the measures in the model.
[6]We set to 20% the significance threshold.

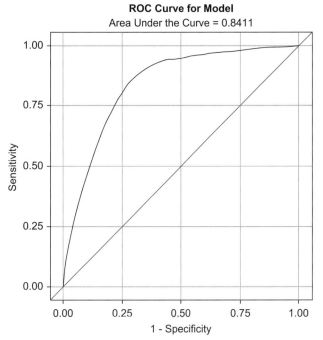

**FIGURE 11.1**
ROC curve for the optimal model.

To ensure the robustness of our model, we first cut the sample in two parts of similar sizes: one for the building of the model, the second as a validation group. To avoid contagion in the data when applying the model on the validation group, we ensure that all instances of a fund are present in only one subsample. We obtain the following values for the Somers' $D$ of the two samples: 0.682 for the modeling sample and 0.606 for the validation sample. Those values are much higher than those obtained by Cogneau and Hübner (2012) on a sample of mutual funds: they get values of 0.400 for the modeling sample and 0.346 for the validation sample.[7] A value of 0.682 implies that the area below the receiver operating characteristic (ROC) curve is almost equal to 85% of the total area. The ROC curve is given in Figure 11.1. We see that after selection of the worst 25% of funds ordered by the model, we have already found more than 80% of the funds that will cease publishing their prices; when we take the first half of the funds with the worst scores, we find around 95% of the target.

In Table 11.4 we present the values of the estimates for each covariate in the model, i.e. each selected measure, by order of entry in the model. We mention the standard error of each measure and its accompanying Wald $\chi^2$ to check whether it is significantly different from 0.

---

[7]When considering only funds issued in US$, the values were slightly higher (i.e., 0.497 for the modeling sample and 0.348 for the validation sample).

| Table 11.4 | Coefficients of the Discriminant Function | | | |
|---|---|---|---|---|
| **Parameter** | **Estimate** | **Standard Error** | **Wald $\chi^2$** | **Pr $> \chi^2$** |
| Intercept | −2.8463 | 0.0277 | 10,592.54 | — |
| Sharpe_SK | −1.4852 | 0.0795 | 348.72 | 0.0000 |
| eSDAR | −0.1703 | 0.0574 | 8.81 | 0.0030 |
| Adj_Skew_Sharpe_3 | 0.1447 | 0.0791 | 3.35 | 0.0672 |
| Fouse_ifl_1 | 0.1864 | 0.0289 | 41.45 | 0.0000 |
| Alpha_mkt_tim_TM | −0.1229 | 0.0259 | 22.43 | 0.0000 |
| Carhart_alpha | −0.4986 | 0.0355 | 197.35 | 0.0000 |
| Jensen_alpha | −0.1266 | 0.0206 | 37.93 | 0.0000 |
| Information_Ratio | −0.1826 | 0.0422 | 18.76 | 0.0000 |
| Hnr_Mrt_3_f_gam_rm | 0.6721 | 0.0269 | 622.68 | 0.0000 |
| Hnr_Mrt_3_f_gam_smb | −0.5922 | 0.0276 | 460.24 | 0.0000 |
| Isr_Infor_Ratio | 0.4596 | 0.0414 | 123.21 | 0.0000 |
| Hnr_Mrt_3_f_alpha | 0.6289 | 0.0357 | 310.40 | 0.0000 |
| SRAP | 0.3371 | 0.0366 | 84.70 | 0.0000 |
| Far_Tib_risk-free_2x2 | 0.2299 | 0.0262 | 77.09 | 0.0000 |
| Trn_Maz_gamma | −0.3768 | 0.0278 | 184.34 | 0.0000 |

The first and the most weighted measure in the model is the Sharpe ratio corrected by adding the ratio skewness/kurtosis. This measure features the advantage of being consistent with an equilibrium framework, which makes it a popular method for fund managers to position themselves, while accounting for the departure from normality of hedge fund returns, which is part of their DNA.

We notice that the eSDAR measure enters in second rank in the model: this relatively unknown measure was already found to be important in the analysis of disappearance for mutual funds by Cogneau and Hübner (2012). We also see the presence in the model of most commonly used measures, such as the alphas of Jensen and Carhart, and the IR.

Some measures show a positive value for the estimated coefficient, while a negative value is in general expected. Most of the time this can be explained by the presence of at least a similar measure having a negative estimate (e.g., adjusted for skewness Sharpe ratio versus Sharpe ratio plus skewness and kurtosis; IR versus Israelsen IR). However, we see some highly significant market-timing measures that do not have equivalent counter-weight: this seems to indicate that a good market timer presents higher risk of stopping the publication of prices.[8]

---

[8]This finding is not surprising as a good market timer will typically report a negative alpha, because it partly stands for the cost of replicating the convex payoff of the portfolio with option-based strategies. Such managers are thus likely to be penalized for their perceived negative intercept.

| Table 11.5 | Somers' $D$ for a Selection of Classical Performance Measures | |
| --- | --- | --- |

| Measure | Somers' $D$ |
| --- | --- |
| $M^2$ | 0.558 |
| Sharpe ratio | 0.532 |
| Calmar | 0.525 |
| Fouse, param = 2, risk-free | 0.513 |
| MorningStar, param = 2 | 0.480 |
| Sterling | 0.473 |
| Sharpe alpha | 0.446 |
| Fama–French alpha | 0.357 |
| Carhart alpha | 0.317 |
| Treynor | 0.295 |
| Jensen alpha | 0.256 |
| IR | 0.251 |
| Henriksson–Merton gamma | 0.034 |
| Farinelli–Tibiletti, $r = 2$, $s = 2$, risk-free | 0.004 |
| Treynor–Mazuy gamma | 0.004 |
| Sortino, with risk-free | 0.002 |
| Moses, Cheney, and Veit | 0.001 |
| Rachev ratio, param = 20% and 5% | 0.000 |
| Bernardo–Ledoit (omega) risk-free | −0.002 |
| Sharpe VaR CF, threshold = 20% | −0.052 |

The added value of 'exotic' performance measures becomes interesting when one considers the use of classical performance measures instead. In Table 11.5, we report the Somers' $D$ of a selection of 20 amongst the most widely used performance measures.

The $M^2$ and Sharpe ratio, although their use for hedge fund performance measurement should be considered with caution, score quite highly on their ability to predict a fund's failure. Surprisingly, the Calmar ratio, which builds on the maximum drawdown − a risk measure that is mostly used by practitioners and that does not derive from the investor's structure of preferences − scores quite highly as well. This finding suggests that the predictive ability of performance measures for hedge funds could be largely related to their perception by investors − conditioning their decision to stay invested or not − rather than on the capacity of these measures to detect persistence in performance. This should be a matter of investigation, as this would imply that the notion of persistence in performance could largely differ from the one of ability to survive in the context of alternative investments in a period of crisis.

The ROC curve for a reduced model with only Jensen's alpha, the Sharpe ratio, the IR, and the Treynor ratio (i.e., four performance measures presented as the 'classical' ones) is represented in Figure 11.2.

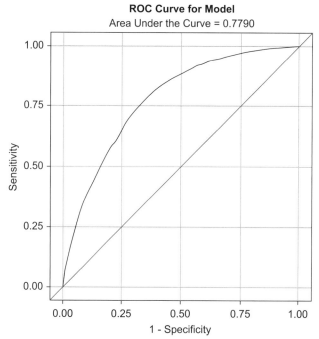

**FIGURE 11.2**
ROC curve for the reduced model.

The Somers' $D$ of this model equals 55.8% for the modeling group and 51.9% for the validation group. Thus, adding other performance measures to the Sharpe ratio does not seem to add any explanatory power.

## 11.4.2. Implications for Portfolio Construction

To show the practical aspect of our research, we perform the following simulation. We consider the performance of all funds living during the period January 2004–December 2006 and we classify them in five quintiles, according to the model described in Section 11.4.1. Then, we consider five portfolios that invested at the beginning of January 2007 the same initial amount of US$1000, on equal weights to all funds of the related quintile. Three months later, we considered the values of each portfolio and we reinvested them similarly, equally weighted on funds ranked by quintiles, according to their performance April 2004–March 2007. This process is repeated until March 2010.

If a fund ceases to publish its prices during one period, its previous contribution to a portfolio is fully reinvested in all other remaining funds in this portfolio at the moment; however, we consider 10 possible levels of penalty that are applied to the last price of the leaving fund: 0%, 1%, 2%, 3%, 5%, 10%, 25%, 50%, 75% and 100%. The final values of the five portfolios are given in the top panel of Table 11.6.

| Quintile | Applied Penalty | | | | | | | | | |
|---|---|---|---|---|---|---|---|---|---|---|
| Portfolio | 0% | 1% | 2% | 3% | 5% | 10% | 25% | 50% | 75% | 100% |
| *Portfolios are rebalanced each quarter* | | | | | | | | | | |
| Q1 | 980.34 | 957.92 | 935.92 | 914.36 | 872.47 | 774.73 | 606.55 | 272.78 | 127.83 | 53.55 |
| Q2 | 945.14 | 930.94 | 916.91 | 903.06 | 875.86 | 810.79 | 692.46 | 418.76 | 264.71 | 160.13 |
| Q3 | 966.70 | 953.41 | 940.26 | 927.27 | 901.72 | 840.32 | 727.66 | 460.52 | 303.99 | 193.18 |
| Q4 | 980.58 | 968.13 | 955.80 | 943.60 | 919.56 | 861.59 | 754.32 | 494.20 | 336.55 | 221.24 |
| Q5 | 975.72 | 960.62 | 945.71 | 930.98 | 902.08 | 832.97 | 707.51 | 418.90 | 258.27 | 150.86 |
| *Portfolios are rebalanced each semester* | | | | | | | | | | |
| Q1 | 911.19 | 898.02 | 884.98 | 872.09 | 846.70 | 785.57 | 672.90 | 403.98 | 247.07 | 138.86 |
| Q2 | 923.78 | 913.89 | 904.08 | 894.35 | 875.10 | 828.27 | 739.99 | 514.96 | 368.18 | 253.21 |
| Q3 | 954.21 | 945.52 | 936.88 | 928.30 | 911.28 | 869.64 | 790.16 | 580.55 | 436.41 | 317.32 |
| Q4 | 955.32 | 946.11 | 936.96 | 927.87 | 909.87 | 865.92 | 782.41 | 564.85 | 417.90 | 298.52 |
| Q5 | 916.60 | 907.10 | 897.66 | 888.29 | 869.75 | 824.54 | 738.89 | 517.90 | 371.20 | 254.53 |

**Table 11.6** Final Values of Rebalanced Quintile Portfolios

We see that the final value of portfolio associated to the first quintile is much lower, especially when the applied penalty is 5% or more. The difference between the four other portfolios is smaller and this can be explained considering the ROC curve in Figure 11.1: after consideration of the worst 20% of funds, we have already discovered 75% of the funds that will cease the publication of prices in the next 3 months.

A period of 3 months could be considered too short, so we simulate a similar process, where the period between two rebalancing dates of the portfolios is 6 months. The results, given in the bottom panel of Table 11.6, present the same two trends: first portfolio performs worst[9] and the difference between the others is weak.

## CONCLUSION

This chapter reproduces a methodology developed in the context of mutual funds within a specific context: during the financial crisis of 2008, many FoHFs experienced some kind of distress resulting in ceasing to report in databases, which was typically a bad sign for their continuation.

Given the vast choice of FoHFs that were available before the crisis and the evidence of capacity effects in this domain, it is logical that the decision of an investor to redeem or not should be related to his/her perception of the fund's capacity to generate performance. On the other hand, the selection of a fund

---

[9]However, the fall in performance between the first quintile portfolio and the others is a little bit less marked; this is probably due to the fact that the model is built to foresee the attrition of funds in the coming 3 months, not 6 months.

manager should be driven by the belief that this manager is able to generate and reproduce past performance. The intersection of these two intuitions leads to a simple explanation of our results: even if persistence in performance did not exist or would be difficult to uncover, the investors' behavior, exacerbated at times of crises, creates a causality effect between the observed past performance and the subsequent decision to invest or divest.

The evidence presented in this chapter, which appears to us to be particularly strong, lends support to an explanation of this type. We do not believe that it would be reproduced with the same strength in times of little or no stress on financial markets. Nevertheless, this study is not necessarily to be considered as a mere exercise of archiving an aspect of the crisis. If another severe crisis occurs, the safe haven reflex of investors will likely be similar and thus constituting one's portfolio with hindsight about the self-fulfilling effect of recorded performance on posterior divestments could be very helpful to save future returns.

# References

Baquero, G., ter Horst, J. R., & Verbeek, M. (2005). Survival, Look-Ahead Bias, and Persistence in Hedge Fund Performance. *Journal of Financial and Quantitative Analysis, 40*(3), 493−517.

Chan, N. T., Getmansky, M., Haas, S. M., & Lo, A. W. (2006). Do Hedge Funds Increase Systematic Risk? Federal Reserve Bank of Atlanta Economic Review. *Fourth Quarter,* 49−80.

Chapman, L., Stevenson, M., & Hutson, E. (2008). *Identifying and Predicting Financial Distress in Hedge Funds.* Working Paper, The 28th International Symposium on Forecasting.

Cogneau, P., & Hübner, G. (2009a). The (More Than) 100 Ways to Measure Portfolio Performance − Part 1: Standardized Risk-Adjusted Measures. *Journal of Performance Measurement, 13*(4), 56−71.

Cogneau, P., & Hübner, G. (2009b). The (More Than) 100 Ways to Measure Portfolio Performance − Part 2: Special Measures and Comparison. *Journal of Performance Measurement, 14*(1), 56−69.

Cogneau, P., & Hübner, G. (2012). *The Prediction of Fund Failure through Performance Diagnostics.* Liège: Working Paper. University of Liège.

Eling, M. (2008). Does the Measure Matter in the Mutual Fund Industry? *Financial Analysts Journal, 64*(3), 54−66.

Eling, M., & Schuhmacher, F. (2007). Does the Choice of Performance Measure Influence the Evaluation of Hedge Funds? *Journal of Banking and Finance, 31*(9), 2632−2647.

Grecu, A., Malkiel, B. G., & Saha, A. (2006). *Why Do Hedge Funds Stop Reporting Their Performance?* Princeton, NJ: Working Paper, CEPS.

Haas Ornelas, J. R., Silva Junior, A. F., & Barros Fernandes, J. L. (2012). Yes, the Choice of Performance Measure Does Matter for Ranking of US Mutual Funds. *International Journal of Finance and Economics, 17*(1), 61−72.

Lee, H. S. (2011). *Dynamic Prediction of Financial Distress in Hedge Funds and Funds-of-Hedge Funds.* Sydney: Working Paper, University of Sydney.

Lobosco, A., & DiBartolomeo, D. (1997). Approximating the Confidence Intervals for Sharpe Style Weights. *Financial Analysts Journal, 53*(4), 80−85.

Liang, B., & Park, H. (2010). Predicting Hedge Fund Failure: A Comparison of Risk Measures. *Journal of Financial and Quantitative Analysis, 45*(1), 199−222.

Malkiel, B. G., & Saha, A. (2005). Hedge Funds: Risk and Return. *Financial Analysts Journal, 61*(6), 80−88.

Ng, M. S. F. (2008). *Development of a Forecasting Model for Hedge Fund Failure: a Survival Analysis Approach.* Thesis. Sydney: University of Sydney.

Plantinga, A., & de Groot, S. (2001). Risk-adjusted performance measures and implied risk-attitudes. *Journal of Performance Measurement, 6*(2), 9–22.

Sharpe, W. F. (1992). Asset Allocation: Management Style and Performance Measurement. *Journal of Portfolio Management, 18*(2), 7–19.

Somers, R. H. (1962). A New Asymmetric Measure of Association for Ordinal Variables. *American Sociological Review, 27*(6), 799–811.

Zakamouline, V. (2011). The Performance Measure You Choose Influences the Evaluation of Hedge Funds. *Journal of Performance Measurement, 15*(3), 48–64.

# APPENDIX

**Table 11.A1**   List of 147 Computed Measures

| Short Name | Long Name |
| --- | --- |
| Adj_Skew_Sharpe_3 | Adjusted for skewness Sharpe ratio (ASSR), taking the value 3 for the investor's relative preference to the skewness of the distribution |
| Aftal_Ponc_2 | Aftalion and Poncet's index, price of the risk = 2 |
| Aftal_Ponc_3 | Aftalion and Poncet's index, price of the risk = 3 |
| Carhart_alpha | Alpha based on Carhart's four-factor model |
| Alpha_cond_alpha | Conditional alpha |
| Alpha_cond_beta | Alpha with conditional betas |
| Trn_Maz_cub_alpha | Alpha in Treynor and Mazuy extended timing measure |
| Fama_French_alpha | Alpha based on Fama and French's three-factor model |
| Hnr_Mrt_3_f_alpha | Alpha in Henriksson and Merton timing measure in a three-factor context |
| Hnr_Mrt_alpha | Alpha in Henriksson and Merton's model |
| Jensen_alpha | Jensen's alpha |
| Alpha_mkt_tim_HM | Market timing alpha in Henriksson and Merton's model |
| Alpha_mkt_tim_TM | Market timing alpha in Treynor and Mazuy's model |
| Alpha_TM_cond_beta | Alpha in the conditional version of Treynor and Mazuy's model |
| Trn_Maz_alpha | Alpha in Treynor and Mazuy's model |
| Bernardo_Ledoit_ifl | Bernardo—Ledoit gain loss ratio, or omega, with inflation rate as reserve return |
| Bernardo_Ledoit_rf | Bernardo—Ledoit gain loss ratio, or omega, with risk-free rate as reserve return |
| Bernardo_Ledoit_zro | Bernardo—Ledoit gain loss ratio, or omega, with zero as reserve return |
| Burke_3 | Burke ratio, where the three largest losses are observed |
| Calmar | Calmar ratio |
| Trn_Maz_cub_delta | Coefficient of cubic term in Treynor and Mazuy's extended timing measure |
| Downsd_risk_Sharpe | Downside-risk Sharpe ratio |
| eSDAR | Excess standard deviation adjusted return (eSDAR) |
| Upsd_pot_ratio_ifl | Upside potential ratio, with inflation rate as reserve return |
| Far_Tib_ifl_1_5x1 | Farinelli—Tibiletti ratio, with inflation rate as reserve return, exponent is 1.5 at numerator and 1 at denominator |

*(Continued)*

**Table 11.A1** List of 147 Computed Measures—cont'd

| Short Name | Long Name |
| --- | --- |
| Far_Tib_ifl_2x2 | Farinelli–Tibiletti ratio, with inflation rate as reserve return, exponent is 2 at numerator and 2 at denominator |
| Far_Tib_ifl_2x3 | Farinelli–Tibiletti ratio, with inflation rate as reserve return, exponent is 2 at numerator and 3 at denominator |
| Upsd_pot_ratio_rf | Upside potential ratio, with risk-free rate as reserve return |
| Far_Tib_rf_1_5x1 | Farinelli–Tibiletti ratio, with risk-free rate as reserve return, exponent is 1.5 at numerator and 1 at denominator |
| Far_Tib_rf_2x2 | Farinelli–Tibiletti ratio, with risk-free rate as reserve return, exponent is 2 at numerator and 2 at denominator |
| Far_Tib_rf_2x3 | Farinelli–Tibiletti ratio, with risk-free rate as reserve return, exponent is 2 at numerator and 3 at denominator |
| Fouse_ifl_1 | Fouse's index, with inflation rate as reserve return and 1 as coefficient of aversion to risk for the investor |
| Fouse_ifl_2 | Fouse's index, with inflation rate as reserve return and 2 as coefficient of aversion to risk for the investor |
| Fouse_ifl_3 | Fouse's index, with inflation rate as reserve return and 3 as coefficient of aversion to risk for the investor |
| Fouse_rf_1 | Fouse's index, with risk-free rate as reserve return and 1 as coefficient of aversion to risk for the investor |
| Fouse_rf_2 | Fouse's index, with risk-free rate as reserve return and 2 as coefficient of aversion to risk for the investor |
| Fouse_rf_3 | Fouse's index, with risk-free rate as reserve return and 3 as coefficient of aversion to risk for the investor |
| Trn_Maz_cub_gamma | Gamma in Treynor and Mazuy extended timing measure |
| Hnr_Mrt_3_f_gam_hml | Gamma for the 'high minus low' risk factor, from Henriksson and Merton timing measure in a three-factor context |
| Hnr_Mrt_3_f_gam_rm | Gamma for the 'market' risk factor, from Henriksson and Merton timing measure in a three-factor context |
| Hnr_Mrt_3_f_gam_smb | Gamma for the 'small minus big' risk factor, from Henriksson and Merton timing measure in a three-factor context |
| Hnr_Mrt_gamma | Henriksson and Merton's coefficient |
| Gamma_TM_cond_beta | Gamma in the conditional version of Treynor and Mazuy's model |
| Trn_Maz_gamma | Treynor and Mazuy's coefficient |
| Gen_Bla_Trn_alpha | Generalized Black–Treynor ratio |
| Gini | Gini ratio |
| Hwang_Satchell | Higher moment measure of Hwang and Satchell |
| Information_Ratio | IR |
| Isr_Infor_Ratio | Israelsen's modified IR |
| Isr_Roy_ifl | Israelsen's modified Roy's measure, with inflation rate as reserve return |
| Isr_Sharpe_ratio | Israelsen's modified Sharpe ratio |
| Isr_Roy_zro | Israelsen's modified Roy's measure, with zero as reserve return |
| M2_Sortino_rf | $M^2$ for Sortino, with risk-free rate as reserve return |
| MAD | Mean absolute deviation (MAD) ratio |
| Martin | Martin ratio or Ulcer performance index |
| Minimax | Minimax |

**Table 11.A1**  List of 147 Computed Measures—cont'd

| Short Name | Long Name |
| --- | --- |
| Modified_Jensen | Modified Jensen |
| Mod_Treynor | Modified Treynor ratio |
| M2 | $M^2$ index, or risk-adjusted performance (RAP) |
| MorningStar_1 | Morningstar risk-adjusted return (MRAR), with gamma $= 1$ |
| MorningStar_2 | Morningstar risk-adjusted return (MRAR), with gamma $= 2$ |
| MorningStar_3 | Morningstar risk-adjusted return (MRAR), with gamma $= 3$ |
| MRAP | Market risk-adjusted performance (MRAP) |
| Moses_Cheney_Veit | Moses, Cheney, and Veit's measure |
| Prosp_rat_ifl_1 | Prospect ratio, with inflation rate as reserve return and coefficient equal to 1 |
| Prosp_rat_ifl_2v25 | Prospect ratio, with inflation rate as reserve return and coefficient equal to 2.25 |
| Prosp_rat_ifl_5 | Prospect ratio, with inflation rate as reserve return and coefficient equal to 5 |
| Prosp_rat_rf_1 | Prospect ratio, with risk-free rate as reserve return and coefficient equal to 1 |
| Prosp_rat_rf_2v25 | Prospect ratio, with risk-free rate as reserve return and coefficient equal to 2.25 |
| Prosp_rat_rf_5 | Prospect ratio, with risk-free rate as reserve return and coefficient equal to 5 |
| Psp_S_K_rt_ifl_1 | Prospect + skewness/kurtosis, with inflation rate as reserve return and coefficient equal to 1 |
| Psp_S_K_rt_ifl_2v25 | Prospect + skewness/kurtosis, with inflation rate as reserve return and coefficient equal to 2.25 |
| Psp_S_K_rt_ifl_5 | Prospect + skewness/kurtosis, with inflation rate as reserve return and coefficient equal to 5 |
| Psp_S_K_rt_rf_1 | Prospect + skewness/kurtosis, with risk-free rate as reserve return and coefficient equal to 1 |
| Psp_S_K_rt_rf_2v25 | Prospect + skewness/kurtosis, with risk-free rate as reserve return and coefficient equal to 2.25 |
| Psp_S_K_rt_rf_5 | Prospect + skewness/kurtosis, with risk-free rate as reserve return and coefficient equal to 5 |
| Rv_avg_dup_ddwn_ifl | Rachev average drawup/down ratio, with inflation rate as reserve return |
| Rv_avg_dup_ddwn_rf | Rachev average drawup/down ratio, with risk-free rate as reserve return |
| Rv_avg_dup_ddwn_zro | Rachev average drawup/down ratio, with zero as reserve return |
| Rv_ifl_v01_v05_v05 | Rachev ratio, with inflation rate as reserve return, threshold is 5% for both the numerator and the denominator; CVaR computed through the EVT with a threshold of 1% |
| Rv_ifl_v01_v5_v2 | Rachev ratio, with inflation rate as reserve return, threshold is 50% for the numerator and 20% for the denominator; CVaR computed through the EVT with a threshold of 1% |
| Rv_max_dup_ddwn_ifl | Rachev maximum drawup/down ratio, with inflation rate as reserve return |
| Rv_max_dup_ddwn_rf | Rachev maximum drawup/down ratio, with risk-free rate as reserve return |

*(Continued)*

**Table 11.A1** List of 147 Computed Measures—cont'd

| Short Name | Long Name |
|---|---|
| Rv_max_dup_ddwn_zro | Rachev maximum drawup/down ratio, with zero as reserve return |
| Rv_rf_v01_v05_v05 | Rachev ratio, with risk-free rate as reserve return, threshold is 5% for both the numerator and the denominator; CVaR computed through the EVT with a threshold of 1% |
| Rv_rf_v01_v2_v05 | Rachev ratio, with risk-free rate as reserve return, threshold is 20% for the numerator and 5% for the denominator; CVaR computed through the EVT with a threshold of 1% |
| Rv_rf_v01_v5_v05 | Rachev ratio, with risk-free rate as reserve return, threshold is 50% for the numerator and 5% for the denominator; CVaR computed through the EVT with a threshold of 1% |
| Rv_rf_v01_v5_v2 | Rachev ratio, with risk-free rate as reserve return, threshold is 50% for the numerator and 20% for the denominator; CVaR computed through the EVT with a threshold of 1% |
| Rv_rf_v01_v5_v5 | Rachev ratio, with risk-free rate as reserve return, threshold is 50% for both the numerator and the denominator; CVaR computed through the EVT with a threshold of 1% |
| Rwd_to_half_variance | Reward to half-variance index |
| Roy_ifl | Roy's measure, with inflation rate as reserve return |
| Sharpe_ratio | Sharpe ratio |
| Roy_zro | Roy's measure, with zero as reserve return |
| RewVaR_rf_v05_v01 | Reward-to-VaR ratio, with risk-free rate as reserve return, threshold is 5%; VaR computed through the EVT with a threshold of 1% |
| RewVaR_rf_v1_v01 | Reward-to-VaR ratio, with risk-free rate as reserve return, threshold is 10%; VaR computed through the EVT with a threshold of 1% |
| Semi_Var_Infor_Ratio | IR based on semi-variance |
| Sharpe_Alpha_1 | Sharpe's alpha, coefficient of aversion to risk for the investor is equal to 1 |
| Sharpe_Alpha_2 | Sharpe's alpha, coefficient of aversion to risk for the investor is equal to 2 |
| Sharpe_Alpha_3 | Sharpe's alpha, coefficient of aversion to risk for the investor is equal to 3 |
| Sharpe_SK | Sharpe + skewness/kurtosis |
| Shp_VaRCF_ifl_v05 | Sharpe ratio based on Cornish−Fisher VaR, with inflation rate as reserve return, threshold is 5% |
| Shp_VaRCF_ifl_v2 | Sharpe ratio based on Cornish−Fisher VaR, with inflation rate as reserve return, threshold is 20% |
| Shp_VaRCF_rf_v05 | Sharpe ratio based on Cornish−Fisher VaR, with risk-free rate as reserve return, threshold is 5% |
| Shp_VaRCF_rf_v2 | Sharpe ratio based on Cornish−Fisher VaR, with risk-free rate as reserve return, threshold is 20% |
| Shp_VaRCF_zro_v05 | Sharpe ratio based on Cornish−Fisher VaR, with zero as reserve return, threshold is 5% |
| Shp_VaRCF_zro_v2 | Sharpe ratio based on Cornish−Fisher VaR, with zero as reserve return, threshold is 20% |

**Table 11.A1**  List of 147 Computed Measures—cont'd

| Short Name | Long Name |
|---|---|
| Shp_CVaR_ifl_v05_v01 | Sharpe ratio based on CVaR or STARR ratio, with inflation rate as reserve return, threshold is 5%; CVaR is computed through the EVT with a threshold of 1% |
| Shp_CVaR_ifl_v1_v01 | Sharpe ratio based on CVaR or STARR ratio, with inflation rate as reserve return, threshold is 10%; CVaR computed through the EVT with a threshold of 1% |
| Shp_CVaR_rf_v05_v01 | Sharpe ratio based on CVaR or STARR ratio, with risk-free rate as reserve return, threshold is 5%; CVaR computed through the EVT with a threshold of 1% |
| Shp_CVaR_rf_v1_v01 | Sharpe ratio based on CVaR or STARR ratio, with risk-free rate as reserve return, threshold is 10%; CVaR computed through the EVT with a threshold of 1% |
| Shp_CVaR_zro_v05_v01 | Sharpe ratio based on CVaR or STARR ratio, with zero as reserve return, threshold is 5%; CVaR computed through the EVT with a threshold of 1% |
| Shp_CVaR_zro_v1_v01 | Sharpe ratio based on CVaR or STARR ratio, with zero as reserve return, threshold is 10%; CVaR computed through the EVT with a threshold of 1% |
| Shp_VaR_ifl_v05_v01 | Sharpe ratio based on the VaR, with inflation rate as reserve return, threshold is 5%; VaR computed through the EVT with a threshold of 1% |
| Shp_VaR_ifl_v1_v01 | Sharpe ratio based on the VaR, with inflation rate as reserve return, threshold is 10%; VaR computed through the EVT with a threshold of 1% |
| Shp_VaR_rf_v05_v01 | Sharpe ratio based on the VaR, with risk-free rate as reserve return, threshold is 5%; VaR computed through the EVT with a threshold of 1% |
| Shp_VaR_rf_v1_v01 | Sharpe ratio based on the VaR, with risk-free rate as reserve return, threshold is 10%; VaR computed through the EVT with a threshold of 1% |
| Shp_VaR_zro_v05_v01 | Sharpe ratio based on the VaR, with zero as reserve return, threshold is 5%; VaR computed through the EVT with a threshold of 1% |
| Shp_VaR_zro_v1_v01 | Sharpe ratio based on the VaR, with zero as reserve return, threshold is 105%; VaR computed through the EVT with a threshold of 1% |
| Sortino_ifl | Sortino ratio, with inflation rate as reserve return |
| Sortino_rf | Sortino ratio, with risk-free rate as reserve return |
| Sortino_zro | Sortino ratio, with zero as reserve return |
| Sortino_SK_ifl | Sortino + skewness/kurtosis ratio, with inflation rate as reserve return |
| Sortino_SK_rf | Sortino + skewness/kurtosis ratio, with risk-free rate as reserve return |
| Sortino_SK_zro | Sortino + skewness/kurtosis ratio, with zero as reserve return |
| Sortino_Sat_ifl_1 | Sortino—Satchell ratio or kappa coefficient of order 1, with inflation rate as reserve return |
| Sortino_Sat_ifl_2 | Sortino—Satchell ratio or kappa coefficient of order 2, with inflation rate as reserve return |
| Sortino_Sat_ifl_3 | Sortino—Satchell ratio or kappa coefficient of order 3, with inflation rate as reserve return |

*(Continued)*

| Table 11.A1 List of 147 Computed Measures—cont'd | |
|---|---|
| **Short Name** | **Long Name** |
| Sortino_Sat_ifl_5 | Sortino—Satchell ratio or kappa coefficient of order 5, with inflation rate as reserve return |
| Sortino_Sat_rf_1 | Sortino—Satchell ratio or kappa coefficient of order 1, with risk-free rate as reserve return |
| Sortino_Sat_rf_2 | Sortino—Satchell ratio or kappa coefficient of order 2, with risk-free rate as reserve return |
| Sortino_Sat_rf_3 | Sortino—Satchell ratio or kappa coefficient of order 3, with risk-free rate as reserve return |
| Sortino_Sat_rf_5 | Sortino—Satchell ratio or kappa coefficient of order 5, with risk-free rate as reserve return |
| Sortino_Sat_zro_1 | Sortino—Satchell ratio or kappa coefficient of order 1, with zero as reserve return |
| Sortino_Sat_zro_2 | Sortino—Satchell ratio or kappa coefficient of order 2, with zero as reserve return |
| Sortino_Sat_zro_3 | Sortino—Satchell ratio or kappa coefficient of order 3, with zero as reserve return |
| Sortino_Sat_zro_5 | Sortino—Satchell ratio or kappa coefficient of order 5, with zero as reserve return |
| SRAP | Style risk-adjusted performance measure (SRAP) |
| Std_Info_Ratio_1 | Standardized IR, version 1 |
| Std_Info_Ratio_2 | Standardized IR, version 2 |
| Std_Info_Ratio_3 | Standardized IR, version 2 |
| Std_Info_Ratio_4 | Standardized IR, version 4 |
| Sterling | Sterling ratio |
| Sterling_Calmar_3 | Sterling—Calmar ratio |
| Stutzer_ifl | Stutzer index of convergence, with inflation rate as reserve return |
| Stutzer_rf | Stutzer index of convergence, with risk-free rate as reserve return |
| Total_risk_alpha | Total risk alpha |
| Treynor | Treynor ratio |

**Table 11.A2** List of 58 Measures Correlated at Less Than 85%

| | | | |
|---|---|---|---|
| Adj_Skew_Sharpe_3 | Gamma_TM_cond_beta* | Modified_Jensen* | Shp_VaRCF_ifl_v2 |
| Aftal_Ponc_2* | Gen_Bla_Trn_alpha* | Moses_Cheney_Veit* | Shp_VaR_ifl_v1_v01 |
| Alpha_TM_cond_beta* | Hnr_Mrt_3_f_alpha* | Rv_avg_dup_ddwn_zro | Sortino_Sat_ifl_2* |
| Alpha_cond_alpha | Hnr_Mrt_3_f_gam_hml* | Rv_ifl_v01_v05_v05* | Stutzer_ifl* |
| Alpha_cond_beta* | Hnr_Mrt_3_f_gam_rm* | Rv_ifl_v01_v5_v2* | Stutzer_rf* |
| Alpha_mkt_tim_HM* | Hnr_Mrt_3_f_gam_smb* | Rv_max_dup_ddwn_ifl | Total_risk_alpha* |
| Alpha_mkt_tim_TM* | Hnr_Mrt_alpha* | Rv_rf_v01_v05_v05 | Trn_Maz_alpha* |
| Std_Info_Ratio_1 | Hnr_Mrt_gamma* | Rv_rf_v01_v2_v05* | Trn_Maz_cub_alpha* |
| Std_Info_Ratio_2* | Hwang_Satchell* | Rv_rf_v01_v5_v05* | Trn_Maz_cub_delta* |
| Std_Info_Ratio_3* | Information_Ratio | Rv_rf_v01_v5_v2* | Trn_Maz_cub_gamma* |
| Carhart_alpha | Isr_Infor_Ratio* | Rv_rf_v01_v5_v5* | Trn_Maz_gamma* |
| Fama_French_alpha* | Jensen_alpha* | SRAP* | Upsd_pot_ratio_rf |
| Far_Tib_rf_2x2 | M2* | Sharpe_SK* | eSDAR* |
| Far_Tib_rf_2x3 | Martin | Shp_CVaR_rf_v1_v01* | |
| Fouse_ifl_1 | Mod_Treynor* | Shp_VaRCF_ifl_v05* | |

*Measure was also selected in Cogneau and Hübner (2012), when considering mutual funds.

# CHAPTER 12

# Does Funds of Hedge Funds Size Matter? Size versus Performance Before, During, and After the Crisis

Jeannine Daniel[*] and François-Serge Lhabitant[†]

[*]Kedge Capital (UK) Ltd, London, UK
[†]Kedge Capital Fund Management, St Helier, Jersey

## 12.1. BACKDROP

Hedge funds are currently managing peak assets of US$2.1 trillion, a quarter of which (US$510 billion) are from funds of hedge funds (FoHFs). These vehicles allow smaller or less sophisticated investors to participate in hedge funds without the various risks associated with investing directly in only one or two. Contextually, aggregate FoHFs assets are down from US$877 billion in mid 2008 when they accounted for 63% of the hedge fund invested universe. The number of FoHFs is also down, at the end of the first quarter of 2012 at 1988 FoHFs versus a 2007 peak of 2462. This trend continues, as FoHFs continue to face redemption pressure as investors opt to invest directly with single hedge fund managers or via intermediaries as consultants and advisors take a bigger role in allocations in exchange for a competitive fee.

The increase in industry concentration is evidenced by a list of the top 5 and 50 FoHFs providers by size, which now account for US$143 and US$500 billion in assets, which equates to 30% and almost 100% of the whole FoHFs industry respectively (see Table 12.1). It is worth noting that the hedge fund industry

Reconsidering Funds of Hedge Funds. http://dx.doi.org/10.1016/B978-0-12-401699-6.00012-5

| Table 12.1 Top 10 Ranking FoHFs Q1 2012 | | | |
| --- | --- | --- | --- |
| **Rank** | | | **Firm/Fund Capital** |
| **2012** | **2011** | **Firm/Fund** | **(US$ million)** |
| 1 | 2 | Blackstone Alternative Asset Management | 39 042 |
| 2 | 1 | HSBC Alternative Investments | 29 670 |
| 3 | 3 | Alternative and Quantitative Investments, UBS | 26 983 |
| 4 | 6 | Goldman Sachs Hedge Fund Strategies | 22 800 |
| 5 | 4 | Grosvenor Capital Management | 22 746 |
| 6 | 5 | Permal Group | 20 000 |
| 7 | 7 | BlackRock Alternative Advisors | 16 785 |
| 8 | 8 | Pacific Alternative Asset Management Co. | 15 070 |
| 8 | 13 | Mesirow Advanced Strategies | 14 267 |
| 10 | 14 | Morgan Stanley Alternative Investment Partners | 13 371 |

Data from Absolute Return + Alpha (2012) Staying Alive: The Top 50 FoHFs Globally. Available at http://www.absolutereturn-alpha.com/Article/3001822/Staying-Alive.html?ArticleId=3001822.

itself is also heavily concentrated, with less than 5% of the managers controlling more than 75% of the assets. The concentration among top FoHFs continues to increase and we will go on to explain why.

Up until 2011, under the 1940 Investment Company Act, certain hedge funds were exempt from Securities and Exchange Commission (SEC) registration and oversight because of an exemption that applied to advisers with fewer than 15 clients — an exemption that counted each fund as a client, as opposed to each investor in a fund.[1] This relieved non-registered hedge funds from having to disclose information pertaining to their investment activities, introducing an element of opacity to the industry. For this reason, among others, many institutional investors concerned about their fiduciary responsibilities and reluctant to build out the necessary infrastructure to analyze and monitor hedge fund managers turned to FoHFs. In return for a fee (typically a 1–2% management fee and a 5–10% performance fee), FoHFs were able to provide investors with a service of asset allocation and manager due diligence, selection, and monitoring. The 'regulatory lite' approach at that time meant that the 'barriers to entry' in establishing a FoHFs business were fairly low, and between 1982 and 2008 the industry grew rapidly (Figures 12.1–12.3).

---

[1]In December 2004, the SEC adopted a new rule and amendments under the Investment Advisers Act of 1940 that would require hedge fund managers to register as investment advisers by 1 February 2006; however, this requirement was subsequently overturned.

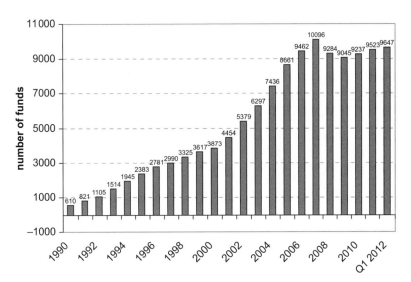

**FIGURE 12.1**
Estimated total number of hedge funds and funds of funds 1990 — Q1 2012.
*Source: Hedge Fund Research.*

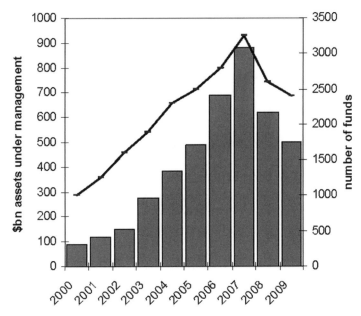

**FIGURE 12.2**
Global fund of funds industry.
*Source: International Financial Services, London estimates.*

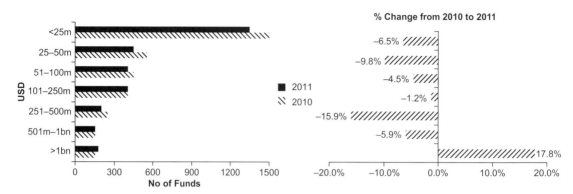

**FIGURE 12.3**
Number of FoHFs by AUM size and percentage change from 2010 to 2011 (excludes 515 funds in 2010 and 522 funds in 2001 that did not report AUM).
*Source: PerTrac.*

## 12.2. FoHFs POST THE 2008 FINANCIAL CRISIS

In the aftermath of 2008, the FoHFs universe has severely contracted. Part of this is 2008 performance related, but the uncovering of the Madoff Ponzi scheme did little to help the industry's popularity. That said, some commentators would argue that the contraction is somewhat expected and a natural evolution, given the knowledge and skill transfer from FoHFs to institutional allocators who have in turn built out their own in-house capabilities. These forces have resulted in fee pressure and forced many FoHFs to adapt their business model in a competitive landscape where the largest survive. From a regulatory development perspective, in June 2011 the SEC adopted the Dodd–Frank Act Amendments to Investment Advisors Act, which required advisers to hedge funds and other private funds to register as investment advisors with the SEC (and file Form ADV disclosures), by no later than March 2012 in the hope that it would provide the Commission, and the public, insight into hedge fund managers who were previously seen as conducting their work under the radar and outside the vision of regulators.

In view of these influences, questions have been raised about the sustainability of FoHFs providers, particularly the small- and medium-sized firms. The consensus has been that FoHFs will continue to exist, but not in their traditional form, and that the rising tide of hedge fund assets has not lifted all players. This fact is only too apparent amidst the current wave of FoHFs consolidation, with most small independent FoHFs reportedly up 'for sale.'

In today's model FoHFs are increasingly being regarded as a solutions provider, one which is used for advice (which infers a lower fee than discretionary mandates) and/or to create satellite funds in more niche strategies to complement an institutional investor's 'core' multistrategy allocation. That said, there are still many instances whereby institutional investors are likely to outsource a hedge fund allocation. FoHFs are still regarded as having a role as the due diligence associated with hedge funds investments is both difficult and expensive, and trustees are keen to outsource the operational cost, and headline and governance risk.[2] For example, a trustee may allocate 5% of their portfolio to hedge funds/FoHFs and operate in the confines of a small budget and investment committee. This rationale is particularly valid given the increasing costs associated with the recent additional regulatory burden of hedge fund investing that we will discuss later. From an individual investor standpoint, FoHFs also provide access to hedge funds with high minimum investment amounts and sophisticated investor requirements that can act as a hurdle to high-net-worth individuals' going direct.

From a behavioral perspective a trustee might not want to assume accountability for running an in-house hedge funds allocation — given the potential for 'blow ups.' Fraud remains an issue and over the past several years, the SEC has brought almost 100 enforcement cases against investment advisers for defrauding hedge fund investors or using hedge funds to defraud others. Another reason is that hedge fund performance is less easy to 'benchmark' versus peers or the market than, say, equities — a much more publicly traded asset class.

In a similar vein, it is often the behavioral instinct associated with a herd mentality that dictates an individual's preference for safety in numbers. Post-2008 investors have in their hordes been allocating to large FoHFs brand names that have established a critical mass. These well-known players (highlighted in Table 12.1) are also more likely to have developed strong relationships with hedge funds managers over the years and thus are able to provide investors with access to managers otherwise closed to new investment.

## 12.3. PERFORMANCE

The analysis of hedge funds and FoHFs performance pre and post the 2008 financial crisis reveals some interesting results.

### 12.3.1. Pre-2008: Small is Supposed to be Beautiful

Prior to the financial crisis, smaller FoHFs were often credited with being nimble and more able to invest in younger, and by definition smaller, hedge funds, which on average were expected to outperform their older peers. The common belief is that in the early years of a hedge fund, managers and employees are supposed to be hungry for success and eager to prove themselves, whereas they may adopt a more conservative investment approach once their performance fees have been invested in the fund (e.g., see Kaiser, 2008). A smaller hedge fund is therefore able to be more flexible in their investment approach, with a focus on exploiting less scalable opportunities, especially in new under-researched markets. In addition, Gregoriou and Rouah (2002) note that the bureaucracy resulting from increased assets under management (AUM) and the demands of

---

[2]The Uniform Prudent Investor Act (1994) permits a fiduciary to delegate investment and management functions, while exercising 'reasonable care, skill, and caution' in selecting a manager and monitoring the manager's performance.

a more institutional investor base (e.g., in terms of transparency) can cause companies to lose their entrepreneurial edge.

While commonly used to promote smaller hedge funds, it is worth noting that the above-mentioned arguments are not systematically supported by academic researchers. In fact, the effective impact of size on hedge fund performance is still not precisely determined. Empirical research provides conflicting results, depending on the sample/period used as well as the type of performance measure considered (see Table 12.2). Survivorship bias should also not be neglected. Simply stated there is a higher mortality rate among younger and smaller funds, and a fund that dies falls out of databases and is no longer observable. Some therefore argue that unconditional performance versus performance conditional on survival might be very different.

This brings us to the impact of fund size on FoHFs performances. There are only a few research papers available on the topic, but here again, their results vary depending on the sample and the timeframe considered (see Table 12.2). Ammann and Moerth (2005) and Brown *et al.* (2008a) infer, however, that the larger FoHFs do outperform their smaller counterparts, and our index data also serves to support this notion. Ammann and Moerth (2005) found that asset-weighted returns of FoHFs were higher than equally weighted returns by an annualized rate of 1.09% from January 1994 to April 2005. The outperformance over the 136-month period is statistically significant at the 5% significance level. One explanation for this is better manager access; another argument is a potentially lower fee structure for larger FoHFs that primarily target large institutional investors.

Brown *et al.* (2008b) find that the alphas of large FoHFs are significantly higher than those of small FoHFs, which they attribute to significant economies of scale. Xiong *et al.* (2009) observe that funds with a larger AUM tend to achieve

**Table 12.2** Illustrating the Research Findings from Academics Examining the Relationship Between Size and Performance at the Hedge Fund Level

| Researchers | Sample Period | Observed Relationship | Performance Measure(s) |
|---|---|---|---|
| Agarwal *et al.* (2004) | 1994–2000 | Linear–negative | Returns |
| Amenc *et al.* (2004) | 1996–2002 | Linear–positive | Alpha |
| Ammann and Moerth (2005) | 1994–2002 | Quadratic–concave | Returns, alpha, Sharpe ratio |
| Ding *et al.* (2009) | 1994–2005 | Linear–negative | Returns |
| Ding *et al.* (2009) | 1994–2005 | Linear–positive | Sharpe ratio |
| Getmansky (2004) | 1994–2002 | Quadratic–concave | Returns |
| Gregoriou and Rouah (2003) | 1994–1999 | No correlation | Returns, Sharpe ratio |
| Guidotti (2009) | 2003–2008 | No clear relation | Alpha |
| Hedges (2004) | 1995–2001 | Quadratic–concave | Alpha |
| Herzberg and Mozes (2003) | 1990–2001 | Linear–negative | Returns, Sharpe ratio |
| Liang (1999) | 1992–1996 | Linear–positive | Returns |
| Xiong *et al.* (2009) | 1995–2006 | Quadratic–concave | Returns, alpha, Sharpe ratio |

higher returns with lower standard deviation and that the smallest 25% of FoHFs underperformed the largest 75% FoHFs by more than 2% *per annum* from January 1995 to November 2006. However, this study does not differentiate between large funds of different ages. Additionally, Heidorn *et al.* (2009) empirically show that the number of drawdowns and the magnitude of maximum drawdowns decrease as a FoHFs manager's experience increases.

Fuss *et al.* (2009) use ordinary least squares and quantile regression on a sample of 649 FoHFs drawn from the Lipper TASS hedge fund database for the time period January 1996–August 2007. They observe that experience and size actually have (i) no significant effect at the median, (ii) a negative effect on performance with a positive curvature at the higher quantiles, and (iii) a positive effect with a negative curvature at lower quantiles.

## 12.3.2. An Index Perspective

Eurekahedge is one of the few hedge fund index providers that calculates indices based on the size of the underlying funds. Over the January 2000–May 2012 period:

- Smaller FoHFs (less than US$100 million of assets) have achieved a compounded annualized return of 3.83% with an annualized standard deviation of 3.89% and a maximum drawdown of −21.12%. They are positive 65.77% of months during the period assessed.
- Medium FoHFs (US$100–500 million of assets) have achieved a compounded annualized return of 5.28% with an annualized standard deviation of 5.02% and a maximum drawdown of −19.15%. They are positive 70.47% of the time.
- Large FoHFs (more than US$1 billion of assets) have achieved a compounded annualized return of 5.69% with an annualized standard deviation of 4.78% and a maximum drawdown of −20.00%. They are positive 73.83% of the time.

These results suggest that larger FoHFs deliver superior returns, with smaller drawdowns than smaller ones from a long-term performance perspective, except when one considers the worst monthly return (Figure 12.4). Interestingly, pre the 2008 crisis, large FoHFs outperformed medium and small FoHFs in a fairly consistent manner. Post-2008, the performance differential between the large and small FoHFs in particular has significantly increased − supporting the notion that FoHFs size post the 2008 crisis is a problem, and that the larger FoHFs are outperforming medium and smaller sized FoHFs.

## 12.3.3. Post-2008: Size Does Matter

While most investors focus on the investment strategy of a hedge fund when considering whether or not to place an investment, an equally important aspect is how the manager operates his hedge fund business. Simply stated, hedge fund operational due diligence (ODD) is the process of reviewing and monitoring the operation and management of hedge fund managers, with the

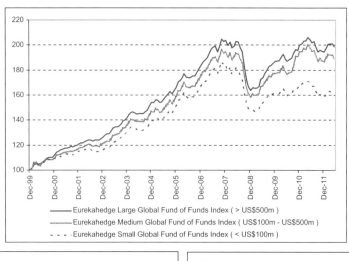

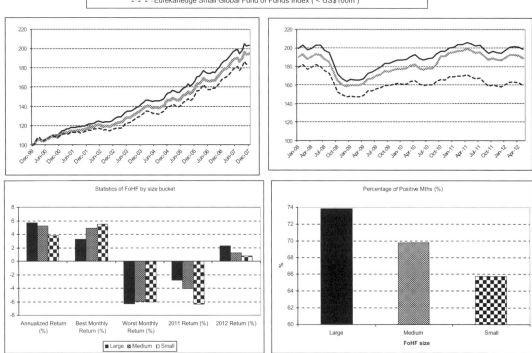

**FIGURE 12.4**
Eurekahedge — index performance pre- and post-2008.

goal of avoiding taking unnecessary *operational risks* such as theft and fraud, deficiencies in controls and procedures, and/or weak business infrastructures and service providers. In 2008 many hedge fund investors learnt the true value of ODD the hard way.

Operational failure is a significant cause of hedge fund liquidations and is a key area as it pertains to an investor wanting to avoid reputational, or headline, risk.

In a study of more than 100 hedge funds liquidations over 20 years, Feffer and Kundro (2003) find that '54% of failed funds had identifiable operational issues and half of all fund failures could be attributed to operational risk alone.'

ODD is one of the services investors have implicitly delegated to FoHFs managers.[3] It is a critical and often very expensive one. The cost and level of due diligence (both operational and financial[4]) are usually correlated and can vary considerably, depending on a number of factors, although available resources usually form a significant driver of this. ODD resources may depend on staffing, budgeting, and, more broadly, a FoHFs philosophy. It is generally the case that larger FoHFs have a higher budget assigned to the area, and are broad and deep in their work. For example, in addition to an in-house dedicated ODD team, some of the largest funds of funds use third-party service providers such as consulting firms, law firms, accounting firms, and even private investigators to conduct full background investigations (criminal, civil, and regulatory actions) to supplement their work internally. Other, more budget-constrained managers may opt only to use consultants or their own industry network for references on a hedge fund manager and the quality of their employees.

From a cost perspective, many would argue that the larger FoHFs are better positioned to absorb the high cost of due diligence and thus have a significant competitive advantage over smaller funds of funds. For instance, Brown *et al.* (2008b) argue that the difference in returns between FoHFs with limited AUM and larger FoHFs represent economies of scale almost entirely attributed to the fixed cost associated with necessary operational due diligence. They conclude that economies of scale in funds of funds can be quite substantial and support the proposition that due diligence is a source of alpha in hedge fund investments. The implications of avoiding poorly performing managers can be more important than selecting top performing hedge funds.

How large are the ODD costs? They can vary depending on the degree of thoroughness and whether, for example, outside specialists such as law firms, accounting firms, consulting firms, or other third-party service providers are employed. According to Anson (2006), a thorough investor should expect to spend 75–100 hours reviewing a hedge fund manager before investing. Assuming a conservative cost of due diligence of US$50 000–100 000 per hedge fund, the cost of performing initial due diligence on 10 hedge funds would be US$500 000 to US$1 million. Also keep in mind that it is highly probable that only a fraction of those funds going under due diligence actually make it into the portfolio and the cost incurred for those that do not make it through is written

---

[3]Note that there are also a few cases of FoHFs that suffered from operational failures, such as Charles Schmitt in Hong Kong and Portus and Norshield in Canada. In all cases, the FoHFs manager created fictitious assets in addition to 'real' third-party hedge fund holdings.
[4]Feffer and Kundro (2003) argues that operational risk as distinct from financial risk accounts for a substantial fraction of fund attrition. Brown *et al.* (2008a, 2008b) attempt to quantify this risk, showing that operational risk associated with conflicts of interest both within the fund and external to the fund can lead to a reduction in return of on average 1.68% on an annualized basis.

off. Furthermore, there are ongoing costs associated with existing hedge fund allocation monitoring.

To put this in further context, approximately 35% of US-domiciled FoHFs have less than US$20 million in AUM. With an annual management fee of 1.5%, which is on the generous side, a FoHF with US$20 million generates US$300 000 in management fees annually — some way off the estimated ODD costs associated with 10 managers. Between starving and doing light due diligence, the choice is obvious.

The cost budget also raises questions about the incentive structure, and the ability of larger FoHFs to attract and retain talented teams versus smaller FoHFs, who may struggle. Post 2008 one could observe a flood of talent from banks and failed FoHFs who prefer the brand and security offered by a larger FoHF.

## CONCLUSION

Since 2008, the FoHFs industry has experienced a series of significant transformations as high-net-worth individuals have reduced their allocations and institutional capital has replaced them. Institutional investors are known to be more demanding and FoHFs are learning this the hard way. In particular, they are asked to do more due diligence, more advisory work, more customized portfolios, and more reporting, and, if possible, for lower fees. Whilst the larger players with well-controlled costs have been able to weather the storm without further undermining the viability of their business, smaller FoHFs players struggle, particularly in Europe.

As a result, the number of FoHFs is shrinking, due to attrition as firms decide to shut down and exit, but also as a consequence of mergers and acquisitions. Indeed, the list of recent FoHFs combination deals is quite long. Let us mention, for instance, SkyBridge Capital/Citi Alternative Investments (April 2010), Nexar/Allianz Alternative Asset Management (September 2010), William Blair/Guidance Capital (January 2011), Nexar/Ermitage Group (May 2011), Arden Asset Management/Robeco Sage (June 2011), Athena Capital Advisors/Stonehorse Capital Management (July 2011), Cantor Fitzgerald/Cadogan Management (December 2011), UBP/Nexar (March 2012), Crestline Investors/Lyster Watson (March 2012), Gottex/Penjing Asset Management (May 2012), and Man Group/FRM (May 2012). This is the tip of the iceberg and some other FoHFs managers are reportedly in discussions about a potential sale of their business.

In our opinion it is clear that, going forward, only larger FoHFs will be able to cater for the increasing requests of institutional investors and their consultants. Boutique firms with a modest team size and appropriately controlled cost base do not have much choice. Either they will have to become specialists with a niche product satisfying an investor's desire for a satellite strategy (typically just one FoHFs) or they may very well end up as takeover targets.

This evolution is Darwinian in nature and there is not much one can do against it. However, it should be noted that size in the FoHFs industry has its own challenges — since capacity in the most successful established blue-chip players is not infinite. The larger players might very well have to overdiversify their portfolios in order to deploy their ever growing asset base. As noted by Brown *et al.* (2012), overdiversification is often synonymous with diluting potential manager alpha. It therefore seems that the recent success of the largest FoHFs in terms of attracting new inflows signifies both an opportunity and a threat to their future success.

## Acknowledgments

The views expressed in this chapter are exclusively those of the authors and do not necessarily represent the views of, and should not be attributed to, the various entities they are or have been affiliated with.

## References

Agarwal, V., Daniel, N., & Naik, N. (2004). *Flows, Performance, and Managerial Incentives in Hedge Funds*. London: Center for Financial Research Working Paper.

Amenc, N., Curtis, S., & Martellini, L. (2004). *The Alpha and Omega of Hedge Fund Performance Measurement*. Nice: EDHEC Working Paper.

Ammann, M., & Moerth, P. (2005). Impact of Fund Size on Hedge Fund Performance. *Journal of Asset Management, 6*(3), 219–238.

Ammann, M., & Moerth, P. (2008). Performance of Funds of Hedge Funds. *Journal of Asset Management, 11*(1), 46–63.

Anson, & Mark, J. P. (2006). *Handbook of Alternative Investments*. New York: John Wiley & Sons Inc.

Brown, S. J., Goetzmann, W. N., Liang, B., & Schwarz, C. (2008a). Mandatory Disclosure and Operational Risk: Evidence from Hedge Fund Registration. *Journal of Finance, 63*(6), 2785–2815.

Brown, S. J., Fraser, T. L., & Liang, B. (2008b). Due Diligence: A Source of Alpha in a Hedge Fund Portfolio Strategy. *Journal of Investment Management, 6*(4). 23–3.

Brown, S. J., Gregoriou, G. N., & Pascalau, R. (2012). Diversification in Funds of Hedge Funds: Is It Possible to Overdiversify? *Review of Asset Pricing Studies, 2*(1), 89–100.

Ding, B., Shawky, H., & Tian, J. (2009). Liquidity Shocks, Size and the Relative Performance of Hedge Fund Strategies. *Journal of Banking and Finance, 33*(5), 883–891.

Feffer, S., & Kundro, C. (2003). *Understanding and Mitigating Operational Risk in Hedge Fund Investments*. Working Paper, The Capital Markets Company Ltd.

Fuss, R., Kaiser, D., & Strittmatter, A. (2009). Measuring Funds of Hedge Funds Performance Using Quantile Regressions: Do Experience and Size Matter? *Journal of Alternative Investments, 12*(2), 41–53.

Getmansky, M. (2004). *The Life Cycle of Hedge Funds: Fund Flows, Size and Performance*. Cambridge, MA: MIT Working Paper.

Guidotti, I. (2009). Trade-off Between Liquidity, Size and Performance. *Hedge Fund Journal*. Available at http://www.thehedgefundjournal.com/node/6752.

Gregoriou, G., & Rouah, F. (2003). Large versus Small Hedge Funds: Does Size Affect Performance? *Journal of Alternative Investments, 5*(3), 75–77.

Hedges, J. (2004). Size vs. Performance in the Hedge Fund Industry. *Journal of Financial Transformation, 10*(1), 14–17.

Heidorn, T., Kaiser, D. G., & Roder, C. (2009). The Risk of Funds of Hedge Funds: An Empirical Analysis of the Maximum Drawdown. *Journal of Wealth Management, 12*(2), 89–100.

Herzberg, M., & Mozes, H. (2003). The Persistence of Hedge Fund Risk: Evidence and Implications for Investors. *Journal of Alternative Investments, 6*(2), 22–42.

Kaiser, D. G. (2008). The Life-Cycle of Hedge Funds. *Journal of Derivatives and Hedge Funds, 14*(2), 127–149.

Liang, B. (1999). On the Performance of Hedge Funds. *Financial Analysts Journal, 55*(4), 72–85.

Xiong, J., Idzorek, T., Chen, P., & Ibbotson, R. (2009). Impact of Size and Flows on Performance for Funds of Hedge Funds. *Journal of Portfolio Management, 35*(2), 118–130.

# CHAPTER 13

# Normalized Risk-Adjusted Performance Measures Revisited: The Performance of Funds of Hedge Funds Before and After the Crisis

**Laurent Bodson**[*], **Laurent Cavenaile**[†], **and Alain Coën**[**]
[*]Head of Asset Management, Gambit Financial Solutions SA,
Liège, Belgium
[†]Department of Economics, New York University, New York, NY, USA
[**]Professor of Finance, Department of Finance, ESG-UQAM, Graduate School of
Business, University of Quebec in Montreal (UQÀM),
Montreal, QC, Canada

**Chapter Outline**

13.1. Introduction  195
13.2. Theoretical Framework  197
    13.2.1. Performance
        Measures  197
    13.2.2. Adaptation of
        Performance Measures
        for Illiquidity  198
    13.2.3. Asset Pricing Model and
        EIVs  200
13.3. Data and Empirical
    Method  201

13.3.1. The Data and Adjusted
        Return Series  201
13.3.2. The Asset Pricing
        Model  201
13.3.3. Empirical Results:
        Stability and
        Persistence
        of Performance
        Measures  202
Conclusion  211
References  212

## 13.1. INTRODUCTION

Since the 2007–2008 financial crisis the performance of portfolio managers in the hedge fund industry has been seriously criticized as long as they seem to have ignored the true level of risk. As well established in the financial literature, this risk can be decomposed into specific and systematic risk. Since the seminal paper of Sharpe (1964), systematic risk has been modeled by single or multi benchmarks or risk factors. As highlighted by Roll (1977) and rigorously demonstrated by Ross (1976), a single risk factor encompasses many drawbacks.

Reconsidering Funds of Hedge Funds. http://dx.doi.org/10.1016/B978-0-12-401699-6.00013-7
Copyright © 2013 Elsevier Inc. All rights reserved.

Thus, the use of multi-factor models stands as a norm in the funds industry. As a consequence, many performance measures are based on these models. As reported by Grinold (1989), the idiosyncratic risk is the key element to measure the skill and the ability of a fund manager to outperform. Measures should include a comparison between specific (or idiosyncratic risk) and total risk. Recently, Bodson *et al.* (2010a) have investigated this point and developed four normalized risk-adjusted performance measures to focus on mutual funds. We focus on funds of hedge funds (FoHFs) where there is a need to shed new light on the accuracy of performance measures.

With respect to mutual funds, hedge funds and FoHFs exhibit recurrent risk characteristics, especially their illiquidity. This idiosyncratic lack of liquidity, estimated by serial correlation in returns, may seriously impact the accuracy and robustness of performance measures. As documented and demonstrated by Cohen *et al.* (1979) and Atchinson *et al.* (1987), among others, the presence of autocorrelation return series may be explained by illiquidity. This problem is associated with smooth returns in the hedge funds industry and implies that reported hedge fund returns are smoother than 'true' returns. Cavenaile *et al.* (2011) report that smoothed returns exhibit a lower volatility than 'true' returns. As a consequence, the level is perceived as lower, inducing biased risk-adjusted performance measures.

Moreover, many performance measures are directly related to asset pricing models and risk factors. The main problem is that true risk factors are often unobserved. In this case ordinary least squares (OLS) estimates suffer from errors-in-variables (EIVs) complications. The use of instrumental variables techniques should be a solution. Carmichael and Coën (2008), Coën and Hübner (2009), and Bodson *et al.* (2010b) have recently analyzed the relevance of Dagenais and Dagenais' higher moment estimator (HME) for linear multifactor asset pricing models. Dagenais and Dagenais' HME, exploiting orthogonality conditions in terms of higher moments, is easily applicable to hedge fund multifactor asset pricing models (for more details, see Coën and Hübner, 2009).

Our contribution is 3-fold.

- We apply series of risk-adjusted performance measures based on multifactor asset pricing models to identify the risk exposures of FoHFs before and after the 2007−2008 financial crisis.
- To take into account the illiquidity feature of FoHFs, we compute unsmoothed return series and adjust measures for risk.
- We use Dagenais and Dagenais' (1997) instrumental variables estimator to deal with the consequences of EIVs for parameter estimates of linear multifactor models and performance measures.

This chapter is organized as follows. Section 13.2 defines the theoretical framework, presenting performance measures, adjustment for illiquidity of FoHFs, and Dagenais and Dagenais' (1997) HME. Section 13.3 presents the data of FoHFs for the period from January 2010 to April 2010 and describes the risk factors used in the asset pricing model. Subsection 13.3.3 reports and analyzes the persistence and the stability of the different performance measures for the two subperiods (before and after the crisis). Conclusions are then drawn.

## 13.2. THEORETICAL FRAMEWORK

### 13.2.1. Performance Measures

Following Bodson *et al.* (2010a), we introduce four normalized risk-adjusted performance measures compared with Jensen's alpha and the information ratio (IR). These different measures exhibit interesting advantages: all are normalized, they are computed from linear multifactor asset pricing models, and the use of a benchmark portfolio is not required. Bodson *et al.* (2010a) have developed and applied these measures to a sample of mutual funds using augmented Fama–French asset pricing models. We suggest the use of these measures for a sample of FoHFs applying a linear Fung–Hsieh asset pricing model adjusted for illiquidity and EIVs.

To formally introduce these measures, we assume a standard linear asset pricing model given by:

$$R_t = \alpha + \sum_{k=1}^{K} \beta_k \cdot \tilde{F}_{kt} + e_t, \tag{13.1}$$

where $\alpha$ is a constant term defined as the security's abnormal return, or Jensen's alpha, $\tilde{F}_{tk}$ is factor $k$ realization in period $t$, $\beta_k$ is factor $k$ loading and $e_t$ is a residual idiosyncratic risk. For each FoHFs $i$, the intercept of the OLS regression (13.1) is our reference performance measure, the well-known Jensen's alpha (1968), $\alpha_i$. It encompasses the three advantages mentioned earlier. A positive metric underlines the ability of portfolio managers to earn returns in excess of their exposure to the different sources of risks modeled in the linear asset pricing model.

The normalized measures are based on the decomposition of total risk into systemic and specific risks, as defined by Sharpe (1964), Lintner (1965), and Mossin (1966). Therefore, we use the variance instead of the standard deviation to capture this dimension: $\sigma^2(R_i) = \sigma^2(\beta_i F) + \sigma^2(e_i)$.

Considering the popular IR, the normalized IR is given by *ratio*1 as:

$$IR_i = \frac{\alpha_i}{\sigma(e_i)} \tag{13.2}$$

$$ratio1_i = \alpha_i \frac{\sigma^2(R_i)}{\sigma^2(e_i)}. \tag{13.3}$$

For *ratio*1 the specific risk is expressed relative to the total risk, assessing the skills of the manager to generate abnormal returns with few specific risks. An increase of idiosyncratic risk induces a lower ratio, *ceteris paribus*, and inversely. The IR can be adapted, replacing the alpha by the mean excess return of the FoHFs to avoid of the main drawback of the alpha — its erratic behavior:

$$ratio2_i = \overline{R}_i \frac{\sigma^2(R_i)}{\sigma^2(e_i)}, \tag{13.4}$$

where $\overline{R}_i$ is the mean of realized returns of FoHFs $i$ in excess of the risk-free rate.

We present now the adaptations of the risk-adjusted Modigliani and Modigliani (1997) measure ($M^2$) developed by Bodson *et al.* (2010a) for a multifactor asset pricing model. The performance is expressed per unit of systematic risk. With these measures, *ratio*3 and *ratio*4, the abnormal and excess returns respectively, are weighted by their proportion of systematic risk in the total FoHFs risk:

$$ratio3_i = \alpha_i \frac{\sigma^2\left(\sum_{k=1}^{K} \beta_{k,i} F_k\right)}{\sigma^2(R_i)} \tag{13.5}$$

$$ratio4_i = \overline{R}_i \frac{\sigma^2\left(\sum_{k=1}^{K} \beta_{k,i} F_k\right)}{\sigma^2(R_i)}. \tag{13.6}$$

Unlike in *ratio*1 and *ratio*2, total risk appears now at the denominator. An increase of systematic (decline in specific risk) risk induces an increase (decline) in the performance measures.

Moreover, Bodson *et al.* (2010a) show that *ratio*3 and *ratio*4 are related to *ratio*1 and *ratio*2, respectively:

$$ratio3_i = \alpha_i \frac{\sigma^2\left(\sum_{k=1}^{K} \beta_{k,i} F_k\right)}{\sigma^2(R_i)} = \alpha_i \frac{\sigma^2(R_i) - \sigma^2(e_i)}{\sigma^2(R_i)} = \alpha_i \cdot \left(1 - \frac{\alpha_i}{ratio1}\right) \tag{13.7}$$

$$ratio4_i = \overline{R}_i \frac{\sigma^2\left(\sum_{k=1}^{K} \beta_{k,i} F_k\right)}{\sigma^2(R_i)} = \overline{R}_i \frac{\sigma^2(R_i) - \sigma^2(e_i)}{\sigma^2(R_i)} = \overline{R}_i \cdot \left(1 - \frac{\alpha_i}{ratio2}\right). \tag{13.8}$$

## 13.2.2. Adaptation of Performance Measures for Illiquidity

The lack of liquidity, statistically estimated by the serial correlation in historical returns, is a recurrent risk characteristic of hedge funds. It materializes through the 'liquidity dates' and appears to have played a significant role in the

2007–2008 financial crisis. We can acknowledge that this problem of illiquidity may vary according to the different hedge fund strategies. Nevertheless, its impact on the performance measurement of FoHFs cannot be ignored and could be corrected, as demonstrated by Brooks and Kat (2002), Kat and Lu (2002), Getmansky et al. (2004), and Okunev and White (2003), among others. The hedge fund returns are indeed too smooth, decreasing the perceived volatility and thus increasing risk-adjusted measures such as the Sharpe ratio, as reported by Lo (2002). Since the seminal work of Geltner (1991, 1993), the presence of serial correlation has been proven to be an indicator of illiquidity as underlined by Okunev and White (2003). According to Getmansky et al. (2004), the problem of autocorrelation in hedge fund returns should be related to the role of non-synchronous trading in the alternative investments industry. As they report, it is one of the reasons, but not the only one.

If the first method to incorporate illiquidity was proposed by Geltner (1991, 1993), several methods have been developed to deal with the impact of serial correlation on performance measures and risk. Recently, Cavenaile et al. (2011) have suggested the use of two methods to deal with these smoother returns and to compute the 'true' returns before analyzing their impact on performance and risk. The first one, developed by Okunev and White (2003), is an adaptation to the hedge fund returns of the method introduced by Geltner (1991, 1993) in real estate economics. The second one is based on Getmansky et al. (2004). As reported by Cavenaile et al. (2011), risk is significantly underestimated by smoothed returns: the Sharpe ratio tends to overestimate the true performance of hedge funds. Interestingly, their results obtained through the Getmansky et al. (GLM) approach are very similar to those obtained with the adjustment of Okunev and White. Therefore, to deal with illiquidity problem in the FoHF, we have decided to focus on one correction method: the GLM approach.

The GLM adjustment to obtain unsmoothed return series may be defined following the method developed by Gallais et al. (2008) and reported in detail in Cavenaile et al. (2011). It is assumed that the reported returns are a weighted average of past 'true' unobserved returns (independently and identically distributed):

$$r_t^o = \theta_0 r_t + \theta_1 r_{t-1} + \dots + \theta_q r_{t-q}. \tag{13.9}$$

Such that:

$$\theta_j \in [0, 1], j = 0, \dots, q \tag{13.10}$$

$$\theta_0 + \theta_1 + \dots + \theta_q = 1, \tag{13.11}$$

where $r_t^o$ is the observed return at time $t$, $r_t$ is the 'true' unobserved return at time $t$, and $\theta$s are 'smoothing parameters' to be estimated.

Using the innovations algorithm of Brockwell and Davis (1991), the estimation method based on a maximum likelihood estimation of a moving average process is applied. Following this approach, de-meaned observed returns are computed as follows:

$$X_t = r_t^o - \bar{r}^o, \tag{13.12}$$

where $\bar{r}^o$ is the expected value of the observed return series.

Therefore, equation (13.9) can be rewritten as an MA($q$):

$$X_t = \theta_0 \, \eta_t + \theta_1 \, \eta_{t-1} + \dots + \theta_q \, \eta_{t-q}, \tag{13.13}$$

with the additional assumption that $\eta_q \sim N(0, \sigma_\eta^2)$. (We acknowledge that this assumption may be criticized since it has already been proven that hedge fund returns are traditionally not normally distributed.)

Getmansky *et al.* (2004) show that the expected return is not affected by the smoothing process; however, the variance of smoothed returns is biased downward when compared to the true variance. More precisely, they establish that the 'true' unobserved variance is a function of the observed variance and of the $\theta$s.

### 13.2.3. Asset Pricing Model and EIVs

It is well known in the financial economic literature that EIVs are important in the estimation of linear asset pricing models. As recently illustrated by Coën and Racicot (2007) and Carmichael and Coën (2008) in a financial context, they induce a correlation between residuals and regressors that lead to biased and inconsistent parameter estimates. In a multifactor asset pricing model given by equation (13.1), if the true factors, $\tilde{F}_{kt}$ are observed, the parameters of the model can be consistently estimated by OLS. On the other hand, if some or all factors $\tilde{F}_{kt}$ are unknown, and estimation and inference are based on observed factors, $F_{kt}$, OLS is no longer consistent (for a demonstration, see Carmichael and Coën, 2008).

A solution is to use instrumental variables. In this paper, following Carmichael and Coën (2008) and Coën and Hübner (2009), we suggest the use of Dagenais and Dagenais' HME. Estimates of EIVs, $\hat{W}$, are computed as the differences between observed factors, $F$, and estimates of the true factors, $\hat{F}$:

$$F - \hat{F} = \hat{W}.$$

As suggested by Davidson and McKinnon (1993, 2004), to compute Dagenais and Dagenais' HME, we may imply two-step artificial regressions. First, estimates of the true factors are constructed using $K$ OLS regressions with $F_{kt}$ as dependent variables and higher moments (own and cross moments) of $F_{kt}$, used as instruments, as regressors.

These instruments are $z_1 = f*f$, $z_2 = f*f*f - 3f[E(f'f/N)*I_K]$, and a constant. $f_{ij}$ are the elements of the matrix $f$ and $f = AF$, where $A = I_N - ii'/N$. The matrix $f$ is the $T \times K$ matrix $F$ calculated in mean deviation, standing for the matrix of $K$ factor loadings where $T$ is here the number of observations. The symbol '*' is the Hadamard element-by-element matrix multiplication operator.

Second, estimates of EIVs are introduced as additional regressors (for more details, see the appendix of Carmichael and Coën, 2008) in the asset pricing equation (13.14) as follows:

$$R_t = \alpha^{HM} + \sum_{k=1}^{K} \beta_k^{HM} \cdot F_{kt} + \sum_{k=1}^{K} \psi_k \cdot \hat{w}_{kt} + \varepsilon_t. \qquad (13.14)$$

Exponent HM stands for Dagenais and Dagenais' HME. To detect the presence of EIVs, we have run a Durbin—Wu—Hausman (DWH)-type test (for more details, see Hausman, 1978)

## 13.3. DATA AND EMPIRICAL METHOD

### 13.3.1. The Data and Adjusted Return Series

We use the BarclayHedge database including 2956 FoHFs for the period from January 1995 to November 2012. To analyze the performance of FoHFs before and after the crisis, we focus on the period from January 2000 to November 2011. Due to the dead funds, we have retained 246 living FoHFs for the complete period from January 2000 to late April 2010 with 124 monthly returns for each fund.

We have divided our sample in two subperiods: before the crisis from January 2000 to June 2007 (90 monthly returns), and during and after the crisis from July 2007 to April 2010 (34 monthly returns). After the computation of unsmoothed returns, using the method described in the previous section, our sample is divided as follows: from May 2000 to June 2007 (86 monthly returns for a sample of 246 FoHFs) for the first subperiod and from July 2007 to April 2010 (34 monthly returns for a sample of 246 FoHFs) for the second subperiod.

Using the computation method developed by Getmansky *et al.* (2004) for unsmoothed returns, we may report that 50 FoHFs do not need an adjustment, 118 FoHFs are corrected for smoothed returns with a MA(1) procedure, 48 FoHFs are corrected with a MA(2) procedure, 22 FoHFs are corrected with a MA(3) procedure, and, finally, eight FoHFs are corrected with a MA(4) procedure.

### 13.3.2. The Asset Pricing Model

Important literature has been devoted to the identification of relevant risk premiums in order to refine the measurement performance by Jensen's alpha (e.g., Schneeweis and Spurgin, 1998; Liang, 1999; Capocci and Hübner, 2004; Agarwal and Naik, 2004; Fung *et al.*, 2008), so the multifactor linear asset pricing model developed by Fung and Hsieh (2001) can reasonably stand as a reference. Therefore, we have decided to use this specification with seven risk premiums given by equation (13.1): three trend-following risk factors (Bond Trend-Following Factor, Currency Trend-Following Factor, and Commodity Trend-Following Factor) from the David Hsieh data library,[1] two equity-oriented risk

---

[1]Available at http://faculty.fuqua.duke.edu/~dah7/DataLibrary/TF-FAC.xls.

factors (Equity Market Factor and Size Spread Factor) from the Kenneth French data library,[2] and two bond-oriented risk factors (Bond Market Factor and Credit-Spread Factor) available at the Board of Governors of the Federal Reserve System.

We have performed different normality tests (Bera–Jarque, Lilliefors, Cramer–von Mises, Watson, and Anderson–Darling) on the smoothed and unsmoothed FoHFs data series and on the seven risk factors (detailed results are available upon request). As expected, the results reject normality. As reported by Carmichael and Coën (2008), Coën and Hübner (2009), and Bodson *et al.* (2010b), this feature makes Dagenais and Dagenais' HME useful to deal with the presence of EIVs.

Parameter estimates with (Dagenais and Dagenais' HME) and without (OLS) corrections for the presence of EIVs are obtained using equations (13.14) and (13.1), for smoothed and unsmoothed FoHFs data series. Then, we compute the six performance measures presented in the previous section for smoothed and unsmoothed FoHFs data series, corrected (Dagenais and Dagenais' HME) and not corrected (OLS) for EIVs. We obtain four series of six performance measures for each subsample period. Their stability and persistence before and after the crisis are analyzed in the following section using rank correlation matrix estimates.

### 13.3.3. Empirical Results: Stability and Persistence of Performance Measures

First, we compute the Kendall rank correlation matrix for the six performance measures, for the two subperiods, using smoothed and unsmoothed returns, and with and without correction for EIVs. Results (all significant at 1%) are reported in the series of Tables 13.1–13.6. As expected, for all measures, we observe a sharp contrast between the period before and the period after the crisis. On the one hand, the rank correlations are significantly negative for Jensen's alpha, IR, *ratio*1, and *ratio*3, highlighting the important impact of this event and the relative inadequacy of these metrics during the transition period. On the other hand, Kendall rank correlations are significantly higher for *ratio*2 and *ratio*4. We may mention that these ratios are based on the mean of realized return series of FoHFs while *ratio*1 and *ratio*3 are adapted from Jensen's alpha. As mentioned by Coën and Racicot (2007) for mutual equity funds and confirmed by Coën and Hübner (2009) for hedge funds indices, EIVs tend to induce significantly different alpha after correction.

To illustrate the relative outperformance of *ratio*2 and *ratio*4 versus the other measures, we compute the differences of the correlation coefficients. The results for *ratio*4 are reported in the series of Tables 13.7–13.11 and for *ratio*2 in the series of Tables 13.12–13.15. All differences are significantly positive (with only

---

[2]Available at http://mba.tuck.dartmouth.edu/pages/faculty/ken.french/data_library.html.

| Table 13.1 | Correlation Measures for Jensen's Alpha (Kendall Rank Correlation, All Significant at 1%) | | | | | | | |
| --- | --- | --- | --- | --- | --- | --- | --- | --- |
|  | a-OLS1 | a-HME1 | au-OLS1 | au-HME1 | a-OLS2 | a-HME2 | au-OLS2 | au-HME2 |
| a-OLS1 | **1.000** | 0.645 | 0.787 | 0.562 | −0.179 | −0.212 | −0.218 | −0.235 |
| a-HME1 | 0.645 | **1.000** | 0.594 | 0.761 | −0.232 | −0.260 | −0.228 | −0.252 |
| au-OLS1 | 0.787 | 0.594 | **1.000** | 0.618 | −0.238 | −0.247 | −0.235 | −0.213 |
| au-HME1 | 0.562 | 0.761 | 0.618 | **1.000** | −0.205 | −0.211 | −0.190 | −0.188 |
| a-OLS2 | −0.179 | −0.232 | −0.238 | −0.205 | **1.000** | 0.623 | 0.783 | 0.481 |
| a-HME2 | −0.212 | −0.260 | −0.247 | −0.211 | 0.623 | **1.000** | 0.597 | 0.744 |
| au-OLS2 | −0.218 | −0.228 | −0.235 | −0.190 | 0.783 | 0.597 | **1.000** | 0.575 |
| au-HME2 | −0.235 | −0.252 | −0.213 | −0.188 | 0.481 | 0.744 | 0.575 | **1.000** |

a, Jensen's alpha; OLS, OLS estimators; HME, higher moment estimators; 1, first subperiod before the crisis (May 2000–June 2007); 2, second subperiod during and after the crisis (July 2007–April 2010); u, unsmoothed returns with GLM method.

| Table 13.2 | Correlation Measures for IR (Kendall Rank Correlation, All Significant at 1%) | | | | | | | |
| --- | --- | --- | --- | --- | --- | --- | --- | --- |
|  | IR-OLS1 | IR-HME1 | IRu-OLS1 | IRu-HME1 | IR-OLS2 | IR-HME2 | IRu-OLS2 | IRu-HME2 |
| IR-OLS1 | **1.000** | 0.606 | 0.729 | 0.485 | −0.130 | −0.160 | −0.152 | −0.188 |
| IR-HME1 | 0.606 | **1.000** | 0.555 | 0.724 | −0.174 | −0.212 | −0.153 | −0.203 |
| IRu-OLS1 | 0.729 | 0.555 | **1.000** | 0.573 | −0.217 | −0.224 | −0.191 | −0.186 |
| IRu-HME1 | 0.485 | 0.724 | 0.573 | **1.000** | −0.176 | −0.192 | −0.136 | −0.152 |
| IR-OLS2 | −0.130 | −0.174 | −0.217 | −0.176 | **1.000** | 0.623 | 0.797 | 0.489 |
| IR-HME2 | −0.160 | −0.212 | −0.224 | −0.192 | 0.623 | **1.000** | 0.608 | 0.756 |
| IRu-OLS2 | −0.152 | −0.153 | −0.191 | −0.136 | 0.797 | 0.608 | **1.000** | 0.575 |
| IRu-HME2 | −0.188 | −0.203 | −0.186 | −0.152 | 0.489 | 0.756 | 0.575 | **1.000** |

OLS, OLS estimators; HME, higher moment estimators; 1, first subperiod before the crisis (May 2000–June 2007); 2, second subperiod during and after the crisis (July 2007–April 2010); u, unsmoothed returns with GLM method.

| Table 13.3 | Correlation Measures for *Ratio*1 (Kendall Rank Correlation, All Significant at 1%) | | | | | | | |
| --- | --- | --- | --- | --- | --- | --- | --- | --- |
|  | r1-OLS1 | r1-HME1 | r1u-OLS1 | r1u-HME1 | r1-OLS2 | r1-HME2 | r1u-OLS2 | r1u-HME2 |
| r1-OLS1 | **1.000** | 0.651 | 0.734 | 0.550 | −0.146 | −0.158 | −0.215 | −0.225 |
| r1-HME1 | 0.651 | **1.000** | 0.572 | 0.759 | −0.208 | −0.233 | −0.226 | −0.250 |
| r1u-OLS1 | 0.734 | 0.572 | **1.000** | 0.620 | −0.236 | −0.242 | −0.231 | −0.207 |
| r1u-HME1 | 0.550 | 0.759 | 0.620 | **1.000** | −0.213 | −0.232 | −0.189 | −0.195 |
| r1-OLS2 | −0.146 | −0.208 | −0.236 | −0.213 | **1.000** | 0.633 | 0.749 | 0.474 |
| r1-HME2 | −0.158 | −0.233 | −0.242 | −0.232 | 0.633 | **1.000** | 0.556 | 0.689 |
| r1u-OLS2 | −0.215 | −0.226 | −0.231 | −0.189 | 0.749 | 0.556 | **1.000** | 0.582 |
| r1u-HME2 | −0.225 | −0.250 | −0.207 | −0.195 | 0.474 | 0.689 | 0.582 | **1.000** |

r1, *ratio*1; OLS, OLS estimators; HME, higher moment estimators; 1, first subperiod before the crisis (May 2000–June 2007); 2, second subperiod during and after the crisis (July 2007–April 2010); u, unsmoothed returns with GLM method.

| Table 13.4 | Correlation measures for the *Ratio2* (Kendall Rank Correlation, All Significant at 1%) |

|          | r2-OLS1 | r2-HME1 | r2u-OLS1 | r2u-HME1 | r2-OLS2 | r2-HME2 | r2u-OLS2 | r2u-HME2 |
|----------|---------|---------|----------|----------|---------|---------|----------|----------|
| r2-OLS1  | **1.000** | 0.940 | 0.802 | 0.775 | 0.020 | 0.017 | 0.032 | 0.032 |
| r2-HME1  | 0.940 | **1.000** | 0.790 | 0.792 | 0.016 | 0.013 | 0.027 | 0.027 |
| r2u-OLS1 | 0.802 | 0.790 | **1.000** | 0.933 | 0.045 | 0.040 | 0.049 | 0.046 |
| r2u-HME1 | 0.775 | 0.792 | 0.933 | **1.000** | 0.044 | 0.038 | 0.046 | 0.043 |
| r2-OLS2  | 0.020 | 0.016 | 0.045 | 0.044 | **1.000** | 0.962 | 0.951 | 0.928 |
| r2-HME2  | 0.017 | 0.013 | 0.040 | 0.038 | 0.962 | **1.000** | 0.934 | 0.939 |
| r2u-OLS2 | 0.032 | 0.027 | 0.049 | 0.046 | 0.951 | 0.934 | **1.000** | 0.961 |
| r2u-HME2 | 0.032 | 0.027 | 0.046 | 0.043 | 0.928 | 0.939 | 0.961 | **1.000** |

r2, ratio2; OLS, OLS estimators; HME, higher moment estimators; 1, first subperiod before the crisis (May 2000–June 2007); 2, second subperiod during and after the crisis (July 2007–April 2010); u, unsmoothed returns with GLM method.

| Table 13.5 | Correlation Measures for *Ratio3* (Kendall Rank Correlation, All Significant at 1%) |

|          | r3-OLS1 | r3-HME1 | r3u-OLS1 | r3u-HME1 | r3-OLS2 | r3-HME2 | r3u-OLS2 | r3u-HME2 |
|----------|---------|---------|----------|----------|---------|---------|----------|----------|
| r3-OLS1  | **1.000** | 0.638 | 0.756 | 0.554 | −0.150 | −0.171 | −0.220 | −0.216 |
| r3-HME1  | 0.638 | **1.000** | 0.585 | 0.768 | −0.210 | −0.240 | −0.222 | −0.242 |
| r3u-OLS1 | 0.756 | 0.585 | **1.000** | 0.616 | −0.234 | −0.232 | −0.238 | −0.202 |
| r3u-HME1 | 0.554 | 0.768 | 0.616 | **1.000** | −0.206 | −0.219 | −0.185 | −0.190 |
| r3-OLS2  | −0.150 | −0.210 | −0.234 | −0.206 | **1.000** | 0.638 | 0.749 | 0.484 |
| r3-HME2  | −0.171 | −0.240 | −0.232 | −0.219 | 0.638 | **1.000** | 0.574 | 0.718 |
| r3u-OLS2 | −0.220 | −0.222 | −0.238 | −0.185 | 0.749 | 0.574 | **1.000** | 0.586 |
| r3u-HME2 | −0.216 | −0.242 | −0.202 | −0.190 | 0.484 | 0.718 | 0.586 | **1.000** |

r3, ratio3; OLS, OLS estimators; HME, higher moment estimators; 1, first subperiod before the crisis (May 2000–June 2007); 2, second subperiod during and after the crisis (July 2007–April 2010); u, unsmoothed returns with GLM method.

| Table 13.6 | Correlation Measures for *Ratio4* (Kendall Rank Correlation, All Significant at 1%) |

|          | r4-OLS1 | r4-HME1 | r4u-OLS1 | r4u-HME1 | r4-OLS2 | r4-HME2 | r4u-OLS2 | r4u-HME2 |
|----------|---------|---------|----------|----------|---------|---------|----------|----------|
| r4-OLS1  | **1.000** | 0.931 | 0.772 | 0.773 | 0.015 | 0.019 | 0.021 | 0.023 |
| r4-HME1  | 0.931 | **1.000** | 0.756 | 0.792 | 0.005 | 0.008 | 0.010 | 0.012 |
| r4u-OLS1 | 0.772 | 0.756 | **1.000** | 0.913 | 0.041 | 0.041 | 0.039 | 0.039 |
| r4u-HME1 | 0.773 | 0.792 | 0.913 | **1.000** | 0.031 | 0.031 | 0.027 | 0.029 |
| r4-OLS2  | 0.015 | 0.005 | 0.041 | 0.031 | **1.000** | 0.959 | 0.948 | 0.935 |
| r4-HME2  | 0.019 | 0.008 | 0.041 | 0.031 | 0.959 | **1.000** | 0.931 | 0.959 |
| r4u-OLS2 | 0.021 | 0.010 | 0.039 | 0.027 | 0.948 | 0.931 | **1.000** | 0.953 |
| r4u-HME2 | 0.023 | 0.012 | 0.039 | 0.029 | 0.935 | 0.959 | 0.953 | **1.000** |

r4, ratio4; OLS, OLS estimators; HME, higher moment estimators; 1, first subperiod before the crisis (May 2000–June 2007); 2, second subperiod during and after the crisis (July 2007–April 2010); u, unsmoothed returns with GLM method.

| Table 13.7 | | Comparison of *Ratio*4 with Jensen's Alpha (Based on Kendall Rank Correlation Coefficients Difference) | | | | | | |
|---|---|---|---|---|---|---|---|---|
| | **OLS1** | **HME1** | **u-OLS1** | **u-HME1** | **OLS2** | **HME2** | **u-OLS2** | **u-HME2** |
| OLS1 | **0.000** | 0.286 | −0.015 | 0.211 | 0.195 | 0.232 | 0.240 | 0.258 |
| HME1 | 0.286 | **0.000** | 0.162 | 0.031 | 0.237 | 0.269 | 0.238 | 0.264 |
| u-OLS1 | −0.015 | 0.162 | **0.000** | 0.294 | 0.279 | 0.288 | 0.274 | 0.252 |
| u-HME1 | 0.211 | 0.031 | 0.294 | **0.000** | 0.236 | 0.242 | 0.217 | 0.217 |
| OLS2 | 0.195 | 0.237 | 0.279 | 0.236 | **0.000** | 0.336 | 0.166 | 0.454 |
| HME2 | 0.232 | 0.269 | 0.288 | 0.242 | 0.336 | **0.000** | 0.334 | 0.216 |
| u-OLS2 | 0.240 | 0.238 | 0.274 | 0.217 | 0.166 | 0.334 | **0.000** | 0.378 |
| u-HME2 | 0.258 | 0.264 | 0.252 | 0.217 | 0.454 | 0.216 | 0.378 | **0.000** |

OLS, OLS estimators; HME, higher moment estimators; 1, first subperiod before the crisis (May 2000–June 2007); 2, second subperiod during and after the crisis (July 2007–April 2010); u, unsmoothed returns with GLM method.

| Table 13.8 | | Comparison of *Ratio*4 with IR (Based on Kendall Rank Correlation Coefficients Difference) | | | | | | |
|---|---|---|---|---|---|---|---|---|
| | **OLS1** | **HME1** | **u-OLS1** | **u-HME1** | **OLS2** | **HME2** | **u-OLS2** | **u-HME2** |
| OLS1 | **0.000** | 0.325 | 0.043 | 0.288 | 0.146 | 0.179 | 0.174 | 0.211 |
| HME1 | 0.325 | **0.000** | 0.201 | 0.068 | 0.179 | 0.220 | 0.163 | 0.214 |
| u-OLS1 | 0.043 | 0.201 | **0.000** | 0.340 | 0.257 | 0.266 | 0.230 | 0.225 |
| u-HME1 | 0.288 | 0.068 | 0.340 | **0.000** | 0.207 | 0.223 | 0.163 | 0.181 |
| OLS2 | 0.146 | 0.179 | 0.257 | 0.207 | **0.000** | 0.336 | 0.151 | 0.445 |
| HME2 | 0.179 | 0.220 | 0.266 | 0.223 | 0.336 | **0.000** | 0.323 | 0.203 |
| u-OLS2 | 0.174 | 0.163 | 0.230 | 0.163 | 0.151 | 0.323 | **0.000** | 0.378 |
| u-HME2 | 0.211 | 0.214 | 0.225 | 0.181 | 0.445 | 0.203 | 0.378 | **0.000** |

OLS, OLS estimators; HME, higher moment estimators; 1, first subperiod before the crisis (May 2000–June 2007); 2, second subperiod during and after the crisis (July 2007–April 2010); u, unsmoothed returns with GLM method.

| Table 13.9 | | Comparison of *Ratio*4 with *Ratio*1 (Based on Kendall Rank Correlation Coefficients Difference) | | | | | | |
|---|---|---|---|---|---|---|---|---|
| | **OLS1** | **HME1** | **u-OLS1** | **u-HME1** | **OLS2** | **HME2** | **u-OLS2** | **u-HME2** |
| OLS1 | **0.000** | 0.280 | 0.037 | 0.223 | 0.161 | 0.177 | 0.236 | 0.247 |
| HME1 | 0.280 | **0.000** | 0.184 | 0.033 | 0.213 | 0.241 | 0.236 | 0.262 |
| u-OLS1 | 0.037 | 0.184 | **0.000** | 0.292 | 0.277 | 0.283 | 0.270 | 0.246 |
| u-HME1 | 0.223 | 0.033 | 0.292 | **0.000** | 0.244 | 0.263 | 0.216 | 0.224 |
| OLS2 | 0.161 | 0.213 | 0.277 | 0.244 | **0.000** | 0.326 | 0.199 | 0.461 |
| HME2 | 0.177 | 0.241 | 0.283 | 0.263 | 0.326 | **0.000** | 0.374 | 0.270 |
| u-OLS2 | 0.236 | 0.236 | 0.270 | 0.216 | 0.199 | 0.374 | **0.000** | 0.371 |
| u-HME2 | 0.247 | 0.262 | 0.246 | 0.224 | 0.461 | 0.270 | 0.371 | **0.000** |

OLS, OLS estimators; HME, higher moment estimators; 1, first subperiod before the crisis (May 2000–June 2007); 2, second subperiod during and after the crisis (July 2007–April 2010); u, unsmoothed returns with GLM method.

| Table 13.10 | Comparison of *Ratio*4 with *Ratio*2 (Based on Kendall Rank Correlation Coefficients Difference) | | | | | | | |
|---|---|---|---|---|---|---|---|---|
| | **OLS1** | **HME1** | **u-OLS1** | **u-HME1** | **OLS2** | **HME2** | **u-OLS2** | **u-HME2** |
| OLS1 | **0.000** | −0.010 | −0.030 | −0.002 | −0.004 | 0.002 | −0.011 | −0.009 |
| HME1 | −0.010 | **0.000** | −0.034 | 0.000 | −0.011 | −0.004 | −0.018 | −0.015 |
| u-OLS1 | −0.030 | −0.034 | **0.000** | −0.021 | −0.004 | 0.002 | −0.010 | −0.007 |
| u-HME1 | −0.002 | 0.000 | −0.021 | **0.000** | −0.013 | −0.007 | −0.018 | −0.014 |
| OLS2 | −0.004 | −0.011 | −0.004 | −0.013 | **0.000** | −0.003 | −0.003 | 0.007 |
| HME2 | 0.002 | −0.004 | 0.002 | −0.007 | −0.003 | **0.000** | −0.003 | 0.020 |
| u-OLS2 | −0.011 | −0.018 | −0.010 | −0.018 | −0.003 | −0.003 | **0.000** | −0.008 |
| u-HME2 | −0.009 | −0.015 | −0.007 | −0.014 | 0.007 | 0.020 | −0.008 | **0.000** |

OLS, OLS estimators; HME, higher moment estimators; 1, first subperiod before the crisis (May 2000–June 2007); 2, second subperiod during and after the crisis (July 2007–April 2010); u, unsmoothed returns with GLM method.

| Table 13.11 | Comparison of *Ratio*4 with *Ratio*3 (Based on Kendall Rank Correlation Coefficients Difference) | | | | | | | |
|---|---|---|---|---|---|---|---|---|
| | **OLS1** | **HME1** | **u-OLS1** | **u-HME1** | **OLS2** | **HME2** | **u-OLS2** | **u-HME2** |
| OLS1 | **0.000** | 0.292 | 0.016 | 0.219 | 0.165 | 0.190 | 0.242 | 0.239 |
| HME1 | 0.292 | **0.000** | 0.171 | 0.024 | 0.215 | 0.248 | 0.232 | 0.253 |
| u-OLS1 | 0.016 | 0.171 | **0.000** | 0.296 | 0.274 | 0.273 | 0.277 | 0.242 |
| u-HME1 | 0.219 | 0.024 | 0.296 | **0.000** | 0.237 | 0.250 | 0.212 | 0.219 |
| OLS2 | 0.165 | 0.215 | 0.274 | 0.237 | **0.000** | 0.321 | 0.200 | 0.451 |
| HME2 | 0.190 | 0.248 | 0.273 | 0.250 | 0.321 | **0.000** | 0.356 | 0.242 |
| u-OLS2 | 0.242 | 0.232 | 0.277 | 0.212 | 0.200 | 0.356 | **0.000** | 0.367 |
| u-HME2 | 0.239 | 0.253 | 0.242 | 0.219 | 0.451 | 0.242 | 0.367 | **0.000** |

OLS, OLS estimators; HME, higher moment estimators; 1, first subperiod before the crisis (May 2000–June 2007); 2, second subperiod during and after the crisis (July 2007–April 2010); u, unsmoothed returns with GLM method.

| Table 13.12 | Comparison of *Ratio*2 with Jensen's alpha (Based on Kendall Rank Correlation Coefficients Difference) | | | | | | | |
|---|---|---|---|---|---|---|---|---|
| | **OLS1** | **HME1** | **u-OLS1** | **u-HME1** | **OLS2** | **HME2** | **u-OLS2** | **u-HME2** |
| OLS1 | **0.000** | 0.295 | 0.015 | 0.213 | 0.199 | 0.229 | 0.251 | 0.267 |
| HME1 | 0.295 | **0.000** | 0.196 | 0.031 | 0.247 | 0.273 | 0.256 | 0.279 |
| u-OLS1 | 0.015 | 0.196 | **0.000** | 0.315 | 0.283 | 0.286 | 0.284 | 0.259 |
| u-HME1 | 0.213 | 0.031 | 0.315 | **0.000** | 0.249 | 0.250 | 0.236 | 0.231 |
| OLS2 | 0.199 | 0.247 | 0.283 | 0.249 | **0.000** | 0.339 | 0.168 | 0.447 |
| HME2 | 0.229 | 0.273 | 0.286 | 0.250 | 0.339 | **0.000** | 0.337 | 0.196 |
| u-OLS2 | 0.251 | 0.256 | 0.284 | 0.236 | 0.168 | 0.337 | **0.000** | 0.387 |
| u-HME2 | 0.267 | 0.279 | 0.259 | 0.231 | 0.447 | 0.196 | 0.387 | **0.000** |

OLS, OLS estimators; HME, higher moment estimators; 1, first subperiod before the crisis (May 2000–June 2007); 2, second subperiod during and after the crisis (July 2007–April 2010); u, unsmoothed returns with GLM method.

| Table 13.13 | Comparison of *Ratio2* with IR (Based on Kendall Rank Correlation Coefficients Difference) | | | | | | | |
|---|---|---|---|---|---|---|---|---|
| | **OLS1** | **HME1** | **u-OLS1** | **u-HME1** | **OLS2** | **HME2** | **u-OLS2** | **u-HME2** |
| OLS1 | **0.000** | 0.334 | 0.072 | 0.290 | 0.150 | 0.176 | 0.185 | 0.220 |
| HME1 | 0.334 | **0.000** | 0.235 | 0.068 | 0.190 | 0.225 | 0.180 | 0.230 |
| u-OLS1 | 0.072 | 0.235 | **0.000** | 0.360 | 0.261 | 0.264 | 0.240 | 0.232 |
| u-HME1 | 0.290 | 0.068 | 0.360 | **0.000** | 0.220 | 0.230 | 0.182 | 0.195 |
| OLS2 | 0.150 | 0.190 | 0.261 | 0.220 | **0.000** | 0.339 | 0.154 | 0.438 |
| HME2 | 0.176 | 0.225 | 0.264 | 0.230 | 0.339 | **0.000** | 0.326 | 0.183 |
| u-OLS2 | 0.185 | 0.180 | 0.240 | 0.182 | 0.154 | 0.326 | **0.000** | 0.386 |
| u-HME2 | 0.220 | 0.230 | 0.232 | 0.195 | 0.438 | 0.183 | 0.386 | **0.000** |

OLS, OLS estimators; HME, higher moment estimators; 1, first subperiod before the crisis (May 2000–June 2007); 2, second subperiod during and after the crisis (July 2007–April 2010); u, unsmoothed returns with GLM method.

| Table 13.14 | Comparison of *Ratio2* with *Ratio1* (Based on Kendall Rank Correlation Coefficients Difference) | | | | | | | |
|---|---|---|---|---|---|---|---|---|
| | **OLS1** | **HME1** | **u-OLS1** | **u-HME1** | **OLS2** | **HME2** | **u-OLS2** | **u-HME2** |
| OLS1 | **0.000** | 0.289 | 0.067 | 0.226 | 0.165 | 0.175 | 0.247 | 0.257 |
| HME1 | 0.289 | **0.000** | 0.218 | 0.033 | 0.224 | 0.246 | 0.253 | 0.277 |
| u-OLS1 | 0.067 | 0.218 | **0.000** | 0.313 | 0.281 | 0.282 | 0.280 | 0.253 |
| u-HME1 | 0.226 | 0.033 | 0.313 | **0.000** | 0.257 | 0.270 | 0.234 | 0.238 |
| OLS2 | 0.165 | 0.224 | 0.281 | 0.257 | **0.000** | 0.328 | 0.202 | 0.454 |
| HME2 | 0.175 | 0.246 | 0.282 | 0.270 | 0.328 | **0.000** | 0.378 | 0.250 |
| u-OLS2 | 0.247 | 0.253 | 0.280 | 0.234 | 0.202 | 0.378 | **0.000** | 0.380 |
| u-HME2 | 0.257 | 0.277 | 0.253 | 0.238 | 0.454 | 0.250 | 0.380 | **0.000** |

OLS, OLS estimators; HME, higher moment estimators; 1, first subperiod before the crisis (May 2000–June 2007); 2, second subperiod during and after the crisis (July 2007–April 2010); u, unsmoothed returns with GLM method.

| Table 13.15 | Comparison of *Ratio2* with *Ratio3* (Based on Kendall Rank Correlation Coefficients Difference) | | | | | | | |
|---|---|---|---|---|---|---|---|---|
| | **OLS1** | **HME1** | **u-OLS1** | **u-HME1** | **OLS2** | **HME2** | **u-OLS2** | **u-HME2** |
| OLS1 | **0.000** | 0.302 | 0.046 | 0.221 | 0.169 | 0.188 | 0.253 | 0.248 |
| HME1 | 0.302 | **0.000** | 0.205 | 0.024 | 0.225 | 0.253 | 0.250 | 0.269 |
| u-OLS1 | 0.046 | 0.205 | **0.000** | 0.317 | 0.278 | 0.271 | 0.287 | 0.248 |
| u-HME1 | 0.221 | 0.024 | 0.317 | **0.000** | 0.249 | 0.258 | 0.231 | 0.233 |
| OLS2 | 0.169 | 0.225 | 0.278 | 0.249 | **0.000** | 0.324 | 0.202 | 0.444 |
| HME2 | 0.188 | 0.253 | 0.271 | 0.258 | 0.324 | **0.000** | 0.359 | 0.222 |
| u-OLS2 | 0.253 | 0.250 | 0.287 | 0.231 | 0.202 | 0.359 | **0.000** | 0.375 |
| u-HME2 | 0.248 | 0.269 | 0.248 | 0.233 | 0.444 | 0.222 | 0.375 | **0.000** |

OLS, OLS estimators; HME, higher moment estimators; 1, first subperiod before the crisis (May 2000–June 2007); 2, second subperiod during and after the crisis (July 2007–April 2010); u, unsmoothed returns with GLM method.

**Table 13.16** Rank Correlation Measures: Performance Measures without GLM Adjustment (Period 1 before the Crisis (Row) versus Period 2 after July 2007 (Column))

|  | Alpha | IR | Ratio1 | Ratio2 | Ratio3 | Ratio4 | a HME | IR HME | r1 HME | r2 HME | r3 HME | r4 HME |
|---|---|---|---|---|---|---|---|---|---|---|---|---|
| Alpha | **-0.179** | -0.183 | -0.178 | -0.109 | -0.179 | -0.106 | -0.212 | -0.208 | -0.197 | -0.113 | -0.206 | -0.114 |
| IR | -0.128 | **-0.130** | -0.127 | -0.092 | -0.129 | -0.088 | -0.169 | -0.160 | -0.154 | -0.095 | -0.161 | -0.095 |
| *Ratio1* | -0.151 | -0.153 | **-0.146** | -0.100 | -0.148 | -0.097 | -0.178 | -0.173 | -0.158 | -0.105 | -0.168 | -0.103 |
| *Ratio2* | 0.224 | 0.219 | 0.234 | **0.020** | 0.233 | 0.024 | 0.192 | 0.185 | 0.222 | 0.017 | 0.205 | 0.028 |
| *Ratio3* | -0.152 | -0.155 | -0.148 | -0.101 | **-0.150** | -0.098 | -0.180 | -0.176 | -0.162 | -0.107 | -0.171 | -0.105 |
| *Ratio4* | 0.227 | 0.223 | 0.236 | 0.011 | 0.235 | **0.015** | 0.187 | 0.179 | 0.211 | 0.008 | 0.196 | 0.019 |
| a HME | -0.232 | -0.233 | -0.241 | -0.087 | -0.242 | -0.089 | **-0.260** | -0.264 | -0.270 | -0.096 | -0.266 | -0.099 |
| IR HME | -0.173 | -0.174 | -0.179 | -0.088 | -0.180 | -0.091 | -0.212 | **0.212** | -0.216 | -0.095 | -0.214 | -0.099 |
| r1 HME | -0.204 | -0.208 | -0.208 | -0.080 | -0.209 | -0.082 | -0.237 | -0.241 | **0.233** | -0.088 | -0.237 | -0.091 |
| r2 HME | 0.220 | 0.214 | 0.230 | 0.016 | 0.229 | 0.020 | 0.186 | 0.179 | 0.216 | **0.013** | 0.199 | 0.023 |
| r3 HME | -0.204 | -0.205 | -0.209 | -0.087 | -0.210 | -0.088 | -0.237 | -0.241 | -0.240 | -0.095 | **-0.240** | -0.097 |
| r4 HME | 0.211 | 0.207 | 0.220 | 0.001 | 0.219 | 0.005 | 0.172 | 0.164 | 0.196 | -0.001 | 0.182 | **0.008** |

Performance measures without acronym HME are estimated with OLS; HME, higher moment estimators; a, Jensen's alpha; r1, *ratio1*; r2, *ratio2*; r3, *ratio3*; r4, *ratio4*.

**Table 13.17** Rank Correlation Measures: Performance Measures with GLM Adjustment (Period 1 before the Crisis (Row) versus Period 2 after July 2007 (Column))

| GLM | Alpha | IR | Ratio1 | Ratio2 | Ratio3 | Ratio4 | a HME | IR HME | r1 HME | r2 HME | r3 HME | r4 HME |
|---|---|---|---|---|---|---|---|---|---|---|---|---|
| Alpha | **−0.235** | −0.212 | −0.238 | −0.081 | −0.244 | −0.076 | −0.213 | −0.203 | −0.210 | −0.086 | −0.212 | −0.083 |
| IR | −0.212 | **0.191** | −0.213 | −0.066 | −0.219 | −0.062 | −0.194 | −0.186 | −0.191 | −0.071 | −0.193 | −0.068 |
| *Ratio1* | −0.229 | −0.203 | **0.231** | −0.076 | −0.238 | −0.072 | −0.208 | −0.197 | −0.207 | −0.083 | −0.208 | −0.079 |
| *Ratio2* | 0.074 | 0.084 | 0.054 | **0.049** | 0.057 | 0.047 | 0.013 | −0.003 | 0.001 | 0.046 | 0.007 | 0.048 |
| *Ratio3* | −0.228 | −0.204 | −0.232 | −0.073 | **−0.238** | −0.069 | −0.202 | −0.192 | −0.201 | −0.080 | −0.202 | −0.076 |
| *Ratio4* | 0.082 | 0.091 | 0.062 | 0.040 | 0.065 | **0.039** | 0.011 | −0.005 | −0.002 | 0.037 | 0.004 | 0.039 |
| a HME | −0.190 | −0.160 | −0.187 | −0.104 | −0.194 | −0.102 | **0.188** | −0.169 | −0.180 | −0.111 | −0.185 | −0.111 |
| IR HME | −0.156 | −0.136 | −0.151 | −0.098 | −0.158 | −0.098 | −0.166 | **0.152** | −0.157 | −0.105 | −0.163 | −0.107 |
| r1 HME | −0.187 | −0.158 | −0.189 | −0.088 | −0.195 | −0.086 | −0.200 | −0.184 | **0.195** | −0.096 | −0.199 | −0.094 |
| r2 HME | 0.060 | 0.068 | 0.039 | 0.046 | 0.042 | 0.044 | −0.001 | −0.016 | −0.013 | **0.043** | −0.008 | 0.045 |
| r3 HME | −0.179 | −0.151 | −0.179 | −0.093 | −0.185 | −0.091 | −0.190 | −0.175 | −0.186 | −0.101 | **0.190** | −0.100 |
| r4 HME | 0.069 | 0.075 | 0.051 | 0.030 | 0.053 | 0.027 | 0.002 | −0.014 | −0.011 | 0.027 | −0.005 | **0.029** |

Performance measures without acronym HME are estimated with OLS; HME, higher moment estimators; a, Jensen's alpha; r1, *ratio1*; r2, *ratio2*; r3, *ratio3*; r4, *ratio4*.

**Table 13.18** Unsmoothed Performance Measures versus Smoothed Performance Measures

| GLM | Alpha | IR | Ratio1 | Ratio2 | Ratio3 | Ratio4 | a HME | IR HME | r1 HME | r2 HME | r3 HME | r4 HME |
|---|---|---|---|---|---|---|---|---|---|---|---|---|
| Alpha | **-0.056** | -0.029 | -0.060 | 0.029 | -0.065 | 0.030 | -0.001 | 0.006 | -0.012 | 0.027 | -0.006 | 0.031 |
| IR | -0.083 | **0.061** | -0.086 | 0.026 | -0.091 | 0.027 | -0.026 | -0.026 | -0.036 | 0.024 | -0.032 | 0.027 |
| Ratio1 | -0.078 | -0.050 | **0.086** | 0.024 | -0.090 | 0.025 | -0.030 | -0.024 | -0.049 | 0.022 | -0.040 | 0.025 |
| Ratio2 | -0.150 | -0.136 | -0.180 | **0.029** | -0.176 | 0.023 | -0.178 | -0.187 | -0.221 | 0.029 | -0.198 | 0.020 |
| Ratio3 | -0.076 | -0.049 | -0.083 | 0.028 | -0.088 | 0.029 | -0.022 | -0.016 | -0.039 | 0.027 | -0.031 | 0.029 |
| Ratio4 | -0.145 | -0.132 | -0.174 | 0.030 | -0.170 | **0.023** | -0.176 | -0.184 | -0.213 | 0.029 | -0.193 | 0.020 |
| a HME | 0.042 | 0.074 | 0.054 | -0.017 | 0.048 | -0.012 | **0.072** | 0.095 | 0.090 | -0.016 | 0.081 | -0.012 |
| IR HME | 0.017 | 0.039 | 0.028 | -0.010 | 0.022 | -0.007 | 0.046 | **0.059** | 0.059 | -0.010 | 0.051 | -0.007 |
| r1 HME | 0.017 | 0.050 | 0.020 | -0.008 | 0.014 | -0.004 | 0.036 | 0.057 | **0.038** | -0.008 | 0.037 | -0.004 |
| r2 HME | -0.160 | -0.146 | -0.191 | 0.030 | -0.187 | 0.024 | -0.187 | -0.196 | -0.229 | **0.030** | -0.207 | 0.022 |
| r3 HME | 0.024 | 0.055 | 0.030 | -0.006 | 0.025 | -0.003 | 0.046 | 0.067 | 0.054 | -0.006 | **0.049** | -0.003 |
| r4 HME | -0.142 | -0.131 | -0.169 | 0.029 | -0.166 | 0.022 | -0.169 | -0.178 | -0.206 | 0.028 | -0.186 | **0.020** |

Performance measures without acronym HME are estimated with OLS; HME, higher moment estimators; a, Jensen's alpha; r1, ratio1; r2, ratio2; r3, ratio3; r4, ratio4.

one exception in Table 13.7). These results tend to underline the importance of normalized risk-adjusted performance measures corrected for illiquidity and EIVs.

To emphasize the relative outperformance of *ratio2* and *ratio4*, we analyze the persistence of rank correlations between the two periods before and after (and during) the crisis. We report the Kendall rank correlation coefficients (all significant at 1%) without and with GLM adjustments, in Tables 13.16 and 13.17, respectively. Kendall rank correlations are significantly negative for four metrics: Jensen's alpha, IR, *ratio1*, and *ratio3*. On the other hand, correlation measures are significantly positive for *ratio2* and *ratio4* even if they are higher without GLM adjustment, as reported in Table 13.18. This table computes the difference between the correlation coefficients for unsmoothed (with GLM adjustment) performance measures and the correlation coefficients for smoothed performance measures (without GLM adjustment).

In this section, we have analyzed the persistence of six performance measures during two subperiods before and after the 2007–2008 financial crisis. Our different results tend to highlight the relative superiority of *ratio2* and *ratio4* to capture the performance of FoHFs during this perturbed transition period. These ratios are less sensitive to model estimation and inference changes than the other four measures. Before, during, and after the crisis *ratio2* and *ratio4* out-performed the other alternative measures, and offer promising applications and research avenues.

## CONCLUSION

The main objective of this chapter was to revisit performance measures in the hedge fund industry, focusing on a sample of FoHFs, after the 2007–2008 financial crisis. We used two subperiods before (from January 2000 to June 2007) and during and after the credit crisis (from July 2007 to April 2010). As performance measures are often developed to analyze the skill and the ability of portfolio managers to outperform, we follow Grinold's (1989) fundamental law of active management. We compare idiosyncratic risk to global risk based on multifactor models. Four metrics developed by Bodson *et al.* (2010a) and initially applied to mutual funds were good candidates for our sample of normalized and risk-adjusted FoHFs.

Moreover, to increase the relevance of our approach, we have added two features of hedge fund performance and risk: their illiquidity and the potential presence of EIVs in linear multifactor models usually used by this industry. We have applied a method to unsmooth returns and used the Dagenais and Dagenais' HME as a solution to EIVs.

Our results, based on Kendall rank correlations, have clearly highlighted the superiority and the relevance of *ratio2* and *ratio4* to capture specific risk of FoHFs returns for the two subperiods of our sample. These ratios outperform the other alternative measures, especially Jensen's alpha and the IR.

Both *ratio*2 and *ratio*4 exhibit significant value-added, and could shed new light on performance measurement in the hedge fund industry. It would be interesting to refine our interpretation of such measures in more global multifactor models, using more accurate econometrics techniques. We leave this promising avenue for future research.

# References

Agarwal, V., & Naik, N. (2004). Risk and Portfolio Decisions Involving Hedge Funds. *Review of Financial Studies, 17*(1), 63−98.

Bodson, L., Cavenaile, L., & Hübner, G. (2010a). *Normalized Risk-Adjusted Performance Measures Based on Multi-Factor Models.* Liege: Working Paper, HEC-ULg, Université de Liège.

Bodson, L., Coën, A., & Hübner, G. (2010b). Dynamic Hedge Fund Style Analysis with Errors-In-Variables. *Journal of Financial Research, 33*(3), 201−221.

Brockwell, P., & Davis, R. (1991). *Time Series: Theory and Methods* (2nd ed.). New York: Springer.

Brooks, C., & Kat, H. (2002). The Statistical Properties of Hedge Fund Index Returns and Their Implications for Investors. *Journal of Alternative Investments, 5*(2), 26−44.

Capocci, D., & Hübner, G. (2004). Analysis of Hedge Fund Performance. *Journal of Empirical Finance, 11*(1), 55−89.

Carmichael, B., & Coën, A. (2008). Asset Pricing Models with Errors-in-Variables. *Journal of Empirical Finance, 15*(4), 778−788.

Cavenaile, L., Coën, A., & Hübner, G. (2011). The Impact of Illiquidity and Higher Moments of Hedge Fund Returns on Their Risk-Adjusted Performance and Diversification Potential. *Journal of Alternative Investments, 13*(4), 9−29.

Coën, A., & Hübner, G. (2009). Risk and Performance Estimation in Hedge Funds Revisited: Evidence from Errors-In-Variables. *Journal of Empirical Finance, 16*(1), 112−125.

Coën, A., & Racicot, F. E. (2007). Capital Asset Pricing Models Revisited: Evidence from Errors in Variables. *Economics Letters, 95*(3), 443−450.

Cohen, K., Maier, S., Schwartz, R., & Whitcomb, D. (1979). On the Existence of Serial Correlation in an Efficient Securities Market. *TIMS Studies in Management Sciences, 11*, 151−168.

Dagenais, M. G., & Dagenais, D. I.. (1997). Higher Moment Estimators for Linear Regression Models with Errors in the Variables. *Journal of Econometrics, 76*(1-2), 193−221.

Fung, W., & Hsieh, D. A. (2001). The Risk in Hedge Fund Strategies: Theory and Evidence from Trend Followers. *Review of Financial Studies, 14*(1), 313−341.

Fung, W., Hsieh, D. A., Naik, N., & Ramodarai, T. (2008). Hedge Funds: Performance, Risk and Capital Formation. *Journal of Finance, 63*(4), 1777−1803.

Gallais, G., Hoang, T., & Nguyen, H. (2008). La Nécessité de Corriger les Rentabilités des Hedge Funds, Preuve Empirique et Méthode de Correction. *Banque et Marchés, 96*, 6−19.

Geltner, D. (1991). Smoothing in Appraised-Based Returns. *Journal of Real Estate Finance and Economics, 4*(3), 327−345.

Geltner, D. (1993). Estimating Market Values from Appraised Values without Assuming an Efficient Market. *Journal of Real Estate Research, 8*(3), 325−345.

Getmansky, M., Lo, A., & Makarov, I. (2004). An Econometric Model of Serial Correlation and Illiquidity in Hedge Fund Returns. *Journal of Financial Economics, 74*(3), 529−609.

Grinold, R. (1989). The Fundamental Law of Active Management. *Journal of Portfolio Management, 15*(3), 30−37.

Hausman, J. A. (1978). Specification Tests in Econometrics. *Econometrica, 46*, 1251−1271.

Kat, H., & Lu, S. (2002). *An Excursion into the Statistical Properties of Hedge Fund Returns.* Working Paper, ISMA Centre, University of Reading.

Liang, B. (1999). On the Performance of Hedge Fund. *Financial Analyst Journal, 55*(4), 72−85.

Lintner, J. (1965). The Valuation of Risk Assets and the Selection of Risky Investments in Stock Portfolios and Capital Budgets. *Review of Economics and Statistics, 47*(1), 13−37.

Lo, A. (2002). The Statistics of Sharpe Ratios. *Financial Analysts Journal, 58*(4), 36−52.

Modigliani, F., & Modigliani, L. (1997). Risk-Adjusted Performance. *Journal of Portfolio Management, 23*(2), 24–33.

Mossin, J. (1966). Equilibrium in a Capital Asset Market. *Econometrica* 768–783.

Okunev, J., & White, D. (2003). *Hedge Fund Risk Factors and Value at Risk of Credit Trading Strategies.* Sydney: Working Paper, University of New South Wales.

Roll, R. (1977). A Critique of the Asset Pricing Theory's Tests: Part I: On the Past and the Potential Testability of the Theory. *Journal of Financial Economics, 4*(2), 129–176.

Ross, S. A. (1976). The Arbitrage Theory and Capital Asset Pricing. *Journal of Economic Theory* 343–362.

Schneeweis, T., & Spurgin, R. (1998). Multifactor Analysis of Hedge Funds, Managed Futures and Mutual Fund Return and Risk Characteristics. *Journal of Alternative Investments, 2*(2), 83–87.

Sharpe, W. F. (1964). Capital Asset Prices: A Theory of Market Equilibrium under Conditions of Risk. *Journal of Finance, 19*(3), 425–442.

CHAPTER 14

# The Impact of the 2008 Financial Crisis on Funds of Hedge Funds

**Na Dai and Hany A. Shawky**
University at Albany, State University of New York, Albany, NY, USA

## 14.1. INTRODUCTION

Funds of hedge funds (FoHFs) assets under management (AUM) have fallen by almost a third since 2007, while direct investment in hedge funds has grown 1%. The number of FoHFs has fallen by a quarter and the value of their investments is still more than 10% below what it was in 2009, while the hedge fund industry has more or less recovered from the 2008 financial crisis. Industry consultants believe that FoHFs need to broaden their business model to remain relevant. Is the FoHFs industry facing a slow death as investors bypass their services and invest directly in hedge funds?

According to a hedge fund research investors are increasingly bypassing FoHFs and investing directly into hedge funds on account of a reduced additional layer of fees. The value of FoHFs total AUM at the end of 2011 had fallen 30%, from US$799 billion to US$564 billion, while hedge funds have staged a full recovery from the crisis. Since the start of the financial crisis, more than 800 FoHFs have been liquidated. The number of hedge funds has also fallen, but only fell by 9% during that same period.

Large minimum investments and costly due diligence for hedge funds makes it difficult for most investors to allocate capital to more than a few funds. Thus, investing in FoHFs is viewed by individual investors and institutional investors as one of the few ways that they can gain exposure to hedge funds without assuming excessive costs or risks. As a result, FoHFs continue to be important players in the hedge fund industry, managing an estimated 43% of the over US$2 trillion in total hedge fund assets.

Moreover, the ability of FoHFs managers to screen and monitor hedge fund managers also helps to attract investors. Aiken *et al.* (2012) find evidence to suggest that FoHFs do play an important role in monitoring their hedge fund investments and disinvesting from those funds that are likely to be poor performers in the future. They show that FoHFs may help investors avoid the most extreme risk in hedge fund investing, which is the 'blow-up' or left-tail risk. They further show that FoHFs select funds that are *ex ante* less likely to fail, thereby suggesting they are adding value through their due diligence process.

On the other hand, the preponderance of evidence suggests that FoHFs do not add value for their investors. Fung *et al.* (2008) find that while most studies document a significant alpha for hedge funds, they generally do not find significant alpha for FoHFs. Brown *et al.* (2004) find that FoHFs do not offer superior performance when compared to selecting a portfolio of hedge funds at random and suggest that their underperformance could be due to an excessive fee structure.

In the context of the hedge fund industry, Shawky *et al.* (2012) provide evidence of a significant relation between diversification and performance. Measuring diversification across four distinct dimensions, they find a significant positive relation between hedge fund performance and diversification across *sectors* and *asset classes*. However, diversification across *styles* and *geographies* exhibits a significant negative association with hedge fund returns.

The literature provides several arguments for the underperformance of FoHFs. For instance, Brown *et al.* (2004) show that the costs charged by FoHFs in providing diversification, oversight, and access come at the cost of increased fees paid by investors. As a result, the performance of individual hedge funds dominates the performance of FoHFs on an after-fee return basis. Brown *et al.* (2008) suggest that since a standard operational due diligence report costs about US$12 500 on a per fund basis, the larger the number of underlying funds, the larger the cost to the FoHF. In a more recent paper, Brown *et al.* (2012) argue that FoHFs are in general overdiversified. They measure diversification as the number of underlying hedge fund managers in a FoHFs as reported by the BarclayHedge database. While on average, FoHFs invest in more than 20 underlying funds, Brown *et al.* (2012) show that on the basis of performance alone, an optimal degree of diversification may be in the range of 10–12 underlying hedge funds.

Failure risk is another hedge fund characteristic that has received a great deal of attention in the recent literature. As documented by Brown *et al.* (1999), Liang (2000), Agarwal and Naik (2000, 2004), and Kosowski *et al.* (2007), the failure risk in the hedge fund industry is high and rather persistent. Moreover, Kim (2008) examines failure risk in the hedge fund industry, and finds that hedge funds and FoHFs fail as poor performance over an extended period of time (typically 6–9 months) leads to significant withdrawals by investors.

Given the significant recent downsizing and the slow recovery of the FoHFs industry, there is increasing doubt from investors about the benefits of investing in FoHFs accompanied by a heated debate on the fate of the FoHFs industry in the future. In this chapter, we examine the performance of FoHFs, its relation to fund size and level of diversification, the risk of FoHFs, and the determinants of survival before and after the financial crisis. Through such a comparison, we aim to shed some light on what has happened to the FoHFs industry during the financial crisis and what we can learn from these changes.

## 14.2. DATA AND SAMPLE STATISTICS

We obtain FoHFs data from Lipper TASS hedge fund database. To address survivorship bias (e.g., see Liang, 1999, 2001; Agarwal and Jorion, 2010), our sample includes both live and dead FoHFs, from March 2004 to December 2010. To avoid backfill bias, we follow the convention of excluding the first 18 monthly observations for each fund (Fung and Hsieh, 2009). Table 14.1 provides summary statistics for the FoHFs sample for both the pre-crisis period (March 2004 to July 2007) and the post-crisis period (August 2007 to December 2010).

**Table 14.1**   Summary Statistics for Pre- and Post-2008 Financial Crisis

| | Pre-Crisis (FoHFs n = 5703) | | Post-Crisis (FoHFs n = 5338) | | Difference | |
|---|---|---|---|---|---|---|
| | Mean | Median | Mean | Median | in Mean | in Median |
| Average AUM (US$ million) | 172.90 | 28.40 | 174.80 | 28.70 | 1.90 | 0.30 |
| Average monthly return (%) | 0.36 | 0.39 | −0.54 | −0.29 | −0.90*** | −0.68*** |
| Average monthly excess return (%) | 0.18 | 0.18 | −0.67 | −0.42 | −0.85*** | −0.60*** |
| Standard deviation of monthly excess return (%) | 2.03 | 1.58 | 3.10 | 2.61 | 1.07*** | 1.03*** |
| Seven-factor alpha | 0.03 | 0.15 | −0.29 | 0.25 | −0.32* | 0.10*** |
| IR | 0.17 | 0.11 | −0.03 | −0.17 | −0.20*** | −0.28*** |
| Average management fees | 1.35 | 1.50 | 1.35 | 1.50 | 0.00 | 0.00 |
| Average incentive fees | 7.42 | 10.00 | 7.24 | 10.00 | −0.18 | 0.00 |

Summary statistics on the various performance measures for FoHFs during the post-crisis period, August 2007–December 2010, and the pre-crisis period, March 2004–July 2007. Differences in the performance measures and other FoHFs characteristics are reported in the last column. Asterisks denote coefficient significant at the *10, and ***1% levels, respectively.

We utilize three different measures of performance in our analysis: the average monthly excess returns, the Fung and Hsieh (2004) seven-factor alpha, and the information ratio (IR) estimated using risk-free rates and the benchmark index. Excess return is calculated as the difference between FoHFs monthly raw returns and risk-free rates.

The Fung and Hsieh seven-factor alpha is estimated with the following model:

$$r_t^i = \alpha^i + \sum_{k=1}^{K} \beta_k^i F_{k,t} + \varepsilon_{i,t}, \tag{14.1}$$

where $r_t^i$ is the excess return (in excess of the risk-free rate) on fund $i$ for month $t$, $\alpha^i$ is the abnormal performance of fund $i$ over the regression time period, $\beta_k^i$ is the factor loading of fund $i$ on factor $k$ during the regression period, $F_{k,t}$ is the return for factor $k$ for month $t$, and $\varepsilon_{i,t}$ is the error term. The Fung and Hsieh (2004) seven-factor model has shown strong explanatory power of the variation in hedge fund returns.[1] The estimated intercept $\hat{\alpha}^i$ is the alpha performance measure or the abnormal performance of fund $i$ over the regression time period.

The IR is a performance measure that is particularly useful as we compare FoHFs with varying degrees of leverage and different diversification strategies. Agarwal and Naik (2000) show that unlike the alpha measure, the IR is invariant to leverage. The IR measures performance relative to an appropriate benchmark. In particular, we calculate the information ratio as:

$$IR_t^i = \frac{E[R_t^i - R_t^b]}{\sigma[R_t^i - R_t^b]}. \tag{14.2}$$

where $R_t^i$ and $R_t^b$ denote the returns on FoHFs $i$ and the benchmark index.

The data in Table 14.1 reveals some important statistics. For every performance measure used, we find that FoHFs performance suffered significantly during the crisis. For instance, based on average excess returns, Fung–Hsieh seven-factor alpha, and IR, FoHFs significantly underperformed during the post-crisis period relative to the pre-crisis period. Furthermore, the standard deviation of monthly returns during the post-crisis period is significantly higher than for the pre-crisis period. Interestingly, however, we find that the average AUM per fund did not change significantly, and the management fees and the incentive fees did not change at all. Consistent with Aiken *et al.* (2012), it must be the case that investors look for reasons other than performance to invest or remain with FoHFs.

---

[1]The Fung and Hsieh factors are the S&P 500 return minus the risk-free rate (*SNPMRF*), the Wilshire small cap minus the large cap return (*SCMLC*), the change in the constant maturity yield of the 10-Year Treasury (*BD10RET*), the change in the spread of Moody's Baa minus the 10-Year Treasury (*BAAMTSY*), the bond PTFS (*PTFSBD*), the currency PTFS (*PTFSFX*), and the commodities PTFS (*PTFSCOM*), where PTFS denotes primitive trend-following strategy.

| Table 14.2 | Changes in AUM of FoHFs by Size Quintile Pre- and Post-2008 Financial Crisis | | |
|---|---|---|---|
| **AUM** | **Pre-Crisis** | **Post-Crisis** | **Difference** |
| Smallest Quintile | 1.9 | 2.9 | 1.0*** |
| Q2 | 11.0 | 11.4 | 0.4* |
| Q3 | 29.3 | 30.5 | 1.3*** |
| Q4 | 75.7 | 77.8 | 2.0 |
| Largest Quintile | 615.0 | 624.0 | 8.9 |

Average AUM (in millions of 2010 US$) for FoHFs by asset size quintiles during the post-crisis period, August 2007–December 2010, and the pre-crisis period, March 2004–July 2007. Differences between pre- and post-crisis period are reported in last the column. Asterisks denote coefficient significant at the *10, and ***1% levels, respectively.

## 14.3. CHANGES IN AUM DURING THE 2008 FINANCIAL CRISIS

In order to explore investor reaction to FoHFs performance during the crisis, we first examine the changes in average AUM that occurred during the crisis. Specifically, we compare average assets held by FoHFs pre- and post-2008 financial crisis for each of the five size quintiles. Table 14.2 presents these comparisons and shows a number of important characteristics for the FoHFs industry. First, average AUM in every size quintile is actually higher after the crisis than before the crisis. Given what has been documented in the literature, i.e., that aggregate FoHFs assets actually declined significantly during the 2008 financial crisis, it is clear that as funds liquidated, some of that capital flowed into other surviving funds, thus raising the average assets managed per fund for the industry. Another possible reason is that small FoHFs are more likely to fail during the financial crisis (as is confirmed in our survival analysis), the surviving funds therefore being larger in size.

## 14.4. ASSET SIZE AND FoHFs PERFORMANCE DURING THE 2008 FINANCIAL CRISIS

Given the overall poor performance of FoHFs during the crisis period, we now explore if such performance was in any way related to fund size. Unlike the documented evidence available on the diseconomies of scale for hedge funds, there is some evidence to suggest that economies of scale may actually exist for FoHFs, at least during the financial crisis period. For a closer look at the characteristics of FoHFs based on their asset size, we sort the FoHFs sample into quintiles based on their AUM. Table 14.3 reports the performance results (excess monthly returns, seven-factor alpha, and IR) for each of the five size quintiles before and after the financial crisis, respectively.

Consistent with Table 14.1, the estimates in Table 14.3 show that the performance of FoHFs was negatively impacted during the financial crisis. For all three

**Table 14.3** Performance of FoHFs by Size Quintiles Pre- and Post-2008 Financial Crisis

| AUM Pre-Crisis | Average Monthly Excess Return (%) | | | Seven-Factor Alpha (%) | | | IR | | |
|---|---|---|---|---|---|---|---|---|---|
| | Pre-Crisis | Post-Crisis | Difference | Pre-Crisis | Post-Crisis | Difference | Pre-Crisis | Post-Crisis | Difference |
| Smallest | −0.013 | −0.736 | −0.723*** | −0.325 | −1.805 | −1.481*** | 0.289 | 0.115 | −0.174 |
| 2 | 0.070 | −0.805 | −0.875*** | −0.543 | −0.328 | 0.215 | 0.146 | −0.064 | −0.209*** |
| 3 | 0.193 | −0.678 | −0.871*** | 0.177 | −0.241 | −0.401* | 0.180 | −0.085 | −0.265*** |
| 4 | 0.295 | −0.725 | −1.019*** | 0.274 | 0.234 | −0.040 | 0.253 | −0.076 | −0.329*** |
| Largest | 0.364 | −0.687 | −1.051*** | 0.395 | 0.189 | −0.206 | 0.275 | −0.065 | −0.339*** |
| Difference | 0.377*** | 0.049 | | 0.720*** | 1.994*** | | −0.014 | −0.180 | |

Performance comparisons for FoHFs by asset size quintiles during the post-crisis period, August 2007−December 2010, and the pre-crisis period, March 2004−July 2007. The performance measures used are the average monthly returns, the seven-factor alpha, and the IR. Differences in performance between pre- and post-crisis periods are reported for each quintile. Asterisks denote coefficient significant at the *10, and ***1% levels, respectively.

performance measures, within every size quintile, FoHFs performance after the crisis was significantly lower than their performance before the crisis. More significantly however, when we measure performance on a risk-adjusted basis using the Fung–Hsieh seven-factor alpha, we find that large FoHFs performed better than small funds both in the pre-crisis period and in the post-crisis period. Indeed, a significant difference between pre- and post-crisis performance is only found for small funds, suggesting that large funds may have been able to weather the crisis better than small funds.

To provide further robustness to our time-series performance estimates, we also employ a cross-sectional regression approach in which we incorporate other FoHFs characteristics to assess performance during the crisis. Table 14.4 presents cross-sectional regression estimates of the relationship between the three performance measures, excess returns, seven-factor alpha, and IR, along with other FoHFs characteristics (AUM, management and incentive fee, leverage, etc.) over the period March 2004–December 2010. The key independent variable of interest in this section is the Post-Crisis Dummy, which is equal to 1 if the performance is estimated during the post-crisis period, and 0 otherwise. More-over, we incorporate an interaction term between the Post-Crisis Dummy and AUM to capture the difference in the impact of size on fund performance before and after the crisis.

**Table 14.4**   FoHFs Performance and Fund Characteristics Pre- and Post-2008 Financial Crisis

| Variables | Excess Return (1) | Excess Return (2) | Alpha (3) | Alpha (4) | IR (5) | IR (6) |
|---|---|---|---|---|---|---|
| Post-crisis | −0.955*** | −0.114 | −0.005* | −0.036*** | −0.271*** | 0.171 |
| | (0.029) | (0.214) | (0.002) | (0.017) | (0.055) | (0.401) |
| Ln(AUM) | 0.028*** | 0.052*** | 0.002*** | 0.001 | −0.005 | 0.008 |
| | (0.006) | (0.009) | (0.001) | (0.001) | (0.012) | (0.016) |
| Post-crisis * Ln(AUM) | | −0.050*** | | 0.002* | | −0.026 |
| | | (0.013) | | (0.001) | | (0.024) |
| Management fee | −0.031 | −0.031 | 0.001 | 0.001 | −0.138*** | −0.138*** |
| | (0.021) | (0.021) | (0.002) | (0.002) | (0.039) | (0.039) |
| Incentive fee | 0.009*** | 0.009*** | 0.000 | 0.000 | 0.004 | 0.004 |
| | (0.002) | (0.002) | (0.000) | (0.000) | (0.004) | (0.004) |
| Leverage | 0.023 | 0.023 | 0.001 | 0.001 | −0.045 | −0.045 |
| | (0.031) | (0.031) | (0.003) | (0.003) | (0.058) | (0.058) |
| Constant | −0.357*** | −0.765*** | −0.032*** | −0.016 | 0.428*** | 0.213 |
| | (0.111) | (0.151) | (0.009) | (0.012) | (0.207) | (0.283) |
| Observations | 7598 | 7598 | 7598 | 7598 | 7574 | 7574 |
| Adjusted $R^2$ | 0.129 | 0.131 | 0.002 | 0.002 | 0.004 | 0.004 |

Cross-sectional regression estimates of the relationship between the three performance measures, excess returns, seven-factor alpha, and the IR and FoHFs characteristics over the period March 2004–December 2010. Dummy variables are used to estimate the post-crisis effect. For each of the performance measures, the second regression model incorporates an interaction term between AUM and the post-crisis period. Asterisks denote coefficient significant at the *10, and ***1% levels, respectively.

The cross-sectional regression estimates of the performance of FoHFs in Table 14.4 are consistent with our earlier time-series results (in Table 14.3). In all six models, FoHFs performance declined significantly after the 2008 financial crisis. When Excess Return is used as the performance measure in models 1 and 2, asset size also plays an important role. In model 1, despite the fact that all funds performed significantly lower in the post-crisis periods, large funds performed better, or at least less poorly, than small funds. Model 2 incorporates an interaction term to capture the difference in the impact of size on performance. The significance of the interaction term indicates that indeed the impact of size on excess return is smaller during the post-crisis period than in the pre-crisis period.

Columns 3 and 4 provide regression results using the Fung–Hsieh seven-factor alpha as the dependent variables. Once again we find that FoHFs performance declined significantly after the crisis and that asset size has a significantly positive effect on the seven-factor alpha. However, when we include the interaction term, the significance of asset size disappears and we observe a significantly positive coefficient on the interaction term. This result suggests that asset size has a greater impact (which is positive) on risk-adjusted alpha during the post-crisis period. The last two columns provide consistent performance estimates for the IR with respect to the crisis. More importantly, unlike other performance measures, we find that management fees are negative and significant for both pre- and post-crisis periods. This suggests that for the FoHFs segment of the industry, management fees represent a significant drag on the performance of FoHFs.

## 14.5. DIVERSIFICATION AND FoHFs PERFORMANCE DURING THE 2008 FINANCIAL CRISIS

The high diversification quintile represents the diversified funds, while the low diversification quintile represents the less diversified or specialized types of funds. We measure FoHFs diversification as the total number of foci, along three dimensions including asset class, sector, and investment approach.[2] As the number of foci increase, the fund is more diversified. TASS updates their data on a monthly basis, overwriting previous cross-sectional focus or diversification data with recent information. Given the nature of the focus variables, our analysis examines the cross-sectional effect of diversification on hedge fund performance. These cross-sectional focus variables are recorded in the year 2010 and for our purposes we take these characteristics as constant over the estimation periods.[3] To ensure that the number of foci identified by individual hedge funds accurately reflect the degree of diversification in that category, it is necessary to modify how we measure three of

---

[2]We exclude geographical focus as it provides a relatively unreliable measure of geographic diversification given the US-centric nature of the FoHF sample.

[3]To examine the robustness of this assumption, we examined the consistency of the focus variables across the years 2008, 2009, and 2010. We found that the consistency of the focus variables in the data between these consecutive years is 98% and 97%, respectively.

| | Table 14.5 | Performance of FoHFs by Diversification Level (Number of Foci) Pre- and Post-2008 Financial Crisis |

| | Average Monthly Excess Return (%) | | | Seven-Factor Alpha (%) | | | IR | | |
|---|---|---|---|---|---|---|---|---|---|
| Quintile | Pre-Crisis | Post-Crisis | Difference | Pre-Crisis | Post-Crisis | Difference | Pre-Crisis | Post-Crisis | Difference |
| Lowest | 0.237 | −0.571 | −0.808*** | 0.023 | −0.121 | −0.144 | 0.195 | 0.150 | −0.045 |
| 2 | 0.134 | −0.766 | −0.900*** | 0.191 | −1.571 | −1.762*** | 0.108 | −0.135 | −0.243*** |
| 3 | 0.175 | −0.743 | −0.918*** | 0.093 | 0.042 | −0.051 | 0.315 | 0.026 | −0.289 |
| 4 | 0.140 | −0.663 | −0.803*** | 0.027 | −0.271 | −0.298 | 0.072 | −0.141 | −0.213*** |
| Highest | 0.178 | −0.642 | −0.820*** | −0.134 | −0.117 | 0.017 | 0.110 | −0.108 | −0.218*** |
| Difference | −0.059 | −0.071 | | −0.157 | 0.004 | | −0.085 | −0.258*** | |

Performance comparisons for FoHFs by level of diversification (number of foci) during the post-crisis period, August 2007–December 2010, and the pre-crisis period, March 2004–July 2007. The performance measures used are the average monthly returns, the seven-factor alpha, and the IR. Differences in performance between pre- and post-crisis periods are reported for each quintile. Asterisks denote coefficient significant at the ***1% levels.

the variables in the TASS database. Specifically, we reclassify the variable listed as 'Diversified' within both the sector focus category and the investment approach category and the variable listed as 'Multistrategy' in the investment focus category so that instead of giving it a value of 1, it is given a number equal to the maximum value reported by all other funds for that category.[4]

Table 14.5 presents performance estimates for pre- and post-2008 crisis periods broken down by quintiles based on their level of diversification. As before, FoHFs performance is significantly lower post the 2008 financial crisis. With the exception of performance based on the Fung–Hsieh seven-factor alpha, there do not appear to be any significant differences in performance based on the diversification quintiles.[5] However, for the seven-factor alpha performance measure, there is some evidence to suggest that less diversified funds performed worse than more diversified funds. More diversified FoHFs may have been able to weather the crisis better than the highly specialized and less diversified FoHFs.

## 14.6. RISK FACTOR ESTIMATES OF FoHFs PRE- AND POST-2008 FINANCIAL CRISIS

We measure the risk profile of FoHFs using the seven-factor betas estimated from the Fung and Hsieh (2004) model. Table 14.6 presents estimates of the risk

---

[4]We verified the appropriateness of these variable reclassifications by examining individual fund characteristics with such classifications. For all the funds for which we were able to obtain further information, the fund characteristics were far more consistent with the reclassified values of these three variables. Further, we also used mean value instead of the maximum value as a replacement in additional robustness checks. The results are qualitatively similar.
[5]While Dai and Shawky (2012) show that more diversified FoHFs outperformed less diversified funds prior to 2008, it is likely that the diversification effect on performance was totally dominated by the underperformance of FoHFs during the 2008 financial crisis.

| Table 14.6 | FoHFs Risk Profiles Pre- and Post-2008 Financial Crisis | | |
|---|---|---|---|
| **Beta** | **Pre-Crisis** | **Post Crisis** | **Difference** |
| *Market* | 0.065 | 0.260 | 0.195*** |
| *Size* | 0.182 | −0.278 | −0.460*** |
| *Credit Spread* | −0.052 | −0.086 | −0.034* |
| *Bond Term* | 0.047 | −0.098 | −0.145*** |
| *PTFSBD* | −0.004 | −0.053 | −0.049*** |
| *PTFSFX* | 0.013 | 0.024 | 0.011*** |
| *PTFSCOM* | 0.008 | −0.021 | −0.029*** |

Factor beta estimates for FoHFs during the post-crisis period, August 2007–December 2010, and the pre-crisis period, March 2004–July 2007. Factor betas are estimated following the Fung and Hsieh (2004) seven-factor model. Asterisks denote coefficient significant at the *10, and ***1% levels respectively.

profile of FoHFs for both the pre- and the post-2008 financial crisis periods. The estimates in Table 14.6 reveal several important observations regarding the risk profile of FoHFs during the crisis. (i) All of the seven risk factors for FoHFs changed significantly during the 2008 financial crisis. (ii) The market or systematic risk factor significantly increased as a result of the crisis. This result is consistent with the notion that during severe crisis, all assets move in the same direction and asset diversification becomes far less effective than in normal market conditions. (iii) The size factor may have become more significant during the crisis. It is possible that larger funds were able to weather the 2008 liquidity crisis slightly better than smaller funds. This may be due to the more diversified sources of capital (individual and institutions) as well as more access to bank lines of credit. Both the credit risk and the term risk appeared to have significantly contributed to the negative FoHFs performance during the crisis period. The foreign exchange and commodity risk factors also contributed to the poor performance of FoHFs during the crisis, but to a much lesser extent than market, asset size, and bond risk.

## 14.7. ATTRITION RATES AND FoHFs SURVIVAL ANALYSIS

Finally, we examine whether attrition rates and the probability of survival for FoHFs have significantly changed around the 2008 crisis period. We first examine the attrition rates over the period 2004–2010. Attrition rates are defined as the ratio of funds exiting in a given year to the sum of the number of existing funds at the start of the year plus the new entries in a given year. As expected, attrition rates increased substantially after the 2008 financial crisis, with 2009 marking the highest attrition rate recorded for FoHFs. Over the period 2007–2010, the total number of funds declined from 4099 to 3142 − a decline of over 23% (Table 14.7).

We then apply the Cox proportional hazards regressions for the pre-crisis 2004–2007 period and the post-crisis 2007–2010 period. The dependent variable is the probability of failure, which reflects the chance of any fund being

| Table 14.7 | Frequency Counts of Entries and Exits of FoHFs (2004–2010) | | | | |
|---|---|---|---|---|---|
| Year | Existing Funds | New Entries | New Exits | Total Funds | Attrition Rate (%) |
| 2004 | 2075 | 657 | 47 | 2685 | 1.72 |
| 2005 | 2685 | 626 | 121 | 3190 | 3.65 |
| 2006 | 3190 | 668 | 132 | 3726 | 3.42 |
| 2007 | 3726 | 599 | 226 | 4099 | 5.23 |
| 2008 | 4099 | 528 | 785 | 3842 | 16.97 |
| 2009 | 3842 | 449 | 860 | 3431 | 20.04 |
| 2010 | 3431 | 219 | 508 | 3142 | 13.92 |

Annual frequency counts of entries and exits of FoHFs during the period from 2004 to 2010. Attrition rates are defined as the ratio of funds exiting in a given year to the sum of the number of existing funds at the start of the year and the new entries in a given year.

| Table 14.8 | Cox Proportional Hazard Analysis Pre- and Post-2008 Financial Crisis | |
|---|---|---|
| | **Pre-Crisis** | **Post-Crisis** |
| Excess return | 0.542*** | 0.707*** |
| | (0.066) | (0.011) |
| Ln(AUM) | 0.867*** | 0.823*** |
| | (0.020) | (0.009) |
| Management fee | 0.820*** | 0.919*** |
| | (0.064) | (0.034) |
| Incentive fee | 1.038*** | 1.016*** |
| | (0.007) | (0.004) |
| Leverage | 0.946 | 0.852*** |
| | (0.112) | (0.047) |
| Beta | | |
| *Market* | 1.002 | 0.720*** |
| | (0.010) | (0.041) |
| *Size* | 0.989 | 0.908*** |
| | (0.007) | (0.040) |
| *Credit Spread* | 2.445*** | 1.525*** |
| | (0.567) | (0.162) |
| *Bond Term* | 0.516*** | 0.617*** |
| | (0.077) | (0.030) |
| *PTFSBD* | 9.396*** | 1.197 |
| | (5.807) | (0.230) |
| *PTFSFX* | 0.001*** | 3.283*** |
| | (0.002) | (1.089) |
| *PTFSCOM* | 0.000*** | 0.681 |
| | (0.000) | (0.208) |
| No. of observations | 3180 | 3556 |
| No. of failures | 326 | 1463 |

Analysis on the factors that contribute to FoHFs failure during the pre-crisis period, March 2004 to July 2007, and the post-crisis period, August 2007 to December 2010. Hazard ratios and standard errors are reported. Asterisks denote coefficient significant at the ***1% levels.

a dead fund by the end of the period. Early studies on hedge funds regard moving to the graveyard fund database as failure because such funds on average have poor performance (see Gregoriou *et al.*, 2003; Malkiel and Saha, 2005). Recent studies point out that 'graveyard' may be a misnomer because funds can be included in the graveyard fund database for reasons other than liquidation, such as funds that stop reporting, unable to contact, closed to new investment, merged into another fund, and dormant funds. These studies (e.g., Getmansky *et al.*, 2004; Baquero *et al.*, 2005) use the drop reason codes provided by TASS and regard only liquidated funds in the graveyard as failed funds.

We conduct survival analysis by defining a dead fund as one that has been liquidated according to TASS. Our primary independent variable is the FoHFs Excess Return and Fund Size. We also control for other fund characteristics such as the incentive structure, leverage as well as betas estimated with the Fung-Hsieh seven-factor model. The estimates are presented in Table 14.8. To simplify the interpretation of the results, we report the hazard ratios rather than the coefficients.

Consistent with the existing literature, the estimates in Table 14.8 show that performance is an important determinant of fund survival. We further show that larger funds are more likely to survive than smaller funds, which is robust for both of the time periods examined. We also find some evidence to suggest that higher incentive fees may encourage risk-taking behavior, which is indicated by a higher probability of failure. Further, increases in leverage and market risk are found to increase the probability of failure, while term risk, foreign exchange risk, and commodity risk are not significant factors in predicting FoHFs failure.

## CONCLUSION

This chapter examines the performance of FoHFs before and after the 2008 financial crisis. We investigate the impact this crisis had on the level and the distribution of AUM within the industry. We further explore if asset diversification among individual FoHFs had any significant effect on performance during the crisis.

Using the Lipper TASS hedge fund database (both live funds and graveyard funds), we extract monthly returns and AUM data over the period March 2004–December 2010. The pre-crisis period examined is March 2004–July 2007 and the post-crisis period August 2007–December 2010. We apply both a quintile ranking methodology and regression analysis to examine our research questions.

Our main findings in this study show that FoHFs performance was severely impacted by the crisis and that in general, large funds suffered less than small funds. Diversification as measured by increased number of foci was not a major factor in preventing poor performance, but to some extent, more diversified funds performed slightly better than less diversified funds during the crisis period. The remarkably high attrition rate for FoHFs during and after the crisis suggests that they were not sufficiently agile to be able to effectively respond to the severe liquidity shortages that were characteristic of the 2008 financial crisis.

# References

Agarwal, R. K., & Jorion, P. (2010). Hidden Survivorship in Hedge Fund Returns. *Financial Analyst Journal, 66*, 69–74.

Agarwal, V., & Naik, N. Y. (2000). Multi-period Performance Persistence Analysis of Hedge Funds. *Journal of Financial and Quantitative Analysis, 53*, 327–342.

Agarwal, V., & Naik, N. Y. (2004). Risk and Portfolio Decisions Involving Hedge Funds. *Review of Financial Studies, 17*, 63–98.

Aiken, A., Clifford, C. P., & Ellis, J. (2012). *Do Fund of Hedge Funds Add Value? Evidence from their holdings.* Working Paper, Quinnipiac University.

Baquero, G., ter Horst, J. R., & Verbeek, M. (2005). Survival, Look Ahead Bias and the Persistence in Hedge Fund Performance. *Journal of Financial and Quantitative Analysis, 40*, 493–518.

Brown, S., Goetzmann, W., & Ibbotson, R. (1999). Offshore Hedge Funds: Survival and Performance, 1989–95. *Journal of Business, 72*, 91–117.

Brown, S., Goetzmann, W., & Liang, B. (2004). Fees on Fees in Funds of Funds. *Journal of Investment Management, 2*(4), 39–56.

Brown, S., Fraser, T., & Liang, B. (2008). Hedge Fund Due Diligence: a Source of Alpha in a Hedge Fund Portfolio Strategy. *Journal of Investment Management, 6*, 23–33.

Brown, S., Gregoriou, G., & Pascalau, R. (2012). Diversification in Funds of Hedge Funds: Is it Possible to Overdiversify? *Review of Asset Pricing Studies, 2*(1), 89–110.

Dai, N., & Shawky, H. (2012). Diversification Strategies and the Performance of Funds of hedge funds. *Journal of Alternative Investments, 15*, 75–85.

Fung, W., & Hsieh, D. (2004). Hedge Fund Benchmarks: A Risk Based Approach. *Financial Analyst Journal, 60*, 65–80.

Fung, W., & Hsieh, D. A. (2009). Measurement Biases in Hedge Fund Performance Data: an Update. *Financial Analyst Journal, 65*, 36–38.

Fung, W., Hsieh, D., Naik, N., & Ramadorai, T. (2008). Hedge Funds: Performance, Risk, and Capital Formation. *Journal of Finance, 63*, 1777–1803.

Getmansky, M., Lo, A., & Makarov, I. (2004). An Econometric Model of Serial Correlation and Illiquidity of Hedge Fund Returns. *Journal of Financial Economics, 74*, 529–610.

Gregoriou, G. N., Karavas, V., & Rouah, F. (Eds.) (2003). *Hedge Funds: Strategies, Risk Assessment and Returns.* Baltimore, MD: Beard Books.

Kim, J. (2008). *Failure risk and the cross-section of hedge fund returns. Working Paper.* Columbus, OH: Ohio State University.

Kosowski, R., Naik, N., & Teo, M. (2007). Do Hedge Funds Deliver Alpha? A Bayesian and Bootstrap Analysis. *Journal of Financial Economics, 84*, 229–264.

Liang, B. (1999). On the Performance of Hedge Funds. *Financial Analyst Journal, 55*, 72–85.

Liang, B. (2000). Hedge Funds: the Living and the Dead. *Journal of Financial and Quantitative Analysis, 35*, 309–327.

Liang, B. (2001). Hedge Fund Performance: 1990–1999. *Financial Analyst Journal, 57*, 11–18.

Malkiel, B., & Saha, A. (2005). Hedge Funds: Risk and Return. *Financial Analyst Journal, 15*, 80–88.

Shawky, H., Dai, N., & Cumming, D. (2012). Diversification in the Hedge Fund Industry. *Journal of Corporate Finance, 18*, 166–178.

## CHAPTER 15

# Forecasting Funds of Hedge Funds Performance: A Markov Regime-Switching Approach

**Szabolcs Blazsek**
School of Business, Universidad Francisco Marroquín, Guatemala

## 15.1. INTRODUCTION

Several papers in the finance literature have investigated the performance of funds of hedge funds (FoHFs). It has been reported that, at least, three advantages of investing in FoHFs are as follows:

- They are diversified since they represent investments in several funds.
- Due diligence: a detailed review of their operation and management is offered to investors.
- They require lower initial investments as hedge funds.

One of the drawbacks of FoFHs, however, is that they may have high management and performance fees, decreasing realized returns.[1] Moreover, it has been reported that returns on FoHFs and hedge funds may be persistent, and therefore historical returns may provide information to forecast future fund performance (e.g., Gregoriou, 2003; Gregoriou *et al.*, 2007; Abdou and Nasereddin, 2011; Jordan and Simlai, 2011; Laube *et al.*, 2011).

In this chapter, we focus on forecasting the performance of FoHFs indices. We compare out-of-sample and multistep ahead forecasts of the performance of five FoHFs indices and 15 hedge fund indices over the period January 2000–March 2012. Index performance is defined as excess return above the MSCI Global Equity market index. Out-of-sample forecasts are computed using data collected from Hedge Fund Research (HFR) for the period January 1990–March 2012. To forecast, we use a large number of competing econometric specifications. These models are: $AR(p)$, $AR(p)$-$GARCH(1,1)$, $MS$-$AR(p)$, $MS$-$AR(p)$-$GARCH(1,1)$, and $MS$-$AR(p)$-$MS$-$GARCH(1,1)$ specifications with $p = 1, ..., 12$ lags. Consideration of the AR (autoregressive) model with several lags is motivated by Pesaran and Timmermann (2004), who show that AR models frequently produce smaller forecast errors than models with more complicated non-linear dynamics or with additional explanatory variables. The MS (Markov-switching) formulation is motivated by Billio *et al.* (2006, 2009) and Blazsek and Downarowicz (2012), who find significant regime-switching dynamics in hedge fund returns. We use the GARCH (generalized autoregressive conditional heteroscedasticity) model, since it is widely applied for modeling volatility in the literature (e.g., Donaldson and Kamstra, 1997; Dunis *et al.*, 2003; Hansen and Lunde, 2005; Preminger *et al.*, 2006; Muzzioli, 2010). Out-of-sample forecasts are estimated by a moving time window approach. The first time window is set for January 1990–December 1999. Then, we extend the time window by adding one more observation and re-estimate all models to forecast fund performance for the subsequent months of 2000. We repeat this approach until out-of-sample forecasts are obtained for each month over the period January 2000–March 2012. Multistep ahead forecasts are provided for the 1-, 3-, 6-, 9-, and 12-month time horizons. The number of specifications used for forecasting is 20 indices × 5 models × 12 AR lags = 1200. We perform diagnostic tests for each model and we forecast only by correctly specified models. Since for each specification there are five different forecast horizons, there may be 1200 × 5 horizons = 6000 out-of-sample forecasts. Forecast accuracy is measured by the root mean squared error (RMSE) loss function. We break down the full forecasting period of January 2000–March 2012 to pre-crisis, crisis, and post-crisis subperiods. RMSEs of different indices are compared in the full forecasting period, as well as in the three subperiods. Moreover, the RMSE of each index is compared among the

---

[1]See Gregoriou and Rouah (2002), Gregoriou (2003), Gregoriou *et al.* (2007), Brown *et al.* (2008), Abdou and Nasereddin (2011), Jordan and Simlai (2011), Laube *et al.* (2011), and Brown *et al.* (2012).

three subperiods. We apply the Diebold—Mariano (DM) (Diebold and Mariano, 1995) of predictive accuracy to see if forecast precision differences are significant.

We find that (i) FoHFs have significant regime-switching dynamics and (ii) the lowest RMSE model is an MS specification for several FoHFs. These results motivate the following question that may be interesting for practitioners: what drives the regime-switching dynamics of FoHFs? To answer, we apply an endogenous switching AR model, where the transition probability of regimes is formulated according to a probit specification. The estimation results of this model identify specific factors driving FoHFs regimes. To the best of our knowledge, MS models with endogenous switching have not been applied yet in the hedge fund literature.

The remaining part of this chapter is organized as follows. Section 15.2 reviews the database applied, provides a data description, and analyzes FoHFs excess return drivers. Section 15.3 gives a brief overview of the econometric models applied. Section 15.4 presents out-of-sample forecasting and model diagnostic procedures, out-of-sample forecasting precision results, out-of-sample forecast accuracy tests, and in-sample determinants of FoHFs regimes. This is followed by the conclusion. Additional figures showing the probability of regimes for exogenous switching and endogenous switching models are presented in Figure 15.A1 in the Appendix.

## 15.2. DATA
### 15.2.1. FoHFs and the Hedge Fund Database

Similarly to Agarwal and Naik (2000), Jagannathan *et al.* (2010), and Blazsek and Downarowicz (2012), we use FoHFs and hedge fund index data obtained from HFR. HFR Monthly Indices (HFRI) are equally weighted performance indices, which are used as benchmarks in the hedge fund industry. As HFR data contain information on when funds actually joined the database, they are corrected for backfill bias. See Ackermann *et al.* (1999) and Brown *et al.* (1999) about backfill bias. Moreover, the HFR database is constructed so as to account for survivorship bias, since if a fund closes, then the fund's last reported performance will be included in the HFRI. Fung and Hsieh (1997) provide a discussion on survivorship bias. Finally, Fung and Hsieh (2000) suggest that data biases may be less severe for FoHF data. They suggest using data on FoHFs, arguing that FoHFs returns are a more accurate representation of the returns earned by hedge fund investors than hedge fund returns. For example, see also Fung and Hsieh (1999), Hedges (2005), Goodworth and Jones (2007), Fung *et al.* (2008), Bollen and Pool (2009), and Straumann (2009).

### 15.2.2. Data Description

The dataset includes $T = 267$ observations of monthly returns of five FoHFs indices and 15 hedge fund indices over the period January 1990—March 2012.

The indices used represent FoHFs and hedge fund performance at various levels. We classify them as follows:

- *HFRI Fund of Funds Composite Index (FF).*
  - *Specific FoHFs strategies*: HFRI FOF Strategic Index (FF1); HFRI FOF Market Defensive Index (FF2); HFRI FOF Diversified Index (FF3); HFRI FOF Conservative Index (FF4).
- *HFRI Fund-Weighted Composite Index (HF).*
  - *Directional funds*: HFRI Emerging Markets: Asia ex-Japan Index (D1); HFRI Emerging Markets (Total) Index (D2); HFRI Equity Hedge (Total) Index (D3); HFRI EH: Short Bias Index (D4); HFRI Macro: Systematic Diversified Index (D5); HFRI Macro (Total) Index (D6); HFRI EH: Quantitative Directional (D7).
  - *Non-directional funds*: HFRI RV: Fixed Income-Corporate Index (ND1); HFRI RV: Fixed Income-Convertible Arbitrage Index (ND2); HFRI EH: Equity Market Neutral Index (ND3); HFRI Relative Value (Total) Index (ND4); HFRI Event-Driven (Total) Index (ND5); HFRI ED: Distressed/ Restructuring Index (ND6); HFRI ED: Merger Arbitrage Index (ND7).

This classification is similar to that for the hedge fund groups defined in several previous studies (e.g., Agarwal and Naik, 2000; Ineichen, 2003; Gregoriou *et al.*, 2007). Description of FoHFs and hedge fund indices is provided by HFR (see http://www.hedgefundresearch.com). See also Chan *et al.* (2005), who provide descriptions of specific hedge fund strategies.

In addition, monthly MSCI Global Equity market index data, obtained from Bloomberg, are used to compute excess returns on FoHFs and hedge fund indices over the MSCI index. MSCI data are collected for the same time span as FoHFs and hedge fund data. We denote the monthly excess returns on FoHFs and hedge fund indices by $y_t$. The MSCI Global Equity market factor is used for two reasons. (i) Several papers evidence that the equity market index is a common risk factor of hedge fund indices (e.g., Agarwal and Naik, 1999, 2004; Liang, 1999; Chan *et al.*, 2005; Billio *et al.*, 2006). (ii) The MSCI index is a global index. Gregoriou (2003) notes that a great majority of FoHFs are geographically diversified and FoHFs managers use the MSCI Global Equity market index to provide a benchmark for investors. As the hedge fund indices provided by HFR correspond to geographically diversified portfolios, we use the MSCI index as a benchmark for hedge fund indices as well.

Figure 15.1 shows the evolution of FoHFs composite and MSCI indices over the period 1990–2012. The initial value of both indices is normalized to 100. The figure shows that there is a significant comovement between the two indices.

Descriptive statistics of $y_t$ are presented in Table 15.1, which shows the mean, maximum, minimum, standard deviation (SD), skewness, and kurtosis estimates for each FoHF and hedge fund index. Table 15.1 also shows the augmented Dickey–Fuller (ADF) unit root test statistic (Dickey and Fuller, 1979). The ADF specification estimated is with a constant term and without

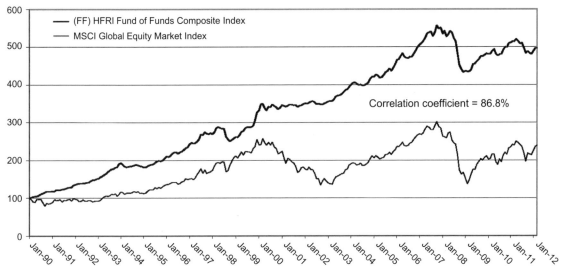

**FIGURE 15.1**
Evolution of FoHFs Composite and MSCI indices over the period 1990 to 2012.

a linear time trend. The ADF statistics indicate that the unit root null hypothesis is rejected for all FoHFs and hedge fund indices at the 1% level of significance (i.e., all time series are covariance stationary). Table 15.1 also shows the Ljung–Box (LB) test statistic computed for 12th-order serial correlation (Ljung and Box, 1978). The LB test is performed since several papers in the hedge fund literature report significant serial correlation of hedge fund returns (e.g., Gregoriou, 2003; Gregoriou *et al.*, 2007; Füss *et al.*, 2007; Abdou and Nasereddin, 2011; Jordan and Simlai, 2011; Kang *et al.*, 2010; Laube *et al.*, 2011). The LB statistics show that the absence of serial correlation null hypothesis is rejected for four directional hedge funds: D1, D2, D5, and D6, while it cannot be rejected for other indices. This result coincides with that of Harri and Brorsen (2004), who show that some hedge fund strategies are more persistent than others.

## 15.2.3. FoHFs Return Drivers

In this section, we evaluate the dynamic relationships among FoHFs returns and some factors that may be considered as FoHFs return drivers. We study some hedge fund return drivers reported in the literature (e.g., Agarwal and Naik, 1999, 2004; Liang, 1999; Chan *et al.*, 2005; Billio *et al.*, 2006; Racicot and Théoret, 2007). The excess return drivers considered are: three factors of the Fama–French (1993) model (i.e., market risk premium factor $(R_m - R_f)$, small minus big (SMB) factor, and high minus low (HML) factor); 1-month US Treasury bill (T-bill) rate; percentage change of monthly EUR/US$ exchange rate; percentage change of monthly crude oil per barrel price; percentage change of monthly volatility VIX index. Return driver data are collected for the same time span as FoHFs and hedge fund data.

**Table 15.1** Descriptive Statistics of $y_t$

| | Mean | Maximum | Minimum | SD | Skewness | Kurtosis | ADF | LB(12) |
|---|---|---|---|---|---|---|---|---|
| *FoHFs* | | | | | | | | |
| (FF) HFRI FOF Composite Index | 0.002 | 0.136 | −0.109 | 0.039 | 0.284 | 4.101 | −15.420*** | 11.162 |
| (FF1) HFRI FOF: Strategic Index | 0.004 | 0.134 | −0.115 | 0.038 | 0.298 | 4.366 | −14.850*** | 13.932 |
| (FF2) HFRI FOF: Market Defensive Index | 0.002 | 0.205 | −0.132 | 0.046 | 0.602 | 4.976 | −14.360*** | 12.728 |
| (FF3) HFRI FOF: Diversified Index | 0.002 | 0.133 | −0.109 | 0.039 | 0.303 | 4.109 | −15.279*** | 11.176 |
| (FF4) HFRI FOF: Conservative Index | 0.001 | 0.132 | −0.106 | 0.040 | 0.328 | 3.636 | −15.798*** | 9.921 |
| *Hedge Funds* | | | | | | | | |
| (HF) HFRI Fund-Weighted Composite Index | 0.005 | 0.122 | −0.091 | 0.033 | 0.269 | 3.888 | −15.803*** | 15.156 |
| *Directional funds* | | | | | | | | |
| (D1) HFRI Emerging Markets: Asia ex-Japan Index | 0.004 | 0.107 | −0.097 | 0.035 | 0.181 | 3.139 | −13.137*** | 28.164*** |
| (D2) HFRI Emerging Markets (Total) Index | 0.007 | 0.101 | −0.083 | 0.034 | −0.055 | 2.929 | −12.215*** | 53.042*** |
| (D3) HFRI Equity Hedge (Total) Index | 0.006 | 0.124 | −0.083 | 0.032 | 0.600 | 4.432 | −15.686*** | 14.383 |
| (D4) HFRI EH: Short Bias Index | −0.003 | 0.329 | −0.253 | 0.092 | 0.397 | 3.675 | −14.763*** | 7.269 |
| (D5) HFRI Macro: Systematic Diversified Index | 0.005 | 0.249 | −0.147 | 0.041 | 0.999 | 8.915 | −14.015*** | 31.954*** |
| (D6) HFRI Macro (Total) Index | 0.006 | 0.207 | −0.122 | 0.043 | 0.506 | 4.952 | −14.129*** | 25.469** |
| (D7) HFRI EH: Quantitative Directional | 0.006 | 0.127 | −0.113 | 0.030 | 0.369 | 4.951 | −15.240*** | 11.075 |
| *Non-directional funds* | | | | | | | | |
| (ND1) HFRI RV: Fixed Income-Corporate Index | 0.002 | 0.102 | −0.153 | 0.039 | −0.035 | 3.883 | −16.934*** | 11.694 |
| (ND2) HFRI RV: Fixed Income-Convertible Arbitrage Index | 0.003 | 0.137 | −0.107 | 0.039 | 0.483 | 3.808 | −16.587*** | 11.267 |
| (ND3) HFRI EH: Equity Market Neutral Index | 0.001 | 0.185 | −0.113 | 0.044 | 0.494 | 4.064 | −15.069*** | 10.629 |
| (ND4) HFRI Relative Value (Total) Index | 0.004 | 0.118 | −0.101 | 0.040 | 0.314 | 3.305 | −16.285*** | 8.676 |
| (ND5) HFRI Event-Driven (Total) Index | 0.005 | 0.111 | −0.107 | 0.035 | 0.111 | 3.674 | −16.802*** | 13.905 |
| (ND6) HFRI ED: Distressed/Restructuring Index | 0.006 | 0.111 | −0.120 | 0.039 | 0.093 | 3.482 | −16.212*** | 18.165 |
| (ND7) HFRI ED: Merger Arbitrage Index | 0.003 | 0.166 | −0.101 | 0.041 | 0.362 | 3.661 | −15.743*** | 7.945 |

Table 15.2 presents the dynamic correlation coefficients between each return driver and the excess return on each FoHFs index. Correlation coefficients are computed for the first lag, contemporaneous value, and first lead of each return driver. Bold numbers in Table 15.2 show that, for all FoHFs indices, significant contemporaneous correlation is evidenced for the market risk premium, percentage change of the VIX index, and percentage change of the EUR/US\$ exchange rate.[2] Furthermore, we find significant correlation between all FoHFs indices and the first lead of market risk premium, SMB factor, and percentage change of the VIX index. Finally, Table 15.2 shows that some FoHFs are correlated with the T-bill rate and the HML factor as well.

## 15.3. FORECASTING MODELS

In this section, five econometric models used for forecasting purposes are presented. For each model, we summarize the econometric specification, conditions of covariance stationarity, parameter estimation procedures, and multistep ahead forecasting formulas.

### 15.3.1. AR($p$) Model

$$y_t = c + \phi_1 y_{t-1} + \cdots + \phi_p y_{t-p} + \omega u_t, \qquad (15.1)$$

where $u_t$ is an $N(0,1)$ distributed i.i.d. (independent and identically distributed) error term. The AR($p$) structure of the mean equation is motivated by possible serial correlation of returns reported in the existing literature (see the references in Section 15.2.2). We consider several specifications of this model by choosing different values for $p = 1, \ldots, 12$.[3] Conditions of covariance stationarity are reported in Hamilton (1994). The parameters of the model are estimated by the maximum likelihood method (see Hamilton, 1994). The formula of $n$-step ahead forecast, $E[y_{t+n}|F_t]$, is reported in Hamilton (1994). $F_{t-1} = (y_1, \ldots, y_t)$ denotes the information set available at time $t$.

### 15.3.2. AR($p$)-GARCH(1,1) Model

$$y_t = c + \phi_1 y_{t-1} + \cdots + \phi_p y_{t-p} + \varepsilon_t, \qquad (15.2)$$

where $\varepsilon_t$ is specified according to the GARCH(1,1) model of Bollerslev (1986) and Taylor (1986). The GARCH(1,1) specification is considered for two reasons. (i) The GARCH(1,1) model is widely applied in the finance literature (e.g., Donaldson and Kamstra, 1997; Dunis *et al.* 2003; Hansen and Lunde, 2005; Preminger *et al.*, 2006; Muzzioli, 2010). (ii) We have found that the forecasting performance of models with GARCH(1,1) error specification is superior to that of alternative GARCH models with more complicated lag structure.

---

[2]The EUR/US\$ data used represent $X$ EUR $= 1$ US\$ (i.e., an increasing exchange rate implies a stronger US\$).

[3]We consider $p = 1, \ldots, 12$ for all models in this chapter.

**Table 15.2** Dynamic Correlation Coefficients of FoHFs and Hedge Fund Returns with Return Drivers

| Return Drivers | (FF) | (FF1) | (FF2) | (FF3) | (FF4) |
|---|---|---|---|---|---|
| $R_m - R_f$ (Fama–French factor 1), lag 1 | −0.019 | 0.006 | −0.089 | −0.016 | −0.033 |
| SMB (Fama–French factor 2), lag 1 | 0.015 | 0.033 | −0.028 | 0.023 | −0.002 |
| HML (Fama–French factor 3), lag 1 | 0.047 | 0.019 | 0.092 | 0.039 | 0.063 |
| $R_f$ (1-month US T-bill rate), lag 1 | 0.094 | 0.129** | 0.094 | 0.087 | 0.088 |
| EUR/US$ % change, lag 1 | −0.058 | −0.053 | −0.048 | −0.052 | −0.069 |
| Crude oil price % change, lag 1 | 0.026 | 0.021 | 0.011 | 0.020 | 0.025 |
| VIX index % change, lag 1 | 0.065 | 0.042 | 0.134*** | 0.063 | 0.076 |
| $R_m - R_f$ (Fama–French factor 1) | −0.808*** | −0.678*** | −0.859*** | −0.805*** | −0.864*** |
| SMB (Fama–French factor 2) | −0.011 | 0.098 | −0.102 | 0.000 | −0.096 |
| HML (Fama–French factor 3) | 0.078 | −0.023 | 0.143** | 0.070 | 0.130** |
| $R_f$ (1-month US T-bill rate) | 0.076 | 0.113* | 0.079 | 0.068 | 0.069 |
| EUR/US$ % change | 0.262*** | 0.277*** | 0.211*** | 0.267*** | 0.243*** |
| Crude oil price % change | 0.051 | 0.048 | 0.024 | 0.053 | 0.032 |
| VIX index % change | 0.441*** | 0.351*** | 0.490*** | 0.441*** | 0.491*** |
| $R_m - R_f$ (Fama–French factor 1), lead 1 | −0.119* | −0.106* | −0.149*** | −0.128** | −0.107* |
| SMB (Fama–French factor 2), lead 1 | −0.129** | −0.113* | −0.146*** | −0.122** | −0.137*** |
| HML (Fama–French factor 3), lead 1 | −0.104 | −0.095 | −0.134** | −0.103 | −0.112* |
| $R_f$ (1-month US T-bill rate), lead 1 | 0.103 | 0.143** | 0.093 | 0.095 | 0.092 |
| EUR/US$ % change, lead 1 | 0.096 | 0.118* | 0.042 | 0.108* | 0.085 |
| Crude oil price % change, lead 1 | −0.070 | −0.083 | −0.089 | −0.064 | −0.096 |
| VIX index % change, lead 1 | 0.207*** | 0.199*** | 0.220*** | 0.210*** | 0.195*** |

HFRI Fund of Funds Composite Index (FF); HFRI FOF Strategic Index (FF1); HFRI FOF Market Defensive Index (FF2); HFRI FOF Diversified Index (FF3); HFRI FOF Conservative Index (FF4). Asterisks denote test statistically significant at the *10%, **5% and ***1% levels, respectively. Data sources of return drivers: Bloomberg, Reuters, and DataStream.

Conditions of covariance stationarity for the GARCH(1,1) model are reported in Bollerslev (1986). The parameters of the model are estimated by the maximum likelihood method (see Hamilton, 1994). The $n$-step ahead forecasting formula is presented in Hamilton (1994).

### 15.3.3. MS-AR($p$) Model

$$y_t = c(s_t) + \phi_1(s_t)y_{t-1} + \cdots + \phi_p(s_t)y_{t-p} + \omega(s_t)u_t, \qquad (15.3)$$

where $u_t$ is an $N(0,1)$ distributed i.i.d. error term. MS models have been developed as a way of allowing data to arise from a combination of two or more distinct data-generating processes (Hamilton, 1989; Kim and Nelson, 1999). At each time $t$, the actual process generating the data is determined by the realization of a latent random discrete variable denoted by $s_t$, which is called a state variable or regime. In the MS models, $s_t$ over $t = 1, \ldots, T$ is assumed to form a Markov process. We consider a two-state MS model (i.e., $s_t = 1$ or 2), where $s_t$ forms a Markov chain with a $2 \times 2$ transition probability matrix, $P = \{\eta_{ij}\}$. The elements of $P$ are given by:

$$\begin{aligned}
\Pr[s_t = 1 | s_{t-1} = 1] &= \eta_{11} \\
\Pr[s_t = 1 | s_{t-1} = 2] &= \eta_{12} \\
\Pr[s_t = 2 | s_{t-1} = 1] &= \eta_{21} \\
\Pr[s_t = 2 | s_{t-1} = 2] &= \eta_{22}
\end{aligned} \qquad (15.4)$$

where $\eta_{11} + \eta_{21} = 1$ and $\eta_{12} + \eta_{22} = 1$ are parameters of the MS model. We assume that $P$ is constant over time; in other words, we consider an exogenous switching model.[4] Francq and Zakoian (2001) give stationarity conditions for the MS-AR($p$) model. The parameters of the model are estimated by the maximum likelihood method (see Kim and Nelson, 1999). The $n$-step ahead forecast is computed by:

$$\begin{aligned}
E[y_{t+n}|F_t] &= E[y_{t+n}|F_t, s_{t+n} = 1] \times \Pr[s_{t+n} = 1|F_t] + E[Y_{t+n}|F_t, s_{t+n} \\
&= 2] \times \Pr[s_{t+n} = 2|F_t]
\end{aligned} \qquad (15.5)$$

For regime $i$, $E[y_{t+n}|F_t, s_{t+n} = i]$ is computed according to Hamilton (1994) and $\Pr[s_{t+n} = i|F_t]$ is computed according to Kim and Nelson (1999).

### 15.3.4. MS-AR($p$)-GARCH(1,1) Model

$$y_t = c(s_t) + \phi_1(s_t)y_{t-1} + \cdots + \phi_p(s_t)y_{t-p} + \varepsilon_t, \qquad (15.6)$$

where $\varepsilon_t$ is specified according to a single regime GARCH(1,1) model. The parameters of the model are estimated by the maximum likelihood method (see Kim and Nelson, 1999). The $n$-step ahead forecast is computed by equation (15.5).

---

[4]In Section 15.4.4, we extend this model and we consider an endogenous switching AR model.

### 15.3.5. MS-AR($p$)-MS-GARCH(1,1) Model

$$y_t = c(s_t) + \phi_1(s_t)y_{t-1} + \cdots + \phi_p(s_t)y_{t-p} + \varepsilon_t(s_t), \qquad (15.7)$$

where $\varepsilon_t(s_t)$ is specified according to the MS-GARCH(1,1) model of Klaassen (2002). Abramson and Cohen (2007) give stationarity conditions for Klaassen's MS-GARCH model. The parameters of the model are estimated by the maximum likelihood method (see Klaassen, 2002). The $n$-step ahead forecast is computed by equation (15.5). Consideration of MS parameters in the volatility equation is motivated, for example, by Diebold (1986), who notes that the GARCH specification can be improved by including regime dummy variables for the conditional variance intercept. Moreover, Friedman and Laibson (1989) note that the GARCH model does not differentiate between the persistence of large and small shocks. We apply the non-path-dependent MS volatility model of Klaassen (2002) for two reasons. (i) The MS-GARCH model of Klaassen (2002) can be estimated more rapidly than path-dependent MS-GARCH models (e.g., Dueker, 1997; Bauwens *et al.*, 2010; Henneke *et al.*, 2011). Therefore, it is more appropriate for repeated out-of sample forecasting purposes. (ii) We have found that the forecasting performance of models with Klaassen's volatility formulation is superior to alternative MS-ARCH (e.g., Hamilton and Susmel, 1994; Cai, 1994) and other non-path-dependent MS-GARCH models (e.g., Gray, 1996; Haas *et al.*, 2004).

## 15.4. RESULTS
### 15.4.1. Out-of-sample Forecasting Procedure and Model Diagnostics

Out-of-sample forecasts of $y_t$ are derived by dividing the full sample period (1990−2012) into two subsamples. The first subsample contains 120 observations from January 1990 to December 1999, which are used to estimate the parameters of competing econometric specifications to produce out-of-sample forecasts of $y_t$ for the year 2000. Next, the dataset is updated by adding the first month of the year 2000 to the previous subsample and the parameters are re-estimated to produce the out-of-sample forecasts for the subsequent months of the year 2000. This procedure is repeated until out-of-sample forecasts are obtained for each month over the period January 2000−March 2012. Multistep ahead forecasts are estimated for 1, 3, 6, 9, and 12 months. More formally, $n$-step ahead forecasts of $y_{t+n}$ with $n = 1, 3, 6, 9,$ and 12 are computed.

In the forecasting procedure, diagnostic tests are performed for each model in four steps. (i) The residuals corresponding to the i.i.d. error terms are computed and the following properties are verified: the mean of residuals is zero and there is no significant autocorrelation among the residuals. We forecast by specifications where these two properties are satisfied. (ii) Stationarity of the dynamic models is verified. We find that the AR($p$) and

MS-AR($p$) specifications are stationary for all indices and for all models. Furthermore, we find that the GARCH(1,1) and MS-GARCH(1,1) models are stationary for all indices and for all models. (iii) When volatility is modeled according to the GARCH(1,1) formulation, we check the significance of the coefficients corresponding to the dynamic terms of the volatility equation. We only consider a specification for forecasting purposes when the dynamic parameters of GARCH are significant. For the MS-GARCH model, in some cases, we find that the dynamic coefficients are significant for one regime, but they are non-significant for the other regime. In these cases, we forecast with the model, since it implies dynamic volatility for one regime and constant volatility for the other regime. (iv) For the MS specifications, we study the significance of parameters in the transition probability matrix (i.e., $\eta_{11}$ and $\eta_{22}$) to see whether two different regimes of the return process exist. For the MS-AR($p$) model, we find significant regime-switching dynamics for all FoHFs indices (i.e., FF, FF1, FF2, FF3, and FF4). Nevertheless, we find significant regime-switching only for the following six hedge fund indices: D3, D4, D5, D6, D7, and ND3 (i.e., most directional hedge funds are regime switching, but most non-directional hedge funds are not regime switching). When more complicated MS-AR($p$)-GARCH(1,1) and MS-AR($p$)-MS-GARCH(1,1) models are considered, we still find significant MS dynamics for all FoHFs indices, but we find regime switching only for the following two hedge funds: D6 and ND3. From these results, it seems that FoHFs are more sensitive to switches in the state variable, $s_t$, than most hedge funds. These results may imply that MS models may produce more accurate forecasts of $y_t$ for FoHFs (see Sections 15.4.2 and 15.4.3). Furthermore, practitioners may be interested in the following question: what drives the regime-switching dynamics of different FoHFs indices? We investigate this question in Section 15.4.4.

## 15.4.2. Out-of-Sample Forecasting Precision

The $n$-step ahead forecasting performance of models is verified using the RMSE loss function. The RMSE is the square root of the MSE, which is given by

$$\text{MSE}_n = (1/n) \sum_{\tau=t+1}^{t+n} \{y_\tau - \text{E}[y_\tau|F_t]\}^2, \qquad (15.8)$$

Table 15.3 reports the RMSE and the best forecasting specification for each index for the period January 2000–March 2012. Table 15.3 shows that, in most cases, an MS specification dominates forecasting performance for FoHFs excess returns. The only exception is the FoHFs Conservative Index (FF4), where the AR($p$) and AR($p$)-GARCH specifications dominate forecast accuracy. We can also see that, in several cases, the MS-AR-GARCH and MS-AR-MS-GARCH specifications are the best forecasters of FoHFs excess returns. However, these models are not the best predictors of hedge fund performance in most cases. Table 15.3 also shows that the single-regime AR and AR-GARCH specifications dominate

**Table 15.3** RMSE (%) for Full Forecasting Period, January 2000–March 2012

| | Out-of-Sample Forecast Horizon | | | | | | | | | |
| --- | --- | --- | --- | --- | --- | --- | --- | --- | --- | --- |
| | 1 Month | | 3 Months | | 6 Months | | 9 Months | | 12 Months | |
| | RMSE | Best Model | RMSE | Best Model | RMSE | Best Model | RMSE | Best Model | RMSE | Best Model |
| *FoHFs* | | | | | | | | | | |
| (FF) HFRI Fund of Funds Composite Index | 3.803 | M3(2) | 3.926 | M4(1) | 3.912 | M3(2) | 3.914 | M4(3) | 3.869 | M4(7) |
| (FF1) HFRI FOF: Strategic Index | 3.590 | M4(2) | 3.567 | M4(2) | 3.598 | M3(7) | 3.650 | M1(3) | 3.525 | M2(8) |
| (FF2) HFRI FOF: Market Defensive Index | 4.873 | M1(3) | 4.881 | M1(1) | 4.869 | M4(8) | 4.697 | M4(12) | 4.720 | M4(8) |
| (FF3) HFRI FOF: Diversified Index | 4.009 | M3(2) | 4.017 | M4(1) | 4.070 | M5(1) | 4.032 | M4(3) | 3.949 | M1(8) |
| (FF4) HFRI FOF: Conservative Index | 4.193 | M3(3) | 4.214 | M1(1) | 4.238 | M2(1) | 4.157 | M2(11) | 4.151 | M1(8) |
| *Hedge funds* | | | | | | | | | | |
| (HF) HFRI Fund Weighted Composite Index | 3.416 | M2(2) | 3.416 | M2(1) | 3.461 | M3(1) | 3.394 | M2(11) | 3.370 | M2(8) |
| *Directional funds* | | | | | | | | | | |
| (D1) HFRI Emerging Markets: Asia ex–Japan Index | 3.134 | M1(1) | 3.221 | M1(3) | 3.270 | M1(3) | 3.369 | M1(8) | 3.171 | M1(8) |
| (D2) HFRI Emerging Markets (Total) Index | 2.903 | M2(1) | 3.000 | M2(1) | 2.985 | M2(1) | 3.141 | M2(3) | 2.835 | M1(8) |

| | Col 1 | Col 2 | Col 3 | Col 4 | Col 5 |
|---|---|---|---|---|---|
| (D3) HFRI Equity Hedge (Total) Index | M2(2) 3.017 | M2(1) 3.009 | M3(1) 3.050 | M2(3) 3.034 | M2(8) 2.982 |
| (D4) HFRI EH: Short Bias Index | M2(1) 9.389 | M2(1) 9.335 | M3(4) 9.317 | M3(10) 9.275 | M3(9) 9.320 |
| (D5) HFRI Macro: Systematic Diversified Index | M1(6) 4.597 | M1(1) 4.631 | M2(3) 4.723 | M2(6) 4.627 | M2(1) 4.646 |
| (D6) HFRI Macro (Total) Index | M4(4) 4.545 | M2(1) 4.623 | M2(7) 4.788 | M4(3) 4.712 | M2(2) 4.635 |
| (D7) HFRI EH: Quantitative Directional | **M2(4) 2.757** | **M2(1) 2.749** | **M3(7) 2.734** | **M3(7) 2.772** | **M2(4) 2.739** |
| *Non-directional funds* | | | | | |
| (ND1) HFRI RV: Fixed Income-Corporate Index | M2(2) 3.960 | M3(1) 4.003 | M1(1) 3.999 | M2(11) 3.884 | M1(8) 3.954 |
| (ND2) HFRI RV: Fixed Income-Convertible Arbitrage Index | M2(1) 4.087 | M2(5) 4.062 | M2(1) 4.110 | M2(11) 3.911 | M1(8) 4.022 |
| (ND3) HFRI EH: Equity Market Neutral Index | M1(3) 4.697 | M1(1) 4.704 | M2(1) 4.761 | M4(1) 4.713 | M3(6) 4.669 |
| (ND4) HFRI Relative Value (Total) Index | M1(1) 4.208 | M1(1) 4.208 | M1(1) 4.231 | M2(9) 4.119 | M1(5) 4.131 |
| (ND5) HFRI Event-Driven (Total) Index | **M2(2) 3.510** | **M1(1) 3.553** | **M2(1) 3.511** | **M2(11) 3.433** | **M1(8) 3.462** |
| (ND6) HFRI ED: Distressed/Restructuring Index | M2(2) 3.859 | M3(1) 3.903 | M2(1) 3.898 | M2(11) 3.777 | M1(8) 3.810 |
| (ND7) HFRI ED: Merger Arbitrage Index | M1(1) 4.401 | M1(1) 4.409 | M2(1) 4.392 | M2(1) 4.328 | M1(8) 4.335 |

M1 = AR($p$); M2 = AR($p$)-GARCH(1,1); M3 = MS-AR($p$); M4 = MS-AR($p$)-GARCH(1,1); M5 = MS-AR($p$)-MS-GARCH(1,1). The value of $p$ is indicated in parentheses. The lowest RMSE is given in bold; the highest RMSE is given in italic.

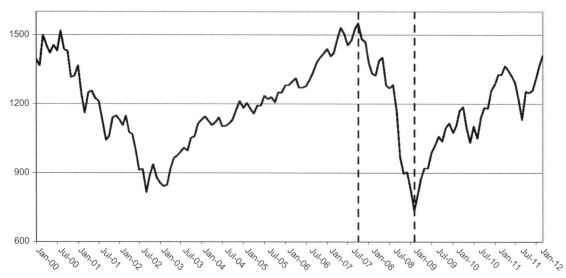

**FIGURE 15.2**
Evolution of the S&P 500 Index over the period 2000 to 2012.

forecasting performance for hedge fund indices. The exception is the Short Bias index (D4), where an MS model dominates predictive accuracy.

We break down the full forecasted period of 2000–2012 to subperiods before, during, and after the US financial crisis to see how forecast accuracy of different models changes in different subperiods. The pre-crisis period is from January 2000 to September 2007; the crisis period is from October 2007 to February 2009; the post-crisis period is from March 2009 to March 2012. We present these subperiods on Figure 15.2, where the evolution of the S&P 500 index is shown over the period January 2000–March 2012.

Tables 15.4, 15.5, and 15.6 report the RMSE and the best forecasting specification for the subperiods before, during, and after the financial crisis, respectively, for all FoHFs and hedge fund indices. In addition to comparing the forecasts of different FoHFs and hedge fund indices, these tables also help to compare forecasting performance among different subperiods. For all FoHFs and hedge fund indices, the results show that forecast accuracy is the lowest during the crisis period. We also find that, although the predictive accuracy improves after the financial crisis, the RMSE is higher in the post-crisis period than in the pre-crisis period for all indices. Tables 15.4, 15.5, and 15.6 also show that the MS specifications dominate forecasting performance for most FoHFs in all subperiods. The only exception is the FoHFs Conservative Index (FF4) for the subperiods before and during the financial crisis, where the AR($p$) model dominates predictive accuracy (see Tables 15.4 and 15.5). In the after crisis subperiod, MS specifications dominate forecast accuracy for all FoHFs indices (see Table 15.6). Furthermore, Tables 15.4 and

**Table 15.4**  RMSE (%) for Pre-crisis Period, January 2000–September 2007

| | Out-of-Sample Forecast Horizon | | | | | | | | | | |
|---|---|---|---|---|---|---|---|---|---|---|---|
| | 1 Month | | 3 Months | | 6 Months | | 9 Months | | 12 Months | |
| | RMSE | Best Model | RMSE | Best Model | RMSE | Best Model | RMSE | Best Model | RMSE | Best Model |
| *FoHFs* | | | | | | | | | | |
| (FF) HFRI Fund of Funds Composite Index | 3.063 | M3(2) | 3.275 | M4(1) | 3.151 | M3(2) | 3.217 | M4(3) | 3.184 | M1(8) |
| (FF1) HFRI FOF: Strategic Index | **2.955** | M3(8) | **2.978** | M3(3) | **2.928** | M3(8) | **2.989** | M2(1) | **2.886** | M2(7) |
| (FF2) HFRI FOF: Market Defensive Index | *4.022* | M5(3) | *4.047* | M3(2) | *4.051* | M1(1) | *3.913* | M4(12) | *3.934* | M5(7) |
| (FF3) HFRI FOF: Diversified Index | 3.332 | M3(2) | 3.329 | M3(2) | 3.330 | M3(1) | 3.301 | M4(3) | 3.217 | M1(8) |
| (FF4) HFRI FOF: Conservative Index | 3.472 | M3(3) | 3.515 | M1(1) | 3.529 | M1(1) | 3.440 | M5(4) | 3.413 | M1(8) |
| *Hedge funds* | | | | | | | | | | |
| (HF) HFRI Fund Weighted Composite Index | 2.772 | M1(8) | 2.820 | M2(2) | 2.835 | M1(8) | 2.759 | M2(6) | 2.782 | M1(8) |
| *Directional funds* | | | | | | | | | | |
| (D1) HFRI Emerging Markets: Asia ex-Japan Index | 2.943 | M1(1) | 3.060 | M1(4) | 2.921 | M1(3) | 3.221 | M2(9) | 3.031 | M1(12) |
| (D2) HFRI Emerging Markets (Total) Index | 2.650 | M2(1) | 2.801 | M2(4) | 2.551 | M2(3) | 2.963 | M2(4) | 2.665 | M2(8) |
| (D3) HFRI Equity Hedge (Total) Index | 2.694 | M3(12) | 2.682 | M3(2) | 2.713 | M3(1) | 2.680 | M3(3) | 2.703 | M2(8) |

*(Continued)*

**Table 15.4** RMSE (%) for Pre-crisis Period, January 2000–September 2007—cont'd

| | Out-of-Sample Forecast Horizon | | | | | | | | | |
|---|---|---|---|---|---|---|---|---|---|---|
| | 1 Month | | 3 Months | | 6 Months | | 9 Months | | 12 Months | |
| | RMSE | Best Model | RMSE | Best Model | RMSE | Best Model | RMSE | Best Model | RMSE | Best Model |
| (D4) HFRI EH: Short Bias Index | *9.061* | M2(1) | *8.981* | M3(1) | *8.747* | M3(4) | *8.801* | M2(11) | *8.871* | M3(4) |
| (D5) HFRI Macro: Systematic Diversified Index | 2.726 | M3(6) | 2.810 | M1(1) | 2.821 | M1(1) | 2.780 | M1(1) | 2.792 | M1(1) |
| (D6) HFRI Macro (Total) Index | 3.641 | M4(4) | 3.682 | M2(3) | 3.697 | M2(12) | 3.678 | M4(3) | 3.688 | M2(1) |
| (D7) HFRI EH: Quantitative Directional | **2.140** | M3(1) | **2.141** | M3(1) | **2.057** | M2(11) | **2.122** | M3(2) | **2.126** | M3(1) |
| *Non-directional funds* | | | | | | | | | | |
| (ND1) HFRI RV: Fixed Income-Corporate Index | 3.503 | M2(2) | 3.506 | M2(5) | 3.594 | M3(1) | 3.444 | M2(11) | 3.511 | M2(1) |
| (ND2) HFRI RV: Fixed Income-Convertible Arbitrage Index | 3.935 | M2(1) | 3.924 | M2(5) | 3.989 | M2(3) | 3.747 | M2(11) | 3.833 | M1(8) |
| (ND3) HFRI EH: Equity Market Neutral Index | 3.984 | M4(2) | 4.013 | M3(1) | 4.014 | M3(1) | 3.941 | M4(1) | 3.920 | M3(5) |
| (ND4) HFRI Relative Value (Total) Index | 3.708 | M3(1) | 3.708 | M3(1) | 3.759 | M1(1) | 3.617 | M2(10) | 3.611 | M1(7) |
| (ND5) HFRI Event-Driven (Total) Index | **2.947** | M2(2) | **3.025** | M3(1) | **3.021** | M3(1) | **2.896** | M2(11) | **2.936** | M1(8) |
| (ND6) HFRI ED: Distressed/Restructuring Index | 3.422 | M2(2) | 3.451 | M3(1) | 3.452 | M1(1) | 3.362 | M2(10) | 3.350 | M1(8) |
| (ND7) HFRI ED: Merger Arbitrage Index | 3.576 | M2(1) | 3.665 | M1(1) | 3.669 | M3(1) | 3.524 | M2(1) | 3.563 | M1(8) |

M1 = AR($p$)-GARCH(1,1); M2 = AR($p$)-GARCH(1,1); M3 = MS-AR($p$); M4 = MS-AR($p$)-GARCH(1,1); M5 = MS-AR($p$)-MS-GARCH(1,1). The value of $p$ is indicated in parentheses. The lowest RMSE is given in bold; the highest RMSE is given in italic.

**Table 15.5**  RMSE (%) for Crisis period, October 2007–February 2009

| | Out-of-Sample Forecast Horizon | | | | | | | | | |
|---|---|---|---|---|---|---|---|---|---|---|
| | 1 Month | | 3 Months | | 6 Months | | 9 Months | | 12 Months | |
| | RMSE | Best Model | RMSE | Best Model | RMSE | Best Model | RMSE | Best Model | RMSE | Best Model |
| *FoHFs* | | | | | | | | | | |
| (FF) HFRI Fund of Funds Composite Index | 5.182 | M3(2) | 5.314 | M3(7) | 5.391 | M3(4) | 5.251 | M3(2) | 5.290 | M3(2) |
| (FF1) HFRI FOF: Strategic Index | **4.652** | M1(3) | **4.547** | M3(7) | **4.694** | M3(4) | **4.812** | M1(3) | **4.680** | M3(3) |
| (FF2) HFRI FOF: Market Defensive Index | 6.090 | M4(8) | 6.328 | M4(7) | 6.984 | M4(8) | 7.022 | M4(8) | 6.648 | M4(8) |
| (FF3) HFRI FOF: Diversified Index | 5.349 | M3(2) | 5.415 | M3(1) | 5.585 | M3(4) | 5.405 | M3(2) | 5.418 | M3(2) |
| (FF4) HFRI FOF: Conservative Index | 5.724 | M1(8) | 5.806 | M3(6) | 5.860 | M1(7) | 5.703 | M5(3) | 5.835 | M1(3) |
| *Hedge funds* | | | | | | | | | | |
| (HF) HFRI Fund Weighted Composite Index | 4.820 | M1(8) | 4.888 | M3(1) | 4.891 | M1(7) | 4.909 | M3(2) | 4.899 | M3(1) |
| *Directional funds* | | | | | | | | | | |
| (D1) HFRI Emerging Markets: Asia ex-Japan Index | 3.712 | M1(4) | 3.750 | M1(3) | 4.227 | M1(12) | 3.961 | M1(12) | 3.781 | M1(8) |
| (D2) HFRI Emerging Markets (Total) Index | **3.289** | M2(11) | 3.593 | M2(1) | 3.776 | M2(12) | 3.441 | M2(12) | 3.354 | M1(4) |
| (D3) HFRI Equity Hedge (Total) Index | 3.860 | M3(2) | 3.860 | M2(6) | 3.855 | M3(4) | 3.882 | M3(11) | 3.825 | M3(5) |
| (D4) HFRI EH: Short Bias Index | *11.034* | M3(1) | *11.115* | M3(1) | *10.930* | M3(11) | *10.982* | M3(11) | *11.016* | M3(4) |
| (D5) HFRI Macro: Systematic Diversified Index | 7.763 | M1(12) | 8.162 | M3(1) | 7.931 | M3(2) | 8.331 | M3(1) | 7.977 | M3(7) |
| (D6) HFRI Macro (Total) Index | 6.719 | M2(11) | 6.953 | M3(8) | 7.187 | M3(3) | 7.030 | M3(4) | 7.128 | M3(2) |
| (D7) HFRI EH: Quantitative Directional | **3.381** | M2(10) | **3.495** | M2(1) | **3.451** | M3(6) | **3.368** | M3(6) | **3.332** | M3(11) |
| *Non-directional funds* | | | | | | | | | | |
| (ND1) HFRI RV: Fixed Income-Corporate Index | 4.985 | M1(8) | 5.062 | M1(6) | 5.145 | M1(1) | 5.140 | M3(2) | 5.119 | M1(4) |
| (ND2) HFRI RV: Fixed Income-Convertible Arbitrage Index | 5.159 | M1(12) | 5.127 | M1(6) | 5.260 | M3(1) | 5.151 | M1(7) | 5.284 | M3(1) |
| (ND3) HFRI EH: Equity Market Neutral Index | 6.671 | M3(3) | 6.815 | M3(1) | 6.906 | M3(8) | 6.777 | M3(3) | 6.741 | M3(2) |
| (ND4) HFRI Relative Value (Total) Index | 5.320 | M1(8) | 5.323 | M1(6) | 5.467 | M1(7) | 5.483 | M1(2) | 5.464 | M1(4) |
| (ND5) HFRI Event-Driven (Total) Index | **4.710** | M1(8) | **4.865** | M1(1) | **4.776** | M3(1) | **4.761** | M3(2) | **4.798** | M1(4) |
| (ND6) HFRI ED: Distressed/Restructuring Index | 4.872 | M1(8) | 5.173 | M3(1) | 5.192 | M3(1) | 5.143 | M3(2) | 5.154 | M1(2) |
| (ND7) HFRI ED: Merger Arbitrage Index | 6.138 | M3(3) | 6.214 | M1(9) | 5.763 | M3(3) | 5.990 | M3(3) | 5.612 | M3(3) |

M1 = AR($p$); M2 = AR($p$)-GARCH(1,1); M3 = MS-AR($p$); M4 = MS-AR($p$)-GARCH(1,1); M5 = MS-AR($p$)-MS-GARCH(1,1). The value of $p$ is indicated in parentheses. The lowest RMSE is given in bold; the highest RMSE is given in italic.

**Table 15.6** RMSE (%) for Post-Crisis Period, March 2009–March 2012

| | 1 Month | | 3 Months | | 6 Months | | 9 Months | | 12 Months | |
|---|---|---|---|---|---|---|---|---|---|---|
| | RMSE | Best Model | RMSE | Best Model | RMSE | Best Model | RMSE | Best Model | RMSE | Best Model |
| *FoHFs* | | | | | | | | | | |
| (FF) HFRI Fund of Funds Composite Index | 4.489 | M5(1) | 4.480 | M2(4) | 4.542 | M5(1) | 4.490 | M4(11) | 4.351 | M4(8) |
| (FF1) HFRI FOF: Strategic Index | **4.245** | M2(1) | **4.081** | M4(4) | **4.415** | M3(7) | **4.401** | M3(8) | **4.106** | M4(9) |
| (FF2) HFRI FOF: Market Defensive Index | *5.136* | M4(2) | *5.111* | M2(1) | 5.045 | M4(8) | 4.879 | M4(12) | 4.718 | M4(12) |
| (FF3) HFRI FOF: Diversified Index | 4.501 | M5(3) | 4.581 | M2(4) | 4.542 | M5(3) | 4.585 | M2(11) | 4.437 | M4(8) |
| (FF4) HFRI FOF: Conservative Index | 4.796 | M5(4) | 4.796 | M5(3) | 4.799 | M5(4) | 4.676 | M5(4) | 4.722 | M2(8) |
| *Hedge funds* | | | | | | | | | | |
| (HF) HFRI Fund Weighted Composite Index | 3.880 | M2(2) | 3.871 | M2(1) | 3.950 | M2(2) | 3.798 | M2(11) | 3.694 | M2(8) |
| *Directional funds* | | | | | | | | | | |
| (D1) HFRI Emerging Markets: Asia ex-Japan Index | 3.252 | M2(1) | 3.286 | M3(2) | 3.489 | M2(8) | 3.257 | M1(8) | 3.127 | M2(8) |
| (D2) HFRI Emerging Markets (Total) Index | **3.101** | M1(9) | 3.109 | M2(1) | 3.384 | M2(1) | **3.096** | M1(9) | **2.934** | M1(4) |
| (D3) HFRI Equity Hedge (Total) Index | 3.188 | M2(3) | **3.102** | M2(4) | **3.228** | M2(4) | 3.162 | M2(11) | 3.036 | M2(8) |
| (D4) HFRI EH: Short Bias Index | *9.184* | M2(6) | *8.994* | M2(6) | *9.518* | M3(10) | *9.457* | M3(10) | *9.126* | M2(2) |
| (D5) HFRI Macro: Systematic Diversified Index | 5.642 | M2(2) | 5.624 | M2(1) | 5.703 | M2(2) | 5.630 | M2(2) | 5.565 | M2(2) |
| (D6) HFRI Macro (Total) Index | 5.112 | M4(4) | 5.119 | M4(1) | 5.494 | M4(1) | 5.366 | M2(2) | 5.098 | M2(2) |
| (D7) HFRI EH: Quantitative Directional | 3.532 | M2(5) | 3.501 | M2(3) | 3.562 | M3(7) | 3.554 | M3(7) | 3.464 | M2(9) |
| *Non-directional funds* | | | | | | | | | | |
| (ND1) HFRI RV: Fixed Income-Corporate Index | 4.275 | M2(2) | 4.360 | M2(1) | 4.281 | M2(1) | 4.105 | M2(11) | 4.191 | M1(9) |
| (ND2) HFRI RV: Fixed Income-Convertible Arbitrage Index | **3.684** | M3(4) | **3.760** | M2(2) | **3.742** | M2(1) | **3.618** | M2(9) | **3.674** | M2(10) |
| (ND3) HFRI EH: Equity Market Neutral Index | *5.015* | M2(3) | *5.004* | M4(1) | *5.044* | M4(2) | *5.020* | M2(11) | *4.880* | M2(8) |
| (ND4) HFRI Relative Value (Total) Index | 4.564 | M2(2) | 4.591 | M2(1) | 4.518 | M2(2) | 4.456 | M2(11) | 4.458 | M2(8) |
| (ND5) HFRI Event-Driven (Total) Index | 3.934 | M2(2) | 3.989 | M2(1) | 3.864 | M2(2) | 3.777 | M2(11) | 3.846 | M1(9) |
| (ND6) HFRI ED: Distressed/Restructuring Index | 4.112 | M2(6) | 4.248 | M2(4) | 4.165 | M2(1) | 3.904 | M2(11) | 4.115 | M1(9) |
| (ND7) HFRI ED: Merger Arbitrage Index | 4.993 | M2(2) | 5.001 | M2(1) | 4.849 | M2(2) | 4.836 | M2(11) | 4.844 | M2(10) |

M1 = AR($p$)-GARCH(1,1); M2 = AR($p$); M3 = MS-AR($p$); M4 = MS-AR($p$)-GARCH(1,1); M5 = MS-AR($p$)-MS-GARCH(1,1). The value of $p$ is indicated in parentheses. The lowest RMSE is given in bold; the highest RMSE is given in italic.

15.6 show that, in most cases, the AR($p$) and AR($p$)-GARCH models are the most accurate forecasters for hedge fund indices in the pre-crisis and post-crisis subperiods. Nevertheless, Table 15.5 shows that for most hedge fund indices the MS models dominate forecasting performance during the crisis period. Forecasting benefits provided by the MS specifications during the financial crisis are especially important for the following directional hedge fund indices: D3, D4, D5, D6, and D7. Moreover, the MS models also perform well during the same period for the next non-directional hedge fund indices: ND3, ND6, and ND7.

## 15.4.3. Out-of-Sample Forecast Accuracy Test for FoHFs

The RMSE metric cannot determine if a given forecasting framework is, in fact, significantly better than another. To evaluate the difference between alternative forecasting models, we perform the predictive accuracy test of Diebold and Mariano (1995). The null hypothesis of this test is that the forecast accuracy of two competing models is equal. The DM statistic is computed for the difference of squared forecast errors of two competing specifications. Positive values of the DM statistic indicate superior forecasting performance of the second specification, while negative values reflect better forecasting performance of the first specification. The DM test statistics for the full forecasting period, pre-crisis period, crisis period, and post-crisis period are presented in Table 15.7. (i) Table 15.7 presents the difference between the predictive accuracy of FoHFs composite and hedge fund composite indices. According to the results, the hedge fund Composite Index can be forecasted significantly more precisely than the FoHFs Composite Index for most forecast horizons. (ii) Table 15.7 compares the forecasting performance among all specific FoHFs indices. The DM test results exhibit that the most precise forecasts are obtained for FF1, followed by FF3, FF4, and FF2 for the full forecasting period, as well as for the three subperiods.

## 15.4.4. In-Sample FoHFs Regime Determinants

The results reported so far have shown that: (i) the evolution of FoHFs excess returns can be modeled by regime-switching models (Section 15.4.1) and (ii) in many cases the most accurate out-of-sample forecasting model of FoHFs excess returns is a regime-switching specification (Section 15.4.2). It may be interesting for practitioners to investigate what are the determinants of FoHFs regime-switching dynamics. To answer this question, we present in-sample estimation results for FoHFs data, over the period 1990–2012, for the following econometric models: MS-AR(1) model with exogenous switching (Section 15.3.3) and MS-AR(1) model with endogenous switching. The endogenous switching model estimated is an extension of the MS-AR(1) model presented in Section 15.3.3. The conditional mean equation of both models is the same: equation (15.3) with $p = 1$. Nevertheless, the transition probability matrix, $P$, of these models is different. In the exogenous switching model, $P$ is given by equation (15.4) (i.e., the elements of $P$ are constant parameters).

**Table 15.7** Diebold–Mariano (1995) Predictive Accuracy Test

| | 1 Month | | 3 Months | | 6 Months | | 9 Months | | 12 Months | |
|---|---|---|---|---|---|---|---|---|---|---|
| | DM | p-value | DM | p-value | DM | p-value | DM | p-value | DM | p-value |
| *Full forecast period* | | | | | | | | | | |
| (FF)–(HF) | 3.215 | 0.001 | 6.519 | 0.000 | 4.265 | 0.000 | 4.824 | 0.000 | 5.442 | 0.000 |
| (FF1)–(FF2) | -4.545 | 0.000 | -4.521 | 0.000 | -3.873 | 0.000 | -3.895 | 0.000 | -4.655 | 0.000 |
| (FF1)–(FF3) | -3.857 | 0.000 | -4.427 | 0.000 | -3.611 | 0.000 | -3.532 | 0.000 | -3.611 | 0.000 |
| (FF1)–(FF4) | -4.225 | 0.000 | -5.109 | 0.000 | -4.397 | 0.000 | -3.591 | 0.000 | -4.922 | 0.000 |
| (FF2)–(FF3) | 3.773 | 0.000 | 3.888 | 0.000 | 3.360 | 0.001 | 3.271 | 0.001 | 3.557 | 0.000 |
| (FF2)–(FF4) | 3.141 | 0.002 | 3.007 | 0.003 | 2.684 | 0.007 | 2.834 | 0.005 | 2.758 | 0.006 |
| (FF3)–(FF4) | -2.209 | 0.027 | -4.124 | 0.000 | -3.079 | 0.002 | -1.518 | 0.129 | -4.109 | 0.000 |
| *Pre-crisis period* | | | | | | | | | | |
| (FF)–(HF) | 1.527 | 0.127 | 4.285 | 0.000 | 2.117 | 0.034 | 3.871 | 0.000 | 4.093 | 0.000 |
| (FF1)–(FF2) | -3.649 | 0.000 | -4.221 | 0.000 | -3.993 | 0.000 | -2.982 | 0.003 | -3.160 | 0.002 |
| (FF1)–(FF3) | -2.586 | 0.010 | -2.475 | 0.013 | -2.577 | 0.010 | -2.181 | 0.029 | -2.101 | 0.036 |
| (FF1)–(FF4) | -2.347 | 0.019 | -2.838 | 0.005 | -2.812 | 0.005 | -1.932 | 0.053 | -3.032 | 0.002 |
| (FF2)–(FF3) | 3.695 | 0.000 | 3.731 | 0.000 | 4.249 | 0.000 | 2.851 | 0.004 | 2.782 | 0.005 |
| (FF2)–(FF4) | 3.087 | 0.002 | 2.636 | 0.008 | 3.453 | 0.001 | 2.405 | 0.016 | 2.360 | 0.018 |
| (FF3)–(FF4) | -1.005 | 0.315 | -1.838 | 0.066 | -2.023 | 0.043 | -0.995 | 0.320 | -2.385 | 0.017 |
| *Crisis period* | | | | | | | | | | |
| (FF)–(HF) | 1.494 | 0.135 | 2.033 | 0.042 | 2.520 | 0.012 | 3.118 | 0.002 | 2.589 | 0.010 |
| (FF1)–(FF2) | -1.905 | 0.057 | -2.464 | 0.014 | -1.636 | 0.102 | -2.721 | 0.007 | -1.902 | 0.057 |
| (FF1)–(FF3) | -2.228 | 0.026 | -2.192 | 0.028 | -2.334 | 0.020 | -1.977 | 0.048 | -2.481 | 0.013 |
| (FF1)–(FF4) | -2.119 | 0.034 | -2.756 | 0.006 | -2.622 | 0.009 | -1.665 | 0.096 | -2.823 | 0.005 |
| (FF2)–(FF3) | 1.073 | 0.283 | 1.834 | 0.067 | 1.314 | 0.189 | 2.687 | 0.007 | 1.473 | 0.141 |
| (FF2)–(FF4) | 0.484 | 0.629 | 1.149 | 0.251 | 1.129 | 0.259 | 2.376 | 0.017 | 1.090 | 0.276 |
| (FF3)–(FF4) | -1.328 | 0.184 | -2.790 | 0.005 | -1.832 | 0.067 | -0.899 | 0.368 | -3.257 | 0.001 |
| *Post-crisis period* | | | | | | | | | | |
| (FF)–(HF) | 3.369 | 0.001 | 4.006 | 0.000 | 3.960 | 0.000 | 3.844 | 0.000 | 3.442 | 0.001 |
| (FF1)–(FF2) | -2.905 | 0.004 | -3.216 | 0.001 | -1.155 | 0.248 | -1.338 | 0.181 | -2.187 | 0.029 |
| (FF1)–(FF3) | -1.630 | 0.103 | -4.149 | 0.000 | -0.763 | 0.445 | -1.310 | 0.190 | -1.920 | 0.055 |
| (FF1)–(FF4) | -2.367 | 0.018 | -3.821 | 0.000 | -1.912 | 0.056 | -1.326 | 0.185 | -3.052 | 0.002 |
| (FF2)–(FF3) | 2.340 | 0.019 | 2.168 | 0.030 | 1.141 | 0.254 | 0.825 | 0.409 | 0.945 | 0.345 |
| (FF2)–(FF4) | 1.158 | 0.247 | 1.313 | 0.189 | 0.579 | 0.563 | 0.473 | 0.636 | -0.014 | 0.989 |
| (FF3)–(FF4) | -2.666 | 0.008 | -1.858 | 0.063 | -3.334 | 0.001 | -0.522 | 0.602 | -4.042 | 0.000 |

HFRI Fund of Funds Composite Index (FF); HFRI FOF Strategic Index (FF1); HFRI FOF Market Defensive Index (FF2); HFRI FOF Diversified Index (FF3); HFRI FOF Conservative Index (FF4).

In the endogenous switching model, we use a probit specification for $s_t$, and the elements of $P$ are modeled as:

$$
\begin{aligned}
\Pr[s_t = 1 | s_{t-1} = 1] &= \Phi[a(s_{t-1} = 1) + Z_t'b(s_{t-1} = 1)] \\
\Pr[s_t = 1 | s_{t-1} = 2] &= \Phi[a(s_{t-1} = 2) + Z_t'b(s_{t-1} = 2)] \\
\Pr[s_t = 2 | s_{t-1} = 1] &= 1 - \Phi[a(s_{t-1} = 1) + Z_t'b(s_{t-1} = 1)] \\
\Pr[s_t = 2 | s_{t-1} = 2] &= 1 - \Phi[a(s_{t-1} = 2) + Z_t'b(s_{t-1} = 2)],
\end{aligned}
\tag{15.9}
$$

where $\Phi$ is the distribution function of the $N(0,1)$ distribution, $Z_t$ is a vector of explanatory variables, $a(s_{t-1})$ is a regime-switching parameter (constant in each regime), and $b(s_{t-1})$ is regime-switching vector of parameters capturing the impact of $Z_t$ on the transition probabilities. We choose the variables in $Z_t$ based on the results reported in Section 15.2.3. As there are significant contemporaneous correlations between each FoHF's excess return and the market risk premium ($b_1$), percentage change in the EUR/US\$ exchange rate ($b_2$), and percentage change in the VIX index ($b_3$), we consider these variables in $Z_t$. We estimate the endogenous switching MS-AR(1) model for all possible combinations of these variables included in $Z_t$. The parameter estimates are obtained by the maximum likelihood method summarized in Kim et al. (2008). The best performing specification is selected by using the Bayesian Information Criterion (BIC).

For the exogenous switching model and the best-performing endogenous switching model, Table 15.8 reports the parameter estimates and the following likelihood-based model performance metrics: log likelihood (LL), BIC, and likelihood ratio (LR) test statistic. For some FoHFs indices, the BIC metric suggests better model performance of the exogenous switching model. Nevertheless, the difference between the BIC measures may not be statistically significant. To validate the use of the endogenous switching model, we apply two tests. (i) We implement the $t$-test suggested by Kim et al. (2008). They suggest testing the significance of the correlation coefficient, $\rho$, which captures the correlation between the error terms of the mean equation and the probit equation. They propose this test since if $\rho$ is non-significant, then the endogenous switching model will reduce to the exogenous switching model. Table 15.8 shows that $\rho$ is significant at the 1% level for all FoHFs indices. This supports the endogenous switching specification. (ii) We apply the LR test to see if there is a significant difference between the LL of the two models. Since the two MS specifications are non-nested models, the non-nested LR approach of Vuong (1989) is used to evaluate the significance of the LR statistic; see Table 15.8. For all FoHFs indices, the LR test statistic is significant, at least, at the 10% level, supporting the endogenous switching model.

For all FoHFs indices and both models, the figures showing the estimated filtered probability of the first regime, $\Pr[s_t = 1 | y_1, \ldots, y_{t-1}]$, are presented in Figure 15.A1A in the Appendix. Notice that, in all figures, the first regime ($s_t = 1$) is the 'low-volatility regime,' while the second regime ($s_t = 2$) is the 'high-volatility regime.' This idea helps to interpret the $b(s_{t-1})$ coefficients of the best endogenous switching specification (see Table 15.8). (i) $b_1(s_{t-1})$ measures the impact of

**Table 15.8**   In-sample Estimation Results of Exogenous Switching and Endogenous Switching AR(1) Models

| | Exogenous Switching AR(1) Model | | | | | | Endogenous Switching AR(1) Model | | | | |
|---|---|---|---|---|---|---|---|---|---|---|---|
| | (FF) | (FF1) | (FF2) | (FF3) | (FF4) | | (FF) | (FF1) | (FF2) | (FF3) | (FF4) |
| $c_1$ | -0.004* | -0.002 | -0.006** | -0.004 | -0.004* | $c_1$ | -0.001 | 0.003 | 0.003 | -0.003 | -0.004 |
| $c_2$ | 0.004 | 0.008 | 0.010 | 0.006 | 0.004 | $c_2$ | -0.005 | -0.008 | -0.005 | -0.001 | 0.003 |
| $\varphi_1$ | -0.243* | 0.002 | -0.227** | -0.110 | -0.154 | $\varphi_1$ | -0.158** | 0.044 | 0.188*** | 0.067* | -0.216*** |
| $\varphi_2$ | 0.073 | 0.081 | 0.192* | 0.078 | 0.053 | $\varphi_2$ | 0.023 | 0.034 | -0.213*** | -0.114*** | 0.145*** |
| $\omega_1$ | 0.018*** | 0.018*** | 0.025*** | 0.021*** | 0.023*** | $\omega_1$ | 0.021 | 0.019 | 0.064* | 0.062* | 0.028 |
| $\omega_2$ | 0.045*** | 0.047*** | 0.062*** | 0.049*** | 0.049*** | $\omega_2$ | 0.056* | 0.052* | 0.026 | 0.023 | 0.060* |
| $\eta_{11}$ | 0.982*** | 0.944*** | 0.934*** | 0.964*** | 0.984*** | $a(1)$ | 3.651*** | 1.434*** | 1.526*** | 0.951*** | 3.746*** |
| $\eta_{22}$ | 0.960*** | 0.929*** | 0.947*** | 0.956*** | 0.973*** | $a(2)$ | -0.927*** | -0.749*** | -1.695*** | -6.291*** | -1.344*** |
| | | | | | | $b_1(1)$ | 4.377*** | 1.536*** | NA | 0.739*** | NA |
| | | | | | | $b_1(2)$ | -0.965*** | -1.216*** | NA | -9.152*** | NA |
| | | | | | | $b_2(1)$ | NA | NA | NA | NA | NA |
| | | | | | | $b_2(2)$ | NA | NA | NA | NA | NA |
| | | | | | | $b_3(1)$ | -0.440*** | NA | NA | NA | -9.453*** |
| | | | | | | $b_3(2)$ | 0.057*** | NA | NA | NA | 0.871*** |
| | | | | | | $\rho$ | 0.702*** | 0.713*** | 0.513*** | 0.766*** | 0.703*** |
| | | | | | | Pr | 0.000 | 0.000 | 0.000 | 0.000 | 0.000 |

*Model performance metrics*

| | (FF) | (FF1) | (FF2) | (FF3) | (FF4) | | (FF) | (FF1) | (FF2) | (FF3) | (FF4) |
|---|---|---|---|---|---|---|---|---|---|---|---|
| LL | 519.280 | 526.719 | 478.093 | 518.834 | 502.718 | | 534.980 | 538.646 | 480.846 | 535.589 | 512.960 |
| BIC | -993.863 | -1008.740 | -911.488 | -992.971 | -960.739 | | -991.738 | -1010.245 | -905.819 | -1004.130 | -958.874 |
| LR | 31.400*** | 23.854*** | 5.506* | 33.510*** | 20.484*** | | | | | | |

HFRI Fund of Funds Composite Index (FF); HFRI FOF Strategic Index (FF1); HFRI FOF Market Defensive Index (FF2); HFRI FOF Diversified Index (FF3); HFRI FOF Conservative Index (FF4). Pr is a parameter capturing the probability of the first regime in the initial period (see Kim et al., 2008, p. 266). Asterisks denote significance at the *10%, ***5%, and ***1% levels, respectively.

the market risk premium on the transition probabilities of $s_t$. The market risk premium is included in the probit equation for the FoHFs Composite (FF), FoHFs Strategic (FF1), and FoHFs Diversified (FF3) indices. We find that $b_1(s_{t-1}=1)$ is positive and $b_1(s_{t-1}=2)$ is negative for the three indices. We can interpret these estimates based on equation (15.9) as follows. If the market risk premium increases, then the probability of staying in the same regime will increase. Moreover, if the market risk premium decreases, then the probability of changing to the other regime will increase. The lowest $b_1(s_{t-1}=2)$ coefficient is observed for the FoHFs Diversified Index (FF3). This shows that if the market risk premium decreases, then the FoHFs Diversified Index will change from the high-volatility regime to the low-volatility regime with a relatively high probability. (ii) We do not report the estimates of $b_2(s_{t-1})$ in Table 15.8, since the best performing specification never includes the EUR/US\$ exchange rate. (iii) $b_3(s_{t-1})$ captures the impact of the percentage change in the VIX volatility index variable on the transition probabilities. The VIX index is included in the probit equation for FoHFs Composite (FF) and FoHFs Conservative (FF4) indices. We find that $b_3(s_{t-1}=1)$ is negative and $b_3(s_{t-1}=2)$ is positive for both indices. According to this result, if market volatility increases, then the probability of changing to the other regime will increase. Furthermore, if market volatility decreases, then the probability of staying in the same regime will increase. Finally, the lowest $b_3(s_{t-1}=1)$ parameter is found for the FoHFs Conservative Index (FF4). This shows that if the VIX volatility index increases, then the FoHFs Conservative Index will change from the low-volatility regime to the high-volatility regime with a relatively high probability.

## CONCLUSION

In this chapter we focus on forecasting the performance of FoHFs indices. We compare the predictive accuracy of out-of-sample and multistep ahead forecasts of the performance of five FoHFs indices and 15 hedge fund indices. The performance of these indices is measured by their excess rate of return above the MSCI Global Equity market index. We use data obtained from HFR for the period January 1990–January 2012. We apply a large number of AR and MS-AR specifications for the conditional mean of excess returns and we use GARCH and MS-GARCH specifications for the conditional volatility of excess returns. We perform diagnostic tests for each model and implement only the correctly specified models for forecasting purposes. The full out-of-sample forecasting period is from January 2000 to March 2012. This period is broken down to three subperiods: before, during, and after the financial crisis. We compare the predictive accuracy of competing models among these subperiods. Out-of-sample forecasts are obtained using a moving time window approach. Multistep ahead forecasts are estimated for the 1, 3, 6, 9, and 12 months time horizons. Forecast precision is measured by the RMSE loss function.

The estimation results show that forecast accuracy is the lowest during the financial crisis for all indices. We also find that, although the predictive accuracy improves after the financial crisis, the RMSE is significantly higher in the post-crisis period than in the pre-crisis period for all indices. We use the DM predictive accuracy test to show significant differences of forecast errors: between FoHFs composite and hedge fund composite indices, and among all specific FoHFs indices.

We provide the following contributions:

- We find that excess returns on all FoHFs indices have regime-switching dynamics.
- We find that, in most cases, an MS specification dominates the predictive accuracy for FoHFs indices.
- We investigate the determinants of FoHFs regimes by using an endogenous switching AR model. The estimation results show that the market risk premium and the VIX volatility index are significant determinants of FoHFs regimes, but their importance depends on the specific FoHFs index.

## APPENDIX

**(a)**

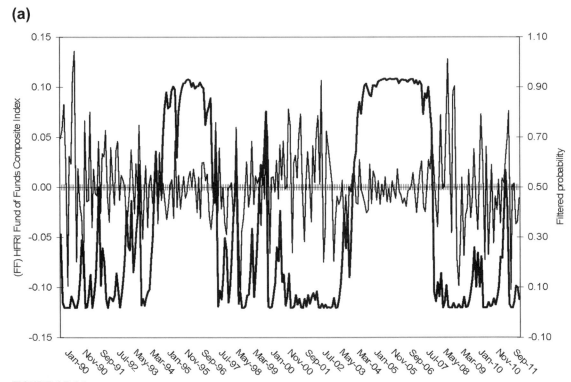

**FIGURE 15.A1**
Filtered probabilities of FoHFs for exogenous switching (a, c, e, g, and i) and endogenous switching (b, d, f, h, and j) models.

**(b)**

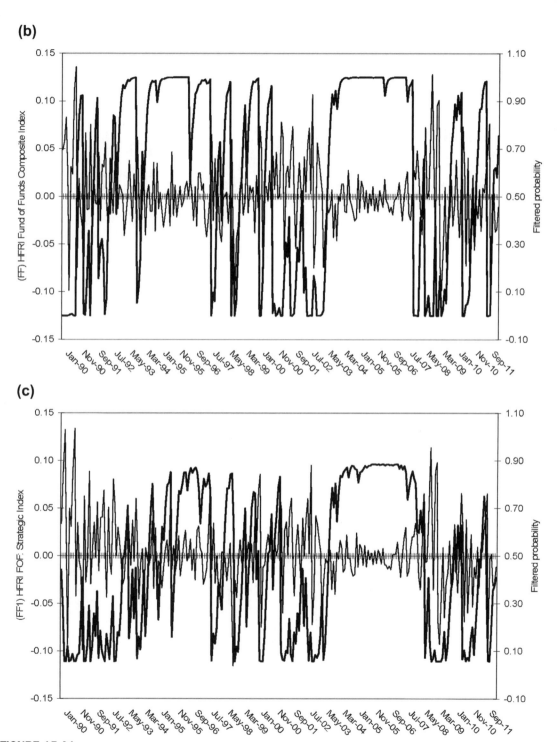

**FIGURE 15.A1**
*Continued.*

**(d)**

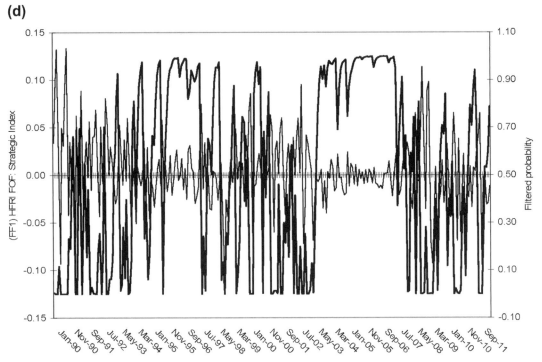

**(e)**

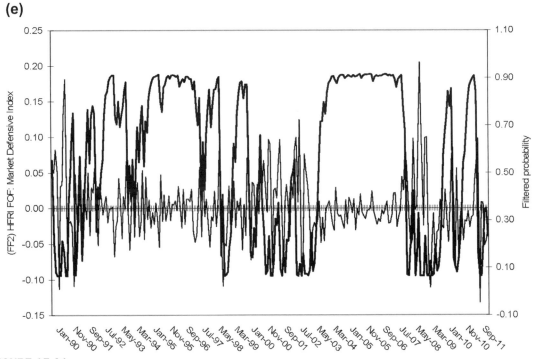

**FIGURE 15.A1**
*Continued.*

**(f)**

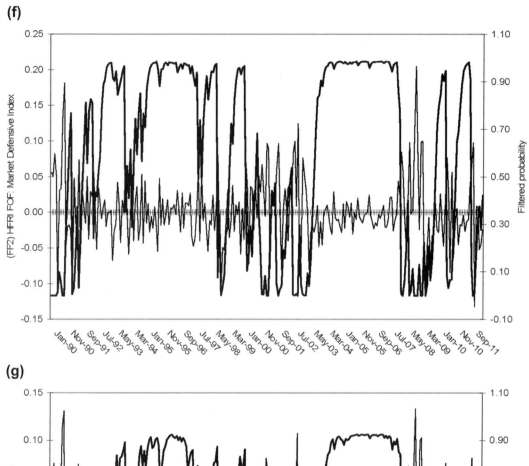

**(g)**

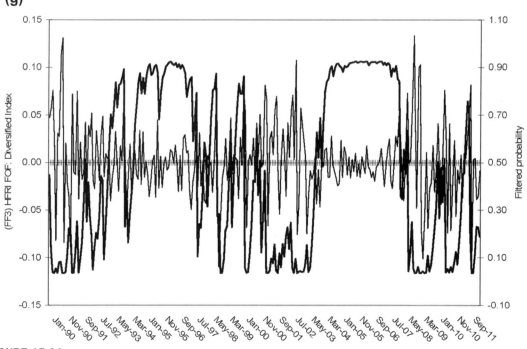

**FIGURE 15.A1**
*Continued.*

**(h)**

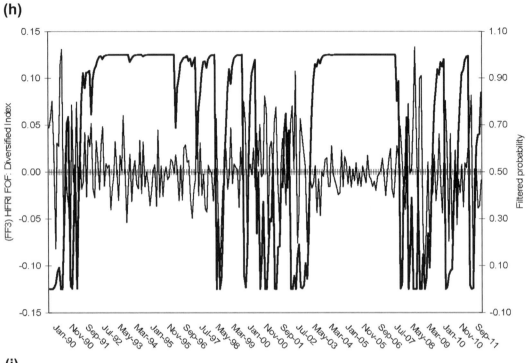

**(i)**

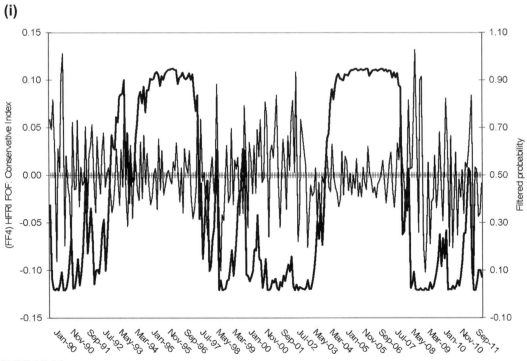

**FIGURE 15.A1**
*Continued.*

(j)

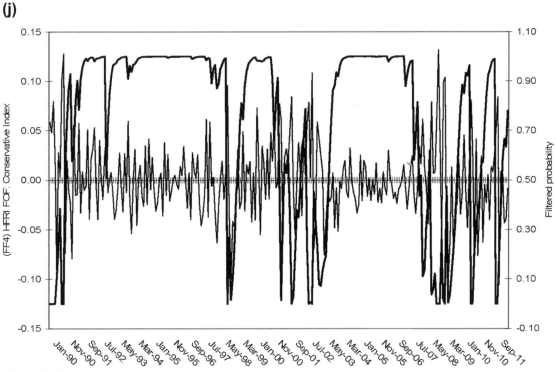

**FIGURE 15.A1**
*Continued.*

# References

Abdou, K., & Nasereddin, M. (2011). The Persistence of Hedge Fund Strategies in Different Economic Periods: A Support Vector Machine Approach. *Journal of Derivatives and Hedge Funds, 17*(1), 2–15.

Abramson, A., & Cohen, I. (2007). On the Stationarity of Markov Switching GARCH Processes. *Econometric Theory, 23*(3), 485–500.

Ackermann, C., McEnally, R., & Ravenscraft, D. (1999). The Performance of Hedge Funds: Risk, Return and Incentives. *The Journal of Finance, 54*(3), 833–874.

Agarwal, V., & Naik, N. Y. (1999). On Taking the 'Alternative' Route: Risks, Rewards and Performance Persistence of Hedge Funds. *The Journal of Alternative Investments, 2*(4), 6–23.

Agarwal, V., & Naik, N. Y. (2000). Multi-Period Performance Persistence Analysis of Hedge Funds. *Journal of Financial and Quantitative Analysis, 35*(3), 327–342.

Agarwal, V., & Naik, N. Y. (2004). Risk and Portfolio Decisions Involving Hedge Funds. *Review of Financial Studies, 17*(1), 63–98.

Bauwens, L., Preminger, A., & Romboust, J. V. K. (2010). Theory and Inference for a Markov Switching GARCH Model. *Econometrics Journal, 13*(2), 218–244.

Billio, M., Getmansky, M., & Pelizzon, L. (2006). Phase-Locking and Switching Volatility in Hedge Funds. In *Working Paper 54/WP/2006, Department of Economics*. Venice: Ca' Foscari University of Venice.

Billio, M., Getmansky, M., & Pelizzon, L. (2009). *Crises and Hedge Fund Risk*. New Haven, CT: Yale School of Management Working Paper AMZ2561, Yale School of Management.

Blazsek, S., & Downarowicz, A. (2012). *Forecasting Hedge Fund Volatility: A Markov Regime-Switching Approach*. The European Journal of Finance. http://www.tandfonline.com/doi/abs/10.1080/1351847X.2011.653576.

Bollen, N. P. B., & Pool, V. K. (2009). Do Hedge Fund Managers Misreport Returns? Evidence from the Pooled Distribution. *The Journal of Finance, 63*(5), 2257–2288.

Bollerslev, T. (1986). Generalized Autoregressive Conditional Heteroskedasticity. *Journal of Econometrics, 31*(3), 307–327.

Brown, S. J., Goetzmann, W. N., & Ibbotson, R. G. (1999). Offshore Hedge Funds: Survival and Performance 1989-1995. *Journal of Business, 72*(1), 91–118.

Brown, S. J., Fraser, T., & Liang, B. (2008). Hedge Fund Due Diligence: A Source of Alpha in a Hedge Fund Portfolio Strategy. *Journal of Investment Management, 6*(4), 22–33.

Brown, S. J., Gregoriou, G. N., & Pascalau, R. (2012). Diversification in Funds of Hedge Funds: Is It Possible to Overdiversify? *The Review of Asset Pricing Studies, 2*(1), 89–110.

Cai, J. (1994). A Markov Model of Switching-Regime ARCH. *Journal of Business and Economic Statistics, 12*(3), 309–316.

Chan, N., Getmansky, M., Hass, S. M., & Lo, A. W. (2005). *Systemic Risk and Hedge Funds. Working Paper 11200.* Cambridge, MA: NBER.

Dickey, D. A., & Fuller, W. A. (1979). Distribution of the Estimators for Autoregressive Time Series with a Unit Root. *Journal of the American Statistical Association, 74*(366), 427–431.

Diebold, F. X. (1986). Modeling the Persistence of Conditional Variances: A Comment. *Econometric Reviews, 5*(1), 51–56.

Diebold, F. X., & Mariano, R. S. (1995). Comparing Predictive Accuracy. *Journal of Business and Economic Statistics, 13*(3), 253–263.

Donaldson, R. G., & Kamstra, M. (1997). An Artificial Neural Network-GARCH Model for International Stock Return Volatility. *Journal of Empirical Finance, 4*(1), 17–46.

Dueker, M. J. (1997). Markov Switching in GARCH Processes and Mean-Reverting Stock-Market Volatility. *Journal of Business and Economic Statistics, 15*(1), 26–34.

Dunis, C. L., Laws, J., & Chauvin, S. (2003). FX Volatility Forecasts and the Informational Content of Market Data for Volatility. *The European Journal of Finance, 9*(3), 242–272.

Fama, E. F., & French, K. R. (1993). Common Risk Factors in the Returns on Stocks and Bonds. *Journal of Financial Economics, 33*(1), 3–56.

Francq, C., & Zakoian, J.-M. (2001). Stationarity of Multivariate Markov-Switching ARMA Models. *Journal of Econometrics, 102*(2), 339–364.

Friedman, B. M., & Laibson, D. I. (1989). Economic Implications of Extraordinary Movements in Stock Prices. *Brookings Papers on Economic Activity, 2*(2), 137–189.

Fung, W., & Hsieh, D. A. (1997). Empirical Characteristics of Dynamic Trading Strategies: The Case of Hedge Funds. *The Review of Financial Studies, 10*(2), 275–302.

Fung, W., & Hsieh, D. A. (1999). A Primer on Hedge Funds. *Journal of Empirical Finance, 6*(3), 309–331.

Fung, W., & Hsieh, D. A. (2000). Performance Characteristics of Hedge Funds and CTA Funds: Natural Versus Spurious Biases. *Journal of Financial and Quantitative Analysis, 35*(3), 291–307.

Fung, W., Hsieh, D. A., Naik, N. Y., & Ramadorai, T. (2008). *Hedge funds* Performance, Risk, and Capital Formation. *The Journal of Finance, 63*(4), 1777–1803.

Füss, R., Kaiser, D. G., & Adams, Z. (2007). Value at Risk, GARCH Modelling and the Forecasting of Hedge Fund Return Volatility. *Journal of Derivatives and Hedge Funds, 13*(1), 2–25.

Goodworth, T. R. J., & Jones, C. M. (2007). Factor-Based, Non-Parametric Risk Measurement Framework for Hedge Funds and Fund-of-Funds. *The European Journal of Finance, 13*(7), 645–655.

Gray, S. (1996). Modeling the Conditional Distribution of Interest Rates as a Regime-Switching Process. *Journal of Financial Economics, 42*(1), 27–62.

Gregoriou, G. N. (2003). Performance Evaluation of Funds of Hedge Funds Using Conditional Alphas and Betas. *Derivatives, Use, Trading and Regulation, 8*(4), 324–344.

Gregoriou, G. N., & Rouah, F. (2002). Pitfalls to Avoid when Constructing a Fund of Hedge Funds. *Derivatives, Use, Trading and Regulation, 8*(1), 59–65.

Gregoriou, G. N., Hübner, G., Papageorgiou, N., & Rouah, F. D. (2007). Funds of Funds versus Simple Portfolios of Hedge Funds: A Comparative Study of Persistence in Performance. *Journal of Derivatives and Hedge Funds, 13*(2), 88−106.

Haas, M., Mittink, S., & Paolella, M. S. (2004). A New Approach to Markov-Switching GARCH Models. *Journal of Financial Econometrics, 2*(4), 493−530.

Hamilton, J. D. (1989). A New Approach to the Economic Analysis of Nonstationary Time Series and the Business Cycle. *Econometrica, 57*(2), 357−384.

Hamilton, J. D. (1994). *Time Series Analysis*. Princeton, NJ: Princeton University Press.

Hamilton, J. D., & Susmel, R. (1994). Autoregressive Conditional Heteroskedasticity and Changes in Regime. *Journal of Econometrics, 64*(1-2), 307−333.

Hansen, P. R., & Lunde, A. (2005). A Forecast Comparison of Volatility Models: Does Anything Beat a GARCH(1,1)? *Journal of Applied Econometrics, 20*(7), 873−889.

Harri, A., & Brorsen, B. W. (2004). Performance Persistence and the Source of Returns for Hedge Funds. *Applied Financial Economics, 14*(2), 131−141.

Hedges, I. V. J. R. (2005). Hedge Fund Transparency. *The European Journal of Finance, 11*(5), 411−417.

Henneke, J. S., Rachev, S. T., Fabozzi, F. J., & Nikolov, M. (2011). MCMC-Based Estimation of Markov Switching ARMA-GARCH Models. *Applied Economics, 43*(3), 259−271.

Ineichen, A. M. (2003). *Absolute Returns − The Risk and Opportunities of Hedge Fund Investing*. London: Wiley.

Jagannathan, R., Malakhov, A., & Novikov, D. (2010). Do Hot Hands Exist Among Hedge Fund Managers? An Empirical Evaluation. *The Journal of Finance, 65*(1), 217−255.

Jordan, A. E., & Simlai, P. (2011). Risk Characterization, Stale Pricing and the Attributes of Hedge Funds Performance. *Journal of Derivatives and Hedge Funds, 17*(1), 16−33.

Kang, B. U., In, F., Kim, G., & Kim, T. S. (2010). A Longer Look at the Asymmetric Dependence between Hedge Funds and the Equity Market. *Journal of Financial and Quantitative Analysis, 45*(3), 763−789.

Kim, C. J., & Nelson, C. R. (1999). *State-Space Models with Regime Switching*. Cambridge, MA: MIT Press.

Kim, C. J., Piger, J., & Startz, R. (2008). Estimation of Markov Regime-Switching Models with Endogenous Switching. *Journal of Econometrics, 143*(2), 263−273.

Klaassen, F. (2002). Improving GARCH Volatility Forecasts with Regime-Switching GARCH. *Empirical Economics, 27*(2), 363−394.

Laube, F., Schiltz, J., & Terraza, V. (2011). On the Efficiency of Risk Measures for Funds of Hedge Funds. *Journal of Derivatives and Hedge Funds, 17*(1), 63−84.

Liang, B. (1999). On Performance of HFs. *Financial Analysts Journal, 55*(4), 72−85.

Ljung, G., & Box, G. (1978). On a Measure of Lack of Fit in Time-Series Models. *Biometrika, 65*(2), 297−303.

Muzzioli, S. (2010). Option-Based Forecasts of Volatility: An Empirical Study in the DAX-Index Options Market. *The European Journal of Finance, 16*(6), 561−586.

Pesaran, M. H., & Timmermann, A. (2004). How Costly is it to Ignore Breaks when Forecasting the Duration of a Time Series? *International Journal of Forecasting, 20*(3), 411−425.

Preminger, A., Ben-Zion, U., & Wettstein, D. (2006). Extended Switching Regression Models with Time-Varying Probabilities for Combining Forecasts. *The European Journal of Finance, 12*(6-7), 455−472.

Racicot, F. É., & Théoret, R. (2007). The Beta Puzzle Revisited: A Panel Study of Hedge Fund Returns. *Journal of Derivatives and Hedge Funds, 13*(2), 125−146.

Straumann, D. (2009). Measuring the Quality of Hedge Fund Data. *The Journal of Alternative Investments, 12*(2), 26−40.

Taylor, S. J. (1986). *Modelling Financial Time Series*. Chichester: Wiley.

Vuong, Q. H. (1989). Likelihood Ratio Tests for Model Selection and Non-Nested Hypotheses. *Econometrica, 57*(2), 303−333.

# CHAPTER 16

# A Panel-Based Quantile Regression Analysis of Funds of Hedge Funds

**David Edmund Allen, Akhmad Kramadibrata, Robert John Powell, and Abhay Kumar Singh**

School of Accounting, Finance and Economics, Edith Cowan University, Joondalup, Western Australia, Australia

## 16.1. INTRODUCTION

In recent decades, hedge funds have become a very popular, growing investment class. For instance, as of September 2012, the BarclayHedge hedge fund database reports 4991 hedge funds in their database. As compared to the time of inception, hedge funds are now more widely accessible, not only to heavily investing individuals, but also to institutional investors like pension funds. Coupled to the growth of hedge funds has been increased academic research interest in the factors involved in their success.

Funds of hedge funds (FoHFs) are investment instruments that enable investing in other hedge funds. After first being introduced in Switzerland in 1969 (Ineichen, 2004), FoHFs have grown considerably in number. For example, as of September 2012, the BarclayHedge FoHFs database alone reports 1353 FoHFs. FoHFs not only enable investor access to hedge fund investments, but also provide benefits like risk diversification, improved liquidity, monitoring service, and higher return. FoHFs data also has certain advantages over hedge fund data,

Reconsidering Funds of Hedge Funds. http://dx.doi.org/10.1016/B978-0-12-401699-6.00016-2

such as being less prone to survivorship bias and backfilled data bias (Fung and Hsieh, 2002; Hutson, 2006).

In this chapter, we evaluate the return-based performance of FoHFs against factor-mimicking portfolios (in the form of financial markets) using panel data analysis tools. We examine the relationship of FoHFs monthly logarithmic returns with the factor-mimicking indices, capturing the effect of size of the FoHFs, world and country-specific market returns, interest rates, currencies, and value premium (Fama and French, 1992, 1993) given by value and growth indices. We use a linear panel analysis model that quantifies the relationship around the mean of the distribution, and contrast the results with a quantile regression panel analysis that provides the relationship for the quantile of interest and is a more comprehensive relationship. There are very few studies that have previously used quantile regression in analyzing hedge funds or FoHFs (e.g., Meligkotsidou *et al.*, 2009; Füss *et al.*, 2009). Our approach is to first use quantile regression in a panel context that evaluates factors other than size and age (Füss *et al.*, 2009) to analyze FoHFs returns across the quantiles.

The factor-based analysis in this chapter is not a new approach. Many previous studies applied Sharpe's (1992) method of analysis to hedge funds and FoHFs, including Goodworth and Jones (2007), Fung and Hsieh (1997), Agarwal and Naik (2000a, 2000b), Duang (2008), Chen (2005), and Assness *et al.* (2004a, 2004b). These factor-based approaches were employed in the past to gain insight into the returns and risk profile of FoHFs. FoHFs are not just studied using factor-based analysis, but also by use of other methods such as survival time analysis (Gregoriou *et al.*, 2008; Gregoriou and Pascalau, 2012; Gregoriou and Rouah, 2002; Brown *et al.*, 2001; Amin and Kat, 2003) and portfolio risk analysis (Gregoriou *et al.*, 2007; Agarwal and Naik, 2004; Davies *et al.*, 2009) among many other areas of academic financial research.

This chapter commences with an overview of quantile regression and quantile regression for panel data. This is followed by a discussion of the data and methodology used, followed by the discussion of major results. We conclude the analysis with a discussion of important findings.

## 16.2. PANEL DATA ANALYSIS AND QUANTILE REGRESSION

Panel data (also known as longitudinal or cross-sectional time series) is a data structure in which the entities and their properties are observed over time. In our case, the entities are FoHFs and we are interested in the monthly returns across a period of 10 years.

The basic linear panel model can be given as:

$$y_{it} = \alpha + x_{it}'\beta + c_i + u_{it}, \qquad (16.1)$$

where $y_{it}$ represents the dependent variable across $i$ entities for time $t$, $x'$ gives the explanatory variables minus the constant, $\alpha$ gives the intercept, $\beta$ is a vector of parameters, $c_i$ gives the individual specific effect, and $u_{it}$ is the error term.

The fixed-effects model and the random-effects model are the two basic models in panel analysis. The individual specific effect in the fixed-effects model is correlated with the explanatory variables (independent variables), whereas in the random-effects model this individual specific effect is uncorrelated with the explanatory variable.

We will not discuss the estimation process of the panel data models, but refer to econometrics textbooks including Baltagi (2001), Wooldridge (2002), Greene (2003), and Stock and Watson (2011) for further comprehensive details.

## 16.2.1. Quantile Regression

The simple ordinary least squares (OLS) regression method assumes a multivariate normal distribution between the dependent and the explanatory variable, which focuses on the mean of the distribution. The assumption of normality makes the computation easy, but is not useful when the variables have skewed distributions and where linear regression is incapable of describing the conditional distribution of the dependent variable.

Koenker and Bassett (1978) introduced quantile regression as an extension of classical OLS estimates of conditional mean models to the estimation of quantile functions for a distribution. Quantile regression enables quantification of the relationship between dependent and independent variables across different quantiles of the conditional distribution of the dependent variable. Quantile regression has advantages over OLS, as it is robust against outliers (Fitzenberger *et al.*, 2001) and it avoids the assumption that the error terms are independent and identically distributed (i.i.d.).

The quantile regression estimation process starts with the central median case in which the median regressor estimator minimizes a sum of absolute errors, as opposed to OLS that minimizes the sum of squared errors. The estimation of other regression quantiles is done by minimizing an asymmetrically weighted sum of absolute errors. Taken together, the ensemble of estimated conditional quantile functions offers a much more comprehensive view of the effect of covariates on the location, scale, and shape of the distribution of the response variable.

As given in Alexander (2008), the quantile regression model is:

$$Y = \alpha_q + \beta_q X + e, \tag{16.2}$$

where $\alpha_q$ and $\beta_q$ for the $q$th quantile can be estimated by solving the following optimization problem:

$$\min_{\alpha,\beta} \sum_{t=1}^{T} (q - 1_{Y_t \leq \alpha + \beta X_t})(Y_t - (\alpha + \beta X_t)), \tag{16.3}$$

where:

$$1_{Y_t \leq \alpha + \beta X_t} = \begin{cases} 1 & \text{if } Y_t \leq \alpha + \beta X_t \\ 0 & \text{Otherwise} \end{cases}. \tag{16.4}$$

We refer the reader to the Koenker (2005) monograph or to Alexander (2008) for a more comprehensive discussion and for mathematical details of quantile regression.

In a panel data structure where the entities are observed over time, equation (16.2) can be rewritten as:

$$Y_{it} = \beta_q X'_{it} + e_{it}, \qquad (16.5)$$

where $i = 1,...,N$ and $t = 1,...,T$ observations.

Quantile regression for panel data with fixed and random effects is a fairly new technique, with the estimation process to include fixed or random effects in a quantile regression panel data model being different to a simple linear quantile regression model. There has been little, but growing, interest in the estimation methods of quantile regression for panel data models (Koenker, 2004; Abrevaya and Dahl, 2008; Bache *et al.*, 2011; Geraci and Bottai, 2007; Canay, 2011; Koenker and Bache 2011; Galvao, 2011; Lamarche, 2010; Rosen, 2009).

It is now well established that hedge fund returns are not normal and are skewed with fat tails (Brooks and Kat, 2002; Gregoriou and Pascalau, 2012). As the FoHFs are constructed using hedge funds we can assume that the statistical properties of hedge funds are true for FoHFs as well and hence in this analysis we use a quantile regression panel estimation model. Quantile regression does not assume normal conditional distribution and its estimates are robust against outliers in heavy tailed distributions.

In this study we use the Penalized Quantile Regression approach for panel data proposed by Koenker (2004) to evaluate the relationship of FoHFs returns with the factors in a fixed effects panel data model.

## 16.3. DATA AND METHODOLOGY

### 16.3.1. Discussion of Data

We use daily logarithmic returns for FoHFs obtained from the BarclayHedge FoHFs database. We use 10 years of monthly data from January 2002 to December 2011, which gives us 119 monthly returns for the analysis. We chose the FoHFs that have data for all the months in the selected time period, which gives us a total of 152 FoHFs to analyze in a panel data setting. The data for explanatory variables is downloaded from BarclayHedge and Datastream databases.

We chose eight different explanatory variables to run the panel regression on: (i) assets under management (AUM), (ii) S&P 500 Composite Index, (iii) FTSE 100 Index, (iv) MSCI World Index, (v) JP Morgan World Government Bond Index, (vi) Russell 1000 Growth Index, (vii) Russell 1000 Value Index, and (viii) Barclay Currency Traders Index. We use the logarithm of AUM and percentage logarithmic returns are used for the rest of the explanatory variables. These independent (or explanatory) variables are chosen as factor-mimicking portfolios for size of FoHFs, market return of United States and United Kingdom, world

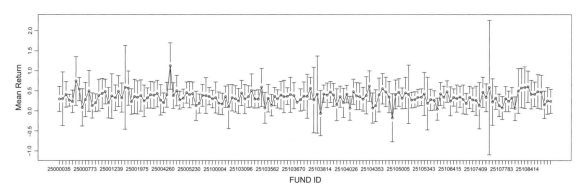

**FIGURE 16.1**
FoHFs Mean logarithmic return plot for the 10-year period from 2002 to 2011.

market return, growth and value portfolios (as analyzed in the Fama–French factor model), and change in currency.

Figure 16.1 gives the average of 10-year returns for each FoHF used in the study, at the 95% confidence interval. It is interesting to note that the average return for all the funds in our data period is positive, which shows the positive returns performance of FoHFs. Table 16.1 gives the descriptive statistics for our dataset. The skewness and excess kurtosis in the descriptive statistics clearly indicate non-normal distribution of the dependent and independent variables.

### 16.3.2. Methodology

We use the following factor model to assess the performance of FoHFs:

$$R_{it} = \beta_1 \log(AUM) + \beta_2(S\&P) + \beta_3(FTSE) + \beta_4(MSCI\ World\ Index)$$
$$+ \beta_5(World\ Government\ Bond\ Index) + \beta_6(Growth\ Index)$$
$$+ \beta_7(Value\ Index) + \beta_8(Currency\ Traders\ Index). \qquad (16.6)$$

We first use the linear panel data model to analyze the effect of explanatory variables in the whole dataset. The analysis is then carried out using quantile regression for panel data at the 1%, 20%, 50%, 80%, and 99% quantiles of interest, ranging from lower to higher quantiles. These quantiles cover the extreme lower to extreme higher tails of the distribution and hence provide a more comprehensive picture of the relationships. The data also exhibits non-normal distribution (as given in Table 16.1). The empirical analysis is conducted in R, using PLM and RQPD packages for linear regression and quantile regression panel data models (R Development Core Team, 2012; Croissant and Millo, 2008). We will now discuss the major results in Section 16.4.

## 16.4. DISCUSSION OF THE RESULTS

We test the model as given in equation (16.6) using a linear panel model to quantify the relationship between the dependent and independent variables

**Table 16.1** Descriptive Statistics for FoHFs Returns and the Explanatory Variables

| | FoHFs Return[1] | Log (AUM)[1] | FTSE 100 | S&P 500 | MSCI World Index | JP Morgan Government Bond Index | Russell 1000 Growth Index | Russell 1000 Value Index | Barclays Currency Traders Index |
|---|---|---|---|---|---|---|---|---|---|
| Minimum | −8.79 | 17.12 | −22.07 | −18.36 | −21.13 | −4.36 | −19.36 | −19.01 | −2.77 |
| Quartile 1 | −0.50 | 18.06 | −3.23 | −2.17 | −2.28 | −0.44 | −1.89 | −1.94 | −0.49 |
| Median | 0.60 | 18.55 | 0.24 | 0.69 | 0.71 | 0.54 | 0.63 | 1.27 | 0.05 |
| Arithmetic mean | 0.34 | 18.45 | 0.11 | 0.07 | 0.16 | 0.57 | 0.21 | 0.33 | 0.25 |
| Quartile 3 | 1.56 | 18.91 | 3.69 | 2.81 | 3.19 | 1.36 | 3.38 | 3.16 | 0.80 |
| Maximum | 4.84 | 19.31 | 16.64 | 14.61 | 10.35 | 5.56 | 10.41 | 10.84 | 6.23 |
| SE mean | 0.18 | 0.06 | 0.54 | 0.47 | 0.46 | 0.14 | 0.44 | 0.45 | 0.12 |
| LCL mean (0.95) | −0.03 | 18.34 | −0.95 | −0.87 | −0.74 | 0.28 | −0.66 | −0.56 | 0.02 |
| UCL mean (0.95) | 0.71 | 18.56 | 1.17 | 1.01 | 1.07 | 0.85 | 1.08 | 1.22 | 0.49 |
| Variance | 4.98 | 0.47 | 34.07 | 26.70 | 24.98 | 2.44 | 23.06 | 24.17 | 1.73 |
| Standard deviation | 2.02 | 0.60 | 5.84 | 5.17 | 5.00 | 1.56 | 4.80 | 4.92 | 1.31 |
| Skewness | −1.41 | −0.45 | −0.48 | −0.83 | −0.97 | 0.39 | −0.81 | −0.94 | 1.30 |
| Kurtosis | 4.95 | −0.21 | 1.83 | 2.11 | 2.15 | 1.24 | 1.61 | 1.82 | 3.99 |

[1]The descriptive statistics for FoHFs returns and AUM are the average of all the FoHFs across the cross-section. The individual descriptive statistics are omitted here to save space.

around the mean (average relationship). We tested for both random and fixed effects in the model. A Hausman test (Hausman, 1978), which compares the two sets of estimates (fixed effects and random effects), rejects the alternate hypothesis of random effects in our model (16.6). We therefore report only the fixed-effects model results from both the linear panel model and quantile regression panel model.

Table 16.2 gives the estimated coefficients from the linear fixed effects panel model. The results show significant coefficients for all the factors chosen in the model. The results show a negative association with the size of FoHFs, which shows that the profits decrease as the FoHFs size grows. This finding is in accordance with other studies on the behavior of hedge funds with size (Agarwal *et al.*, 2004; Harri and Brorsen, 2004; Goetzmann *et al.*, 2003).

The FoHFs sample in our dataset shows positive association with the S&P 500 and the FTSE 100, which suggests that the majority of FoHFs follow these two market returns. The highest positive association (direct relationship) is with the MSCI World Index, which shows that FoHFs closely follow global markets. The highest negative association (inverse relationship) is with the Value Index ($\beta_7$), which shows that FoHFs inversely follow the stocks with lower expected growth rate.

Table 16.3 gives the coefficient estimates from the quantile regression panel data analysis. The coefficients are estimated for five quantiles (0.01, 0.2, 0.5, 0.8, and 0.99), which covers the extreme left and right tails of the distribution. Figure 16.2 plots the estimated coefficients across quantiles for each factor in the model.

It is clearly evident from Table 16.3 and Figure 16.2 that the factor coefficients for FoHFs are not same across the distribution. All the factors give different relationships for the extreme quantile. The effect of the size of the FoHFs as quantified by the linear panel model is negative to the return (Table 16.2), whereas in Table 16.3, the quantile regression panel model presents a completely different picture. Here, the effect is negative for the lower quantiles,

**Table 16.2** Estimated Coefficients for the Linear Panel Model (Fixed Effect)

| Explanatory Factors | Estimate | SE | *t*-value | Pr(>|t|) |
|---|---|---|---|---|
| Log(AUM) ($\beta_1$) | −0.1069 | 0.0188 | −5.6788 | 0.0000 |
| S&P 500 ($\beta_2$) | 0.0535 | 0.0056 | 9.6329 | 0.0000 |
| FTSE 100 ($\beta_3$) | 0.0358 | 0.0049 | 7.3373 | 0.0000 |
| MSCI World Index ($\beta_4$) | 0.6686 | 0.0119 | 56.0058 | 0.0000 |
| JP Morgan Government Bond Index ($\beta_5$) | −0.0305 | 0.0108 | −2.8247 | 0.0047 |
| Russell 1000 Growth Index ($\beta_6$) | −0.0544 | 0.0091 | −6.0026 | 0.0000 |
| Russell 1000 Value Index ($\beta_7$) | −0.4184 | 0.0096 | −43.3955 | 0.0000 |
| Barclays Currency Traders Index ($\beta_8$) | 0.1065 | 0.0113 | 9.3936 | 0.0000 |

The Pr(>|t|) value of <0.05 shows significance of the coefficients at the 95% level or higher.

**Table 16.3** Estimated Coefficients for the Quantile Regression Panel Model (Fixed Effect)

| Explanatory Factors | Estimate | SE | t-value | Pr(>\|t\|) |
|---|---|---|---|---|
| Quantile = 0.01 | | | | |
| Log(AUM) ($\beta_1$) | −0.24769 | 0.02699 | −9.17679 | 0 |
| S&P 500 ($\beta_2$) | −0.23214 | 0.03722 | −6.23726 | 0 |
| FTSE 100 ($\beta_3$) | 0.33407 | 0.03429 | 9.74114 | 0 |
| MSCI World Index ($\beta_4$) | 0.77788 | 0.15247 | 5.10174 | 0 |
| JP Morgan Government Bond Index ($\beta_5$) | −0.15233 | 0.09718 | −1.56751 | 0.11701 |
| Russell 1000 Growth Index ($\beta_6$) | −0.06909 | 0.08434 | −0.81918 | 0.4127 |
| Russell 1000 Value Index ($\beta_7$) | −0.37686 | 0.13767 | −2.73746 | 0.0062 |
| Barclays Currency Traders Index ($\beta_8$) | 0.18317 | 0.12993 | 1.40969 | 0.15865 |
| Quantile = 0.2 | | | | |
| Log(AUM) ($\beta_1$) | −0.0299 | 0.00168 | −17.7484 | 0 |
| S&P 500 ($\beta_2$) | 0.05827 | 0.00407 | 14.30579 | 0 |
| FTSE 100 ($\beta_3$) | 0.04499 | 0.00366 | 12.29357 | 0 |
| MSCI World Index ($\beta_4$) | 0.66186 | 0.02476 | 26.73028 | 0 |
| JP Morgan Government Bond Index ($\beta_5$) | −0.02967 | 0.01025 | −2.89484 | 0.0038 |
| Russell 1000 Growth Index ($\beta_6$) | −0.09469 | 0.01228 | −7.7094 | 0 |
| Russell 1000 Value Index ($\beta_7$) | −0.36271 | 0.01577 | −23.0004 | 0 |
| Barclays Currency Traders Index ($\beta_8$) | 0.052 | 0.01022 | 5.08603 | 0 |
| Quantile = 0.5 | | | | |
| Log(AUM) ($\beta_1$) | 0.02271 | 0.00054 | 41.7722 | 0 |
| S&P 500 ($\beta_2$) | 0.07207 | 0.00345 | 20.88111 | 0 |
| FTSE 100 ($\beta_3$) | 0.0071 | 0.00337 | 2.10481 | 0.03532 |
| MSCI World Index ($\beta_4$) | 0.54509 | 0.02027 | 26.89657 | 0 |
| JP Morgan Government Bond Index ($\beta_5$) | −0.04216 | 0.00864 | −4.87885 | 0 |
| Russell 1000 Growth Index ($\beta_6$) | −0.06865 | 0.00987 | −6.95697 | 0 |
| Russell 1000 Value Index ($\beta_7$) | −0.3078 | 0.01177 | −26.1619 | 0 |
| Barclays Currency Traders Index ($\beta_8$) | 0.12648 | 0.01045 | 12.09938 | 0 |
| Quantile = 0.8 | | | | |
| Log(AUM) ($\beta_1$) | 0.06842 | 0.00144 | 47.5769 | 0 |
| S&P 500 ($\beta_2$) | 0.07345 | 0.00432 | 16.99124 | 0 |
| FTSE 100 ($\beta_3$) | −0.01128 | 0.00349 | −3.23544 | 0.00122 |
| MSCI World Index ($\beta_4$) | 0.55685 | 0.02271 | 24.52289 | 0 |
| JP Morgan Government Bond Index ($\beta_5$) | −0.03113 | 0.01194 | −2.6075 | 0.00913 |
| Russell 1000 Growth Index ($\beta_6$) | −0.04967 | 0.00971 | −5.11646 | 0 |
| Russell 1000 Value Index ($\beta_7$) | −0.35865 | 0.01385 | −25.887 | 0 |
| Barclays Currency Traders Index ($\beta_8$) | 0.18827 | 0.00976 | 19.29853 | 0 |
| Quantile = 0.99 | | | | |
| Log(AUM) ($\beta_1$) | 0.23876 | 0.02486 | 9.60496 | 0 |
| S&P 500 ($\beta_2$) | 0.09692 | 0.04506 | 2.15084 | 0.0315 |
| FTSE 100 ($\beta_3$) | −0.07299 | 0.03724 | −1.95971 | 0.05005 |
| MSCI World Index ($\beta_4$) | 0.90672 | 0.1789 | 5.06842 | 0 |
| JP Morgan Government Bond Index ($\beta_5$) | −0.08546 | 0.08536 | −1.00113 | 0.31678 |
| Russell 1000 Growth Index ($\beta_6$) | −0.22067 | 0.11876 | −1.85817 | 0.06316 |
| Russell 1000 Value Index ($\beta_7$) | −0.5328 | 0.10488 | −5.08005 | 0 |
| Barclays Currency Traders Index ($\beta_8$) | 0.29098 | 0.08456 | 3.44098 | 0.00058 |

The Pr(>\|t\|) value of <0.05 shows significance of the coefficients at the 95% level or higher.

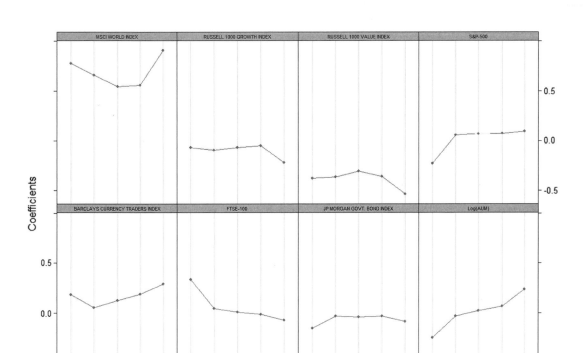

**FIGURE 16.2**
Quantile regression estimates for the factor coefficients across quantiles.

but becomes positive for the higher quantiles (after the median quantile), which indicates that profits do not necessarily decrease with the growing FoHFs size, and for a FoHF with higher AUM the profits can increase. The same contrast can be drawn for the S&P 500, where in the quantile regression panel model, the relationship is negative (inverse) for the extreme left tail (1% quantile) of the FoHFs returns. In the case of the FTSE 100, this relationship is completely opposite, and the FTSE 100 exhibits negative association in higher quantiles and positive association in lower quantiles, showing that the FTSE 100 has a negative effect on higher FoHFs returns.

The MSCI World Index maintains its positive effect across the quantiles, but is highly positively related to the FoHFs returns in extreme quantiles, which shows that FoHFs follow the world index more closely during times of extreme loss or high gain than during normal times. The JP Morgan Government Bond Index has a negative association across quantiles and is also not significant for extreme quantiles. The rest of the factors maintain the same relationship (positive or negative) as for the linear panel model, with different levels. The results from the quantile regression panel model clearly show that the relationship between

FoHFs returns and the factors in our model not only change across quantiles, but can be opposite for extreme tails.

## CONCLUSION

The increasing number of FoHFs and their ease of availability to a wide range of investors, has increased academic and institutional interest in the factors affecting their performance. In this study we analyzed FoHFs returns against eight factors that are frequently used to assess the return-based performance of financial assets. We employed linear panel data analysis to examine monthly percentage logarithmic returns of 152 FoHFs for a period of 10 years. We also used a new approach of quantile regression panel analysis to evaluate the factor model across the distribution of FoHFs returns.

Our results clearly show that the relationships between FoHFs returns and the factors used in this study are not constant across the distribution as quantified by the linear panel model. This empirical analysis provides insights into FoHFs performance and how the returns generated by them are related to the factors. This study adds to the few previous studies that used quantile regression in hedge funds or FoHFs research and demonstrates the capability of quantile regression panel models to quantify the factor model relationships.

Quantile regression is a robust regression tool with critical advantages over OLS, including robustness to outliers, no normal distribution assumption, and quantification of relationships across the complete distribution of the dependent variable. In financial risk, modeling the left tail (or lower quantiles) of the return distribution quantifies the extreme risk of the financial instrument. Quantile regression has the distinct advantage of modeling the desired quantile of interest and hence proves to be an efficient tool in risk modeling.

The study provides a comprehensive picture of the factor model examined in the empirical exercise, but can be furthered by testing other factors like the age of the FoHFs. Not only could the study be furthered with additional factors, but it also could be done over smaller time periods to evaluate the relationship across the distribution and time series.

## Acknowledgments

We thank the Australian Research Council for funding support.

## References

Abrevaya, J., & Dahl, C. M. (2008). The Effects of Birth Inputs on Birthweight. *Journal of Business and Economic Statistics, 26*(4), 379–397.

Agarwal, V., & Naik, N. Y. (2000a). Multi-period performance persistence analysis of hedge funds. *Journal of Financial and Quantitative Analysis, 35*(3), 327–342.

Agarwal, V., & Naik, N. Y. (2000b). *Performance Evaluation of Hedge Funds with Option Based and Buy-and-Hold Strategies*. Working Paper, Georgia State University and London Business School, Institute of Finance and Accounting.

Agarwal, V., Daniel, N. D., & Naik, N. Y. (2004). *Flows, Performance, and Managerial Incentives in Hedge Funds.* Working Paper, Georgia State University.

Agarwal, V., & Naik, N. Y. (2004). Risks and Portfolio Decisions Involving Hedge Funds. *Review of Financial Studies, 17*(1), 63−98.

Alexander, C. (Ed.) (2008). *Market Risk Analysis: Practical Financial Econometrics* (Volume II). Hoboken, NJ: Wiley.

Amin, G., & Kat, H. (2003). Welcome to the Dark Side: Hedge Fund Attrition and Survivorship Bias over the Period 1994−2001. *Journal of Alternative Investments, 6*(1), 57−73.

Bache, S. H., Dahl, C., & Kristensen, J. T. (2011). *Headlights on Tobacco Road to Low Birthweight Outcomes − Evidence from a Battery of Quantile Regression Estimators and a Heterogeneous Panel.* Working Paper, School of Economics and Management, University of Aarhus.

Baltagi, B. (2001). *Econometric Analysis of Panel Data* (3rd ed.). Chichester: Wiley.

Brooks, C., & Kat, H. (2002). The Statistical Properties of Hedge Fund Index Returns and Their Implications For Investors. *Journal of Alternative Investments, 5*(2), 26−44.

Brown, S. J., Goetzmann, W., & Park, J. (2001). Careers and Survival: Competition and Risk in the Hedge Fund and CTA Industry. *Journal of Finance, 56*(5), 1869−86.

Canay, I. A. (2011). A Simple Approach to Quantile Regression for Panel Data. *The Econometrics Journal, 14*(3), 368−386.

Croissant, Y., & Millo, G. (2008). Panel Data Econometrics in R: The plm Package. *Journal of Statistical Software, 27*(2), 1−43.

Davies, R. J., Kat, H. M., & Lu, S. (2009). Fund of Hedge Funds Portfolio Selection: A Multiple-Objective Approach. *Journal of Derivatives & Hedge Funds, 15*(2), 91−115.

Fama, E. F., & French, K. R. (1992). The Cross-Section of Expected Stock Returns. *Journal of Finance, 47*(2), 427−486.

Fama, E. F., & French, K. R. (1993). Common Risk Factors in the Returns on Stocks and Bonds. *Journal of Financial Economics, 33*(1), 3−56.

Fitzenberger, B., Koenker, R., & Machado, J. A. F. (2001). Editorial. *Empirical Economics, 26*(1), 1−5.

Fung, W., & Hsieh, D. A. (2002). Benchmarks of Hedge Funds Performance: Information Content and Measurement Bias. *Financial Analyst Journal, 58*(1), 22−34.

Fung, W., & Hsieh, D. A. (1997). Empirical Characteristics of Dynamic Trading Strategies: The Case of Hedge Funds. *The Review of Financial Studies, 70*(2), 275−302.

Füss, R., Kaiser, D. G., & Strittmatter, A. (2009). Measuring Funds of Hedge Funds Performance Using Quantile Regressions: Do Experience and Size Matter? *The Journal of Alternative Investments, 12*(2), 41−53.

Galvao, A. F., Jr. (2011). Quantile Regression for Dynamic Panel Data With Fixed Effects. *Journal of Econometrics, 164*(1), 142−157.

Geraci, M., & Bottai, M. (2007). Quantile Regression for Longitudinal Data using the Asymmetric Laplace Distribution. *Biostatistics, 8*(1), 140−154.

Goodworth, T. R. J., & Jones, C. M. (2007). Factor-Based, Non-Parametric Risk Measurement Framework for Hedge Funds and Fund-of-Funds. *European Journal of Finance, 13*(7), 645−655.

Greene, W. (2003). *Econometric Analysis.* Upper Saddle River, NJ: Prentice Hall.

Gregoriou, G. N., & Pascalau, R. (2012). A Joint Survival Analysis of Hedge Funds and Funds of Funds Using Copulas. *Managerial Finance, 38*(1), 82−100.

Gregoriou, G. N., & Rouah, F. (2002). Large versus Small Hedge Funds: Does Size Affect Performance? *Journal of Alternative Investments, 5*(4), 75−77.

Gregoriou, G. N., Hubner, G., Papageorgiou, N., & Rouah, D. F. (2007). Funds of Funds Versus Simple Portfolios of Hedge Funds: A Comparative Study of Persistence in Performance. *Journal of Derivatives and Hedge Funds, 13*(2), 88−106.

Gregoriou, G. N., Kooli, M., & Rouah, F. D. (2008). Survival of Strategic, Market Defensive, Diversified and Conservative Fund of Hedge Funds: 1994−2005. *Journal of Derivatives and Hedge Funds, 13*(4), 273−286.

Goetzmann, W. N., Ingersoll, J. E., & Ross, S. A. (2003). High-Water Marks and Hedge Fund Management Contract. *Journal of Finance, 58*(4), 1685−1718.

Harri, A., & Brorsen, B. W. (2004). Performance Persistence and the Source of Returns for Hedge Funds. *Applied Financial Economics, 14*(2), 131−141.

Hausman, J. (1978). Specification Tests in Econometrics. *Econometrica, 46*(6), 1251–1271.

Hutson, E. (2006). Funds of Hedge Funds: Not the Poor Cousins of the Hedge Fund Industry. *JASSA, 4,* 22–26.

Ineichen, A. M. (2004). European Hedge Funds. *Journal of Portfolio Management, 30*(4), 254–267.

Koenker, R., & Bassett, G., Jr. (1978). Regression Quantiles. *Econometrica, 46*(1), 33–50.

Koenker, R. (2005). Quantile Regression. *Econometric Society Monograph Series.* Cambridge: Cambridge University Press.

Koenker, R. (2004). Quantile Regression for Longitudinal Data. *Journal of Multivariate Analysis, 91*(1), 74–89.

Koenker, R., & Bache, S. H. (2011). rqpd: Regression Quantiles for Panel Data. *R package version 0.5/r9.* Available at http://R-Forge.R-project.org/projects/rqpd.

Lamarche, C. (2010). Robust Penalized Quantile Regression Estimation for Panel Data. *Journal of Econometrics, 157*(2), 396–408.

Meligkotsidou, L., Vrontos, I. D., & Vrontos, S. D. (2009). Quantile Regression Analysis of Hedge Fund Strategies. *Journal of Empirical Finance, 16*(2), 264–279.

R Development Core Team. (2012). *R: A Language and Environment for Statistical Computing.* Vienna: R Foundation for Statistical Computing. http://www.R-project.org/.

Rosen, A. (2009). *Set identification Via Quantile Restrictions in Short Panels.* London: Working Papers, Centre for Microdata Methods and Practice.

Sharpe, W. F. (1992). Asset Allocation: Management Style and Performance Measurement. *Journal of Portfolio Management, 18*(2), 7–19.

Stock, J. H., & Watson, M. W. (2011). *Introduction to Econometrics.* Upper Saddle River, NJ: Pearson Addison-Wesley.

Wooldridge, J. (2002). *Econometric Analysis of Cross-Section and Panel Data.* Cambridge, MA: MIT Press.

# SECTION 4
# Fund of Hedge Fund Alpha

# CHAPTER 17

# Reward-to-Risk Ratios of Funds of Hedge Funds

**Yigit Atilgan**\*, **Turan G. Bali**†, and **K. Ozgur Demirtas**\*\*
\*Assistant Professor of Finance, Sabanci Universitesi, İstanbul, Turkey
†Robert S. Parker Chair Professor of Business Administration,
Georgetown University, Washington, DC, USA.
\*\*Professor of Finance, Sabanci Universitesi, İstanbul, Turkey

## Chapter Outline

## 17.1. INTRODUCTION

Investors base their portfolio asset allocation decisions on the interactions between risks and returns of available financial securities. The assumption of risk aversion implies that securities with greater risk should demand greater return. Although the tradeoff between risk and return is well-established in financial economics, the ability to generate higher expected returns per unit risk can vary from one security to another. This chapter compares various reward-to-risk ratios for the funds of hedge funds (FoHFs) index with those of several bond and stock market indices.

Traditional risk measures used in portfolio performance measurement assume that returns are normally distributed and therefore the standard deviation of the empirical return distribution is a sound measure of risk only if the underlying return distribution is close to normal. The first measure of reward-to-risk that we use is the Sharpe ratio (1966), defined as the ratio of the mean excess return of a portfolio to its standard deviation. The Sharpe ratio is the most common measure of how well the return of a portfolio compensates the investor for the risk taken. However, a common criticism is that it is too broad since it includes the total risk of a portfolio in its denominator. Another potential issue regarding

Reconsidering Funds of Hedge Funds. http://dx.doi.org/10.1016/B978-0-12-401699-6.00017-4

the calculation of Sharpe ratios for the FoHFs index is the non-normality of hedge fund return distributions.

The hedge fund literature provides evidence that distributions of hedge fund returns tend to deviate from normality. Malkiel and Saha (2005) report that the distribution of hedge fund returns generally has high kurtosis and negative skewness. The documented deviation from normality can be traced to the unique investment strategies that hedge funds follow. Bali *et al.* (2011, 2012) provide evidence for hedge funds' superior performance for detecting shifts in financial markets, and their ability to timely adjust their positions to those changes in financial and economic conditions. Fung and Hsieh (1997) observe that hedge fund managers are flexible to choose among a diverse set of asset classes, and they can use dynamic trading strategies that involve short sales, leverage, and derivatives. Such strategies have the potential to induce option-like payouts and exposure to tail events for hedge funds. In a follow-up study, Fung and Hsieh (2001) focus on hedge funds that use trend-following strategies. They construct several trend-following factors that can replicate key features of hedge fund returns such as skewness and positive returns during extreme market movements. Mitchell and Pulvino (2001) investigate merger arbitrage strategies and conjecture that returns to risk arbitrage are related to market returns in a non-linear way. Their results indicate that merger risk arbitrage is similar to writing uncovered index put options. Agarwal and Naik (2004) find that non-linear payoff structures exist for a wide range of hedge fund strategies including equity-oriented positions. They state that ignoring the downside risk of hedge funds can result in significantly higher losses during large market downturns. Brown *et al.* (2012) look at the diversification effect of investing in FoHFs and find that the magnitude of skewness is an increasing function of diversification offered by FoHFs. Their finding suggests that downside risk exposure may not be diversifiable. Finally, Bali *et al.* (2007) and Liang and Park (2007) provide direct evidence that downside risk measures such as value at risk (VaR), expected shortfall, and tail risk can explain the cross-section of hedge fund returns.

Downside risk is a function of the higher order moments of a return distribution and even without the existence of non-linear payoffs, higher-order moments such as skewness and kurtosis have been found to play an important role in asset pricing. The mean–variance portfolio theory of Markowitz (1952) has been extended by Arditti (1967) and Kraus and Litzenberger (1976) to incorporate the effect of skewness. These studies present three-moment asset pricing models with investors that hold concave preferences and prefer positive skewness. The main implication of these models is that assets that increase a portfolio's skewness are more desirable and should command lower expected returns. Harvey and Siddique (2000) extend these unconditional pricing models and incorporate conditional coskewness. Again, the implication is that risk-averse investors prefer positively skewed assets to negatively skewed assets. As far as the fourth moment is concerned, Dittmar (2002) builds on the theoretical works of Kimball (1993) and Pratt and Zeckhauser (1987), and finds preference for lower kurtosis. Asset distributions with lower probability mass in their tails are preferred, and therefore assets that increase a portfolio's kurtosis are less desirable and should command higher expected returns.

Downside risk increases with kurtosis and decreases with skewness (Cornish and Fisher, 1937). Given the importance of these return moments for asset pricing and the prevalence of downside risk in hedge fund returns, we place special emphasis on the concept of downside risk in our reward-to-risk analysis. To investigate how much expected return each index commands per unit of downside risk, we use both a non-parametric and parametric measure of VaR in the construction of the alternative reward-to-risk ratios. For the non-parametric *VaRSharpe* ratio, the denominator is the absolute value of the minimum index return over various past sample windows. For the parametric reward-to-downside risk measure (*PVaRSharpe*), the denominator is based on the lower tail of Hansen's (1994) skewed *t*-density.

The results indicate that the FoHFs index outperforms the bond and stock market indices based on traditional Sharpe ratios on average. Although the Sharpe ratios decrease for every index as the sampling window for the calculation of standard deviation is extended and this decline is most pronounced for the FoHFs index, it has the highest Sharpe ratio regardless of the sampling window. When we take downside risk into account through non-parametric and parametric VaR, the results are similar. The FoHFs index has higher downside risk-adjusted Sharpe ratios compared to all bond and stock market indices and this result is especially strong at shorter sampling windows for VaR measurement.

The chapter is organized as follows. Section 17.2 discusses the methodology for calculating the reward-to-risk ratios. Section 17.3 explains the data and presents the summary statistics. Section 17.4 discusses the empirical results, followed by conclusions.

## 17.2. METHODOLOGY

We estimate three reward-to-risk ratios that differ from each other based on the risk measure used in the denominator. The first of these ratios is the standard Sharpe ratio:

$$Sharpe_{i,t} = \frac{R_{i,t} - R_{f,t}}{StDev_{i,t}}, \tag{17.1}$$

where $R_{i,t}$ denotes the return for the month indexed by $t$ on the fund of funds, bond, or stock market index $i$, $R_f$ is the risk-free rate as measured by the 1-month Treasury bill return. The standard deviation for index $i$ is computed using the squared deviations of monthly returns from their means. For each month $t$ and index $i$, past $k$ months are used to compute the standard deviation where $k$ takes the alternative values of 12, 24, 36, or 48. Specifically:

$$StDev_{i,t} = \sqrt{\frac{1}{k-1} \sum_{j=0}^{k} (R_{i,t-j} - \overline{R}_i)^2}, \tag{17.2}$$

In order to take downside risk into account, we first use a non-parametric measure of VaR that measures how much the value of a portfolio could decline in a fairly extreme outcome. In our analysis, we use the minimum index returns observed during past $k$ months of daily data where $k$ again takes the alternative values of 12, 24, 36, or 48. These original VaR measures are multiplied by $-1$ before the construction of the reward-to-risk ratios so that higher magnitudes of the measure correspond to greater downside risk. After we calculate non-parametric VaR measures each month using rolling windows, Sharpe ratios that incorporate these non-parametric VaR estimates are computed. Specifically, *VaRSharpe* is defined as:

$$VaRSharpe_{i,t} = \frac{R_{i,t} - R_f}{VaR_{i,t}}, \tag{17.3}$$

where $VaR_{i,t}$ is the non-parametric VaR.

Finally, for the parametric measure of VaR, we use the skewed $t$-density, which accounts for skewness and excess kurtosis in the data. Hansen (1994) introduces a generalization of the Student $t$-distribution where asymmetries may occur, while maintaining the assumption of a zero mean and unit variance. This skewed $t$ (ST)-density is given by:

$$f(z_t; \mu, \sigma, v, \lambda) = \begin{cases} bc\left(1 + \frac{1}{v-2}\left(\frac{bz_t + a}{1 - \lambda}\right)^2\right)^{-\frac{v+1}{2}} & \text{if } z_t < -a/b \\ bc\left(1 + \frac{1}{v-2}\left(\frac{bz_t + a}{1 + \lambda}\right)^2\right)^{-\frac{v+1}{2}} & \text{if } z_t \geq -a/b \end{cases} \tag{17.4}$$

where $z_t = (R_t - \mu)/\sigma$ is the standardized excess market return, and the constants $a$, $b$, and $c$ are given by:

$$a = 4\lambda c\left(\frac{v-2}{v-1}\right), \quad b^2 = 1 + 3\lambda^2 - a^2, \quad c = \frac{\Gamma\left(\frac{v+1}{2}\right)}{\sqrt{\pi(v-2)}\Gamma\left(\frac{v}{2}\right)}. \tag{17.5}$$

The parametric approach to calculating VaR is based on the lower tail of the ST distribution. Specifically, we estimate the parameters of the skewed $t$-density $(\mu, \sigma, v, \lambda)$ using the past 12, 24, 36, or 48 months of return data and then find the corresponding percentile of the estimated distribution. Assuming that $R_t = f_{v,\lambda}(z)$ follows a skewed $t$-density density, parametric VaR is the solution to:

$$\int_{-\infty}^{\Gamma_{ST}(\Phi)} f_{v,\lambda}\left(z\right) dz = \Phi, \tag{17.6}$$

where $\Gamma_{ST}(\Phi)$ is the VaR threshold based on the skewed $t$-density with a loss probability of $\Phi$. Sharpe ratios that incorporate parametric VaR are defined as:

$$PVaRSharpe_{i,t} = \frac{R_{i,t} - R_f}{PVaR_{i,t}}. \tag{17.7}$$

## 17.3. DATA AND DESCRIPTIVE STATISTICS

We gather the data for the FoHFs index returns from the Hedge Fund Research (HFR) database. The database reports monthly index values for various hedge fund strategies beginning January 1990 and the sample period used in the following analysis extends until December 2011. HFR indices are broken down into four main strategies, each with multiple substrategies. These strategies include Equity Hedge (equity market neutral, quantitative directional, short bias, etc.), Event Driven (distressed/restructuring, merger arbitrage, etc.), Macro (commodity, currency, etc.) and Relative Value (convertible arbitrage, fixed-income corporate, etc.). HFR also reports a Fund of Funds Composite index which includes over 650 constituent funds. FoHFs invest with multiple managers through funds or managed accounts and their main benefit is designing a diversified portfolio of managers to reduce the risk of investing with an individual manager. The Fund of Funds Composite index is an equally weighted index and it is commonly used by hedge fund managers as a performance benchmark. A fund needs to report monthly gross returns and returns net of all fees to be included in the index. Moreover, the assets need to be reported in US$ and the fund needs to have at least US$50 million under management or have been actively trading for at least 12 months. Funds are included in the composite index the month after their addition to the database.

We also collect data for various bond and stock market indices for comparison purposes. Specifically, we collect price data for indices that track Treasury bonds with maturities of 5, 10, 20, and 30 years. For equities, we focus on the S&P 500 index and the NYSE/AMEX/NASDAQ index with distributions. All the data for the bond and stock market indices come from the Center for Research in Security Prices (CRSP). The yield for the 1-month Treasury bill that is used to proxy for the risk-free rate is downloaded from Kenneth French's online data library.

Table 17.1 reports the descriptive statistics for all indices. A comparison of means shows that the NYSE/AMEX/NASDAQ index has the highest monthly return (0.78%); however, the S&P 500 index has not generated as high an average return (0.58%). This difference can be explained by the greater returns generated by small stocks historically. The mean returns on the bond indices increase by time to maturity with the 5-year bond index delivering 0.56% per month and the 30-year bond index delivering 0.73% per month. In terms of means, the FoHFs index sits somewhere in the middle in this picture with a monthly mean return of 0.61%. The medians tell a similar story with the biggest difference being that both stock market indices have generated higher median returns than all other indices. The NYSE/AMEX/NASDAQ index had a median return of 1.34% over the sample period, whereas the S&P 500 index had a median return of 1.01%. Again, the median returns for the bond indices increase by time to maturity and vary from 0.58% to 0.89%. The FoHFs index still positions itself in the middle with a median return of 0.77%.

With respect to the standard deviations, we find that the stock market indices are generally more volatile compared to the bond market indices. NYSE/AMEX/

**Table 17.1** Descriptive Statistics for Fund of Hedge Funds, Bond, and Equity Indices

| | Mean | Standard Deviation | Minimum | 25th Percentile | Median | 75th Percentile | Maximum | Skew | Kurtosis |
|---|---|---|---|---|---|---|---|---|---|
| FoHFs | 0.0061 | 0.0171 | −0.0747 | −0.0021 | 0.0077 | 0.0159 | 0.0685 | −0.6718 | 6.7061 |
| 5-Year bond | 0.0056 | 0.0128 | −0.0338 | −0.0020 | 0.0058 | 0.0145 | 0.0452 | −0.1755 | 3.3092 |
| 10-Year bond | 0.0063 | 0.0203 | −0.0668 | −0.0058 | 0.0071 | 0.0190 | 0.0854 | −0.0719 | 4.0789 |
| 20-Year bond | 0.0077 | 0.0286 | −0.1059 | −0.0084 | 0.0087 | 0.0244 | 0.1445 | 0.0619 | 5.7720 |
| 30-Year bond | 0.0073 | 0.0290 | −0.1474 | −0.0134 | 0.0089 | 0.0270 | 0.1741 | 0.2930 | 6.7463 |
| S&P 500 | 0.0058 | 0.0439 | −0.1694 | −0.0195 | 0.0101 | 0.0340 | 0.1116 | −0.5630 | 3.9987 |
| NYSE/AMEX/NASDAQ | 0.0078 | 0.0455 | −0.1846 | −0.0189 | 0.0134 | 0.0385 | 0.1153 | −0.6827 | 4.2297 |

Descriptive statistics for the returns of various FoHFs, bond, and equity indices in the United States. The four bond market indices are based on 5-, 10-, 20-, and 30-year maturity Treasury bonds. The two equity indices are the S&P 500 index and the NYSE/AMEX/NASDAQ Composite index. The descriptive statistics that are presented in the table are the mean, standard deviation, minimum, 25th percentile, median, 75th percentile, maximum, skewness and kurtosis.

NASDAQ, and S&P 500 indices have monthly standard deviations of 4.55% and 4.39%, respectively. The standard deviations of the bond market indices increase from 1.28% for the 5-year bond index to 2.90% for the 30-year bond index. This finding is in line with the higher interest rate sensitivities associated with bonds of longer durations. The FoHFs index has the second lowest standard deviation, which is equal to 1.71%.

The patterns for standard deviations also manifest themselves when we look at the maximum and minimum returns. The highest (lowest) maximum (minimum) returns belong to the equity indices and the bond indices with longer times to maturity. For example, there has been a month in which the NYSE/AMEX/NASDAQ index gained 11.53% in value and the 30-year bond index gained 17.41% in value. Similarly, there has been a month during which the NYSE/AMEX/NASDAQ index lost 18.46% of its value and the 30-year bond index lost 14.74% of its value. The extreme returns for the FoHFs index are milder with a minimum monthly return of −7.47% and a maximum monthly return of 6.85%. This finding is consistent with the diversification effects inherent in fund of funds strategies as argued in Fung and Hsieh (2000).

Finally, we compare the higher-order moments of the indices. The FoHFs index has the second most negative skewness statistic (−0.67) after the NYSE/AMEX/NASDAQ index (−0.68). The other stock market index, S&P 500, also has negative skewness (−0.56). This is consistent with earlier findings in the literature that the tails of the hedge fund and equity return distributions are longer on the left side compared to the right side. The negative skewness associated with these indices was also foreshadowed by their higher medians compared to the means. For the bond market indices, the skewness statistic increases with time to maturity. The 5-year bond index has a skewness statistic of −0.18, whereas the 30-year bond index distribution is positively skewed with a statistic of 0.29.

The kurtosis of the FoHFs index is again substantial and equal to 6.71. In other words, the FoHFs return distribution has more mass on its tails compared to the normal distribution and thus is leptokurtic. Kurtosis again increases with time to maturity for the bond market indices from 3.31 to 6.75. The kurtosis for stock market indices lies somewhere in the middle among the bond market indices with a kurtosis statistic for the NYSE/AMEX/NASDAQ (S&P 500) index equal to 4.00 (4.23).

## 17.4. EMPIRICAL RESULTS

Table 17.2 presents the traditional Sharpe ratios that incorporate the standard deviation of a portfolio in its denominator. We calculate these monthly Sharpe ratios in a rolling-window fashion and use different sampling windows to calculate the standard deviations. The length of the sampling windows ranges from 12 to 48 months. We present both the time-series mean and the standard deviations of the reward-to-risk ratios for all indices.

| Table 17.2 | Standard Deviation-Based Sharpe Ratios for FoHFs, Bond, and Equity Indices | | | | | | |
|---|---|---|---|---|---|---|---|
| | Sharpe12 | | Sharpe24 | | Sharpe36 | | Sharpe48 |
| FoHFs | 0.3516 | (0.5182) | 0.2979 | (0.3166) | 0.2629 | (0.2363) | 0.2357 | (0.1517) |
| 5-Year bond | 0.2223 | (0.3709) | 0.2127 | (0.2823) | 0.2088 | (0.2338) | 0.2037 | (0.1857) |
| 10-Year bond | 0.1801 | (0.3278) | 0.1676 | (0.2080) | 0.1630 | (0.1592) | 0.1561 | (0.1123) |
| 20-Year bond | 0.1949 | (0.3024) | 0.1766 | (0.1639) | 0.1724 | (0.1204) | 0.1674 | (0.0821) |
| 30-Year bond | 0.1397 | (0.3072) | 0.1252 | (0.1576) | 0.1231 | (0.1119) | 0.1179 | (0.0744) |
| S&P 500 | 0.1653 | (0.3601) | 0.1292 | (0.2472) | 0.1104 | (0.1988) | 0.1054 | (0.1719) |
| NYSE/AMEX/NASDAQ | 0.2324 | (0.3703) | 0.1904 | (0.2443) | 0.1679 | (0.1967) | 0.1583 | (0.1656) |

Standard deviation-based Sharpe ratios for various FoHFs, bond, and equity indices in the United States. The four bond market indices are based on 5-, 10-, 20-, and 30-year maturity Treasury bonds. The two equity indices are the S&P 500 index and the NYSE/AMEX/NASDAQ Composite index. The numerator of the standard deviation-based Sharpe ratio is equal to the monthly return of the index minus the risk-free rate. The denominator is equal to the standard deviation of monthly returns over the past 12, 24, 36, or 48 months. Each row reports the means of each ratio and the standard deviations are presented in parentheses.

When the standard deviation is calculated from the most recent year's data, the FoHFs index generates the highest excess return per unit risk. The Sharpe ratio for FoHFs is equal to 0.352, which implies that the index demands an extra 35 basis points of expected return per 1% increase in standard deviation. The comparison between the bond and stock market indices does not present any clear pattern. Although the NYSE/AMEX/NASDAQ index has a superior Sharpe ratio (0.232) compared to all the bond indices, the S&P index lags behind most of the bond indices with a Sharpe ratio of 0.165. There is a declining pattern for the bond indices with Sharpe ratios of 0.222 for the 5-year bond index and 0.140 for the 30-year bond index. Another point to note is that the FoHFs index also has the highest variation in Sharpe ratios. We observe this pattern for the other ratios as well.

Extending the sampling window for calculating standard deviations to 24 months does not dramatically alter the results. The Sharpe ratio of the FoHFs index declines to 0.298 from 0.352, but it is still the index that generates the highest excess return per unit risk. Note that the reduction in the Sharpe ratio is mechanical due to the positive relation between standard deviation and time horizon, and this reduction is encountered for all indices. The NYSE/AMEX/NASDAQ index has a greater Sharpe ratio (0.190) compared to all bond indices except the 5-year bond index (0.213). On the other hand, the S&P 500 index has a smaller Sharpe ratio (0.129) compared to all bond indices except the 30-year bond index (0.125). For sampling windows of 36 and 48 months, the results are similar except that S&P 500 now has the lowest Sharpe ratios and the 20-year bond index begins to outperform the NYSE/AMEX/NASDAQ index. Most importantly, the FoHFs index has the highest Sharpe ratio regardless of the sampling window for the standard deviation.

One final point is that the decrease in the Sharpe ratios as the sampling window increases is sharper for the FoHFs index compared to the other indices. For the

12-month window, the Sharpe ratio of the FoHFs index exceeds its closest follower by 0.120 (0.352 versus 0.232), whereas the difference is reduced to 0.038 (0.236 versus 0.204) for the 48-month window.

These results collectively suggest that the FoHFs index generates a higher excess return per unit risk when risk is measured by standard deviation. However, there is enough evidence in the literature to believe that the standard deviation is an incomplete measure of risk for hedge fund returns whose distribution deviates from normality. This is also evidenced by the negatively skewed and leptokurtic behavior of the FoHFs index returns in Table 17.1. Therefore, to take the non-linearities hedge fund returns into account, we calculate alternative Sharpe ratios based on non-parametric and parametric VaR.

Table 17.3 presents Sharpe ratios that are based on non-parametric VaR. These *VaRSharpe* ratios scale expected excess returns by the absolute value of the minimum return of a portfolio during a recent sample window where the length of the window varies between 12 and 48 months. When we focus on *VaRSharpe12*, we find that the FoHFs index generates the highest excess return per unit downside risk. The ratio for the FoHFs index is equal to 2.207 and exceeds those of the other indices multiple-fold. We again note that the time-series standard deviation of the *VaRSharpe* measure is the greatest for the FoHFs index. In other words, although the FoHFs index easily outperforms the other indices based on this particular metric, this outperformance seems to be variable through time. *VaRSharpe12* for the NYSE/AMEX/NASDAQ index is equal to 0.254 and greater than those of all bond market indices except the 5-year bond index, which has a *VaRSharpe12* of 0.320. We observe that the downside risk-adjusted Sharpe ratio has a declining pattern for the bond market indices as the time to maturity increases and the 30-year bond index has a *VaRSharpe12* of 0.239. The S&P 500 index has a similar performance with a *VaRSharpe12* of 0.245. To summarize, the

**Table 17.3**  Non-parametric VaR-Based Sharpe Ratios for FoHFs, Bond, and Equity Indices

|  | VaRSharpe12 | | VaRSharpe24 | | VaRSharpe36 | | VaRSharpe48 | |
|---|---|---|---|---|---|---|---|---|
| FoHFs | 2.2073 | (5.8254) | 0.9947 | (3.9006) | 0.2004 | (0.2793) | 0.1306 | (0.1267) |
| 5-Year bond | 0.3198 | (0.6192) | 0.1565 | (0.2003) | 0.1260 | (0.1352) | 0.1104 | (0.0973) |
| 10-Year bond | 0.2187 | (0.4049) | 0.1128 | (0.1402) | 0.0936 | (0.0974) | 0.0779 | (0.0612) |
| 20-Year bond | 0.2473 | (0.8470) | 0.1055 | (0.1091) | 0.0825 | (0.0676) | 0.0738 | (0.0415) |
| 30-Year bond | 0.2387 | (1.4856) | 0.0778 | (0.1037) | 0.0585 | (0.0631) | 0.0497 | (0.0364) |
| S&P 500 | 0.2452 | (0.6728) | 0.0831 | (0.1398) | 0.0608 | (0.1050) | 0.0513 | (0.0825) |
| NYSE/AMEX/ NASDAQ | 0.2544 | (0.4572) | 0.1206 | (0.1473) | 0.0897 | (0.1124) | 0.0742 | (0.0874) |

Non-parametric value at risk-based Sharpe ratios for various FoHFs, bond, and equity indices in the United States. The four bond market indices are based on 5-, 10-, 20-, and 30-year maturity Treasury bonds. The two equity indices are the S&P 500 index and the NYSE/AMEX/NASDAQ Composite index. The numerator of the non-parametric value at risk-based Sharpe ratio is equal to the monthly return of the index minus the risk-free rate. The denominator is equal to the minimum monthly index return over the past 12, 24, 36, or 48 months. Each row reports the means of each ratio and the standard deviations are presented in parentheses.

FoHFs index is the superior performer based on *VaRSharpe12* and neither the bond nor the stock market indices clearly dominate each other.

When we extend the sampling window to calculate non-parametric VaR, the *VaRSharpe* ratios again decline mechanically. The reason is that the absolute value of the minimum return during the last 48 months has to be equal to or greater than that during the last 12 months. Analyzing the longer horizon *VaRSharpe* ratios makes some patterns apparent. (i) The FoHFs index continues to be the best performer regardless of the sampling window. (ii) The 5-year bond index continues to have the highest *VaRSharpe* ratio after the FoHFs index, and for the 36-month and 48-month horizons, the 10-year bond index also outperforms the NYSE/AMEX/NASDAQ index. (iii) The S&P 500 index continues to have the lowest excess return per unit downside risk after the 30-year bond index. (iv) Similarly to the results from the traditional Sharpe ratio analysis, the margin by which the *VaRSharpe* ratio of the FoHFs index exceeds those of the other indices declines as the sampling window increases. For example, *VaRSharpe12* of the FoHFs index is 7 times that of the 5-year bond index, which is its closest follower. However, as the sampling window is extended to 48 months, the difference between the *VaRSharpe* ratios decreases substantially. This is due to the fact that the reduction in the VarSharpe ratios is much steeper for the FoHFs index compared to the other indices. *VaRSharpe48* measures for the FoHFs and the 5-year bond indices are equal to 0.131 and 0.110, respectively.

Next, we investigate the reward-to-risk ratios that have parametric VaR-based on Hansen's (1994) skewed *t*-density in their denominators. Table 17.4 presents the results. The inference from the analysis of *PVaRSharpe* ratios corroborates the findings from Table 17.3. When we focus on the 12-month sampling horizon for the construction of the parametric downside risk measure, we find that the FoHFs index again has the highest reward-to-risk ratio with a *PVaRSharpe12* of

**Table 17.4**   Parametric VaR-Based Sharpe Ratios for FoHFs, Bond, and Equity Indices

| | PVaRSharpe12 | | PVaRSharpe24 | | PVaRSharpe36 | | PVaRSharpe48 | |
|---|---|---|---|---|---|---|---|---|
| FoHFs | 1.1037 | (4.3839) | 0.6146 | (1.7954) | 0.2264 | (0.4187) | 0.1365 | (0.1729) |
| 5-Year bond | 0.2456 | (0.7375) | 0.1326 | (0.1711) | 0.1168 | (0.1265) | 0.1082 | (0.0956) |
| 10-Year bond | 0.6431 | (7.6812) | 0.0971 | (0.1222) | 0.0877 | (0.0916) | 0.0782 | (0.0597) |
| 20-Year bond | 0.2614 | (1.4548) | 0.1058 | (0.1848) | 0.0840 | (0.0739) | 0.0761 | (0.0422) |
| 30-Year bond | 0.1306 | (0.2904) | 0.0924 | (0.3949) | 0.0606 | (0.0755) | 0.0525 | (0.0409) |
| S&P 500 | 0.1314 | (0.2936) | 0.0722 | (0.1218) | 0.0554 | (0.0942) | 0.0490 | (0.0769) |
| NYSE/AMEX/ NASDAQ | 0.1666 | (0.2965) | 0.1035 | (0.1253) | 0.0833 | (0.0993) | 0.0726 | (0.0799) |

Parametric value at risk-based Sharpe ratios for various FoHFs, bond, and equity indices in the United States. The four bond market indices are based on 5-, 10-, 20-, and 30-year maturity Treasury bonds. The two equity indices are the S&P 500 index and the NYSE/AMEX/ NASDAQ Composite index. The numerator of the parametric value at risk-based Sharpe ratio is equal to the monthly return of the index minus the risk-free rate. The denominator is equal to the first percentile of Hansen's (1994) skewed *t*-density estimated using the monthly returns from over the past 12, 24, 36, or 48 months. Each row reports the means of each ratio and the standard deviations are presented in parentheses.

1.104. One can also see that the 10-year bond index also performs well for this metric with a *PVaRSharpe12* of 0.643. The stock market indices (i.e., the NYSE/AMEX/NASDAQ and S&P 500 indices) have *PVaRSharpe* ratios of 0.167 and 0.131, respectively. These values are lower than those of all bond market indices with the exception of the 30-year bond index. The extension of the sampling window again reduces the reward-to-risk ratios for all indices. The FoHFs index continues to be the best performer regardless of the length of the sampling window. However, as observed for the traditional and non-parametric VaR-based Sharpe ratios, the decline in the *PVaRSharpe* ratio is steeper than with the other indices. For example, the ratio of *PVaRSharpe12* of the FoHFs index to that of the 5-year bond index is more than 4 when the 12-month sampling window is used, whereas for the 48-month sampling window, the FoHFs and 5-year bond indices have *PVaRSharpe* ratios of 0.137 and 0.108, respectively. A closer look at the results reveals that the bond market indices generally outperform the stock market indices and there is a downward trend in the reward-to-risk ratios among the bond market indices especially for longer sampling windows.

Figures 17.1 and 17.2 present plots of traditional and non-parametric VaR-based Sharpe ratios, respectively. For these figures, we choose only one bond market and one stock market index to show the relative performance of the FoHFs index to keep the exposition clean. To be conservative, we focus on the 5-year bond and NYSE/AMEX/NASDAQ indices, which have proved to be the bond and stock market indices that have performed the best over the sample period. Moreover, we present the graphs for the reward-to-risk measures that use standard deviation and non-parametric VaR calculated from a 48-month sampling window since the superior performance of the FoHFs index becomes less pronounced as the sampling window is extended.

Figures 17.1 and 17.2 show that the FoHFs index had a superior performance at the beginning of the sample period based on both reward-to-risk metrics, but

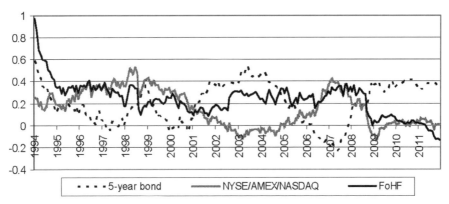

**FIGURE 17.1**
Standard deviation-based Sharpe ratios for the FoHFs, 5-year bond, and NYSE/AMEX/NASDAQ between January 1994 and December 2011. The numerator of the standard deviation-based Sharpe ratio is equal to the monthly return of the index minus the risk-free rate. The denominator is equal to the standard deviation of monthly returns over the past 48 months.

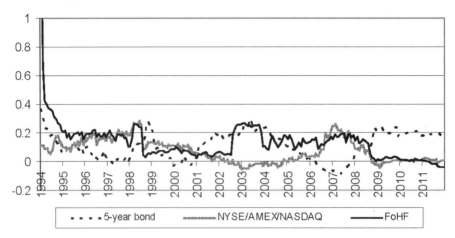

**FIGURE 17.2**
Non-parametric VaR-based Sharpe ratios for the FoHFs, 5-year bond, and NYSE/AMEX/NASDAQ between January 1994 and December 2011. The numerator of the non-parametric VaR-based Sharpe ratio is equal to the monthly return of the index minus the risk-free rate. The denominator is equal to the minimum monthly index return over the past 48 months.

the Sharpe ratios dropped to the level of the NYSE/AMEX/NASDAQ index by 1996. We see that the superior performance of the FoHFs index is not uniform through time. This observation is consistent with the large volatility associated with the reward-to-risk ratios of the FoHFs index uncovered in the earlier analysis. There have been periods in which either the 5-year bond or the NYSE/ AMEX/NASDAQ or both have outperformed the FoHFs index. One such period is the period after the recent global financial crisis and it can clearly be seen that the reward-to-risk ratios took a downward turn in the second half of 2008. During this period, the performance of the stock market has also been dismal and the 5-year bond index has generated higher returns per unit risk. Figures 17.1 and 17.2 also capture the stock market crash of the early last decade after the internet bubble burst as evidenced by the steep decline in the reward-to-risk ratios of the NYSE/AMEX/NASDAQ after 2000.

## CONCLUSION

We investigate whether the FoHFs portfolios outperform various bond and stock market indices in terms of being able to generate higher returns per unit risk. Due to the potential non-normality associated with hedge fund returns, we give special emphasis to the concept of downside risk in our analysis. Consequently, apart from the traditional Sharpe ratio, we also construct reward-to-risk ratios that use non-parametric or parametric measures of VaR in their denominator for various indices. Our main finding is that the FoHFs index has superior reward-to-risk ratios compared to all bond and stock market indices. Although this superior performance is more pronounced when the risk measures are calculated using data from the last 12 months, the ability of the FoHFs index to generate higher returns per unit risk is robust regardless of the sampling window. We also find that the documented outperformance is not a phenomenon that has been observed consistently through time and there have been periods in which the FoHFs index has lagged behind the other indices.

# References

Agarwal, V., & Naik, N. Y. (2004). Risks and Portfolio Decisions Involving Hedge Funds. *Review of Financial Studies, 17*(1), 63–98.

Arditti, F. D. (1967). Risk and the Required Return on Equity. *Journal of Finance, 22*(1), 19–36.

Bali, T. G., Gokcan, S., & Liang, B. (2007). Value at Risk and the Cross Section of Hedge Fund Returns. *Journal of Banking and Finance, 31*(4), 1135–1166.

Bali, T. G., Brown, S. J., & Caglayan, M. O. (2011). Do Hedge Funds' Exposures to Risk Factors Predict Their Future Returns? *Journal of Financial Economics, 101*(1), 36–68.

Bali, T. G., Brown, S. J., & Caglayan, M. O. (2012). Systematic Risk and the Cross Section of Hedge Fund Returns. *Journal of Financial Economics, 106*(1), 114–131.

Brown, S. J., Gregoriou, G., & Pascalau, R. (2012). Diversification in Funds of Hedge Funds: Is It Possible to Overdiversify? *Review of Asset Pricing Studies, 2*(1), 89–110.

Cornish, E. A., & Fisher, R. A. (1937). Moments and Cumulants in the Specification of Distributions. In *La Revue de l'Institute International de Statistique, 4*. Reprinted in Fisher, R.A. (1950). In: Contributions to Mathematical Statistics. New York, NY: Wiley.

Dittmar, R. F. (2002). Non-linear Pricing Kernels, Kurtosis Preference, and Evidence from the Cross Section of Equity Returns. *Journal of Finance, 57*(1), 369–403.

Fung, W., & Hsieh, D. A. (1997). Empirical Characteristics of Dynamic Trading Strategies: The Case of Hedge Funds. *Review of Financial Studies, 10*(2), 275–302.

Fung, W., & Hsieh, D. A. (2000). Performance Characteristics of Hedge Funds and CTA Funds: Natural versus Spurious Biases. *Journal of Financial and Quantitative Analysis, 35*(3), 291–307.

Fung, W., & Hsieh, D. A. (2001). The Risk in Hedge Fund Strategies: Theory and Evidence from Trend Followers. *Review of Financial Studies, 14*(2), 313–341.

Hansen, B. E. (1994). Autoregressive Conditional Density Estimation. *International Economic Review, 35*(3), 705–730.

Harvey, C. R., & Siddique, A. (2000). Conditional Skewness in Asset Pricing Tests. *Journal of Finance, 55*(3), 1263–1295.

Kimball, M. (1993). Standard Risk Aversion. *Econometrica, 61*(3), 589–611.

Kraus, A., & Litzenberger, R. H. (1976). Skewness Preference and the Valuation of Risk Assets. *Journal of Finance, 31*(4), 1085–1100.

Liang, B., & Park, H. (2007). Risk Measures for Hedge Funds: A Cross-sectional Approach. *European Financial Management, 13*(2), 333–370.

Malkiel, B. G., & Saha, A. (2005). Hedge Funds: Risk and Return. *Financial Analysts Journal, 61*(6), 80–88.

Markowitz, H. (1952). Portfolio Selection. *Journal of Finance, 7*(1), 77–91.

Mitchell, M., & Pulvino, T. (2001). Characteristics of Risk and Return in Risk Arbitrage. *Journal of Finance, 56*(6), 2135–2175.

Pratt, J., & Zeckhauser, R. (1987). Proper Risk Aversion. *Econometrica, 55*(1), 143–154.

Sharpe, W. F. (1966). Mutual Fund Performance. *Journal of Business, 39*(1), 119–138.

## CHAPTER 18

# The Short-Run Performance Persistence in Funds of Hedge Funds

**David Ardia**[*] **and Kris Boudt**[†]
[*]University Laval, Québec City, Québec, Canada
[†]KU Leuven, Leuven, Belgium

## 18.1. INTRODUCTION

In this chapter, we study the stability of risk exposure and performance of funds of hedge funds (FoHFs) over recent years. Our research universe consists of the Hedge Fund Research (HFR) database over a period ranging from January 2005 to June 2011, thus covering the pre-crisis period (January 2005–August 2007), crisis period (September 2007–February 2009), and post-crisis period (March 2009–June 2011).

There is extensive empirical evidence that FoHFs quickly change their investment bets as a function of the changing market conditions (e.g., see Fung and Hsieh, 2004; Patton and Ramadorai, 2012). Through a subsample analysis, we show that FoHFs have increased their exposure significantly to the aggregate equity and bond market risk in the post-crisis period. During the crisis period over 10% of FoHFs were significantly negatively exposed to the credit spread risk of the bond market.

Reconsidering Funds of Hedge Funds. http://dx.doi.org/10.1016/B978-0-12-401699-6.00018-6

We analyze also the persistence in relative performance through an analysis of the return-to-risk characteristics of a systematic allocation strategy that dynamically selects FoHFs as a function of the fund's alpha or the fund's Sharpe ratio. Since most FoHFs are characterized by high minimum investments and limitations on the entry and exit of the investment, such a momentum strategy is clearly not feasible in practice. However, it allows us to indirectly test the presence of so-called 'hot hands' among fund of funds managers.

Starting with Hendricks *et al.* (1993) introducing the concept of 'hot hands,' an extensive body of research has investigated the short-run persistence of relative performance of mutual funds. In particular, Carhart (1997) and Wermers (1997) show that the 'hot hands' result is mostly driven by the 1-year momentum effect of Jegadeesh and Titman (1993). Further, Sirri and Tufano (1998) document large inflows of money into last years' best performing mutual funds and withdrawals from last years' losers.

A more recent stream of literature has investigated the presence of 'hot hands' in the hedge funds and FoHFs industry. For example, Jagannathan *et al.* (2010) find significant performance persistence among top hedge funds, but little evidence of persistence among inferior funds. Capocci and Hübner (2004) find limited evidence of persistence in performance, but not for extreme performers. In addition, Fung *et al.* (2008) show that during the 1995−2004 period, alpha-producing funds were not as likely to liquidate as those that did not deliver alpha, and experienced far greater and steadier capital inflows than their less fortunate counterparts. However, these capital inflows attenuated their ability to continue to deliver alpha in the future.

We contribute to this literature by investigating the performance of a systematic allocation strategy that invests in the top quintile of the highest performance FoHFs. We study four measures of (risk-adjusted) performance: 1-year trailing mean return, Sharpe ratio, alpha based on the Carhart four-factor model, and alpha based on the Fung−Hsieh model.

A study of the transition probability matrix between portfolio quintiles gives insights in how stable the relative performance of FoHFs is. The highest resiliency is found if we focus on predicting return using the 1-year trailing returns: 86% (82%) of the top (worst) performing funds are in the top (bottom) quintile of the next period. The stability for the alpha factors is significantly lower: 75% (72%) of the top (worst) performing funds are in the top (bottom) quintile of the next period. We thus find a slightly lower persistence in performance of the inferior funds compared to the top funds.

Finally, we consistently find that using risk-adjusted return measures improves the risk-adjusted performance of the momentum investment strategy. This finding holds for the financial crisis period as well as the pre- and post-crisis periods.

The remainder of this chapter is organized as follows. Section 18.2 describes our dataset. Sections 18.3 and 18.4 empirically investigate the time variation in

FoHFs risk exposures and performance. The key contribution is in Section 18.5 where we evaluate the performance of a systematic allocation strategy that invests in the top quintile of highest performance funds. We then summarize our main findings and point out some directions for further research.

## 18.2. DATA

Our data source is the HFR database, which is one of the largest commercial hedge fund datasets available. As of October 2011, the database comprised 6953 hedge funds and FoHFs. We focus our analysis on FoHFs and rely only on the US$ share class. Our analysis considers monthly returns from January 2005 to June 2011, thus covering the pre-crisis period (January 2005–August 2007), crisis period (September 2007–February 2009), and post-crisis period (March 2009–June 2011). Excluding funds with missing observations and duplicates, this leads to a filtered database of 401 funds with 80 observations. The database does not contain dead funds. However, since we focus on relative performance, the analysis is robust against survivorship bias.

For the factor model, we choose the seven asset-based style factors suggested by Fung and Hsieh (2004):

- Two equity-oriented risk factors: the US aggregate market factor (*Market*) and the small minus big factor (*SMB*) from the website of Kenneth French.[1]
- An aggregate and credit risk bond-oriented risk factors. The first is the monthly change in the 10-year treasury constant maturity yield (*10Y*). The credit spread factor is the monthly change of the difference between Moody's Baa yield and the 10-year treasury constant maturity yield. Both series are available at the website of the Board of Governors of the Federal Reserve System.
- The bond, currency, and commodity trend-following risk factors suggested by Fung and Hsieh (2001); these are available from David Hsieh's data library.[2]

As a robustness check, we also consider the four-factor model of Carhart (1997), which is standard in the analysis of mutual funds performance. The factors are retrieved from Kenneth French's website.

## 18.3. TIME VARIATION IN FoHFs RISK EXPOSURE

A distinguishing characteristic of FoHFs compared to mutual funds is the speed at which they can alter their investments in response to market conditions. The subsample analysis of Fung and Hsieh (2004) illustrated the time variation of hedge fund risk exposure over the period January 1994–December 2002. They study vendor-provided fund-of-fund indices and

---

[1]Available at http://mba.tuck.dartmouth.edu/pages/faculty/ken.french/data_library.html.
[2]Available at http://faculty.fuqua.duke.edu/~dah7/DataLibrary/TF-Fac.xls.

perform a modified-CUSUM test to find structural break points in fund factor loadings. They note that the break points coincide with extreme market events, such as the collapse of LTCM in September 1998 and the peak of the technology bubble in March 2000. For further information, see also Criton and Scaillet (2011) and Patton and Ramadorai (2012) as well as references therein for empirical evidence on time-varying risk exposure.

In Table 18.1 we estimate the Fung–Hsieh risk model for the pre-crisis, crisis, and post-crisis periods. Regarding the market factor, we find a positive and significant exposure for 61% of the FoHFs in the post-crisis period compared to 38% and 36% in the pre-crisis and crisis periods. This suggests a significant increase in the number of aggregate equity market bets made by FoHFs in the post-crisis periods. The average market exposure is 0.25 in the crisis period and around 0.3 in the pre-crisis and post-crisis periods. This is relatively low compared to the beta of usual mutual fund strategies, confirming the well-known diversification benefits of including FoHFs in the portfolio. In the pre-crisis period 15% of FoHFs have a significant positive exposure to the SMB equity risk factor, but this proportion shrinks to less than 5% in the periods thereafter.

| Table 18.1 | Regression of the Fund of Hedge Funds Monthly Returns on Seven Hedge Fund Risk Factors | | | | | | | |
|---|---|---|---|---|---|---|---|---|
| | **Alpha** | **Market** | **SMB** | **10Y** | **CredSprd** | **BdOpt** | **FxOpt** | **ComOpt** |
| *Pre-crisis period: January 2005–August 2007 (Average $R^2 = 41.03\%$)* | | | | | | | | |
| Ave. coef. | 0.0074 | 0.2999 | 0.1509 | 1.2316 | 0.1785 | 0.0116 | 0.0076 | 0.0134 |
| Ave. SE | 0.0053 | 0.2238 | 0.2003 | 2.0992 | 2.1125 | 0.0406 | 0.0235 | 0.0214 |
| Pos. signif. (%) | 38.2 | 38 | 15.2 | 4.7 | 3.5 | 4.7 | 4.2 | 7.7 |
| Neg. signif. (%) | 0.5 | 2 | 1.5 | 1.25 | 1.5 | 1.5 | 2 | 2.5 |
| *Crisis period: September 2007–February 2009 (Average $R^2 = 61.16\%$)* | | | | | | | | |
| Ave. coef. | 0.0037 | 0.2481 | −0. 2306 | −0.5299 | −0.7351 | −0.0396 | −0.0372 | 0.0415 |
| Ave. SE | 0.0091 | 0.1667 | 0.3984 | 3.1754 | 1.2403 | 0.0894 | 0.0611 | 0.0755 |
| Pos. signif. (%) | 8.2 | 36 | 1 | 1.5 | 1 | 1.3 | 1 | 7.2 |
| Neg. signif. (%) | 1 | 2.5 | 3.5 | 2.7 | 12.5 | 8.2 | 5.5 | 0.5 |
| *Post-crisis period: March 2009–June 2011 (Average $R^2 = 52.34\%$)* | | | | | | | | |
| Ave. coef. | 0.0048 | 0.3058 | −0.0766 | 0.9585 | −0.3898 | 0.0191 | 0.0089 | 0.0114 |
| Ave. SE | 0.0050 | 0.1171 | 0.1699 | 2.0270 | 1.4215 | 0.0354 | 0.0407 | 0.0493 |
| Pos. signif. (%) | 22.1 | 61 | 4.7 | 10.9 | 2.2 | 11.9 | 4.9 | 6.5 |
| Neg. signif. (%) | 1.3 | 2.9 | 8.7 | 1.5 | 3.7 | 1.3 | 3.9 | 4.5 |

We report the equally weighted cross-sectional mean regression coefficient (Ave. coef.), Newey–West standard error (Ave. SE), and percentage of positive and negative coefficients that are statistically different from zero at the 5% level (Pos./Neg. signif.). *Market* and *SMB* are the Fama and French (1993) market and small minus big factors for the US stock market. *10Y* is the month-end to month-end change in the US Federal Reserve 10-year constant maturity yield; *CredSprd* is the month-end to month-end change in the difference between Moody's Baa yield and the Federal Reserve's 10-year constant-maturity yield; *BdOpt* is the return of a portfolio of lookback straddles on bond futures; *FxOpt* is the return of a portfolio of lookback straddles on currency futures; *ComOpt* is the return of a portfolio of lookback straddles on commodity futures.

The remaining columns in Table 18.1 describe the exposure of FoHFs to risks other than equity market risk. We see that few funds have a bond risk exposure in the pre-crisis periods. In the crisis period 13% of the funds have a significant negative exposure to the credit spread, but this number dwindles again to only 3% in the post-crisis period, where around 10% of funds are positively exposed to the aggregate bond and bond trend-following risks. Finally, we see that the percentage of funds making commodity trend-following bets remains stable during the three periods.

Note that our exposure analysis does not distinguish the change of exposure of the FoHFs from the change of exposure of the underlying hedge funds. While this is a relevant question, this does not affect the impact of the final investor, which invests in the FoHFs and therefore faces the top-down exposure.

## 18.4. TIME VARIATION IN PERFORMANCE

It is often argued by FoHF managers that their aim is not to track and try to beat a given asset class benchmark, but rather to focus on pure performance generation. Empirically, this would imply a series of 'absolute alpha,' without much effect of the crisis period. We analyze this statement in Figures 18.1 and 18.2, where we plot the estimated Sharpe ratio and alpha on rolling 1-year samples for

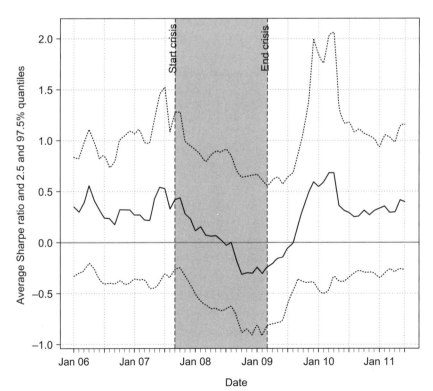

**FIGURE 18.1**
Average (bold line) and 2.5%, 97.5% quantiles (dotted lines) of estimated Sharpe on rolling 1-year samples.

**FIGURE 18.2**
Average (bold line) and 2.5%, 97.5% quantiles (dotted lines) of estimated alpha on rolling 1-year samples.

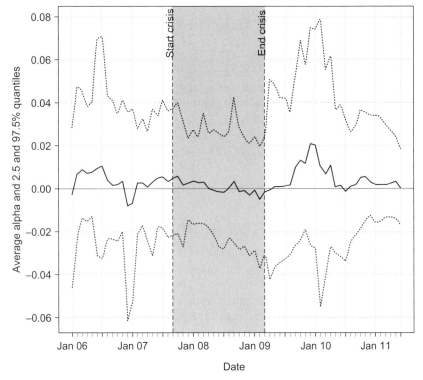

the period ranging from January 2006 to June 2011. The bold line reports the average value of the various FoHFs, while the dotted lines indicate the 2.5% and 97.5% empirical percentiles. Note that the plotted alphas take into account the time variation in the FoHFs risk exposure, since they are based on rolling samples.

The average Sharpe ratio is clearly negatively impacted by the crisis and positively affected by the subsequent market recovery. This is in contrast to the series of average alpha, which is indeed stable and seems to be little affected by the crisis, and increases temporarily at the beginning of the post-crisis period. The increase in average fund alpha in the post-crisis period is, however, short-lived. The confidence intervals indicate a wide cross-sectional variation in performance across the funds for both measures.

## 18.5. BACK-TEST ON SHORT-RUN PERFORMANCE PERSISTENCE

The aim of this section is to test the hypothesis of persistence in performance. Similarly to Carhart (1997) and Capocci and Hübner (2004), all funds are ranked based on their performance in the previous year. While Carhart (1997) and Capocci and Hübner (2004) limit their study to ordering funds using the return, we also study performance of ordering funds based on risk-adjusted performance measures.

Our back-test begins in January 2006 and uses the last 12 months (rolling window) of data to compute the average return, Sharpe ratio, Fung–Hsieh alpha, and Carhart alpha of the various FoHFs. We then rank funds and construct equal-weighted quintile portfolios, which are held over 1 month. The ranking is updated every month, thus leading to a monthly rebalancing of the portfolio.

A crucial requirement for performance persistence is the stability of the quintile portfolios. Table 18.2 reports the transition matrices of these quintile portfolios. We see that effectively there is a high short-run persistence in performance. Interestingly, this persistence is the highest for the return ranking, followed by the Sharpe ratio ranking. Rankings based on alphas are the least stable. More precisely, for the return-based portfolios, 86% (82%) of the top (worst) performing funds are in the top (bottom) quintile of the next period. For the Sharpe ratio ordered portfolios, 82% of the top/bottom quintile funds are in the top/bottom quintile of the next period. The stability for the alpha factors is significantly lower: 75% (72%) of the top (worst) performing funds are in the top (bottom) quintile of the next period. When ordering using the return or fund alpha, we thus find a slightly lower persistence in performance of the inferior funds compared to the top funds.

Table 18.3 reports summary performance statistics of the equally weighted quintile portfolios. Performance is evaluated using the return, standard deviation, Sharpe ratio, Carhart and Fung–Hsieh alpha, as well as the Cornish–Fisher value at risk (VaR). As shown by Boudt *et al.* (2008), Favre and Galeano (2002), Gregoriou and Gueyie (2003), and Amenc *et al.* (2003), the latter measures the downside risk of the investment accounting for the non-normality of the return series. This is necessary, because of the skewness and excess kurtosis typically observed in FoHFs return series.

An important caveat in interpreting these performance results is that in absolute terms they probably provide an overly optimistic image, due to bias (e.g., see Amenc *et al.*, 2003). In fact, the decision to post the performance in the HFR database is purely voluntary and only a certain number of funds decide to participate. This leads to a *self-reporting bias*. HFR also uses certain selection criteria to include FoHFs in the database. This creates a *selection bias*. Furthermore, since hedge funds that have performed poorly exit the industry, the funds that are still present in the database tend to be funds that have performed better than the average of the entire population. In this case we refer to the *survivorship bias*. Finally, when a fund is added to the database, all or part of its historical data is recorded ex-post in the data base, leading to an *instant history bias*. In spite of all these sources of bias, we feel confident that the analysis of the relative differences in performance of the quintile portfolios is still indicative of the strength of the persistence of performance of FoHFs.

**Table 18.2** Transition Matrix Quintile Portfolios Based on Trailing 1-year Return, Sharpe ratio, Carhart alpha, and Fung–Hsieh alpha

| | Transition matrix return quintiles | | | | | Transition matrix Sharpe ratio quintiles | | | | | Transition matrix Carhart alpha quintiles | | | | | Transition matrix Fung–Hsieh alpha quintiles | | | | |
|---|---|---|---|---|---|---|---|---|---|---|---|---|---|---|---|---|---|---|---|---|
| | Q1 | Q2 | Q3 | Q4 | Q5 | Q1 | Q2 | Q3 | Q4 | Q5 | Q1 | Q2 | Q3 | Q4 | Q5 | Q1 | Q2 | Q3 | Q4 | Q5 |
| Q1 | 85.77 | 12.4 | 1.1 | 0.48 | 0.23 | 82.25 | 15.38 | 2.0 | 0.31 | 0.08 | 79.60 | 16.00 | 2.80 | 1.20 | 0.77 | 74.90 | 16.29 | 3.92 | 2.23 | 2.65 |
| Q2 | 12.00 | 68.1 | 16.0 | 2.85 | 1.06 | 15.40 | 62.73 | 18.8 | 2.75 | 0.36 | 14.5 | 61.00 | 18.4 | 4.60 | 1.87 | 16.58 | 53.67 | 19.42 | 6.88 | 3.44 |
| Q3 | 1.35 | 16.0 | 63.1 | 17.37 | 2.13 | 1.81 | 18.81 | 57.6 | 20.38 | 1.38 | 2.8 | 18 | 57.1 | 18.0 | 4.31 | 3.17 | 19.92 | 51.85 | 19.37 | 5.69 |
| Q4 | 0.46 | 2.5 | 17.6 | 64.60 | 14.83 | 0.50 | 2.87 | 20.1 | 60.21 | 16.29 | 1.6 | 4 | 18.2 | 60.9 | 15.27 | 2.58 | 6.54 | 19.40 | 54.69 | 16.79 |
| Q5 | 0.42 | 1.0 | 2.1 | 14.53 | 81.98 | 0.04 | 0.21 | 1.5 | 16.14 | 82.11 | 1.4 | 2 | 3.4 | 15.1 | 78.06 | 2.74 | 3.53 | 5.34 | 16.62 | 71.78 |

**Table 18.3** Summary Statistics of Monthly Returns of Momentum Strategies Using the 1-year Trailing Average Return, Sharpe Ratio, Carhart alpha and Fung–Hsieh alpha

| | Pre-Crisis Period | | | | | Crisis Period | | | | | Post-Crisis Period | | | | |
|---|---|---|---|---|---|---|---|---|---|---|---|---|---|---|---|
| | Q1 | Q2 | Q3 | Q4 | Q5 | Q1 | Q2 | Q3 | Q4 | Q5 | Q1 | Q2 | Q3 | Q4 | Q5 |
| *One-year trailing average return* | | | | | | | | | | | | | | | |
| Ann. mean | 0.16 | 0.11 | 0.10 | 0.08 | 0.12 | 0.09 | −0.04 | −0.07 | −0.15 | −0.26 | 0.15 | 0.11 | 0.10 | 0.11 | 0.15 |
| Ann. SD | 0.08 | 0.05 | 0.04 | 0.03 | 0.04 | 0.10 | 0.08 | 0.09 | 0.10 | 0.17 | 0.09 | 0.06 | 0.05 | 0.06 | 0.09 |
| 95% Cornish–Fisher VaR | 0.03 | 0.02 | 0.01 | 0.01 | 0.01 | 0.04 | 0.04 | 0.05 | 0.07 | 0.11 | 0.03 | 0.02 | 0.02 | 0.01 | 0.01 |
| Ann. Sharpe | 1.43 | 1.14 | 1.17 | 1.12 | 1.64 | 0.69 | −0.74 | −1.09 | −1.69 | −1.69 | 1.66 | 1.87 | 1.91 | 1.91 | 1.58 |
| Ann. Carhart alpha | 0.13 | 0.08 | 0.07 | 0.05 | 0.07 | 0.21 | 0.04 | 0.00 | −0.06 | −0.17 | 0.16 | 0.09 | 0.08 | 0.08 | 0.07 |
| Ann. Fung–Hsieh alpha | 0.17 | 0.12 | 0.10 | 0.09 | 0.13 | 0.14 | 0.01 | 0.01 | −0.02 | −0.04 | 0.15 | 0.09 | 0.07 | 0.06 | 0.00 |
| *One-year trailing Sharpe ratio* | | | | | | | | | | | | | | | |
| Ann. mean | 0.13 | 0.11 | 0.12 | 0.10 | 0.11 | 0.08 | −0.06 | −0.11 | −0.17 | −0.19 | 0.11 | 0.12 | 0.17 | 0.13 | 0.08 |
| Ann. SD | 0.05 | 0.05 | 0.04 | 0.05 | 0.05 | 0.09 | 0.09 | 0.11 | 0.12 | 0.12 | 0.05 | 0.07 | 0.09 | 0.07 | 0.05 |
| 95% Cornish–Fisher VaR | 0.01 | 0.02 | 0.01 | 0.02 | 0.02 | 0.03 | 0.05 | 0.07 | 0.08 | 0.08 | 0.01 | 0.02 | 0.02 | 0.02 | 0.02 |
| Ann. Sharpe | 1.68 | 1.26 | 1.57 | 0.95 | 1.19 | 0.76 | −0.83 | −1.20 | −1.51 | −1.80 | 2.44 | 1.87 | 1.84 | 1.73 | 1.58 |
| Ann. Carhart alpha | 0.11 | 0.09 | 0.09 | 0.05 | 0.06 | 0.17 | 0.05 | −0.03 | −0.05 | −0.13 | 0.12 | 0.10 | 0.12 | 0.09 | 0.07 |
| Ann. Fung–Hsieh alpha | 0.15 | 0.13 | 0.11 | 0.10 | 0.11 | 0.11 | 0.06 | 0.01 | 0.00 | −0.04 | 0.11 | 0.08 | 0.07 | 0.07 | 0.03 |
| *One-year trailing Carhart alpha* | | | | | | | | | | | | | | | |
| Ann. mean | 0.16 | 0.11 | 0.09 | 0.10 | 0.11 | 0.04 | −0.05 | −0.09 | −0.15 | −0.18 | 0.17 | 0.11 | 0.09 | 0.11 | 0.13 |
| Ann. SD | 0.06 | 0.04 | 0.04 | 0.04 | 0.07 | 0.09 | 0.08 | 0.08 | 0.10 | 0.12 | 0.08 | 0.05 | 0.05 | 0.05 | 0.08 |
| 95% Cornish–Fisher VaR | 0.02 | 0.01 | 0.01 | 0.01 | 0.02 | 0.03 | 0.04 | 0.05 | 0.07 | 0.08 | 0.02 | 0.02 | 0.02 | 0.02 | 0.02 |
| Ann. Sharpe | 1.90 | 1.43 | 1.03 | 1.35 | 0.88 | 0.26 | −0.86 | −1.51 | −1.65 | −1.70 | 2.17 | 2.11 | 1.72 | 2.00 | 1.77 |
| Ann. Carhart alpha | 0.14 | 0.08 | 0.06 | 0.06 | 0.05 | 0.16 | 0.04 | −0.02 | −0.08 | −0.09 | 0.14 | 0.10 | 0.07 | 0.08 | 0.11 |
| Ann. Fung–Hsieh alpha | 0.21 | 0.12 | 0.10 | 0.09 | 0.08 | 0.16 | 0.05 | 0.01 | −0.02 | −0.05 | 0.11 | 0.08 | 0.05 | 0.06 | 0.07 |
| *One-year trailing Fung–Hsieh alpha* | | | | | | | | | | | | | | | |
| Ann. mean | 0.14 | 0.11 | 0.10 | 0.09 | 0.12 | 0.02 | −0.07 | −0.08 | −0.11 | −0.19 | 0.19 | 0.12 | 0.09 | 0.09 | 0.12 |
| Ann. SD | 0.07 | 0.04 | 0.04 | 0.04 | 0.06 | 0.09 | 0.09 | 0.08 | 0.09 | 0.12 | 0.09 | 0.06 | 0.05 | 0.05 | 0.06 |
| 95% Cornish–Fisher VaR | 0.02 | 0.01 | 0.01 | 0.01 | 0.02 | 0.03 | 0.05 | 0.05 | 0.06 | 0.08 | 0.02 | 0.02 | 0.02 | 0.02 | 0.02 |
| Ann. Sharpe | 1.34 | 1.41 | 1.40 | 1.16 | 1.19 | 0.03 | −1.00 | −1.37 | −1.44 | −1.75 | 2.08 | 2.05 | 1.84 | 1.94 | 1.83 |
| Ann. Carhart alpha | 0.13 | 0.08 | 0.07 | 0.05 | 0.06 | 0.14 | 0.03 | 0.02 | −0.03 | −0.10 | 0.15 | 0.09 | 0.08 | 0.08 | 0.09 |
| Ann. Fung–Hsieh alpha | 0.20 | 0.12 | 0.10 | 0.07 | 0.12 | 0.13 | 0.05 | 0.00 | 0.00 | −0.03 | 0.12 | 0.06 | 0.07 | 0.06 | 0.06 |

In terms of generating the highest *ex post* return, we observe that, except for the Sharpe ratio portfolio in the post-crisis period, the highest return is obtained when investing in the funds with the highest 1-year trailing (risk-adjusted) return (i.e., the Q1 portfolio). Since these are typically also the lower risk portfolio, the Q1 portfolio tends to have also a higher Sharpe ratio and alpha than the Q2, Q3, Q4, and Q5 portfolios.

Note also that in the crisis period the return on each of the portfolios tends to be lower than in the pre-crisis and post-crisis periods, and the risk tends to be

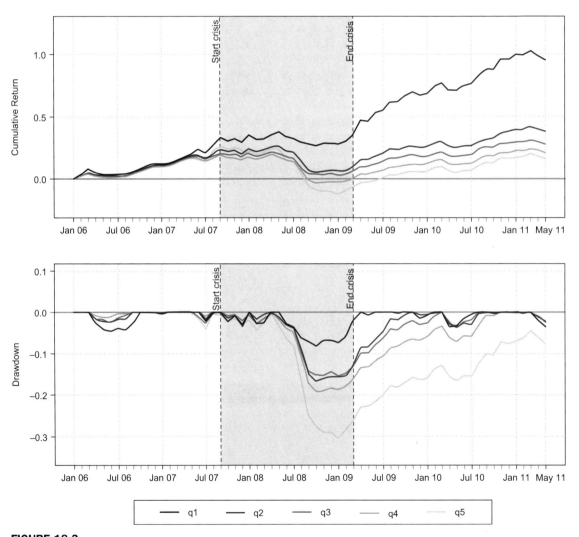

**FIGURE 18.3**
Cumulative return (top panel) and drawdown (bottom panel) of portfolios investing in the funds belonging to the *x*th quintile of highest Sharpe ratios in the previous month.

higher. The return on the Q1 portfolio is for all periods positive, while Q2—Q5 has a negative return in the crisis period. Over a period ranging from 2005 to 2011, we consistently find that using risk-adjusted return measures improves the risk-adjusted performance of the momentum investment strategy. This finding holds for the financial crisis period as well as the pre- and post-crisis periods.

In Figures 18.3 and 18.4 we study the compounded return of the quintile portfolios based on the Sharpe ratio and Fung—Hsieh alpha ranking, respectively. Over the period January 2006—June 2011, all quintile portfolios have

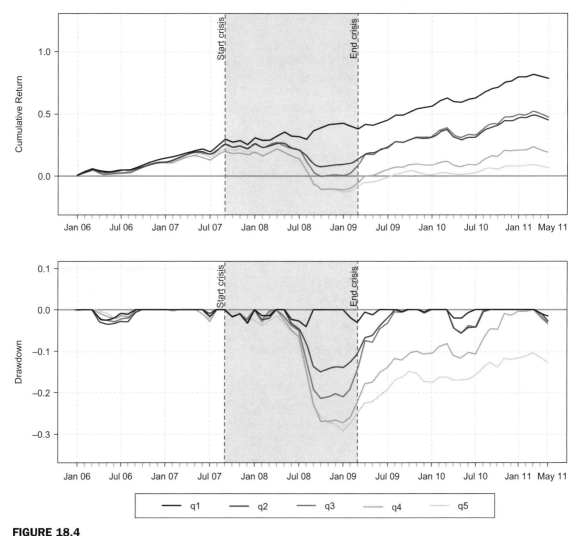

**FIGURE 18.4**
Cumulative return (top panel) and drawdown (bottom panel) of portfolios investing in the funds belonging to the *x*th quintile of highest Fung—Hsieh alphas in the previous month.

a positive return, but dynamically investing in the past winners clearly pays off. The winner quintile (loser quintile) portfolio has a total return of 79% (6%) and 95% (16%) for the Sharpe ratio and alpha strategy, respectively.

In the bottom panels of Figures 18.3 and 18.4 we study the drawdowns of the quintile portfolio. As expected, investing in the previous winners leads out-of-sample to lower drawdowns. The drawdown of the alpha-based winner portfolio is somewhat higher than that of the Sharpe ratio-based portfolio.

Finally, note that similar conclusions are obtained with alternative rolling window lengths or a larger number of portfolios (e.g., percentile portfolios).

## CONCLUSION

This chapter analyzed the risk exposure and the short-run persistence in relative performance of FoHFs over the period ranging from January 2005 to June 2011, thus covering the pre-crisis, crisis, and post-crisis periods. Our results indicate that the risk exposure of FoHFs has faced great changes over the three subperiods. We found a positive and significant exposure for 61% of the funds in the post-crisis period compared to 38% and 36% in the pre-crisis and crisis periods, respectively. Also, we found that using risk-adjusted return measures improves the risk-adjusted performance of a systematic momentum investment strategy. This finding holds for the financial crisis period as well as the pre- and post-crisis periods.

In the future, we plan to study the same strategies but with various holding periods, to see at which horizon the performance persistence dies out. Also, it would be interesting to investigate potential combinations of the risk-adjusted performance measures for building the quintile portfolios.

## Acknowledgments

Financial support from aeris CAPITAL AG and the Dutch Science Foundation is gratefully acknowledged. The views expressed in this chapter are the sole responsibility of the authors and do not necessarily reflect those of aeris CAPITAL AG or any of its affiliates. Any errors or shortcomings are the authors' responsibility.

## References

Amenc, N., Martellini, L., & Vaissié, M. (2003). Benefits and Risks of Alternative Investment Strategies. *Journal of Asset Management, 4*(2), 96–118.

Boudt, K., Peterson, B., & Croux, C. (2008). Estimation and Decomposition of Downside Risk for Portfolios with Non-normal Returns. *Journal of Risk, 11*(2), 79–103.

Capocci, D., & Hübner, G. (2004). Analysis of Hedge Fund Performance. *Journal of Empirical Finance, 11*(1), 55–89.

Carhart, M. (1997). On Persistence in Mutual Fund Performance. *Journal of Finance, 52*(1), 57–82.

Criton, G., & Scaillet, O. (2011). Time-varying Analysis in Risk and Hedge Fund Performance. *How Forecast Ability Increases Estimated Alpha*, Working Paper, Lombard Odier Darier. Geneva: Hentsch and Cie.

Favre, L., & Galeano, J. A. (2002). Portfolio Allocation with Hedge Funds: Case Study of a Swiss Institutional Investor. *Journal of Financial Transformation, 4*(2), 57–63.

Fung, W., & Hsieh, D. A. (2001). The Risk in Hedge Fund Strategies: Theory and Evidence from Trend Followers. *Review of Financial Studies, 14*(2), 313–341.

Fung, W., & Hsieh, D. A. (2004). Hedge Fund Benchmarks: A Risk Based Approach. *Financial Analysts Journal, 60*(5), 65–80.

Fung, W., Hsieh, D., Naik, N. Y., & Ramadorai, R. (2008). Hedge Funds: Performance, Risk, and Capital Formation. *Journal of Finance, 63*(4), 1777–1803.

Gregoriou, G., & Gueyie, J.-P. (2003). Risk Adjusted Performance of Funds of Hedge Funds. Using a Modified Sharpe Ratio. *Journal of Wealth Management, 6*(2), 51–56.

Hendricks, D., Patel, J., & Zeckhauser, R. (1993). Hot Hands in Mutual Funds: Short-Run Persistence of Relative Performance, 1974–1988. *Journal of Finance, 48*(1), 93–130.

Jagannathan, R., Malakhov, A., & Novikov, D. (2010). Do Hot Hands Exist Among Hedge Fund Managers? An Empirical Evaluation. *Journal of Finance, 65*(1), 217–255.

Jegadeesh, N., & Titman, S. (1993). Returns to Buying Winners and Selling Losers: Implications for Stock Market Efficiency. *Journal of Finance, 48*(1), 65–91.

Patton, A. J., & Ramadorai, T. (2012). On the High-frequency Dynamics of Hedge Fund Risk Exposures. *Journal of Finance, forthcoming.*

Sirri, E. R., & Tufano, P. (1998). Costly Search and Mutual Fund Flows. *Journal of Finance, 53*(5), 1589–1622.

Wermers, R. (1997). *Momentum Investment Strategies of Mutual Funds, Performance Persistence, and Survivorship Bias.* Denver, CO: Working Paper, University of Colorado.

# CHAPTER 19

# 'Seeking Alpha': The Performance of Funds of Hedge Funds

**Willi Semmler, Christian Proaño, and Raphaële Chappe**
New School For Social Research, Economics Department,
New York, NY, USA

## 19.1. INTRODUCTION

One of the fastest growing sectors in the hedge funds industry is the funds of hedge funds (FoHFs) — hedge funds that invest in other hedge funds.[1] The value delivered to investors by FoHFs is the ability to perform due diligence and screen funds, select the best-performing hedge funds, and diversify across funds. To the extent many hedge funds are opaque, FoHFs investors have access to information on constituent funds that would be difficult and costly to obtain on an individual basis.

As for other active investment portfolios, hedge fund returns are often characterized through the use of a model featuring alpha and beta coefficients, as

---

[1]FoHFs are also called 'feeder funds' since they allocate (feed) assets from original investors to hedge funds.

Reconsidering Funds of Hedge Funds. http://dx.doi.org/10.1016/B978-0-12-401699-6.00019-8

a direct application of the Capital Asset Pricing Model (CAPM) theory. Roughly, the beta and alpha terms measure the passive and active components of the return, respectively. The beta return component is viewed as a 'passive' in that it could be achieved through a static well-diversified portfolio. The alpha component determines the skill of the fund manager.

Normally the beta should be the right benchmark for a hedge fund. Reasonable investors would expect to be paying fees to the hedge fund manager only for the alpha. However, this is not the case, as the compensation structure of hedge funds is quite unique, typically a 1–2% management fee based on assets under management (AUM) and a 20% performance fee on total return (the carry). FoHFs typically receive a 1% management fee and a 5–10% carry. In addition to these fees, FoHFs typically pass on to investors fees charged by the underlying hedge funds, resulting in a double-fee structure. The major disadvantage for investors is that diversification across funds actually has a cost. For example, it is possible that some underlying funds will generate positive returns while there is overall negative return at the FoHFs level. These funds will attract carry in spite of the fact that a FoHF has negative performance. Brown *et al.* (2004) argue that the more diversified the FoHF, the greater the likelihood that the investor will incur underlying hedge funds carry regardless of overall FoHFs performance. For this reason, Brown *et al.* (2004) argue that there is a significant probability that the carry on underlying funds will be so large as to absorb all of the FoHFs return.

Presumably, it is the ability to deliver high alphas that is responsible for the rise of the hedge fund industry. This issue is even more critical for FoHFs in light of the double-free structure. Our goal is to test this hypothesis and determine whether we can confirm statistically significant positive alphas for FoHFs. The chapter is structured as follows. In Section 19.2, we review the theoretical approaches to modeling hedge fund returns. In Section 19.3, we outline our linear regression model and data (as well as some data bias issues). Our results are given in Section 19.4, followed by our conclusions.

## 19.2. THEORETICAL APPROACHES TO MODEL HEDGE FUND RETURNS

### 19.2.1. Single-Asset Models

Index models are statistical models designed to estimate the breakdown of a security's risk between firm-specific risk and systematic risk. Note that the approach is very general in nature and not particularly targeted at hedge fund investment strategies. Typically the single-asset model identifies one broad market index (such as the S&P 500) to capture the influence of macroeconomic events. This model can be estimated with a regression:

$$R_i = \alpha_i + \beta_i R_m + e_i, \tag{19.1}$$

where $R_i$ denotes the security's return in excess of the risk-free rate, $R_i = r_i - r_f$, and $R_m$ is the excess return on a market index, $R_m = r_m - r_f$. In this model, the firm's beta measures the response of the particular security to changes in the market return (i.e., systematic risk). The alpha term measures the security return in excess of the return induced by the market. On average, securities with higher alphas are more attractive in that they offer higher expected returns to investors. Finally, the error term $e_i$ measures the impact of firm-specific events and as such is a measure of firm-specific risk. The expected value of $e_i$ is zero since on average the impact of unanticipated firm-specific events must even out.

This approach originates with the CAPM of Sharpe (1964), and was subsequently applied to the mutual fund industry (Treynor, 1965; Sharpe, 1966; Jensen, 1968, 1969). The very simple estimation regression in equation (19.1) can also be applied to hedge funds. One example of this approach can be found in Goetzmann and Ross (2000). They compute Jensen's alpha with respect to the average performance of hedge fund managers in excess of the Treasury bill (T-bill) rate, once the amount due to systematic factor exposures has been subtracted. Although their paper does not actually spell out the actual regression in equation form, we understand that they estimated Jensen's alpha as:

$$\alpha_i = R_i - \beta_i R_m,$$

where $R_i$ and $R_m$ are, respectively, the hedge fund and market returns in excess of the risk-free rate. This was achieved by regressing the excess hedge fund returns (excess over the T-bill rate) against the excess market return (S&P 500 return in excess of the US 30-day T-bill) on the basis of equation (19.1). The time series had 77 periods (monthly returns from 1994 to 2000). For each period, the equal-weighted index is computed by taking monthly returns for single funds and calculating equal-weighted aggregates. In addition, Goetzmann and Ross (2000) run separate regressions for each investment strategy (i.e. computing an equal-weighted index only for those funds using a specific investment strategy). Their findings show that the alpha is 0.3 for the full universe of hedge funds and varies from −0.17 to 1.01 depending on the investment strategy.

Note that lagged models can also be used. For instance, working on individual returns for 2024 funds (including defunct funds to avoid survivorship bias) over the period 1996−2003, obtained from the TASS database, Malkiel and Saha (2004) run regressions of monthly individual excess hedge fund returns for a particular strategy against excess returns for the S&P 500. To allow for the possibility that hedge funds hold illiquid assets that are not synchronously priced with a stock index, they introduced lags in the estimation process (lagged excess S&P 500 returns). They ran the following regression:

$$(R_{i,t} - R_{F,t}) = \alpha_1 + \beta_{0,i}(R_{m,t} - R_{F,t}) + \beta_{1,i}(R_{m,t-1} - R_{F,t-1})$$
$$+\beta_{2,i}(R_{m,t-2} - R_{F,t-2}) + \beta_{3,i}(R_{m,t-3} - R_{F,t-3}) + \varepsilon_{i,t},$$

where $R_{i,t}$ is the fund return for a particular investment strategy for period $t$, $R_{m,t}$ the S&P 500 return for period $t$, $R_{F,t}$ the risk-free rate for period $t$, and $\varepsilon_{i,t}$ the error term. Malkiel and Saha (2004) estimate for the entire hedge fund universe an alpha of 0.0368, a beta of 0.231 with contemporaneous S&P 500 returns, and a beta of 0.393 (summed betas $\beta_0 + \beta_1 + \beta_2 + \beta_3$) with lagged S&P returns.

## 19.2.2. Multifactor Models

Single-factor models based on an equity index are very limited to the extent that they fail to capture the great varieties of asset classes that hedge fund may invest in. Hedge funds have different stated investment styles and invest in a vast array of financial assets, from equity instruments and derivatives (e.g., stock options), fixed-income instruments (bonds and loans), and derivatives (e.g., interest rate derivatives such as credit default swaps) to other classes of assets, such as foreign exchange futures and commodity derivatives. As a result funds may have significant exposures to various market factors such as credit conditions, currency exchange rates, commodities, volatility, and bonds. The multifactor approach is helpful to capture the sensitivity of different hedge fund investment strategies to different indices, as these different strategies result in very different risk exposures depending on the types of assets being invested in, and whether the fund is pursuing a directional or non-directional strategy.

The multifactor approach was pioneered in Sharpe (1992) and was originally applied in the context of the mutual fund industry. Sharpe (1992) identifies 12 asset classes (factors) that mutual funds may invest in, and uses twelve asset classes as potential independent variables in the regression (see Table 19.A1 in the Annex for a list of asset classes and corresponding indexes). Sharpe's model is:

$$R_i = (b_{i1}F_1 + b_{i2}F_2 + \cdots + b_{in}F_n) + e_i,$$

where $R_i$ represents the return on asset $i$, $F_1$ represents the value of factor 1, $F_n$ the value of the $n$th factor (with $n \leq 12$), and $e_i$ the error term. The return of each asset class is represented by a market capitalization weighted index of the returns on a large number of securities.[2]

The approach has been applied to the hedge funds industry. The models are typically linear in nature, with hedge fund returns regressed against various ($K$) assets/indices:

$$R_{it} = \alpha_i + \beta_{i1} Factor1_t + \cdots + \beta_{iK} FactorK_t + e_{it}.$$

The betas measure the sensitivity of hedge fund returns to each factor. The residual error $e_{it}$ term measures the non-systematic (fund specific) risk. The $\alpha_i$ term measures the average performance of the fund above the return of systematic factors. Hence, this model allows for the decomposition of a hedge fund return into the beta sources of return, and the manager-specific alpha separate from the identifiable risk factors. We can characterize the fund's expected return and variance:

$$E[R_{it}] = \alpha_i + \beta_{i1}E[Factor1_t] + \cdots + \beta_{iK}E[FactorK_t] \qquad (19.2)$$

---

[2]Further, there is the constraint that the weights must add up to 1. This yields a portfolio weights interpretation for the betas.

$$Var[R_{it}] = \beta_{i1}^2 Var[Factor1_t] + \ldots + \beta_{iK}^2 Var[FactorK_t] + Var[e_{it}] + Covariances,$$
$$(19.3)$$

where the 'Covariances' term is the sum of all cross covariances between the factor terms weighted by the product of their respective beta coefficients. Equation (19.2) shows that the fund's expected return can be decomposed between the 'beta returns' (expected return of the risk factors multiplied by the betas) and the manager-specific alpha. Equation (19.3) shows that the variance of the fund can be decomposed into the variance attributable to the risk factors (multiplied by the squared beta coefficient), the variance of the residual $e_{it}$, and the weighted covariances between factors.

We can see many applications of this type of multifactor model in the literature. For instance, Agarwal and Naik (2000) regress hedge fund returns (by investment strategy) against a variety of stock, bond, and commodity indices. They run the following regression for each separate hedge fund strategy:

$$R_t = \alpha + \sum_{k=1}^{K} b_k F_{kt} + u_t,$$

where $R_t$ is the return of the Hedge Fund Research index for a particular investment strategy for period $t$, $\alpha$ the abnormal return, $b_k$ a factor coefficient, $F_{kt}$ the return on the $k$th asset (or index) for period $t$, and $u_t$ the error term. The independent variables $F_{kt}$ used are the following eight indices: S&P 500 Composite Index, MSCI World Index excluding the United States, MSCI Emerging Markets Index, Salomon Brothers Government and Corporate Bond Index, Salomon Brothers World Government Bond Index, Lehman High Yield Composite Index, Federal Reserve Trade-Weighted Dollar, and Gold Price Index. They estimate alpha coefficients ranging from 0.54 to 1.25 depending on the hedge fund strategy, and find that directional strategies exhibit substantial exposures to US equities, emerging markets equities, and currencies, while non-directional strategies show substantial exposures to currencies and bond indices. Fung and Hsieh (2004) use a similar asset-based style approach with seven risk factors.

Hasanhodzic and Lo (2007) construct 'linear clones' of individual hedge funds for the purpose of determining whether these clones can provide similar risk exposures and return as hedge funds, with lower fees and more transparency. Portfolio weights are estimated by regressing individual hedge fund returns on six risk factors chosen so as to give a reasonably broad cross-section of risk exposures for typical hedge funds, roughly stocks, bonds, currencies, credit, commodities, and volatility: a US$ index return, the return on the Lehman Corporate AA Intermediate Bond Index, the spread between the Lehman BAA Corporate Bond Index and the Lehman Treasury Index, the S&P 500 total return, the Goldman Sachs Commodity Index total return, and the first-difference of the end-of-month value of the CBOE Volatility Index (VIX). For the entire sample of 1610 funds, Hasanhodzic and Lo (2007) find that 61% of the average total return is attributable to manager-specific alpha and 39% to the risk premia from the risk factors. This said, there is considerable variation in the manager-specific alpha between fund strategies. For example, the alpha accounts for over 80% of the average total return for Equity Market Neutral funds, while, for Managed Futures funds, the alpha is actually negative (−0.275).

It is also possible to use multifactor models with lagged independent variables. Ibbotson and Chen (2005) estimate a breakdown of return between the management and performance fees, and the alpha and beta returns. Forming an equally weighted index for the total hedge fund universe as well as for each subcategory based on investment strategy, using monthly return data for 3000 funds, they run a regression the hedge fund index (for the total universe as well as for each investment subcategory) against three asset classes: S&P 500 total returns (including both concurrent and with 1-month lag), US Intermediate-Term Government Bond returns (including 1-month lag), and cash (US T-bills). They estimate the pre-fee return from the fund to be 12.8%, which is split into a fee (3.8%), an alpha return (3.7%), and a beta return (5.4%). The reason for this relatively limited use of factors is that the authors are mostly interested in the value-added by hedge fund to investors that hold portfolios allocated to only traditional stocks, bonds, and cash. Note that, as in Sharpe (1992), they impose the constraint that all factor loads must add up to one.

### 19.2.3. Some Issues in Linear Regression Models

Hedge funds have unique features that may not be well identified by traditional risk management tools such as alpha and beta measures. There can be significant illiquidity exposure, as lock-in periods and other investment restrictions allow hedge funds to hold more illiquid assets than mutual funds. Further, by design hedge funds have enormous flexibility in trading (quickly moving in and out of positions with high-frequency trading, etc.) and are empowered to invest in a large variety of positions and strategies (short-selling, complex hedged positions, high use of leverage, etc.). For this reason, Lo (2001) has identified the need for a new set of risk analytics better suited to address these unique features.

*ILLIQUIDITY EXPOSURE AND SERIAL CORRELATION*

Illiquidity exposure can induce serially correlated returns (see Getmansky *et al.*, 2004). The reason for this is that mark-to-market accounting requires that a market value be assigned to portfolio securities, even when there is no active market and comparable transactions, as is the case for illiquid investments. There is some flexibility on the part of the fund manager in computing the most accurate mark for the security. Returns computed on the basis of such computations typically exhibit lower volatility and higher serial correlation than true economic returns. There are many potential sources of serial correlation. Serial correlation is induced to the extent hedge fund managers might obtain different quotes for a given illiquid security from different broker-dealers and pick a linear average as the most accurate mark, thereby minimizing volatility ('smoothed' returns). There is also the practice of performance smoothing, where hedge fund managers deliberately fail to report a portion of gains in profitable months to offset potential future losses.

Further, if broker-dealers do not frequently update their quotes, as is likely the case when there is a low trading volume, funds might not accurately mark securities for several months. This would result in a low degree of correlation between reported fund returns and factor returns, with potentially some underestimation of the true factor betas, and lagged relations between factor returns and fund returns. This problem would seem to support the use of lagged variables in the regression. Asness *et al.* (2001) show that using a lagged market return as an independent variable will result in higher market expo-sures (higher betas) for hedge funds in the aggregate. Using a single factor model:

$$R_t = \mu + \beta \wedge_t + \varepsilon_t,$$
where:
$$E[\wedge_t] = E[\varepsilon_t] = 0$$
$$Var[R_t] = \sigma^2$$

Getmansky *et al.* (2004) consider situations where the information driving a fund's performance is not immediately reflected in observed returns, but instead takes many periods to be incorporated, with the observed return each period a weighted average of true returns over the most recent $k + 1$ periods

$$R_t^o = \theta_0 R_t + \theta_1 R_{t-1} + \cdots + \theta_k R_{t-k},$$
where:
$$\theta_0 + \theta_1 + \cdots + \theta_k = 1$$
$$\theta_j \in [0, 1], j = 0, \dots, k$$

The smoothed returns will not affect the expected value of $R_t^o$, but will reduce the variance:

$$E[R_t^o] = \mu$$
$$Var[R_t^o] = c_\sigma^2 \leq \sigma^2,$$
where:
$$c_\sigma^2 = \theta_0^2 + \theta_1^2 + \cdots + \theta_k^2$$

Getmansky *et al.* (2004) outline two estimation procedures (maximum likeli-hood and linear regression) on the basis of a linear single-factor model to take the issue of smoothed returns into account.

## NON-LINEARITIES

The traditional measures of alphas, betas, and Sharpe ratios are static in nature (i.e., based on return distributions at a given point in time). This is because these measures are based on the CAPM framework for conventional portfolio analysis, which assumes stable risk profiles over time. To the extent fund managers have considerable trading flexibility to improve their performance, this assumption may not be justified in the context of the hedge fund industry. For this reason, the alpha estimate of the standard linear multifactor model may be biased, as the factor loads may be changing over time.

To incorporate the dynamic aspect of a manager's investment process, Lo (2008) puts forward a decomposition (the 'AP decomposition') of a fund's expected return into two components: a component that depends on the average values of portfolio weights and assets returns (which measures the value of passive management), and another component that depends on the correlation between portfolio weights and returns (which measures the value of active management). The rationale behind this approach is that portfolio weights are the result of decisions taken by the portfolio manager on the basis of prior information. The ability of the fund's manager to use prior information to appropriately select weights to generate returns is characteristic of active portfolio management. A passive portfolio, on the other hand, is one where weights are uncorrelated with return. In a situation where a manager invests in assets with positive premia and yields positive returns, weights will be uncorrelated with return (weights are not changing) — the only source of return is the risk premia on the underlying risk factors (asset classes the manager is investing in). On the other hand, if weights have some forecasting power, there will be some relationship between the variability of portfolio weights and returns, measured by the correlation of portfolio weights and returns at date $t$. This provides a new way of thinking about passive and active investing: if the beta exposure is time-varying rather than fixed, it may be considered a genuine source of active value for the fund.

Hence, for a portfolio invested in n securities, and defined by its weights $\omega_{it}$ in those securities at date $t$, where $R_{it}$ is the return of security $i$ at date $t$, and $R_{pt} = \sum_{i=1}^{n} \omega_{it}R_{it}$ is the portfolio's return between dates $t-1$ and $t$, Lo (2008) provides for the following decomposition:

$$E[R_{pt}] = \delta_p + v_p,$$

where:

$$\delta_p \equiv \sum_{i=1}^{n} Cov[\omega_{it}, R_{it}] \text{ (Active Component)}$$

$$v_p \equiv \sum_{i=1}^{n} E[\omega_{it}]E[R_{it}] \text{ (Passive Component)}$$

$$\theta_p \equiv \frac{\delta_p}{\delta_p + v_p} \text{ (Active Ratio)}$$

Note that, importantly, the Lo (2008) approach is applicable even if asset returns follow a linear factor model. In this situation, the portfolio's expected return can even be decomposed into three components. The beta terms are a measure of risk premia. The alpha term can be decomposed into a security selection component, and a factor-timing ability component (see Lo, 2008, p. 12). This said, the AP decomposition requires information regarding portfolio weights at each date $t$, which is unlikely to exist since hedge fund managers typically do not provide investors with position-level transparency. Lo (2008) does provide for an alternative computation method for $\delta_p$ that only requires average weights and average returns for the portfolio, which is more likely to be disclosed by a fund manager (unless the average weights do not vary much over time, in which case it is suggested that investors should reconsider paying management fees, etc.).

Another criticism of the alpha, beta, and Sharpe ratios measures is that hedge funds may display non-linearities that are not captured by linear regression models. Brooks and Kat (2002) have found that published hedge fund indexes exhibit high kurtosis, indicating that the distribution has 'fat' tails. Malkiel and Saha (2004) have confirmed that hedge fund returns are characterized by high kurtosis and that many hedge fund categories have considerable negative skewness, implying an asymmetric distribution.

## 19.3. REGRESSION ANALYSIS

### 19.3.1. Factor Model Specification

We adopt a simple linear multifactor model similar to Hasanhodzic and Lo (2007). We believe that the multifactor approach is appropriate given the variety of financial assets the underlying hedge funds are investing in. We perform a time-series regression by ordinary least squares (OLS) for each of the 5509 FoHFs in our sample, regressing FoHFs' monthly returns against eight indices, mainly: the S&P 500 total return (*S&P 500*); a US$ index return DXY (*USD*); the return on the FINRA BLP Active Investment Grade US Corporate Bond Total Return Index (*BOND*), the Goldman Sachs Commodity Index total return (*CMDTY*), the end-of-month value of the CBOE VIX (*VIX*), the MSCI World Index (*WORLD*), the MSCI Emerging Market Index (*EMERGING*), and the Morgan Stanley REIT Index RMS (*REIT*).

Our model is as follows, for the $i$th FoHF:

$$R_{it} = \alpha_i + \beta_{i1}S\&P500_t + \beta_{i2}USD_t + \beta_{i3}BOND_t + \beta_{i4}CMDTY_t + \beta_{i5}VIX_t$$
$$+ \beta_{i6}WORLD_t + \beta_{i7}EMERGING_t + \beta_{i8}REIT_t.$$

We also use one lag to allow for the possibility of illiquidity resulting in lagged relations between factor returns and fund returns.

### 19.3.2. Data Bias Issues

The hedge fund industry has been largely unregulated until now. Hedge funds were under no obligation to report net asset values or income statements. Hedge fund managers have reported performance information to different databases on a purely voluntary basis. This has given rise to several biases and the issue of distorted data, which we examine below. We note that the recent Dodd–Frank Act (signed into law on 21 July 2010) provides for new registration requirements for investment advisers in relation to private funds with

AUM of US$150 million or more. Hedge fund managers will have to register with the Securities and Exchange Commission and disclose financial statements. Further, hedge funds will also have to have assets audited by public accountants. All of this should hopefully reduce, going forward, the issue of biases in the data.

Survivorship bias originates from lower returns being excluded from performance studies if the hedge fund has failed (only surviving funds are analyzed). There are different studies and estimates of survivorships bias in the literature, analyzing different years and different funds. Amin and Kat (2003) estimate survivorship bias at about 2% per year. Fung and Hsieh (2000) have calculated that the survivorship bias is 3% annually with a 15% dropout rate. Malkiel and Saha (2004) find a bias averaging 3.74% per year. Note, however, that survivorship bias differs for hedge funds and FoHFs. Fung and Hsieh (2000) find that part of the reported underperformance of FoHFs may be attributed to lower survivorship bias. Liang (2003) estimates an annual survivorship bias of 1.18% a year for FoHFs, and 2.32% per year for hedge funds. One explanation for the smallest survivorship bias for FoHFs is the fact that they actually incur losses of underlying hedge funds that have shut down (Brown *et al.*, 2004). Hence, non-surviving funds will affect the continued performance of FoHFs. For this reason, Fung and Hsieh (2000) argue that FoHFs are possibly a better source of hedge fund performance in the aggregate.

Self-selecting bias is generated to the extent that hedge fund managers report performance after the fact and only have an incentive to do so if the hedge fund has performed well. Hedge funds might wait for a good track record before they start to report to a database. Underperforming funds might decide to stop reporting to a database. It is typically the case that hedge funds stop reporting during their last months. One example of self-selecting bias is the backfill bias (also called instant history bias), which appears when hedge fund managers add historical results to their files to give a more comprehensive view of the fund's performance once the fund begins reporting to a database. Since fund managers have an incentive to begin reporting only with a good track record, backfilled returns tend to be higher than contemporaneously reported returns. The backfill bias has been estimated on the basis of different databases at different times. Fung and Hsieh (2000) estimated the backfill bias to be 1.4% for the TASS database over the period 1994–1998. Also on the basis of the TASS database, Posthuma and Van der Sluis (2003) have found that backfilled returns are on average 4% higher annually than normal returns.

### 19.3.3. Data Description

In this chapter, we work with individual hedge fund data rather than with fund indices. Working with individual fund returns rather than indices eliminates the issue of the choice of index weights and its potential impact on regression coefficients. We use monthly returns for 3545 active and 3170 inactive FoHFs in the Bloomberg database.[3] Note that we combine the data for active and inactive funds to minimize survivorship data. Our data ranges from November 2002 to February 2012. Our combined database is of 6715 funds in total (quite a large sample of funds[4]), but we eliminate 1206 funds with insufficient observations, bringing our sample to 5509 FoHFs. These FoHFs have different strategy styles: Emerging Market, Equity Directional, Equity Market Neutral, Event Driven, Fixed Income Directional, Fixed Income Relative Value, Global Macro, Managed Futures, and Multistrategy. Table 19.1 classifies the various FoHFs into nine investment styles, reports the number of FoHFs in each category in our sample, and provides some performance statistics: for the mean and for the standard deviation, as well as Sharpe ratios. We note that the large majority of FoHFs are 'Multistrategy', which makes sense considering that many FoHFs are diversifying across funds and investment styles.

## 19.4. RESULTS

Table 19.2 summarizes the results of the linear regressions of monthly returns of FoHFs against the eight indices, estimated by OLS for each FoHF, grouped in accordance with their strategy style. We report different summary statistics (minimum, median, mean, and maximum) for the intercept and the beta coefficients of each of the 16 regression factors (including lagged factors) for all regressions in each strategy style. In Table 19.3, we show the explanatory power of the regression for each FoHF investment category, reporting the summary statistics for the adjusted $R^2$ and the probability of the $F$-statistic $p(F)$. Table 19.4 shows for each regression factor (and the intercept) the number of funds in each strategy for which the coefficient was statistically significant. Overall, the adjusted $R^2$ statistics for investment strategies are consistent with similar regressions in the literature, except for the 'Managed Futures' strategy, which has a very poor fit.

We note that the regression coefficients for the regression factors are broadly consistent with the strategy styles. The negative mean of the beta coefficients for the S&P 500 for all fund strategies would seem to indicate that, on average, funds have tended to short the S&P 500 from November 2002 to February 2012. If so it is logical that the 'Equity Directional' strategy would be the most negatively correlated to the S&P 500, with the highest beta mean in absolute value $(-0.355)$, since this strategy would logically attempt to take advantage of long-term negative market trends (by shorting). Interestingly, the mean for

---

[3]There are about 1511 active and 1798 inactive funds organized in the Americas (Bermuda/Cayman Islands/British Virgin Islands, etc.), and 1819 active and 1329 inactive funds organized in Western Europe (Gibraltar/Guernsey/Malta/Luxembourg/Switzerland/Ireland/Jersey). In terms of management location, there are 455 active and 1275 inactive funds managed in the United States, and 2771 active and 1866 inactive funds managed in Western Europe. The rest of the funds are organized and managed in miscellaneous locations.

[4]Hasanhodzic and Lo (2007), Ibbotson and Chen (2005), and Malkiel and Saha (2004) work with returns for 1610, 3000, and 2024 funds respectively. Agarwal and Naik (2000) work with returns for 1000 funds, using a database of indices compiled by Hedge Fund Research.

**Table 19.1** Summary Statistics for Monthly Returns of Funds of Hedge Funds from November 2002–February 2012

| Category | Sample size | Mean (%) | | SD (%) | | SR (%) | | | | |
|---|---|---|---|---|---|---|---|---|---|---|
| | | Mean | SD | Mean | SD | Mean | SD | Median | Skewness | Kurtosis |
| Emerging Market | 69 | 0.000331 | -0.005589 | 0.032631 | 0.020596 | 0.052554 | 0.267851 | 0.007842 | 2.917973 | 12.515566 |
| Equity Directional | 482 | 0.000390 | 0.004987 | 0.026027 | 0.023363 | 0.053302 | 0.140217 | 0.062604 | 0.027762 | 2.064063 |
| Equity Market Neutral | 95 | 0.000217 | 0.005598 | 0.026027 | 0.023363 | 0.087143 | 0.206113 | 0.069465 | 0.455967 | 0.186245 |
| Event Driven | 102 | 0.000246 | 0.007467 | 0.027255 | 0.029812 | 0.080239 | 0.195813 | 0.091782 | -0.256103 | -0.691361 |
| Fixed Income Directional | 109 | -0.002476 | 0.009345 | 0.021798 | 0.021253 | -0.005769 | 0.303383 | -0.032539 | 1.069548 | 7.707655 |
| Fixed Income Relative Value | 80 | 0.001491 | 0.003849 | 0.018971 | 0.017991 | 0.197880 | 0.409222 | 0.096344 | 3.089158 | 11.913544 |
| Global Macro | 228 | 0.000635 | 0.006375 | 0.024640 | 0.024366 | 0.084236 | 0.180704 | 0.096886 | 0.013152 | 1.479688 |
| Managed Futures | 186 | 0.002116 | 0.004402 | 0.028724 | 0.021067 | 0.074901 | 0.157358 | 0.094011 | -0.232063 | 1.748741 |
| Multi-Strategy | 4158 | 0.000143 | 0.019013 | 0.026269 | 0.117588 | 0.039575 | 0.179665 | 0.042222 | 0.005099 | 1.713706 |
| Total | 5509 | 0.000217 | 0.016778 | 0.026117 | 0.102840 | 0.046955 | 0.187989 | 0.050681 | 0.750072 | 8.711779 |

**Table 19.2** Summary Statistics for Multivariate Linear regressions of Monthly Returns of FoHFs from February 2002 to February 2012: Regression Coefficients

| Category | Sample size | Statistic | Minimum | Median | Mean | Maximum | SD |
|---|---|---|---|---|---|---|---|
| *S&P 500* | | | | | | | |
| Emerging Market | 69 | beta | −1.386032 | −0.266833 | −0.272771 | 1.504171 | 0.373698 |
| | | t-stat | −3.934157 | −1.044151 | −1.125467 | 1.643862 | 1.056136 |
| Equity Directional | 482 | beta | −2.697439 | −0.325762 | −0.355147 | 0.918121 | 0.400743 |
| | | t-stat | −5.823214 | −1.602316 | −1.660071 | 2.096280 | 1.312265 |
| Equity Market Neutral | 95 | beta | −7.522637 | −0.126599 | −0.177239 | 2.540991 | 0.933982 |
| | | t-stat | −3.723686 | −0.791767 | −0.908323 | 2.891983 | 1.230987 |
| Event Driven | 102 | beta | −0.680968 | −0.198818 | −0.113235 | 2.401215 | 0.377405 |
| | | t-stat | −3.226521 | −1.039724 | −0.886291 | 1.149727 | 0.993192 |
| Fixed Income Directional | 109 | beta | −4.757311 | −0.107484 | −0.160712 | 0.797801 | 0.532372 |
| | | t-stat | −2.472319 | −0.551032 | −0.470634 | 1.772905 | 0.927641 |
| Fixed Income Relative Value | 80 | beta | −0.527020 | −0.127854 | −0.116994 | 1.063919 | 0.213498 |
| | | t-stat | −2.617702 | −0.701859 | −0.696222 | 2.298863 | 0.962538 |
| Global Macro | 228 | beta | −7.866970 | −0.219084 | −0.229184 | 3.771929 | 0.878075 |
| | | t-stat | −3.925852 | −0.977428 | −0.892330 | 2.041004 | 1.202436 |
| Managed Futures | 186 | beta | −4.250377 | −0.160840 | −0.201661 | 2.560291 | 0.679547 |
| | | t-stat | −3.452080 | −0.335987 | −0.542431 | 1.992625 | 1.124579 |
| Multistrategy | 4158 | beta | −117.461300 | −0.226994 | −0.264071 | 30.847800 | 2.026007 |
| | | t-stat | −5.319845 | −1.224531 | −1.196765 | 3.836359 | 1.247741 |
| *S&P 500(−1)* | | | | | | | |
| Emerging Market | 69 | beta | −2.306515 | −0.089953 | −0.156367 | 0.874864 | 0.548116 |
| | | t-stat | −2.718282 | −0.369764 | −0.277132 | 2.110685 | 1.069082 |
| Equity Directional | 482 | beta | −3.448084 | −0.084514 | −0.112661 | 1.392002 | 0.396173 |
| | | t-stat | −3.069894 | −0.400337 | −0.357281 | 2.603040 | 0.881722 |
| Equity Market Neutral | 95 | beta | −9.035378 | −0.036433 | −0.110460 | 2.023817 | 1.119314 |
| | | t-stat | −2.224584 | −0.296484 | −0.308676 | 1.854910 | 0.940549 |
| Event Driven | 102 | beta | −5.028908 | −0.141292 | −0.187279 | 5.550888 | 0.801684 |
| | | t-stat | −4.095113 | −0.548879 | −0.634615 | 1.273096 | 0.896923 |
| Fixed Income Directional | 109 | beta | −3.909181 | −0.215864 | −0.299856 | 0.272101 | 0.439447 |
| | | t-stat | −2.589887 | −0.987013 | −0.964650 | 1.699385 | 0.931347 |
| Fixed Income Relative Value | 80 | beta | −1.417236 | −0.077794 | −0.125879 | 0.758001 | 0.357791 |
| | | t-stat | −2.797331 | −0.469708 | −0.454538 | 2.362270 | 0.873621 |

*(Continued)*

**Table 19.2** Summary Statistics for Multivariate Linear regressions of Monthly Returns of FoHFs from February 2002 to February 2012: Regression Coefficients—cont'd

| Category | Sample size | Statistic | Minimum | Median | Mean | Maximum | SD |
|---|---|---|---|---|---|---|---|
| Global Macro | 228 | beta | −9.530159 | 0.068058 | 0.110083 | 2.899727 | 0.838927 |
| | | t-stat | −2.412619 | 0.193259 | 0.363085 | 3.901601 | 1.142983 |
| Managed Futures | 186 | beta | −2.494621 | 0.275419 | 0.446590 | 4.443062 | 0.843179 |
| | | t-stat | −2.100540 | 0.551559 | 0.838321 | 3.687189 | 1.294453 |
| Multistrategy | 4158 | beta | −11.076980 | −0.029852 | 0.040285 | 289.986100 | 4.591626 |
| | | t-stat | −3.455344 | −0.157047 | −0.123711 | 5.055431 | 0.989332 |
| *USD* | | | | | | | |
| Emerging Market | 69 | beta | −1.052715 | 0.141837 | 0.180087 | 1.214323 | 0.304175 |
| | | t-stat | −1.870047 | 1.219238 | 1.111797 | 7.562502 | 1.400721 |
| Equity Directional | 482 | beta | −0.989058 | 0.205229 | 0.195913 | 1.475328 | 0.263658 |
| | | t-stat | −1.605247 | 2.014504 | 2.048849 | 8.242568 | 1.658084 |
| Equity Market Neutral | 95 | beta | −2.114650 | 0.073785 | 0.048876 | 5.538395 | 0.729908 |
| | | t-stat | −3.528904 | 1.000678 | 0.796364 | 4.388824 | 1.585652 |
| Event Driven | 102 | beta | −4.808031 | 0.117924 | 0.015098 | 0.506885 | 0.628944 |
| | | t-stat | −1.698653 | 1.180507 | 1.239422 | 4.962891 | 1.446639 |
| Fixed Income Directional | 109 | beta | −0.870540 | 0.071842 | 0.155520 | 4.021779 | 0.434864 |
| | | t-stat | −2.187879 | 0.843571 | 0.969887 | 4.198018 | 1.305771 |
| Fixed Income Relative Value | 80 | beta | −0.594471 | 0.054829 | 0.077527 | 0.661332 | 0.200874 |
| | | t-stat | −3.193676 | 0.644703 | 0.593085 | 3.110031 | 1.352730 |
| Global Macro | 228 | beta | −2.018558 | −0.020510 | −0.010103 | 3.765596 | 0.479845 |
| | | t-stat | −4.002226 | −0.118528 | 0.064224 | 5.778937 | 1.815117 |
| Managed Futures | 186 | beta | −3.026264 | −0.176241 | −0.282562 | 2.441883 | 0.593622 |
| | | t-stat | −6.938476 | −0.805975 | −0.859799 | 3.213531 | 1.515763 |
| Multistrategy | 4158 | beta | −43.621780 | 0.106288 | 0.108341 | 7.091864 | 0.795753 |
| | | t-stat | −4.146748 | 1.146952 | 1.122064 | 9.574645 | 1.631312 |
| *USD(−1)* | | | | | | | |
| Emerging Market | 69 | beta | −0.587026 | 0.051677 | 0.090427 | 1.889908 | 0.303970 |
| | | t-stat | −1.296891 | 0.367213 | 0.366841 | 3.387144 | 0.976053 |
| Equity Directional | 482 | beta | −1.229473 | 0.000704 | 0.007134 | 1.336369 | 0.180273 |
| | | t-stat | −2.523755 | 0.006995 | 0.119522 | 3.377926 | 0.957737 |
| Equity Market Neutral | 95 | beta | −0.277439 | −0.009084 | 0.061554 | 3.700804 | 0.400024 |
| | | t-stat | −2.201450 | −0.136552 | 0.071905 | 2.734356 | 0.929053 |
| Event Driven | 102 | beta | −0.986762 | 0.056924 | 0.104782 | 2.426766 | 0.307649 |
| | | t-stat | −2.179664 | 0.493441 | 0.518352 | 3.466350 | 1.156243 |

| | | | | | | | |
|---|---|---|---|---|---|---|---|
| Fixed Income Directional | 109 | beta | −0.793278 | 0.086994 | 0.106892 | 1.192062 | 0.221862 |
| | | t-stat | −1.463209 | 0.879538 | 0.940226 | 4.264346 | 1.173236 |
| Fixed Income Relative Value | 80 | beta | −0.501039 | 0.042271 | 0.059205 | 0.912977 | 0.176622 |
| | | t-stat | −2.451789 | 0.539638 | 0.446257 | 2.808669 | 1.012136 |
| Global Macro | 228 | beta | −3.286894 | −0.025711 | −0.010249 | 4.802261 | 0.539622 |
| | | t-stat | −3.570505 | −0.226927 | −0.270913 | 2.549595 | 1.036946 |
| Managed Futures | 186 | beta | −3.639167 | −0.092715 | −0.016460 | 3.464381 | 0.700279 |
| | | t-stat | −3.790145 | −0.560114 | −0.504350 | 3.590857 | 1.345608 |
| Multistrategy | 4158 | beta | −142.970600 | −0.004058 | −0.041806 | 12.644700 | 2.286872 |
| | | t-stat | −4.957396 | −0.044614 | −0.023935 | 4.274445 | 0.999153 |
| *BOND* | | | | | | | |
| Emerging Market | 69 | beta | −0.904396 | 0.126475 | 0.258054 | 4.319487 | 0.673618 |
| | | t-stat | −2.034794 | 0.609786 | 0.840995 | 5.623200 | 1.486664 |
| Equity Directional | 482 | beta | −3.883958 | 0.006745 | 0.007867 | 13.035750 | 0.711969 |
| | | t-stat | −3.498139 | 0.061892 | 0.127769 | 5.339740 | 1.106551 |
| Equity Market Neutral | 95 | beta | −2.253279 | 0.001752 | −0.118927 | 3.222545 | 0.623222 |
| | | t-stat | −4.994372 | 0.021847 | −0.253381 | 3.427484 | 1.528036 |
| Event Driven | 102 | beta | −3.076266 | 0.013839 | −0.067862 | 2.313097 | 0.535347 |
| | | t-stat | −3.587220 | 0.144228 | 0.070247 | 4.265916 | 1.493205 |
| Fixed Income Directional | 109 | beta | −4.281753 | 0.031140 | 0.096969 | 3.415503 | 0.733668 |
| | | t-stat | −2.475516 | 0.217987 | 0.717528 | 5.139878 | 1.872114 |
| Fixed Income Relative Value | 80 | beta | −0.946025 | 0.004847 | 0.073694 | 1.380469 | 0.371001 |
| | | t-stat | −3.415834 | 0.056015 | 0.543690 | 4.447196 | 1.860605 |
| Global Macro | 228 | beta | −7.642492 | 0.043206 | 0.060820 | 5.214611 | 0.994582 |
| | | t-stat | −3.562686 | 0.276754 | 0.423722 | 5.150938 | 1.331774 |
| Managed Futures | 186 | beta | −2.362070 | −0.009216 | 0.522352 | 11.087281 | 1.639549 |
| | | t-stat | −5.150938 | −0.035005 | 0.176464 | 5.967330 | 1.448366 |
| Multistrategy | 4158 | beta | −66.459120 | 0.032190 | 0.038359 | 16.928230 | 1.213876 |
| | | t-stat | −5.593823 | 0.282821 | 0.381398 | 7.017641 | 1.383775 |
| *BOND(−1)* | | | | | | | |
| Emerging Market | 69 | beta | −0.702193 | 0.031742 | 0.044921 | 1.438039 | 0.308901 |
| | | t-stat | −1.761986 | 0.198913 | 0.222704 | 2.147795 | 0.943410 |
| Equity Directional | 482 | beta | −1.214316 | 0.076879 | 0.066851 | 6.712532 | 0.391209 |
| | | t-stat | −2.493586 | 0.708603 | 0.753381 | 5.943416 | 1.260333 |
| Equity Market Neutral | 95 | beta | −0.429576 | 0.036509 | 0.060740 | 3.057952 | 0.340143 |
| | | t-stat | −2.323730 | 0.276160 | 0.319470 | 3.275885 | 1.179828 |
| Event Driven | 102 | beta | −3.545080 | 0.163134 | 0.084920 | 3.401128 | 0.671802 |
| | | t-stat | −1.495568 | 1.469617 | 1.346922 | 5.997768 | 1.319386 |

(Continued)

**Table 19.2** Summary Statistics for Multivariate Linear regressions of Monthly Returns of FoHFs from February 2002 to February 2012: Regression Coefficients—cont'd

| Category | Sample size | Statistic | Minimum | Median | Mean | Maximum | SD |
|---|---|---|---|---|---|---|---|
| Fixed Income Directional | 109 | beta | −1.025324 | 0.040158 | 0.082524 | 3.101950 | 0.414612 |
| | | t-stat | −1.218692 | 0.527543 | 0.426843 | 2.381924 | 0.807369 |
| Fixed Income Relative Value | 80 | beta | −0.559607 | 0.055248 | 0.072127 | 0.595702 | 0.195643 |
| | | t-stat | −3.178391 | 0.521121 | 0.558795 | 4.976239 | 1.236851 |
| Global Macro | 228 | beta | −10.007090 | 0.060863 | 0.043066 | 1.949784 | 0.954049 |
| | | t-stat | −1.674327 | 0.479101 | 0.522029 | 4.524410 | 1.193874 |
| Managed Futures | 186 | beta | −1.024765 | 0.128384 | 0.372699 | 4.366595 | 0.757818 |
| | | t-stat | −4.195272 | 0.666507 | 0.640649 | 4.088881 | 1.040490 |
| Multistrategy | 4158 | beta | −11.220020 | 0.073589 | 0.105002 | 80.935710 | 1.322381 |
| | | t-stat | −4.100830 | 0.697938 | 0.819440 | 7.910288 | 1.317918 |
| *CMDTY* | | | | | | | |
| Emerging Market | 69 | beta | −0.084726 | 0.036807 | 0.050785 | 0.560194 | 0.089234 |
| | | t-stat | −1.553637 | 0.853317 | 0.817834 | 4.076170 | 1.082800 |
| Equity Directional | 482 | beta | −0.334654 | 0.024068 | 0.032948 | 2.458856 | 0.138758 |
| | | t-stat | −3.308826 | 0.718151 | 0.735108 | 3.801617 | 1.171448 |
| Equity Market Neutral | 95 | beta | −0.561183 | 0.005823 | 0.008702 | 1.853827 | 0.223410 |
| | | t-stat | −2.301382 | 0.154758 | 0.250944 | 3.452224 | 1.277354 |
| Event Driven | 102 | beta | −1.276376 | 0.032551 | 0.030490 | 0.327668 | 0.149504 |
| | | t-stat | −1.715528 | 0.910466 | 1.098636 | 5.779843 | 1.338598 |
| Fixed Income Directional | 109 | beta | −0.271254 | 0.036293 | 0.046329 | 0.540046 | 0.115754 |
| | | t-stat | −3.314652 | 0.955703 | 0.692367 | 4.082468 | 1.703299 |
| Fixed Income Relative Value | 80 | beta | −0.288409 | 0.013960 | 0.023411 | 0.295914 | 0.081816 |
| | | t-stat | −2.411011 | 0.654141 | 0.595632 | 3.168584 | 1.333615 |
| Global Macro | 228 | beta | −0.773471 | 0.033321 | 0.042658 | 0.979084 | 0.153504 |
| | | t-stat | −3.677923 | 0.818413 | 0.634689 | 3.829830 | 1.181660 |
| Managed Futures | 186 | beta | −0.855377 | 0.034108 | 0.071614 | 0.981983 | 0.208755 |
| | | t-stat | −2.862082 | 0.469319 | 0.649607 | 6.921268 | 1.677449 |
| Multistrategy | 4158 | beta | −5.355858 | 0.032047 | 0.055684 | 34.981210 | 0.573267 |
| | | t-stat | −3.770385 | 1.038972 | 0.995283 | 5.690315 | 1.382587 |
| *CMDTY(−1)* | | | | | | | |
| Emerging Market | 69 | beta | −0.510320 | 0.020655 | 0.025526 | 0.632000 | 0.119356 |
| | | t-stat | −2.099774 | 0.450992 | 0.413781 | 3.488592 | 1.074488 |
| Equity Directional | 482 | beta | −0.275108 | −0.014065 | −0.012297 | 0.487037 | 0.063019 |
| | | t-stat | −2.695420 | −0.404651 | −0.378512 | 3.829194 | 0.935612 |

| Strategy | n | | | | | | |
|---|---|---|---|---|---|---|---|
| Equity Market Neutral | 95 | beta | −0.358187 | −0.005696 | −0.009367 | 2.090439 | 0.232094 |
| | | t-stat | −3.038378 | −0.383086 | −0.219392 | 2.246045 | 1.164558 |
| Event Driven | 102 | beta | −0.197073 | 0.000324 | 0.025328 | 0.797703 | 0.136569 |
| | | t-stat | −2.902508 | 0.010941 | 0.066080 | 2.974469 | 0.995396 |
| Fixed Income Directional | 109 | beta | −0.144664 | 0.002310 | 0.021163 | 0.587041 | 0.090239 |
| | | t-stat | −2.821887 | 0.077186 | 0.150799 | 3.001151 | 1.097416 |
| Fixed Income Relative Value | 80 | beta | −0.494678 | 0.008850 | 0.009172 | 0.167035 | 0.080843 |
| | | t-stat | −1.807455 | 0.374527 | 0.266447 | 2.687273 | 0.993247 |
| Global Macro | 228 | beta | −1.142879 | 0.006617 | 0.019409 | 2.430823 | 0.214725 |
| | | t-stat | −3.216865 | 0.106314 | 0.179269 | 3.086217 | 0.967278 |
| Managed Futures | 186 | beta | −1.218579 | −0.005009 | 0.051983 | 1.100153 | 0.233975 |
| | | t-stat | −2.656183 | −0.111497 | −0.064538 | 3.181176 | 1.143333 |
| Multistrategy | 4158 | beta | −21.215800 | −0.000347 | 0.000719 | 7.322513 | 0.377394 |
| | | t-stat | −3.990841 | −0.010977 | 0.017301 | 4.143225 | 0.999838 |
| **VIX** | | | | | | | |
| Emerging Market | 69 | beta | −0.004061 | −0.000160 | −0.000429 | 0.000455 | 0.000825 |
| | | t-stat | −2.735578 | −0.555135 | −0.318866 | 3.960865 | 1.181290 |
| Equity Directional | 482 | beta | −0.012984 | 0.000018 | −0.000152 | 0.008671 | 0.001521 |
| | | t-stat | −3.724569 | 0.101579 | 0.095483 | 3.524974 | 1.082890 |
| Equity Market Neutral | 95 | beta | −0.001585 | −0.000016 | 0.000422 | 0.015421 | 0.002233 |
| | | t-stat | −2.931292 | −0.171474 | −0.097503 | 3.942151 | 1.159772 |
| Event Driven | 102 | beta | −0.015140 | −0.000039 | −0.000967 | 0.002062 | 0.002729 |
| | | t-stat | −2.215587 | −0.261012 | −0.352519 | 1.610540 | 0.800340 |
| Fixed Income Directional | 109 | beta | −0.010566 | −0.000081 | −0.000344 | 0.002161 | 0.001331 |
| | | t-stat | −2.353472 | −0.493102 | −0.363018 | 7.738418 | 1.156144 |
| Fixed Income Relative Value | 80 | beta | −0.005500 | −0.000057 | −0.000255 | 0.001443 | 0.000827 |
| | | t-stat | −2.342033 | −0.499781 | −0.531385 | 1.039181 | 0.751495 |
| Global Macro | 228 | beta | −0.014138 | −0.000167 | −0.000314 | 0.038967 | 0.003748 |
| | | t-stat | −4.030750 | −0.598429 | −0.589778 | 2.766981 | 1.043500 |
| Managed Futures | 186 | beta | −0.025888 | −0.000421 | −0.001372 | 0.008520 | 0.003587 |
| | | t-stat | −5.008568 | −0.830645 | −0.720581 | 2.705547 | 1.204412 |
| Multistrategy | 4158 | beta | −0.049143 | −0.000045 | −0.000195 | 0.456050 | 0.007283 |
| | | t-stat | −6.241159 | −0.311094 | −0.337136 | 9.003303 | 1.057114 |
| **VIX(−1)** | | | | | | | |
| Emerging Market | 69 | beta | −0.000699 | 0.000305 | 0.000772 | 0.010095 | 0.001746 |
| | | t-stat | −0.845125 | 1.317766 | 1.166241 | 3.976391 | 1.088999 |
| Equity Directional | 482 | beta | −0.011335 | 0.000104 | 0.000185 | 0.016524 | 0.001357 |
| | | t-stat | −2.557723 | 0.601716 | 0.611837 | 13.299190 | 1.190479 |

(Continued)

**Table 19.2** Summary Statistics for Multivariate Linear regressions of Monthly Returns of FoHFs from February 2002 to February 2012: Regression Coefficients—cont'd

| Category | Sample size | Statistic | Minimum | Median | Mean | Maximum | SD |
|---|---|---|---|---|---|---|---|
| Equity Market Neutral | 95 | beta | −0.005267 | 0.000040 | −0.000152 | 0.001297 | 0.000999 |
| | | t-stat | −3.490970 | 0.381449 | 0.274703 | 2.669179 | 1.078845 |
| Event Driven | 102 | beta | −0.014607 | 0.000045 | −0.000063 | 0.015635 | 0.002327 |
| | | t-stat | −1.959556 | 0.182490 | 0.177708 | 3.822898 | 1.004745 |
| Fixed Income Directional | 109 | beta | −0.002865 | 0.000072 | 0.000185 | 0.008340 | 0.001244 |
| | | t-stat | −3.795331 | 0.149713 | 0.327353 | 3.511667 | 1.152832 |
| Fixed Income Relative Value | 80 | beta | −0.001839 | 0.000027 | 0.000054 | 0.001830 | 0.000487 |
| | | t-stat | −2.672627 | 0.235144 | 0.183153 | 2.780450 | 0.990081 |
| Global Macro | 228 | beta | −0.023029 | 0.000152 | 0.000336 | 0.010977 | 0.002332 |
| | | t-stat | −2.983087 | 0.655224 | 0.653080 | 6.395911 | 1.080500 |
| Managed Futures | 186 | beta | −0.003382 | 0.000353 | 0.001459 | 0.015020 | 0.002629 |
| | | t-stat | −2.988159 | 0.804132 | 0.854060 | 4.648004 | 1.044809 |
| Multistrategy | 4158 | beta | −1.981165 | 0.000099 | −0.000223 | 0.074486 | 0.030783 |
| | | t-stat | −7.004497 | 0.560328 | 0.588061 | 9.821796 | 1.014531 |
| *WORLD* | | | | | | | |
| Emerging Market | 69 | beta | −1.550304 | 0.267551 | 0.265840 | 1.654658 | 0.469099 |
| | | t-stat | −1.657810 | 0.946106 | 0.986887 | 3.427268 | 1.048413 |
| Equity Directional | 482 | beta | −2.536202 | 0.476653 | 0.469953 | 2.995080 | 0.588905 |
| | | t-stat | −2.155199 | 2.019725 | 2.094394 | 7.826357 | 1.535864 |
| Equity Market Neutral | 95 | beta | −2.799690 | 0.216836 | 0.194702 | 6.719867 | 1.014859 |
| | | t-stat | −2.205200 | 1.091212 | 1.054921 | 4.083042 | 1.278310 |
| Event Driven | 102 | beta | −6.412665 | 0.320564 | 0.182115 | 1.133774 | 0.883394 |
| | | t-stat | −1.208571 | 1.402756 | 1.392148 | 4.239508 | 1.343094 |
| Fixed Income Directional | 109 | beta | −2.600056 | 0.174121 | 0.265841 | 9.332728 | 0.951493 |
| | | t-stat | −1.280122 | 0.699608 | 0.743645 | 3.140292 | 0.949591 |
| Fixed Income Relative Value | 80 | beta | −1.074446 | 0.144888 | 0.165378 | 1.575879 | 0.302983 |
| | | t-stat | −2.370226 | 0.805040 | 0.757961 | 2.460967 | 0.915114 |
| Global Macro | 228 | beta | −3.211516 | 0.225568 | 0.253252 | 7.466799 | 0.924450 |
| | | t-stat | −2.522594 | 0.881865 | 0.882714 | 5.193665 | 1.327151 |
| Managed Futures | 186 | beta | −3.269861 | 0.135469 | 0.174574 | 4.237425 | 0.744367 |
| | | t-stat | −2.662491 | 0.303638 | 0.475231 | 4.106744 | 1.207053 |

| | | | | | | | |
|---|---|---|---|---|---|---|---|
| Multistrategy | 4158 | beta | −26.424490 | 0.314736 | 0.323475 | 21.642550 | 0.932212 |
| | | t-stat | −3.291884 | 1.353522 | 1.400925 | 7.002658 | 1.382443 |
| **WORLD(−1)** | | | | | | | |
| Emerging Market | 69 | beta | −0.582311 | 0.134796 | 0.281068 | 2.913916 | 0.636506 |
| | | t-stat | −1.892130 | 0.522894 | 0.525289 | 3.071492 | 1.015727 |
| Equity Directional | 482 | beta | −1.675916 | 0.190532 | 0.217659 | 2.428935 | 0.415174 |
| | | t-stat | −2.887076 | 0.779512 | 0.749414 | 2.800526 | 0.861594 |
| Equity Market Neutral | 95 | beta | −1.405351 | 0.106218 | 0.188766 | 5.458973 | 0.848398 |
| | | t-stat | −1.636472 | 0.651375 | 0.603289 | 2.544495 | 0.952892 |
| Event Driven | 102 | beta | −2.016587 | 0.308911 | 0.335024 | 4.909122 | 0.629412 |
| | | t-stat | −1.180642 | 0.836021 | 0.996364 | 3.345068 | 1.006616 |
| Fixed Income Directional | 109 | beta | −0.275870 | 0.306770 | 0.348628 | 2.800785 | 0.387123 |
| | | t-stat | −1.301033 | 1.225186 | 1.160078 | 3.345728 | 1.024096 |
| Fixed Income Relative Value | 80 | beta | −1.363054 | 0.136568 | 0.148292 | 1.959199 | 0.494053 |
| | | t-stat | −2.009252 | 0.680228 | 0.544428 | 3.128042 | 1.070106 |
| Global Macro | 228 | beta | −5.677376 | −0.010309 | −0.093431 | 4.957445 | 0.818553 |
| | | t-stat | −3.182317 | −0.027234 | −0.139214 | 2.703042 | 1.106282 |
| Managed Futures | 186 | beta | −4.261891 | −0.161201 | −0.316782 | 6.061162 | 1.036666 |
| | | t-stat | −3.820644 | −0.327422 | −0.568388 | 3.660250 | 1.314406 |
| Multistrategy | 4158 | beta | −350.917500 | 0.110085 | 0.009566 | 6.968760 | 5.564167 |
| | | t-stat | −4.190403 | 0.479308 | 0.422773 | 3.776146 | 0.988541 |
| **EMERGING** | | | | | | | |
| Emerging Market | 69 | beta | −0.135170 | 0.216728 | 0.229335 | 1.034713 | 0.184476 |
| | | t-stat | −1.686818 | 2.665767 | 2.987501 | 10.144270 | 2.591164 |
| Equity Directional | 482 | beta | −0.777654 | 0.070375 | 0.108408 | 1.607152 | 0.199594 |
| | | t-stat | −2.813053 | 1.371016 | 1.455413 | 9.149550 | 1.505399 |
| Equity Market Neutral | 95 | beta | −0.950324 | 0.014492 | 0.007026 | 0.729645 | 0.163905 |
| | | t-stat | −2.388818 | 0.331768 | 0.514498 | 5.765963 | 1.161378 |
| Event Driven | 102 | beta | −0.745410 | 0.028107 | 0.045651 | 0.561260 | 0.151317 |
| | | t-stat | −3.172772 | 0.504315 | 0.427745 | 3.223054 | 0.988039 |
| Fixed Income Directional | 109 | beta | −0.611491 | 0.016706 | 0.027538 | 0.693198 | 0.142955 |
| | | t-stat | −1.604402 | 0.381746 | 0.518246 | 2.940343 | 0.840148 |
| Fixed Income Relative Value | 80 | beta | −0.426926 | 0.023519 | 0.020226 | 0.395358 | 0.109588 |
| | | t-stat | −1.980395 | 0.609646 | 0.398540 | 3.195102 | 1.066948 |
| Global Macro | 228 | beta | −0.747667 | 0.041850 | 0.038566 | 0.797174 | 0.173015 |
| | | t-stat | −3.015988 | 0.635824 | 0.866757 | 7.539781 | 1.611957 |
| Managed Futures | 186 | beta | −0.621789 | −0.019348 | −0.054054 | 0.657775 | 0.173856 |
| | | t-stat | −2.175274 | −0.223720 | −0.054345 | 4.152239 | 1.107211 |

(Continued)

322 SECTION 4 Fund of Hedge Fund Alpha

**Table 19.2** Summary Statistics for Multivariate Linear regressions of Monthly Returns of FoHFs from February 2002 to February 2012: Regression Coefficients—cont'd

| Category | Sample size | Statistic | Minimum | Median | Mean | Maximum | SD |
|---|---|---|---|---|---|---|---|
| Multistrategy | 4158 | beta | −6.762128 | 0.052448 | 0.062898 | 5.672284 | 0.231280 |
| | | t-stat | −3.011620 | 0.982304 | 1.064442 | 9.351035 | 1.357809 |
| *EMERGING(−1)* | | | | | | | |
| Emerging Market | 69 | beta | −0.508711 | −0.008146 | −0.035021 | 0.265246 | 0.127043 |
| | | t-stat | −2.644558 | −0.173148 | −0.238679 | 2.505622 | 0.992467 |
| Equity Directional | 482 | beta | −1.867738 | −0.036340 | −0.046521 | 0.490148 | 0.157501 |
| | | t-stat | −3.298636 | −0.659664 | −0.667268 | 2.968810 | 0.964062 |
| Equity Market Neutral | 95 | beta | −0.818103 | −0.015471 | −0.019255 | 0.419704 | 0.148687 |
| | | t-stat | −2.669863 | −0.416052 | −0.338202 | 2.713970 | 1.002673 |
| Event Driven | 102 | beta | −1.361714 | −0.034424 | −0.070768 | 0.362897 | 0.246406 |
| | | t-stat | −2.775007 | −0.595745 | −0.570870 | 2.217752 | 1.031510 |
| Fixed Income Directional | 109 | beta | −0.777570 | −0.009055 | −0.011956 | 0.444976 | 0.138413 |
| | | t-stat | −2.485618 | −0.196562 | −0.201400 | 1.977393 | 0.925864 |
| Fixed Income Relative Value | 80 | beta | −0.522834 | 0.002109 | 0.000253 | 0.547944 | 0.101806 |
| | | t-stat | −1.936332 | 0.082374 | −0.125582 | 1.609882 | 0.799281 |
| Global Macro | 228 | beta | −1.039578 | −0.022531 | −0.004194 | 2.558440 | 0.279624 |
| | | t-stat | −2.749369 | −0.310872 | −0.306330 | 2.587481 | 0.861100 |
| Managed Futures | 186 | beta | −1.306477 | −0.031458 | −0.085973 | 0.954623 | 0.239340 |
| | | t-stat | −3.683299 | −0.321485 | −0.446438 | 1.682641 | 0.963749 |
| Multistrategy | 4158 | beta | −5.087918 | −0.022608 | −0.013790 | 50.883950 | 0.833196 |
| | | t-stat | −3.692003 | −0.440467 | −0.399906 | 2.936131 | 0.897063 |
| *REIT* | | | | | | | |
| Emerging Market | 69 | beta | −0.084726 | 0.036807 | 0.050785 | 0.560194 | 0.089234 |
| | | t-stat | −1.553637 | 0.853317 | 0.817834 | 4.076170 | 1.082800 |
| Equity Directional | 482 | beta | −0.334654 | 0.024068 | 0.032948 | 2.458856 | 0.138758 |
| | | t-stat | −3.308826 | 0.718151 | 0.735108 | 3.801617 | 1.171448 |
| Equity Market Neutral | 95 | beta | −0.561183 | 0.005823 | 0.008702 | 1.853827 | 0.223410 |
| | | t-stat | −2.301382 | 0.154758 | 0.250944 | 3.452224 | 1.277354 |
| Event Driven | 102 | beta | −1.276376 | 0.032551 | 0.030490 | 0.327668 | 0.149504 |
| | | t-stat | −1.715528 | 0.910466 | 1.098636 | 5.779843 | 1.338598 |
| Fixed Income Directional | 109 | beta | −0.271254 | 0.036293 | 0.046329 | 0.540046 | 0.115754 |
| | | t-stat | −3.314652 | 0.955703 | 0.692367 | 4.082468 | 1.703299 |
| Fixed Income Relative Value | 80 | beta | −0.288409 | 0.013960 | 0.023411 | 0.295914 | 0.081816 |
| | | t-stat | −2.411011 | 0.654141 | 0.595632 | 3.168584 | 1.333615 |

| | | | | | | | |
|---|---|---|---|---|---|---|---|
| Global Macro | 228 | beta | −0.773471 | 0.033321 | 0.042658 | 0.979084 | 0.153504 |
| | | t-stat | −3.677923 | 0.818413 | 0.634689 | 3.829830 | 1.181660 |
| Managed Futures | 186 | beta | −0.855377 | 0.034108 | 0.071614 | 0.981983 | 0.208755 |
| | | t-stat | −2.862082 | 0.469319 | 0.649607 | 6.921268 | 1.677449 |
| Multistrategy | 4158 | beta | −5.355858 | 0.032047 | 0.055684 | 34.981210 | 0.573267 |
| | | t-stat | −3.770385 | 1.038972 | 0.995283 | 5.690315 | 1.382587 |
| *REIT(−1)* | | | | | | | |
| Emerging Market | 69 | beta | −1.057193 | −0.028817 | −0.042438 | 0.254985 | 0.139656 |
| | | t-stat | −2.641958 | −0.624735 | −0.640858 | 2.292830 | 0.971181 |
| Equity Directional | 482 | beta | −0.593237 | −0.015941 | −0.012351 | 0.425869 | 0.078369 |
| | | t-stat | −3.592356 | −0.605327 | −0.503989 | 4.235638 | 1.062174 |
| Equity Market Neutral | 95 | beta | −0.489651 | −0.005477 | 0.014968 | 1.856601 | 0.209684 |
| | | t-stat | −2.438209 | −0.381551 | −0.269501 | 2.546807 | 0.933488 |
| Event Driven | 102 | beta | −2.061385 | −0.008507 | 0.008716 | 1.310397 | 0.291221 |
| | | t-stat | −2.449879 | −0.239837 | −0.106601 | 3.508897 | 1.084334 |
| Fixed Income Directional | 109 | beta | −0.320246 | −0.005453 | −0.009733 | 0.605723 | 0.102299 |
| | | t-stat | −3.577737 | −0.352376 | −0.315862 | 1.714518 | 1.136955 |
| Fixed Income Relative Value | 80 | beta | −0.143287 | −0.002652 | 0.007357 | 0.258267 | 0.070038 |
| | | t-stat | −2.384320 | −0.114281 | −0.077119 | 3.496080 | 1.189637 |
| Global Macro | 228 | beta | −5.572068 | −0.008406 | −0.005209 | 2.722757 | 0.429669 |
| | | t-stat | −2.700822 | −0.199586 | −0.225015 | 4.588663 | 1.051714 |
| Managed Futures | 186 | beta | −2.561154 | −0.009462 | −0.045132 | 1.274597 | 0.333803 |
| | | t-stat | −3.686823 | −0.190976 | −0.116187 | 5.280157 | 1.172636 |
| Multistrategy | 4158 | beta | −1.870969 | −0.010252 | −0.002877 | 3.181232 | 0.143319 |
| | | t-stat | −4.433839 | −0.368538 | −0.320474 | 5.761099 | 1.154393 |

| | | | Significance (%) | | | |
|---|---|---|---|---|---|---|
| **Table 19.3** | | Summary Statistics for Multivariate Linear Regressions of Monthly Returns of FoHFs from November 2002 to February 2012: Explanatory Power | | | | |

| Category | Sample size | Statistic | Minimum | Median | Mean | Maximum |
|---|---|---|---|---|---|---|
| Emerging Market | 69 | adj. $R^2$ | −0.191144 | 0.597483 | 0.530538 | 0.961636 |
| | | $p(F)$ | 9.04E-37 | 0.000001 | 0.058506 | 0.977448 |
| Equity Directional | 482 | adj. $R^2$ | −0.367760 | 0.567359 | 0.491671 | 0.974916 |
| | | $p(F)$ | 3.2E-28 | 3.33E−07 | 0.071195 | 0.999919 |
| Equity Market Neutral | 95 | adj. $R^2$ | −0.212856 | 0.281051 | 0.283779 | 0.794722 |
| | | $p(F)$ | 6.39E-20 | 0.004541 | 0.152119 | 0.970343 |
| Event Driven | 102 | adj. $R^2$ | −0.407803 | 0.505607 | 0.429257 | 0.819363 |
| | | $p(F)$ | 2.92E-22 | 0.000045 | 0.090305 | 0.991927 |
| Fixed Income Directional | 109 | adj. $R^2$ | −0.327964 | 0.396889 | 0.363257 | 0.880191 |
| | | $p(F)$ | 7.45E-18 | 0.001647 | 0.130459 | 0.986769 |
| Fixed Income Relative Value | 80 | adj. $R^2$ | −0.145958 | 0.292699 | 0.282662 | 0.789927 |
| | | $p(F)$ | 1.49E-16 | 0.006718 | 0.141141 | 0.988870 |
| Global Macro | 228 | adj. $R^2$ | −2.272564 | 0.307198 | 0.289782 | 0.900542 |
| | | $p(F)$ | 1.98E-33 | 0.006860 | 0.187814 | 0.990051 |
| Managed Futures | 186 | adj. $R^2$ | −0.703659 | 0.120821 | 0.175143 | 0.829050 |
| | | $p(F)$ | 2.51E-31 | 0.208904 | 0.291516 | 0.999390 |
| Multistrategy | 4158 | adj. $R^2$ | −0.364087 | 0.454629 | 0.405484 | 0.980435 |
| | | $p(F)$ | 3.14E-17 | 0.000052 | 0.101779 | 0.999976 |

WORLD and EMERGING indices is positive for most strategies, meaning that, on average, FoHFs were taking long positions on foreign equity markets. On the other hand, it is surprising that the 'Equity Market Neutral' strategy does not have an average beta close to zero for the S&P 500, WORLD, and EMERGING indices, as we would expect with market neutral status.

The measures of standard deviation, minimum, and maximum for the beta coefficients also indicate that there are funds that are far more correlated to the S&P 500 than the average beta would suggest. This is particularly apparent with the 'Multistrategy' investment style, where the average beta mean for the S&P 500 is −0.264, but the standard deviation is high and some funds have a beta as high as 30.84 and as low as −117.46. This suggests that looking at the average beta alone is somewhat misleading and does not capture the full extent of FoHFs exposure to S&P500 movements. This also holds for the WORLD and EMERGING indices, where we also see some large deviations around the mean, and potentially wide discrepancies among funds.

We find that the 'Multistrategy' style (which is the largest sample) bears systematic exposure to all asset classes. In a sample of 4158 funds, we find statistical significance for 1171 (S&P 500), 1387 (USD), 631 (BOND), 1099

**Table 19.4** Multivariate Linear Regressions of Monthly Returns of FoHFs November 2002–February 2012: Number of Funds with a Statistically Significant Coefficient

| Category | Sample size | C | SP 500 | SP 500(-1) | USD | USD (-1) | BOND | BOND (-1) | CMDTY | CMDTY (-1) | VIX | VIX (-1) | WORLD | WORLD (-1) | EMERGING | EMERGING (-1) | REIT | REIT (-1) |
|---|---|---|---|---|---|---|---|---|---|---|---|---|---|---|---|---|---|---|
| Emerging Market | 69 | 6 | 9 | 4 | 16 | 4 | 14 | 1 | 8 | 13 | 8 | 11 | 13 | 3 | 41 | 3 | 12 | 6 |
| Equity Directional | 482 | 8 | 45 | 4 | 47 | 1 | 8 | 14 | 12 | 4 | 5 | 8 | 54 | 4 | 36 | 11 | 40 | 6 |
| Equity Market Neutral | 95 | 17 | 24 | 11 | 29 | 7 | 18 | 10 | 13 | 9 | 4 | 4 | 19 | 7 | 6 | 4 | 8 | 2 |
| Event Driven | 102 | 16 | 9 | 6 | 29 | 11 | 18 | 34 | 20 | 4 | 2 | 2 | 38 | 17 | 5 | 10 | 14 | 6 |
| Fixed Income Directional | 109 | 7 | 6 | 15 | 27 | 28 | 30 | 3 | 34 | 10 | 8 | 12 | 13 | 24 | 6 | 2 | 4 | 11 |
| Fixed Income Relative Value | 80 | 15 | 10 | 4 | 14 | 5 | 25 | 13 | 16 | 3 | 1 | 6 | 9 | 11 | 1 | 0 | 3 | 8 |
| Global Macro | 228 | 33 | 42 | 34 | 56 | 3 | 27 | 22 | 25 | 10 | 17 | 22 | 45 | 18 | 52 | 11 | 50 | 23 |
| Managed Futures | 186 | 26 | 23 | 44 | 43 | 29 | 25 | 12 | 38 | 18 | 19 | 21 | 26 | 5 | 14 | 12 | 16 | 14 |
| Multistrategy | 4158 | 378 | 1171 | 197 | 1387 | 208 | 631 | 672 | 1099 | 191 | 270 | 326 | 1381 | 256 | 963 | 171 | 1013 | 407 |

We test for a positive intercept at the 5% degree of significance (one-sided test). For all other coefficients, we test for statistical significance at the 5% degree of significance.

(CMDTY), 270 (VIX), 1381 (WORLD), 963 (EMERGING), and 1013 funds (REIT). This is consistent with the variety of strategies and asset classes encompassed within this all-encompassing classification. The statistical significance drops for the lagged values, except for BOND. Most strategies bear some exposure to the US$, but the 'Global Macro,' 'Event Driven,' and 'Fixed Income Directional' strategies bear the highest exposure in terms of the percentage of funds in the sample for which there is statistical relevance. All strategies bear some exposure to BOND and CMDTY indices.

Table 19.2 shows that, on average, FoHFs have not delivered positive manager-specific alphas, which would suggest that active management at the FoHFs level may not add, on average, much value for investors. This said, a small percentage of FoHFs do deliver statistically significant positive alphas (see Table 19.4). For the 'Multistrategy' investment style, we find statistically significant positive alphas for 378 funds out of 4158. In the total sample of 5509 FoHFs, 506 funds have statistically significant positive alphas.[5] This would suggest that investors should not automatically assume that all FoHFs are able to select the best-performing hedge funds, but instead should carefully pick those FoHFs that will create statistically significant positive alphas.

These results provide support for the idea that the returns of FoHFs can be replicated with basic liquid indices by constructing passive portfolios of common risk factors. With the exception of volatility, each risk factor is easily tradable via exchange-traded funds (ETFs) or derivative instruments. This would allow investors to avoid high management fees, limited liquidity, potential redemption fees, and ultimately the lack of transparency associated with hedge funds. This result is consistent with some recent results in the literature. For instance, Hasanhodzic and Lo (2007) study how linear clones of hedge funds can replicate some of the fund risk exposures and derive similar risk premia from those exposures. Gilli *et al.* (2010) show it may be possible to replicate the attractive features of hedge fund returns using liquid assets.[6] The issue of lowering costs is particularly relevant for FoHFs in that, as we have described, there is a double-fee structure (passing-on fees charged by the underlying hedge funds) with a corresponding potential inherent inefficiency if there is a high degree of diversification across underlying hedge funds (Brown *et al.*, 2004).

While some papers have confirmed statistically significant positive alphas, others have shown that a substantial part of the return can be explained by simple stock, bond, and cash betas. Agarwal and Naik (2000) find alphas ranging from 0.54 to 1.25 depending on hedge fund strategy (using a database

---

[5]Note that the MSCI World Index (WORLD) has a high correlation with the MSCI Emerging Market Index (EMERGING) and the S&P 500, suggesting a possible issue of multicollinearity. We run the same regression dropping the WORLD factor, but we do not find that the explanatory power of the model is enhanced, and there is no change in the lack of statistical significance of the intercept.

[6]They are able to construct a portfolio that closely follows the CSFB/Tremont Hedge Fund Index, but is less sensitive to adverse equity market movements.

of indices rather than individual returns). Goetzmann and Ross (2000) find an alpha of 0.3 for the full universe of hedge funds (also working with an equal-weighted index rather than individual returns), varying from −0.17 to 1.01 depending on the investment strategy.[7] Hasanhodzic and Lo (2007) find that estimates of manager-specific alpha (the mean for all multivariate linear regressions of individual funds returns) are significant in most cases (for most fund strategies), ranging from 0.42 (Managed Futures) to 1.41 (Emerging Markets) − although they also acknowledge that a large portion of a hedge fund's expected return can be obtained through the factor risks (passive diversification) rather than manager-specific alpha. Note that all these empirical studies are not specifically focused on FoHFs, but rather on hedge funds. For the FoHFs investment strategy (a sample of 355 FoHFs), Hasanhodzic and Lo (2007) find an alpha mean of 0.43. Ibbotson and Chen (2005), using an equally weighted index, find that overall alphas are significantly positive (0.037), which also holds true in each strategy subcategory (all 10 subcategories had positive alphas, with five of the alphas statistically significant).[8] On the other hand, working with an index of FoHFs, Fung and Hsieh (2004) find an alpha of 0.00477 (in itself not very high), but the significance level (and magnitude) drop as soon as the sample period is split into two subperiods (the authors conclude that there is a 'vanishing alpha'). Fung and Hsieh (2004) find that the seven regression factors can explain up to 80% of monthly return variations.

Running a Chow stability test to understand the impact of the 2007−2008 financial crisis, we find that there are 1752 funds that display a structural break as of August 2008, 1731 funds with parameter stability, and 2026 funds where we cannot run the test because of insufficient data for both the pre- and the post-crisis period.[9] We can thus conclude that the financial crisis has had a significant impact on half of those FoHFs that were in existence (and had been for some time) as of August 2008. Given that the hedge fund industry experienced losses and redemptions in 2008, with US$155 billion of net outflows,[10] it is very likely that both underlying hedge funds in which FoHFs invest and FoHFs themselves may have had to significantly readjust their positions and/or reconsider their investment strategies.

## CONCLUSION

The linear 'asset class risk factors' model can explain a significant part of the returns of FoHFs. The FoHFs return can be analyzed in terms of common market risk factor exposures and corresponding risk premia. We find that about 10% of FoHFs in our sample deliver statistically significant manager-specific alpha, but

[7]Note that the only explanatory variable is the excess market (S&P 500) return.
[8]They also compare the management fees charged relative to the amount of alpha that hedge funds add.
[9]All estimation results and statistics for the Chow test are available from the authors upon request. We use a 5% statistical significance level.
[10]*HFR Global Hedge Fund Industry Report* Q4 2008.

that, on average, manager-specific alpha is not statistically significant. Given that FoHFs typically have a double-fee structure (passing-on fees charged by the underlying hedge funds) and that fees on underlying funds might absorb a large share of the return at the FoHFs level if there is a high degree of diversification across underlying hedge funds, investors should exercise great scrutiny when selecting a FoHF to ensure that there is a significant manager-specific alpha.

Although our results provide some support for the conclusion that the returns of FoHFs can be replicated with basic indices, such as with fixed-weights portfolios of the factors used in our regression (though the risk factors in our model are not necessarily unique — other market indices could produce similar results), we should proceed with caution. We should keep in mind the inherent limitations of a linear model in light of the nonlinearities of many fund strategies. Non-linear models may be able to yield better adjusted $R_2$ coefficients and evidence manager-specific alpha that is not captured in linear models. Specifically, segmented linear regression models with thresholds effects could display better goodness of fit and possibly a better estimation of the intercept. Further research will be required on this point, and more refinements should be carried out to improve the explanatory power of the model.

## ANNEX

**Table 19.A1**  Different Asset Classes from Sharpe (1992)

| Class | Description | Index |
|---|---|---|
| Bills | Cash-equivalents with less than 3 months to maturity | Salomon Brothers 90-Day Treasury Bill Index |
| Intermediate-Term Government Bonds | Government bonds with less than 10 years to maturity | Lehman Brothers Intermediate-term Government Bond Index |
| Long-Term Government Bonds | Government bonds with more than 10 years to maturity | Lehman Brothers Long-term Government Bond Index |
| Corporate Bonds | Corporate bonds with ratings of at least Baa by Moody's or BBB by S&P | Lehman Brothers Corporate Bond Index |
| Mortgage-Related Securities | Mortgage-backed and related securities | Lehman Brothers Mortgage-Backed Securities Index |
| Large-Capitalization Value Stocks | Stocks in S&P 500 stock index with high book-to-price ratios | Sharpe/BARRA Value Stock Index |
| Large-Capitalization Growth Stocks | Stocks in S&P 500 stock index with low book-to-price ratios | Sharpe/BARRA Growth Stock Index |
| Medium-Capitalization Stocks | Stocks in the top 80% of capitalization in the US equity universe after the exclusion of stocks in S&P 500 stock index | Sharpe/BARRA Medium Capitalization Stock Index |

*(Continued)*

| Table 19.A1 | Different Asset Classes from Sharpe (1992)—cont'd | |
| --- | --- | --- |
| **Class** | **Description** | **Index** |
| Small-Capitalization Stocks | Stocks in the bottom 20% of capitalization in the US equity universe after the exclusion of stocks in S&P 500 stock index | Sharpe/BARRA Small Capitalization Stock Index |
| Non-US Bonds | Bonds outside the United States and Canada | Salomon Brothers Non-US Government Bond Index |

# References

Agarwal, V., & Naik, N. (2000). On Taking the 'Alternative' Route: The Risks, Rewards, and Performance of Persistence of Hedge Funds. *Journal of Alternative Investments, 2*(4), 6–23.

Amin, G., & Kat, H. (2003). Stocks, Bonds and Hedge Funds: Not a Free Lunch! *Journal of Portfolio Management, 29*(4), 113–118.

Asness, C., Krail, R., & Liew, J. (2001). *Do Hedge Funds Hedge? Working Paper*. Greenwich, CT: AQR Capital Management LLC.

Brooks, C., & Kat, H. (2002). The Statistical Properties of Hedge Fund Index Returns and Their Implications for Investors. *Journal of Alternative Investments, 5*(3), 26–44.

Brown, S., Goetzmann, W., & Liang, B. (2004). *Fees on Fees in Funds of Funds. Working Paper 02-33*. New Haven, CT: Yale School of Management International Center for Finance.

Fung, W., & Hsieh, D. (2000). Performance Characteristics of Hedge Funds and Commodity Funds: Natural vs. Spurious Biases. *Journal of Financial and Quantitative Analysis, 35*(3), 291–307.

Fung, W., & Hsieh, D. (2004). Hedge Fund Benchmarks: A Risk-Based Approach. *Financial Analysts Journal, 60*(5), 291–307.

Getmansky, M., Lo, A., & Makarov, I. (2004). An Econometric Analysis of Serial Correlation and Illiquidity in Hedge-Fund Returns. *Journal of Financial Economics, 74*(3), 529–609.

Gilli, M., Schumann, E., Cabej, G., & Lula, J. (2010). Replicating Hedge Fund Indices with Optimization Heuristics. *Working Paper*. Switzerland: University of Geneva.

Goetzmann, W., & Ross, S. (2000). *Hedge Funds: Theory and Performance, Working Paper F-52B*. New Haven, CT: Yale School of Management.

Hasanhodzic, & Lo. (2007). Can Hedge-Fund Returns Be Replicated?: The Linear Case. *Journal of Investment Management, 5*(2), 5–45.

Ibbotson, R., & Chen, P. (2005). *Sources of Hedge Fund Returns: Alphas, Betas, and Costs. Working Paper 05-17*. New Haven, CT: Yale School of Management, International Center for Finance.

Jensen, M. (1968). The Performance of Mutual Funds in the Period 1945–1964. *Journal of Finance, 23*(2), 389–416.

Jensen, M. (1969). Risk, the Pricing of Capital Assets, and the Evaluation of Investment Portfolios. *Journal of Business, 42*(2), 167–247.

Liang, B. (2003). *On the Performance of Alternative Investments: CTAs, Hedge Funds, and Funds-of-Funds. Working Paper*. Amherst, MA: University of Massachusetts.

Lo, A. (2001). Risk Management for Hedge Funds: Introduction and Overview. *Financial Analysts Journal, 57*(6), 16–33.

Lo, A. (2008). Where do Alphas Come From? A New Measure of the Value of Active Investment Management. *Journal of Investment Management, 6*(3), 6–34.

Malkiel, B., & Saha, A. (2004). *Hedge Funds: Risk and Return. Working Paper 104, Center for Economic Policy Studies*. NJ: Princeton University.

Posthuma, N., & Van der Sluis, P. (2003). *A Reality Check on Hedge Fund Returns. Working Paper*. Amsterdam: Free University.

Sharpe. (1964). Capital Asset Prices: A Theory of Market Equilibrium Under Conditions of Risk. *Journal of Finance, 19*, 425–442.

Sharpe, W. (1966). Mutual Fund Performance. *Journal of Business, 39*(1), 119–138.

Sharpe, W. (1992). Asset Allocation: Management Style and Performance Measurement. *Journal of Portfolio Management, 18*(2), 7–19.

Treynor, J. (1965). How to Rate Management of Investment Funds. *Harvard Business Review, 43*(1), 63–75.

# CHAPTER 20

# Quantitative Insight into Management of Funds of Hedge Funds and Consequences on Fund Alpha Performance

**Justina Dambrauskaite**[*], **Haidar Haidar**[†], **Bernard Minsky**[*], **and Qi Tang**[†]
[*]International Asset Management Ltd., London, UK
[†]University of Sussex, Department of Mathematics, Brighton, UK

## 20.1. INTRODUCTION

Many statistical models have been developed to predict future returns of different asset classes during the last 40 years. In this respect, we develop a slightly different idea in this chapter. Instead of looking at predictions, we classify funds of hedge funds (FoHFs) using risk measures of historical data. We expect that in a risk controlled environment (hedge funds and investment funds) and risk control squared environment (FoHFs), the risk classification is good enough to reflect management quality through quantitative description of consistency and aggression in management styles. In this chapter, we investigate FoHFs and further claim similar results for hedge funds. It is interesting to note that the recent paper by Ben-Dor and Xu (2012) discusses the issue of consistency from various management points of view. We argue a similar issue from a quantitative analysis point of view not for a single fund, but rather a portfolio of hedge funds. In Dewaele *et al.* (2011), the authors use a different classification method to categorize FoHFs; however, they did not give a very clear indication on how their classes behave in terms of long-term return performance.

It is well known that the investment community has various opinions regarding the quality of risk measures. Issues of consistency and usefulness are constantly under discussion, and the use of one particular risk measure may not reflect all aspects of an asset. In this chapter, we combine nine popular and standard risk measures (annual return, alpha, trend correlation, maximum drawdown, volatility, Sortino ratio, up capture, down capture, and winning runs), and apply them to historical returns of FoHFs. We then produce a ranking of each asset according to each statistic calculated among all other assets used in the test. In addition, we determine the ranking order (ascending or descending in terms of risk values) according to the natural preference of a rational investor. When using a basket of statistics all based on returns, it seems likely that there would be a considerable degree of codependence as evidenced by the correlation between the ranks of the statistics. For this reason we restrict ourselves to nine risk measures against a much larger set of readily available risk measures. The statistical dependence is performed separately and statistics that are extremely highly correlated with at least one of the other statistics are removed.

Subsequently, we compute the principal components of these ranking vectors. Owing to the significant proportion of the total variance of the original ranking vectors explained by the principal components, we concentrate on the first and second principal components, denoted as PC1 and PC2, respectively.

By inspecting the factor loadings, we infer that PC1 represents the consistency of the FoHFs and PC2 represents the aggression of the FoHFs. We note that if PC is a principal component, any scaling of PC, $\alpha * PC$, is also a principal component, for any given non-zero constant $\alpha$. We note that any principal component may be replaced by its mirror image without impacting the overall mathematical results (the mirror image principal component will have the same variance and will be uncorrelated with all the other principal components). Therefore, we have chosen factor loadings such that increasing factor score corresponds to increasing the strength of the style inferred.

We first obtain 4024 live and dead FoHFs that reported for at least a 24-month period during the January 2003 to December 2011 period in the International Asset Management (IAM) database. At any given point in time during the investigative period, the number of FoHFs reporting to the database is between 1453 and 2196. Therefore, for any 24-month period (12-month for historical statistic computation and 12-month for future return computation) under investigation, we deal with a subset of funds that has reported for the entire period. Consequently, for any period of time, the number of FoHFs under investigation is a varying number. We use 12-month returns for each rolling-year period of historical data to produce a matrix of the risk statistic ranks, with number of rows corresponding to number of FoHFs in the sample and nine columns corresponding to nine risk statistics used. We then produce the principal components of the rankings and plot, for fund $i$, the point:

$$
\begin{aligned}
(x_{i1}, x_{i2}) = (&(\text{ann return}_i, \text{ ann volatility}_i, \text{ correlation}_i, \text{ max drawdown}_i, \\
&\text{ann sortino}_i, \text{ up capture}_i, \text{ down capture}_i, \text{ winning runs}_i) * \text{PC1}, \\
&(\text{ann return}_i, \text{ ann volatility}_i, \text{ correlation}_i, \text{ max drawdown}_i, \\
&\text{ann sortino}_i, \text{ up capture}_i, \text{ down capture}_i, \text{ winning runs}_i) * \text{PC2}),
\end{aligned}
$$

where $\text{risk}_i$ is the ranking number of the $i$th asset under that risk statistic, the $*$ represents the scalar product between two vectors, and PC1 and PC2 are the factor loadings calculated for the first two principal components for that window.

In Section 20.2, we describe how principal components analysis (PCA) is applied to the dataset. In Section 20.3, we present the data, calculate the required variables to be used in the model, discuss the results, and interpret the role of principal components analysis. In Section 20.4, we discuss the classification and consequence on FoHFs performance. In Section 20.5, we investigate the migration rate of FoHFs and draw conclusions that FoHFs are pro-active in investment management; subsequently, we make some comments on whether the pro-active nature affects the returns. Section 20.6 is dedicated to discussions relating to the financial crisis of 2008 and subsequent European turbulence. An overall summary is then given.

## 20.2. PRINCIPAL COMPONENTS ANALYSIS

PCA is a statistical variable reduction technique that linearly transforms a set of variables by rotation where the images of the transformation are new uncorrelated factors. Each new factor is a linear combination of the original variables. The complete set of new factors preserves as much variation as the original variables presented. It was first presented by Pearson in 1901 and developed by Hotelling in 1933 (see relevant discussions in Dunteman, 1989; Jolliffe, 2002). The covariance matrix measures the variation of the contributed information of the data. The information that is preserved after the transformation is represented in the variances of the uncorrelated factors. The factors are sorted in a descending order according to the amount of variation explained in their variances and, generally, the first few principal components explain most of the variation, indicating that the effective dimensionality of the original set of variables is considerably less than the total number of variables. The remaining components are associated with eigenvalues that are close to zero and have little explanatory power. PCA has been applied to study bond returns (Litterman and Scheinkman, 1991). The method of classifying funds into classes and observing their performances has been previously

looked at by Brown and Goetzmann (2003) using generalized style classifications by comparing returns data to index portfolios and corresponding
loading factors. Further studies have been carried out in Gibson and Gyger
(2007); however, our risk analysis is risk measure based, while the effect of the
'market' or 'indices' has not been taken into account.

We denote the matrix of RankStatistics by $RS$ where each row of $RS$ corresponds
to a RankStatistic and we denote the new factors by $F$. In each time window, we
have nine variables and $N$ (the number of FoHFs reporting to the database
across that window) observations. It is common to normalize a dataset before
calculating principal components to correct for differences in scale between the
original variables. However, there is no need to normalize the data in our case as
each RankStatistic is a permutation of the numbers from 1 to $N$ and thus all the
RankStatistics have the same mean and variance. The technique was reduced to
a singular value decomposition (SVD) problem as follows:

Let $F_{9\times N} = V_{9\times 9}(RS_{9\times N} - \overline{RS}_{9\times N}) = V_{9\times 9}(\hat{RS}_{9\times N})$ for some $V$ to be chosen
later. Here, the mean matrix:

$$\overline{RS}_{9\times N} = \begin{bmatrix} g & \cdots & g \\ \vdots & \ddots & \vdots \\ g & \cdots & g \end{bmatrix},$$

and:

$$g = \frac{1}{N}\sum_{i=1}^{N} RS_{k\times i} = \frac{1}{N}\sum_{i=1}^{N} i.$$

In our sample, $N$ is the number of FoHFs, $g = (N+1)/2$:

$$Cov(F) = \frac{1}{N-1}F \times F^{\mathrm{T}} = \frac{1}{N-1}\left(V \times \hat{RS}\right) \times \left(\hat{RS}^{\mathrm{T}} \times V^{\mathrm{T}}\right)$$

$$= V \times Cov\left(\hat{RS}\right) \times V^{\mathrm{T}}.$$

Now choose $V_{9\times 9}$ to be the matrix whose columns are the orthonormal
eigenvectors of $Cov\left(\hat{RS}\right)$ such that $V^{-1} = V^{\mathrm{T}}$ and sort the columns in a descending order according to the value of the corresponding eigenvalue $\lambda_k$.
Then:

$$Cov(F) = \begin{bmatrix} \lambda_1 & \cdots & 0 \\ \vdots & \ddots & \vdots \\ 0 & \cdots & \lambda_9 \end{bmatrix},$$

is a diagonal matrix where $\lambda_1 \geq \lambda_2 \geq \ldots \geq \lambda_9$ are the diagonal entries. The
eigenvalue of the factor directly measures the explanatory power of the factor to
the complete variation of the original dataset.

## 20.3. DATA AND THE NATURE OF THE FIRST TWO PRINCIPAL COMPONENTS

A set of FoHFs is used as the subject of our test at any single time period under investigation. The data are downloaded from the IAM proprietary database of hedge fund and FoHFs performance, which is collated from a variety of sources including Hedge Fund Research, Eurekahedge, Altvest, Bloomberg, and proprietary sources. The number of FoHFs analyzed in a period varies between 1453 and 2196. We use 12-month historical risk statistics based on monthly return data to rank the FoHFs. A set of 108 monthly returns from January 2003 to December 2011 is used in the calculations. A rolling window of 12 consecutive months is used to compute the risk statistics at each time step. A new time series of 97 periods is generated for each of the nine risk statistics.

The risk measures used in the model are listed and defined in Table 20.1. The assets are ranked for each statistic from the best performing to the worst according to the sign of the statistic, which represents the preference of the rational investor as shown in Table 20.2. For example, the plus (+) sign for annual return implies that the investor prefers higher returns to lower returns. In contrast, the minus (−) sign for volatility implies that the investor prefers lower volatility.

The set of ranked statistics is referred to as the RankStatistics $RS$ in the rest of this chapter where $RS_{k,t}$ is an $N \times 1$ vector corresponding to the $k$ risk statistic at time $t$. The risk statistics were standardized and made comparable by looking at their $RS$ rather than their quantities. Timeline 1 shows that the returns, $r_t$, were transformed into RankStatistics, $RS_{k,t}$, by calculating the 12-period trailing risk statistics for each of the 97 time subperiods and then ranked according to the investor preference sign. Example 20.1 below displays how a risk statistic with a negative investor preference sign is ranked in ascending order with lowest score ranked number 1 and highest score ranked number 8, whereas if it has a positive sign it is ranked in descending order with the highest score ranked 1:

**Timeline 1**

| Data | Sign | Order | Funds | | | | | | | |
|------|------|-------|-------|------|------|------|-------|-------|-------|------|
| Stats score | | | −0.2 | 0.07 | 0.33 | 0.02 | −0.22 | −0.11 | −0.05 | 0.14 |
| RankStatistics | − | ascending | 2 | 6 | 8 | 5 | 1 | 3 | 4 | 7 |
| | + | descending | 7 | 3 | 1 | 4 | 8 | 6 | 5 | 2 |

**Table 20.1** Definition of the Risk Statistics

| Statistic | Formula | Comment |
|---|---|---|
| 1 Annualized return | $\left\{\displaystyle\prod_{i=1}^{n}(1+r_i)\right\}^{12/n} - 1$ | Annualizing monthly returns, $r_i$ |
| 2 Alpha | $\hat{\alpha} = \overline{(r-f)} - \hat{\beta} \times \overline{(m-f)}$ | Intercept of the regression of excess returns over risk-free rate $(r_i - f_i)$ against market excess returns over risk-free rate $(m_i - f_i)$ |
| 3 Trend correlation | $(-1)^k \times \dfrac{\sum_{i=1}^{n}(r_i - \bar{r}) \times (m_i - \bar{m})}{\sqrt{\sum_{i=1}^{n}(r_i - \bar{r})^2} \times \sqrt{\sum_{i=1}^{n}(m_i - \bar{m})^2}}$ | $k = \begin{cases} 0, & \text{if Market Return over } (0,\ T) \text{ is non-negative} \\ 1, & \text{if Market Return over } (0,\ T) \text{ is negative} \end{cases}$ |
| 4 Maximum drawdown | $\displaystyle\max_{i,j} \dfrac{P_{i\in(0,T)} - P_{j\in(i,T)}}{P_i}$ | $P_t =$ Asset price at time $t$ in the interval $(0,T)$ |
| 5 Volatility | $\sqrt{\dfrac{\sum_{i=1}^{n}(r_i - \bar{r})^2}{n-1}} \times \sqrt{12}$ | Annualized standard deviation |
| 6 Sortino ratio | $\dfrac{\left\{\prod_{i=1}^{n}(1+r_i)\right\}^{12/n} - \left\{\prod_{i=1}^{n}(1+f_i)\right\}^{12/n}}{\sqrt{\frac{1}{n} \times \sum_{i=1}^{n} l_i^2} \times 12}$ | Annualized excess returns over risk-free rate/downside deviation; $l_i = \begin{cases} 0, & \text{if } r_i \geq 0 \\ r_i, & \text{if } r_i < 0 \end{cases}$ |
| 7 Up capture | $\dfrac{\prod_{i=1}^{n}\{1+u_i\} - 1}{\prod_{i=1}^{n}\{1+\max(m_i,0)\} - 1}$ | $u_i = \begin{cases} r_i, & \text{if } m_i \geq 0 \\ 0, & \text{if } m_i < 0 \end{cases}$ |
| 8 Down capture | $\dfrac{\prod_{i=1}^{n}\{1+d_i\} - 1}{\prod_{i=1}^{n}\{1+\min(m_i,0)\} - 1}$ | $d_i = \begin{cases} 0, & \text{if } m_i \geq 0 \\ r_i, & \text{if } m_i < 0 \end{cases}$ |
| 9 Winning runs | $\dfrac{\sum_{i=1}^{n-1} A_{i,i+1}}{n-1}$ | $A_{i,i+1} = \begin{cases} 1, & \text{if } r_i \text{ and } r_{i+1} > 0 \\ -1, & \text{if } r_i \text{ and } r_{i+1} < 0 \\ 0, & \text{otherwise} \end{cases}$ |

| Table 20.2 | Relation with Natural Investor Preference | |
| --- | --- | --- |
| **Statistic Index** | **Statistic Name** | **Sign** |
| 1 | Annual return | + |
| 2 | Alpha | + |
| 3 | Trend correlation | + |
| 4 | Maximum drawdown | − |
| 5 | Volatility | − |
| 6 | Sortino ratio | + |
| 7 | Up capture | + |
| 8 | Down capture | − |
| 9 | Winning runs | + |

A positive (negative) sign implies the higher (lower) the measure of the function the better the investor's expectations.

As previously stated we interpret PC1 as a reflection of consistency and PC2 as aggression. In Tables 20.3 and 20.4 we summarize the factor loadings for PC1 and PC2 over time. Table 20.3 shows the mean, median, and standard deviation for the first principal component, PC1. Table 20.4 shows the mean, median, and standard deviation for the second principal component, PC2. It is important to note that with the + and − classification obtained in Table 20.2, the rational investor preferences have been respected. Hence, for the first factor, PC1, we see that all median or mean coefficients are positive, but the trend correlation and up capture have the smallest weights. As these factors represent exploiting trending or bull markets and the other factors represent performance in all types of environments and avoid poor performance, it seems reasonable to define PC1 as a measure of consistency. For the second factor, PC2, as the median or mean weights for volatility, drawdown, and down capture are negative or near zero, while positive for the other factors and the greatest weight attached to up capture, PC2 appears to reflect aggression.

| Table 20.3 | Mean, Median, and Standard Deviation of Cross-Sectional, Time Series Factor Loadings for PC1 | | |
| --- | --- | --- | --- |
| **Statistic** | **Mean** | **Median** | **Standard Deviation** |
| Annualized return (%) | 36.42 | 40.30 | 13.58 |
| Annualized volatility (%) | 15.83 | 18.39 | 17.89 |
| Annualized alpha (%) | 38.51 | 41.67 | 9.72 |
| Trend correlation (%) | 4.77 | 0.81 | 16.19 |
| Maximum drawdown (%) | 32.74 | 35.44 | 14.83 |
| Annualized sortino ratio (%) | 39.77 | 44.20 | 9.47 |
| Up capture (%) | 12.53 | 14.37 | 19.58 |
| Down capture (%) | 32.68 | 36.78 | 16.11 |
| Winning runs (%) | 34.34 | 36.55 | 8.24 |

| Table 20.4 | Mean, Median, and Standard Deviation of Cross-Sectional, Time Series Factor Loadings for PC2 | | |
|---|---|---|---|
| **Statistic** | **Mean** | **Median** | **Standard Deviation** |
| Annualized return (%) | 12.41 | 18.02 | 29.70 |
| Annualized volatility (%) | **−6.78** | **−31.38** | 44.56 |
| Annualized alpha (%) | 14.55 | 14.24 | 22.89 |
| Trend correlation (%) | 2.95 | 6.44 | 29.09 |
| Maximum drawdown (%) | **0.79** | **−13.92** | 31.39 |
| Annualized sortino ratio (%) | 17.82 | 13.85 | 20.02 |
| Up capture (%) | 19.06 | 51.51 | 46.99 |
| Down capture (%) | **−2.33** | **−16.73** | 28.81 |
| Winning runs (%) | 11.44 | 10.66 | 14.32 |

First, we place more stress on median weights because the BL = (low consistency, low aggression), BR = (high consistency, low aggression), TL = (low consistency, high aggression), TR = (high consistency, high aggression) definitions refer to the number of funds placed into the category. Second, the effect on long-term performance may tell a different story from the consistency and aggression we observe, which leads us to reveal an interesting management style of FoHFs collectively.

## 20.4. CLASSIFICATION AND ALPHA PERFORMANCE EVALUATION IN THE RECENT FINANCIAL CRISIS

For a given 12-month period, we evaluate, for each of the existing FoHFs (the precise number varies as per our explanation in Section 20.1) the points:

$$x_i = (x_{i1}, x_{i2}) = ((\text{ann return}_i, \text{ann volatility}_i, \text{correlation}_i, \text{max drawdown}_i,$$
$$\text{ann Sortino}_i, \text{up capture}_i, \text{down capture}_i, \text{winning runs}_i) * PC1,$$
$$(\text{ann return}_i, \text{ann volatility}_i, \text{correlation}_i, \text{max drawdown}_i,$$
$$\text{ann Sortino}_i, \text{up capture}_i, \text{down capture}_i, \text{winning runs}_i) * PC2),$$

and plot these points on the (PC1, PC2) plane (Figure 20.1). Each dot represents a point $x_i$ corresponding to the $i$th FoHFs. We draw a square from the bottom-left of the plane and push it to include 7% of the total points and define all FoHFs falling in this region to form the BL class. Note we use 7% because we aim to retain approximately 100–150 funds in each class. Correspondingly, BR is the bottom-right, TR is the top-right, and TL is the top-left (see Figure 20.1 for self-evident explanations).

After classification, we compare class average returns against the Index of FoHFs. In the universe of FoHFs, the Index of FoHFs can be regarded as risk-free returns. We mainly observe the excessive alpha returns and make corresponding remarks on management styles (for definition of alpha returns in the particular context of FoHFs, the reader can refer to Philipp et al., 2009).

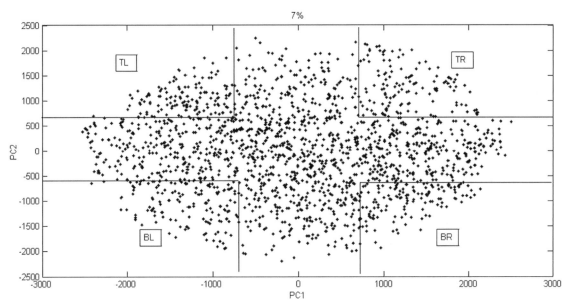

**FIGURE 20.1**
Distribution of assets using PC1 and PC2.

For the funds in the BL class, we calculate the forward 12-month return and corresponding investment value of each dollar invested using equal weights on its constituents and the corresponding return is recorded at the end of the time period concerned. We repeat this at the end of every month to obtain a returns table together with the corresponding ending month and then calculate the average of 12 of them as the yearly return. For example, to obtain the return for January 2004–December 2004, we average the returns in January 2004, February 2004, ..., December 2004, then record the annual return January 2004–December 2004 at December 2004.

We carry out similar computations for BR, TL, and TR classes, and plot these against the Index of FoHFs (called Market in the graphs) and the results are shown in Figure 20.2.

From Table 20.5, it is clear that both BL and BR have considerable advantage over TL and TR. According to the definition, the BL and BR classes are defined to be 'less aggressive' than TL and TR in our framework. We can conclude that during this particular period, aggression (as measured by the PC2 component) is less helpful to gain longer-term wealth accumulation. PC1, in contrast, seems to be more relevant to long-term wealth accumulation.

In Figure 20.3, the accumulated portfolio asset values appear to more precise. If we look at the portfolio asset values in Figure 20.3, the BL class has performed significantly better and BR slightly outperformed the market, while TL and TR underperformed most of the time.

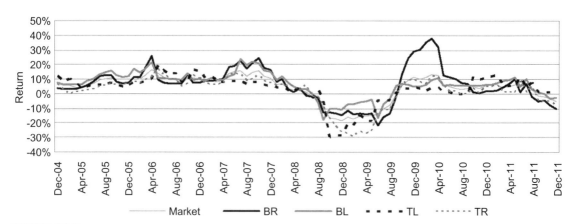

**FIGURE 20.2**
Average 12-month returns.

| Table 20.5 | Statistics for Figure 20.2 | | |
| --- | --- | --- | --- |
| | **Mean** | **Median** | **Standard Deviation** |
| Market (%) | 4.21 | 6.12 | 8.85 |
| BR (%) | 6.19 | 7.12 | 12.30 |
| BL (%) | 6.52 | 7.31 | 8.26 |
| TL (%) | 3.27 | 5.49 | 9.82 |
| TR (%) | 1.88 | 5.45 | 10.51 |

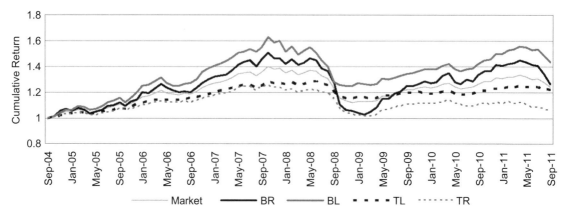

**FIGURE 20.3**
Portfolio asset values.

The advantage of BL against BR is clear during the depth of the crisis: BL outperforms BR dramatically, and although the subsequent recovery is not as strong, BL still maintains its advantage. There is a clear indication that, with rigorous risk control, the FoHFs in the BL category present better opportunities for the longer term investors.

In order to obtain a closer look at the effect of the financial crisis, we divide the time interval into various subperiods (Figures 20.4–20.13). We observe that:

- The TL class, which according to our definition, has strong aggression and weak consistency, demonstrates some bright spots in 2004 and 2010–2011, but is one of the worst asset classes in pre-crisis 2008–2009. During the 2008–2009 financial crisis, we can easily conclude that the TL class suffered early asset value fall and was very late to recover. The consolation is that this 'long-term' reaction to the crisis is not very dramatic in terms of percentage performance.
- The TR class has mostly been an underdog despite having strong consistency and strong aggression according to our definition.
- The BL class, which was very weak in both consistency and aggression by our definition, behaved remarkably well.
- The BR class, which performed poorly in the pre–2008 crisis and recovered very strongly in the recovery market after March 2009, again performed very poorly in the secondary European crisis during 2010 and 2011. Although it corresponds to low aggression and high consistency according to our definition, it is actually very aggressive and quick to respond to events.

From these remarks, we notice that if we apply quantitative risk analysis concepts to FoHFs, a FoHF that scores highly on both principal components, PC1 and PC2, in one year seems to have poorest returns in the immediate year after. The opposite regarding a FoHF that scores low on PC1 and PC2 in one year seems to have better returns in the immediate year after. It prompts us to make an investigation in the following section and reveal an interesting insight into the management mentality of FoHFs as a group from a purely quantitative point of view.

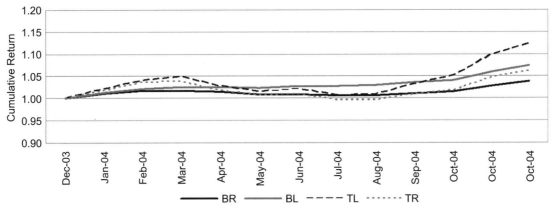

**FIGURE 20.4**
December 2003–December 2004 asset accumulation.

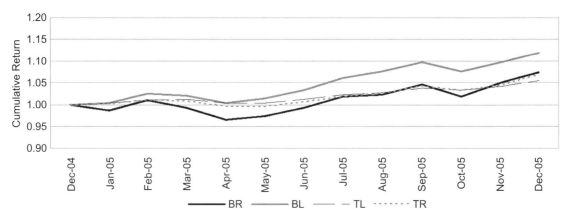

**FIGURE 20.5**
December 2004–December 2005 asset accumulation.

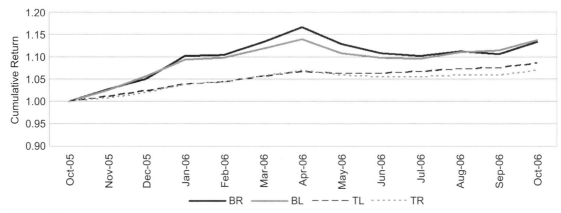

**FIGURE 20.6**
October 2005–October 2006 asset accumulation.

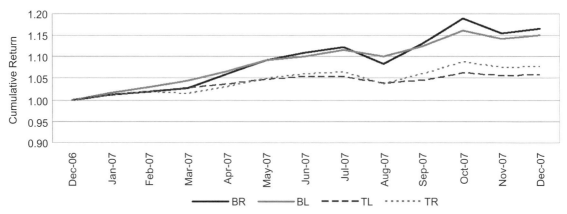

**FIGURE 20.7**
December 2006–December 2007 asset accumulation.

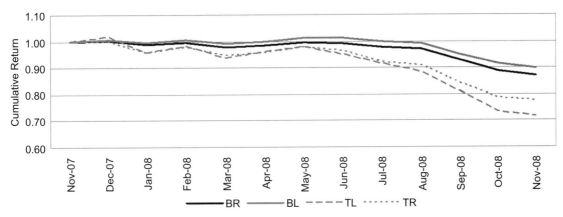

**FIGURE 20.8**
November 2007–November 2008 asset accumulation.

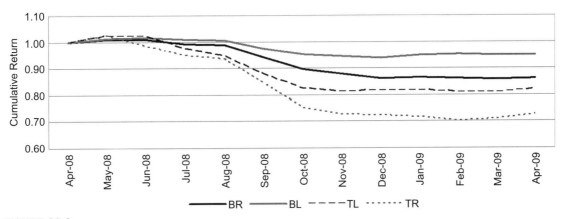

**FIGURE 20.9**
April 2008–April 2009 asset accumulation. Just before the bottom of the financial crisis, BR underperforms BL by more than 10%, while BL remains stable.

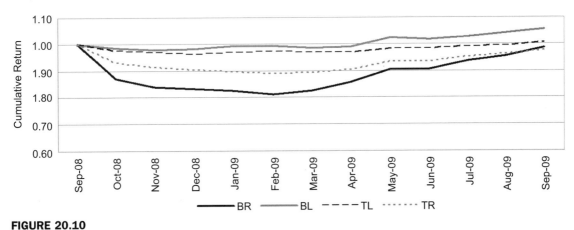

**FIGURE 20.10**
September 2008–September 2009 asset accumulation. This is the bottom behavior; the center is placed at March 2009, when the stock market bottomed; BR is the most exhilarating class while others maintain relative stability; BL is by far the best asset class.

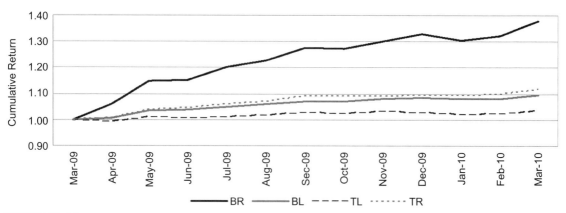

**FIGURE 20.11**
March 2009—March 2010 asset accumulation. In the recovery phase, since BR tanked the most beforehand, its recovery has been very exciting.

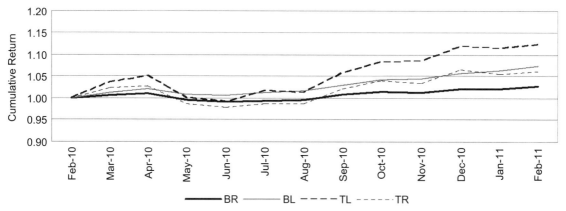

**FIGURE 20.12**
February 2010—February 2011 asset accumulation. After the initial recovery, TL forms the best asset class, in response to its much earlier pre-crisis underperformance of 2008—2009.

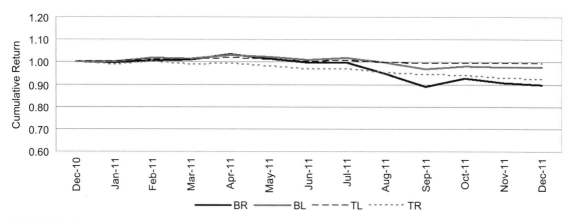

**FIGURE 20.13**
December 2010—December 2011 asset accumulation. After the initial recovery, TL forms the best asset class, in response to its much earlier pre-crisis underperformance of 2008—2009.

## 20.5. THE 'PRO-ACTIVE' NATURE OF FoHFs

We follow the same discussions as in the previous section, but we now look at another piece of information: on a time-rolling basis, whereby we calculate the risk measures using 1-year data (e.g., 2007), we then classify them into BL, BR, TL, TR, and remainder. We then look at the percentage of the funds that are in each of the classes BL, BR, TL, and TR that continue to remain in the same class in the immediate year after (e.g., 2008). We compare the average return of BL, BR, TL, and TR against the average returns of those FoHFs that remained in the same class and the average returns of those FoHFs that did not remain in the same class.

Figures 20.14–20.17 depict returns and show that:

- The overall BR, BL, TL, and TR class average returns are almost the same as the corresponding 'out' class average returns, suggesting that most of the funds 'pro-actively' move out of their existing situation. Therefore, FoHFs seem to be actively managing portfolios.
- The FoHFs in BR and TR classes are better off moving out of their existing position, as those staying in are the underperforming ones. This implies that if historical data dictates that a fund is 'consistent,' then change is needed.
- The TL class is a mixed bag. During most of the time periods, staying in the class proved to be a better strategy, suggesting that if the fund's historical data indicates that it is aggressive but not consistent, then staying in the same class during the turbulent times of 2008–2009 crisis and the subsequent European crisis is a better option. The fact that FoHFs were locked into gated or suspended investments in 2008 witnessed many funds recovering in the bull market run after the market bottomed in March 2009.
- For the BL class, staying in is the best option since it is the best performing class.

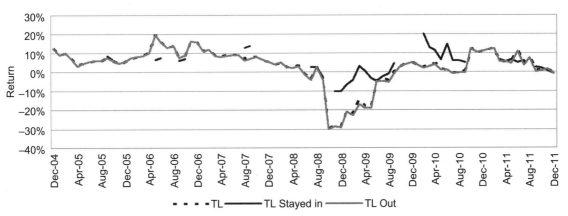

**FIGURE 20.14**
Migration performance analysis for TL class.

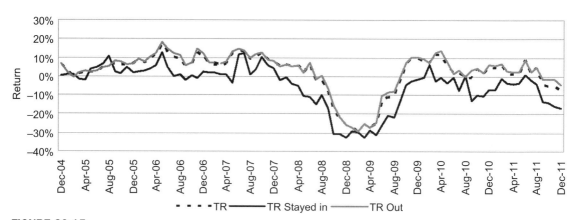

**FIGURE 20.15**
Migration performance analysis for TR class.

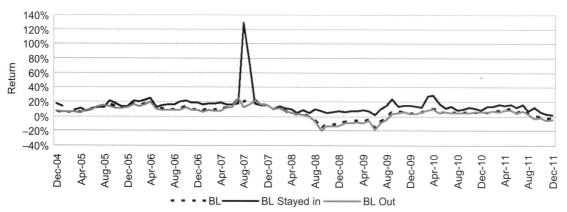

**FIGURE 20.16**
Migration performance analysis for BL class.

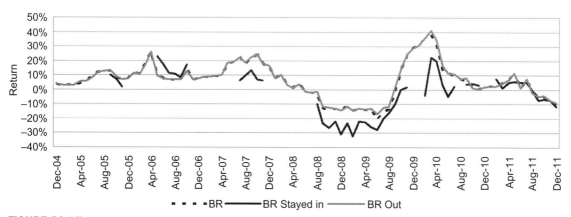

**FIGURE 20.17**
Migration performance analysis for BR class.

Finally, we note an alternative argument: the seemingly high rate of FoHFs moving out of their existing class may be caused by the underlying holdings of hedge funds, which cannot be independently verified here. Future investigation is needed to clarify this possibility.

## 20.6. THE STORY OF THE FINANCIAL CRISIS OF 2008–2009 AND SUBSEQUENT DEVELOPMENTS

In this section, we look at the number of funds reporting, the changes in management styles, and the asset returns of the classified classes.

### 20.6.1. Total Number of Funds in Existence for Reporting

The number of funds declined significantly from the peak of mid 2008 and it appears that the FoHFs industry has been going into a gradual decline since 2008 (Figure 20.18).

### 20.6.2. Change in 'Staying in Class' Mentality

Figures 20.19–20.22 illustrate the migration rates in the four classes. Immediately after the Lehman bankruptcy in September 2008 a significant proportion of hedge funds and FoHFs experienced very high redemption rates that they were unable to meet. As a consequence, the funds and FoHFs gated or suspended redemptions for at least 12 months. This meant that the FoHFs were unable to manage their portfolios actively. Many of the hedge funds that suspended redemptions were able to participate in the bull market rally after 2009. Shortly before the market bottoming out in March 2009, the rate of migration between the classes decreased significantly. This might not have been caused by deliberate actions of FoHFs, but might have been the result of market turbulence causing hedge funds and FoHFs to suspend redemptions, and, consequently, finding it

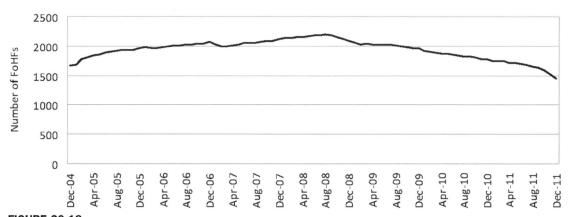

**FIGURE 20.18**
Number of funds reporting.

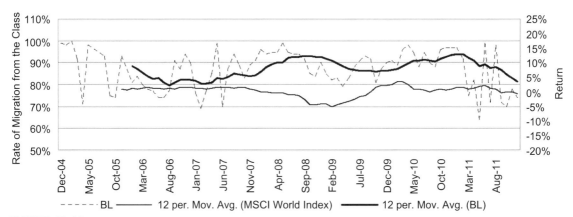

**FIGURE 20.19**
Migration analysis for BL class.

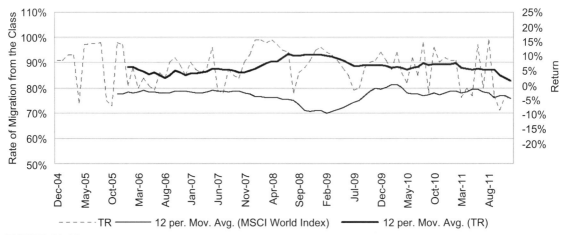

**FIGURE 20.20**
Migration analysis for TR class.

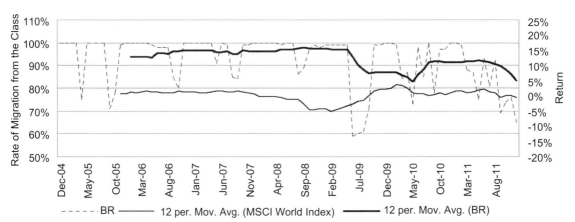

**FIGURE 20.21**
Migration analysis for BR class.

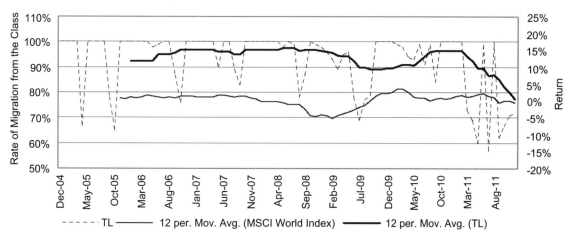

**FIGURE 20.22**
Migration analysis for TL class.

much more difficult to trade in and out of the positions. After the 2008–2009 crisis the migration rates started moving towards historical levels.

The migration rates in BL and TR classes show some cyclicality with rates falling until the end of 2006, rising until the beginning of the crisis, and then falling through the 2009 recovery and rising in 2010. The 12-month moving averages, shown in Figures 20.19 and 20.20, illustrate this phenomenon. The peaks of the migration rates coincide with the turbulent equity markets. In contrast, Figures 20.21 and 20.22 indicate that the BR and TL classes showed an increasing migration rate trend until the crisis, but since then the migration rates have tended to fall.

## CONCLUSION

In the risk control squared environment of FoHFs, it is interesting to observe the pro-active management activities in changing the risk profiles of themselves, most of the time to replicate better results of the past. We believe the idea of classification is of great help in the risk controlled and risk control squared environments. Our belief is that we could work out a precise rating system using this idea for the fund industry. This will be the aim of our future work.

From our observation, it is clear that PC1 has a much stronger impact on long-term performances; PC2, in contrast, should be kept at a relatively low level for long-term performance purposes, but could present fantastic investment opportunities in the short-term recovery phase.

A final interesting remark is that the BL class boasts an excessive return of between 2% and 3% *per annum* over the period of investigation. If we apply the same analysis to hedge funds, the excessive return of the BL class is well over 10% *per annum*.

## Acknowledgments

The author list is alphabetically ordered.

## References

Ben-Dor, A., & Xu, J. (2012). *Performance Persistence in Hedge Funds — Identifying Future Outperformers Using a Measure of Manager Skill (MMS)*. New York: Barclays Cross Asset Research Quantitative Portfolio Strategy.

Brown, S. J., & Goetzmann, W. N. (2003). Hedge Funds with Style. *Journal of Portfolio Management, 29*(2), 101–112.

Dewaele, B., Pirotte, H., Tuchschmid, N., & Wallerstein, E. (2011). *Assessing the Performance of Funds of Hedge Funds*. Available at SSRN: http://ssrn.com/abstract=1929097.

Dunteman, G. H. (1989). *Principal Components Analysis*. Thousand Oaks, CA: Sage.

Gibson, R., & Gyger, S. (2007). The Style Consistency of Hedge Funds. *European Financial Management, 13*(2), 287–308.

Litterman, R., & Scheinkman, J. (1991). Common Factors Affecting the Bond Returns. *Journal of Fixed Income, 1*(1), 54–61.

Jolliffe, I. T. (2002). *Principal Component Analysis*. New York: Springer.

Philipp, M., Ruckstuhl, A., Manz, P., Dettling, M., Durr, F., & Meier, P. (2009). *Performance Rating of Funds of Hedge Funds*. Available at: http://www.sml.zhaw.ch/fileadmin/user_upload/management/zai/forschung/pdf/studie_performance_rating_zai.pdf.

# CHAPTER 21

# Selecting Top Funds of Hedge Funds Based on Alpha and Other Performance Measures

**Ying-Lin Hsu**[*], **Chung-Ming Kuan**[†], **and Stéphane M. F. Yen**[**]

[*]Department of Applied Mathematics and Institute of Statistics, National Chung Hsing University, Taichung, Taiwan (R.O.C.)
[†]National Taiwan University, Department of Finance, Taipei, Taiwan (R.O.C.)
[**]National Cheng Kung University, Department of Accounting and Institute of Finance and Banking, Tainan, Taiwan (R.O.C.)

## 21.1. INTRODUCTION AND LITERATURE REVIEW

The hedge fund industry suffered from a significant downfall in assets under management (AUM) along with its reputation due to the financial tsunami and the Madoff Ponzi scheme fraud, respectively, during the 2007—2009 period. The Hedge Fund Research (HFR) hedge fund dataset reports a total of 653 funds of hedge funds (FoHFs) that had survived for at least 6 years and managed total assets of US$20 million or more as of June 2008; only 368 of them remained functional by the end of 2011. Despite the troubling period from 2007 to 2009, the hedge fund industry started to regain its strength in late 2009. Hedge funds

Reconsidering Funds of Hedge Funds. http://dx.doi.org/10.1016/B978-0-12-401699-6.00021-6

remain as a substantial part of the portfolio of large institutional investors, such as pension funds and endowment funds, in the aftermath of the crisis. For instance, the Yale endowment fund includes hedge funds as component assets of their portfolio, which accounted for 24.3%, 21.0%, and 17.5% of their total asset as of June in 2009, 2010, and 2011, respectively.[1] As relatively few FoHFs are able to survive a crisis as catastrophic as the credit crisis in 2008, it is of great interest, based on an ex ante analysis, to screen and identify those FoHFs that turn out to be successful crisis survivors. Brown *et al.* (2012) find that 22% of FoHFs shut down during the 2008−2009 crisis − a number larger than hedge fund closures.

There is a wide variety of quantitative and qualitative approaches to tackle the fund-selection issue. Traditional quantitative metrics used by practitioners to evaluate the performance of a hedge fund include average monthly returns (in excess of the risk-free rate), the Sharpe ratio, the alpha given by a multifactor model, and information ratio, among others. A recently developed quantitative metric is the manipulation-proof performance measure introduced by Goetzmann *et al.* (2007) (GIS MPPM). However, all these measures are likely to suffer from data-snooping bias, which tends to manifest itself in the existence of a large universe of models being tested together. In the context of testing a certain category of hedge funds performance with respect to a benchmark, an individual null hypothesis is that a particular fund is not able to outperform the benchmark. However, multiple individual tests of this kind result in the data-snooping bias. For instance, let the significance level for a conventional t-test for the significance of each fund's alpha be 5%. For a mere 100 funds of the same category tested together, assuming that these funds are independent, the probability of falsely rejecting at least one correct null hypothesis is $1 - (0.95)^{100}$, i.e. 0.994. Increasing the number of funds to 1000 extends the probability to nearly 1. Therefore, it is highly likely that an individual test would incorrectly suggest a model that outperforms the benchmark, even though the performance is not significantly different. An appropriate method to control for such data-snooping bias is necessary to avoid spurious inference about the performance of a large set of hedge funds examined together.

There exist in the literature various approaches to controlling for the data-snooping bias. For example, one may apply Bonferroni's inequality to determine the significance of a test. However, this method suffers from serious reduction in its testing power as the number of models tested increases. In light of this drawback, many bootstrap techniques, such as the Bootstrap Reality Check (BRC) of White (2000), the test for Superior Predictive Ability (SPA test) of Hansen (2005), the stepwise Reality Check (SRC) of Romano and Wolf (2005), and the stepwise SPA procedure of Hsu *et al.* (2010), have been proposed in the literature. While variant in details, all these approaches aim to bootstrap one single null distribution for testing the significance of either just the best model or

---

[1]See the 2011 report of the Yale endowment fund.

all outperforming models. In contrast, Kosowski *et al.* (2006) introduce a different approach called the cross-sectional alpha bootstrap. Kosowski *et al.*'s (2006) contribution in this regard has been credited by mainstream finance literature on fund performance evaluation. Their approach aims to bootstrap the null distribution for each individual fund among a large universe. Kosowski *et al.* (2006) show that mutual funds ranking at both ends of the performance spectrum tend to show the 'hot-hand' (performance persistence) effect. Basing on Kosowski *et al.*'s (2006) method, Kosowski *et al.* (2007) also document that well- and poorly performing hedge funds tend to persist across time in performance.

The cross-sectional alpha bootstrap of Kosowski *et al.* (2006) is computationally demanding because it needs to bootstrap the null distribution for each single model. This is in sharp contrast to all the other approaches mentioned above that bootstrap only one null distribution. Moreover, the Kosowski *et al.* (2006) approach might not be informative enough from the perspective of portfolio management because it tends to identify too many outperforming models or funds. For example, 303 out of 332 original uncategorized hedge funds in the HFR hedge fund database during the February 2000–December 2007 period can be selected as outperforming funds based on the standardized alpha as the test statistic under the 10% significance level. On the contrary, only 13 funds are identified under the stepwise SPA procedure with a family-wise error (FWE) rate[2] of 10% for the same timespan. Given that a typical hedge fund requires an initial investment of US$1 million or more, it is unlikely for retail investors or even institutional investors to meet the expense of a portfolio of 300 hedge funds. Due diligence comes at a heavy cost of US$12 500 per hedge fund manager (Brown *et al.*, 2009, 2012), which will dig into the portfolio's management fees on small FoHFs. In this regard, the stepwise SPA procedure is relatively more selective in evaluating fund performance. Therefore, this study aims to employ the stepwise SPA procedure to control for the data-snooping bias and to identify as many 'elite' FoHFs as possible from a large universe of FoHFs.

In this chapter, we study the FoHFs in the HFR hedge funds dataset, including defunct funds as of December 2011, for a period of 163 months from June 1998 to December 2011. In particular, we apply the stepwise SPA procedure to test multiple hypotheses that all FoHFs are no better than the relevant benchmark. Via this procedure, we identify all 'elite' FoHFs (i.e., funds that outperform the benchmark in a statistical sense) during four in-sample periods: June 1998–May 2008, June 2003–May 2008, June 1999–May 2009, and June 2004–May 2009. The turning point in the hedge fund industry occurred in May 2008 as a result of the subprime crisis. Our stepwise SPA procedure suggests that these selected 'elite' funds yield a statistically significant, positive Sharpe ratio, average

---

[2]A FWE rate denotes the probability of rejecting at least one true null hypothesis for any underlying probability mechanism.

monthly excess return, or GIS MPPM. They also significantly outperform the Fung and Hsieh (2004) seven-factor model during the in-sample periods above. However, the effect of the subprime crisis is obvious in that the number of selected in-sample outperformers greatly reduces if the 1-year aftermath is included in the in-sample period. Using the stepwise SPA procedure, for instance, 16 FoHFs showed a significant, positive Sharpe ratio during the period June 1998–May 2008, while none of the FoHFs was able to do so during the period June 1999–May 2009.

We also examine the performance of these selected 'elite' funds in the wake of the crisis. Our results show that the portfolio of in-sample outperformers formed in May 2008 and May 2009, respectively, was generally able to provide a positive mean return, Sharpe ratio, GIS MPPM, alpha, or Studentized alpha in the aftermath of the crisis through the end of 2011. To highlight the practical usefulness of our stepwise procedure, we compare the portfolio of selected in-sample elites to its unselected counterpart for their performance during the out-of-sample periods: June 2008–December 2010, June 2009–December 2010, June 2008–December 2011, and June 2009–December 2011, respectively. We find that the portfolio of FoHFs, which outperforms the benchmark before May 2008 or May 2009, is still able to offer better performance in the aftermath of the crisis than the portfolio of in-sample non-outperformers. Obviously, the subprime crisis does not eliminate the hot-hand effect among best FoHFs if they are appropriately selected in-sample.

## 21.2. IMPACT OF THE SUBPRIME CRISIS

How did the subprime crisis exert an effect on the ebb and flow of funds of hedge funds? Despite the depth and breadth of the effect, a comparison of the numbers of FoHFs going defunct before and after the crisis might provide a simple answer to this question. According to the HFR dead funds database, 218 and 228 FoHFs ceased to exist during the post-crisis periods from June 2008 to December 2010 and from June 2008 to December 2011, respectively. In contrast, a mere 74 and 84 FoHFs, respectively, died in the June 2009–December 2010 and June 2009–December 2011 periods. This means 148 FoHFs died during June 2008–May 2009, accounting for 65% of the defunct FoHFs in the aftermath until the end of 2011. To avoid the effect of the survivorship bias on our empirical results, we include the dead funds in our sample periods. Table 21.1 shows the numbers of dead and surviving funds for our chosen pre-crisis and post-crisis sample periods. Note that these numbers are recorded as of the end of each sample period.

## 21.3. PERFORMANCE METRICS

In contrast to mutual funds that are generally relative performers to market index, most hedge funds claim to pursue absolute returns. A natural benchmark of hedge fund performance is the risk-free rate. We use the 1-month Treasury bill (T-bill) returns reported by Ibbotson and Associates, Inc., which

| Table 21.1 | Numbers of Dead and Live Funds for Pre-Crisis and Post-Crisis Sample Periods | | | |
|---|---|---|---|---|
| | | | **Number of FoHFs** | |
| **Sample Period** | | | Dead | Surviving |
| In-sample | pre-crisis | (i) 5 years: 2003/06−2008/05 | 285 | 368 |
| | | (ii) 10 years: 1998/06−2008/05 | 67 | 138 |
| | including 1-year | (iii) 5 years: 2004/06−2009/05 | 130 | 428 |
| | aftermath | (iv) 10 years: 1999/06−2009/05 | 41 | 147 |
| Out-of-sample | | (a) 2008/06−2010/12 | 61 | 654 |
| (post-crisis) | | (b) 2009/06−2010/12 | 65 | 706 |
| | | (c) 2008/06−2011/12 | 0 | 633 |
| | | (d) 2009/06−2011/12 | 0 | 693 |

are available from the data library of Kenneth French.[3] The resulting performance measure is the fund's expected excess return over the risk-free rate. Other popular metrics include the Sharpe ratio, factor alpha, and Studentized factor alpha (in the same spirit of information ratio). Among these metrics, the seven-factor model of Fung and Hsieh (2004) is one of the most commonly adopted benchmarks (e.g., Kosowski *et al.*, 2007). To account for different fund styles, the seven factors consist of two equity-oriented risk factors (the equity market and size spread factors), two bond-oriented factors (the bond market and credit spread factors), and three trend-following factors (the bond trend-following, currency trend-following, and commodity trend-following factors).[4] We refer to Fung and Hsieh (2004) for more details on factor construction.

Given the Fung and Hsieh (2004) seven-factor model, we are able to estimate the factor alpha (also known as abnormal return in the literature of asset pricing) and its Studentized ratio by dividing the estimated alpha by the corresponding estimated standard error. However, the traditional ordinary least squares (OLS) estimate of the standard error for the alpha estimate is inefficient in the context of time-series returns characterized by autocorrelation and heteroscedasticity (HA). We apply the kernel estimation technique to give an HA-consistent estimate for the standard error by using a quadratic spectral kernel with the bandwidth determined using the selection method of Andrews (1991).

As noted by Goetzmann *et al.* (2007), the Sharpe ratio and the factor alpha (and, arguably, the Studentized factor alpha) are subject to the manipulation behavior

---

[3]Available at http://mba.tuck.dartmouth.edu/pages/faculty/ken.french/data_library.html
[4]Instructions on construction of the first four factors and monthly data on the last three factors are available from the data library of David A. Hsieh: http://faculty.fuqua.duke.edu/~dah7/HFRFData. htm.

of fund managers who seek (higher) incentive incomes. As a result, we also employ a more robust measure, GIS MPPM, introduced by Goetzmann *et al.* (2007). Based on GIS MPPM, the stepwise SPA procedure can identify skilled managers who are clear of the performance manipulation problem. In a nutshell, we employ two non-risk-adjusted measures (the expected excess return and GIS MPPM) and three risk-adjusted measures (Sharpe ratio, factor alpha, and Studentized factor alpha).

The GIS MPPM is characterized by the following requirements: (i) this measure gives a single-valued score for ranking portfolios, (ii) the score's value is not dependent upon the portfolio's dollar value, and (iii) an uninformed investor cannot expect to enhance his estimated score by deviating from the benchmark portfolio. An informed investor should be able to form a portfolio with a higher score and can always do so by exploiting arbitrage opportunities. (iv) This measure is consistent with standard financial market equilibrium conditions. These four requirements are enough to devise a unique MPPM. In particular, the first requirement eliminates measures leading to only partial rankings. The second requirement implies that returns are sufficient statistics rather than dollar gains or losses. The third and fourth requirements specify the structure. To meet the requirements above, an MPPM must be increasing in returns, concave, time separable to prevent dynamic manipulation of the estimated statistic, and have a power form to be consistent with an economic equilibrium. Goetzmann *et al.*, (2007) suggest the following functional form:

$$\hat{\Theta} \equiv \frac{1}{(1-\rho)\Delta t}\ln\left\{\frac{1}{T}\sum_{t=1}^{T}[(1+r_t)/(1+r_{\mathrm{f}t})]^{1-\rho}\right\},$$

where $T$ is the total number of observations, $\Delta t$ is the time interval between observations, and $r_t$ and $r_{\mathrm{f}t}$ denote, respectively, the unannualized rate of return of the portfolio and that of the risk-free asset at time t. The coefficient $\Delta$ should be selected to make holding the benchmark optimal for uninformed investors. The $\hat{\Theta}$ -statistic is an estimate of the portfolio's premium return after adjusting for risk (i.e., the portfolio has the same score as a risk-free asset whose continuously compounded return surpasses the risk-free rate by $\hat{\Theta}$ per time period). Stated otherwise, a risk-free portfolio earning $\exp(\ln(1 + r_{\mathrm{f}t}) + \hat{\Theta}\,\Delta t)$ each time period will have an MPPM of $\hat{\Theta}$.[5]

In a nutshell, we have three model-free measures (the expected excess return, the Sharpe ratio, and the GIS MPPM) and two model-dependent measures (the Fung–Hsieh seven-factor alpha and its Studentized version).

---

[5]As noted in Goetzmann *et al.* (2007), the GIS MPPM is identical in substance and almost in form to the Morningstar Risk Adjusted Rating (Morningstar, 2009) which was introduced in July 2002. The Morningstar ranking is motivated directly as a representative utility function rather than from the manipulation-proof properties Goetzmann *et al.* (2007) addressed.

## 21.4. SUMMARY STATISTICS OF FoHFs BEFORE AND AFTER THE SUBPRIME CRISIS

Prior to examining the performance of the FoHFs universe in the HFR dataset, we report their summary statistics during the pre-crisis and post-crisis periods. In particular, Table 21.2 reports the mean, maximum, and minimum values of five statistics: average monthly excess return, Sharpe ratio, GIS MPPM, factor alpha, and Studentized alpha given by the seven-factor model of Fung and Hsieh (2004). Note that any FoHF should have at least 1-year pre-sample data to be included in any of our four sample periods. We exclude the 12 monthly returns prior to an in-sample period from analysis to account for the well-known incubation/backfill bias of hedge fund data. We intend to provide results useful to the general FoHF investors; moreover, FoHFs with AUM less than US$20 million are also removed from the universe under investigation. The results related to these small FoHFs will not bring forth any economic implications since common investors invest little or even nothing with these small FoHFs.

As shown by the results in Table 21.2, the maximum—minimum range of all five performance metrics is less for the 10-year in-sample period than for the 5-year in-sample period, irrespective of whether the 1-year aftermath is included in the comparison. This result is not surprising since a long-surviving FoHF is supposed to perform to an extent more steadily than a relatively short-lived FoHF. The means of these five metrics characterize how the average FoHF performs. The means of all five metrics are positive during all four in-sample periods. Having survived the 1-year aftermath of the crisis, the average FoHF is still able to generate positive performance evaluated by all five metrics; see the means of these five metrics for in-sample periods (iii) and (iv). However, the crisis did jeopardize the overall performance of the FoHF universe in that the means of the average monthly excess return, Sharpe ratio, and GIS MPPM turn negative if the 1-year aftermath is included in the out-of-sample period, such as (a) and (c) of Table 21.2. Only 1 year after the crisis did the remaining FoHFs managers start to resume their lost territory of performance. This can be seen by the positive means of all five metrics for out-of-sample (b) and (d) of Table 21.2.

Turning back to the in-sample analysis, the crisis seems to enhance the performance of long-surviving FoHFs relative to the relatively short-lived FoHFs. In particular, the mean values of all five metrics are all larger for the 10-year period from June 1999 to May 2009 than for the 5-year period from June 2004 to May 2009. This is not the case, however, if we focus on the pre-crisis periods. The means of all three model-free[6] metrics (i.e., average monthly excess return,

---

[6]Model-free means being independent of any factor-based linear regression model, while model-dependent means dependence upon a factor-based linear regression model such as the Fung—Hsieh seven-factor model.

**Table 21.2** Summary Statistics of FoHFs Before and After the Crisis

| | Sample Period | | **Average Monthly Excess Return** | | | |
|---|---|---|---|---|---|---|
| | | | **HFRI FOF Index** | **FoHF Universe** | | |
| | | | | **Mean** | **Max.** | **Min.** |
| In-sample | pre-crisis | (i) 5 Years: 2003/06–2008/05 | 0.403 | 0.442 | 2.378 | −0.369 |
| | | (ii) 10 Years: 1998/06–2008/05 | 0.271 | 0.424 | 1.708 | −0.278 |
| | including 1-year aftermath | (iii) 5 Years: 2004/06–2009/05 | −0.011 | 0.305 | 2.876 | −1.010 |
| | | (iv) 10 Years: 1999/06–2009/05 | 0.180 | 0.552 | 2.035 | −0.089 |
| Out-of-sample (post-crisis) | | (a) 2008/06–2010/12 | −0.198 | −0.023 | 2.509 | −1.601 |
| | | (b) 2009/06–2010/12 | 0.614 | 0.723 | 3.841 | −0.713 |
| | | (c) 2008/06–2011/12 | −0.279 | −0.117 | 2.027 | −1.408 |
| | | (d) 2009/06–2011/12 | 0.188 | 0.272 | 2.657 | −0.678 |

| | Sample Period | | **Sharpe Ratio** | | | |
|---|---|---|---|---|---|---|
| | | | **HFRI FOF Index** | **FoHF Universe** | | |
| | | | | **Mean** | **Max.** | **Min.** |
| In-sample | pre-crisis | (i) 5 Years: 2003/06–2008/05 | 1.098 | 1.042 | 5.771 | −0.882 |
| | | (ii) 10 Years: 1998/06–2008/05 | 0.560 | 0.877 | 2.905 | −0.295 |
| | including 1-year aftermath | (iii) 5 Years: 2004/06–2009/05 | −0.021 | 0.521 | 2.529 | −0.564 |
| | | (iv) 10 Years: 1999/06–2009/05 | 0.355 | 0.977 | 2.276 | −0.079 |
| Out-of-sample (post-crisis) | | (a) 2008/06–2010/12 | −0.307 | −0.010 | 4.669 | −2.065 |
| | | (b) 2009/06–2010/12 | 1.871 | 1.929 | 7.633 | −2.382 |
| | | (c) 2008/06–2011/12 | −0.476 | −0.165 | 4.946 | −1.466 |
| | | (d) 2009/06–2011/12 | 0.494 | 0.662 | 6.322 | −1.308 |

| | Sample Period | | **GIS MPPM** | | | |
|---|---|---|---|---|---|---|
| | | | **HFRI FOF Index** | **FoHF Universe** | | |
| | | | | **Mean** | **Max.** | **Min.** |
| In-sample | pre-crisis | (i) 5 Years: 2003/06–2008/05 | 0.046 | 0.049 | 0.252 | −0.095 |
| | | (ii) 10 Years: 1998/06–2008/05 | 0.029 | 0.044 | 0.165 | −0.045 |
| | including 1-year aftermath | (iii) 5 Years: 2004/06–2009/05 | −0.006 | 0.029 | 0.270 | −0.181 |
| | | (iv) 10 Years: 1999/06–2009/05 | 0.018 | 0.058 | 0.182 | −0.030 |

*(Continued)*

| Table 21.2 | Summary Statistics of FoHFs Before and After the Crisis—cont'd |
|---|---|

|  |  |  | GIS MPPM | | | |
|---|---|---|---|---|---|---|
|  |  |  | **HFRI FOF Index** | **FoHF Universe** | | |
| **Sample Period** | | | | **Mean** | **Max.** | **Min.** |
| Out-of-sample (post-crisis) | | (a) 2008/06–2010/12 | −0.030 | −0.012 | 0.238 | −0.259 |
|  | | (b) 2009/06–2010/12 | 0.072 | 0.083 | 0.445 | −0.088 |
|  | | (c) 2008/06–2011/12 | −0.038 | −0.022 | 0.197 | −0.218 |
|  | | (d) 2009/06–2011/12 | 0.020 | 0.028 | 0.307 | −0.094 |

|  |  |  | Fung–Hsieh Seven-Factor Alpha | | | |
|---|---|---|---|---|---|---|
|  |  |  | **HFRI FOF Index** | **FoHF Universe** | | |
| **Sample Period** | | | | **Mean** | **Max.** | **Min.** |
| In-sample | pre-crisis | (i) 5 Years: 2003/06–2008/05 | 0.225 | 0.279 | 2.217 | −0.653 |
|  |  | (ii) 10 Years: 1998/06–2008/05 | 0.224 | 0.385 | 1.519 | −0.329 |
|  | including 1-year aftermath | (iii) 5 Years: 2004/06–2009/05 | 0.202 | 0.483 | 2.958 | −0.603 |
|  |  | (iv) 10 Years: 1999/06–2009/05 | 0.239 | 0.597 | 1.953 | 0.016 |
| Out-of-sample (post-crisis) | | (a) 2008/06–2010/12 | −0.096 | 0.069 | 3.954 | −1.589 |
|  | | (b) 2009/06–2010/12 | 0.157 | 2.993 | −1.160 | 0.224 |
|  | | (c) 2008/06–2011/12 | −0.135 | 0.386 | 3.746 | −1.500 |
|  | | (d) 2009/06–2011/12 | 0.163 | 0.215 | 2.738 | −1.111 |

|  |  |  | Fung–Hsieh Seven-Factor Studentized Alpha | | | |
|---|---|---|---|---|---|---|
|  |  |  | **HFRI FOF Index** | **FoHF Universe** | | |
| **Sample Period** | | | | **Mean** | **Max.** | **Min.** |
| In-sample | pre-crisis | (i) 5 Years: 2003/06–2008/05 | 1.452 | 1.519 | 12.190 | −1.668 |
|  |  | (ii) 10 Years: 1998/06–2008/05 | 1.618 | 2.642 | 10.550 | −1.391 |
|  | including 1-year aftermath | (iii) 5 Years: 2004/06–2009/05 | 1.355 | 2.104 | 6.151 | −0.897 |
|  |  | (iv) 10 Years: 1999/06–2009/05 | 1.902 | 3.548 | 6.592 | 0.049 |
| Out-of-sample (post-crisis) | | (a) 2008/06–2010/12 | −0.436 | 0.358 | 8.263 | −2.789 |
|  | | (b) 2009/06–2010/12 | 0.945 | 0.987 | 8.148 | −3.245 |
|  | | (c) 2008/06–2011/12 | −0.740 | 0.257 | 10.120 | −3.058 |
|  | | (d) 2009/06–2011/12 | 1.945 | 1.248 | 9.582 | −4.912 |

Sharpe ratio, and GIS MPPM) are all less for the 10-year period from June 1998 to May 2008 than for the 5-year period from June 2003 to May 2008. Note that the universe of the 10-year FoHFs is a subset of the 5-year FoHFs as of May 2008 or May 2009. These results show that the relatively short-lived FoHFs, such as those surviving for 5 years as of May 2009, are adversely affected by the subprime crisis in terms of performance.

The performance seems to be subject to the choice of metrics. For instance, the means of the seven-factor alpha of Fung and Hsieh (2004) and of its Studentized version are positive in both out-of-sample periods including the 1-year aftermath (see (a) and (c) of Table 21.2), although other three metrics show a negative mean for the same sample periods and this inconsistency justifies why we employ both model-free and model-dependent metrics to evaluate FoHF performance.

Finally, 2011 was a bad year for FoHF managers due to the impact of the European sovereign debt problems. The means of average monthly excess return, Sharpe ratio, and GIS MPPM are all smaller during the post-crisis periods ending in 2011 ((c) and (d) of Table 21.2) relative to the post-crisis periods ending in 2010 ((a) and (b) of Table 21.2).

## 21.5. HOW DOES ONE SELECT 'ELITE' FoHFs?

In line with Wolf and Wunderli (2009), we address the challenge of fund selection from a statistical perspective. The main thrust of this chapter is to document a formal statistical analysis for selecting as many elite FoHFs as possible, while excluding all the lucky ones, based on their track records (observed monthly returns). We state the problem by formulating the following hypothesis including a large number of individual null hypotheses in the lingo of Wolf and Wunderli (2009):

$H_0^i \alpha_i \leq 0$, $i = 1, ..., m$ (non-skilled or potentially lucky FoHFs managers).
$H_1^i \alpha_i > 0$ (skilled FoHFs managers) for some $i$.

The tests of such multiple hypotheses must control a proper FWE rate and include, e.g., the tests of White (2000), Hansen (2005), Romano and Wolf (2005), and Hsu et al. (2010). Given the better power property of the stepwise SPA procedure of Hsu et al. (2010), this test is employed in our research to select elite FoHFs. By controlling the FWE rate of $\sigma = 10\%$, we can be 90% sure that all identified managers are truly skilled at any given point of time. Using the seven-factor alpha of Fung and Hsieh (2004) as the performance measure, the stepwise SPA procedure is based on the following assumptions.[7]

Let $\hat{\alpha} = (\hat{\alpha}_1, ..., \hat{\alpha}_m)$ be the estimator of $\alpha$ and the procedure imposes high-level assumptions on $\hat{\alpha}$.

---

[7]It is straightforward to amend this procedure to be applied to the other four performance measures.

**Assumption 1**: Let $\hat{\alpha}$ be an estimator of $\alpha$ satisfying:

$$\sqrt{n}(\hat{\alpha} - \alpha) \xrightarrow{D} N(0, \, \Omega) \equiv \Psi,$$

and there exists a consistent estimator $\hat{\Omega}$ of $\Omega$, where the $(i,j)$th element of $\Omega$:

$$\omega_{ij} = cov(\sqrt{n}(\hat{\alpha}_i - \alpha_i), \sqrt{n}(\hat{\alpha}_j - \alpha_j)).$$

Additionally, we assume there is a simulated distribution $\Psi^u = (\psi_1^u, \psi_2^u, ..., \psi_m^u)$ satisfying the following.

**Assumption 2**: $\Psi^u \xrightarrow{D} \Psi$ conditional on the sample path with probability approaching 1. Following Romano and Wolf (2005, 2007) and Hsu *et al.* (2010), we adopt the bootstrap methods to obtain $\Psi^u$. Hansen (2005) suggests adding a recentering vector $\hat{d}$, where $\hat{d}_i = \hat{\alpha}_i \cdot 1_{\{\sqrt{n}\hat{\alpha}_i \leq a_n \hat{\sigma}_i\}}$ for $i = 1$, ..., $m$, to the bootstrapped distribution of $\Psi^u$ to yield a better approximation to the null distribution of $\Psi$. The recentered distribution of $\Psi^u$ is given by $\Psi^u + \sqrt{n}\hat{d}$. In particular, we use:

$$\sqrt{n}\max\{\max[\hat{\alpha}_1(b) - \hat{\alpha}_1 \cdot 1_{\{\sqrt{n}\hat{\alpha}_1 \leq a_n \hat{\sigma}_1\}}, ..., \hat{\alpha}_m(b) - \hat{\alpha}_1 \cdot 1_{\{\sqrt{n}\hat{\alpha}_m \leq a_n \hat{\sigma}_m\}}], 0\},$$

for $b = 1$, ..., $B$ ($B =$ number of bootstrap resamples[8]) to form an empirical distribution that better approximates the null distribution of $\Psi$ (see also Hsu *et al.*, 2010).

**Assumption 3**: Let $\{a_n\}$ be a sequence of negative numbers that diverges to $-\infty$. As an example, $a_n = -\sqrt{2\log\log n}$. Let the critical value $\hat{q}_1 = \max(\tilde{q}_1(\delta), 0)$, where $\tilde{q}_1(\delta)$ is the $(1 - \delta)$th quantile of $\max_{i=1,...,m}(\psi_i^u + \sqrt{n}\hat{d}_i)$. The stepwise SPA procedure proceeds as:

1. Relabel all FoHFs in descending order of corresponding $\hat{\alpha}_i$, $i = 1$, ..., $m$.
2. Reject individual hypothesis $i$ (i.e., identifying the **i**-fund manager as truly skilled) if $\sqrt{n}\hat{\alpha}_i > \hat{q}_1$.
3. If none of the null hypotheses is rejected, the procedure stops. If the first $i_1$ hypotheses are rejected in the previous step (which is called the first round of the procedure), we remove those $i_1$ funds from the universe and treat all remaining funds as the original data.
4. Like $\hat{q}_1$, we use the remaining data to construct $\hat{q}_2$ and reject the $i$th hypothesis if $\sqrt{n}\hat{\alpha}_i > \hat{q}_2$. If there are no further rejections, stop; otherwise, go to the next step.
5. Repeat previous steps until no further rejections occur.

## 21.6. IDENTIFIED FoHFs MANAGERS WITH GENUINE SKILL

Using the stepwise SPA procedure of Hsu *et al.* (2010), we are able to select those FoHFs whose good performance relative to the benchmark was not due

---

[8]We apply the Politis and Romano (1994) stationary bootstrap for data resampling.

| Table 21.3 | Numbers of Identified Elite Funds Under Five Performance Metrics |

| In-Sample Period | Number of HFR FoHFs | Average Monthly Excess Return | GIS MPPM | Sharpe Ratio | Alpha | Studentized Alpha |
|---|---|---|---|---|---|---|
| (i) 5 Years: 2003/06–2008/05 | 653 | 9 | 4 | 16 | 1 | 1 |
| (ii) 10 Years: 1998/06–2008/05 | 205 | 1 | 1 | 13 | 6 | 8 |
| (iii) 5 Years: 2004/06–2009/05 | 558 | 1 | 0 | 0 | 5 | 0 |
| (iv) 10 Years: 1999/06–2009/05 | 188 | 1 | 0 | 0 | 4 | 0 |

The FWE is fixed at 10% for the stepwise SPA procedure under all five performance metrics. The identified elite fund based on average monthly excess return is identical for periods (iii) and (iv).

to chance, but rather to genuine management skill. These identified FoHFs are referred to as 'elite' funds (managers). Given that the FWE rate is controlled at the 10% level, we have 90% of confidence to claim that the managers of all identified elite FoHFs possessed genuine skill to manage their funds. The results in Table 21.3 show that the stepwise SPA procedure is able to identify at least one elite fund during the pre-crisis periods, namely 5 and 10 years through May 2008, respectively (see in-sample periods (i) and (ii) of Table 21.3). Moving these in-sample windows one year forward to include the one-year aftermath into the analysis substantially reduces the number of identified elite funds. Using three performance metrics (Sharpe ratio, GIS MPPM, and Studentized alpha), the stepwise SPA procedure is not able to reject any null hypothesis for the in-sample periods through May 2009 (see in-sample periods (iii) and (iv)).

## 21.7. OUT-OF-SAMPLE PERFORMANCE OF IN-SAMPLE 'ELITE' FoHFs FUNDS

In this section, we test whether the stepwise SPA procedure provides any value for FoHF investors. We examine the out-of-sample performance of those in-sample elites as a whole relative to their in-sample followers as a whole. The out-of-sample analysis is undertaken twofold: one is to test how the pre-crisis elite funds perform relative to their followers during the post-crisis periods, the other is to conduct the same comparison, but for the periods starting from June 2009. The second comparison might bring implications for investors seeking investment opportunities in the FoHFs universe during the largest drawdown of the hedge fund industry.

To test if good performance of in-sample elite funds relative to the benchmark persists over time, we compute the same performance metric during the out-of-sample period. For instance, assume a portfolio of elite funds is selected using the Sharpe ratio to form the test statistic under the stepwise SPA procedure. We compute the portfolio's Sharpe ratio for the out-of-sample period, whereby a positive Sharpe ratio will imply consistent outperformance of the portfolio of in-sample elite funds relative to the benchmark during the out-of-sample period. Similarly, all other four metrics need a positive value to imply outperformance of the selected elite funds against the benchmark of either the risk-free rate or the seven-factor model of Fung and Hsieh (2004). As shown by the results contained in Table 21.4, we can see that the in-sample elite funds tend to generate a positive average monthly excess return and Fung—Hsieh seven-factor alpha. This result is robust to the choice of in-sample and out-of-sample periods. It appears that the subprime crisis does not eliminate the hot-hand effect of the FoHFs if we focus only on the elite funds. With regard to the GIS MPPM used to form the test statistic for the procedure, the elite group is able to show a positive value during the out-of-sample period despite the fact that including the 1-year aftermath renders no rejection of the null hypothesis, suggesting that the hot-hand effect of elite FoHFs is not a result of performance manipulation. Based on the risk-adjusted metrics (i.e., the Sharpe ratio and Studentized alpha), the in-sample elite group is not able to produce a positive value of either of these two metrics for all combinations of in-sample and out-of-sample periods. If we apply the stepwise SPA procedure to select elite FoHFs, we should not consider these two metrics.

To highlight how an investor can benefit from using the fund selecting procedure, in particular, we also compute the same performance metric for the in-sample followers (i.e., those that are not identified as outperformers relative to the benchmark.). Hopefully, the in-sample elite funds are able to also outperform their in-sample followers during the out-of-sample period. This is generally what we find from the results of Table 21.4: the elite funds provide performance better than their followers during the out-of-sample periods. The only four exceptions occur in the following scenarios. As shown by the results for the 5-year and 10-year in-sample periods through May 2009 in Table 21.4, the elite FoHF,[9] selected based on the average monthly excess return, trails its followers during the out-of-sample period from June 2009 to December 2010. The elite FoHF generates an average monthly excess return of 0.48% during the out-of-sample period from June 2009 to December 2010, while its followers generate 0.65% and 0.69% for the same out-of-sample period if they come from the in-sample periods of June 2004—May 2009 and of June 1999—May 2009, respectively. Moreover, the elite fund[10] selected using the Studentized alpha to form

---

[9]The elite FoHF selected using the average monthly excess return as the performance measure under the stepwise SPA procedure is the same for both in-sample periods from June 2004 to May 2009 and from June 1999 to May 2009. Similarly, there is only one FoHF identified as an elite fund using the Studentized alpha as the performance measure for the in-sample period from June 2003 to May 2008.
[10]Only one FoHF is identified as an elite fund for this in-sample period under the performance measure of Studentized alpha.

**Table 21.4**   Out-of-sample Performance of Elite Group versus Followers under Five Performance Metrics

| Out-of-Sample period | In-Sample Period | Elites[1] versus Followers | Out-of-Sample performance | | | | |
| --- | --- | --- | --- | --- | --- | --- | --- |
| | | | Average Monthly Excess Return | Sharpe Ratio | GIS MPPM | Alpha | Studentized Alpha |
| (a) 2008/ 06–2010/12 | (i) 5 Years: 2003/ 06–2008/05 | Elites | 0.41 | −0.21 | 0.04 | 1.86 | NA[2] |
| | | Followers | −0.16 | −0.24 | −0.02 | −0.06 | −0.27 |
| | (ii) 10 Years: 1998/ 06–2008/05 | Elites | 1.17 | −0.02 | 0.03 | 1.07 | −0.34 |
| | | Followers | −0.13 | −0.21 | −0.02 | −0.05 | −0.07 |
| (b) 2009/ 06–2010/12 | (iii) 5 Years: 2004/ 06–2009/05 | Elites | 0.48 | | | 1.29 | |
| | | Followers | 0.65 | | | 0.18 | |
| | (iv) 10 Years: 1999/ 06–2009/05 | Elites | 0.48 | | | 0.51 | |
| | | Followers | 0.69 | | | 0.19 | |
| (c) 2008/ 06–2011/12 | (i) 5 Years: 2003/ 06–2008/05 | Elites | 0.20 | −0.34 | 0.04 | 1.81[3] | NA[2] |
| | | Followers | −0.23 | −0.41 | −0.03 | −0.10[3] | −0.59[3] |
| | (ii) 10 Years: 1998/ 06–2008/05 | Elites | 1.6 | −0.23 | 0.10 | 0.92[3] | −0.34[3] |
| | | Followers | −0.22 | −0.36 | −0.03 | −0.10[3] | −0.38[3] |
| (d) 2009/ 06–2011/12 | (iii) 5 Years: 2004/ 06–2009/05 | Elites | 1.34 | | | 0.99[3] | |
| | | Followers | 0.25 | | | 0.19[3] | |
| | (iv) 10 Years: 1999/ 06–2009/05 | Elites | 1.34 | | | 0.35[3] | |
| | | Followers | 0.28 | | | 0.21[3] | |

[1] 'Elites' and 'Followers' refer to equal-weighted portfolios of those identified outperforming FoHFs and their non-identified counterparts, respectively, by the stepwise SPA procedure.

[2] The only elite fund, TS Multi-Strategy Fund, L.P. Class B (Unleveraged), selected during the 5-year in-sample period from June 2003 to May 2008 actually chose not to report performance data any more from August 2010

[3] As data on three of the Fung–Hsieh seven factors (BdOpt, FxOpt, and ComOpt) were updated only until June 2011, both the Fung–Hsieh seven-factor alpha and the Studentized alpha are calculated using data until June 2011.

the statistic of the stepwise SPA procedure from the pre-crisis in-sample period of June 2003 through May 2008 chose not to report performance data any more from August 2010. The lack of reporting makes it impossible to compute the fund's Studentized alpha. As a result, even the negative Studentized alpha of the group of the followers is regarded as better than the elite fund which no longer reported its returns.

## CONCLUSION

In this chapter, we examined the performance of the FoHFs reported by the HFR hedge fund dataset for 163 months from June 1998 to December 2011. Based on the Hsu *et al.* (2010) stepwise SPA procedure, we test multiple hypotheses that all FoHFs are no better than the corresponding benchmark. We identify as many 'elite' FoHFs as possible during different in-sample periods either ending in May 2008 or 1 year after. Those selected 'elite' funds yield a statistically significant, positive Sharpe ratio, average monthly excess return, or GIS MPPM score. Alternatively, they significantly outperform the Fung and Hsieh (2004) seven-factor model during the in-sample periods. The main thrust of this chapter is to examine how the identified 'elite' funds perform relative to their followers in the wake of the crisis.

Our results show that the equal-weighted portfolio of those elites selected in May 2008 and May 2009, respectively, is generally able to perform better than that of their followers in the aftermath of the crisis through the end of 2010 or 2011. To name but a few, the elite portfolios selected from all four pre-crisis in-sample periods generate a positive Fung–Hsieh seven-factor alpha in all four out-of-sample periods ending in 2010 or 2011. On the contrary, the portfolio of in-sample followers tends to generate an alpha either negative or less than from the corresponding elite portfolio in all four out-of-sample periods. Obviously, the subprime debt crisis did not annihilate the hot-hand effect among appropriately selected FoHFs. The results of this study might provide economic implications for institutional investors: they can apply the stepwise SPA procedure to form their portfolio of elite FoHFs based on their chosen performance measure and such a portfolio is very likely to remain outperforming relative to their followers in the future, whether promising or weak.

## Acknowledgments

Ying-Lin Hsu and Meng-Feng Yen thank their research assistant, Shuo-Wun Chang, who did the programming for the stepwise SPA procedure.

## References

Andrews, D. W. K. (1991). Heteroskedasticity and Autocorrelation Consistent Covariance Matrix Estimation. *Econometrica, 59*(3), 817–858.

Brown, S. J., Goetzmann, W. N., Liang, B., & Schwarz, C. (2009). Estimating Operational Risk for Hedge Funds: The ω Score. *The Financial Analysts Journal, 65*(1), 43–53.

Brown, S. J., Gregoriou, G., & Pascalau, R. (2012). Diversification in Funds of Hedge Funds: Is It Possible to Overdiversify? *Review of Asset Pricing Studies, 2*(1), 89−110.

Fung, W., & Hsieh, D. (2004). Hedge Funds Benchmarks: A Risk-Based Approach. *Financial Analyst Journal, 60*(5), 65−80.

Goetzmann, W. N., Ingersoll, J., & Spiegel, M. (2007). Portfolio Performance Manipulation and Manipulation-Proof Performance Measures. *The Review of Financial Studies, 20*(5), 1503−1546.

Hansen, P. R. (2005). A Test for Superior Predictive Ability. *Journal of Business and Economic Statistics, 23*(1), 365−380.

Hsu, P.-H., Hsu, Y.-C., & Kuan, C.-M. (2010). Testing the Predictive Ability of Technical Analysis Using a New Stepwise Test without Data-Snooping Bias. *Journal of Empirical Finance, 17*(3), 471−484.

Kosowski, R., Naik, N. Y., & Teo, M. (2007). Do Hedge Funds Deliver Alpha? A Bayesian and Bootstrap Analysis. *Journal of Financial Economics, 84*(1), 229−264.

Kosowski, R., Timmermann, A., Wermers, R., & White, H. (2006). Can Mutual Fund 'Stars' Really Pick Stocks? New Evidence from a Bootstrap Analysis. *Journal of Finance, 61*(6), 2551−2596.

Morningstar (2009). The Morningstar Rating™ Methodology Morningstar Methodology Paper, available online at http://corporate.morningstar.com/no/documents/MethodologyDocuments/MethodologyPapers/MorningstarFundRating-Methodology.pdf

Politis, D. N., & Romano, J. P. (1994). The Stationary Bootstrap. *Journal of American Statistical Association, 89*(2), 1303−1313.

Romano, J. P., & Wolf, M. (2005). Stepwise Multiple Testing as Formalized Data Snooping. *Econometrica, 73*(4), 1237−1282.

Romano, J. P., & Wolf, M. (2007). Control of Generalized Error Rates in Multiple Testing. *Annals of Statistics, 35*(4), 1378−1408.

White, H. (2000). A Reality Check for Data Snooping. *Econometrica, 68*(5), 1097−1126.

Wolf, M., & Wunderli, D. (2009). *Fund-of-Funds Construction by Statistical Multiple Testing Methods. IEW Working Paper 445. Institute for Empirical Research in Economics*. University of Zurich.

# CHAPTER 22

# Funds of Hedge Funds Strategies and Implications for Asset Management: Is Diversification Enough?

**Simone Siragusa**
Università della Svizzera Italiana, Lugano, Switzerland

## 22.1. INTRODUCTION AND LITERATURE REVIEW

Selling a fund of hedge funds (FoHF) to investors requires that the manager perform due diligence with each underlying hedge fund manager and simultaneously provide proper diversification of hedge fund strategies. The simple time-tested and appealing concept of diversification of 'Don't put all your eggs in one basket' stills holds true today. However, diversification proved not to be enough to protect investor capital during the recent extreme negative market event of 2008–2009. Many FoHFs lagged single-manager hedge funds, hedge funds, and FoHFs indexes, resulting in disastrous results with many funds shutting down because they were below their high watermark. Recent academic research has examined the optimal number of underlying hedge funds in FoHFs, suggesting that fewer underlying hedge funds result in less exposure to tail risk (Brown *et al.*, 2012). Brown *et al.* (2008) further document that FoHFs due diligence comes at a heavy cost whereby funds with limited assets under management (AUM) are highly penalized due to economies of scale induced by the due diligence process. Brown *et al.* (2012) report that, according to the most recent Lipper TASS database, 22% of FoHFs and 30% of all multistrategy funds failed during the recent credit crunch crisis —

a fraction as large or larger than the fraction of failures in any other hedge fund category.

Modern Portfolio Theory's goal is not to entirely eliminate risk, but to reduce it. The only way to mitigate systematic risk is to hedge part of the risk brought into a portfolio. While diversification lowers operational risk and/or fraud risk, many believe that diversification provides protection in market downturns. This old adage is incorrect, because in extreme negative market movements, correlation of assets tends to increase to unity, making diversification of little value.

The first goal of this chapter is to examine various Hedge Fund Research (HFR) FOF Indexes and observe their added value in a strategic asset allocation framework. Our findings suggest that while finding a new 'alpha provider' is important, chasing alpha is a difficult task. Despite this, given the relatively stable risk profile of hedge funds strategies we are going to provide evidence that FoF can add value to a portfolio. Our findings are similar to those of Kat and Menexe (2002), where the authors find no persistence in mean returns while they find stable correlation and stable volatility of hedge fund strategies with respect to stock and bond markets, implying that hedge funds have a relatively stable risk profile. We compute the value-added of different FoHFs strategies using Certainty Equivalence Return Maximization as in Ang *et al.* (2005), Kandel and Stambaugh (1996), and Campbell and Viceira (1999). This permits us to take into account different levels of investor preferences and investment conditions (i.e., non-normal returns).[1] Employing Certainty Equivalence Return Maximization based on power utilities gives us the great flexibility to take into account multiple utility functions, different levels of risk aversion and higher moments. The Certainty Equivalent principle determines how much utility a new investment should add to an existing portfolio to convince investors to consider adding it to the portfolio.[2]

The remainder of the chapter is organized as follows. In Section 22.2, we present the univariate statistics of the data, and apply models to analyze higher comoments and market neutrality with respect to the stock market. In Section 22.3, we introduce various exogenous risk factors. In Section 22.4, we compute Jensen's alpha to rank investment possibilities. In Section 22.5 we set up the Certainty Equivalence analysis to gain the best information by applying different utility functions and taking into account higher moments; this is followed by our conclusions.

---

[1] Many popular measures such as the omega ratio, the Sortino index, and expected shortfall are incompatible with expected utility maximization.
[2] Consider an existing portfolio of government bonds paying 3%, in order to analyze the possibility of adding a stock with a 6% return; the Certainty Equivalence is the basis for determining how much the company has to pay in order to convince the investor to add the stock to his/her initial portfolio.

## 22.2. DATA

We proxy FoHF strategies using various HFR FOF Indexes. In particular, we use the HFR Multi-Strategy Index, where FoHFs invest in all the possible alternative strategies, such as managed futures, private equity, and venture capital. Next, we use the HFR FOF Conservative Index, which generally focuses on strategies such as Equity Market Neutral, Fixed Income Arbitrage, and Convertible Arbitrage. The HFR FOF Diversified Index exhibits one or more of the following characteristics: invests in a variety of strategies among multiple managers, historical annual return, and/or a standard deviation generally similar to the HFRI FOF Composite index. The HFR FOF Market Defensive Index invests in funds that normally use short-biased strategies such as short selling and managed futures that display negative correlation to general market benchmarks such as the S&P 500. A fund in the FOF Market Defensive Index exhibits higher returns during down markets than during up markets.

The HFR FOF Strategic Index seeks superior returns by primarily investing in funds that focus on opportunistic strategies such as Emerging Markets, Sector Specific, and Equity Hedge.

Finally, we divide the HFR Indexes per geographical area: HFR FOF Composite (Offshore) represents multiple managers or managed accounts operating offshore while the HFR FOF Composite (Onshore) focuses on managers based in the United States. We note that both HFR FOF Indexes exhibit high and positive autocorrelation for most of the strategies (see last column of Table 22.1). With few exceptions, autocorrelations are substantially high. Lo (2001) and Getmansky *et al.* (2004) suggest that such a high autocorrelation in hedge fund returns is likely to be an indication of illiquidity exposure.[3] In order to take into account this bias we filter the data.[4] We apply the Blundell/Ward Filter to the data. In particular we regress the return time series ($r_t$) on the lagged time series ($r_{t-1}$) running the regression script:

$$r_t = \alpha_0 + \beta_1 r_{t-1} + \varepsilon_t.$$

Finally, we obtained the new filtered time series transforming the data with the formula:

$$ur_t = \frac{1}{(1-\beta_1)r_t} - \frac{\beta_1}{(1-\beta_1)r_{t-1}},$$

where $ur_t$ is the new uncorrelated time series, $r_t$ and $r_{t-1}$ are respectively the original time series at time $t$ and lagged time series at time $t-1$, $\beta_1$ is the coefficient of the standard regression of the return on the lagged time series. Using this filter we reduce the first-order autocorrelation (AC1) while keeping

---

[3]This is also a well-known stylized fact, and it is usually traced back to stale prices and investment in illiquid assets.
[4]Another explanation could be return smoothing done by hedge fund managers for the purpose of lowering the reported standard deviation.

**Table 22.1** Univariate Statistics of the Barclay FoHF from January 1997 to February 2012

| Index | Mean (Annualized %) | Standard Deviation (Annualized %) | Skewness | Excess Kurtosis | VaR 99% | Autocorrelation (%) |
|---|---|---|---|---|---|---|
| HFR FOF Multi-Strategy | 7.17 | 5.23 | −0.98 | 4.26 | 4.42 | 38.67** |
| HFR FOF Conservative | 5.27 | 4.16 | −1.75 | 7.15 | 3.74 | 48.53** |
| HFR FOF Diversified | 5.24 | 6.23 | 0.47 | 3.92 | 5.45 | 37.66** |
| HFR FOF Defensive | 7.06 | 5.63 | −0.03 | 0.44 | 2.83 | 4.59 |
| HFR FOF Strategic | 6.25 | 8.72 | 0.55 | 3.79 | 7.11 | 32.21** |
| HFR FOF Offshore | 4.85 | 6.56 | −0.52 | 3.66 | 5.74 | 36.81** |
| HFR FOF Onshore | 6.78 | 5.59 | −1.07 | 4.46 | 5.61 | 36.07** |

Significant at 95% (*) and 99% (**) confidence level.

the same mean of the returns. Regarding higher moments we observe that all Indexes report negative skewness and positive excess kurtosis. Generally speaking we can say that a rational investor would have preference for positive odd moments and aversion for positive even moments. In our database we can count five out of seven strategies that are negatively skewed and almost every index has positive kurtosis.

Furthermore, kurtosis is also positive for all strategies. Looking for historical 1-month value at risk (VaR) at the 99% confidence level (VaR 99% in Table 22.1), we observe that the broader indexes (i.e. Multi-Strategy Diversified) experience higher values with respect to FoHFs with a much clear strategic asset allocation. We do not report here the Jarque–Bera normality test, which is rejected for all FoHF Indexes except for the HFR FOF Defensive Index.

Given the high non-normality of data, we search for other models that enable us to analyze risk premia and particularly in the case of coskewness or cokurtosis. We use a cubic capital asset pricing model (CAPM) similar to that used by Barone-Adesi et al. (2004) and Ranaldo and Favre (2005) to obtain further insight into higher-moment risks. We apply the following model:

$$r_i - r_F = a_{i,1} + b_{i,1}[r_M - r_F] + b_{i,2}[r_M - r_F]^2 + b_{i,3}[r_M - r_F]^3 + \varepsilon_i,$$

where $r_i$ is the return of the FoHF Index, $r_M$ is the market return, represented by S&P 500, $r_F$ is the risk-free rate, represented by the 1-month Treasury bill rate, $a_1$ indicates the intercept of the model, and $b_1$, $b_2$, and $b_3$ are, respectively, the

| Table 22.2 | | Four-Moment CAPM of HFR FOF Indexes from January 1994 to February 2012 | | |

| Index | $a_1$ (%) | Covariance $(b_1)$ (%) | Coskewness $(b_2)$ | Coexcess Kurtosis $(b_3)$ |
|---|---|---|---|---|
| HFR FOF Multi-Strategy | 0.54* | 5.03 | −0.06 | −2.01 |
| HFR FOF Conservative | 0.42* | 4.31 | −0.11 | −0.56 |
| HFR FOF Diversified | 0.45* | 2.43 | −0.22 | 0.08 |
| HFR FOF Defensive | 0.53* | 4.37 | 0.03 | −0.68 |
| HFR FOF Strategic | 0.48 | 4.41 | −0.12 | −2.26 |
| HFR FOF Offshore | 0.42 | 3.62 | −0.28 | −1.21 |
| HFR FOF Onshore | 0.52* | 1.97 | 0.10 | 2.03 |

Significant at 95% (*) and 99% (**) confidence level.

covariance, coskewness, and cokurtosis sensitivity of the hedge fund strategy compared to the stock market. A rational investor, considering higher moments, will always prefer to add to his/her existing portfolio an asset that has positive coskewness and negative cokurtosis with the aim to improve the skewness and kurtosis of the existing portfolio. In doing this we lower the probability of reporting negative months (positive coskeweness) and the likelihood of extreme events (low cokurtosis). In Table 22.2 we report the result of the model, using the market as single-risk premia.

The four-moment CAPM model reports that only in a few cases the alternative strategies are desirable diversifiers. Only the HFR FOF Defensive Index reports a positive coskewness and negative cokurtosis parameter, despite non-significance. In addition, only the HFR FOF Defensive Index has a significant alpha. The Multi-Strategy, Conservative, Strategic, and Offshore Indexes report negative cokurtosis, and it is important to note that only in a few cases is the parameter positive and significant for covariance and cokurtosis.

Another aspect to investigate is whether the strategies/indexes are market-neutral and independent of the market. For this purpose we apply a model that tests mean-neutrality. As in Patton (2009), Agarwal and Naik (2004), Asness *et al.* (2001), Mitchell and Pulvino (2001), and Fung and Hsieh (1997), we employ piecewise linear regression and run the following model:

$$r_{it} = \alpha_o + \beta_{it}^- Ir_{mt}\{r_{mt} \leq 0\} + \beta_{it}^+ Ir_{mt}\{r_{mt} > 0\} + \varepsilon_{it},$$

where $r_i$ are the HFR FOF Indexes to be analyzed, $r_m$ represent the stock market, and $\beta^-$ and $\beta^+$ are, respectively, the sensitivity of the hedge fund with respect to negative or positive movements of the stock market. Table 22.3 reports the findings.

In Table 22.3, we see that the intercept is positive for all HFR FOF Indexes, but significant only for the HFR FOF Defensive Index. In addition, none of the FOF

| Table 22.3 | Market Neutrality of the HFR FOF Indexes with Respect to the Stock Market from January 1997 to February 2012 | | |
|---|---|---|---|
| **Index** | $\alpha$ (%) | $\beta^-$ (%) | $\beta^+$ (%) |
| HFR FOF Multi-Strategy | 0.49 | 2.06 | 5.36 |
| HFR FOF Conservative | 0.40 | 4.18 | 4.17 |
| HFR FOF Diversified | 0.40 | 3.17 | 3.09 |
| HFR FOF Defensive | 0.51** | 2.71 | 4.93 |
| HFR FOF Strategic | 0.37 | 0.21 | 6.15 |
| HFR FOF Offshore | 0.36 | 3.14 | 3.88 |
| HFR FOF Onshore | 0.48 | 2.36 | 4.34 |

Significant at 95% (*) and 99% (**) confidence level.

Indexes are able to protect the mean value of the portfolio when the market drops, despite the fact that we do not find any significant parameter. Contrarily, when we analyze the sensitivity of the HFR FOF Indexes by taking into account market upturns, we observe that every FOF Index has a positive and significant parameter.

## 22.3. FACTOR MODEL (RISK FACTORS)

When it comes to analyzing hedge funds, a reasonable and investable opportunity set must be constructed, and existing literature suggests using different risk factors. In this chapter, we would like to keep them as simple as possible, avoiding the use of spreads or strategies. Similarly to Hasanhodzic and Lo (2007), we use a stock market risk factor, a bond risk factor, a credit risk high-yield bond factor, and an emerging market factor. In order to keep the model simple and investable we add a simple option strategy. Our complete list[5] includes:

- *Stock risk factor*: the S&P 500 total return represents the equity market risk factor.
- *Bond risk factor*: Fidelity Government Income Fund (FGOVX). The fund invests in instruments related to US government securities, and allocates assets across different market sectors and maturities. The credit quality is high (AAA) and the modified duration of the fund is medium/low.
- *Credit risk factor*: Vanguard High Yield Corporate (VWEHX). The fund invests in a diversified group of high-yielding, higher-risk corporate bonds with medium- and lower-range credit quality ratings. At least 80% of assets are corporate bonds that are rated below Baa by Moody's or equivalent. The fund may not invest more than 20% of assets in bonds with credit ratings lower than B or equivalent, convertible securities, and preferred stocks. The interest rate sensitivity is classified as medium.
- CBOE S&P 500 95–110 Collar Index (CLL). The CBOE S&P 500 Collar Index measures the total return of the CBOE S&P 500 Collar Strategy. This is a passive

---

[5]Note that contrarily to Hasanhodzic and Lo (2007), we do not use the credit spread, but simply a credit factor. Contrarily to Barone-Adesi and Siragusa (2011), the currency risk factor, the commodity risk factor, and the volatility risk factor are omitted.

| Table 22.4 | Statistics from January 1997 to February 2012 | | | | | |
|---|---|---|---|---|---|---|
| **Index** | **Mean (Annualized%)** | **Standard Deviation (Annualized %)** | **Skewness** | **Excess Kurtosis** | **Historical VaR 99% CL** | **Autocorrelation (%)** |
| S&P 500 | 5.56 | 16.56 | −0.58 | 0.66 | 11.68 | 10.40 |
| FGOVX | 7.35 | 9.37 | −0.02 | 2.69 | 6.95 | −2.72 |
| VWEHX | 6.52 | 8.26 | −1.58 | 11.63 | 5.99 | 21.99** |
| CLL | 4.17 | 11.55 | −0.13 | −0.55 | 7.75 | 9.15 |
| FEMKX | 7.82 | 27.95 | −0.91 | 2.23 | 24.56 | 17.76* |
| EW S + B | 6.46 | 8.69 | −0.68 | 2.13 | 6.48 | −0.43 |
| EW ALT BETA | 6.24 | 14.02 | −0.87 | 2.12 | 11.42 | 41.97** |

Significant at 95% (*) and 99% (**) confidence level.

strategy that consists of (a) holding the S&P 500 portfolio and collecting dividends, (b) buying 5% out-of-the-money SPX puts that expire in the March quarterly cycle, and (c) selling 10% out-of-the-money SPX calls on a monthly basis. The collar permits stopping loss and the cost of the put is covered by selling an out-of-the-money call with shorter maturity. The result is a more compact distribution of returns with shorter left and right tails; in other words, less risk and less return.[6]

- *Emerging markets risk factor*: Fidelity Emerging Markets Fund (FEMKX). The fund invests normally at least 80% of assets in securities (common stocks) of issuers in emerging markets and other investments that are economically tied to emerging markets.

In Table 22.4 we report the univariate statistics for every asset class and the statistics for an equally weighted portfolio that contains stocks and bonds (denominated EW S + B) and an equally weighted portfolio that represents the Alternative Beta Strategies that is formed by an emerging market factor (FEMKX in the table, representing emerging market exposure), high yield factor (VWEHX, representing credit risk exposure), and options strategy factor (CLL in the table, added to capture a stock market non-linear sensitivity). The EW portfolio of the above mentioned alternative factors is denominated EW ALT BETA. Similarly to Hedge Funds strategies, notice the higher autocorrelation and kurtosis and negative skewness of the alternative factors and the EW ALR BETA portfolio formed by the same factors.

## 22.4. PORTFOLIO ALLOCATION WITH HEDGE FUNDS AND FoHFs

Jensen's alpha is a standard selection technique used by the investment industry in order to rank asset classes and investments while building optimal portfolios.

---

[6]For further information, see http://www.cboe.com/micro/cll/newcollardescriptionoct1909.pdf.

| Table 22.5 | Regression of HFR FOF Indexes versus Equally Weighted Portfolio of Stocks and Bonds from January 1997 to February 2012 | | |
|---|---|---|---|
| **Index** | **Alpha (%)** | **Beta (%)** | **Adjusted $R^2$ (%)** |
| Tremont Hedge Fund Index | 0.11 | 1.17** | 81.22 |
| HFR FOF Multi-Strategy | 0.01 | 1.08** | 87.01 |
| HFR FOF Conservative | −0.05 | 0.90** | 71.51 |
| HFR FOF Diversified | −0.20 | 1.29** | 89.73 |
| HFR FOF Defensive | 0.20** | 0.70** | 72.08 |
| HFR FOF Strategic | −0.28* | 1.60** | 79.93 |
| HFR FOF Offshore | −0.28** | 1.33** | 89.07 |
| HFR FOF Onshore | 0.01 | 1.12** | 84.89 |

Significance at 95% (*) and 99% (**) confidence level.

Jensen's alpha relies on the fact that returns on the investments to be analyzed and the portfolio are jointly normal distributed and investor has constant absolute risk tolerance. Unfortunately, we notice in Table 22.1 that joint normality is non-existent for the HFR FOF Indexes. We then use Jensen's alpha knowing the measure could be biased, given high non-normality present in hedge fund returns. In Table 22.5, we regress the return of each FOF Index against an equally weighted portfolio of stocks and bonds (EW S + B in Table 22.4). The intercept (alpha) and slope (beta) are reported in Table 22.5.

In Table 22.5 only the HFR FOF Defensive Index has positive and significant alpha. We see also that the picture is much more uncertain when we examine the Tremont Hedge Fund Index. The HFR FOF Strategic and Offshore Indexes instead report negative and significant alphas. When we compare the HFR FOF Onshore and Offshore Indexes, it is apparent that FoHF location seems a discriminatory factor to take into account. We also include the Tremont Hedge Fund Index, which reports an insignificant alpha.

## 22.5. CERTAINTY EQUIVALENCE AND PORTFOLIO ALLOCATION WITH FoHFs

In order to judge the economic impact of adding a hedge fund or a FoHFs position to a set of benchmark assets, we compute the percentage increase in the Certainty Equivalent Return (CER), similarly to Kandel and Stambaugh (1996), Campbell and Viceira (1999), Ang and Bekaert (2002), and Ang et al. (2005).[7] The CER is the appropriate monetary payment a risk-averse investor

---

[7]In particular, Ang et al. (2005) examine the value-added by comparing Certainty Equivalent of different portfolios with and without FoHFs and Indexes taking into account the exact advantage given by adding alternatives by computing: $100 \times [(1 + CE^*)/(1 + CE) - 1]$, where $CE^*$ is the Certainty Equivalent Return with the alternative investment and CE is the Equivalent Return without any exposure to hedge funds.

must receive to get compensated for not investing in the optimal risky position. For example, if the CER is 7%, then 7% is the equivalent return that an investor must receive in order to compensate the investor not to hold the optimal portfolio.[8]

Notice that the Certainty Equivalent concept reflects the investor's view, personal risk attitude, and investment constraints. A rational investor should prefer the investments (assets mix) that give a maximum CER. To obtain meaningful results we use a constrained portfolio (positive weights and adding up to 1). Given the high non-normality and that quadratic utility is less appealing because of the presumption of absolute risk aversion and relative risk aversion increase with wealth, we examine different types of utility functions. Following Pézier (2010), we choose the power utility function. This function gives us the possibility to include exponential, hyperbolic, logarithmic, and square root utility functions. Pézier (2010, p. 21) approximates the expected utility for the first four moments of a return distribution with the following formula:

$$CE(P4) \cong 0.5\lambda S^2 \left\{ 1 + \frac{S(1+\eta)\xi}{3} - \frac{S^2[(1+\eta)(1+2\eta)k + 3\eta(2\eta - 1)]}{12} \right\}$$

where $\lambda$ is the level of risk aversion, $\eta$ is the sensitivity to changes in wealth of the investor, $S$ is the ratio of the mean of the portfolio above the volatility of the portfolio, $\xi$ is the skewness of the portfolio, and $k$ is the excess kurtosis. Table 22.6 reports the optimized weights for exponential ($\eta = 0$), hypergeometric ($\eta = 0.5$), logarithmic ($\eta = 1$), and square root utility ($\eta = 2$) functions.

We see in Table 22.6 that the CER increases when we add a FOF Index. Despite this, the strategic asset allocation that focuses more on hedging extreme events displays excellent results, with the higher CER for every utility function. We report in Table 22.7 the equally weighted portfolio of stocks and bonds and alternative assets for every FOF Index.

Table 22.7 shows that the HFR FOF Defensive Index proves to be the best 'hedger' when we consider risk-adjusted returns. In fact, the HFR FOF Defensive Index reports lower volatility, higher skewness, and lower kurtosis and historical monthly VaR. The HFR FOF Offshore Index appears to be the worst performer, confirming our previous findings. This is a simple robustness check that supports the findings of previous models.

---

[8]Certainty Equivalent is simply the level of the utility function at the optimal portfolio weight. In standard mean–variance space with expected return on the $y$-axis and volatility or variance on the $x$-axis, the Certainty Equivalent represents the point where the utility indifference curve crosses the $y$-axis and corresponds to the value of the quadratic utility function.

| Table 22.6 | Asset Allocation (No Short Sales) and CER for Exponential, Hypergeometric, Logarithmic, and Square Root Utility taking into Account the Four Moments from January 1997 to February 2012 |

| | Asset Class Weights (%) | | | |
|---|---|---|---|---|
| **CER** | $\eta = 0$ | $\eta = 0.5$ | $\eta = 1$ | $\eta = 2$ |
| EW S + B | 72.54 | 60.71 | 51.12 | 36.57 |
| EW ALT | 27.46 | 39.29 | 48.88 | 63.43 |
| *CE* | *5.25* | *4.17* | *3.31* | *2.12* |
| EW S + B | 33.29 | 19.25 | 7.02 | 0.00 |
| EW ALT | 21.10 | 23.72 | 26.45 | 33.72 |
| HFR FOF MS | 45.61 | 57.03 | 66.53 | 66.28 |
| *CE** | *6.12* | *5.37* | *4.64* | *3.24* |
| EW S + B | 56.22 | 37.91 | 24.30 | 5.07 |
| EW ALT | 24.24 | 30.07 | 34.84 | 40.50 |
| HFR FOF Conservative | 19.54 | 32.02 | 40.87 | 54.43 |
| *CE** | *5.35* | *4.40* | *3.61* | *2.52* |
| EW S + B | 62.60 | 44.71 | 32.31 | 15.20 |
| EW ALT | 25.00 | 28.01 | 30.60 | 34.93 |
| HFR FOF Diversified | 12.40 | 27.28 | 37.09 | 49.87 |
| *CE** | *5.32* | *4.49* | *3.81* | *2.78* |
| EW S + B | 16.68 | 14.48 | 12.17 | 5.87 |
| EW ALT | 10.53 | 10.55 | 10.72 | 12.02 |
| HFR FOF Defensive | 72.79 | 74.97 | 77.11 | 82.11 |
| *CE** | *10.99* | *10.72* | *10.07* | *7.76* |
| EW S + B | 65.88 | 48.55 | 36.15 | 18.68 |
| EW ALT | 26.21 | 31.05 | 34.83 | 40.94 |
| HFR FOF Strategic | 7.91 | 20.40 | 29.02 | 40.37 |
| *CE** | *5.29* | *4.40* | *3.68* | *2.64* |
| EW S + B | 72.54 | 50.97 | 37.06 | 19.03 |
| EW ALT | 27.46 | 31.10 | 33.20 | 36.75 |
| HFR FOF Offshore | 0.00 | 17.92 | 29.74 | 44.22 |
| *CE** | *5.25* | *4.27* | *3.54* | *2.52* |
| EW S + B | 37.97 | 24.38 | 12.67 | 0.00 |
| EW ALT | 21.77 | 25.23 | 28.78 | 36.03 |
| HFR FOF Onshore | 40.26 | 50.40 | 58.55 | 63.97 |
| *CE** | *6.00* | *5.17* | *4.37* | *2.98* |

| Table 22.7 | Equally Weighted Portfolio versus all HFR FOF Indexes from January 1997 to February 2012 |

| Index | Mean (Annualized %) | Standard Deviation (Annualized %) | Skewness | Excess Kurtosis | Historical Monthly VaR 99% CL |
|---|---|---|---|---|---|
| EW S + B/EW ALT BETA | 5.56 | 8.05 | −0.61 | 1.44 | 6.54 |
| HFR FOF Multi-Strategy | 5.88 | 6.99 | −0.51 | 1.23 | 5.61 |
| HFR FOF Conservative | 5.30 | 6.80 | −0.62 | 1.64 | 5.82 |
| HFR FOF Diversified | 5.39 | 7.40 | −0.42 | 1.31 | 5.93 |
| HFR FOF Defensive | 5.94 | 6.44 | −0.36 | 0.83 | 4.67 |
| HFR FOF Strategic | 5.63 | 8.00 | −0.47 | 1.56 | 6.22 |
| HFR FOF Offshore | 5.17 | 7.45 | −0.45 | 1.38 | 5.84 |
| HFR FOF Onshore | 5.89 | 7.09 | −0.57 | 1.45 | 6.19 |

## CONCLUSION

Our chapter attempts to analyze if FoHFs can provide value when added to an existing portfolio. We first examined univariate statistics of various HFR FOF Indexes to analyze market neutrality and higher moments with respect to the stock market (S&P 500). Ranking investments by the information ratio and alpha will likely lead to drawbacks due to the non-normality of hedge fund returns. In addition, the performance measures do not consider the investment constraints and the risk attitudes of the investor. In order to take into account all aspects, this chapter uses the Certainty Equivalence principle to compare a balanced portfolio and an alternative portfolio with FoHF and hedge fund indexes. To properly evaluate non-normal returns, we use the power utility function where we easily account for higher moments and discover that FoHFs add value. In their landmark study, Brinson *et al.* (1986, 1991) argue that approximately 90% of portfolio performance can be explained by asset allocation. In addition, Kat and Menexe (2002) find no persistency in mean returns, but find both stable correlation and volatility of hedge fund strategies with respect to stock and bond markets, implying that hedge funds have a much more stable risk-to-return profile. The FoHFs manager who is able to think 'out of the box' looking for real hedging and not only chasing alpha is able to obtain better risk-adjusted returns.

## References

Agarwal, V., & Naik, N. (2004). Risk and Portfolio Decisions Involving Hedge Funds. *Review of Financial Studies, 17*(1), 63–98.

Ang, A., & Bekaert, G. (2002). International Asset Allocation with Regime Shifts. *Review of Financial Studies, 15*(4), 1137–1187.

Ang, A., Rhodes-Kropf, M., & Zhao, R. (2005). Do Funds-of-Funds Deserve Their Fees-on-Fees? Working Paper. *AFA 2007 Chicago Meetings Paper.*

Asness, C., Krail, R., & Liew, J. (2001). Do Hedge Funds Hedge? *Journal of Portfolio Management, 28*(1), 6–19.

Barone-Adesi, G., Gagliardini, P., & Urga, G. (2004). A test of the homogeneity hypothesis on asset pricing models. In E. Jurczenko, & B. Maillett (Eds.), *Multi-Moment CAPM and Related Topics.* Berlin: Springer.

Brown, S., Goetzmann, W., & Liang, B. (2004). Fees-on-Fees in Funds-of-Funds. *Journal of Investment Management, 2*(4), 39–56.

Brown, S. J., Fraser, T. L., & Liang, B. (2008). Hedge Fund Due Diligence: A Source of Alpha in a Diversified Hedge Fund Strategy. *Journal of Investment Management, 6,* 23–33.

Brown, S. J., Gregoriou, G. N., & Pascalau, R. (2012). Diversification in Funds of Hedge Funds: Is It Possible to Overdiversify? *Review of Asset Pricing Studies, 2*(1), 89–110.

Brinson, G. P. L., Hood, R., & Beebower, G. L. (1986). Determinants of Portfolio Performance. *The Financial Analysts Journal, July/August, 42*(4), 39–44.

Brinson, G. P. L., Hood, R., & Beebower, G. L. (1991). Determinants of Portfolio Performance II: An Update. *The Financial Analysts Journal, 74*(3), 40–48.

Barone Adesi, G., Siragusa, S. (2011). Linear Model for Passive Hedge Fund Replication. Included in The Handbook of Hedge Fund Replication. Palgrave, MacMillan, December, 2011.

Campbell, J. Y., & Viceira, L. (1999). Consumption and Portfolio decision when expected returns are time varying. *Quarterly Journal of Economics, 114*(1), 433–495.

Fung, W., & Hsieh, D. A. (1997). Empirical Characteristics of Dynamic Trading Strategies: the Case of Hedge Funds. *Review of Financial Studies, 10*(2), 275–302.

Getmansky, M., Lo, A., & Makarov, I. (2004). An econometric model of serial correlation and illiquidity in hedge fund returns. *Journal of Financial Economics, 74*(3), 529–609.

Hasanhodzic, J., & Lo, A. W. (2007). Can Hedge-Fund Returns Be Replicated?: The Linear Case. *Journal of Investment Management, 5*(2), 5–45.

Kandel, S., & Stambaugh, R. S. (1996). On the predictability of Stock Returns: An Asset Allocation Perspective. *Journal of Finance, 51*(2), 385–424.

Kat, H. M., & Menexe, F. (2002). *Persistence in Hedge Fund Performance: The True Value of a Track Record. Research Paper.* Cass Business School.

Lo, A. W. (2001). Risk Management for Hedge Funds: Introduction and Overview. *Financial Analysts Journal, 57*(6), 16–33.

Patton, A. J. (2009). Are 'Market Neutral' Hedge Funds Really Market Neutral? *Review of Financial Studies, 22*(7), 2495–2530.

Pulvino, T., & Mitchell, M. (2001). Characteristics of Risk and Return in Risk Arbitrage. *Journal of Finance, 56*(6), 2135–2175.

Pézier, J. P. (2010). Maximum Certainty Equivalent Excess Returns and Equivalent Preference Criteria, Working Paper, ICMA Centre. *The Henley Business School.* Reading University.

Ranaldo, A., & Favre, L. (2005). How to Price Hedge Funds: From Two- to Four-Moment CAPM. *UBS Research Paper.*

# SECTION 5
# Tail Risk

# CHAPTER 23

# The Intertemporal Relation between Tail Risk and Funds of Hedge Funds Returns

**Yigit Atilgan**[*], **Turan G. Bali**[†], and **K. Ozgur Demirtas**[**]

[*]Assistant Professor of Finance, Sabanci Universitesi, İstanbul, Turkey
[†]Robert S. Parker Chair Professor of Business Administration, Georgetown University, Washington, DC, USA
[**]Professor of Finance, Sabanci Universitesi, İstanbul, Turkey

## 23.1. INTRODUCTION

Merton (1981) and Dybvig and Ross (1985) were among the first studies that suggested that managed portfolios may exhibit option-like payoffs even when the managers do not trade in derivatives. Glosten and Jagannathan (1994) use excess returns of various stock index options as additional factors in performance measurement. Bali *et al.* (2011) provide evidence for the ability of hedge funds to dynamically adjust their positions to changes in financial and economic conditions. Hedge funds are especially relevant from this perspective because their opportunistic trading behavior induces a substantial portion of their returns to be driven by state-contingent bets. The resulting non-linear, option-like returns of hedge funds have been an active question of research in financial economics.

Hedge fund managers face very few restrictions when they choose the constituents of their portfolios, and they can use dynamic trading strategies that can involve short selling, high leverage, and derivatives. Due to these reasons, Fung and Hsieh (1997a) argue that it may not be possible to explain hedge fund returns using traditional asset pricing factors. In particular, tail risk becomes an important factor to understand the non-linear hedge fund returns. To capture such non-linear relationships, Fung and Hsieh (2001) model them using trend-following strategies. These strategies are shown to be uncorrelated with standard equity, bond, and commodity strategies, and they bring high returns during periods in which world equity markets perform both the worst and the best (Fung and Hsieh, 1997b). A simple trend-following strategy such as a lookback straddle on various asset classes can replicate fundamental features of trend-following hedge fund returns such as large skewness and high returns during extreme value gains and losses in world equity markets. The superior explanatory power of these primitive trend-following factors over standard benchmarks lends support to the idea that trend-following funds have non-linear and option-like strategies with high levels of tail risk exposure.

Mitchell and Pulvino (2001) focus on merger arbitrage strategies rather than trend-following strategies. Although it is possible that the documented profitability of such strategies may be due to the systematic inefficiencies in the way that firms involved in a merger are priced, it is also possible that the abnormal returns are just compensation for extraordinary risk. Standard asset pricing models that impose linear relations between returns and factors may fail to account for some dimensions of risk such as tail risk. The analysis shows that the market beta of a merger risk arbitrage portfolio is close to zero in flat and appreciating markets; however, it increases to 0.50 when the equity market experiences large drops in value. In other words, a merger risk arbitrage strategy is akin to writing an uncovered index put option and therefore it is more suitable to follow a contingent claims approach that accounts for tail risk. In addition to trend followers and risk arbitrageurs, a wide range of hedge fund strategies such as those taking equity-oriented positions also exhibit non-linear and option-like payoffs. Agarwal and Naik (2004) investigate the returns from a large number of equity-oriented strategies and find that their returns also resemble those from writing a put option on the stock market index. Their analysis, which relies on a mean-conditional value at risk (VaR) framework, also shows that expected tail losses of traditional mean–variance optimal portfolios can be substantially underestimated. In other words, big losses can arise during large market downturns if the valuation procedure ignores the tail risk of hedge funds.

Given the potential importance of tail risk in explaining hedge fund returns, a natural question is whether this risk can be diversified away. Brown *et al.* (2012) investigate this question and focus on funds of hedge funds (FoHFs) that invest in a diverse selection of hedge funds. FoHFs stress the importance of the concept of diversification as they market their strategies. Although there may be diversification benefits of investing in FoHFs, it is still possible that they do not protect the investors against significant left tail market risk that many hedge funds face. This kind of exposure has been explained by Lo (2001) with the conjecture that hedge funds earn rents from liquidity provision and thus their losses are heavy during liquidity crises. Brown *et al.* (2012) indeed find that the magnitude of negative skewness for FoHFs is an increasing function of the level of diversification. Thus, if there is a common liquidity factor that affects many hedge fund strategies, tail risk may not be diversifiable.

Bali *et al.* (2007) provide direct tests of the presence and significance of a cross-sectional relation between hedge fund returns and tail risk as measured by VaR. The univariate and bivariate portfolio analysis as well as the fund-level regression results from their study indicate that there is a significantly positive relation between VaR and the cross-section of expected returns of hedge funds. Even after controlling for factors such as size, liquidity, and age, funds with high tail risk outperform those with low tail risk. Liang and Park (2007) extend these results to alternative tail risk measures such as the expected shortfall and semideviation.

Our emphasis in this chapter is not on examining whether tail risk can explain the cross-sectional distribution of hedge fund returns, but, rather, on investigating whether there is an intertemporal relation between tail risk and expected returns of FoHFs at the index level. Motivated by the expected utility framework of Levy and Sarnat (1972) and Arzac and Bawa (1977) which deal with safety-first investors who aim to maximize their expected return subject to a maximum loss constraint, Bali *et al.* (2009) apply this kind of intertemporal analysis to several US broad market indices, and find that tail risk as measured by VaR can predict future stock market returns and is a superior measure of risk when compared to traditional risk measures. We extend their results to the FoHFs context and the first main finding of this chapter is that there is a positive and significant relation between tail risk and future FoHFs portfolio returns.

Once we uncover this predictive relation, we seek to understand its source. It has been shown that tail risk is an increasing function of variance and kurtosis, and a decreasing function of skewness by Cornish and Fisher (1937). The moments of the return distribution have important implications for asset pricing. The literature on the relation between skewness and expected returns dates back to Arditti (1967). Arditti shows that, in a Taylor series expansion of the utility function around expected future wealth, the third moment of future wealth that can be interpreted as a measure of coskewness becomes a priced risk factor. For a risk-averse investor with non-increasing absolute risk aversion, this factor needs to be negatively related to expected returns. In other words, there is a preference for positive skewness and risk-averse investors would be more (less) reluctant to take investments that might bring large losses (gains) with limited gains (losses). Thus, assets that make portfolio returns more right-skewed are more desirable and they would demand lower expected returns from investments with higher coskewness. Rubinstein (1973) and Kraus and Litzenberger (1976) develop more elaborate general equilibrium models in which the marginal rate of substitution between expected return and skewness times the risky asset's marginal contribution to the skewness of the market portfolio becomes a component of the expected return of the risky asset. Harvey and Siddique (2000) introduce a similar model that focuses on conditional coskewness, and also document a negative relationship between individual securities' expected returns and the returns on a factor-mimicking portfolio based on conditional coskewness. More recently, idiosyncratic skewness has also gained attention in the asset pricing literature. Barberis and Huang (2008) model investors that use a transformed probability weighting function in the spirit of the cumulative prospect theory of Tversky and Kahneman (1992), and Brunnermeier *et al.* (2007) set up a model of optimal expectations to argue that idiosyncratic skewness has valuation effects. The fourth moment of the return distribution, kurtosis, which measures how much a distribution is weighted toward its tails, has also been put forward as an asset pricing factor. Following Kimball (1993) and Pratt and Zeckhauser (1987), Dittmar (2002) builds on the three-moment asset pricing model and finds preference for lower kurtosis (i.e., investors are averse to kurtosis and prefer stocks with lower probability mass in the tails of the distribution to stocks with higher probability mass in the tails of the distribution). In other words, assets that make portfolio returns more leptokurtic are less desirable and should command higher expected returns.

Our analysis of the intertemporal relationship between the individual moments of the FoHFs return distribution and expected FoHFs index returns reveals that although variance and skewness cannot predict future FoHFs returns, there is a significantly positive relation between kurtosis and FoHFs returns. In other words, investors demand higher returns from hedge funds that expose them to this particular dimension of tail risk.

A study that is similar to ours is Bali *et al.* (2012) that investigates the relation between systematic risk and the cross-section of hedge fund returns. They argue that cross-sectional dispersion in measures of skewness and kurtosis can be important factors explaining differences in hedge fund expected returns. They generate monthly rolling-window estimates of volatility, skewness, and kurtosis for individual funds, and they regress hedge fund expected returns on these individual moments. Although they find a negative (positive) cross-sectional link between the skewness (kurtosis) of hedge funds and their returns, these relations are statistically insignificant. In this chapter, as explained before, we conduct a time-series predictability analysis at the index level and our results differ from Bali *et al.* (2012) in that both VaR and kurtosis have significantly positive intertemporal relations with FoHF index returns.

The chapter is organized as follows. Section 23.2 discusses the methodology and explains the data. Section 23.3 discusses the empirical results from the regression analysis, followed by our conclusions.

## 23.2. DATA AND METHODOLOGY

We first measure tail risk using a non-parametric measure of VaR that indicates how much the value of a portfolio could decline in a fairly extreme outcome if one were to rank order possible outcomes from best to worst. In other words, VaR attempts to measure how much an investor can expect to lose on a portfolio in a given time period at a given level of probability. In our analysis, we use the minimum FoHFs index returns observed during the past year and estimate alternative VaR measures from the lower tail of the empirical return distribution in a rolling-window fashion. These VaR measures are multiplied by $-1$ before they are included in the regressions so that higher magnitudes of the measures correspond to greater downside risk.

Next, we also calculate a parametric measure of VaR that accounts for skewness and excess kurtosis in the data. Hansen (1994) introduces a generalization of the Student $t$-distribution where asymmetries may occur, while maintaining the assumption of a zero mean and unit variance. This skewed $t$ (ST)-density is given by:

$$
f(z_t; \mu, \sigma, v, \lambda) = \begin{cases} bc\left(1 + \dfrac{1}{v-2}\left(\dfrac{bz_t + a}{1-\lambda}\right)^2\right)^{-\frac{v+1}{2}} & \text{if } z_t < -a/b \\[4mm] bc\left(1 + \dfrac{1}{v-2}\left(\dfrac{bz_t + a}{1+\lambda}\right)^2\right)^{-\frac{v+1}{2}} & \text{if } z_t \geq -a/b \end{cases} , \qquad (23.1)
$$

where $z_t = (R_t - \mu)/\sigma$ is the standardized excess market return, and the constants $a$, $b$, and $c$ are given by:

$$
a = 4\lambda c\left(\frac{v-2}{v-1}\right), \quad b^2 = 1 + 3\lambda^2 - a^2, \ c = \frac{\Gamma\left(\dfrac{v+1}{2}\right)}{\sqrt{\pi(v-2)}\Gamma\left(\dfrac{v}{2}\right)}. \qquad (23.2)
$$

Hansen (1994) shows that this density is defined for $2 < v < \infty$ and $-1 < \lambda < 1$. This density has a single mode at $-a/b$, which is of opposite sign to the parameter $\lambda$. Thus, if $\lambda > 0$, the mode of the density is to the left of zero and the variable is skewed to the right, and *vice versa* when $\lambda < 0$. Furthermore, if $\lambda = 0$, Hansen's distribution reduces to the traditional standardized t distribution. If $\lambda = 0$ and $v = \infty$, it reduces to a normal density.[1]

A parametric approach to calculating VaR is based on the lower tail of the ST distribution. Specifically, we estimate the parameters of the skewed $t$-density $(\mu, \sigma, v, \lambda)$ using data from the most recent year and then find the corresponding percentile of the estimated distribution. Assuming that $R_t = f_{v,\lambda}(z)$ follows skewed $t$-density, parametric VaR is the solution to:

$$
\int_{-\infty}^{\Gamma_{ST}(\Phi)} f_{v,\lambda}(z)\, dz = \Phi, \qquad (23.3)
$$

where $\Gamma_{ST}(\Phi)$ is the VaR threshold based on the skewed $t$-density with a loss probability of $\Phi$. Equation (23.3) indicates that VaR can be calculated by integrating the area under the probability density function of the skewed $t$-density

---

[1]The parameters of the skewed $t$-density are estimated by maximizing the log-likelihood function of $R_t$ with respect to the parameters $\mu$, $\sigma$, $v$, and $\lambda$:

$$
\log L = n\ln b + n\ln\Gamma\left(\frac{v+1}{2}\right) - \frac{n}{2}\ln\pi - n\ln\Gamma(v-2) - n\ln\Gamma\left(\frac{v}{2}\right) - n\ln\sigma - \left(\frac{v+1}{2}\right)\sum_{t=1}^{n}\ln\left(1 + \frac{d_t^2}{(v-2)}\right),
$$

where $d_t = (bz_t + a)/(1 - \lambda s)$ and $s$ is a sign dummy taking the value of 1 if $bz_t + a < 0$ and $s = -1$ otherwise.

distribution. Specifically, to compute a quantile of a distribution, we utilize the Cornish–Fisher expansion, which is a moment-based approximation motivated by the theory of estimating functions, saddle-point approximations, and Fourier-inversion.

To investigate the intertemporal relation between VaR and expected FoHF index returns, we use the following regression specification:

$$R_{t+1} = \alpha + \gamma \cdot VaR_t + \varepsilon_{t+1} \tag{23.4}$$

where $R_{t+1}$ is the excess monthly return on the FoHF index at time $t+1$ and $VaR_t$ is the time $t$ measure of either non-parametric or parametric VaR.

Next, we use FoHF index returns to estimate monthly time-series measures of variance, skewness, and kurtosis:

$$VOL_t = \frac{1}{n-1} \sum_{t=1}^{n} (R_t - \bar{R}_i)^2$$

$$SKEW_t = \frac{1}{n} \sum_{t=1}^{n} \left( \frac{R_t - \bar{R}_i}{\sigma_t} \right)^3 \tag{23.5}$$

$$KURT_t = \frac{1}{n} \sum_{t=1}^{n} \left( \frac{R_t - \bar{R}_i}{\sigma_t} \right)^4 - 3,$$

where $R_t$ is the excess return on the FoHF index in month $t$, $\bar{R}_i$ is the sample mean of excess returns on the FoHF index over the past $n$ months ($n = 24$ or $48$), $VOL_t$, $SKEW_t$, and $KURT_t$ are, respectively, the sample variance, skewness, and kurtosis of excess returns on the FoHF index over the past $n$ months, and $\sigma_t$ is the sample standard deviation of excess returns on the FoHF index over the past $n$ months, defined as the square root of the variance. Using these estimates, we regress 1-month ahead FoHF index returns on the conditional moments:

$$R_{t+1} = \alpha + \gamma_1 \cdot VOL_t + \gamma_1 \cdot SKEW_t + \gamma_1 \cdot KURT_t + \theta \cdot X_t + \varepsilon_{t+1}, \tag{23.6}$$

where $R_{t+1}$ is the excess monthly return on the FoHF index at time $t+1$, and $VOL_t$, $SKEW_t$, $KURT_t$ are defined in equation (23.5). $X_t$ denotes a set of macroeconomic variables associated with business cycle fluctuations. There is a large body of literature indicating that aggregate returns can be predicted by such macroeconomic variables that affect future investment opportunities and these variables also control for the hedging demand component in Merton's (1973) ICAPM. Ross (1976) argues that securities affected by systematic risk factors should earn risk premiums in risk-averse economies and macroeconomic variables are ideal candidates for these risk factors because unexpected changes in macroeconomic variables can impact fundamentals of the firms that constitute the economy. Aggregate production, term spread, and default spread have been shown to be among economic indicators that determine securities' equilibrium expected returns by Chan *et al.* (1985) and Chen *et al.* (1986). Fama and Schwert (1977), Keim and Stambaugh (1986), Campbell and Shiller (1988), and Fama and French (1989) find that short-term interest rates, dividend yield, term spread, default spread, and lagged stock returns can predict the expected returns of bonds and stocks.

In our time-series regressions, we also control for a large set of macroeconomic variables. *DEF* is the change in the default spread calculated as the difference between the yields on BAA- and AAA-rated corporate bonds. *TERM* is the term spread calculated as the change in the difference between the yields on the 10-year Treasury bond and 1-month Treasury bill (T-bill). *RREL* is the detrended riskless rate defined as the yield on the 1-month T-bill minus its 1-year backward moving average. The time-series data on 10-year Treasury bond yields and BAA- and AAA-rated corporate bond yields are available at the Federal Reserve Statistical Release website. Yields on the 1-month T-bill are downloaded from Kenneth French's online data library. *DP* is the aggregate dividend yield calculated by using the returns on the S&P 500 index with and without dividends following Fama and French (1988). IP and *UR* are the monthly growth rate of industrial production and the unemployment rate, respectively. The data for these variables are obtained from the Bureau of Labor Statistics. We also include *LAGRET*, the 1-month lagged return of the FoHF index in the regressions.

We gather the data for the FoHF index returns from the Hedge Fund Research (HFR) database. The sample covers the period from January 1990 to December 2011. HFR indices are broken down into four main strategies: Equity Hedge, Event Driven, Macro, and Relative Value. Each of these main strategies also has multiple substrategies. HFR reports an equally weighted FOF Composite index that includes over 650 constituent funds and is commonly used by hedge fund managers as a performance benchmark. To be included in the index, a fund needs to report monthly gross and net returns, disclose the assets under management in US$, have at least US$50 million under management, and have been actively trading for at least 12 months.

## 23.3. EMPIRICAL RESULTS

Table 23.1 presents the results from the regressions of 1-month ahead FoHF index returns on non-parametric and parametric measures of VaR. All the regression results reported in the tables are based on Newey and West (1987) adjusted standard errors. We expect a positive coefficient for the VaR measures since they reflect the amount of left tail risk and investors would demand a higher expected return from investments with greater tail risk. The findings confirm our expectations. Non-parametric VaR has a coefficient of 0.1187 with a *t*-statistic of 1.82, which is significant at the 7% level. The economic interpretation of this coefficient is that if the minimum return of the FoHFs index over the last 12 months declines by 1%, the investors demand about 12 more

| Table 23.1 | Intertemporal Relation between VAR and FoHFs Returns | |
|---|---|---|
| **Constant** | **Non-parametric VaR** | **Parametric VaR** |
| 0.0081 | 0.1187 | |
| (5.15) | (1.82) | |
| 0.0085 | | 0.1039 |
| (5.23) | | (1.99) |

Results from the time-series regressions of the excess return of the FoHF index on non-parametric or parametric VaR. Non-parametric value at risk is equal to the minimum monthly return over the past year. Parametric value at risk is equal to the first percentile of Hansen's (1994) skewed $t$-density estimated using the monthly returns from over the past year. In each regression, the dependent variable is the 1-month ahead excess FoHF index return. For each regression, the first row gives the intercepts and slope coefficients. The second row presents the Newey–West adjusted $t$-statistics.

basis points of expected returns. The coefficient of parametric VaR is equal to 0.1039 and it is significant at the 5% level with a $t$-statistic of 1.99. Overall, the results from alternative measures of non-parametric and parametric VaR turn out to be similar, indicating a significantly positive relation between tail risk and expected fund of hedge fund returns. Next, we investigate what the source of this positive relation is. Specifically, we recognize that VaR is a function of the moments of the return distribution and regress 1-month ahead FoHF index returns on variance, skewness, and kurtosis.

Table 23.2 presents the results. We provide two sets of regression results that differ from each other based on the length of the sampling window used to calculate the variance, skewness, and kurtosis measures. When we focus on the index returns from the past 24 months, we find that variance has a significantly negative and kurtosis has a significantly positive relation with 1-month ahead FoHF index returns. The coefficient of variance is $-10.2524$ with a $t$-statistic of $-2.19$, whereas the coefficient of kurtosis is equal to 0.0035 with a $t$-statistic of 2.43. The negative coefficient of variance is surprising since one would expect to find a positive relation between the volatility of hedge fund returns and their

| Table 23.2 | Intertemporal Relation between Variance, Skewness, Kurtosis, and FoHFs Returns | | | | | |
|---|---|---|---|---|---|---|
| **Constant** | *VOL24* | *SKEW24* | *KURT24* | *VOL48* | *SKEW48* | *KURT48* |
| −0.0034 | −10.2524 | 0.0012 | 0.0035 | | | |
| (−0.65) | (−2.19) | (0.53) | (2.43) | | | |
| 0.0001 | | | | −21.6172 | 0.0004 | 0.0025 |
| (0.01) | | | | (−4.07) | (0.25) | (2.75) |

Results from the time-series regressions of the excess return of the FoHF index on conditional variance, skewness, and kurtosis. Variance, skewness, and kurtosis measures are constructed from monthly FoHF index data over either the past 24 or 48 months. In each regression, the dependent variable is the 1-month ahead excess FoHF index return. For each regression, the first row gives the intercepts and the slope coefficients. The second row presents the Newey–West adjusted $t$-statistics.

expected values. However, in subsequent analysis, we will see that the negative relation between variance and future FoHF index returns is not robust to the inclusion of macroeconomic variables in the specification. Skewness does not have any meaningful relation with expected FoHFs returns as its coefficient is equal to 0.0012 and insignificant with a $t$-statistic of 0.53. When we extend the sampling window for measuring the return moments to 48 months, the results are the same. The $t$-statistics of variance and kurtosis increase in absolute value to $-4.07$ and 2.75, respectively, whereas the coefficient of skewness is still insignificant with a $t$-statistic of 0.25.

Next, we investigate whether the results from Table 23.2 still hold when we augment the regressions using macroeconomic variables. In Table 23.3, default and term premia, detrended riskless rate, and lagged FoHF index returns are added to the specifications. Again, two sets of regressions results are presented separately for sampling windows of 24 and 48 months. In regression (1), we see that only the lagged FoHFs returns and the term premium can significantly predict 1-month ahead returns. $LAGRET$ is highly significant with a coefficient of 0.3377 and a $t$-statistic of 8.74 indicating positive serial correlation in monthly FoHF index returns. $TERM$ has a coefficient of $-0.1479$ with a $t$-statistic of $-3.13$. More importantly, we find that variance loses its significance at the 5% level with a $t$-statistic of $-1.85$. On the other hand, kurtosis retains its ability to significantly predict future FoHF index returns. Its coefficient is equal to 0.0036

| Table 23.3 | Controlling for Lagged FoHFs Returns, Default and Term Premia, and Detrended Riskless Rate | | | |
|---|---|---|---|---|
| | (1) | | (2) | |
| VOL24 | −9.9674 | (−1.85) | | |
| SKEW24 | 0.0012 | (0.62) | | |
| KURT24 | 0.0036 | (3.24) | | |
| VOL48 | | | −15.1460 | (−2.34) |
| SKEW48 | | | −0.0001 | (−0.08) |
| KURT48 | | | 0.0026 | (4.54) |
| LAGRET | 0.3377 | (8.74) | 0.3476 | (8.31) |
| DEF | 0.3203 | (1.83) | 0.1380 | (0.82) |
| TERM | −0.1479 | (−3.13) | −0.1671 | (−2.37) |
| RREL | 0.1726 | (1.36) | 0.1376 | (1.12) |
| Constant | −0.0056 | (−1.17) | −0.0023 | (−0.61) |

Results from the time-series regressions of the excess return of the fund of hedge fund (FoHF) index on conditional variance, skewness, and kurtosis, and various macroeconomic variables. Variance, skewness, and kurtosis measures are constructed from monthly FoHF index data over either the past 24 or 48 months. LAGRET is equal to the lagged return of the FoHF index. DEF is the change in the default spread calculated as the change in the difference between the yields of BAA- and AAA-rated corporate bonds. TERM is change in the term spread calculated as the change in the difference between the yields on the 10-year Treasury bond and the 1-month T-bill. RREL is the detrended riskless rate defined as the 1-month T-bill rate minus its 1-year backward moving average. In each regression, the dependent variable is the 1-month ahead excess FoHF index return. For each regression, the first column gives the intercepts and the slope coefficients. The second column presents the Newey–West adjusted t-statistics.

with a $t$-statistic of 3.24. Skewness still has no relation with 1-month ahead FoHFs returns. When the sampling window is extended to 48 months, the coefficient of kurtosis decreases to 0.0026 but increases its statistical significance as its $t$-statistic becomes 4.54. Lagged return (term premium) retains its significantly positive (negative) relation with expected fund of hedge fund portfolio returns.

Table 23.4 presents the final set of regression results that add the dividend yield, industrial production growth rate, and unemployment rate to the specification. Several results are apparent from the first regression. (i) Both variance and skewness have insignificant coefficients. (ii) Kurtosis has a positive and significant relation with expected FoHF index returns since its coefficient is 0.0033 with a $t$-statistic of 3.45. (iii) Lagged return and term premium continue to be significant predictors of future FoHFs portfolio returns. Lagged return (term premium) has a coefficient of 0.3399 ($-0.2281$) with a $t$-statistic of 9.02 ($-3.97$). (iv) Among the newly added macroeconomic variables, only the monthly industrial production growth rate has a significant relation with expected FoHF index returns and its coefficient is positive with a $t$-statistic of

| Table 23.4 | Controlling for Dividend Yield, Industrial Production Growth Rate, and Unemployment Rate | | | |
|---|---|---|---|---|
| | (1) | | (2) | |
| VOL24 | −8.1275 | (−1.85) | | |
| SKEW24 | 0.0015 | (0.68) | | |
| KURT24 | 0.0033 | (3.45) | | |
| VOL48 | | | −11.7610 | (−1.82) |
| SKEW48 | | | 0.0005 | (0.45) |
| KURT48 | | | 0.0024 | (4.85) |
| LAGRET | 0.3399 | (9.02) | 0.3471 | (8.15) |
| DEF | 0.5963 | (1.70) | 0.4548 | (1.49) |
| TERM | −0.2281 | (−3.97) | −0.2435 | (−2.99) |
| RREL | 0.0676 | (0.70) | 0.0341 | (0.41) |
| DP | 0.1702 | (1.21) | 0.1222 | (0.57) |
| IP | 0.4539 | (1.96) | 0.5119 | (2.70) |
| UR | −0.0038 | (−0.76) | −0.0016 | (−0.33) |
| Constant | −0.0105 | (−2.08) | −0.0069 | (−1.12) |

Results from the time-series regressions of the excess return of the FoHF index on conditional variance, skewness, and kurtosis, and various macroeconomic variables. Variance, skewness, and kurtosis measures are constructed from monthly FoHF index data over either the past 24 or 48 months. LAGRET is equal to the lagged return of the FoHF index. DEF is the change in the default spread calculated as the change in the difference between the yields of BAA- and AAA-rated corporate bonds. TERM is change in the term spread calculated as the change in the difference between the yields on the 10-year Treasury bond and the 1-month T-bill. RREL is the detrended riskless rate defined as the 1-month T-bill rate minus its 1-year backward moving average. DP is the aggregate dividend price ratio obtained by using the S&P 500 index return with and without dividends. IP and UR represent the monthly industrial production growth rate and the unemployment rate, respectively. In each regression, the dependent variable is the 1-month ahead excess FoHF index return. For each regression, the first column gives the intercepts and the slope coefficients. The second column presents the Newey–West adjusted $t$-statistics.

1.96. The results from the second regression in which a 48-month sampling window is used are similar. To summarize, in the presence of macroeconomic variables, kurtosis has a positive and significant relation with future FoHFs returns, whereas variance and skewness lack predictive power.

## CONCLUSION

This chapter investigates whether any predictive relation exists between tail risk and FoHFs returns. We find that measures of tail risk such as non-parametric and parametric VaR positively predict future fund of funds returns. Since VaR is a function of the moments of the return distribution, we examine the driving force behind this positive relation. Although variance and skewness lack predictive power, we find that there is a significant and positive relation between kurtosis and expected fund of funds returns. These findings are robust after a diverse set of macroeconomic variables and past fund of fund returns are included in the regressions. Some macroeconomic variables such as term premium and industrial production growth rate also predict future fund of funds returns.

## References

Agarwal, V., & Naik, N. Y. (2004). Risks and Portfolio Decisions Involving Hedge Funds. *Review of Financial Studies, 17*(1), 63–98.

Arditti, F. D. (1967). Risk and the Required Return on Equity. *Journal of Finance, 22*(1), 19–36.

Arzac, E. R., & Bawa, V. S. (1977). Portfolio Choice and Equilibrium in Capital Markets with Safety-First Investors. *Journal of Financial Economics, 4*(3), 277–288.

Bali, T. G., Gokcan, S., & Liang, B. (2007). Value at Risk and the Cross Section of Hedge Fund Returns. *Journal of Banking and Finance, 31*(4), 1135–1166.

Bali, T. G., Demirtas, K. O., & Levy, H. (2009). Is There an Intertemporal Relation between Downside Risk and Expected Returns? *Journal of Financial and Quantitative Analysis, 44*(4), 883–909.

Bali, T. G., Brown, S. J., & Caglayan, M. O. (2011). Do Hedge Funds' Exposures to Risk Factors Predict Their Future Returns? *Journal of Financial Economics, 101*(1), 36–68.

Bali, T., Brown, S. J., & Caglayan, M. O. (2012). Systematic Risk and the Cross Section of Hedge Fund Returns. *Journal of Financial Economics, 106*(1), 114–131.

Barberis, N., & Huang, M. (2008). Stocks as Lotteries: The Implications of Probability Weighting for Security Prices. *American Economic Review, 98*(5), 2066–2100.

Brown, S. J., Gregoriou, G., & Pascalau, R. (2012). Diversification in Funds of Hedge Funds: Is It Possible to Overdiversify? *Review of Asset Pricing Studies, 2*(1), 89–110.

Brunnermeier, M. K., Gollier, C., & Parker, J. A. (2007). Optimal Beliefs, Asset Prices and the Preference for Skewed Returns. *American Economic Review, 97*(2), 159–165.

Campbell, J. Y., & Shiller, R. J. (1988). Stock Prices, Earnings and Expected Dividends. *Journal of Finance, 43*(3), 661–676.

Chan, K. C., Chen, N. F., & Hsieh, D. A. (1985). An Exploratory Investigation of the Firm Size Effect. *Journal of Financial Economics, 14*(3), 451–471.

Chen, N. F., Roll, R., & Ross, S. A. (1986). Economic Forces and the Stock Market. *Journal of Business, 59*(3), 383–403.

Cornish, E. A., & Fisher, R. A. (1937). Moments and Cumulants in the Specification of Distributions. In *La Revue de l'Institute International de Statistique, 4. Reprinted in Fisher, R.A. (1950). In: Contributions to Mathematical Statistics.* New York, NY: Wiley.

Dittmar, R. F. (2002). Non-linear Pricing Kernels, Kurtosis Preference, and Evidence from the Cross Section of Equity Returns. *Journal of Finance, 57*(1), 369–403.

Dybvig, P. H., & Ross, S. A. (1985). Differential Information and Performance Measurement Using a Security Market Line. *Journal of Finance, 40*(2), 383–399.

Fama, E. F., & French, K. R. (1988). Dividend Yields and Expected Stock Returns. *Journal of Financial Economics, 22*(1), 3–25.

Fama, E., & French, K. R. (1989). Business Conditions and Expected Returns on Stocks and Bonds. *Journal of Financial Economics, 25*(1), 23–49.

Fama, E., & Schwert, G. W. (1977). Asset Returns and Inflation. *Journal of Financial Economics, 5*(2), 115–146.

Fung, W., & Hsieh, D. A. (1997a). Empirical Characteristics of Dynamic Trading Strategies: The Case of Hedge Funds. *Review of Financial Studies, 10*(2), 275–302.

Fung, W., & Hsieh, D. A. (1997b). Survivorship Bias and Investment Style in the Returns of CTAs. *Journal of Portfolio Management, 24*(1), 30–41.

Fung, W., & Hsieh, D. A. (2001). The Risk in Hedge Fund Strategies: Theory and Evidence from Trend Followers. *Review of Financial Studies, 14*(2), 313–341.

Glosten, L. R., & Jagannathan, R. (1994). A Contingent Claim Approach to Performance Evaluation. *Journal of Empirical Finance, 1*(2), 133–160.

Hansen, B. E. (1994). Autoregressive Conditional Density Estimation. *International Economic Review, 35*(3), 705–730.

Harvey, C. R., & Siddique, A. (2000). Conditional Skewness in Asset Pricing Tests. *Journal of Finance, 55*(3), 1263–1295.

Keim, D., & Stambaugh, R. (1986). Predicting Returns in the Stock and Bond Markets. *Journal of Financial Economics, 17*(2), 357–390.

Kimball, M. (1993). Standard Risk Aversion. *Econometrica, 61*(3), 589–611.

Kraus, A., & Litzenberger, R. H. (1976). Skewness Preference and the Valuation of Risk Assets. *Journal of Finance, 31*(4), 1085–1100.

Levy, H., & Sarnat, M. (1972). Safety First – An Expected Utility Principle. *Journal of Financial and Quantitative Analysis, 7*(3), 1829–1834.

Liang, B., & Park, H. (2007). Risk Measures for Hedge Funds: A Cross-sectional Approach. *European Financial Management, 13*(2), 333–370.

Lo, A. W. (2001). Risk Management for Hedge Funds: Introduction and Overview. *Financial Analysts Journal, 57*(6), 16–33.

Merton, R. C. (1973). An Intertemporal Asset Pricing Model. *Econometrica, 41*(5), 867–887.

Merton, R. C. (1981). On Market Timing and Investment Performance I: An Equilibrium Theory of Value for Market Forecasts. *Journal of Business, 54*(3), 363–406.

Mitchell, M., & Pulvino, T. (2001). Characteristics of Risk and Return in Risk Arbitrage. *Journal of Finance, 56*(6), 2135–2175.

Newey, W. K., & West, K. D. (1987). A Simple, Positive Semi-Definite, Heteroscedasticity and Autocorrelation Consistent Covariance Matrix. *Econometrica, 55*(3), 703–708.

Pratt, J., & Zeckhauser, R. (1987). Proper Risk Aversion. *Econometrica, 55*(1), 143–154.

Rubinstein, M. (1973). The Fundamental Theory of Parameter-Preference Security Valuation. *Journal of Financial and Quantitative Analysis, 8*(1), 61–69.

Ross, S. A. (1976). The Arbitrage Theory of Capital Asset Pricing. *Journal of Economic Theory, 13*(3), 341–360.

Tversky, A., & Kahneman, D. (1992). Advances in Prospect Theory: Cumulative Representation of Uncertainty. *Journal of Risk and Uncertainty, 5*(4), 297–323.

# CHAPTER 24

# Tail Risk Protection for Funds of Hedge Funds

**Oliver A. Schwindler**
HF-Analytics GmbH, Bamberg, Germany

## 24.1. INTRODUCTION

The events unfolding during the last decade clearly show the importance of controlling portfolio exposures to fat-tail events like the capital markets turmoil after the bankruptcy of Lehman Brothers and its contagion effects on worldwide financial markets. Although funds of hedge funds (FoHFs) were supposed to be absolute return funds, the financial crisis in 2008 clearly shows that these FoHFs are not immune to tail risk events.

Basically, there are three methods available for hedging tail risks or protecting portfolios during market sell-offs. Historically, market stress causes 'flights to quality' where investors buy high-quality, very liquid instruments, which usually results in Treasuries or bonds rallying. Therefore, short-term cash and Treasuries are simple instruments for protecting portfolios, not just during tail risk events, but also during normal market corrections. The second method is to buy contingent claims, or option-like securities, that provide insurance by an exponential price appreciation. One example would be out-of-the-money tranches on CDX or iTraxx indices, or more simply put options on the S&P 500 or call options on the Chicago Board Options Exchange (CBOE) Volatility Index (VIX). The third approach to tail risk mitigation is to invest in strategies that are negatively correlated to tail risk, like systematic, trend-following managed futures. Fung and Hsieh (2001) provide evidence that trend-following strategies empirically behave like a long position in look-back straddles and hence are an indirect hedging instrument against tail risks. Bhansali (2008) correctly points out that a dynamic adjustment of exposures, which would be more or less a zero-cost tail hedge solution, is heavily based on the assumption that liquidity will be present during financial stress. When it comes to tail risk hedging for FoHFs, only a solution based on derivatives is technically possible, besides a small allocation to trend-following managed futures strategies. For FoHFs, a tail risk hedging strategy by shifting assets directly into cash investments or Treasuries is technically not feasible due to the redemption frequencies offered by hedge funds.

Several empirical studies (e.g., Fung and Hsieh, 1997; Asness *et al.*, 2001; Agarwal and Naik, 2004; Bali *et al.*, 2011) show that hedge fund returns are exposed to market factors. Interestingly enough, Titman and Tiu (2011) argue that hedge funds with low $R^2$ values are the real alpha generators. Furthermore, Fung and Hsieh (2001) and Mitchell and Pulvino (2001) show that dynamic trading and arbitrage strategies exhibit significant tail risks. In addition, Brown and Spitzer (2006) document that hedge funds are more sensitive to market risk when the market declines and Adrian *et al.* (2013) confirm that sensitivities between hedge fund styles increase during tail risk events. Intuitively, investors would expect that FoHFs should be able to mitigate specific tail risks by diversification. However, Brown *et al.* (2012) provide evidence that FoHFs exhibit a much higher tail risk exposure than individual hedge funds. Their results suggest that tail risk exposure of FoHFs might not be diversifiable.

Given these findings, tail risk hedging is an important exercise for FoHFs managers, and investors should be concerned when tail risks are not managed in an active and proper manner. In order to protect FoHFs against tail risks, derivatives seem to be the most appropriate instrument due to their embedded leverage and their low capital requirements. The VIX is widely regarded as an indicator of investor sentiment and appetite for risk. Whaley (2000, p. 17) terms it the 'investor fear gauge.' Given its properties, which will be described in Section 24.2, the VIX is a natural fit as an underlying for a derivative strategy used for tail hedging of FoHFs. First, simply because during tail risk events, the fear of investors increases and they lose their appetite for risk, which in the end will drive up the VIX. Second, derivatives are flexible securities that do not weaken the liquidity position of a FoHF due to their implemented leverage.

## 24.2. VIX, VIX FUTURES, VIX OPTIONS, AND THE VVIX

Originally, Whaley (1993) introduced the VIX as an index of implied volatility from options on the S&P 100. In 2003, the CBOE modified the methodology for the VIX so that it now estimates implied volatility of 30-day S&P 500 options (Chicago Board Options Exchange, 2003). The new calculation methodology is not dependent on an option pricing model and uses the prices of the front month and next-to-front month at-the-money (ATM) and out-of-money (OTM) call and put options on the S&P 500. Basically, it is the expected volatility by market participants over the next 30 days of the S&P 500 (see Whaley, 2009).

It has been widely documented that VIX is negatively correlated to equity markets, but as Szado (2009) points out, that this relationship is extremely dynamic. This inverse relationship seems also to be the case for hedge funds (see Kazemi *et al.*, 2003; Amenc *et al.*, 2003). Several studies have documented the potential diversification benefits of spot VIX for equity portfolios and hedge funds (e.g., see Daigler and Rossi, 2006; Dash and Moran, 2005). The empirical study of Black (2006) suggests that the skewness and excess kurtosis of many hedge fund strategies can be eliminated by a small long exposure to spot VIX.

However, spot VIX is not directly investable. To invest in VIX, an investor can take a long position in VIX futures, which started trading at the Chicago Futures Exchange (CFE) in May 2004. Whereas spot VIX is an indicator for the expected volatility of the S&P 500 over the next 30 days, the price of the VIX future represents the current expectation of what the expected 30-day volatility will be at the expiration date. Although, VIX futures always converge to the spot VIX at expiration, there are significant disconnects between spot VIX and VIX futures. VIX futures have a number of unique characteristics when compared with other financial futures contracts. While spot VIX returns are driven by changes in the level of implied volatilities, VIX futures returns are influenced by the expectations of implied volatilities. Since spot VIX is not replicable, which means there is no cost-of-carry arbitrage between them possible, the relationship between spot VIX and VIX futures cannot be characterized by a typical cost-of carry model. Moreover, Szado (2009) documents that the returns of VIX futures exhibit a lower volatility than spot VIX, which can be attributed to the fact that volatility trends to a mean-reverting process.

Due to the skewed distribution of spot VIX levels, displayed in Figure 24.1, and due to the asymmetric return distribution of spot VIX, the normal expectation of future implied volatility levels is above the current spot VIX level. This is why VIX

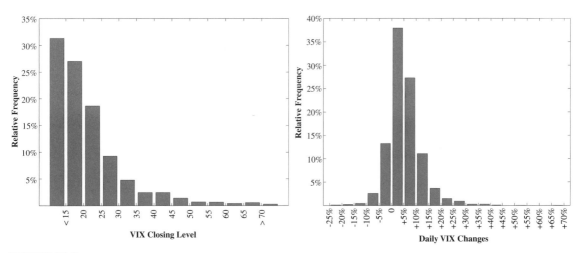

**FIGURE 24.1**
Histogram of daily closing VIX values (left) and daily VIX changes (right).
*Data from CBOE. Based on daily data from January 2004 to May 2012.*

futures trade most of the time in contango. However, during tail risk events the VIX futures market falls into backwardation as the expectation of the mean reverting kicks in.

Figure 24.2 displays two term structures that illustrate the contango situation on 22 August 2008 and the backwardation situation on 24 October 2008. On 22 August 2008, before the crash of 2008 occurred, the VIX futures market was still trading in contango, as the spot VIX was slightly below 19 while the front month VIX future was trading around 21.5 and future contracts with longer maturity were trading above these levels. However, during the financial crisis the VIX futures market traded in a hefty backwardation (e.g., on 24 October 2008). Although the spot VIX closed slight below 80, VIX futures with the shortest maturity traded around 55 and futures with a longer maturity even further below. During that period most market participants expected volatility to revert back to its mean − it was just a question of timing when such a move would occur.

The shape of the term structure determines whether investors earn more or less while holding a VIX future versus a theoretical investment in spot VIX. Figure 24.3 illustrates the performance of a theoretical investment in spot VIX (which has no roll losses) versus an investment in a fully collateralized constantly rolled front month VIX future with a daily rehedged exposure of 100%.

The difference between the two is quite significant. Holding a long position in the VIX future with the shortest maturity, rehedging such position on a daily basis in order to have 100% notional exposure, and rolling the future over every month into the new contract would have cost investors 51.88% *per annum*, whereas the evolution of the VIX does not show that kind of loss. The rationality behind these hefty roll losses is a risk premium called the volatility premium. Speculators who sell investors VIX futures contracts expect compensation

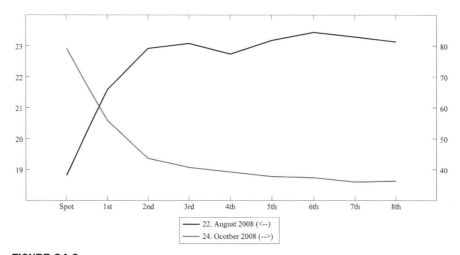

**FIGURE 24.2**
Term structure of VIX futures market.

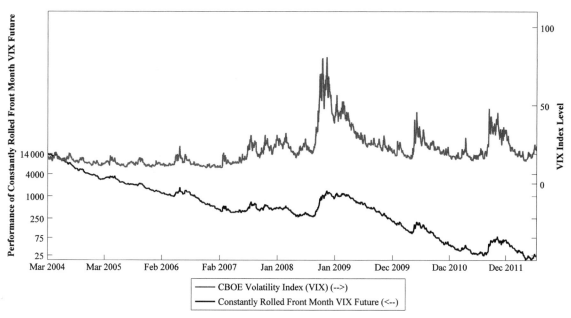

**FIGURE 24.3**
Theoretical investment in spot VIX versus VIX futures, March 2004–May 2012.

(an insurance premium or rather the volatility premium) for providing insurance against volatility spikes. As Warren (2012) points out, given these high roll losses it is prudent for long-term investors to invest in VIX futures with a higher maturity because they have lower roll losses. However, that comes at a cost and these instruments have a lower sensitivity to spot VIX.

VIX options also have unique characteristics that distinguish them from options on other financial indices. When pricing VIX options, one has to deal with the absence of a typical cost-of-carry model and, furthermore, these options should be priced in a manner that reflects the mean reverting nature of volatility. Somewhat surprisingly, several theoretical approaches to price VIX options appeared in the academic literature long before they could be traded (e.g., Whaley, 1993; Grunbichler and Longstaff, 1996; Detemple and Osakwe, 2000). Wang and Daigler (2011) come to the conclusion that the most convenient pricing model is that one of Whaley (1993). Mencia and Entana (2011) point out that one could alternatively price VIX options with the Black (1976) model like options on VIX futures, although these are options on spot VIX. However, Wang and Daigler (2011) point out that this convenience comes at a cost: OTM call (put) VIX options are underpriced (overpriced) resulting in an implied volatility skew of VIX options, which is opposite to the skew for index options. However, it is important to point out that the Whaley (1993) model for pricing VIX options is consistent with the mean reverting nature of volatility.

The CBOE began publishing the VVIX, which is a measure for the expected volatility of the 30-day forward price of the VIX, in March 2012 (Chicago Board

Options Exchange, 2012b). That new volatility index tracks the implied volatilities of nearby VIX options. The calculation method, which is the same as for the VIX, is applied to the prices of a portfolio of liquid ATM and OTM VIX options. Figure 24.4 shows a graph of the time series of the VVIX and the VIX between May 2006 and May 2012. The VVIX ranges between 60 and 145 around an average of 86, whereas the VIX ranges between 10 and 81 around an average of 24. Figure 24.4 clearly shows that VVIX exhibits the same mean reverting nature as the VIX.

In addition, Figure 24.4 shows also that both indices are positively correlated with each other. In fact, the correlation coefficient between the changes of VIX and VVIX is 0.6096. However, the conditional correlations between the two time series reveal an interesting finding. Figure 24.5 shows that as long as the VIX stays below 15, there is almost no correlation between VIX and VVIX as the coefficient is at 0.1686. However, if the VIX rises above 15, the correlation between the two indices increases to around 0.71 until VIX breaches the threshold of 30. When that happens the correlation increases even further to 0.7947, and rises up to 0.836 when the VIX moves between 35 and 40. In case the VIX trades between 40 and 45 the correlation drops off to 0.6604, but rises again up to 0.8069 when VIX breaches the level of 45. For VIX levels above 50 the correlation drops again to 0.6692.

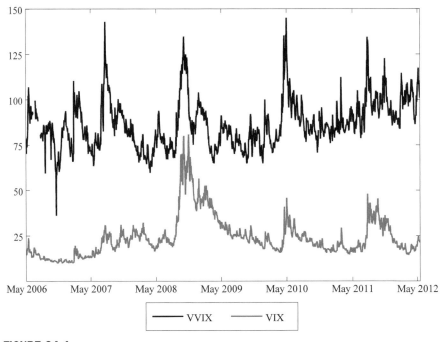

**FIGURE 24.4**
CBOE VVIX and VIX, May 2006–May 2012.
*Data from CBOE. Based on daily data from June 2006 to May 2012.*

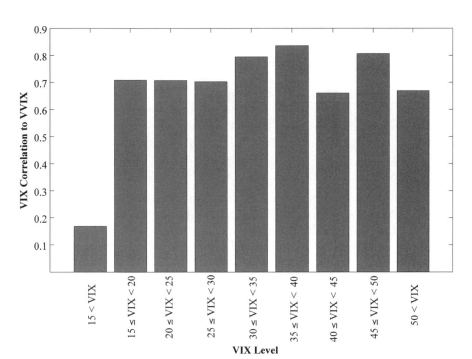

**FIGURE 24.5**
Conditional correlation between VIX and VVIX, June 2006–May 2012.
*Data from CBOE. Based on daily data from June 2006 to May 2012.*

## 24.3. TAIL RISK HEDGING

Daigler and Rossi (2006) and Chen *et al.* (2011) provide evidence that the VIX is suitable for diversification for portfolio of stocks, and Dash and Moran (2005) document that adding VIX to FoHFs reduces the portfolio volatility as well as the downside deviation of the portfolio. Black (2006) emphasizes that adding VIX to a portfolio reduces especially the kurtosis of portfolios of hedge funds. Given the fact that VIX is neither investable nor replicable, investors should rely on empirical studies that use VIX futures and options as an investment vehicle to get exposure to volatility rather than on studies that use spot VIX. Moran and Dash (2007) and Szado (2009) provide evidence that the diversification benefits are still valid for VIX futures and options as well, when it comes to portfolios of stocks. However, Alexander and Korovilas (2011) point out that investors should not underestimate the complications of adding VIX futures to an investment portfolio, as VIX futures can cause excessive roll losses which can reduce the hedging benefits to a minimum. In addition, Jones (2011) shows that a dynamic usage of VIX futures is promising.

In July 2011, the CBOE launched a new index called the CBOE VIX Tail Hedge Index (VXTH), which uses VIX call options for protecting equity portfolios against tail risks (Chicago Board Options Exchange, 2012a). The VXTH tracks the performance of a portfolio that overlays 1-month OTM VIX call options with a delta of 0.3 on the S&P 500 index. The VIX call options are held until expiration and rolled every month on the day of expiration into the next month. In order to reduce roll losses, the weight of the VIX call options in the portfolio depends on the price of the front month VIX future on expiration. In the case that the 1-month forward value of the VIX is below 15, no position in VIX call options is taken. The portfolio contains the full allocation of 1% in VIX call options when the VIX future with the shortest maturity trades above 15 or 30 at most on the expiration date. Quotes for the VIX future above 30 or 50 at most trigger a lower allocation of 50 basis points in VIX call options. In the case that the 1-month forward value of VIX trades above 50 on the expiration date, no position in VIX call options is taken.

Although the strategy endures roll losses on a standalone basis, the combination with an investment in the S&P 500 and the implemented profit taking on VIX options by the monthly rebalancing leads to an obvious outperformance of VXTH compared to the S&P 500. Looking at Figure 24.6, which displays the relative performance of VXTH versus the S&P 500 index, it is obvious that during calm periods the VXTH underperforms the S&P 500 due to the protection premium paid. However, during tail risk events the protection by VIX call options pays off.

For example, during October 2008 the 1% allocation in VIX call options purchased in September returned 2260%, which amounts to a return contribution of 22.60% at the portfolio level. On the bottom line, VXTH earned 1.48% while the S&P 500 lost 21.36% during October 2008.

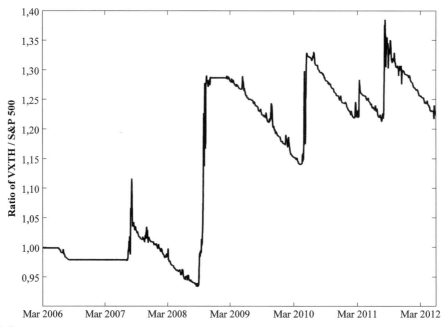

**FIGURE 24.6**
Relative performance of VXTH versus S&P 500 index, March 2006–May 2012.
*Data from S&P and CBOE. Based on daily data from March 2006 to May 2012.*

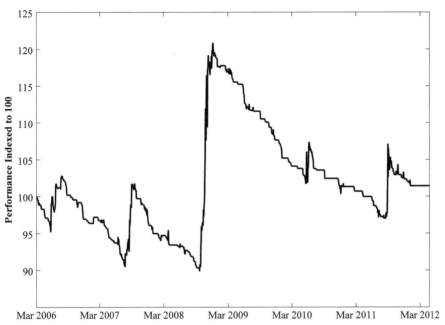

**FIGURE 24.7**
Performance of dynamic tail risk hedging strategy (standalone), March 2006–March 2012.

This chapter proposes a more dynamic tail risk hedging strategy that is also profitable on a standalone basis by minimizing the roll losses. The goal to reduce roll losses while providing protection during tail risk events is not an easy task. While analyzing the term structure of the VIX futures market it turned out that during sharp VIX explosions the futures market trades in backwardation. Given this finding, it makes sense to buy VIX call options when the VIX futures market changes from contango into backwardation (signal day). At the closing of a signal day a mixed portfolio of ATM and OTM VIX call options is purchased, where each option makes up 0.5% of the portfolio. ATM options are defined as the first strike price below the current VIX futures price of the front month and OTM options exhibit a delta of 30. The long position in VIX call options is closed out, when the VIX futures market trades back into contango. Given the short maturity of the VIX call options, profits are normally taken at expiration of the contracts. While a position is held until maturity unless the market moves back into contango, a new position is taken in ATM and OTM call options based on the current market conditions on the last trading day at closing prices. Figure 24.7 displays the performance of that strategy on a standalone basis, where no interest is earned on cash, trades are done on the closing bid and ask prices at a signal day, daily valuation is done at closing bid prices, and transaction costs are set at US$5 per options contract (half turn). In contrast to the standalone version of the VXTH options strategy, that dynamic tail hedging strategy would have been positive over the sample period from March 2006 to March 2012 and even would have returned 0.23% *per annum*.

## 24.4. TAIL RISK PROTECTION FOR FoHFs

We use the FoHF Index from EDHEC-Risk Institute to represent the FoHFs industry. Clearly, the position sizing is too big for the purpose of tail risk hedging of FoHFs, since they lost 12% during September and October 2008 while the strategy would have contributed approximately 30% at the portfolio level with a position size of 1% in VIX call options. Therefore, the VIX call option position size is set to 25 basis points for each, ATM and OTM, options for the tail risk protection strategy for FoHFs. Furthermore, the harvested gain from the option positions is invested on the month end of the following month. Moreover, as most FoHFs nowadays normally hold cash between 5% and 10% of the portfolio, we model the option strategy as an overlay strategy. The strategy can be implemented in reality in the same way, as long as the cash drawdown is not too deep. Figure 24.8 displays the cash drawdown of the strategy, whereas the drawdown value is set to zero every time a tail risk event occurs.

Figure 24.8 clearly shows that the hardest time was from December 2008 to May 2010. During that period the strategy would have drawn slightly over 7% from the cash reserves. Figure 24.9 plots the cumulative returns of EDHEC-Risk (FoHF Index and the same index in combination with the dynamic tail risk hedging strategy as overlay over 6 years ending in March 2012). Table 24.1 displays the characteristics of the two portfolios.

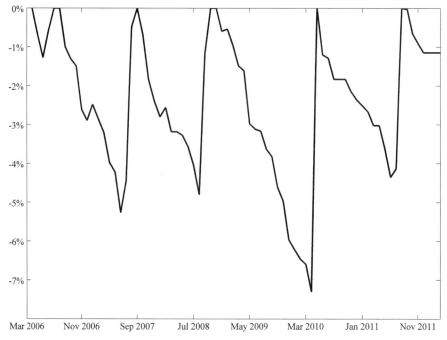

**FIGURE 24.8**
Cash drawdown of dynamic tail hedging strategy, March 2006—March 2012.

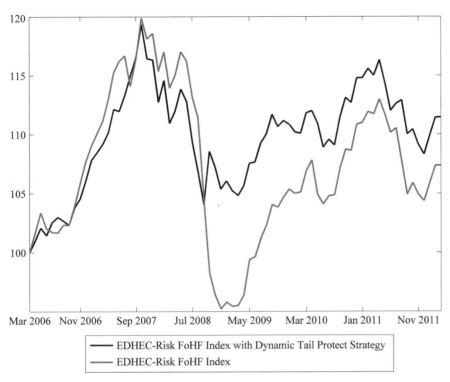

**FIGURE 24.9**
Cumulative returns of EDHEC-Risk FoHF Index with tail protection, March 2006–March 2012.

| Table 24.1 | Characteristics of the Tail Risk-Protected EDHEC-Risk FoHF Index | |
| --- | --- | --- |
| | **EDHEC-Risk FoHF Index** | **Tail Risk-Protected EDHEC-Risk FoHF Index** |
| Annualized return (% *per annum*) | 1.18 | 1.80 |
| Volatility (% *per annum*) | 6.11 | 5.09 |
| Loss volatility (% *per annum*) | 4.77 | 3.53 |
| Maximum drawdown (%) | 20.59 | 12.83 |
| Sharpe ratio | 0.15 | 0.30 |
| Sortino ratio | 0.25 | 0.51 |
| Skewness | −1.32 | −0.34 |
| Kurtosis | 5.62 | 3.25 |

Data from EDHEC-Risk Institute, CBOE. Based on monthly returns from March 2006 to March 2012. The Sharpe ratio is calculated with a risk-free rate of 0.25%, while the Sortino ratio uses a minimum return threshold of 0%.

As can be seen from both exhibits, adding the dynamic tail risk protection overlay improves the performance of FoHFs meaningfully, as the tail-protected version clearly has outperformed the EDHEC-Risk FoHF Index, although the means are not statically significant different from each other. Nevertheless, the hedged portfolio has a higher annualized return of 60bps *per annum* with a lower volatility of 5.09% compared to 6.11% for the EDHEC-Risk FoHF Index. Moreover, the maximum drawdown can be significantly reduced from 20.59% for the EDHEC-Risk FoHF Index to just 12.83% while adding VIX call options in a dynamic manner. The doubled values for both the Sharpe ratio and the Sortino ratio document the improved risk-to-return profile of the tail risk-protected portfolio. Furthermore, the skewness and kurtosis of the monthly return distribution for the hedged version is considerably lower than the statistics for the EDHEC-Risk FoHF Index.

Looking at Figure 24.9 it is obvious that the tail-protected strategy would have had a positive month in October 2008. One explanation for the unorthodox finding could be the late stale pricing of hedge funds, which gets even worse on the FoHFs level. Portfolios of FoHFs are normally priced with a certain delay, whereas the VIX options are priced without a delay.

## CONCLUSION

Protecting FoHFs against tail risks is an important task for portfolio managers as well as investors. However, as Brown *et al.* (2012) document, overdiversification across different hedge funds is not the right way to go because increased diversification leads to a higher tail risk, at least for FoHFs. This study shows that a dynamic tail hedging strategy can alleviate the roll losses normally associated with investments in volatility and even add value in different types of forms. The proposed strategy increases FoHFs returns while it reduces the volatility and, more importantly the strategy enables FoHFs to decrease their maximum drawdown significantly.

## References

Adrian, T., Brunnermeier, M. K., & Nguyen, H.-L. (2013). Hedge Fund Tail Risk. In J. G. Haubrich, & A. W. Lo (Eds.), *Quantifying Systemic Risk*. Chicago, IL, forthcoming: University of Chicago Press.

Agarwal, V., & Naik, N. Y. (2004). Risks and Portfolio Decisions Involving Hedge Funds. *Review of Financial Studies, 17*(1), 63−98.

Alexander, C., & Korovilas, D. (2011). *The Hazards of Volatility Diversification. Working Paper*. Reading: ICMA Centre.

Amenc, N., El Bied, S., & Martellini, L. (2003). Predictability in Hedge Fund Returns. *Financial Analysts Journal, 59*(5), 32−46.

Asness, C. S., Krail, R., & Liew, J. M. (2001). Do Hedge Funds Hedge? *Journal of Portfolio Management, 28*(1), 6−19.

Bali, T. G., Brown, S. J., & Caglayan, M. O. (2011). Do hedge funds' exposures to risk factors predict their future returns? *Journal of Financial Economics, 101*(1), 36−68.

Bhansali, V. (2008). Tail Risk Management. *The Journal of Portfolio Management, 34*(4), 68−75.

Black, F. (1976). The Pricing of Commodity Contracts. *Journal of Financial Economics, 3*(1−2), 167−179.

Black, K. (2006). Improving Hedge Fund Risk Exposures by Hedging Equity Market Volatility, or How the VIX Ate My Kurtosis. *Journal of Trading, 1*(2), 6–15.

Brown, S. J., & Spitzer, J. F. (2006). *Caught by the Tail: Tail Risk Neutrality and Hedge Fund Returns. Working Paper.* Available at SSRN: http://ssrn.com/abstract=1852526.

Brown, S. J., Gregoriou, G., & Pascalau, R. (2012). Is it Possible to Overdiversify? The Case of Funds of Hedge Funds. *Review of Asset Pricing Studies, 2*(1), 89–110.

Chicago Board Options Exchange (2003). *The CBOE Volatility Index – VIX. Working Paper.* Chicago, IL: CBOE.

Chicago Board Options Exchange (2012a). *CBOE VIX Tail Hedge Index. Working Paper.* Chicago, IL: CBOE.

Chicago Board Options Exchange (2012b). *Double the Fun With CBOE's VVIX Index. Working Paper.* Chicago, IL: CBOE.

Chen, H.-C., Chung, S.-L., & Ho, K.-Y. (2011). The Diversification Effects of Volatility-Related Assets. *Journal of Banking and Finance, 35*(5), 1179–1189.

Daigler, R. T., & Rossi, L. (2006). A Portfolio of Stocks and Volatility. *Journal of Investing, 15*(2), 99–106.

Dash, S., & Moran, M. T. (2005). VIX as a Companion for Hedge Fund Portfolios. *Journal of Alternative Investments, 8*(3), 75–80.

Detemple, J., & Osakwe, C. (2000). The Valuation of Volatility Options. *European Finance Review, 4*(1), 21–50.

Fung, W., & Hsieh, D. (1997). Empirical Characteristics of Dynamic Trading Strategies: The Case of Hedge Funds. *Review of Financial Studies, 10*(2), 275–302.

Fung, W., & Hsieh, D. (2001). The Risk of Hedge Fund Strategies: Theory and Evidence from Trend Followers. *Review of Financial Studies, 14*(2), 313–341.

Grunbichler, A., & Longstaff, F. A. (1996). Valuing Futures and Options on Volatility. *Journal of Banking and Finance, 20*(6), 985–1001.

Jones, T. L. (2011). A Look at the Use of VIX Futures in Investment Portfolios: Buy-and-Hold versus Tactical Allocation. *Journal of Trading, 6*(2), 22–29.

Kazemi, H., Schneeweis, T., & Martin, G. (2003). Understanding Hedge Fund Performance: Research Issues Revised – Part II. *Journal of Alternative Investments, 5*(4), 8–30.

Mencia, J., & Entana, E. (2011). *Valuation of VIX Derivatives. Working Paper.* London: Centre for Economic Policy Research.

Mitchell, M., & Pulvino, T. (2001). Characteristics of risk and return in risk arbitrage. *Journal of Finance, 56*(6), 2135–2175.

Moran, M. T., & Dash, S. (2007). VIX Futures and Options Pricing and Using Volatility Products to Manage Downside Risk and Improve Efficiency in Equity Portfolios. *Journal of Trading, 2*(3), 96–105.

Szado, E. (2009). VIX Futures and Options: A Case Study of Portfolio Diversification During the 2008 Financial Crisis. *Journal of Alternative Investments, 12*(9), 68–85.

Titman, S., & Tiu, C. (2011). Do the Best Hedge Funds Hedge? *Review of Financial Studies, 24*(1), 123–168.

Wang, Z., & Daigler, R. T. (2011). The Performance of VIX Option Pricing Models: Empirical Evidence Beyond Simulation. *Journal of Futures Markets, 31*(3), 251–281.

Warren, G. J. (2012). Can Investing in Volatility Help Meet Your Portfolio Objectives? *Journal of Portfolio Management, 38*(2), 82–98.

Whaley, R. E. (1993). Derivatives on Market Volatility: Hedging Tools Long Overdue. *Journal of Derivatives, 1*(1), 71–84.

Whaley, R. R. (2000). The Investor Fear Gauge. *Journal of Portfolio Management, 26*(3), 12–17.

Whaley, R. E. (2009). Understanding the VIX. *The Journal of Portfolio Management, 35*(3), 98–105.

# CHAPTER 25

# Autocorrelation, Bias, and Fat Tails: An Analysis of Funds of Hedge Funds

**Martin Eling**

Professor Dr. Martin Eling, Institute of Insurance Economics I.VW-HSG, University of St. Gallen, St.Gallen, Switzerland

## 25.1. INTRODUCTION

Funds of hedge funds (FoHFs) have become an increasingly popular investment vehicle in the past decade, especially due to their low correlation with stocks and bond markets. However, there have also been substantial setbacks for this new asset class, especially during the financial crisis, when some funds could not meet investor expectations. When evaluating the performance of FoHFs using the classical Sharpe ratio, these funds appear to offer a remarkable opportunity, but using the Sharpe ratio ignores a number of important characteristics of this asset class, especially the existence of autocorrelation, bias, and fat tails. In this chapter, we build on the work of Eling (2006) to analyze the performance of FoHFs when these three important qualities are taken into account. We extend Eling's (2006) paper by focusing on FoHFs, considering different subperiods in order to analyze the effect of the financial crisis and using a long time horizon in the analysis.

Both hedge funds and FoHFs have been the subject of much research since the mid 1990s. In the literature, hedge funds' performance is often evaluated using classical performance measures such as the Sharpe ratio, under which they appear to be very attractive (e.g., see Ackermann *et al.*, 1999; Liang, 1999; Gregoriou and Rouah, 2002; Nicholas, 2004). However, a number of researchers discover problems concerning hedge fund returns that make their attractiveness more ambiguous (e.g., see Asness *et al.*, 2001; Lo, 2001; Favre and Galéano, 2002; Fung and Hsieh, 2002; Amin and Kat, 2003; Gregoriou, 2002; Kouwenberg, 2003; Amenc *et al.*, 2003). When hedge fund returns are compared to those of traditional investments, they exhibit significant autocorrelation, contain systematic estimation errors called bias, and tend to stronger deviations from normally distributed returns. As we show in this chapter, FoHFs are affected by these types of problems as well.

Each of these problems has been analyzed in the literature. For example, Kat and Lu (2002) and Getmansky *et al.* (2004) examine the statistics of hedge fund returns and discuss, among other issues, the autocorrelation of returns. Cappochi and Huebner (2004) and Ammann and Moerth (2005) analyze hedge fund performance using multifactor models and provide a detailed bias discussion. Favre and Galéano (2002) use a modified value at risk (VaR) for hedge fund evaluation with consideration of the higher moments of return distribution so as to incorporate the fat-tail problem in performance measurement. Gregoriou and Gueyie (2003) rely on this latter approach to develop a modified Sharpe ratio that takes the higher moments of the return distribution into account.

Eling (2006) analyzes all three problems in one integrated performance measurement framework. For this purpose an adjusted version of the modified Sharpe ratio presented by Gregoriou and Gueyie (2003) is developed. In this chapter, we build on these works to analyze the performance of FoHFs. We consider the performance of FoHF indices provided by Hedge Fund Research (HFR) over the period 1994–2011. Different subperiods are considered in order to analyze the effect of the financial crisis on performance measurement. Moreover, hedge fund indices, as well as traditional benchmark indices, are included in the analysis so as to compare the performance of FoHFs with other relevant asset classes.

The remainder of this chapter is structured as follows. We first discuss the data and the strategies reflected in the data. We then present classical performance measurement using the Sharpe ratio and highlight its inherent problems. Building on these observations, we then integrate the three above-discussed problems in the performance measurement of funds of hedge funds. Finally, we present the implications for the evaluation of hedge funds by integrating all problems in one common framework and measuring the adjusted performance of FoHFs. Here we also discuss the performance of FoHFs in different subperiods.

## 25.2. DATA AND STRATEGIES

In the empirical analysis, we consider monthly returns of the HFR indices over the period from January 1994 to December 2011. HFR sorts both hedge funds and FoHFs into four strategy groups depending on their investment focus. For the hedge funds, these groups are Equity Hedge, Event Driven, Macro, and Relative Value. For FoHFs, the four categories are Conservative, Diversified, Market Defensive, and Strategic. Various hedge fund and FoHFs strategies are thus reflected in the indices. We also consider two aggregate indices: the Fund Weighted Composite and the FOF Composite. In Table 25.1, the individual strategies are presented and a brief description of each is provided (for the strategy description, see Hedge Fund Research, 2012).

All funds included in the HFR indices report returns net of all fees in US$. Furthermore, HFR requires all funds to have a minimum of US$50 million under management or have been actively trading for at least 12 months. The HFR database underlying the indices tracks the performance of more than 6500 funds and FoHFs, and is one of the large hedge funds databases frequently used in academia and practice (e.g., see Deuskar *et al.*, 2011). The HFR indices also are often considered in academic literature (e.g., see Jagannathan *et al.*, 2010).

The hedge fund indices are compared with four benchmark indices — two measuring stock performance and two measuring bond performance. We consider one world index (MSCI World) and one index with a focus on the US capital market (S&P 500) for the stocks. For the bonds, one index tracks the performance of government bonds (BofA/ML Global Government Bond) and one the performance of corporate bonds (BofA/ML Global Broad Corporate Bond). Here, also, one index is worldwide (the government index), while the other focuses on the US capital market (the corporate bond index). All indices were calculated on a US$ basis and thus it is the perspective of a US investor that is modeled. To measure returns from price changes and dividends, we consider performance indices. The data for the benchmark indices was collected from the Datastream database.

## 25.3. CLASSICAL PERFORMANCE MEASUREMENT

When we discuss risk-adjusted performance in this chapter, we always assume that the fund's return is related to a suitable risk measure. Traditionally, when hedge fund performance is analyzed, the Sharpe ratio is chosen as the performance measure and a comparison is made between the Sharpe ratios of other funds or market indices (e.g., see Ackermann *et al.* 1999). The Sharpe ratio measures the mean excess return over the risk-free interest rate and relates it to the standard deviation of the returns. Using historical monthly returns $r_{i1}, \ldots, r_{iT}$ for security $i$, the Sharpe ratio ($SR$) is given as:

$$SR_i = \frac{r_i^d - r_f}{\sigma_i},$$

where $r_i^d = (r_{i1} + \cdots + r_{iT})/T$ is the average monthly return for security $i$, $r_f$ the risk-free monthly interest rate, and $\sigma_i = (((r_{i1} - r_i^d)^2 + \cdots + (r_{iT} - r_i^d)^2)/(T-1))^{0.5}$

| Table 25.1 | Hedge Fund Strategies | |
|---|---|---|
| **Strategy Group** | **Index** | **Description** |
| Hedge funds | Fund Weighted Composite | Aggregated index comprising the performance of all the hedge fund strategies |
| | Equity Hedge (Total) | Positions both long and short in primarily equity and equity derivative securities |
| | Event Driven (Total) | Positions in companies currently or prospectively involved in corporate transactions of a wide variety, including, but not limited to, mergers, restructurings, financial distress, tender offers, shareholder buybacks, and other capital structure adjustments |
| | Macro (Total) | Broad range of strategies in which the investment process is predicated on movements in underlying economic variables and the impact these have on equity, fixed income, currency, and commodity markets |
| | Relative Value (Total) | Positions in which the investment thesis is predicated on realization of a valuation discrepancy in the relationship between multiple securities |
| FoHFs | FOF Composite | Aggregated index comprising the performance of all the funds of hedge funds strategies |
| | Conservative | Investing in funds that engage in more 'conservative' strategies such as equity market neutral, fixed-income arbitrage, and convertible arbitrage |
| | Diversified | Investing in a variety of strategies among multiple managers |
| | Market Defensive | Investing in funds that engage in short-biased strategies such as short selling and managed futures |
| | Strategic | Investing in funds that engage in more opportunistic strategies such as emerging markets, sector specific, and equity hedge |
| Benchmark indices | S&P 500 | Aggregated index comprising the performance of 500 large US stocks |
| | MSCI World | Aggregated index comprising the performance of stocks from 24 countries |
| | BofA/ML Global Government Bond | Aggregated index comprising the performance of government bonds |
| | BofA/ML Global Broad Corporate Bond | Aggregated index comprising the performance of corporate bonds |

BofA/ML, Bank of America/Merrill Lynch.

the estimated standard deviation of the monthly return generated by security *i*. The returns are calculated at the end of each month. In light of the historically low interest rates of the last few years, we decided to use a constant risk-free interest rate of 0% per month. Alternatively, a rolling interest rate, an average interest rate for the period under consideration, or the interest rate at the beginning of the investigation period could be used. Any of these alternatives will yield different numbers, but the conclusions derived from the numbers are unaffected by this variation. Performance measurement results based on the Sharpe ratio are shown in Table 25.2.

When the Sharpe ratio is used as the performance measure, both hedge funds and FoHFs on average yield a better performance than traditional investments; the performance of the aggregated Fund Weighted Composite index (0.35) is higher than the maximum performance of the traditional investments (0.34, regarding the BofA/ML Global Broad Corporate Bond). Event Driven (0.42) and Relative Value hedge funds (0.54) achieve a much higher performance than stocks and bonds. Considering the FOF Composite index, the performance is on average lower (0.25), but selected FoHFs strategies such as Conservative (0.35) or Market Defensive (0.36) perform, again, far better than traditional investments. Thus, based on the traditional Sharpe ratio, we conclude that both hedge fund and FoHF indices exhibit better performance than traditional investment indices. Note, also, that the performance of the aggregated FoHF index is lower than the performance of the aggregated hedge fund index. One reason for this could be the additional fees required by FoHFs managers. We do not examine the statistical significance in the differences of the Sharpe ratios on the basis of the widespread Jobson and Korkie (1981) statistic, as this test assumes normally distributed and not autocorrelated returns. As shown in the following, neither condition is usually present in the case of hedge funds.

## 25.4. PROBLEMS OF CLASSIC PERFORMANCE MEASUREMENT

The results for the classical Sharpe ratio presented in the last section can be found in comparable form in many academic and practitioner publications. However, the literature points out that there are a number of problems with hedge fund performance measurement. We concentrate on three of these in the following, specifically that the returns of hedge funds are autocorrelated, systematically distorted, and deviate from normally distributed returns. We provide an overview of each of these problems in the following paragraphs.

Autocorrelation results from difficulties in the monthly valuation of the investments. If, for example, a valuation is impossible because of illiquid positions, the hedge fund manager takes the return of the last month or an estimation of the market value (see Kat, 2002, p. 110). Table 25.3 (part A) gives the first-order autocorrelation value and the Ljung and Box (1978) statistic,

**Table 25.2** Performance Measurement Results for the Sharpe Ratio

| Index | Hedge Funds | | | | | FoHFs | | | | | Benchmark Indices | | | |
|---|---|---|---|---|---|---|---|---|---|---|---|---|---|---|
| | Fund Weighted Composite | Equity Hedge (Total) | Event Driven (Total) | Macro (Total) | Relative Value (Total) | FOF Composite | Conservative | Diversified | Market Defensive | Strategic | S&P 500 | MSCI World | BofA ML Global Government Bond | BofA ML Global Broad Corporate Bond |
| Monthly return ($r_i^-$) (%) | 0.74 | 0.85 | 0.84 | 0.70 | 0.68 | 0.44 | 0.42 | 0.42 | 0.58 | 0.49 | 0.72 | 0.60 | 0.53 | 0.55 |
| Standard deviation ($\sigma_i$) (%) | 2.09 | 2.73 | 2.01 | 1.93 | 1.26 | 1.76 | 1.21 | 1.81 | 1.63 | 2.53 | 4.53 | 4.54 | 1.95 | 1.61 |
| Sharpe ratio ($SR_i$) | 0.35 | 0.31 | 0.42 | 0.36 | 0.54 | 0.25 | 0.35 | 0.23 | 0.36 | 0.20 | 0.16 | 0.13 | 0.27 | 0.34 |

**Table 25.3** Autocorrelation and Higher Moments of the Return Distribution

| Index | Hedge Funds | | | | | FoHFs | | | | | Benchmark Indices | | | |
|---|---|---|---|---|---|---|---|---|---|---|---|---|---|---|
| | Fund Weighted Composite | Equity Hedge (Total) | Event Driven (Total) | Macro (Total) | Relative Value (Total) | FOF Composite | Conservative | Diversified | Market Defensive | Strategic | S&P 500 | MSCI World | BofA ML Global Government Bond | BofA ML Global Broad Corporate Bond |
| *(A) Autocorrelation* | | | | | | | | | | | | | | |
| Autocorrelation ($\rho_i$) | 0.28 | 0.26 | 0.10 | 0.10 | 0.49 | 0.37 | 0.49 | 0.38 | 0.05 | 0.32 | 0.09 | 0.13 | 0.10 | 0.20 |
| Ljung–Box statistic (LB) | 16.94 *** | 14.99 *** | 31.00 *** | 2.01 | 52.54 *** | 30.12 *** | 51.92 *** | 31.28 *** | 0.44 | 22.94 *** | 1.96 | 3.94 ** | 2.38 | 8.81 ** |
| *(B) Higher moments of return distribution* | | | | | | | | | | | | | | |
| Skewness ($S_i$) | −0.62 | −0.21 | −1.26 | 0.18 | −2.84 | −0.66 | −1.71 | −0.45 | −0.04 | −0.53 | −0.63 | −0.71 | 0.11 | −0.91 |
| Excess ($E_i$) | 2.39 | 1.88 | 3.89 | 0.91 | 15.43 | 3.51 | 6.74 | 3.69 | 0.36 | 3.58 | 0.84 | 1.41 | 0.42 | 4.80 |
| Jarque–Bera statistic ($JB_i$) | 65.48 *** | 33.45 *** | 193.6 *** | 8.51 *** | 2433.7 *** | 126.4 *** | 513.2 *** | 129.8 *** | 1.24 | 125.40 *** | 20.86 *** | 36.08 *** | 2.09 | 237.5 *** |

Significant at *10%, **5%, and ***1%.

which is used to check the statistical significance of the autocorrelation values. Here, the first-order autocorrelation ($\rho_i$) of security $i$ is calculated as:

$$\rho_i = \sum_{t=2}^{T}\left(r_{it}-r_i^d\right)\left(r_{it-1}-r_i^d\right) \Big/ \sum_{t=1}^{T}\left(r_{it}-r_i^d\right)^2.$$

The Ljung and Box statistic ($LB_i$) of security $i$ is given by:

$$LB_i = (T \times (T+2))/(T-1) \times \rho_i^2.$$

$LB_i$ is $\chi^2$-distributed with 1 degree of freedom.

Four out of the five FoHF indices are highly autocorrelated. Exactly the same result is observed for the hedge fund indices. Apart from Macro and Market Defensive, all hedge fund and FoHFs strategies exhibit statistically significant test values. It thus seems that FoHFs are subject to autocorrelation to the same extent as are hedge funds. The degree of autocorrelation is much smaller for the traditional indices. The returns of the corporate bond indices are, however, also autocorrelated. One consequence of the autocorrelation for performance measurement is that it might lead to an underestimation of the standard deviation of returns (see Asness et al., 2001, p. 10). In this case, the Sharpe ratio will be overestimated (see Lo, 2002, p. 37).

The database of the hedge fund indices exhibits systematic distortions, which can affect the measurement result in the sense that index returns are too high (see Ackermann et al., 1999, pp. 863−865). We typically distinguish among two forms of this distortion: survivorship bias and backfilling bias.[1] Survivorship bias arises because an index considers only those funds that are alive and report data to the database vendor. Unsuccessful funds that have been discontinued, perhaps due to bad performance, and removed from the database, are not considered. The database thus may provide an unrealistically positive picture of the reality. Backfilling bias exists because many hedge fund data providers integrate past returns of new funds in their databases. However, only successful funds have an incentive to report past performance. Thus, backfilling can also lead to an unrealistically positive representation of the reality. HFR, however, only allows funds to submit data following the integration into an index so that this sort of bias should not be a problem for the HFR indices.

Many hedge funds use derivative instruments, which might lead to an asymmetric return distribution and fat tails also for FoHFs. For this reason, it cannot generally be assumed that fund returns are well described by a normal distribution. In this case, the higher moments of the returns (skewness and excess) deviate from zero. A negative skewness and positive excess kurtosis are

---

[1]There are three other types of bias (selection, liquidation, and double counting) that are not discussed here in detail because they typically cannot be quantified. See Lhabitant (2002, pp. 133−136).

unattractive features for risk-adverse investors because they generally indicate a higher probability of large losses than for normally distributed returns (see Kat, 2003, p. 75; Favre and Signer, 2002, p. 35). Using the Jarque and Bera (1987) statistic, we test whether the values of skewness and excess are consistent with the assumption of normally distributed returns. The values of skewness, excess, and the Jarque–Bera statistic are shown in part (B) of Table 25.3. The skewness ($S_i$) and excess ($E_i$) of security $i$ are given by:

$$S_i = \left(\frac{1}{T}\sum_{t=1}^{T}\left(r_{it} - r_i^{\mathrm{d}}\right)^3\right) \Big/ \sigma_i^3 \text{ and } E_i = \left(\frac{1}{T}\sum_{t=1}^{T}\left(r_{it} - r_i^{\mathrm{d}}\right)^4\right) \Big/ \sigma_i^4 - 3.$$

The Jarque–Bera statistic ($JB_i$) of security $i$ is:

$$JB_i = \frac{T}{6}\left(S_i^2 + \frac{1}{4}E_i^2\right).$$

$JB_i$ is $\chi^2$-distributed with 2 degrees of freedom.

In light of the fact that FoHFs represent portfolios of single hedge funds, it could be expected that FoHFs are closer to a normal distribution. However, this expectation is not met by our data. In fact, according to the results of this test, only a few indices fulfill the assumption of normally distributed returns. The returns of all hedge fund indices display the unattractive combination of negative skewness and positive excess kurtosis, with only Macro as an exception. This combination also occurs for three of the four market indices, but their values for skewness and excess kurtosis are less extreme than those shown for many of the hedge funds. On the basis of the Jarque–Bera statistic, the assumption of normally distributed hedge fund returns is valid only for the Market Defensive strategy. However, it is not only the hedge fund indices that display these characteristics; the monthly returns of the S&P 500, the MSCI World, and the BofA/ML Global Government Bond index also fail to display a normal distribution.

The higher moments of the return distribution are not considered by the classical Sharpe ratio. Thus, the higher probability of large losses for some hedge funds is disregarded and their risk possibly underestimated.

## 25.5. INTEGRATING THE PROBLEMS IN PERFORMANCE MEASUREMENT

We now consider approaches for integrating the above-described three performance measurement problems. An easy way of integrating autocorrelation is to calculate the standard deviation not on the basis of monthly returns, but on the basis of quarterly returns (see Asness *et al.*, 2001, p. 11) (another approach to dealing with autocorrelation is unsmoothing the returns; see Kat and Lu, 2002, p. 16). Then, the monthly and quarterly values are annualized in order to compare them. The annual standard deviation of security $i$ can be calculated as (see Dorfleitner, 2002, pp. 228–229):

$$\sigma_i^{\tau} = \sqrt{\left(\left(1+r_i^d\right)^2+\sigma_i^2\right)^{\tau}-\left(1+r_i^d\right)^{2\tau}},$$

where $\tau$ denotes the number of considered time intervals (with monthly returns (quarterly returns) $\tau = 12\ (4)$). Table 25.4 (part A) shows the results.

Without autocorrelation, the standard deviation should remain unchanged. However, it instead rises for most of the strategies (e.g., Conservative $(+43.64\%)$ or Strategic $(+27.75\%)$) and remains almost unchanged for a few strategies (e.g., Macro $(+4.96\%)$). The standard deviation also rises for the traditional indices (e.g., MSCI World $(+35.18\%)$).

Systematic distortion of the database (bias problem) cannot be eliminated. To consider it nonetheless, however, results from investigation of the bias problem are used to estimate distortion of the database in this case. Estimations of survivorship bias range from 0.01 to 0.36 percentage points and are on average about 0.18 percentage points per month.[2] The estimations of backfilling bias range from 0.00 to 0.12 percentage points and are on average about 0.08 percentage points per month.[3] As there is no backfilling bias for CSFB, only the survivorship bias can be considered in our investigation.[4]

To consider the fat-tail problem in the performance measurement, a risk measure that shows the skewness and excess of the return distribution is needed. We consider the modified VaR presented by Favre and Galéano (2002) for this purpose. Under this approach, the well-known formula for the standard VaR, $VaR_i = -(z_\alpha\sigma_i + r_i^d)w$, where $w$ denotes the value of the investment, is modified in such a way that the alpha quantile of the standard normal distribution $z_\alpha$ is replaced by the value of the Cornish–Fisher expansion, i.e., $MVaR_i = -(z_{CFi}\sigma_i + r_i^d)w$.

The value of the Cornish–Fisher expansion is calculated as the alpha quantile of the standard normal distribution plus adjustments for skewness and excess:

$$\left(z_{CF_i} = z_\alpha + \frac{1}{6}\left(z_\alpha^2-1\right)S_i + \frac{1}{24}\left(z_\alpha^3-3z_\alpha\right)E_i-\frac{1}{36}\left(2z_\alpha^3-5z_\alpha\right)S_i^2\right).$$

---

[2]This average value results from the arithmetic mean of the estimated values from 16 investigations of the survivorship bias problem. See Eling (2006) for more details.

[3]This average value results from the arithmetic mean of the estimated values from five investigations of the backfilling bias problem. See Eling (2006) for more details.

[4]See Amenc et al. (2003) and Christiansen et al. (2003), who correct the hedge fund returns by about 0.21 and 0.25 percentage points per month. Liang (2000, pp. 322–325) and Edwards and Caglayan (2001, p. 1007) point out that the distortion can differ between different hedge fund strategies. In addition, Ammann and Moerth (2005, p. 230) show that the distortion can differ between small and large funds. However, documenting the distortion for different strategies or fund size is not possible here due to missing data.

**Table 25.4** Annual Standard Deviation and Modified Sharpe Ratio

| Index | Fund Weighted Composite | Hedge Funds | | | | FoHFs | | | | | Benchmark Indices | | | |
|---|---|---|---|---|---|---|---|---|---|---|---|---|---|---|
| | | Equity Hedge (Total) | Event Driven (Total) | Macro (Total) | Relative Value (Total) | FOF Composite | Conservative | Diversified | Market Defensive | Strategic | S&P 500 | MSCI World | BofA ML Global Government Bond | BofA ML Global Broad Corporate Bond |
| *(A) Annual standard deviation* | | | | | | | | | | | | | | |
| Annual σ (monthly) (%) | 7.86 | 10.41 | 7.64 | 7.23 | 4.71 | 6.41 | 4.39 | 6.57 | 6.02 | 9.27 | 17.08 | 16.88 | 7.16 | 5.91 |
| Annual σ (quarterly) (%) | 10.56 | 13.87 | 11.40 | 7.59 | 7.93 | 8.42 | 6.30 | 8.57 | 6.62 | 11.84 | 21.56 | 22.82 | 9.32 | 7.81 |
| *(B) Modified Sharpe ratio* | | | | | | | | | | | | | | |
| VaR ($VaR_i$) | 4.12 | 5.50 | 3.83 | 3.79 | 2.26 | 3.65 | 2.39 | 3.79 | 3.21 | 5.39 | 9.82 | 9.96 | 3.99 | 3.19 |
| Modified VaR ($MVaR_i$) | 5.94 | 7.08 | 6.32 | 3.93 | 5.61 | 5.66 | 4.49 | 5.81 | 3.40 | 8.23 | 12.14 | 12.96 | 4.01 | 5.57 |
| ($MVaR_i/VaR_i$) − 1 (%) | 44.17 | 28.68 | 64.98 | 3.62 | 148.84 | 55.03 | 87.76 | 53.37 | 5.90 | 52.61 | 23.64 | 30.16 | 0.52 | 74.58 |
| Modified Sharpe ratio ($MSR_i$) (%) | 0.12 | 0.12 | 0.13 | 0.18 | 0.12 | 0.08 | 0.09 | 0.07 | 0.17 | 0.06 | 0.06 | 0.05 | 0.13 | 0.10 |

We then follow Gregoriou and Gueyie (2003) and calculate a modified Sharpe ratio (MSR), in which the standard deviation is replaced by the modified VaR:

$$MSR_i = \frac{r_i^d - r_f}{MVaR_i}.$$

The results of the standard VaR, the modified VaR, and the modified Sharpe ratio are given in part (B) of Table 25.4, where the VaR is calculated for a confidence level of 1% ($z_\alpha = 2.326$) and $w = 100$ US$. We also show the change in risk by comparing the value at risk in the standard and the modified versions.

The risk of FoHFs is much higher with the modified value at risk. For the Conservative strategy, the risk increases by 88%; the Strategic index incurs a risk increase of 53%. In contrast, risk rises only moderately for the market indices (i.e., 24% for the S&P 500 and only 1% for the government bond index). Only the corporate bond index shows a larger increase. The modified Sharpe ratio relativizes the outperformance of FoHFs in relation to stocks and bonds. For example, the Conservative strategy now shows worse performance than the bond indices. The performance of the Market Defensive index still looks very good, since it has only a very slight increase in risk. The modified Sharpe ratio of the aggregated FoHF index is 0.08%, in comparison to 0.13%, the maximum for the traditional investments.

Note that the results depend on the confidence level chosen, since the confidence level determines (over the Cornish–Fisher expansion) the influence of the higher moments on the modified VaR. We consider a confidence level of 99%; in the literature, the modified VaR is typically evaluated for a confidence level of either 95% or 99% (see Favre and Galéano, 2002; Favre and Signer, 2002; Gregoriou and Gueyie, 2003; Gregoriou, 2004).

## 25.6. ADJUSTED HEDGE FUND PERFORMANCE MEASUREMENT

We now examine all three problems of hedge fund performance measurement in one common framework. We use the three-step approach presented in Eling (2006). First, the autocorrelation problem is mitigated by using the standard deviation based on quarterly returns instead of monthly returns. The recalculated version of the annual standard deviation of quarterly returns on a monthly basis is called the adjusted standard deviation ($\sigma_{Ai}$). Therefore, the annual standard deviation (on a quarterly basis) is divided by the root of 12. The bias problem is then dealt with by reducing the hedge fund returns using the estimated bias adjustment of 0.18 percentage points per month. The reduced monthly returns are denoted as adjusted monthly returns ($r_{Ai}^d$). As an intermediate step, we can now calculate an adjusted Sharpe ratio, given as $ASR_i = (r_{Ai}^d - r_f)/\sigma_{Ai}$, based on the adjusted monthly returns and their standard deviation, which incorporates autocorrelation and bias in the hedge fund performance measurement. Finally, the fat-tail problem is dealt with by calculating the modified Sharpe ratio on the basis of the adjusted monthly returns and their standard deviation. This ratio is called the adjusted modified Sharpe ratio and is calculated as $AMSR_i = (r_{Ai}^d - r_f)/AMVaR_i$, with $AMVaR_i = -(z_{CFi}\sigma_{Ai} + r_{Ai}^d)w$. The results of this adjusted performance measurement are shown in Table 25.5.

Table 25.5 shows that the adjusted Sharpe ratio (i.e., considering the autocorrelation and bias problem) leads to a lower outperformance of funds of hedge funds compared to traditional investments. For example, only the Conservative (0.13) and the Market Defensive (0.21) indices are close to the performance of the best traditional investments, which are the government and corporate bond indices.

This effect is heightened when additionally considering the fat-tail problem by looking at the adjusted modified Sharpe ratio. In this case, only the Market Defensive strategy, with a performance of 0.09, might be considered competitive with the other indices. Thus, for most strategies, the largest part of the original outperformance compared to stocks disappears when considering autocorrelation, bias, and fat tails. Again, we also find that performance of the aggregated FoHF index is lower than the performance of the aggregated hedge fund index.

## 25.7. ANALYSIS OF SUBPERIODS (PRE-CRISIS AND POST-CRISIS)

We now consider the performance of FoHFs in different subperiods. For this purpose, the time horizon from 1994 to 2011 is subdivided into two different periods. The pre-crisis period ranges from January 1994 to August 2008; the post-crisis period goes from September 2008 to December 2011. Table 25.6 shows the performance measurement results for the different subperiods. In addition to the Sharpe ratio, Table 25.6 also includes the modified Sharpe ratio and the adjusted modified Sharpe ratio.

FoHFs look much more attractive in the pre-crisis period. In this period, FoHFs had relatively high performance compared to many of the traditional investments. In the post-crisis period, however, the performance of FoHFs is very poor. It is noteworthy that the performance of the FoHFs is always superior to the performance of the single hedge funds — a finding that, again, could reflect the additional costs of these funds for investors.

Figure 25.1 graphically illustrates this result by plotting the performance of four indices over the period January 1994–December 2011. Figure 25.1 shows the development of the aggregated FoHF index and compares it with the aggregated hedge fund index and the two global stock and bond indices (MSCI World and BofA/ML Global Government Bond). The hedge fund and FoHF indices are represented by the thick lines; the stock and bond indices by the thin lines.

**Table 25.5**   Performance Measurement Results for the Adjusted Modified Sharpe Ratio

| Index | Hedge Funds | | | | | FoHFs | | | | | Benchmark Indices | | | |
|---|---|---|---|---|---|---|---|---|---|---|---|---|---|---|
| | Fund Weighted Composite | Equity Hedge (Total) | Event Driven (Total) | Macro (Total) | Relative Value (Total) | FOF Composite | Conservative | Diversified | Market Defensive | Strategic | S&P 500 | MSCI World | BofA ML Global Government Bond | BofA ML Global Broad Corporate Bond |
| Adjusted mean monthly return ($\hat{r}_{Ai}$) (%) | 0.56 | 0.67 | 0.66 | 0.52 | 0.50 | 0.26 | 0.24 | 0.24 | 0.40 | 0.31 | 0.54 | 0.42 | 0.35 | 0.37 |
| Adjusted standard deviation of monthly returns ($\sigma_{Ai}$) (%) | 3.05 | 4.00 | 3.29 | 2.19 | 2.29 | 2.43 | 1.82 | 2.47 | 1.91 | 3.42 | 6.22 | 6.59 | 2.69 | 2.25 |
| Adjusted Sharpe ratio ($ASR_i$) | 0.18 | 0.17 | 0.20 | 0.24 | 0.22 | 0.11 | 0.13 | 0.10 | 0.21 | 0.09 | 0.09 | 0.06 | 0.13 | 0.16 |
| Adjusted modified Sharpe ratio ($AMSR_i$) | 0.06 | 0.06 | 0.06 | 0.11 | 0.05 | 0.03 | 0.03 | 0.03 | 0.09 | 0.03 | 0.03 | 0.02 | 0.06 | 0.04 |

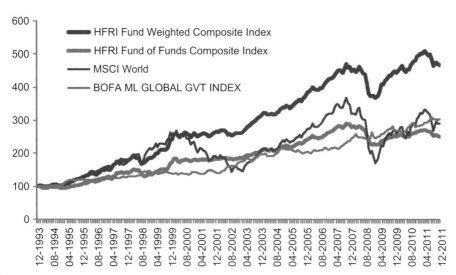

**FIGURE 25.1**
Performance of FoHFs and benchmark indices.

Until the beginning of the financial crisis, FoHFs had steady returns on a level comparable to those for stocks, but with a much lower variation. This is also reflected by the much higher Sharpe ratio of FoHFs (0.35) compared to stocks (0.18) documented in the pre-crisis period (panel B of Table 25.6). In the post-crisis period, however, the aggregated hedge fund index declined by 16% from August 2008 to December 2012 and is still recovering. So, although the standard deviation of the returns is on a very low level, the Sharpe ratio in the post-crisis period is still negative. The results confirm the findings from other papers that FoHFs delivered superior performance only in the pre-crisis period (see Edelman *et al.* 2012).

## CONCLUSION

Evaluating FoHFs performance requires consideration of autocorrelation, bias, and fat tails. In this chapter we rely on the performance measurement framework introduced in Eling (2006) to provide such an evaluation. When the performance of FoHFs is considered under the modified performance measurement framework, many FoHFs become less attractive. This is illustrated by comparing the classical Sharpe ratio to an adjusted version of the modified Sharpe ratio proposed by Gregoriou and Gueyie (2003).

Indeed, only a few strategies appear to be attractive investment options under the modified measurement framework. One of these is the market conservative strategy, which exhibits a relatively good performance even after addressing all three of these problems. If, however, performance since the financial crisis is considered in isolation, all FoHFs strategies look relatively unattractive. It thus seems that many FoHFs are still recovering from financial crisis losses.

**Table 25.6** Performance Measurement Results for Different Subperiods

| Index | Hedge Funds | | | | | FoHFs | | | | | Benchmark Indices | | | |
|---|---|---|---|---|---|---|---|---|---|---|---|---|---|---|
| | Fund Weighted Composite | Equity Hedge (Total) | Event Driven (Total) | Macro (Total) | Relative Value (Total) | FOF Composite | Conservative | Diversified | Market Defensive | Strategic | S&P 500 | MSCI World | BofA ML Global Government Bond | BofA ML Global Broad Corporate Bond |
| *(A) Full time period (January 1994–December 2011)* | | | | | | | | | | | | | | |
| Monthly return ($r_i^S$) (%) | 0.74 | 0.85 | 0.84 | 0.70 | 0.68 | 0.44 | 0.42 | 0.42 | 0.58 | 0.49 | 0.72 | 0.60 | 0.53 | 0.55 |
| Standard deviation ($\sigma_i$) (%) | 2.09 | 2.73 | 2.01 | 1.93 | 1.26 | 1.76 | 1.21 | 1.81 | 1.63 | 2.53 | 4.53 | 4.54 | 1.95 | 1.61 |
| Sharpe Ratio ($SR_i$) | 0.35 | 0.31 | 0.42 | 0.36 | 0.54 | 0.25 | 0.35 | 0.23 | 0.36 | 0.20 | 0.16 | 0.13 | 0.27 | 0.34 |
| Modified Sharpe ratio ($MSR_i$) (%) | 0.12 | 0.12 | 0.13 | 0.18 | 0.12 | 0.08 | 0.09 | 0.07 | 0.17 | 0.06 | 0.06 | 0.05 | 0.13 | 0.10 |
| Adjusted modified Sharpe ratio ($AMSR_i$) (%) | 0.06 | 0.06 | 0.06 | 0.11 | 0.05 | 0.03 | 0.03 | 0.03 | 0.09 | 0.03 | 0.04 | 0.03 | 0.09 | 0.07 |
| *(B) Pre-crisis (January 1994–August 2008)* | | | | | | | | | | | | | | |
| Monthly return ($r_i^S$) (%) | 0.86 | 1.03 | 0.97 | 0.80 | 0.74 | 0.58 | 0.56 | 0.54 | 0.69 | 0.64 | 0.81 | 0.70 | 0.53 | 0.50 |
| Standard deviation ($\sigma_i$) (%) | 1.98 | 2.52 | 1.81 | 2.01 | 0.92 | 1.68 | 0.99 | 1.77 | 1.61 | 2.54 | 4.06 | 3.86 | 1.83 | 1.33 |
| Sharpe ratio ($SR_i$) | 0.44 | 0.41 | 0.53 | 0.40 | 0.79 | 0.35 | 0.56 | 0.31 | 0.43 | 0.25 | 0.20 | 0.18 | 0.29 | 0.38 |
| Modified Sharpe ratio ($MSR_i$) (%) | 0.16 | 0.19 | 0.17 | 0.19 | 0.18 | 0.12 | 0.21 | 0.10 | 0.20 | 0.08 | 0.08 | 0.07 | 0.16 | 0.17 |
| Adjusted modified Sharpe ratio ($AMSR_i$) (%) | 0.10 | 0.13 | 0.10 | 0.14 | 0.09 | 0.07 | 0.10 | 0.06 | 0.13 | 0.05 | 0.07 | 0.06 | 0.11 | 0.17 |
| *(C) Post-crisis (September 2008–December 2011)* | | | | | | | | | | | | | | |
| Monthly return ($r_i^S$) (%) | 0.20 | 0.09 | 0.29 | 0.26 | 0.44 | -0.15 | -0.18 | -0.13 | 0.10 | -0.17 | 0.33 | 0.14 | 0.57 | 0.74 |
| Standard deviation ($\sigma_i$) (%) | 2.48 | 3.44 | 2.67 | 1.50 | 2.20 | 2.01 | 1.78 | 1.90 | 1.63 | 2.43 | 6.23 | 6.82 | 2.40 | 2.51 |
| Sharpe ratio ($SR_i$) | 0.08 | 0.03 | 0.11 | 0.18 | 0.20 | -0.07 | -0.10 | -0.07 | 0.06 | -0.07 | 0.05 | 0.02 | 0.24 | 0.30 |
| Modified Sharpe ratio ($MSR_i$) (%) | 0.03 | 0.01 | 0.04 | 0.11 | 0.06 | -0.02 | -0.03 | -0.02 | 0.03 | -0.02 | 0.02 | 0.01 | 0.10 | 0.10 |
| Adjusted modified Sharpe ratio ($AMSR_i$) (%) | 0.00 | -0.01 | 0.02 | 0.07 | 0.04 | -0.07 | -0.09 | -0.07 | -0.05 | -0.07 | 0.03 | 0.01 | 0.22 | 0.13 |

# References

Ackermann, C., McEnally, R., & Ravenscraft, D. (1999). The Performance of Hedge Funds: Risk, Return, and Incentives. *Journal of Finance, 54*(3), 833–874.

Amenc, N., Martellini, L., & Vaissié, M. (2003). Benefits and Risks of Alternative Investment Strategies. *Journal of Asset Management, 4*(2), 96–118.

Amin, G. S., & Kat, H. M. (2003). Stocks, Bonds, and Hedge Funds. *Journal of Portfolio Management, 30*(4), 113–119.

Ammann, M., & Moerth, P. (2005). Impact of Fund Size on Hedge Fund Performance. *Journal of Asset Management, 6*(3), 219–238.

Asness, C., Krail, R., & Liew, J. (2001). Do Hedge Funds Hedge? *Journal of Portfolio Management, 28*(1), 6–19.

Capocci, D., & Hübner, G. (2004). Analysis of Hedge Fund Performance. *Journal of Empirical Finance, 11*(1), 55–89.

Christiansen, C. B., Madsen, P. B., & Christensen, M. (2003). *Further Evidence on Hedge Fund Performance*. Working Paper, Department of Finance. Aarhus School of Business.

Deuskar, P., Pollet, J. M., Wang, Z. J., & Zheng, L. (2011). The Good or the Bad? Which Mutual Fund Managers Join Hedge Funds? *Review of Financial Studies, 24*(9), 3008–3024.

Dorfleitner, G. (2002). Stetige versus diskrete Renditen: Überlegungen zur richtigen Verwendung beider Begriffe in Theorie und Praxis. *Kredit und Kapital, 35*(2), 216–241.

Edelman, D., Fung, W., Hsieh, D. A., & Naik, N. Y. (2012). Funds of Hedge Funds: Performance, Risk and Capital Formation 2005 to 2010. *Financial Markets and Portfolio Management, 26*(1), 87–108.

Edwards, F. R., & Caglayan, M. O. (2001). Hedge Fund Performance and Manager Skill. *Journal of Futures Markets, 21*(11), 1003–1028.

Eling, M. (2006). Autocorrelation, Bias, and Fat Tails — Are Hedge Funds Really Attractive Investments? Derivatives Use. *Trading & Regulation, 12*(1), 28–47.

Favre, L., & Galéano, J. A. (2002). Mean-Modified Value-at-Risk Optimization with Hedge Funds. *Journal of Alternative Investments, 5*(2), 21–25.

Favre, L., & Signer, A. (2002). The Difficulties of Measuring the Benefits of Hedge Funds. *Journal of Alternative Investments, 5*(1), 31–42.

Fung, W., & Hsieh, D. A. (2002). Hedge-Fund Benchmarks: Information Content and Biases. *Financial Analysts Journal, 58*(1), 22–34.

Getmansky, M., Lo, A. W., & Makarov, I. (2004). An Econometric Model of Serial Correlation and Illiquidity in Hedge Fund Returns. *Journal of Financial Economics, 74*(3), 529–609.

Gregoriou, G. N. (2002). Hedge Fund Survival Lifetimes. *Journal of Asset Management, 3*(3), 237–252.

Gregoriou, G. N. (2004). Performance of Canadian Hedge Funds Using a Modified Sharpe Ratio. *Derivatives Use, Trading & Regulation, 10*(2), 149–155.

Gregoriou, G. N., & Gueyie, J. P. (2003). Risk-Adjusted Performance of Funds of Hedge Funds Using a Modified Sharpe Ratio. *Journal of Alternative Investments, 6*(3), 77–83, Winter.

Gregoriou, G. N., & Rouah, R. (2002). The Role of Hedge Funds in Pension Fund Portfolios: Buying Protection in Bear Markets. *Journal of Pensions Management, 7*(3), 237–245.

Hedge Fund Research (2012). *HFR Strategy Classification System*. Available at https://www.hedgefundresearch.com

Jagannathan, R., Malakhow, A., & Novokov, A. (2010). Do Hot Hands Exist Among Hedge Fund Managers? An Empirical Evaluation. *Journal of Finance, 65*(1), 217–255.

Jarque, C. M., & Bera, A. K. (1987). A Test for Normality of Observations and Regression Residuals. *International Statistical Review, 55*(2), 163–172.

Jobson, D., & Korkie, B. (1981). Performance Hypothesis Testing with the Sharpe and Treynor Measures. *Journal of Finance, 36*(4), 888–908.

Kat, H. M. (2002). Some Facts About Hedge Funds. *World Economics, 3*(2), 93–123.

Kat, H. M. (2003). 10 Things that Investors Should Know About Hedge Funds. *Journal of Wealth Management, 5*(4), 72–81.

Kat, H. M., & Lu, S. (2002). *An Excursion into the Statistical Properties of Hedge Fund Returns*. Working Paper 0016. City University London: Alternative Investment Research Centre, Cass Business School.

Kouwenberg, R. (2003). Do Hedge Funds Add Value to a Passive Portfolio? Correcting for Non-Normal Returns and Disappearing Funds. *Journal of Asset Management, 3*(4), 361–382.

Lhabitant, F. S. (2002). *Hedge Funds: Myths and Limits*. Chichester: Wiley.

Liang, B. (1999). On the Performance of Hedge Funds. *Financial Analysts Journal, 55*(4), 72–85.

Liang, B. (2000). Hedge Funds: The Living and the Dead. *Journal of Financial and Quantitative Analysis, 35*(3), 309–326.

Ljung, G. M., & Box, G. E. P. (1978). On a Measure of Lack of Fit in Time Series Models. *Biometrika, 65*(2), 297–303.

Lo, A. W. (2001). Risk Management for Hedge Funds: Introduction and Overview. *Financial Analysts Journal, 57*(6), 16–33.

Lo, A. W. (2002). The Statistics of Sharpe Ratios. *Financial Analysts Journal, 58*(4), 36–52.

Nicholas, J. G. (2004). *Hedge Fund of Funds Investing*. New York: Bloomberg Press.

# CHAPTER 26

# Crises and Funds of Hedge Funds Tail Risk

**Monica Billio**[*], **Kaleab Y. Mamo**[†], **and Loriana Pelizzon**[*]
[*]Dipartimento di Economia, Università Ca' Foscari Venezia,
Venezia, Italy
[†]University of Toronto, Toronto, Ontario, Canada

## 26.1. INTRODUCTION

The recent financial crises had a major global impact on worldwide markets. Although hedge funds are expected to have the capability to reduce the impact of such crises by hedging against market movements, the Long-Term Capital Management (LCTM) crisis in 1998 and the global meltdown in 2008 showed otherwise. During the recent crises, most hedge funds suffered large losses. At the same time, the number of funds of hedge funds (FoHFs)[1] has increased

---

[1]FoHFs description from the Hedge Fund Research (HFR) website:
Funds of Funds invest with multiple managers through funds or managed accounts. The strategy designs a diversified portfolio of managers with the objective of significantly lowering the risk (volatility) of investing with an individual manager. The Fund of Funds manager has discretion in choosing which strategies to invest in for the portfolio. A manager may allocate funds to numerous managers within a single strategy, or with numerous managers in multiple strategies. The minimum investment in a Fund of Funds may be lower than an investment in an individual hedge fund or managed account. The investor has the advantage of diversification among managers and styles with significantly less capital than investing with separate managers.

Reconsidering Funds of Hedge Funds. http://dx.doi.org/10.1016/B978-0-12-401699-6.00026-5

substantially over the last decade. Nearly every financial institution, endowment fund, and pension fund increased its exposure to alternative investments almost through FoHFs. The key element of this instrument is the design of a diversified portfolio of managers with the objective of significantly lowering the risk of investing with an individual manager. The aim is not only to reduce the volatility of the investment but also the tail risk of such investment.

In this chapter we investigate whether this aim is indeed reached by investing in FoHFs, mostly when tail risk reduction is of extreme importance to investors, i.e., during crisis periods. We analyze FoHF index data provided by BarclayHedge and HFR, and study FoHF tail risk using a multifactor Markov regime switching model (RSM) to capture the non-linear exposure of hedge funds to systematic risk factors and switching in volatility in the specific risk of the different FoHF indexes. The analysis shows that for almost all FoHF indexes the tail risk increases during crisis. Moreover, using a decomposition approach, this chapter shows that the main contribution to tail risk during the crisis is credit risk and momentum.

This chapter is largely related to Brown *et al.* (2012), who investigated excess diversification that could generate tail risks, and Billio *et al.* (2008, 2011) and Billio and Pelizzon (2000), who first applied RSM to hedge funds and proposed a new methodology to calculate value at risk (VaR) for RSM.

The rest of the chapter is organized as follows. In Section 26.2, we develop a theoretical framework for measuring tail risks using RSM. Section 26.3 describes data and presents results, and is followed by our conclusions.

## 26.2. METHODOLOGY

### 26.2.1. The Model

Conventional asset pricing models, such as the Fama and French (1993) three-factor model or the Carhart (1997) four-factor model, have had limited success in explaining hedge fund returns. This phenomenon is usually attributed to the dynamic nature and non-linear payoff structure of hedge funds trading strategies (e.g., Agarwal and Naik, 2004; Fung and Hsieh, 1997, 2002a, 2002b, 2004; Billio *et al.*, 2008, 2011). This problem naturally extends to FoHFs, since they are portfolios of hedge funds.

The literature has developed some methods to tackle this problem. Fung and Hsieh (1997, 2002a, 2002b, 2004) have developed asset-based risk factors that are specifically designed to capture the non-linear payoff structure of hedge fund trading strategies. Billio *et al.* (2008, 2011) have implemented the RSM, which was first proposed by Hamilton (1994), to capture the non-linear exposure of hedge funds to systematic risk factors. In this chapter, we follow the second group of studies and apply the Markov RSM to FoHFs.

The RSM is designed to capture the time-varying distribution of FoHFs returns that results from the dynamic trading strategies of the underlying hedge funds as well as the FoHFs. It assumes that FoHFs returns are drawn from a mixture of distributions, where each distribution is characterized by state-dependent idiosyncratic and systematic components. For instance, the distribution of FoHFs returns is characterized by low (or negative) mean and high volatility during crises periods, as was observed during the 2008 crisis, while the distribution is characterized by high mean and low volatility during non-crises periods. Since these shifts in location and dispersion of the distribution have first-order importance for tail risk, a model that captures these shifts is necessary to study FoHFs tails.

The simplest form of the RSM is:

$$r_t = \mu(S_t) + \sigma(S_t)\varepsilon_t, \qquad (26.1)$$

where $r_t$ is return on a financial asset, $S_t$ is a hidden Markov chain with two states, and $\varepsilon_t$ is an independent and identically distributed (i.i.d.) process drawn from standard normal distribution. Thus, $\mu(S_t)$ is the state-dependent mean and $\sigma(S_t)$ is the state-dependent volatility of the returns. The Markov chain $S_t$ is defined as:

$$S_t = \begin{cases} 0, & \text{with probability} = p_0 \\ 1, & \text{with probability} = p_1 \end{cases}. \qquad (26.2)$$

The state $S_t = 0$ is characterized by low volatility and high mean (the normal regime) and the state $S_t = 1$ is characterized by high volatility and low mean (the crisis regime). Equations (26.1) and (26.2) imply the distribution of $r_t$ is given by:

$$r_1 \sim \begin{cases} N(\mu_0, \sigma_0), & \text{if } S_t = 0 \\ N(\mu_1, \sigma_1), & \text{if } S_t = 1 \end{cases}. \qquad (26.3)$$

The state dynamics is characterized by transition probabilities. A transition probability is the probability of switching from regime $i$ at time $t-1$ to regime $j$ at time $t$ and it is denoted by $P_{ij}$. The transition matrix:

$$\Pi = \begin{pmatrix} P_{00} & P_{10} \\ P_{01} & P_{11} \end{pmatrix} = \begin{pmatrix} P_{00} & 1-P_{11} \\ 1-P_{00} & P_{11} \end{pmatrix} \qquad (26.4)$$

provides a way to compute conditional probabilities of the regimes at time $t$, given information up to time $t-1$. Let $p_{t-1} = (p_{0,t-1}, p_{1,t-1})'$ denote the filtered probabilities of the two regimes at time $t-1$ (i.e., the probabilities of the two regimes in $t-1$ conditional to the available information in $t-1$). Then, the conditional probabilities at $t$, given the available information in $t-1$, are given by $p_t = \Pi p_{t-1}$.[2] Hamilton (1994) shows that the parameters $\{\mu_0, \mu_1, \sigma_0, \sigma_1, P_{00}, P_{11}\}$ can be estimated using quasi maximum likelihood estimation techniques. Moreover, the conditional probabilities of the states are obtained using Hamilton's filter. While the simple RSM is non-linear and has

---

[2]The unconditional probabilities of regimes are given by the vector $\left( \dfrac{1-P_{11}}{1-P_{00}-P_{11}}, \dfrac{1-P_{00}}{1-P_{00}-P_{11}} \right)'$.

time-varying parameters, it does not take into account the exposure of FoHFs to systematic risk factors.

We thus extend the simple RSM to better model the time varying non-linear exposure of FoHFs to systematic risk factors. For a time series of FoHFs returns $r_{it}$, the extended multifactor RSM is given by:

$$
\begin{aligned}
r_{mt} &= \mu_m(S_t) + \sigma_m(S_t)\eta_t \\
r_{it} &= \alpha_i(Z_t^i) + \beta_i(S_t)' F_t + \sigma_i(Z_t^i)\varepsilon_t,
\end{aligned}
\tag{26.5}
$$

where $r_{mt}$ is the market excess return, $S_t$ is a Markov chain characterizing market wide regimes, $r_{it}$ is the FoHFs return, $F_t$ is a vector of risk factors, $\beta_i(S_t)$ is a state-dependent vector of factor loadings, $Z_t^i$ is a Markov chain characterizing the idiosyncratic regimes, $\alpha_i(Z_t^i)$ is the state-dependent (idiosyncratic) constant term, $\sigma_i(Z_t^i)$ is the state-dependent idiosyncratic volatility, and $\eta_t$ and $\varepsilon_t$ are independent random variables, with i.i.d. standard normal distribution, representing market-wide and fund-level shocks respectively. With the assumption that both Markov chains have two states, the multifactor RSM implies that:

$$
r_{it} \sim N\left(\mu_i\left(S_t, Z_t^i\right),\ \sigma_i^2\left(S_t, Z_t^i\right)\right),
$$

where:

$$
\mu_i\left(S_t, Z_t^i\right) = \alpha_i\left(Z_t^i\right) + \beta_i(S_t)' \mu_F
$$

$$
\sigma_i^2\left(S_t, Z_t^i\right) = \beta_i(S_t)'\ Var(F_t)\beta_i(S_t) + \sigma_i^2\left(Z_t^i\right)
$$

$$
\left(S_t, Z_t^i\right) \in \{(0,0),\ (0,1),\ (1,0),\ (1,1)\}.
$$

with $\mu_F$ and $Var(F_t)$ representing the mean and variance of the vector $F_t$. Further assumptions are made in the estimation of the model. First, we assume that the systematic and idiosyncratic regimes are independent. This assumption allows us to estimate the market part of equation (26.5) first (i.e., $r_{mt} = \mu_m(S_t) + \sigma_m(S_t)\eta_t$) and plug the filtered probabilities into the FoHFs return equation. Another implication of this assumption is that the probabilities of the combined states of $(S_t, Z_t^i)$ are obtained by simply multiplying the probabilities of the states of the two Markov chains. Second, we assume that the risk factors in the vector $F_t$ are independent.

This assumption implies:

$$
\beta_i(S_t)'\ Var(F_t)\beta_i(S_t) = \sum_{j=1}^{J}\left[\beta_{i,j}^2(S_t)\sigma_{F_{jt}}^2\right].
$$

While the main purpose of these two assumptions is to reduce the computational complexity, we believe that they are not too unrealistic.

Once we estimate the parameters, which also includes the 'filtered probabilities' of the states of the two Markov chains, we can obtain the distribution for each FoHF index conditional on information available at time $t$.[3] It is just a mixture of the normal distributions characterizing each state weighted by the filtered probabilities of the states. The resulting distributions are then used to compute the tail risk measures as discussed in the next subsection.

## 26.2.2. Tail Risk Measures

We use the two common tail risk measures: VaR and Expected Shortfall (ES).[4] The VaR is theoretically defined as the maximum amount of loss FoHFs can incur over a given horizon at a certain confidence level. The VaR for a FoHF over the horizon $h$ with confidence level $\alpha$ is analytically defined as $Pr(r_{t+h} < VaR(\alpha, h)) = \alpha$ or equivalently $\Phi(VaR(\alpha, h)) = \alpha$, where $\Phi$ is the probability distribution function. Using the probability density function the VaR is defined as:

$$\alpha = \int_{-\infty}^{VaR(\alpha,h)} \varphi(x)\mathrm{d}x. \tag{26.6}$$

The expected shortfall measures the expected loss conditional to the loss exceeding the VaR, i.e., $ES(\alpha, h) = E[r_{t+h}|r_{t+h} < VaR(\alpha, h)]$. Analytically, it is defined as:

$$ES(\alpha h) = \frac{\int_{-\infty}^{VaR(\alpha,h)} x\varphi(x)\,\mathrm{d}x}{\int_{-\infty}^{VaR(\alpha,h)} \varphi(x)\,\mathrm{d}x} = \frac{1}{\alpha} \int_{-\infty}^{VaR(\alpha,h)} x\varphi(x)\,\mathrm{d}x. \tag{26.7}$$

Since our model characterizes returns with a mixture of distributions, the definition of the VaR in equation (26.6) is thus equivalent to:

$$\alpha = \sum_{(Z_{t+h}^i, S_{t+h}) \in S} \left\{ p\big((Z_{t+h}^i, S_{t+h})\big|I_t\big) \int_{-\infty}^{VaR(\alpha,h)} \varphi\big(x\big|Z_{t+h}^i, S_{t+h}, I_t\big)\mathrm{d}x \right\}, \tag{26.8}$$

where $S = \{(0,0), (0,1), (1,0), (1,1)\}$ and $I_t$ denotes all the available information at time $t$. Similarly, the ES is given by:

$$ES(\alpha, h) = \frac{1}{\alpha} \sum_{(Z_{t+h}^i, S_{t+h}) \in S} \left\{ p\big((Z_{t+h}^i, S_{t+h})\big|I_t\big) \int_{-\infty}^{VaR(\alpha,h)} x\varphi\big(x\big|Z_{t+h}^i, S_{t+h}, I_t\big)\mathrm{d}x \right\}.$$
$$\tag{26.9}$$

---

[3]Details of the estimation methodology and the filtering technique used to obtain the probabilities of the states can be obtained in Billio *et al.* (2011) and Hamilton (1994).
[4]More discussion on the advantages and disadvantages of VaR and ES can be found in Artzner *et al.* (1998), Jorion (2003), Acerbi and Tasche (2002), and Inuia and Kijima (2005).

The closed form solution for $ES(\alpha, h)$, which can be derived by integrating the right-hand side of (26.9), is given by:

$$
\begin{aligned}
ES(\alpha, h) = \frac{1}{\alpha} \sum_{(Z^i_{t+h}, S_{t+h}) \in S} \frac{1}{2} \Bigg\{ & p\big((Z^i_{t+h}, S_{t+h})|I_t\big) \\
\times \Bigg[ & \mu(Z^i_{t+h}, S_{t+h}) \Phi\left(\frac{VaR(\alpha, h) - \mu(Z^i_{t+h}, S_{t+h})}{\sigma(Z^i_{t+h}, S_{t+h})}\right) \\
- & \sigma(Z^i_{t+h}, S_{t+h}) \varphi\left(\frac{VaR(\alpha, h) - \mu(Z^i_{t+h}, S_{t+h})}{\sigma(Z^i_{t+h}, S_{t+h})}\right) \Bigg] \Bigg\}.
\end{aligned}
\qquad (26.10)
$$

We use a numerical procedure to estimate the VaR using (26.8) and plug the estimated VaR in (26.10) to obtain the ES.

## 26.3. EMPIRICAL RESULTS
### 26.3.1. Data

We use a sample of monthly returns on six FoHF indices for a sample period of January 1997–December 2011. The data is obtained from BarclayHedge and HFR hedge fund databases. The BarclayHedge FoHF index is calculated every month, and is a simple arithmetic average of the net returns of all FoHFs that report their net returns in that particular month and includes only funds that report net returns.

HFR provides one composite FoHF index and four FoHF indices classified based on their portfolio selection strategies: the Conservative index, the Market Defensive index, the Strategic index, and the Diversified index. The BarclayHedge FoHF index and the HFRI indices are equally weighted. However, HFR does not include all reporting funds in the index calculation. To be included in an HFRI index, FoHFs must report monthly returns net of all fees, report assets in US$, and have at least US$50 million of assets under management, or have been actively trading for at least 12 months. FoHFs are eligible for inclusion in an HFRI index 1 month after their addition to the HFR database. If a fund liquidates or closes, that fund's performance will be included in the index computation as of that fund's last reported performance update. In cases where a manager lists mirrored-performance funds, only the fund with the larger asset size is included in the HFRI. HFRI indices include both domestic and offshore funds.

The HFRI *Conservative* index is composed of FoHFs that seek consistent returns by primarily investing in hedge funds that generally engage in more 'conservative' strategies. The HFRI *Market Defensive* index is composed of FoHFs that invest in hedge funds that generally engage in short-biased strategies. The HFRI *Strategic* index consists of FoHFs that seek superior returns by primarily investing in funds that generally engage in more opportunistic strategies. The HFRI *Diversified* index is composed of FoHFs that invest in a variety of strategies among multiple managers. The HFRI *Composite index* includes all the FoHFs in the four strategy indices.

We provide simple summary statistics of the FoHF indices in Table 26.1. The first panel shows that all FoHF indices, except the market defensive index, exhibit negative skewness and excess kurtosis. This finding rules out the possibility of using a Gaussian distribution to describe the FoHFs returns. The second panel presents the correlations among the six FoHF indices. It is apparent that the indices are highly correlated with each other and with the market. Moreover, as expected from the definitions of the strategies, the Conservative index has the lowest mean return and volatility, while the Strategic index has the highest volatility. The Market Defensive index exhibits high mean return, moderate volatility, virtually no skewness, low kurtosis, and low correlation with the market. It is surprising that the strategy that focuses on short-biased hedge funds appears to have the best characteristics. Conversely, the Diversified index is highly correlated with the market and all the other indices. This casts some doubt on the FoHFs managers' ability to hedge systematic risk.

## 26.3.2. Expanding Window Estimation Procedure

The empirical tests for the tail risk measures require an estimation of the model for a period of time as opposed to a point in time. To this end, we employ an expanding window estimation procedure. The complete sample contains 180 monthly observations for each FoHF index. The first estimation window contains the first 84 observations (January 1997–December 2004) to estimate the parameters and tail risk measures for December 2004. The next estimation window contains the first 85 observations (January 1997–January 2005) to estimate the parameters and tail risk measures for January 2005. This process is repeated, each time including one more observation, until we obtain the results for the last observation (December 2011).

In this way we are able to investigate tail risk measures for a significant period before the Subprime crisis of August 2007, and during the Subprime crisis of 2007, the global crisis of 2008–2009, and the most recent period.

Note that the last step of this procedure uses all the available data and for this reason we report only the model parameters for the last iteration. Through this procedure, we are able to estimate and forecast the tail risk measures for 84 months (January 2005–December 2011).

## 26.3.3. Results

In this subsection, we present the results of our empirical analysis. (i) We present the estimation results for the multifactor RSM described in equation (26.5). (ii) We show the distribution of the FoHF indices implied by the model. (iii) We show the tail risk measures estimated from these distributions. (iv) We present a decomposition of the tail risk measures into idiosyncratic and systematic components.

Table 26.2 presents the parameters for the second part of equation (26.5) estimated using the whole sample period. This is the estimation of the two-state RSM for the market index. As discussed earlier, the two components of equation

**Table 26.1** Summary Statistics

| | (A) Simple Summary Statistics | | | | | | | (B) Correlation Matrix | | | | | |
| --- | --- | --- | --- | --- | --- | --- | --- | --- | --- | --- | --- | --- | --- |
| FoHF Indices | Mean | Standard Deviation | Minimum | Median | Maximum | Skewness | Kurtosis | Barclay Hedge | HFRI Composite | HFRI Conservative | HFRI Market Defensive | HFRI Strategic | HFRI Diversified |
| BarclayHedge | 0.48 | 1.69 | −6.79 | 0.595 | 6.05 | −0.76 | 3.98 | | | | | | |
| HFRI Composite | 0.42 | 1.83 | −7.47 | 0.655 | 6.85 | −0.66 | 3.70 | 0.98 | | | | | |
| HFRI Conservative | 0.37 | 1.27 | −5.91 | 0.55 | 3.96 | −1.67 | 6.65 | 0.93 | 0.93 | | | | |
| HFRI Market Defensive | 0.55 | 1.61 | −5.42 | 0.585 | 4.93 | −0.07 | 0.78 | 0.63 | 0.65 | 0.56 | | | |
| HFRI Strategic | 0.46 | 2.60 | −12.11 | 0.73 | 9.47 | −0.52 | 4.06 | 0.94 | 0.97 | 0.86 | 0.60 | | |
| HFRI Diversified | 0.41 | 1.89 | −7.75 | 0.525 | 7.73 | −0.45 | 3.79 | 0.96 | 0.99 | 0.89 | 0.63 | 0.95 | |
| S&P 500 | 0.40 | 4.83 | −16.69 | 0.89 | 11.25 | −0.50 | 3.49 | 0.60 | 0.60 | 0.56 | 0.14 | 0.64 | 0.56 |

Panel (A) presents the simple summary statistics of the six FoHF indices for the sample period January 1997–December 2011. Panel (B) shows the correlation of the FoHF indices among each other and with the equity market.

**Table 26.2**  Parameter Estimates Market Regimes

| | Mean | | Volatility | | |
|---|---|---|---|---|---|
| | Estimate | t-Statistic | Estimate | t-Statistic | In-Sample Proportion |
| Tranquil regime | 0.764 | 2.342 | 2.175 | 9.039 | 0.344 |
| Crisis regime | 0.256 | 0.524 | 5.515 | 15.677 | 0.656 |

Maximum likelihood estimates of the two-state simple RSM for the market index.

(26.5) can be estimated independently because of the independence of the two Markov chains. Table 26.2 shows that the market can be characterized by two regimes — one with high mean of 0.76 and low volatility of 2.18 (tranquil regime) and another with low mean of 0.26 and high volatility of 5.51 (crisis regime). We plot in Figure 26.1 the distributions of the market index conditional on different months that are selected to emphasize the difference among the two states. The graphs show that the distribution of the market index exhibits significant variations across time depending on the whether we are in tranquil or crises regimes. The main distinguishing feature of this variation over time is volatility; the distribution of the market index has the smallest volatility before crises (February 2005) and the highest volatility in the middle of the crises (October 2008). While the volatility is decreasing after the crises (December 2011), it is still higher than the level in February 2005.

We insert the estimated probabilities of the regimes in the first part of equation (26.5) to obtain the results in Table 26.3. Table 26.3 presents the parameter estimates for the first part of equation (26.5), which are obtained using the entire sample period. Table 26.3 shows that all FoHF indices have significant market exposure in at least one of the market regimes. Except for the Strategic and BarclayHedge FoHF indices, there exists at least a 30% difference between the betas in the two regimes. The Conservative and the Strategic indices are not significantly related to the market during the tranquil regime, whereas they show a significant correlation during the crisis regime. This may indicate that these FoHFs do not benefit from the up market during tranquil regimes, but they are exposed to the down-side risk during crises periods. In fact, all FoHF indices, except for the Market Defensive and the Diversified indices, are significantly exposed to downside market risk. The Market Defensive index is positively (negatively, but not significantly) correlated with the market during the tranquil (crisis) regime. This indicates that the strategy of these FoHFs to focus on short biased hedge funds is more prevalent during crises periods. The Diversified index is also not significantly correlated with the market during the crises regime, indicating that diversified FoHFs may be able to avoid downside market risk.

For almost all FoHF indices the market beta in the crisis regime is smaller than the beta in the tranquil regime. This may be evidence of FoHFs managers' efforts to avoid market risk during crises. FoHF indices, with few exceptions, exhibit a significant correlation with the other relevant risk factors in the crises regime. This might indicate that while some FoHFs manage to limit their tail risk by

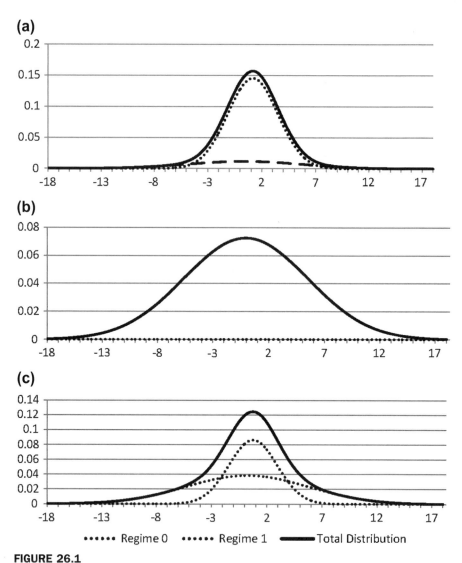

**FIGURE 26.1**
S&P 500 index distributions: the distribution of the market index at different times, chosen to reflect different market conditions, as captured by our simple two-state RSM for the market index. (a) February 2005, (b) October 2008, and (c) December 2011.

minimizing or avoiding a positive exposure to the market during the crises regime, they are significantly exposed to other sources of risk during this regime. Credit spread, momentum, and VIX (volatility index) are among the important factors in this regard. Except for the Market Defensive index, all indices are significantly negatively correlated with credit spread in the crisis regime. This indicates that, like hedge funds, FoHFs are significantly exposed to credit risk during crisis periods. The magnitude of the coefficients indicates the importance of credit risk for FoHFs. The momentum factor exhibits an interesting

**Table 26.3** Multi-factor Regime Switching Model for FoHFs

| Variable | HFR Composite Index | | HFR Conservative Index | | HFR Market Defensive Index | |
|---|---|---|---|---|---|---|
| | Coefficient | t-Statistic | Coefficient | t-Statistic | Coefficient | t-Statistic |
| $\alpha(Z_t=0)$ | 1.10 | 5.52 | 1.31 | 6.45 | 1.11 | 3.84 |
| $\alpha(Z_t=1)$ | 1.18 | 3.03 | 1.00 | 2.66 | 1.00 | 2.64 |
| $\beta_{SP}\ (S_t=0)$ | 0.15 | 2.10 | 0.10 | 1.63 | 0.20 | 1.87 |
| $\beta_{SP}\ (S_t=1)$ | 0.10 | 3.27 | 0.06 | 2.11 | -0.08 | -1.60 |
| $\theta_{LMS}\ (S_t=0)$ | 0.08 | 1.55 | 0.08 | 2.15 | 0.14 | 1.68 |
| $\theta_{LMS}\ (S_t=1)$ | 0.07 | 2.55 | 0.00 | 0.09 | 0.05 | 1.32 |
| $\theta_{VMG}\ (S_t=0)$ | | | 0.09 | 1.70 | 0.19 | 2.00 |
| $\theta_{VMG}\ (S_t=1)$ | | | -0.04 | -2.09 | -0.01 | -0.31 |
| $\theta_{LGC}\ (S_t=0)$ | | | | | 0.50 | 2.53 |
| $\theta_{LGC}\ (S_t=1)$ | | | | | 0.27 | 2.30 |
| $\theta_{TS}\ (S_t=0)$ | -0.23 | -3.25 | -0.24 | -4.09 | -0.32 | -2.71 |
| $\theta_{TS}\ (S_t=1)$ | -0.01 | -0.08 | 0.12 | 1.79 | -0.20 | -1.44 |
| $\theta_{CS}\ (S_t=0)$ | -0.59 | -2.10 | -0.76 | -2.93 | -0.88 | -2.08 |
| $\theta_{CS}\ (S_t=1)$ | -0.79 | -3.73 | -1.02 | -4.28 | -0.02 | -0.05 |
| $\theta_{EmD}\ (S_t=0)$ | -0.07 | -1.16 | -0.13 | -2.28 | -0.39 | -2.74 |
| $\theta_{EmD}\ (S_t=1)$ | 0.08 | 2.30 | 0.10 | 2.75 | 0.05 | 0.88 |
| $\theta_{EmS}\ (S_t=0)$ | 0.17 | 5.23 | 0.09 | 3.07 | 0.22 | 4.03 |
| $\theta_{EmS}\ (S_t=1)$ | 0.12 | 4.88 | 0.04 | 2.12 | 0.09 | 2.28 |
| $\theta_{UMD}\ (S_t=0)$ | -0.03 | -0.86 | -0.02 | -0.57 | -0.05 | -0.83 |
| $\theta_{UMD}\ (S_t=1)$ | 0.08 | 5.58 | 0.02 | 1.93 | 0.09 | 4.07 |
| $\theta_{VIX}\ (S_t=0)$ | 0.07 | 1.31 | 0.02 | 0.45 | | |
| $\theta_{VIX}\ (S_t=1)$ | 0.08 | 2.54 | 0.07 | 3.12 | | |
| $\sigma(Z_t=0)$ | 0.56 | 13.38 | 0.42 | 11.46 | 0.87 | 12.91 |
| $\sigma(Z_t=1)$ | 1.88 | 6.34 | 1.50 | 6.86 | 1.63 | 11.07 |
| $P^Z_{00}$ | 0.94 | 32.90 | 0.93 | 27.62 | 0.98 | 71.14 |
| $P^Z_{11}$ | 0.79 | 6.33 | 0.76 | 6.74 | 0.99 | 62.89 |

| Variable | HFR Strategic Index | | HFR Diversified Index | | BarclayHedge Index | |
|---|---|---|---|---|---|---|
| | Coefficient | t-Statistic | Coefficient | t-Statistic | Coefficient | t-Statistic |
| $\alpha(Z_t=0)$ | 0.53 | 1.70 | 0.79 | 3.15 | 1.35 | 6.35 |
| $\alpha(Z_t=1)$ | 1.30 | 3.35 | 1.07 | 3.15 | 1.42 | 5.33 |
| $\beta_{SP}\ (S_t=0)$ | 0.07 | 0.92 | 0.19 | 2.54 | 0.06 | 0.97 |
| $\beta_{SP}\ (S_t=1)$ | 0.09 | 2.28 | 0.06 | 1.54 | 0.06 | 1.87 |
| $\theta_{LMS}\ (S_t=0)$ | 0.06 | 1.04 | 0.06 | 1.17 | 0.07 | 1.58 |
| $\theta_{LMS}\ (S_t=1)$ | 0.14 | 3.90 | 0.07 | 2.34 | 0.04 | 1.77 |
| $\theta_{VMG}\ (S_t=0)$ | 0.00 | -0.04 | | | | |
| $\theta_{VMG}\ (S_t=1)$ | -0.10 | -2.92 | | | | |
| $\theta_{LGC}\ (S_t=0)$ | | | | | -0.08 | -0.96 |
| $\theta_{LGC}\ (S_t=1)$ | | | | | 0.22 | 2.74 |
| $\theta_{TS}\ (S_t=0)$ | -0.21 | -2.56 | -0.21 | -3.00 | -0.17 | -2.64 |
| $\theta_{TS}\ (S_t=1)$ | 0.23 | 1.76 | 0.08 | 0.82 | -0.11 | -1.31 |
| $\theta_{CS}\ (S_t=0)$ | 0.12 | 0.30 | -0.27 | -0.82 | -0.99 | -3.50 |

*(Continued)*

| Table 26.3 | Multi-factor Regime Switching Model for FoHFs—cont'd | | | | | |
|---|---|---|---|---|---|---|
| | **HFR Strategic Index** | | **HFR Diversified Index** | | **BarclayHedge Index** | |
| **Variable** | **Coefficient** | **t-Statistic** | **Coefficient** | **t-Statistic** | **Coefficient** | **t-Statistic** |
| $\theta_{CS}$ $(S_t=1)$ | −1.09 | −3.44 | −0.80 | −2.94 | −0.77 | −3.36 |
| $\theta_{EmD}$ $(S_t=0)$ | −0.14 | −1.88 | −0.07 | −1.21 | | |
| $\theta_{EmD}$ $(S_t=1)$ | 0.13 | 3.02 | 0.11 | 2.94 | | |
| $\theta_{EmS}$ $(S_t=0)$ | 0.28 | 7.18 | 0.16 | 4.74 | 0.15 | 5.70 |
| $\theta_{EmS}$ $(S_t=1)$ | 0.12 | 3.20 | 0.11 | 3.40 | 0.13 | 4.85 |
| $\theta_{UMD}$ $(S_t=0)$ | −0.04 | −0.84 | −0.01 | −0.39 | 0.00 | −0.13 |
| $\theta_{UMD}$ $(S_t=1)$ | 0.08 | 4.09 | 0.07 | 4.39 | 0.08 | 5.39 |
| $\theta_{VIX}$ $(S_t=0)$ | | | 0.08 | 1.56 | | |
| $\theta_{VIX}$ $(S_t=1)$ | | | 0.05 | 1.71 | | |
| $\sigma(Z_t=0)$ | 0.64 | 13.69 | 0.55 | 13.58 | 0.48 | 9.46 |
| $\sigma(Z_t=1)$ | 1.96 | 10.46 | 1.66 | 10.07 | 1.28 | 10.34 |
| $P^Z_{00}$ | 0.98 | 84.11 | 0.98 | 58.30 | 0.97 | 45.21 |
| $P^Z_{11}$ | 0.98 | 50.02 | 0.97 | 30.33 | 0.98 | 37.42 |

Quasi maximum likelihood estimates of the RSM, which is described in equation (26.5). $Z_t$ is the idiosyncratic Markov chain affecting the constant term $\alpha$ and the idiosyncratic volatility $\sigma$. The coefficients of the risk factors are functions of the systematic Markov chain $S_t$. $\beta_{SP}$ represents the coefficient of the market index, in this case the S&P 500 composite index. To differentiate the market beta from the coefficients of the other factors, we use $\theta$ to represent the coefficients of the other risk factors. LMS, large minus small. VMG, value minus growth. LGC, Lehmann Government Credit index. TS and CS, respectively term spread and credit spread. EmD and EmS, respectively Emerging Markets Bond and Equity indices. UMD, the momentum factor. VIX, monthly change in the VIX index. $P^Z_{00}$ and $P^Z_{11}$, respectively probabilities of staying in regime 0 and 1 for the idiosyncratic Markov chain $Z_t$.

relationship to the FoHF indices. While no FoHF index is significantly associated with the momentum factor during the tranquil regime, all indices are significantly positively associated with the momentum factor. This indicates the persistence of FOHF's poor performance (or good performance for market defensive funds) during crisis periods, and thus persistently high tail risk during these periods. The change in VIX also loads significantly during the crisis regime, although only for three indices.

Another important factor in capturing the difference in risk exposure across crisis and tranquil regimes is the Term Spread, which is significantly negatively correlated with all indices in the tranquil regime but only with two indices in the crises regime. In general, market risk, credit risk, liquidity risk, and momentum are the important factors in determining the differential risk exposures of FOHFs during tranquil and crises regimes.

Moreover, Table 26.3 shows that each FoHF index exhibits two distinct idiosyncratic regimes characterized by low and high volatility. The evolution of the idiosyncratic regimes combined with that of the exposures to the systematic risk factors will determine the characteristics of the underlying distribution of FoHFs returns. In addition to the idiosyncratic parameters presented in Table 26.3, we also filter out the time-varying probabilities of the idiosyncratic regimes. Figure 26.3 presents plots of the filtered probabilities of the high volatility idiosyncratic regime for all the FoHF indices. We observe that all the FoHF

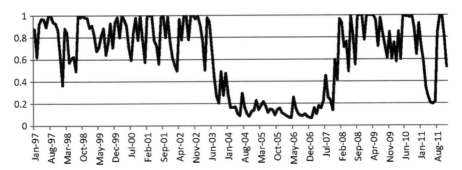

**FIGURE 26.2**
Filtered probabilities of S&P 500 regimes: filtered probability of the high-volatility idiosyncratic regime (i.e., the probability of $S_t = 1$).

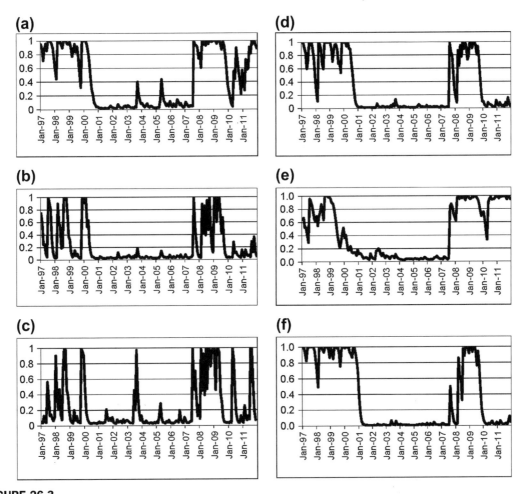

**FIGURE 26.3**
Filtered probabilities of FoHFs regimes: filtered probabilities of the high-volatility idiosyncratic regime (i.e., the probability of regime 1) for all FoHF indices. (a) BarclayHedge, (b) Composite, (c) Conservative, (d) Diversified, (e) Defensive, and (f) Strategic.

indices switch between high and low idiosyncratic volatility regimes. Both these regimes exhibit some level of persistence, with the low volatility regime being more persistent. The two most common high idiosyncratic volatility periods are 1997–2000 and 2007–2010, which coincide with the two global liquidity crises. This high volatility should be added to the high-volatility regime that FoHFs face because of their dynamic exposure to systematic risk factors during high-volatility regimes of the stock market as reported in Figure 26.2.

The parameters in Table 26.2 together with the filtered probabilities characterize the underlying distributions of the FoHF indices in any given month. Figure 26.4

**(a)**

February 2005

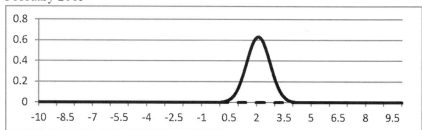

October 2008

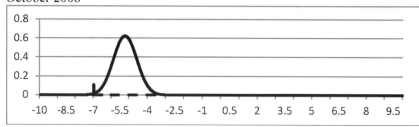

December 2011

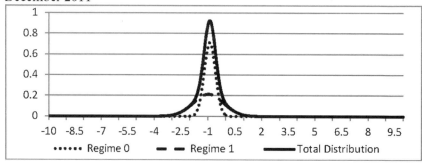

**FIGURE 26.4**

FoHF index distributions: the distribution of the FoHF indices at different times, chosen to reflect different market conditions, as captured by our RSM described in equation (26.5). (a) Composite, (b) Conservative, and (c) Defensive.

**(b)**

February 2005

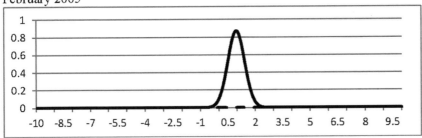

October 2008

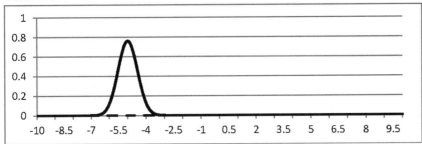

December 2011

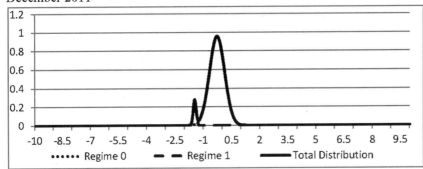

**FIGURE 26.4**
*Continued.*

presents the conditional distributions of selected FoHF indices for three selected months: February 2005 (pre-crisis period), October 2008 (crisis period), and December 2011 (post-crisis). Figure 26.4 shows that FoHF indices exhibit significant time variation in their distribution. These variations are characterized by shifts in the location of the distribution and changes in the dispersion of the distribution, both of which have first-order importance for tail risk. It is apparent from Figure 26.4 that the tail risk of FoHFs was exceptionally high during the crises and has declined to lower levels in the post-crisis period. However, FoHFs tail risk remains higher than the pre-crisis (February 2005) levels.

**(c)**

February 2005

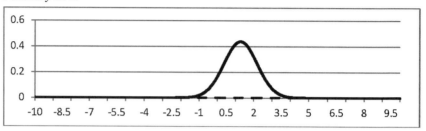

October 2008

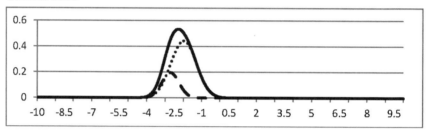

December 2011

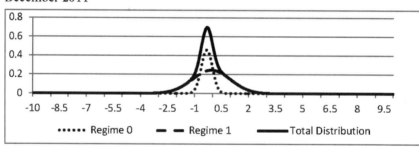

**FIGURE 26.4**
*Continued.*

We then estimate the VaR and ES for each FoHF index for the period January 2005—December 2011. Figure 26.5 presents the results. Both tail risk measures exhibit significant variation over time. The pre-crisis and post-crisis periods are characterized by low tail risk compared to the crisis period. While the FoHFs tail risk has decreased in the post-crisis period, it is still higher (and less stable) than the pre-crisis levels. This is not surprising given that financial markets and economic conditions are yet to show stable recovery. The only exception to this pattern in the FoHFs tail risk is the for the Market Defensive index. The tail risk for Market Defensive FoHFs is high during non-crisis periods and low during the crisis period. This is perfectly in line with their strategy of investing in

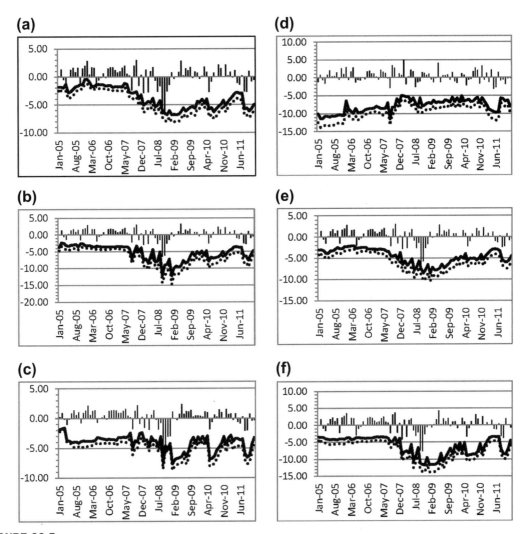

**FIGURE 26.5**
Tail risk estimates: the 95% VaR (solid lines), 95% ES (dotted lines), and FoHFs return (bars) for each FoHFs index.
(a) BarclayHedge, (b) Composite, (c) Conservative, (d) Defensive, (e) Diversified, and (f) Strategic.

short-biased hedge funds, which results in negative correlation with the market. Thus Market Defensive FoHFs are exposed to higher risk during bull markets.

In order to understand the sources of tail risk in FoHFs, we use the multifactor structure of our model to decompose the VaR into an idiosyncratic part and a systematic part, which can be further decomposed into parts created by the exposure of FoHFs to different risk factors. The results of this decomposition as percentages of total VaR are presented in Figure 26.6 and Table 26.4. The graphs

**(a)**

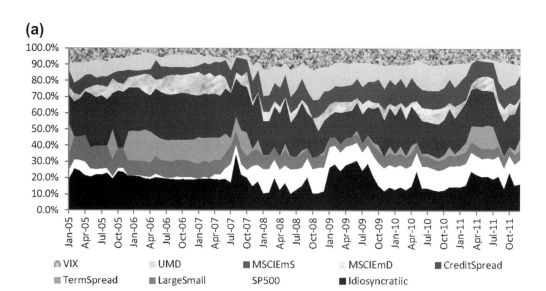

**(b)**

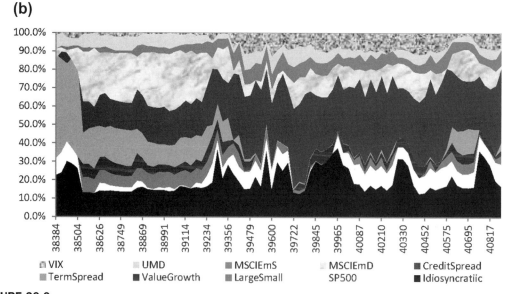

**FIGURE 26.6**
Factor contributions to tail risk estimates: the contribution of the idiosyncratic and the systematic VaR towards the total VaR for each FoHF index. (a) Composite, (b) Conservative, and (c) Market Defensive.

in Figure 26.6 also include the idiosyncratic and total VaR estimates for comparison.

Figure 26.6(a) presents the percentage contributions for the Composite index. The graphs show that the idiosyncratic component is relatively small compared to the systematic component, especially in the pre-crisis period. However, if we

**(c)**

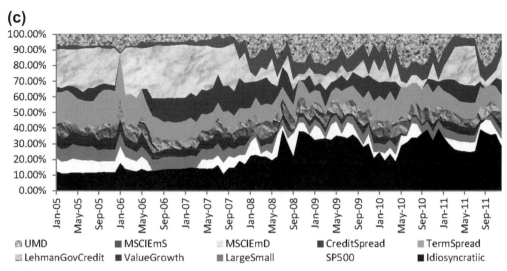

**FIGURE 26.6**
*Continued.*

include the alpha component, the contribution of the idiosyncratic component to the total VaR is negative in the pre-crisis period. This supports the hypothesis that FoHFs are able to reduce tail risk through fund-specific portfolio strategies. However, this comes to an end during the crisis, as the contribution of the idiosyncratic component becomes positive. These results show that FoHFs are able to reduce tail risk, but mainly during non-crisis periods (results are provided upon request). The graphs also show the contribution of each risk factor to the FoHFs tail risk. Credit risk is by far the most important factor for FoHFs tail risk, followed by emerging markets risk, term spread, market risk, and momentum. This follows both from the graphs and the average contributions reported in Table 26.4. Conversely, we observe from Figure 26.6(b and c) that there are some differences in the tail risk exposures of the FoHF strategy indices. While there is some evidence of a negative idiosyncratic contribution to tail risk for the Conservative index indicating that these FoHFs have some ability to reduce tail risk, there is very little evidence of such tail risk reduction ability for the Market Defensive index.

Moreover, Table 26.4 presents the contribution of each risk factor to the tail risk of the six FoHF indices. By far the most important factor is credit risk during the last crisis, with an average contribution of 26%. The other important factors include emerging markets, term spread, and momentum. To drive the point home, we perform a regression analysis of the 95% VaR for each FoHF index on the risk factors. The results, reported in Table 26.5, show that credit spread and term spread are the most important factors in explaining FoHFs tail risk.

**Table 26.4** Average Factor Contribution to Tail Risk

| Risk Factors | BarclayHedge Index | HFRI Composite Index | HFRI Conservative Index | HFRI Diversified Index | HFRI Market Defensive Index | HFRI Strategic Index | Overall Average |
|---|---|---|---|---|---|---|---|
| *(A) Whole sample* | | | | | | | |
| Idiosyncratic | 0.285 | 0.193 | 0.203 | 0.232 | 0.212 | 0.246 | 0.228 |
| S&P 500 | 0.079 | 0.087 | 0.060 | 0.052 | 0.079 | 0.078 | 0.073 |
| Large − small | 0.070 | 0.083 | 0.039 | 0.055 | 0.108 | 0.078 | 0.072 |
| Value − growth | | | 0.037 | 0.045 | 0.050 | | 0.044 |
| Lehman Government Credit | 0.040 | | | 0.082 | | | 0.061 |
| Term spread | 0.098 | 0.061 | 0.095 | 0.129 | 0.065 | 0.030 | 0.080 |
| Credit spread | 0.216 | 0.240 | 0.268 | 0.085 | 0.138 | 0.234 | 0.197 |
| MSCI Emerging Debt | | 0.064 | 0.142 | 0.161 | 0.113 | 0.065 | 0.109 |
| MSCI Emerging Stock | 0.116 | 0.097 | 0.052 | 0.068 | 0.119 | 0.112 | 0.094 |
| Momentum | 0.095 | 0.098 | 0.050 | 0.091 | 0.117 | 0.105 | 0.093 |
| VIX | | 0.077 | 0.054 | | | 0.052 | 0.061 |
| *(B) January 2005–July 2007 subsample* | | | | | | | |
| Idiosyncratic | 0.320 | 0.207 | 0.170 | 0.134 | 0.189 | 0.258 | 0.213 |
| S&P 500 | 0.073 | 0.028 | 0.036 | 0.053 | 0.060 | 0.042 | 0.049 |
| Large − small | 0.108 | 0.110 | 0.061 | 0.076 | 0.120 | 0.094 | 0.095 |
| Value − growth | | | 0.045 | 0.064 | 0.033 | | 0.047 |

| | | | | | | | |
|---|---|---|---|---|---|---|---|
| Lehman Government Credit | 0.024 | 0.105 | 0.216 | 0.075 | 0.146 | 0.041 | 0.050 |
| Term spread | 0.163 | 0.272 | 0.149 | 0.162 | 0.042 | 0.295 | 0.139 |
| Credit spread | 0.144 | 0.083 | 0.220 | 0.085 | 0.171 | 0.037 | 0.164 |
| MSCI Emerging Debt | | 0.065 | 0.030 | 0.269 | 0.099 | 0.079 | 0.156 |
| MSCI Emerging Stock | 0.106 | 0.075 | 0.060 | 0.026 | 0.141 | 0.078 | 0.068 |
| Momentum | 0.061 | 0.055 | 0.014 | 0.056 | | 0.076 | 0.078 |
| VIX | | | | | | | 0.048 |
| *(C) July 2007–December 2011 subsample* | | | | | | | |
| Idiosyncratic | 0.264 | 0.185 | 0.222 | 0.290 | 0.225 | 0.239 | 0.238 |
| S&P 500 | 0.082 | 0.123 | 0.074 | 0.052 | 0.091 | 0.099 | 0.087 |
| Large – small | 0.048 | 0.068 | 0.026 | 0.044 | 0.101 | 0.068 | 0.059 |
| Value – growth | | | 0.032 | 0.033 | 0.061 | | 0.042 |
| Lehman Government Credit | 0.049 | 0.034 | 0.024 | 0.086 | 0.017 | 0.024 | 0.068 |
| Term spread | 0.061 | 0.220 | 0.338 | 0.109 | 0.194 | 0.199 | 0.045 |
| Credit spread | 0.259 | 0.052 | 0.097 | 0.085 | 0.079 | 0.081 | 0.216 |
| MSCI Emerging Debt | | 0.116 | 0.065 | 0.098 | 0.130 | 0.132 | 0.081 |
| MSCI Emerging Stock | 0.122 | 0.112 | 0.044 | 0.092 | 0.102 | 0.120 | 0.109 |
| Momentum | 0.116 | 0.090 | 0.078 | 0.111 | | | 0.101 |
| VIX | | | | | | 0.038 | 0.069 |

Contributions of the idiosyncratic and systematic parts in equation (26.5) to the total tail risk (measured by 95% VaR) of the FoHF indices. The columns represent the FoHF indices. The first row contains the idiosyncratic contributions to the total VaR and the rest of the rows contain the systematic part decomposed into the different risk factors that are significantly associated with the FoHF indices.

**Table 26.5** Regression Analysis of FoHF Index VaR

| | Dependent Variables | | | | | |
|---|---|---|---|---|---|---|
| | VaR of BarclayHedge FoHF Index | VaR of HFRI Composite Index | VaR of HFRI Conservative Index | VaR of HFRI Diversified Index | VaR of HFRI Market Defensive Index | VaR of HFRI Strategic Index |
| *(A) Entire sample* | | | | | | |
| S&P 500 | −0.06 | −0.05 | −0.01 | −0.06 | 0.08 | −0.03 |
| | (−1.28) | (−0.67) | (−0.21) | (−1.29) | (1.15) | (−0.45) |
| Large − small | 0.02 | −0.01 | 0.02 | −0.02 | 0.05 | 0.02 |
| | (0.42) | (−0.21) | (0.37) | (−0.38) | (0.57) | (0.30) |
| Term spread | −0.93*** | −0.41*** | −0.12 | −0.39*** | 0.72*** | −0.78*** |
| | (−11.46) | (−4.76) | (−1.50) | (−4.65) | (5.84) | (−5.64) |
| Credit spread | −1.58*** | −2.27*** | −1.12*** | −1.88*** | 0.62* | −3.09*** |
| | (−6.24) | (−6.84) | (−5.10) | (−7.89) | (1.73) | (−7.89) |
| Emerging Debt | −0.06 | −0.06 | −0.06 | −0.02 | −0.07 | 0.04 |
| | (−0.67) | (−0.67) | (−1.20) | (−0.39) | (−0.55) | (0.48) |
| Emerging Stock | 0.04 | 0.02 | −0.01 | 0.04 | −0.04 | 0.02 |
| | (1.54) | (0.59) | (−0.46) | (1.48) | (−0.80) | (0.59) |
| Momentum | −0.01 | 0.02 | 0.04 | 0.00 | 0.00 | 0.03 |
| | (−0.28) | (0.66) | (1.51) | (0.14) | (0.05) | (0.86) |
| VIX | −0.09 | −0.09 | −0.07 | −0.06 | | |
| | (−1.51) | (−1.51) | (−1.56) | (−1.32) | | |
| Lehman Government Credit | −0.15 | | | | 0.22 | |
| | (−1.46) | | | | (1.17) | |
| Value − growth | | | 0.05 | | −0.07 | −0.04 |
| | | | (0.90) | | (−0.67) | (−0.42) |
| Constant | −1.46*** | −3.10*** | −3.65*** | −2.71*** | −11.31*** | −1.91*** |
| | (−5.14) | (−9.00) | (−14.73) | (−10.54) | (−24.76) | (−5.38) |
| No. of observations | 84 | 84 | 84 | 84 | 84 | 84 |
| Adjusted $R^2$ | 0.78 | 0.71 | 0.42 | 0.69 | 0.34 | 0.74 |
| *(B) January 2005–July 2007 subsample* | | | | | | |
| S&P 500 | −0.08 | 0.06 | −0.02 | 0.00 | −0.15* | 0.00 |
| | (−1.12) | (1.19) | (−0.24) | (0.06) | (−1.88) | (0.13) |
| Large − small | 0.00 | 0.04 | −0.03 | −0.04 | 0.07 | −0.01 |
| | (0.02) | (1.66) | (−0.52) | (−1.17) | (0.57) | (−0.22) |

| | (1) | (2) | (3) | (4) | (5) | (6) |
|---|---|---|---|---|---|---|
| Term spread | −0.24 (−0.78) | 0.45*** (2.71) | −0.06 (−0.23) | −0.69*** (−3.86) | −1.84*** (−6.75) | −0.27*** (−3.42) |
| Credit spread | −0.88 (−0.49) | 0.26 (0.17) | −5.26*** (−3.33) | −1.09 (−1.26) | −2.35 (−0.95) | −1.74*** (−3.08) |
| Emerging Debt | | 0.03 (0.62) | 0.07 (0.65) | −0.09 (−1.19) | −0.25 (−1.36) | −0.02 (−0.47) |
| Emerging Stock | 0.04 (1.21) | −0.02 (−1.12) | −0.03 (−0.72) | 0.02 (0.50) | 0.06 (1.16) | −0.01 (−0.45) |
| Momentum | −0.13* (−1.72) | −0.01 (−0.22) | 0.09 (1.03) | 0.04 (0.68) | 0.06 (0.58) | 0.00 (0.15) |
| VIX | | 0.03 (0.78) | 0.04 (0.67) | −0.07 (−1.44) | | |
| Lehman Government Credit | | | | | 0.05 (0.23) | |
| Value – growth | −0.18 (−1.24) | | −0.15* (−1.94) | | −0.03 (−0.18) | −0.01 (−0.37) |
| Constant | −1.88 (−1.16) | −5.39*** (−3.91) | 0.05 (0.04) | −3.03*** (−3.73) | −8.44*** (−3.79) | −2.91*** (−5.55) |
| No. of observations | 31 | 31 | 31 | 31 | 31 | 31 |
| Adjusted $R^2$ | −0.08 | 0.25 | 0.29 | 0.43 | 0.59 | 0.11 |

*(C) July 2007–December 2011 subsample*

| | (1) | (2) | (3) | (4) | (5) | (6) |
|---|---|---|---|---|---|---|
| S&P 500 | −0.05 (−1.05) | | −0.00 (−0.00) | −0.08 (−1.49) | 0.05 (0.61) | −0.02 (−0.24) |
| Large – small | 0.08* (1.93) | | 0.07 (1.10) | −0.02 (−0.23) | −0.06 (−1.08) | 0.05 (0.52) |
| Term spread | −0.25* (−1.88) | | −0.08 (−0.43) | 0.19 (1.27) | 0.08 (0.35) | −0.26 (−0.89) |
| Credit spread | −1.28*** (−7.05) | | −0.94*** (−4.17) | −1.84*** (−7.01) | 0.22 (0.79) | −2.90*** (−7.19) |
| Emerging Debt | 0.03 (1.29) | | −0.05 (−0.91) | 0.02 (0.33) | 0.06 (0.66) | 0.09 (0.93) |
| Emerging Stock | | | −0.01 (−0.45) | 0.03 (0.99) | −0.04 (−0.72) | 0.00 (0.04) |
| Momentum | 0.02 (1.40) | | 0.05* (1.85) | 0.02 (0.54) | 0.00 (0.01) | 0.05 (1.10) |
| VIX | −0.09 (−1.22) | | −0.06 (−1.22) | −0.07 (−1.30) | | |

*(Continued)*

**Table 26.5**   Regression Analysis of FoHF Index VaR—cont'd

| | Dependent Variables | | | | | |
|---|---|---|---|---|---|---|
| | VaR of BarclayHedge FoHF Index | VaR of HFRI Composite Index | VaR of HFRI Conservative Index | VaR of HFRI Diversified Index | VaR of HFRI Market Defensive Index | VaR of HFRI Strategic Index |
| Lehman Government Credit | 0.03 (0.46) | | | | −0.20 (−1.09) | |
| Value − growth | | | 0.07 (0.89) | | 0.09 (0.93) | −0.09 (−0.64) |
| Constant | −3.97*** (−10.31) | −4.56*** (−7.27) | −4.07*** (−7.16) | −4.43*** (−9.81) | −8.48*** (−12.39) | −3.79*** (−5.01) |
| No. of observations | 53 | 53 | 53 | 53 | 53 | 53 |
| Adjusted $R^2$ | 0.55 | 0.57 | 0.34 | 0.56 | −0.11 | 0.56 |

Regression analysis of the VaR for each FoHF index in our sample. The regression equation is of the form $VaR_{i,t} = \alpha + \beta' F_{i,t} + \varepsilon_t$, where $F_{i,t}$ is a vector of relevant risk factors for index $i$. The relevant risk factors are those factors that were used in the RSM as presented in Table 26.3.
Significant at *10%, **5%, and ***1%.

## CONCLUSION

In this chapter, we study the effects of financial crises on FoHFs tail risk. We analyze crisis-dependent risk exposures for various FoHF index strategies and identify common risk factors on tail risks, especially during crises. We have two main results. (i) We show that FoHFs present large and fat left-hand tails. Using our multifactor switching regime approach we find that Credit Risk is by far the most important factor for tail risk of FoHFs during the recent crisis. Other important factors include term spread and momentum. (ii) Idiosyncratic risk in the FoHF indexes plays a reduced role, mostly during crisis periods. Understanding risk exposures of FoHFs tail risk is important for investors and risk managers. It shows that even if diversification is able to reduce the volatility of a FoHF, it is not able to reduce tail risk, mostly during crises periods; the only exception is the FoHFs Market Defensive index strategy.

## References

Acerbi, C., & Tasche, D. (2002). On the Coherence of Expected Shortfall. *Journal of Banking and Finance, 26*(7), 1487–1503.

Agarwal, V., & Naik, N. Y. (2004). Risk and Portfolio Decision Involving Hedge Funds. *The Review of Financial Studies, 17*(1), 62–98.

Artzner, P., Delbaen, F., Eber, J. M., & Heath, D. (1998). Coherent Measures of Risk. *Mathematical Finance, 9*(3), 203–228.

Billio, M., Getmansky, M., & Pelizzon, L. (2008). *Crises and Hedge Fund Risk*. London: Working Paper, Yale School of Management's Financial Research Network.

Billio, M., Getmansky, M., & Pelizzon, L. (2011). Dynamic Risk Exposures in Hedge Funds. *Computational Statistics & Data Analysis, 56*(11), 3517–3532.

Billio, M., & Pelizzon, L. (2000). Value-at-Risk: A Multivariate Switching Regime Approach. *Journal of Empirical Finance, 7*(5), 513–554.

Brown, S., Gregoriou, G. N., & Pascalau, R. (2012). Diversification in Funds of Hedge Funds: Is It Possible to Overdiversify? *Review of Asset Pricing Studies, 2*(1), 89–100.

Carhart, M. M. (1997). On Persistence in Mutual Fund Performance. *Journal of Finance, 52*(1), 57–82.

Fama, E. F., & French, K. R. (1993). Common Risk Factors in the Returns on Stocks and Bonds. *Journal of Financial Economics, 33*(1), 3–56.

Fung, W. K. H., & Hsieh, D. A. (1997). Empirical Characteristics of Dynamic Trading Strategies: The Case of Hedge Funds. *The Review of Financial Studies, 10*(2), 275–303.

Fung, W. K. H., & Hsieh, D. A. (2002a). Risk in Fixed Income Hedge Fund Styles. *Journal of Fixed Income, 12*(2), 6–27.

Fung, W. K. H., & Hsieh, D. A. (2002b). Asset-Based Style Factors for Hedge Funds. *Financial Analyst Journal, 58*(4), 16–27.

Fung, W. K. H., & Hsieh, D. A. (2004). Hedge Fund Benchmarks: A Risk Based Approach. *Financial Analyst Journal, 60*(2), 60–80.

Hamilton, J. D. (1994). *Time Series Analysis*. Princeton, NJ: Princeton University Press.

Inuia, K., & Kijima, M. (2005). On the Significance of Expected Shortfall as a Coherent Risk Measure. *Journal of Banking and Finance, 29*(4), 853–864.

Jorion, P. (2003). *Financial Risk Manager Handbook*. Hoboken, NJ: Wiley.

# CHAPTER 27

# Funds of Hedge Funds, Efficient Portfolios, and Investor Clienteles: Empirical Evidence from Growth and Financial Crisis Periods

451

Wolfgang Bessler and Philipp Kurmann
Justus-Liebig-University, Giessen, Germany

## 27.1. INTRODUCTION

It has long been argued that hedge funds as an alternative asset class provide positive risk-adjusted returns with rather low correlations to traditional asset classes, suggesting significant diversification benefits in a portfolio context (Fung and Hsieh, 1999). Consequently, institutional investors such as university endowments, pension funds, insurance companies, but also high-net-worth individuals have allocated capital to hedge funds, contributing to the remarkable growth of the hedge fund industry over time (Lerner *et al.*, 2008). Assets under management (AUM) in the hedge fund industry increased from US$345

Reconsidering Funds of Hedge Funds. http://dx.doi.org/10.1016/B978-0-12-401699-6.00027-7

billion in 2000 to almost US$2.2 trillion in 2011 (BarclayHedge). Among these assets, funds of hedge funds (FoHFs), i.e., hedge funds investing in other single-strategy hedge funds, accounted for about 25% (US$509 billion) in 2011. In addition, a recent survey documented that for nearly two-thirds of FoHFs institutional capital represented the majority of their total AUM, reflecting the prominence of institutional investors in the hedge funds industry (Deutsche Bank, 2012).

However, during the recent financial crisis the FoHFs industry experienced significant outflows and an overall decline in its asset base. In fact, AUM decreased by about 60% between 2007 and 2011. Among the driving forces were liquidity problems and substandard due diligence on risky investments. Overall, FoHFs expected diversification benefits from investing in single-strategy hedge funds, i.e., across individual managers and strategies, did not materialize and provided insufficient risk reduction, resulting in a severe decline of investor confidence. Consequently, demand for more transparent FoHFs structures in the form of 'Undertaking in Collective Investment in Transferable Securities' (UCITS) funds emerged. Moreover, investors became well aware of the additional layer of fees charged by FoHFs. This resulted in a substantial reallocation of funds from the FoHFs industry to single-strategy hedge funds. In fact, almost half of the institutions engaged in the hedge funds industry redirected more than 50% of their historical FoHFs allocations towards single-strategy hedge funds (Deutsche Bank, 2012). During the financial crisis, FoHFs AUM continuously decreased while investments into equities and bonds recovered after 2008 (Figure 27.1). Hence, the benefits of FoHFs has become a highly debated topic in the recent years.

To gain insights into their value-added in terms of generating superior returns and diversification benefits, we analyze the contribution of five FoHFs strategies to portfolio efficiency for the period between December 2002 and December 2011. We explicitly differentiate between a growth (2002–2007) and a crisis (2007–2011) period to investigate the benefits of FoHFs in different market environments and in light of the recent decline of their AUM. As illustrated in Figure 27.2, we analyze the value of adding FoHFs to a well-diversified portfolio of traditional and alternative asset classes such as equities, bonds, real estate, and commodities ('Benchmark Portfolio').

Our empirical analysis is based on the mean-variance framework that allows us to conduct spanning tests as proposed by Huberman and Kandel (1987) and Kan and Zhou (2012). Spanning tests explicitly address the question whether FoHFs significantly improve portfolio efficiency, thereby providing a rationale for the 'Alternative Portfolio' (see Figure 27.2). Importantly, the technique of Kan and Zhou (2012) provides evidence on the contribution of FoHFs for individual positions along the efficient frontier, i.e., the Global Minimum Variance (GMV) portfolio and the tangency portfolio. Therefore, we are able to derive recommendations for two different investor clienteles labeled 'Conservative' and 'Aggressive'. Conservative investors are considered to be more risk-averse, thereby

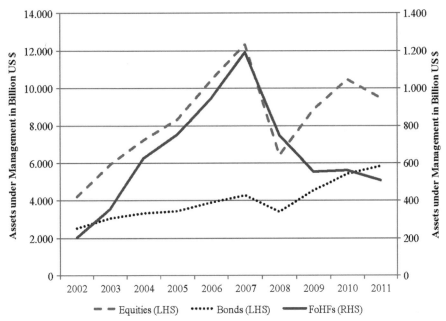

**FIGURE 27.1**
AUM of different asset classes (worldwide equity mutual funds (Equities), international bond mutual funds (Bonds), and FoHFs) between December 2002 and December 2011.
*Data from BarclayHedge and EFAMA.*

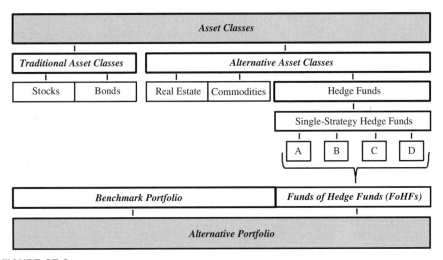

**FIGURE 27.2**
Investment opportunity set considered in the empirical analysis. Asset classes are differentiated between Traditional Asset Classes (Stocks and Bonds) and Alternative Asset Classes (Real Estate, Commodities, and Hedge Funds). The Benchmark Portfolio includes Stocks, Bonds, Real Estate, and Commodities. The Alternative Portfolio additionally includes FoHFs.

focusing on diversification and risk reduction instead of alpha generation. For these objectives, the position of the GMV portfolio is of particular interest. In contrast, aggressive investors are supposed to seek positive risk-adjusted returns (alpha) while diversification benefits along low volatility levels are less relevant. Hence, they strive for changes in the tangency portfolio. Given that hedge fund returns are usually serially correlated as a result of illiquid portfolio holdings, return variances may be significantly downward-biased and mean-variance spanning tests might yield rather inaccurate results. Moreover, FoHFs returns are often not normally distributed, suggesting the relevance to account for higher-moment risk when analyzing their portfolio contribution. Therefore, we additionally control for potential return smoothing and deviations from normality in our empirical setup.

Our results indicate that FoHFs significantly improve the position of the GMV portfolio, hence providing an attractive asset class for conservative investor clienteles even during the recent crisis period. Importantly, this result holds irrespective of the particular FoHFs strategy. The tangency portfolio, however, is more sensitive to the state of the economy. In the bull market period we find evidence that the majority of FoHFs strategies generate diversification benefits for aggressive investor clienteles by providing positive risk-adjusted returns. In contrast, our empirical findings suggest little potential for FoHFs to improve the tangency portfolio during the financial crisis period. Moreover, after controlling for kurtosis and tail risk the evidence for FoHFs' contribution to portfolio efficiency is reduced, but still highly significant for the position of the GMV portfolio. These results even hold after controlling for return smoothing.

The rest of this chapter proceeds as follows. In Section 27.2, we review the relevant literature on FoHFs in terms of their performance and contribution to portfolio efficiency. Section 27.3 discusses our data sample and the identification of individual subperiods, while Section 27.4 introduces the methodology. In Section 27.5, we present and discuss our empirical results, followed by our conclusions.

## 27.2. LITERATURE REVIEW

FoHFs seem to provide a number of advantages compared to individual (single-strategy) hedge funds. Their investment approach is similar to that of funds of mutual funds (FoMFs) in terms of offering investors an investment opportunity in a multi-manager/multi-strategy portfolio. FoHFs invest in different individual hedge funds, thereby diversifying over a variety of hedge fund managers and hedge fund strategies. They allow individual investors to get access to the most prominent and leading single-strategy hedge funds that otherwise might not be available for direct investments (Edelman *et al.*, 2012). In general, monitoring, operational due diligence, and risk management activities are valuable services that individual investors and especially retail investors usually cannot perform themselves. As the initial investment amount in FoHFs is often lower than for single-strategy hedge funds they represent attractive investment vehicles for a relatively large investor group. Recent studies also argue that analyzing FoHFs implicitly controls for realistic investment restrictions such as lock-up periods, redemption periods, and notice periods (Fung et al., 2008; Dewaele et al., 2011). In addition, FoHFs returns usually include the return information of single-strategy hedge funds that are close to collapse and therefore might stop reporting their negative performance to conventional hedge fund databases several months before distress. From a statistical perspective, FoHFs data is less affected by well-known biases, hence providing a more accurate picture of returns of diversified hedge fund investments (Fung and Hsieh, 2000).

## 27.2.1. FoHFs Performance

Hedge funds are well known for engaging in flexible long-short investment strategies that offer them the opportunity to provide positive returns independent of the respective market environment (Holler, 2012). As discussed before, individual hedge funds expose investors to a number of restrictions and constraints so that FoHFs became the preferred vehicle for investors seeking exposure to hedge fund strategies. The funds' objectives are to provide alpha with diversified, less risky portfolios, consisting of single-strategy hedge funds. However, successfully selecting alpha-generating single-strategy hedge funds while still providing sufficient due diligence at reasonable costs is one of the paramount tasks and challenges for FoHFs managers.

Empirical studies analyzing FoHFs' ability to provide significantly positive risk-adjusted returns yield rather mixed results. Fung and Hsieh (2004) report smaller alphas for FoHFs than for single-strategy hedge funds when applying their seven-factor asset-based style (ABS) model. However, they only analyze a diversified FoHF index provided by Hedge Fund Research (HFR). Nevertheless, they conclude that the relative underperformance of FoHFs might be driven by too many inefficient FoHFs in the index rather than by other factors such as the additional layer of fees. A similar result in terms of FoHFs performance is reported by Denvir and Hutson (2006), although they also argue that FoHFs exhibit characteristics that might offset their apparent underperformance. In fact, compared to individual hedge funds, FoHFs returns appear to be less negatively skewed. Moreover, the authors argue that the relative under-performance documented for FoHFs is likely to be a result of the overstatement of single-strategy hedge fund returns in combination with an underestimation of their risk in common indices.

For the period between 1995 and 2004, Fung et al. (2008) find that returns on FoHFs are predominantly driven by their exposure to the seven risk factors proposed by Fung and Hsieh (2004). In general, FoHFs do not generate significant alpha, although this conclusion is partially reversed when taking the cross-section of FoHFs into account. On average, 22% of individual FoHFs deliver significantly positive alphas, although this percentage strongly fluctuates over time, suggesting that the ability of FoHFs to generate alpha depends on market conditions. Edelman et al. (2012) extend the initial sample period of Fung et al. (2008) and document that the average proportion of 'have-alpha'

FoHFs dramatically decreased from 22% to 2% for the period between 2005 and 2010. Their findings are in line with the tendency towards market equilibrium following the theoretical work of Berk and Green (2004) and the empirical evidence for mutual funds provided in Bessler *et al.* (2011, 2012c).

Moreover, Dewaele *et al.* (2011) point out that the proportion of truly alpha-generating FoHFs is highly dependent on the choice of the particular factor model. By applying the false discoveries (FD) technique of Barras *et al.* (2010), they find a proportion of about 22% 'skilled' funds when using a 16-factor model and only 5.56% when using a 13-factor hedge fund index model. Hence, the authors conclude that from a pure investment perspective, and without accounting for potential diversification properties and due diligence activities, any fund-picking skills of FoHFs managers seem to be outweighed by their additional layer of fees.

### 27.2.2. FoHFs and Asset Allocation

Nevertheless, the strong surge of investments in FoHFs over the last decade was only partly driven by the belief of investors in getting positive and significant abnormal returns. Diversification benefits from combining hedge funds with other asset classes are among the most important reasons for investors seeking exposure to hedge fund strategies (Deutsche Bank, 2012). The majority of empirical studies that analyze the diversification benefits of FoHFs in a portfolio context support this idea. Applying four different optimization techniques, Gueyié and Amvella (2006) find that FoHFs improve the risk-return profile of conventional stock/bond portfolios. In a similar vein, Denvir and Hutson (2006) conclude that FoHFs exhibit relatively low correlations with equity indices, suggesting their attractiveness when combined with equity portfolios. By investigating the contribution of single-strategy hedge funds and a FoHF index in the context of different benchmark portfolios, Kooli (2007) reports that FoHFs are beneficial for improving the position of the GMV portfolio, while the evidence for single-strategy hedge funds is less supportive. Similar results are reported by Bessler *et al.* (2012a) within a Bayesian framework. They document that investors allocating assets into a diversified single-strategy hedge fund index (i.e., implicitly taking the perspective of a FoHFs investor) achieve significant improvements of the GMV portfolio in different market environments. Their results indicate that hedge funds are particularly relevant for reducing portfolio volatility in periods of market distress. Consequently, they represent a relatively attractive asset class during market downturns.

Gregoriou and Rouah (2002) further emphasize the relevance of FoHFs in pension fund portfolios as they represent a unique opportunity for reducing capital losses in bear markets. An economic rationale for the attractiveness of FoHFs during times when diversification is most needed is provided by Darolles and Vaissié (2012). They conclude that strategic asset allocation is the only step in the investment process where FoHFs consistently add value. Importantly, strategic asset allocation decisions help mitigate the downside risk that originates from higher correlations with traditional asset classes in periods of market distress while tactical allocation and fund selection are of minor importance.

However, these diversification benefits might be reduced due to increased correlations with traditional asset classes when the number of individual hedge funds in FoHFs portfolios becomes large (Lhabitant and Learned, 2002). Recently, Brown *et al.* (2012) reported that overdiversification in FoHFs holding more than 20 individual hedge funds might even lead to diminished returns and higher tail risk exposure, thereby effectively reducing diversification benefits. Their rather aggregate diversification measure is further differentiated by Shawky *et al.* (2012). Based on four individual dimensions of portfolio diversification, the authors support the empirical findings of Brown *et al.* (2012) as the majority of diversification dimensions have shared a negative relation to FoHFs performance in recent years.

Overall, while the empirical evidence on FoHFs' ability to generate significantly positive alphas is rather mixed, a number of authors document positive diversification benefits. However, these advantages might be reduced in light of crisis periods and inefficient portfolio construction techniques. Therefore, our study provides a detailed analysis of individual FoHF strategies and their ability to enhance the efficient investment opportunity set for both growth and crisis market environments. We explicitly differentiate between a 'Composite' FoHF index and more focused individual single-strategy FoHF indices to shed light on the question whether potential excess diversification has a significant effect on the value-added of FoHFs in a portfolio context. In addition, we investigate whether the contribution of FoHFs differs for particular investor clienteles by focusing on conservative (low-volatility) and more aggressive (high-risk) portfolios.

## 27.3. DATA

### 27.3.1. FoHFs and Benchmark Assets

We analyze the time period between December 2002 and December 2011, which covers both a 'growth period' or 'non-crisis period' (2002–2007) and a 'crisis period' (2007–2011). Our analysis starts in December 2002 subsequent to a number of economic and financial downturn periods as proposed by Billio *et al.* (2010). These involve the Asian, Russian, and Argentinean crises, the default of Long-Term Capital Management (LTCM), the internet bubble, and the September 11 terrorist attacks as well as critical US accounting scandals in the second half of 2002. The period from 2002 to 2007 was accompanied by positive returns for almost all asset classes and sustained growth rates in their respective assets under management as documented in Figures 27.1 and 27.3. With the beginning of the financial crisis these dynamics significantly changed, allowing us to analyze the contribution of FoHFs to portfolio efficiency in bull as well as bear markets.

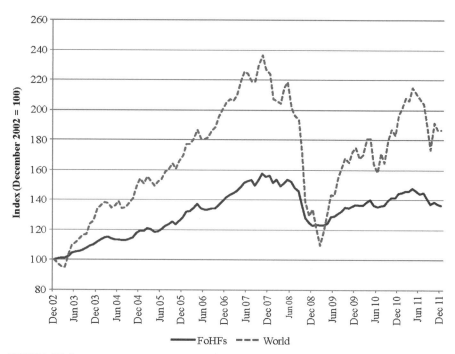

**FIGURE 27.3**
Performance of the Composite FoHFs strategy and the equity market (MSCI World Total Return Index)
between December 2002 and December 2011.
*Data from Thomson Reuters Datastream.*

Our sample data is provided by HFR and includes an index for the aggregate
FoHFs universe ('Composite') as well as four subindices designed to measure the
performance of FoHFs with different investment strategies. The composite index
is equally weighted including FoHFs from different styles that have at least
US$50 million AUM or have been actively traded for at least 12 months. The
subindices are labeled 'Conservative', 'Diversified', 'Market Defensive', and
'Strategic'. The definitions are provided in Table 27.1, while Figure 27.4 further
clarifies the respective investment opportunity set of each index.

The benefits from adding FoHFs to an existing portfolio are evaluated in the
context of a well-diversified multi-asset benchmark portfolio that includes
equities, bonds, real estate, and commodities (see Figure 27.2). Equity markets
are represented by the MSCI World Total Return index (World) and the MSCI
Emerging Markets Total Return index (Emerging). Bond market investments are
approximated by the performance of a total return index replicating an investment in constant 10-year maturity US government bonds (Gov) while the
performance of corporate bonds is captured by the Bank of America/Merrill
Lynch US BBB-A Total Return index (Corp). Moreover, the S&P GSCI Total
Return index (GSCI) is used to reflect the returns on a diversified portfolio of
commodities, the FTSE/NAREIT Total Return index (REIT) represents real estate
investments, and the S&P GSCI Gold Spot index (Gold) measures the returns of

**Table 27.1**  Definition and investment focus of the HFRI FOF Subindices

| | | |
|---|---|---|
| (1) | **Diversified** | Exhibits one or more of the following characteristics: invests in a variety of strategies among multiple managers; historical annual return and/or a standard deviation generally similar to the HFRI FOF Composite index; demonstrates generally close performance and returns distribution correlation to the HFRI FOF Composite index. A fund in the HFRI FOF Diversified index tends to show minimal loss in down markets while achieving superior returns in up markets. |
| (2) | **Conservative** | Exhibits one or more of the following characteristics: seeks consistent returns by primarily investing in funds that generally engage in more 'conservative' strategies such as Equity Market Neutral, Fixed Income Arbitrage, and Convertible Arbitrage; exhibits a lower historical annual standard deviation than the HFRI FOF Composite index. A fund in the HFRI FOF Conservative index shows generally consistent performance regardless of market conditions. |
| (3) | **Market Defensive** | Exhibits one or more of the following characteristics: invests in funds that generally engage in short-biased strategies such as short selling and managed futures; shows a negative correlation to the general market benchmarks (S&P). A fund in the HFRI FOF Market Defensive index exhibits higher returns during down markets than during up markets. |
| (4) | **Strategic** | Exhibits one or more of the following characteristics: seeks superior returns by primarily investing in funds that generally engage in more opportunistic strategies such as Emerging Markets, Sector Specific, and Equity Hedge; exhibits a greater dispersion of returns and higher volatility compared to the HFRI FOF Composite index. A fund in the HFRI FOF Strategic index tends to outperform the HFRI FOF Composite index in up markets and underperform the index in down markets. |

https://www.hedgefundresearch.com.

an investment in gold. The benchmark data is denominated in US$ and provided by Thomson Reuters Datastream.

## 27.3.2. Definition of Individual Subperiods

To analyze the benefits of adding FoHFs to the benchmark portfolio in a time-varying framework, we divide our sample into a period before and subsequent to the beginning of the recent financial crisis. The separation of both subperiods can be motivated from two perspectives. First, Figures 27.1 and 27.3 clearly indicate that the FoHFs industry exhibited sustained growth rates in terms of AUM as well as performance levels until 2007. However, beginning with the default of two hedge funds managed by Bear Stearns in July 2007, performance started to decline, leading to profound losses for FoHFs investors

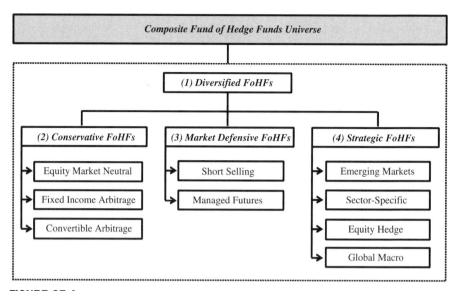

**FIGURE 27.4**
Classification of the FoHFs universe. The Composite FoHFs universe is differentiated into the four subindices and the respective underlying strategies.

throughout 2008. As discussed above, their inferior performance combined with their poor due diligence and unattractive fee structures led to significant outflows and contributed to the reduction of AUM in the FoHFs industry over recent years. Therefore, we set the breakpoint for our empirical analysis in July 2007.

However, to verify the validity of our approach, we apply a Chow test to examine the existence of a structural break in FoHFs returns with July 2007 as breakpoint. Therefore, we run separate regressions (equation 27.1) for the full sample as well as for both individual subperiods, regressing FoHFs returns ($R_t$) on the return vector of our set of benchmark assets ($F_t$):

$$R_t = \alpha_t + \beta F_t + \varepsilon_t. \tag{27.1}$$

The test statistic (equation 27.2) focuses on the sum of squared residuals $S$ of each regression and follows an $F$-distribution with $k$ and $N_1 + N_2 + 2k$ degrees of freedom where $k$ is the total number of estimated parameters, and $N_1$ and $N_2$ are the number of observations in each subperiod:

$$Chow = \frac{\dfrac{S_F - (S_1 + S_2)}{k}}{\dfrac{S_1 + S_2}{N_1 + N_2 - 2k}}, \tag{27.2}$$

where $S_F$, $S_1$, and $S_2$ represent the sum of squared residuals for the full sample, the first subperiod, and the second subperiod. The null hypothesis of this test

| Table 27.2 | Chow Test for Structural Break in July 2007 | | | | |
|---|---|---|---|---|---|
| | **Conservative** | **Diversified** | **Market Defensive** | **Strategic** | **Composite** |
| Chow test | 5.124 | 4.366 | 1.702 | 4.610 | 4.353 |
| $p$-value | 0.000 | 0.000 | 0.108 | 0.000 | 0.000 |

Results for the Chow structural break test. The breakpoint is set to July 2007. 'Chow test' represents the respective test statistic; '$p$-value' provides information on the associated statistical significance.

assumes equality of the regression parameters in both subperiods. If the null hypothesis is rejected there is evidence for the presence of a structural break in the time-series of FoHFs returns. The results are reported in Table 27.2.

For the majority of FoHF indices (four out of five), the null hypothesis of equality of regression parameters in the two subperiods is rejected at conventional significance levels. For the Market Defensive index the Chow test is marginally insignificant with a $p$-value of 10.8%. This result, however, is not surprising as defensive strategies usually outperform during crisis periods. Hence, compared to the other subindices, their returns tend to move in the opposite direction, thus providing a hedge during market downturns and exhibiting rather small exposures to conventional risk factors. Overall, these findings support our initial hypothesis that July 2007 represents a reasonable breakpoint for analyzing FoHFs' contribution to portfolio efficiency for the periods before and subsequent to the beginning of the financial crisis.

While Edelman *et al.* (2012) define an additional period, reflecting the timespan after the financial crisis (April 2009–December 2010), we argue that even though the crisis originated in the US subprime mortgage market, its effects spread widely across the globe and are far from being resolved. For instance, the crisis is still prevalent and noticeable in Europe with a number of countries experiencing severe sovereign debt problems. As FoHFs usually diversify across regions and/or asset classes (Shawky *et al.*, 2012), it is reasonable to assume that structural problems in the US as well as in other countries and continents matter for their investment strategies. Therefore, we define the 'growth period' or 'non-crisis period' from December 2002 to July 2007 and the 'crisis period' from August 2007 to December 2011.

## 27.3.3. Descriptive Statistics

The descriptive statistics of the hedge fund indices and the benchmark assets are provided in Tables 27.3 and 27.4, respectively. In line with the existing literature, the majority of FoHF indices have lower standard deviations than the benchmark assets over the full period as well as for both individual subperiods. Only funds in the Strategic index exhibit a similar or even higher return volatility than corporate bonds. However, these relatively low volatility levels only yield a convincingly superior risk-return tradeoff for FoHFs in the growth period. Here, except for Market Defensive funds, Sharpe ratios range between 0.51 and 0.56. In contrast, during the financial crisis period the majority of

| | Mean | Sdev | Skew | Kurt | Sharpe | MDD | JB |
|---|---|---|---|---|---|---|---|
| **Table 27.3** Descriptive Statistics of the HFRI FOF Indices | | | | | | | |
| *(A) Full period (December 2002–December 2011)* | | | | | | | |
| Conservative | 0.23 | 1.33 | −2.16 | 9.84 | −0.02 | 20.36 | 294.12*** |
| Diversified | 0.31 | 1.59 | −1.44 | 6.42 | 0.04 | 21.75 | 90.10*** |
| Market Defensive | 0.41 | 1.60 | 0.07 | 2.76 | 0.10 | 8.06 | 0.35 |
| Strategic | 0.37 | 2.08 | −1.27 | 5.52 | 0.06 | 26.80 | 57.76*** |
| Composite | 0.30 | 1.65 | −1.43 | 6.39 | 0.03 | 22.20 | 88.65*** |
| *(B) First subperiod (December 2002–July 2007)* | | | | | | | |
| Conservative | 0.63 | 0.68 | −0.35 | 2.55 | 0.56 | 1.34 | 1.61 |
| Diversified | 0.78 | 1.03 | −0.55 | 3.06 | 0.51 | 2.80 | 2.79 |
| Market Defensive | 0.58 | 1.33 | −0.14 | 2.38 | 0.25 | 6.18 | 1.06 |
| Strategic | 0.98 | 1.38 | −0.71 | 3.13 | 0.53 | 4.38 | 4.61* |
| Composite | 0.78 | 1.03 | −0.53 | 2.93 | 0.52 | 2.70 | 2.59 |
| *(C) Second subperiod (August 2007–December 2011)* | | | | | | | |
| Conservative | −0.19 | 1.68 | −1.58 | 6.04 | −0.26 | 20.36 | 42.28*** |
| Diversified | −0.18 | 1.91 | −1.10 | 4.65 | −0.23 | 21.75 | 16.59*** |
| Market Defensive | 0.24 | 1.84 | 0.29 | 2.69 | −0.01 | 8.06 | 0.97 |
| Strategic | −0.26 | 2.47 | −0.90 | 4.09 | −0.21 | 26.80 | 9.83** |
| Composite | −0.20 | 2.00 | −1.03 | 4.47 | −0.22 | 22.20 | 14.10*** |

Descriptive statistics for the full sample period as well as both subperiods for the composite FoHF index and its four subindices. Mean, Sdev, Skew, and Kurt denote the average monthly return, its standard deviation, skewness, and kurtosis. Sharpe represents the Sharpe ratio assuming a risk-free interest rate of 3% per year while MDD and JB represent the maximum drawdown and the Jarque–Bera test statistic. Statistical significance at the ***1%, **5%, and *10% level.

FoHFs generate negative mean returns with Market Defensive funds being the sole exception. This result is consistent with their investment style focusing on short-biased strategies that usually provide positive returns during market downturns.[1] The maximum drawdown of 'Conservative', 'Diversified', 'Strategic', and 'Composite' FoHFs ranges between 20.36% and 26.80%, supporting the notion that FoHFs generated substantial losses for investors in the crisis period. This observation is also documented in Figure 27.3, which highlights the recent increase in the comovement of FoHFs returns with common stock returns. In fact, the correlation between Composite FoHFs and developed market equities amounts to 0.77 between 2002 and 2011, and the correlations are rather similar for the growth (0.74) and the crisis (0.78) periods.

As documented in the literature, the hypothesis of normally distributed returns does not hold for FoHFs as well as for the benchmark assets over the full sample period. While FoHFs returns follow a normal distribution during the growth period, their return distributions tend to exhibit significantly negative skewness and excess kurtosis between July 2007 and December 2011. For the benchmark

---

[1]However, their negative Sharpe ratio is driven by the significant rebound of almost all asset classes during the more recent period.

| **Table 27.4** | Descriptive Statistics of the Benchmark Assets | | | | | | |
|---|---|---|---|---|---|---|---|
| | **Mean** | **Sdev** | **Skew** | **Kurt** | **Sharpe** | **MDD** | **JB** |
| *(A) Full period (December 2002–December 2011)* | | | | | | | |
| World | 0.70 | 4.79 | −0.82 | 5.15 | 0.09 | 53.65 | 32.84*** |
| Emerging | 1.55 | 7.12 | −0.76 | 4.76 | 0.18 | 61.44 | 24.35*** |
| Gov | 0.51 | 2.39 | 0.21 | 5.16 | 0.11 | 9.36 | 21.86*** |
| Corp | 0.50 | 1.95 | −1.45 | 9.39 | 0.13 | 17.63 | 221.62*** |
| REIT | 1.08 | 7.36 | −0.91 | 7.39 | 0.11 | 67.89 | 101.54*** |
| GSCI | 0.53 | 7.44 | −0.65 | 4.17 | 0.04 | 67.64 | 13.68*** |
| Gold | 1.56 | 5.55 | −0.43 | 3.84 | 0.24 | 26.34 | 6.43** |
| *(B) First subperiod (December 2002–July 2007)* | | | | | | | |
| World | 1.47 | 2.59 | 0.22 | 3.15 | 0.47 | 4.94 | 0.49 |
| Emerging | 2.82 | 4.66 | −0.68 | 3.24 | 0.55 | 11.17 | 4.36* |
| Gov | 0.23 | 2.06 | −0.77 | 4.99 | −0.01 | 8.20 | 14.46*** |
| Corp | 0.39 | 1.43 | −0.58 | 4.30 | 0.10 | 4.41 | 6.97** |
| REIT | 1.58 | 4.61 | −1.35 | 5.19 | 0.29 | 21.30 | 27.70*** |
| GSCI | 1.17 | 6.43 | −0.34 | 2.71 | 0.14 | 26.41 | 1.25 |
| Gold | 1.32 | 4.39 | 0.12 | 2.71 | 0.24 | 9.52 | 0.32 |
| *(C) Second subperiod (August 2007–December 2011)* | | | | | | | |
| World | −0.11 | 6.24 | −0.46 | 3.25 | −0.06 | 53.65 | 1.99 |
| Emerging | 0.24 | 8.84 | −0.39 | 3.54 | 0.00 | 61.44 | 2.01 |
| Gov | 0.81 | 2.69 | 0.53 | 4.47 | 0.21 | 9.36 | 7.22** |
| Corp | 0.61 | 2.38 | −1.60 | 8.41 | 0.15 | 17.63 | 87.24*** |
| REIT | 0.57 | 9.42 | −0.60 | 5.28 | 0.03 | 63.19 | 14.69*** |
| GSCI | −0.13 | 8.37 | −0.68 | 4.20 | −0.04 | 67.64 | 7.26** |
| Gold | 1.80 | 6.57 | −0.63 | 3.58 | 0.24 | 26.34 | 4.27* |

Descriptive statistics for the full sample period as well as both subperiods for the benchmark assets. Mean, Sdev, Skew, and Kurt denote the average monthly return, its standard deviation, skewness, and kurtosis. Sharpe represents the Sharpe ratio assuming a risk-free interest rate of 3% per year, while MDD and JB represent the maximum drawdown and the Jarque–Bera test statistic. Statistical significance at the ***1%, **5%, and *10% level.

assets the differences between both periods are less pronounced. Overall, these results strongly suggest that it is essential to consider higher moment risk in a multi-asset portfolio context over time.

## 27.4. METHODOLOGY
### 27.4.1. Mean-Variance Optimization

In our empirical analyses we apply the traditional mean-variance approach to obtain optimal portfolio weights by solving the following minimization problem:

$$\min_{wt} w'_t \cdot \sum_{t+1} \cdot w_t = \sigma^2_{P,t} \qquad (27.3)$$

subject to $R_{P,t+1} = w'_t \cdot R_{i,t+1}$ and $\iota' \cdot w_t = 1$, where $w_t$ is a vector of portfolio weights for time period $t$, $\sigma^2_{P,t}$ is the portfolio variance, $\sum_{t+1}$ is the expected covariance matrix that is approximated by the in-sample variances and covariances of asset returns, $R_{i,t+1}$ is a vector of expected returns for all assets, $R_{P,t+1}$ is the portfolio's expected return, and $\iota$ is a vector of ones. Given that mean-variance optimal allocations are highly sensitive to variations of the input parameters such as expected returns and variances, small variations might lead to economically implausible and infeasible changes in portfolio weights (Michaud, 1989; Bessler *et al.*, 2012b). Therefore, we restrict the minimization problem in equation (27.3) by imposing short-selling constraints as well as minimum and maximum portfolio weights. Including investment restrictions is equivalent to shrinking the covariance matrix, thereby providing more precise estimates of its respective elements (Jagannathan and Ma, 2003). As mentioned before, each asset class has a non-negative, minimum portfolio weight. Moreover, we impose a set of realistic investment restrictions in the form of an allocation to developed market equities, government bonds, and corporate bonds of at least 10% each. The weights also may not exceed 30% for developed market equities and 50% for each fixed-income instrument. The alternative asset classes including hedge funds, emerging market equities, commodities, real estate, and gold are allowed a maximum weight of 20% each, while alternatives as an aggregate may not exceed 50% of the portfolio value. Hence, we ensure that optimal portfolio allocations are sufficiently diversified and realistic from an institutional investor's perspective.

## 27.4.2. Mean-Variance Spanning Tests

The benefits from adding individual asset classes to an existing portfolio are often evaluated in terms of shifts of the efficient frontier. However, such qualitative analyses do not allow to draw further conclusions on the statistical significance of potential changes in the efficient investment opportunity set. Huberman and Kandel (1987) propose a simple regression-based mean-variance spanning test to identify asset classes that significantly improve the risk-return tradeoff. In terms of spanning, Cheung *et al.* (2009) argue that redundant asset classes should receive zero portfolio weights due to the existence of residual risk that might be associated with the additional asset class. In the framework of Huberman and Kandel (1987), $[R'_{Kt}, R'_{Nt}]'$ denote the vectors of returns on risky assets where subscript 'K' ('N') denotes the returns on the benchmark assets (test assets). They suggest projecting $R_{Nt}$ on $R_{Kt}$ in the form of a linear regression:

$$R_{Nt} = \alpha + \beta R_{Kt} + \varepsilon_t, \tag{27.4}$$

with $E(\varepsilon_t) = 0_N$ and $E(\varepsilon_t R'_{Kt}) = 0_{N \times K}$, where $0_N$ is an $N$-vector of zeros and $0_{N \times K}$ is an $N \times K$ matrix of zeros. Under the null hypothesis of 'no spanning' the conditions $\alpha = 0$ and $\delta = 1_N - \beta 1_K = 0$ hold, where $1_N$ is an $N$-vector of ones and $1_K$ is an $K$-vector of ones. Kan and Zhou (2012) show that the first condition is a test of whether the tangency portfolio has zero weights in the test assets while the second condition is a test of whether the GMV portfolio has zero weights in the test assets. To analyze this combined null hypothesis, Huberman and Kandel (1987) employ a likelihood ratio test.

Kan and Zhou (2012) suggest a step-down procedure by first testing $\alpha = 0$ and then testing $\delta = 0$ conditional on the constraint $\alpha = 0$. Under this procedure the hypothesis of mean-variance spanning is rejected if at least one of the tests is rejected at conventional significance levels. If the rejection is driven by the first test, we infer that it is due to the significant difference between the two tangency portfolios. This position is of particular relevance for more aggressive investor clienteles. If the rejection is due to the second test, then the two GMV portfolios are significantly different. In this case the step-down spanning test provides an economic rationale even for 'Conservative' investors to allocate wealth to hedge funds. The second test implicitly assumes that $\alpha = 0$ and indicates diversification opportunities in the position of the GMV portfolio. Note that the GMV portfolio is particularly important because it is not sensitive to expected returns which usually involve considerable estimation risk (Michaud, 1989). Hence, the step-down procedure of Kan and Zhou (2012) allows us to separately test for the statistical significance of potential benefits associated with adding FoHFs to the 'Benchmark Portfolio' for conservative as well as aggressive investor clienteles.

The general test statistics of Kan and Zhou (2012) are derived under the assumption that $\varepsilon_t$ in equation (27.4) is normally distributed and its variance is not time-varying as a function of $R_{Kt}$ (i.e., $\varepsilon_t$ is conditionally homoscedastic). However, stock returns often depart from the normality assumption and may be conditionally heteroscedastic so that the variance of $\varepsilon_t$ becomes a time-varying function of $R_{Kt}$. In this case, Kan and Zhou (2012) recommend Hansen's (1982) Generalized Method of Moments (GMM). Kan and Zhou (2012) propose the multivariate elliptical distribution for modeling asset returns as it accounts for potential excess kurtosis and fat tails in return distributions and, therefore, allows for a more accurate description of asset returns. We follow their approach and conduct spanning tests under the general framework as well as the alternative framework taking potential excess kurtosis and fat tails in asset return distributions into account.

### 27.4.3. Return Smoothing
As hedge fund returns are usually serially correlated due to investments in illiquid and inactively traded securities (Sadka, 2010), their observed returns tend to be smoother than 'true' unobserved returns (Getmansky et al., 2004; Bollen and Pool, 2008). Dubrana (2010) argues that smoothed returns originate primarily for reasons such as marking illiquid assets to market using extrapolation, time-varying expected returns, and time-varying leverage. Hence, conventional risk measures such as the standard deviation of returns are likely to be underestimated, leading to inaccurate reflections of their risk-return tradeoff and thereby potentially affecting inferences on the spanning tests discussed above. In fact, return smoothing might have a significant effect on the spanning inferences for the GMV portfolio and, therefore, for the conservative investor clientele given its sensitivity to the volatility of the FoHF indices. Hence, we follow the approach proposed by Getmansky et al. (2004) and desmooth FoHFs returns as a robustness check. In their model, the

observable return $R_t^0$ is a finite moving average of the $k$-periods unobservable 'true' economic returns $R_t$:

$$R_t^0 = \mu + \theta_0 R_t + \theta_1 R_{t-1} + \theta_2 R_{t-2} + \varepsilon_t, \qquad (27.5)$$

with constraints $\theta_k \in [0, 1]$, $k = 0, 1, 2$, and $\theta_0 + \theta_1 + \theta_2 = 1$. Of particular interest is the coefficient $\theta_0$, which serves as an indicator for return smoothing or illiquidity of the return time series. In other words, a value for $\theta_0 < 1$ suggests that observable returns do not fully incorporate all the available economic return information (Cici *et al.*, 2011). Recent studies document that the adjustment usually leads to an increase in return volatility for alternative asset classes such as hedge funds or private equity (Cumming *et al.*, 2012).

## 27.5. EMPIRICAL RESULTS

In this section, we empirically analyze the contribution of five FoHF indices to portfolio efficiency for two investor clienteles, i.e., conservative and aggressive investors. We first analyze the full sample period (Section 27.5.1) and then separately investigate the growth or non-crisis period (Section 27.5.2) and the crisis period (Section 27.5.3). As a robustness check, we analyze whether potential return smoothing affects our empirical results (Section 27.5.4).

### 27.5.1. Full Period (2002–2011)

Our first major finding is that all FoHFs strategies lead to a change of the GMV portfolio compared to the optimal benchmark allocation (Base) as documented in Figure 27.5. Therefore, conservative investors seem to particularly benefit from adding FoHFs to their benchmark allocation. The strongest shift in terms of the GMV portfolio is observed for FoHFs following conservative investment strategies ('Conservative') while rather aggressive FoHFs in the 'Strategic' subgroup lead to a smaller but still remarkable reduction in return volatility. Overall, these findings are consistent with the underlying investment approaches of these indices. The changes of the tangency portfolio in Figure 27.6, however, seem to be less favorable when adding FoHFs to the benchmark portfolio. Among all strategies, only 'Diversified' and 'Composite' indices encompass a rightward shift of the tangency portfolio, although neither strategy leads to a leftward and upward shift, suggesting that changes in the tangency portfolio are only marginal.

The regression results encompassing the mean-variance spanning tests in panel (A) of Table 27.5 suggest that the multi-asset benchmark model captures a significant fraction of FoHFs return variation over the full sample period. The seven-factor model yields adjusted $R^2$ values between 69% and 83%, while returns of short-biased strategies ('Market Defensive') are less accurately explained by the benchmark assets. This result is not surprising given that rather defensive hedge fund strategies usually exhibit small and mostly insignificant factor exposures to asset classes such as stocks and bonds. Hence, among the set of traditional and alternative asset classes, only real estate and gold have

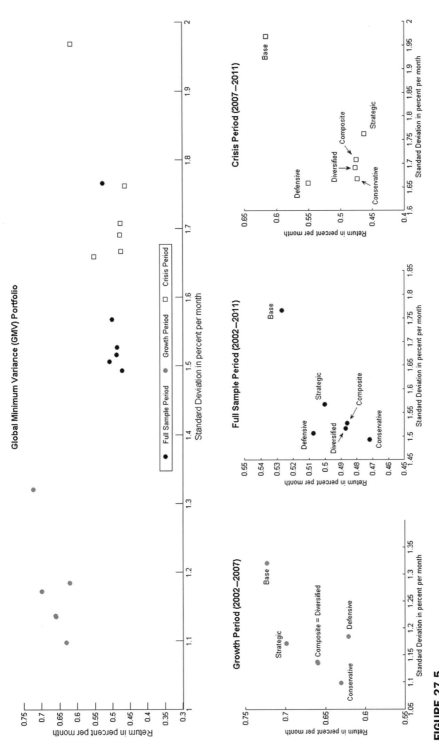

**FIGURE 27.5**
GMV portfolio for the full sample and both subperiods, without (Base) and with FoHFs in the optimal asset allocations.

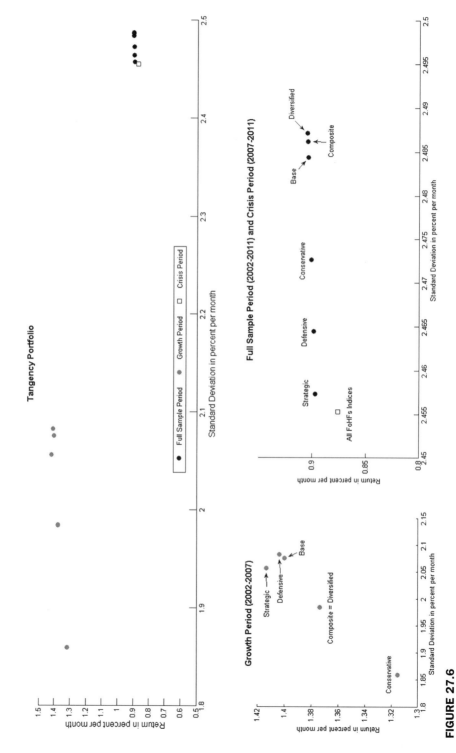

**FIGURE 27.6**
Tangency portfolio for the full sample and both subperiods, without (Base) and with FoHFs in the optimal asset allocations.

| Table 27.5 | Regression Results for the Full Sample and Both Subperiods | | | | | | | | |
|---|---|---|---|---|---|---|---|---|---|
| | **Alpha** | **World** | **Emerging** | **Gov** | **Corp** | **REIT** | **GSCI** | **Gold** | $R^2$ (%) |
| *(A) Full period (December 2002–December 2011)* | | | | | | | | | |
| Conservative | 0.001 | 0.09** | 0.03 | −0.23*** | 0.29*** | −0.04*** | 0.04*** | 0.01 | 69 |
| Diversified | 0.001 | 0.11** | 0.09*** | −0.20*** | 0.23*** | −0.06*** | 0.02* | 0.02 | 73 |
| Market Defensive | 0.002 | 0.11 | 0.05 | 0.05 | −0.09 | −0.08*** | 0.02 | 0.10*** | 30 |
| Strategic | 0.000 | 0.14*** | 0.16*** | −0.18*** | 0.19*** | −0.07*** | 0.02 | 0.03* | 83 |
| Composite | 0.001 | 0.11** | 0.10*** | −0.19*** | 0.23*** | −0.06*** | 0.03** | 0.03* | 77 |
| *(B) First subperiod (December 2002–July 2007)* | | | | | | | | | |
| Conservative | 0.003*** | 0.07 | 0.05* | −0.20 | 0.31* | −0.02 | 0.01 | 0.02 | 43 |
| Diversified | 0.002** | 0.14** | 0.11*** | −0.08 | 0.14 | −0.02 | 0.01 | 0.02 | 64 |
| Market Defensive | 0.000 | 0.11 | 0.09* | −0.06 | 0.23 | −0.01 | 0.03 | 0.08** | 46 |
| Strategic | 0.002* | 0.18*** | 0.18*** | 0.00 | 0.00 | −0.01 | 0.02 | 0.02 | 77 |
| Composite | 0.002** | 0.13** | 0.11*** | −0.08 | 0.14 | −0.02 | 0.01 | 0.02 | 65 |
| *(C) Second subperiod (August 2007–December 2011)* | | | | | | | | | |
| Conservative | −0.002 | 0.07 | −0.01 | −0.24*** | 0.35*** | −0.04** | 0.09*** | 0.00 | 79 |
| Diversified | −0.002 | 0.10 | 0.05 | −0.24*** | 0.30*** | −0.07*** | 0.06*** | 0.01 | 81 |
| Market Defensive | 0.002 | 0.15 | 0.00 | −0.04 | −0.07 | −0.11** | 0.05 | 0.10** | 26 |
| Strategic | −0.003** | 0.13* | 0.11*** | −0.23*** | 0.28*** | −0.08*** | 0.05** | 0.03 | 88 |
| Composite | −0.002 | 0.11* | 0.06 | −0.23*** | 0.29*** | −0.07*** | 0.06*** | 0.02 | 85 |

Regression results in terms of alpha and beta coefficients for the five HFRI FOF indices for the full sample period as well as both subperiods, respectively. $R^2$ denotes the sample adjusted $R^2$. Statistical significance at the ***1%, **5%, and *10% level.

significant factor coefficients for defensive FoHFs. While the returns of real estate investments are negatively related to any FoHFs strategy, the exposures and significance levels for the remaining asset classes are comparable for FoHFs in the conservative, diversified, strategic, and composite indices. Moreover, none of the estimated seven-factor alphas is significantly positive, which might result from including both bull and bear markets in the overall sample.

The spanning tests in panel (A) of Table 27.6 confirm our visual findings in that all FoHFs strategies significantly enhance the efficient investment opportunity set over the full sample period. As expected, their contribution is solely driven by the improvement in the GMV portfolio, underlining their relevance for conservative investor clienteles that strive for assets that stabilize portfolio returns. Importantly, these findings still hold after controlling for excess kurtosis and fat tails in the return distributions, although the respective $F_1$ and $F_2$ statistic is smaller in magnitude. Hence, controlling for non-normality in asset returns provides a more conservative view on the benefits of adding FoHFs to the benchmark portfolio.

So far, we have gained insights on the ability of different FoHFs strategies to significantly improve portfolio efficiency for conservative and aggressive investor clienteles between 2002 and 2011. However, in the context of the recent dynamics underlying the FoHFs industry and the existence of time-varying investment opportunities (Goetzmann *et al.*, 2005; Chan *et al.*, 2011) we now

| Table 27.6 | Spanning Tests for the Full Sample and Both Subperiods | | | | | |
|---|---|---|---|---|---|---|
| | **LR** | **$F_1$** | **$F_2$** | **$W_{ellip}$** | **$F_{1, ellip}$** | **$F_{2, ellip}$** |
| **(A) Full period (December 2002–December 2011)** | | | | | | |
| Conservative | 165.46*** | 1.49 | 359.52*** | 166.28*** | 1.13 | 106.25*** |
| Diversified | 143.50*** | 1.19 | 275.90*** | 138.43*** | 0.92 | 86.63*** |
| Market Defensive | 84.31*** | 1.96 | 115.24*** | 65.88*** | 1.56 | 39.37*** |
| Strategic | 122.32*** | 0.12 | 212.11*** | 108.83*** | 0.09 | 67.71*** |
| Composite | 146.49*** | 0.58 | 288.83*** | 144.36*** | 0.45 | 90.57*** |
| **(B) First subperiod (December 2002–July 2007)** | | | | | | |
| Conservative | 74.27 | 11.63*** | 100.47*** | 121.95*** | 7.90*** | 45.46*** |
| Diversified | 53.67 | 4.58** | 68.05*** | 69.61*** | 3.09* | 30.51*** |
| Market Defensive | 22.17 | 0.09 | 23.69*** | 22.28*** | 0.06 | 10.77*** |
| Strategic | 44.00 | 3.29* | 51.84*** | 50.66*** | 2.21 | 23.01*** |
| Composite | 54.68 | 4.71** | 69.91*** | 71.79*** | 3.18* | 31.37*** |
| **(C) Second subperiod (August 2007–December 2011)** | | | | | | |
| Conservative | 91.33*** | 2.21 | 199.64*** | 139.11*** | 1.72 | 68.02*** |
| Diversified | 82.97*** | 1.52 | 166.92*** | 118.59*** | 1.19 | 58.61*** |
| Market Defensive | 44.59*** | 0.88 | 58.65*** | 42.90*** | 0.70 | 21.97*** |
| Strategic | 75.90*** | 4.37** | 129.58*** | 105.25*** | 3.44* | 46.13*** |
| Composite | 86.24*** | 2.48 | 175.89*** | 129.68*** | 1.95 | 61.89*** |

Results of mean–variance spanning tests for the five HFRI FOF indices for the full sample period as well as for both subperiods, respectively. $LR$, $F_1$, and $F_2$ denote the likelihood ratio test statistic, the test statistic associated with changes in the tangency portfolio, and the test statistic associated with changes in the GMV portfolio, respectively. $W_{ellip}$, $F_{1, ellip}$, and $F_{2, ellip}$ represent the Wald test statistic and both test statistics following the step-down procedure of Kan and Zhou (2012) assuming elliptically distributed returns, and thereby controlling for potential excess kurtosis and tail risk. Statistical significance at the ***1%, **5%, and *10% level.

separately analyze their contribution to the benchmark portfolio for the growth or non-crisis period as well as for the crisis period.

## 27.5.2. Growth Period (2002–2007)

For the growth period, we find substantial changes in the GMV portfolio. This indicates that FoHFs are an attractive investment opportunity for the optimal asset allocation of conservative investors. Again, conservative FoHFs following strategies such as Equity Market Neutral, Fixed Income Arbitrage, and Convertible Arbitrage are associated with the strongest improvement of the GMV portfolio according to Figure 27.5. In contrast, defensive funds provide the least attractive shift of the GMV portfolio. This is not surprising given that the first subperiod can be characterized as a bull market for most asset classes. Consequently, short-biased strategies may have experienced more difficulties in finding profitable investment opportunities than the remaining set of FoHFs. This is also evident in Figure 27.6 in that any strategy except 'Market Defensive' seems to improve the tangency portfolio, which suggests that adding FoHFs to the benchmark portfolio is beneficial for more aggressive investor clienteles. Compared to the results for the full sample period, the respective positions are not similarly aligned but rather shifted leftwards and upwards in a parallel fashion.

According to the regression analyses, FoHFs are predominantly affected by equity market risk (panel (B) of Table 27.5). For most of the strategies, both developed and emerging equity factor exposures are similar in magnitude. They range between 0.07 and 0.18 (MSCI World) and between 0.05 and 0.18 (MSCI Emerging Markets). Not surprisingly, FoHFs in the 'Strategic' subgroup exhibit the highest exposure, although the absolute differences from other indices are relatively small. Among the set of other asset classes only returns on gold highlight their positive association with defensive FoHFs strategies. Compared to the full sample analysis, adjusted $R^2$ values are smaller except for the 'Market Defensive' funds and range between 43% ('Conservative') and 77% ('Strategic'), the latter again indicating that the benchmark assets explain returns for more aggressive FoHFs strategies reasonably well. Moreover, alpha estimates are significantly positive for the majority of indices, suggesting that FoHFs generate state-dependent excess returns, thereby being consistent with the existing literature (Fung *et al.*, 2008).

The spanning tests in panel (B) of Table 27.6 support the first indications in Figures 27.5 and 27.6. While the GMV portfolio is now superior, we also document significant changes of the tangency portfolio for all subindices except 'Market Defensive'. Therefore, conservative as well as aggressive investors are likely to benefit from adding FoHFs to their portfolio during bull markets. However, after controlling for non-normality, there is less evidence for a favorable shift of the tangency portfolio, suggesting the inherent exposure to less favorable tail risk.

### 27.5.3. Crisis Period (2007–2011)

Since the beginning of the recent financial crisis period, FoHFs have effectively reduced portfolio volatility, thereby leading to a leftward shift of the GMV portfolio, suggesting strong benefits for conservative investors (see Figure 27.5). However, aggressive investor clienteles focusing on positive risk-adjusted returns and changes in the tangency portfolio do not benefit from investing in FoHFs (see Figure 27.6). Irrespective of the FoHFs strategy, we do not find empirical evidence for any change in this position along the efficient frontier. This aspect is further analyzed with regression-based spanning tests.

Overall, the beta exposures for the majority of FoHFs increase on an absolute level during the crisis period (panel (C) of Table 27.5). This observation is consistent with empirical findings by Lo (2001), Edwards and Caglayan (2001), and Bollen (2011). In fact, Lo (2001) terms this observation 'phase-locking', suggesting that hedge funds exhibit asymmetric correlations with conventional asset classes such as stocks. The seven-factor model exhibits adjusted $R^2$ values between 79% and 88% for 'Conservative', 'Diversified', 'Strategic', and 'Composite' indices, while the attractiveness of defensive strategies is reflected in their relatively low return comovement. In fact, only short-biased FoHFs generate positive, albeit insignificant excess returns during this period of market distress. More aggressive strategic FoHFs even generate a significantly negative alpha, consistent with their tendency to provide high (low) returns in bull (bear) markets. Similarly to the full and the pre-crisis periods, 'Market Defensive' FoHFs returns are significantly positively exposed to gold. This finding is theoretically consistent with empirical studies indicating that gold provides a safe haven (Baur and McDermott, 2010) in periods of stock market turmoil (Baur and Lucey, 2010) so that rather defensive strategies should be expected to exhibit positive gold exposures. Among the remaining FoHF indices, bonds, real estate, and commodities exhibit significant factor coefficients, underlining the pronounced increase of return comovement in the recent years.

Spanning tests in panel (C) of Table 27.6 confirm our visual interpretations. The improvement of the GMV portfolio is highly significant irrespective of the FoHF index and suggests strong diversification benefits from adding FoHFs to the benchmark allocation for conservative investor clienteles. However, for FoHFs in the 'Strategic' index we find evidence for a change of the tangency portfolio in terms of the significant $F_1$ test statistic which is not documented in Figure 27.6. This result is likely to be related to the implicit assumption made by our regression-based spanning tests that short positions are not restricted. Hence, the 'Strategic' index represents a candidate for a short position that is obviously not feasible. In contrast, Figure 27.6 indicates changes in portfolio efficiency by incorporating a set of investment restrictions including short-selling constraints, among others, as discussed in Section 27.4.1. Comparable to the growth period, we again find evidence for the presence of higher moment risk so that the benefits from adding FoHFs to the tangency portfolio are reduced after controlling for tail risk.

## 27.5.4. Return Smoothing

As expected, we find strong and significant evidence for smoothing in the time series of FoHFs returns (Table 27.7). Except for the 'Market Defensive' index, standard deviations increase in the range between 43% and 67%. The largest increase is observed for FoHFs that follow conservative strategies, suggesting that their investments exhibit the strongest exposure to illiquid portfolio positions. In contrast, FoHFs with rather defensive and short-biased investment styles such as managed futures experience relatively small adjustments of their volatility with standard deviation ratios ranging between 1.05 and 1.07. This finding is consistent with results reported in Getmansky et al. (2004). Overall, given this profound evidence of return smoothing among the majority of FoHF indices, it is necessary to further analyze how this affects our results of the mean-variance spanning tests for different investor clienteles. Here, the increase in FoHFs return volatility is most relevant for the position of the GMV portfolio as it might lead to significantly smaller benefits from adding FoHFs to the portfolios of conservative investor clienteles.

However, Table 27.8 shows that even after adjusting for return smoothing, FoHFs significantly improve the position of the GMV portfolio. This result also holds after controlling for excess kurtosis and fat tails in terms of the step-down

**Table 27.7**   Mean and Standard Deviation of Smoothed and Unsmoothed Returns

| | Mean Smoothed | Mean Unsmoothed | Sdev Smoothed | Sdev Unsmoothed | Sdev Ratio |
|---|---|---|---|---|---|
| *(A) Full period (December 2002–December 2011)* | | | | | |
| Conservative | 0.23 | 0.23 | 1.33 | 2.06 | 1.55 |
| Diversified | 0.31 | 0.31 | 1.59 | 2.39 | 1.50 |
| Market Defensive | 0.41 | 0.41 | 1.60 | 1.70 | 1.06 |
| Strategic | 0.37 | 0.37 | 2.08 | 2.97 | 1.43 |
| Composite | 0.30 | 0.30 | 1.65 | 2.42 | 1.47 |
| *(B) First subperiod (December 2002–July 2007)* | | | | | |
| Conservative | 0.63 | 0.63 | 0.68 | 1.14 | 1.67 |
| Diversified | 0.78 | 0.78 | 1.03 | 1.60 | 1.55 |
| Market Defensive | 0.58 | 0.58 | 1.33 | 1.40 | 1.05 |
| Strategic | 0.98 | 0.98 | 1.38 | 2.02 | 1.46 |
| Composite | 0.78 | 0.78 | 1.03 | 1.55 | 1.51 |
| *(C) Second subperiod (August 2007–December 2011)* | | | | | |
| Conservative | −0.19 | −0.19 | 1.68 | 2.66 | 1.59 |
| Diversified | −0.18 | −0.19 | 1.91 | 2.93 | 1.54 |
| Market Defensive | 0.24 | 0.24 | 1.84 | 1.96 | 1.07 |
| Strategic | −0.26 | −0.26 | 2.47 | 3.63 | 1.47 |
| Composite | −0.20 | −0.20 | 2.00 | 3.02 | 1.50 |

Mean returns and standard deviations for the HFRI FOF indices for the full sample period as well as both individual subperiods. Mean Smoothed and Sdev Smoothed denote mean returns and standard deviations of the original time series while Mean Unsmoothed and Sdev Unsmoothed indicate mean returns and standard deviations after the procedure of Getmansky et al. (2004) was applied to estimate unsmoothed returns. Sdev Ratio represents the ratio between Sdev Smoothed and Sdev Unsmoothed.

test statistics assuming elliptically distributed returns. Although the respective test statistics are considerably reduced, they are still significant at the 1% level. In contrast, return smoothing reduces the benefits for the tangency portfolio remarkably because none of the associated test statistics is significant. Consistent with results in Bessler et al. (2012a), this position is highly sensitive to changes in the input parameters such as the distributional characteristics of the return series, but also in light of particular portfolio weight constraints. Overall, we find that FoHFs' contribution to the GMV portfolio is robust before and after the financial crisis, which underlines their importance for investors seeking diversification benefits in low-risk portfolios irrespective of the market environment.

## CONCLUSION

The purpose of this chapter is to analyze the contribution of five FoHF indices to portfolio efficiency for the period between December 2002 and December 2011. We explicitly differentiate the contribution of hedge funds for the full period, and a growth or non-crisis period between 2002 and 2007 as well as a crisis period between 2007 and 2011. We use constrained mean-variance optimizations and mean-variance spanning tests, controlling for potential excess

**Table 27.8** Spanning Tests with Unsmoothed Returns

| | LR | $F_1$ | $F_2$ | $W_{ellip}$ | $F_{1, ellip}$ | $F_{2, ellip}$ |
|---|---|---|---|---|---|---|
| **(A) Full period (December 2002–December 2011)** | | | | | | |
| Conservative | 67.91*** | 0.09 | 88.25*** | 42.21*** | 0.07 | 26.83*** |
| Diversified | 60.81*** | 0.00 | 76.36*** | 39.53*** | 0.00 | 24.45*** |
| Market Defensive | 76.26*** | 1.50 | 100.62*** | 57.21*** | 1.19 | 34.38*** |
| Strategic | 45.31*** | 0.39 | 52.04*** | 29.21*** | 0.31 | 17.03*** |
| Composite | 60.83*** | 0.05 | 76.32*** | 40.34*** | 0.04 | 24.57*** |
| **(B) First subperiod (December 2002–July 2007)** | | | | | | |
| Conservative | 36.01*** | 1.03 | 42.40*** | 38.84*** | 0.69 | 18.89*** |
| Diversified | 28.14*** | 0.00 | 32.06*** | 28.14*** | 0.00 | 14.09*** |
| Market Defensive | 20.09*** | 0.31 | 20.71*** | 19.97*** | 0.21 | 9.41*** |
| Strategic | 24.23*** | 0.25 | 26.17*** | 23.35*** | 0.16 | 11.36*** |
| Composite | 29.69*** | 0.00 | 34.35*** | 30.17*** | 0.00 | 15.10*** |
| **(C) Second subperiod (August 2007–December 2011)** | | | | | | |
| Conservative | 31.99*** | 0.02 | 38.08*** | 24.97*** | 0.02 | 13.26*** |
| Diversified | 32.19*** | 0.01 | 38.41*** | 26.19*** | 0.01 | 13.76*** |
| Market Defensive | 40.58*** | 0.80 | 51.21*** | 37.36*** | 0.64 | 19.17*** |
| Strategic | 24.33*** | 0.37 | 26.21*** | 19.51*** | 0.29 | 9.60*** |
| Composite | 31.81*** | 0.10 | 37.65*** | 26.40*** | 0.08 | 13.61*** |

Mean–variance spanning test results for the five HFRI FOF indices for the full sample period as well as both subperiods, respectively, after the procedure of Getmansky *et al.* (2004) was applied to estimate unsmoothed returns. $LR$, $F_1$, and $F_2$ denote the likelihood ratio test statistic, the test statistic associated with changes in the tangency portfolio, and the test statistic associated with changes in the GMV portfolio, respectively. $W_{ellip}$, $F_{1, ellip}$, and $F_{2, ellip}$ represent the Wald test statistic and both test statistics following the step-down procedure of Kan and Zhou (2012) assuming elliptically distributed returns, and thereby controlling for potential excess kurtosis and tail risk. Statistical significance at the ***1% level.

kurtosis and tail risk in asset returns. By differentiating between changes in the positions of the GMV portfolio and the tangency portfolio, we are able to distinguish between the contribution of FoHFs for different investor clienteles (i.e., conservative and aggressive investors). Further, we check for the robustness of our results by desmoothing FoHFs returns to control for their rather illiquid portfolio holdings, usually leading to strong autocorrelations in returns and, therefore, the tendency to underestimate return variances.

Overall, our results indicate that FoHFs exhibit relatively low standard deviations even after desmoothing returns. Consistent with the literature we find that FoHFs significantly improve the position of the GMV portfolio. Hence, hedge funds provide a relatively safe asset class over the business cycle, suggesting strong diversification benefits for more conservative investors. Importantly, this result holds irrespective of the particular FoHF index. The tangency portfolio, however, is more sensitive to the state of the economy. In the growth period we find evidence that the majority of FoHF indices generate diversification benefits for aggressive investor clienteles which focus on positive risk-adjusted returns. During the recent financial crisis, however, only defensive FoHFs produce a positive although insignificant alpha, while strategic FoHFs significantly underperform the benchmark model. Hence, our empirical findings suggest little potential to improve the tangency portfolio during the crisis period.

Our results have interesting implications for the investment strategies of institutional investors seeking exposure to the hedge fund industry with a certain degree of intermediation services. Given that FoHFs consistently improve the GMV portfolio, investors do not necessarily need to diversify over a large set of individual strategies as represented by the equally weighted Composite index. In light of the recent study by Brown *et al.* (2012), which indicates that over-diversification might actually reduce portfolio performance and increase tail risk exposure, our results suggest that investors can achieve similar portfolio benefits when considering FoHF subindices for enhancing portfolio efficiency. This argument is further supported by Shawky *et al.* (2012), who find significant differences between individual diversification dimensions and their relation to FoHFs performance. They document that sector diversification is the only dimension exhibiting a positive relation to FoHFs performance. Hence, FoHFs managers may well diversify across sectors, but still keep track of their strategic investment approach in which they may have already acquired substantial knowledge and expertise (e.g., in developed and emerging market equities).

Finally, our findings suggest that investors seeking exposure to FoHFs strategies should consider the respective diversification profile in terms of the number of funds in the portfolio as well as their strategic focus when making investment decisions. Given that hedge funds and FoHFs often lack transparency regarding their portfolio holdings and investment approaches, the recent surge of UCITS funds should improve information disclosure and enable investors to more efficiently screen potential investment opportunities.

# References

Barras, B., Scaillet, O., & Wermers, R. (2010). False Discoveries in Mutual Fund Performance: Measuring Luck in Estimated Alphas. *Journal of Finance, 65*(1), 179—216.

Baur, D. G., & Lucey, B. M. (2010). Is Gold a Hedge or a Safe Haven? An Analysis of Stocks, Bonds and Gold. *The Financial Review, 45*(2), 217—229.

Baur, D. G., & McDermott, T. K. (2010). Is Gold a Safe Haven? International Evidence. *Journal of Banking and Finance, 34*(8), 1886—1898.

Berk, J. B., & Green, R. (2004). Mutual Fund Flows and Performance in Rational Markets. *Journal of Political Economy, 112*(6), 1269—1295.

Bessler, W., Blake, D., Lückoff, P., & Tonks, I. (2011). *Why does Mutual Fund Performance not Persist? The Impact and Interaction of Fund Flows and Manager Changes.* Giessen: Working Paper, University of Giessen.

Bessler, W., Holler, J., & Kurmann, P. (2012a). Hedge Funds and Optimal Asset Allocation: Bayesian Expectations and Spanning Tests. *Financial Markets and Portfolio Management, 26*(1), 109—141.

Bessler, W., Opfer, H., & Wolff, D. (2012b). *Multi-Asset Portfolio Optimization and Out-of-Sample Performance: An Evaluation of Black—Litterman, Mean Variance and Naïve Diversification Approaches.* Giessen: Working Paper, University of Giessen.

Bessler, W., Kryzanowski, L., Kurmann, P., & Lückoff, P. (2012c). *Capacity Effects and Winner Fund Performance: The Relevance and Interactions of Fund and Family Characteristics.* Giessen: Working Paper, University of Giessen.

Billio, M., Getmansky, M., & Pelizzon, L. (2010). *Crises and Hedge Fund Risk*. Venice: Working Paper, University of Venice.

Bollen, N. P. B. (2011). The Financial Crisis and Hedge Fund Returns. *Review of Derivatives Research, 14*(2), 117–135.

Bollen, N. P. B., & Pool, V. K. (2008). Conditional Return Smoothing in the Hedge Fund Industry. *Journal of Financial and Quantitative Analysis, 43*(2), 267–298.

Brown, S. J., Gregoriou, G. N., & Pascalau, R. (2012). Diversification in Funds of Hedge Funds: Is It Possible to Overdiversify? *Review of Asset Pricing Studies, 2*(1), 89–110.

Chan, K. F., Treepongkaruna, S., Brooks, R., & Gray, S. (2011). Asset Market Linkages: Evidence from Financial Commodity and Real Estate Assets. *Journal of Banking and Finance, 35*(6), 1415–1426.

Cheung, C. S., Kwan, V. C. Y., & Mountain, D. C. (2009). On the Nature of Mean–Variance Spanning. *Finance Research Letters, 6*(2), 106–113.

Cici, G., Kempf, A., & Pütz, A. (2012). *The Valuation of Hedge Funds' Equity Positions*. Cologne: Working Paper, CFR Working Paper 10-15, University of Cologne.

Cumming, D., Haß, L. H., & Schweizer, D. (2012). Strategic Asset Allocation and the Role of Alternative Investments. *European Financial Management, forthcoming*.

Darolles, S., & Vaissié, M. (2012). The Alpha and Omega of Fund of Hedge Fund Added Value. *Journal of Banking and Finance, 36*(4), 1067–1078.

Denvir, E., & Hutson, E. (2006). The Performance and Diversification Benefits of Funds of Hedge Funds. *Journal of International Financial Markets, Institutions and Money, 16*(1), 4–22.

Dewaele, B., Pirotte, H., Tuchschmid, N., & Wallerstein, E. (2011). *Assessing the Performance of Funds of Hedge Funds*. Brussels: Working Paper, Solvay Brussels School of Economics and Management, Université Libre de Bruxelles.

Deutsche Bank. (2012). *Tenth Annual Alternative Investment Survey*. Frankfurt: Deutsche Bank.

Dubrana, L. (2010). Review of Econometric Models Applicable to Hedge Fund Returns Capturing Serial Correlation and Illiquidity. *Journal of Alternative Investments, forthcoming*.

Edelman, D., Fung, W., Hsieh, D. A., & Naik, N. Y. (2012). Funds of Hedge Funds: Performance, Risk and Capital Formation 2005 to 2010. *Financial Markets and Portfolio Management, 26*(1), 87–108.

Edwards, F. R., & Caglayan, M. O. (2001). Hedge Fund and Commodity Fund Investments in Bull and Bear Markets. *Journal of Portfolio Management, 27*(4), 97–108.

Fung, W., & Hsieh, D. A. (1999). A Primer on Hedge Funds. *Journal of Empirical Finance, 6*(3), 309–331.

Fung, W., & Hsieh, D. A. (2000). Performance Characteristics of Hedge Funds and CTA Funds: Natural versus Spurious Biases. *Journal of Financial and Quantitative Analysis, 35*(3), 291–307.

Fung, W., & Hsieh, D. A. (2004). Hedge Fund Benchmarks: A Risk-Based Approach. *Financial Analysts Journal, 60*(5), 65–80.

Fung, W., Hsieh, D. A., Naik, N. Y., & Ramadorai, T. (2008). Hedge Funds: Performance, Risk, and Capital Formation. *Journal of Finance, 63*(4), 1777–1803.

Getmansky, M., Lo, A. W., & Makarov, I. (2004). An Econometric Model of Serial Correlation and Illiquidity in Hedge Fund Returns. *Journal of Financial Economics, 74*(3), 529–610.

Goetzmann, W. N., Li, L., & Rouwenhorst, K. G. (2005). Long-Term Global Market Correlations. *Journal of Business, 78*(1), 1–38.

Gregoriou, G. N., & Rouah, F. (2002). The Role of Hedge Funds in Pension Fund Portfolios: Buying Protection in Bear Markets. *Journal of Pensions Management, 7*(3), 237–245.

Gueyié, J.-P., & Amvella, S. P. (2006). Optimal Portfolio Allocation using Funds of Hedge Funds. *Journal of Wealth Management, 9*(2), 85–95.

Hansen, L. P. (1982). Large Sample Properties of the Generalized Method of Moments. *Econometrica, 50*(4), 1029–1054.

Holler, J. (2012). *Hedge Funds and Financial Markets: An Asset Management and Corporate Governance Perspective*. Wiesbaden: Gabler Research.

Huberman, G., & Kandel, S. (1987). Mean-Variance Spanning. *Journal of Finance, 42*(4), 873–888.

Jagannathan, R., & Ma, T. (2003). Risk Reduction in Large Portfolios: Why Imposing the Wrong Constraints Helps. *Journal of Finance, 58*(4), 1651–1683.

Kan, R., & Zhou, G. (2012). Tests of Mean-Variance Spanning. *Annals of Economics and Finance,* *13*(1), 139−187.

Kooli, M. (2007). The Diversification Benefits of Hedge Funds and Funds of Hedge Funds. *Derivatives Use, Trading and Regulation, 12*(4), 290−300.

Lerner, J., Schoar, A., & Wang, J. (2008). Secrets of the Academy: The Drivers of University Endowment Success. *Journal of Economic Perspectives, 22*(3), 207−222.

Lhabitant, F. S., & Learned, M. (2002). Hedge Fund Diversification: How Much is Enough? *Journal of Alternative Investments, 5*(3), 23−49.

Lo, A. W. (2001). Risk Management for Hedge Funds: Introduction and Overview. *Financial Analysts Journal, 57*(6), 16−33.

Michaud, R. O. (1989). The Markowitz Optimization Enigma: Is 'Optimized' Optimal? *Financial Analysts Journal, 45*(1), 31−42.

Sadka, R. (2010). Liquidity Risk and the Cross-Section of Hedge-Fund Returns. *Journal of Financial Economics, 98*(1), 54−71.

Shawky, H. A., Dai, N., & Cumming, D. (2012). Diversification in the Hedge Fund Industry. *Journal of Corporate Finance, 18*(1), 166−178.

# SECTION 6
# Regulation

# CHAPTER 28

# Regulation: Threat or Opportunity for the Funds of Hedge Funds Industry?

**Serge Darolles**[*] and **Mathieu Vaissié**[†]

[*]Université Paris-Dauphine, DRM-Finance, Paris, France
[†]Research Associate, EDHEC-Risk Institute, Senior Portfolio Manager, Lyxor Asset Management Tours Société Générale, Paris, France.

## 28.1. INTRODUCTION

The world financial system has recently been experiencing a series of crises as bad as any since the great depression of 1929. Systemic risk issues have thus resurfaced for the first time since the Russian debt crisis and the collapse of LTCM (Long-Term Capital Management), back in 1998. Against this backdrop, it is no surprise that strong winds of regulation are blowing on financial markets (e.g., Basel III, Dodd—Frank, EMIR, MIFID II, AIFMD, FATCA).

The relationship between regulation and financial markets is complex. On the one hand, it can make them operate more effectively; on the other hand, it may induce additional costs, some would even say bear the seeds of future crisis. Regulation is therefore more often than not seen as a source of risk(s) by practitioners. This is particularly true in the hedge fund world where regulation has been historically poor and investment flexibility a clear edge in the search for alpha. Regulation is bound to have a major impact on both the buy and sell sides. Furthermore, since hedge funds have been in the line of fire for a while they will not be spared this time around. Not to mention the fact that such a large shift toward more regulation is taking place at a time when the

Reconsidering Funds of Hedge Funds. http://dx.doi.org/10.1016/B978-0-12-401699-6.00028-9

performance of hedge funds, and, in turn, of funds of hedge funds (FoHFs), is seriously challenged. Indeed, while FoHFs have been very resilient in the aftermath of the tech bubble, they also suffered in the wake of the Lehman Brothers collapse. In addition, apart from a strong beta-driven rally in 2009, they have been struggling to perform in the 'new normal,' as famously dubbed by Bill Gross, the world renowned bond trader and co-chief investment officer at PIMCO. It is fair to say that FoHFs did not live up to investors' expectations. If a few powerhouses are benefiting from the industry consolidation, most FoHFs are still experiencing outflows. Their aggregated assets under management are as a result approximately 20% off their peak, even though single hedge funds have already reached new highs. The additional regulatory burden could very well be the tipping point for many FoHFs managers. Many pundits are calling for the end of the FoHFs industry.

We argue in this chapter that, unlike conventional wisdom, regulation could be a unique opportunity for the FoHFs industry. In an attempt to make our point, we elaborate in Section 28.2 on one specific case, namely the European insurance regulation, and show that the standard approach does not properly calibrate the risk of FoHFs. We propose in Section 28.3 an amendment to the standard formula that is inspired from the Basel framework and that makes it possible to take into account the diversification benefits of FoHFs. Finally, we show in Section 28.4 that the calibration of FoHFs risk obtained with the granularity adjustment is consistent with empirical evidence.

## 28.2. FoHFs AND SOLVENCY II

In order for the discussion to be as concrete as possible, we focus in this chapter on one specific regulation, namely the European insurance regulation. Here, we give a brief overview of the Solvency II directive, with particular attention paid to the treatment reserved for hedge fund investments.

The Solvency II directive is a principle-based regulatory system that lays the foundations for the new prudential framework for EU (re)insurance companies and EU branches or subsidiaries of non-EU-based groups. It is aimed at establishing harmonized solvency requirements that account for the multitude of risks insurers face nowadays, both on the liabilities and on the assets side. The objective of the directive at the macro level is to mitigate systemic risks and at the micro level to detect fault lines that could prevent an insurance company from absorbing significant unforeseen losses, and as a result impair its capacity to satisfy its future commitments. In other words, the objective of the Solvency II directive is to improve the understanding and the management of the different dimensions of risk.

The Solvency II framework is organized around three pillars. The first pillar deals with the quantitative dimension and sets the Solvency Capital Requirement (SCR). The SCR is calibrated in such a way that the probability for an insurer to default over the next 12 months remains below 0.5%, at any point in time.

From a technical standpoint this comes down to computing a 12-month value at risk (VaR)[1] with a confidence level of 99.5%. The second pillar deals with the qualitative dimension, and defines the standards for the governance and risk management of insurance companies. Finally, the third pillar deals with market discipline and it sets out disclosure requirements to increase transparency.

It is worth mentioning at this stage that each insurance company will technically have the possibility to opt for the standard formula or implement its own internal evaluation model. The latter should remain the privilege of large institutions given the additional burden it will imply (administration, compliance, IT, etc.). The specification of the standard formula is therefore critical for the vast majority.

The pre-requisite for a suitable risk calibration is a 'reliable' risk-to-return analysis. While the exercise is fairly straightforward for traditional asset classes, it may require an overlay of expert judgment for more exotic asset classes (e.g., emerging market equities, commodities) or alternative investment strategies (hedge funds, private equity, etc.). A proper analysis may even be difficult to do for practical reasons. Data on hedge funds has, for example, been sketchy historically and the quality thereof subject to controversy (Liang, 2003; Straumann, 2009; Schneeweis et al., 2011). The information disclosed by the different databases available on the market (e.g., BarclayHedge, Eurekahedge, Hedge Fund Research, Lipper, Morningstar) is consequently impacted by various performance measurement biases (Fung and Hsieh, 2000, 2002). Given the challenges of performing a reliable analysis and the difficulty of defining a capital charge specific to emerging market equities, commodities, hedge funds, or private equity, the Committee of European Insurance and Occupational Pensions Supervisions (EIOPA) considers that a single category and, in turn, a single stress for all of them is appropriate. This category is named 'Other Equities' and the recommended SCR is the highest possible, namely 49% — very far away from the empirically calculated hedge fund stress.

In an attempt to cope with the specific features of the alternative arena, and obtain a true and fair representation of the risk inherent to hedge fund investing, Vaissié (2012) opts for an internal model approach and applies the two-step methodology advocated for equities in EIOPA Consultation Paper 69 to a series of hedge fund strategy indices made up of managed accounts.[2] Figure 28.1 plots the stress level against the risk-adjusted performance for a series of hedge fund strategies, the hedge fund composite index, and an equity index. The hedge fund composite is a capitalization-weighted index made up of the different hedge fund strategy indices available on the Lyxor managed account platform.

---

[1]The limits of this measure have been largely discussed in the literature, but a critique of VaR is beyond the scope of this chapter. The interested reader can refer to Artzner et al. (1999) for greater details on coherent risk measures.
[2]See Giraud (2005) for greater details on the benefits of managed accounts in terms of the quantity and quality of information.

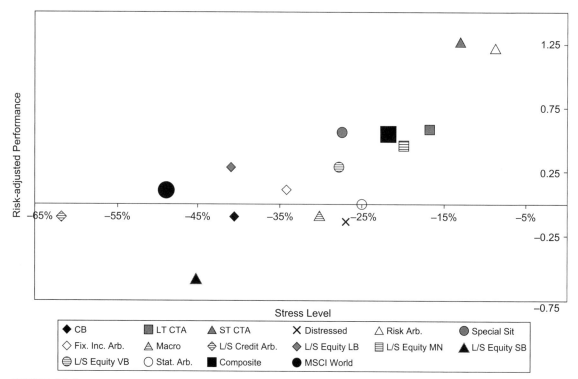

**FIGURE 28.1**
Hedge fund strategies capital efficiency.
*(Vaissié, 2012)*

The index is made up of over 100 single hedge funds that have been selected through a rigorous due diligence process;[3] it can thus be used as a proxy for a diversified FoHF.[4]

The moderate level of stress exhibited by the composite index in Figure 28.1 clearly shows the diversification benefits that can be achieved within the hedge fund world. With a stress test that is inferior to 25% (i.e., only 50% of the capital charge recommended in the standard formula for hedge funds), the composite index presents a level of risk that is dramatically lower than the one of most of its constituents (e.g. Long/Short Credit Arbitrage, Long/Short Equity Short Bias, Long/Short Equity Long Bias, Convertible Bond Arbitrage).

It should also be noted that a capital charge of 25% for a diversified FoHF as suggested in Vaissié (2012) would compare very well with the SCR currently recommended in the Solvency II framework for insurers' typical performance-

---

[3]Detailed information on the index can be downloaded at www.lyxorhedgeindices.com.
[4]One could argue that a FoHF index would have been a better proxy. However, the quality and the quantity of the information available on such indices is not sufficient to carry out the two-step methodology recommended by the regulator to calibrate the SCR.

seeking asset, namely developed market equities (i.e., 39%). This result corroborates the findings of previous studies on the benefits of hedge fund strategies in asset liability management (Martellini and Ziemann, 2006; Darolles and Vaissié, 2011) and it calls for a greater role of alternative investments in insurers' portfolios. A prudential framework such as the Solvency II directive could be instrumental in the rise of alternative investment strategies in the global allocation of institutional investors.

The heterogeneity of hedge fund strategies both in terms of risk-to-return profile and of capital requirement (see Figure 28.1) makes it challenging for insurance companies, with limited expertise and/or resources, to design optimal hedge fund portfolios. This creates opportunities for FoHFs managers that are more than happy to leverage on their capabilities to design customized investment solutions. Moreover, since reports have to be produced on a regular basis to the supervisor, and given the data-intensive nature of the task, the monitoring and reporting costs are liable to be paramount. The capacity of FoHFs managers to mutualize these costs and eventually control the capital efficiency of an allocation through active risk management is another cutting edge. For these reasons, the Solvency II framework could help FoHFs firms regain the confidence of investors.

## 28.3. FINE-TUNING SOLVENCY II STANDARD FORMULA

We have seen in Section 28.2 that the standard formula is mis-specified and overestimates the risk(s) inherent to hedge fund investing by roughly 50%. A suitable calibration for FoHFs risk can be obtained with an internal model approach. Unfortunately, as previously mentioned, many insurers will have no choice but to stick to the standard formula. We therefore propose in this section the implementation of the granularity adjustment, first introduced for application in the Basel framework, in order to take into account the diversification benefits of FoHFs and, in turn, reconcile the outcome of the standard formula with empirical evidence.

Any prudential framework involves a tradeoff between simplicity and complexity. From one point of view, a basic typology of risk(s) is liable to bring clarity, but it will probably not allow for a good cartography of risks, each category being somewhat heterogeneous. The 'Other Equities' category in the Solvency II framework is a perfect illustration. Conversely, a very detailed classification is liable to offer a better understanding of the different facets of risk, but it may at the same time create confusion.

In an attempt to recognize the complexity of risk(s) within a simple framework, we build on Gordy (2003) and propose the implementation of a risk disaggregation technique that separates the common part of risk from the idiosyncratic component. By so doing, we have the possibility to identify different sources of risk within a specific category and analyze their dependence structure. For the sake of simplicity, we use in this chapter the Linear Single Risk Factor Model introduced by

Gordy (2003) for application in the Basel framework (for an extension to dynamic multi-factor models, see Gagliardini and Gouriéroux, 2010).

Let us assume that the individual risk $y_i$ (e.g., the return stream of a portfolio constituent) depends on a single common equity factor plus individual specific effects:

$$y_i = \beta F + u_i,$$

where $y_i$ denotes the individual return, $F$ the unobservable systematic equity factor, $\beta$ the sensitivity between 'Equity' and 'Other Equities,' and $u_i$ the idiosyncratic term. Note that in our specification, individual returns have sensitivity to the systematic factor (referred to as beta) not necessarily equal to 1, as it is in the case of Gordy (2003). This difference allows us to discuss in Section 28.4 different choices of the parameter $\beta$.

In the Linear Single Risk Factor Model of Gordy (2003), variables $F$ and $u_i$ satisfy the following distributional assumptions:

**Assumptions**: For any portfolio size $n$,

> **A1** $F$ and $(u_1, \ldots, u_n)$ are independent;
> **A2** $F \approx N(0, \eta^2)$;
> **A3** $u_1, \ldots, u_n$ are independent and identically normally distributed, $u_i \approx N(0, \sigma^2)$.

The two parameters $\eta$ and $\sigma$ have a financial interpretation. The first one measures the 'Equity' systematic risk level, while the second captures the additional risk associated with the 'Other Equities' category.

Let us now consider a homogeneous[5] portfolio made up of $n$ constituents. This homogeneity assumption means that variables $y_1, \ldots, y_n$ are independently identically distributed (i.i.d.) conditional on the factor $F$. However, when the unobservable systematic factor is integrated out, individual returns are dependent. In particular, we get for any $i \neq j$, $corr(y_i, y_j) = \beta^2 \eta^2 / (\beta^2 \eta^2 + \sigma^2)$ (i.e., a positive dependence between returns when $\eta \neq 0$).

The overall portfolio return is thus equal to:

$$y = \frac{1}{n} \sum_{i=1}^{n} y_i.$$

In general, the distribution of $y$ is unknown in closed-form due to the risk dependences. The density of $y$ does indeed involve integrals with a large dimension. The quantiles (i.e., VaR involved in the definition of the SCR) of the

---

[5]The homogeneity assumption corresponds to the choice of a unique SCR for all the assets belonging to the 'Other Equities' category. The case of non-homogeneous portfolios is left for future research.

distribution of $y$ can as a consequence also be difficult to compute. With Assumptions A1–A3, we have:

$$y \approx N\left(0, \beta^2\eta^2 + \frac{\sigma^2}{n}\right). \qquad (28.1)$$

We can therefore obtain a closed-form formula and solve the problem for a diversified portfolio (i.e., a large $n$). As shall be seen from equation (28.2), when $n$ is large, the VaR of $y$ is approximated by a function of the two volatility parameters $\eta$ and $\sigma$, and the sensitivity level $\beta$. We deduce from equation (28.1):

$$VaR(\alpha) = \sqrt{\beta^2\eta^2 + \frac{\sigma^2}{n}}\ \Phi^{-1}(\alpha) \approx \beta\eta\Phi^{-1}(\alpha) + \frac{1}{n}\frac{\sigma^2}{2\beta\eta}\ \Phi^{-1}(\alpha), \qquad (28.2)$$

where $\alpha$ denotes the level of risk (i.e., 0.5% in the Solvency II framework). The first term of equation (28.2) is usually called the cross-sectional asymptotic (CSA) risk measure and in our case captures the non-diversifiable effect of the 'Equity' systematic risk on the portfolio (Vasicek, 1991). As a risk measure, it neglects the impact of the risks associated with the 'Other Equities' for a portfolio of finite size. The second term is referred to as the granularity adjustment in the Basel framework and measures the impact of the individual risks of the 'Other Equities' when the portfolio size is large, but finite. Let us point out that the second term in the expansion is of order $1/n$ and not $1/\sqrt{n}$ as in typical asymptotic expansions. This means that the approximation proposed is accurate even for small values of $n$.

Despite its simplicity, the Linear Single Risk Factor Model could be too restrictive to capture the complexity of risks, and, in particular, potential cross-effects between the 'Other Equities' and the 'Equity' risks. Indeed, in non-linear model specifications, the granularity adjustment could depend on possible leverage effects (Black, 1976) and eventually turn negative. However, as shown in Gagliardini and Gouriéroux (2010), any portfolio risk measure (not only the VaR) can be easily decomposed as the sum of two components, under a set of assumptions that could be much more general than the basic ones used in this section. For the sake of simplicity, we only consider the linear case in Section 28.4, but the generalization is technically possible.

## 28.4. AN APPLICATION TO FoHFs

As already mentioned, hedge fund strategies show very different risk-to-return profiles. The same holds true for their stress level and, as a result, for their potential capital charge. Ignoring this diversity and considering hedge funds as a homogeneous asset class is therefore a critical error. In an attempt to take into account the heterogeneity of hedge fund strategies and, in turn, the diversification properties of FoHFs, we propose to implement the granularity adjustment to hedge fund investments. The same approach would also make sense for other constituents of the 'Other Equities' category such as commodities.

Practical implementation requires the calibration of three parameters, namely $\eta$, $\sigma$, and $\beta$. We propose two approaches to calibrate them; we label them Granularity Adjustment 1 and Granularity Adjustment 2. We first retain the assumption that $\beta = 1$ and only discuss the calibration of the two remaining parameters. We subsequently consider different values for the sensitivity parameter $\beta$.

For Granularity Adjustment 1, we start with the SCR recommended by the regulator for the 'Equity' and 'Other Equities' categories (i.e., 39% and 49%, respectively), and calibrate the two risk parameters $\eta$ and $\sigma$ through a reverse engineering process *à la* Black and Litterman (1990, 1992), with $\alpha = 0.5\%$ and $\beta = 1$. It is worth stressing that the latter assumption is more conservative than the one made by the regulator in the standard formula, since it assumes no diversification potential at all between the two aforementioned categories.

- *Calibration Step 1.* For $\alpha = 0.5\%$ and $\beta = 1$, we recover the equity SCR when the 'Other Equity' risk parameter $\sigma$ is set to 0. In this particular case, we obtain from equation (28.2) that the standard formula — with the granularity adjustment — is equal to:

$$VaR(0.5\%) = \eta\Phi^{-1}(0.5\%) = -39\%. \qquad (28.3)$$

  We therefore get $\eta = 11.86\%$ for the 'Equity' risk parameter. In other words, an equity volatility of around 12% leads to the SCR calibrated for this asset class.
- *Calibration Step 2.* The SCR of the 'Other Equities' category corresponds in our framework to a non-diversified portfolio of a single asset, i.e., $n = 1$. From equation (28.2) and taking into account the 'Other Equities' capital charge, we obtain:

$$VaR(0.5\%) = \eta\Phi^{-1}(0.5\%) + \frac{\sigma^2}{2\eta}\,\Phi^{-1}(0.5\%) = -49\%,$$

where the only unknown parameter is $\sigma$. By so doing, we obtain $\sigma = 8.5\%$ for the 'Other Equities' risk parameter. This number corresponds to the volatility level of the idiosyncratic risk, filtered from the Solvency framework.

**Definition 1 (Granularity Adjustment 1).** Under Assumptions A1–A3, the capital charge for a diversified FoHF of size $n$ is:

$$SCR(n) = \eta\Phi^{-1}(0.5\%) + \frac{1}{n}\frac{\sigma^2}{2\eta}\,\Phi^{-1}(0.5\%),$$

where $\eta = 11.86\%$ and $\sigma = 8.5\%$.

We simply need to set different values for $n$ to study the impact of the level of diversification on the capital charge. As we shall see from Figure 28.2, the stress level converges with exponential decay from 49% to 39% as $n$ increases from 1 to 20. In line with previous research (Henker, 1998; Learned and Lhabitant, 2004; Brown *et al.*, 2012) we observe that the bulk of the diversification benefits are achieved with a limited number of constituents (i.e., $n = 5$). This being said,

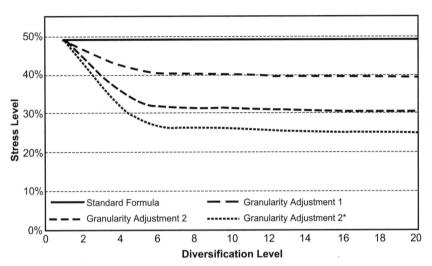

**FIGURE 28.2**
Hedge fund capital charge depending on the diversification level.

it is important to bear in mind that it is the quality rather than the quantity that really matters when it comes to diversification (Darolles *et al.*, 2012). This is particularly true in the case of heterogeneous portfolios.

By making the assumption that part of the idiosyncratic component of the total risk can be diversified away at the portfolio level, the capital charge decreases mechanically, even if one considers that there is no diversification potential between the 'Equity' and 'Other Equities' categories. However, with Granularity Adjustment 1 the capital requirement for hedge fund investments is floored at 39% (i.e., the SCR of Equities).

In order to include the level of correlation between the 'Equity' and 'Other Equities' categories in the analysis, we relax the assumption $\beta = 1$. The regulator proposes to use a correlation of 75%. We therefore use this value to study the diversification effect.

- *Calibration Step 1.* This step is not modified by the new assumption and we obtain the same volatility parameter $\eta = 11.86\%$ when using the 'Equity' SCR.
- *Calibration Step 2.* The 'Other Equities' category corresponds to $n = 1$, but this time the sensitivity parameter $\beta$ is set to 0.75. This choice has a direct impact on the calibration procedure, as we have to solve the following equation:

$$VaR(0.5\%) = \beta\eta\Phi^{-1}(0.5\%) + \frac{\sigma^2}{2\beta\eta} \Phi^{-1}(0.5\%) = -49\%.$$

We then obtain $\sigma = 11.92\%$ from the 'Other Equities' capital charge value. The sensitivity parameter influences the risk disaggregation procedure directly, by putting more weight on the idiosyncratic component. We then understand that the smaller the $\beta$, the better the impact of diversification. The case of $\beta = 1$ considered previously is clearly the worst-case scenario.

**Definition 2 (Granularity Adjustment 2).** Under Assumptions A1–A3, the capital charge for a diversified FoHF of size $n$ is:

$$SCR(n) \ = \ \beta\eta\Phi^{-1}(0.5\%) + \frac{1}{n}\frac{\sigma^2}{2\beta\eta}\ \Phi^{-1}(0.5\%),$$

where $\beta = 0.75$, $\eta = 11.86\%$, and $\sigma = 11.92\%$.

Here, again, we simply need to set different values for $n$ to study the impact of the level of diversification on the capital charge. As we shall see from Figure 28.2, the stress level converges with exponential decay from 49% to 30% as $n$ increases from 1 to 20. The bulk of the diversification benefits are still achieved with a limited number of constituents (i.e., $n = 6$).

In an attempt to fine-tune Granularity Adjustment 2, we finally take as an input the observed sensitivity instead of the one recommended by the regulator. We use the Lyxor Hedge Fund Index as a proxy for the hedge fund industry and the MSCI World Index as a proxy for the equity market. For the capital charge to be conservative, we computed the betas on different rolling windows (see Figure 28.3), we took the highest historical value and majored it by 20%. We

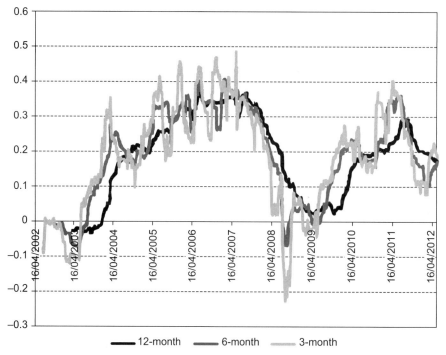

**FIGURE 28.3**
Hedge fund industry equity beta.

therefore end up with a beta of 0.6. We label this approach Granularity Adjustment 2*.

As we can see from Figure 28.2, this time around the stress level converges with exponential decay from 49% to 25% as $n$ increases from 1 to 20. This result gives weight to the previous study by Vaissié (2012) showing that 25% is a suitable capital requirement for a diversified FoHF. The bulk of the diversification benefits are achieved this time again with a limited number of underlyings (i.e., $n = 6$).

## CONCLUSION

Alternative diversification has arguably become part of mainstream investment practices. Making the case for hedge fund strategies is indeed straightforward when looking at their long-term risk-to-return profile. However, many investors are newcomers in the brave new world of hedge funds and their experience has been somewhat dissonant with the long-term view. Indeed, most of them first considered hedge fund investing after the burst of the tech bubble and only made the great leap a few years later, close to the top of the latest bull market. Market conditions have since then been extremely challenging, and the performance of hedge funds and, in turn, FoHFs, fell short of historical standards. Although there is some evidence in the academic literature that FoHFs add value over the long run (Darolles and Vaissié, 2012), investors are progressively climbing up the learning curve and consequently starting to question the rationale behind paying a double-fee structure.

Under these circumstances, FoHFs have no choice but to reinvent themselves. The challenge for them is to do so at a time when a wave of new regulations is set to be a game-changer. We argue in this chapter that, unlike conventional wisdom, such a tidal change toward more regulation could turn out to be a great opportunity for the FoHFs industry. However, there is only one necessary condition for that to exist: a fair treatment of hedge fund investments.

The role of regulation is not only to control risk(s), but it is also aimed at triggering behavior changes. With the benefit of hindsight, it is clear that institutional investors have to rethink their long-term investment policy and pay greater attention to risk management. In this respect, prudential frameworks should give incentives to improve portfolio diversification. However, with the current draft of the Solvency II directive, the regulator is doing nothing but orchestrating a massive move of insurers from equity-linked products to fixed-income instruments (i.e., exchanging one risk for another). The implementation of the granularity adjustment — first introduced for application in the Basel framework — is an attempt to better calibrate the capital charge of FoHFs and make it possible for insurers to leverage on alternative diversification. In line with Vaissié (2012), we find that 25% appears to be a suitable capital requirement for a diversified fund of hedge funds — a very competitive capital charge compared with the ones of traditional performance-seeking assets.

Will insurers increase their allocation to alternative investment strategies? Industry surveys suggest that some of them are already inclined to do so. The others might be forced to follow later on so that they can control their funding ratio efficiently. Will they go direct? Only the largest insurers will have the capacity to manage customized allocations that are optimal from an investment and a regulatory perspective, notwithstanding the fact that monitoring and reporting costs might be dissuasive for many. FoHFs thus have a role to play in the rise of alternative investments in institutional investor portfolios. However, for this they need to adapt their value proposition, from mere gatekeepers to investment stewards. Regulation could very well be the tipping element if representatives from the FoHFs industry succeed in making their voice audible.

# References

Artzner, P. F., Delbaen, F., & Eber, J. M. (1999). Coherent Measures of Risk. *Mathematical Finance, 9*(3), 203–228.

Black, F. (1976). Studies of Stock Price Volatility Changes. *Proceedings of the 1976 Meeting of the American Statistical Association, Business and Economics Statistics Section*, 177–181.

Black, F., & Litterman, R. (1990). *Asset Allocation: Combining Investor Views with Market Equilibrium.* London: Working Paper, Goldman Sachs Fixed Income Research.

Black, F., & Litterman, R. (1992). Global Portfolio Optimization. *Financial Analysts Journal, 48*(5), 28–43.

Brown, S. J., Gregoriou, G. N., & Pascalau, R. (2012). Diversification in Funds of Hedge Funds: Is It Possible to Overdiversify? *Review of Asset Pricing Studies, 2*(1), 89–110.

Darolles, S., & Vaissié, M. (2011). *Diversification at a Reasonable Price: Revisiting Alternative Diversification from the Perspective of Institutional Investors.* Nice: Working Paper, EDHEC-Risk Institute.

Darolles, S., & Vaissié, M. (2012). The Alpha and Omega of Funds of Hedge Funds Added Value: A 'Post' Crisis Analysis'. *Journal of Banking and Finance, 36*(4), 1067–1078.

Darolles, S., Keller, S., & Vaissié, M. (2012). *Diversification: It Is All About Quality, Not Quantity!* Nice: Working Paper, EDHEC-Risk Institute.

Fung, W., & Hsieh, D. (2000). Performance Characteristics of Hedge Funds and Commodity Funds: Natural Versus Spurious Biases. *Journal of Financial and Quantitative Analysis, 35*(3), 291–307.

Fung, W., & Hsieh, D. (2002). Benchmark of Hedge Fund Performance, Information Content and Measurement Biases. *Financial Analysts Journal, 58*(1), 22–34.

Gagliardini, P., & Gouriéroux, C. (2010). *Granularity Adjustment for Risk Measures: Systematic vs Unsystematic Risks.* Paris: Working Paper, CREST.

Giraud, J.R. (2005). Mitigating Hedge Funds' Operational Risks: Benefits and Limitations of Managed Account Platforms. Working Paper, EDHEC-Risk Institute.

Gordy, M. (2003). A Risk Factor Model Foundation for Rating-Based Bank Capital Rules. *Journal of Financial Intermediation, 12*(3), 199–232.

Henker, T. (1998). Naïve Diversification for Hedge Funds. *Journal of Alternative Investments, 1*(3), 33–38.

Learned, M., & Lhabitant, F. S. (2004). Finding the Sweet Spot of Hedge Fund Diversification. *Journal of Financial Transformation, 10*, 31–39.

Liang, B. (2003). The Accuracy of Hedge Fund Returns. *Journal of Portfolio Management, 29*(3), 111–122.

Martellini, L., & Ziemann, V. (2006). The Benefits of Hedge Funds in Asset Liability Management. *Journal of Financial Risk Management, 3*(2), 38–55.

Schneeweis, T., Kazemi, H., & Szado, E. (2011). Hedge Fund Database 'Deconstruction': Are Hedge Fund Databases Half Full or Half Empty? *Journal of Alternative Investments, 14*(2), 65–88.

Straumann, D. (2009). Measuring the Quality of Hedge Fund Data. *Journal of Alternative Investments, 12*(2), 26–40.

Vaissié, M. (2012). Solvency II. Regulation Change and Hedge Fund Evolution. *Journal of Alternative Investments.* doi:10.3905/jai.2012.2012.1.02 0.

Vasicek, O. (1991). *Limiting Loan Loss Probability Distribution.* San Francisco, CA: Working Paper, KMV Corporation.

# CHAPTER 29

# Funds of Hedge Funds and the Principles of Fiduciary Investing Following the Global Financial Crisis

**Paul U. Ali**

Melbourne University Law School, Melbourne, Australia

## 29.1. INTRODUCTION

Funds of hedge funds (FoHFs) are an increasingly common way for institutional investors as well as high-net-worth individuals to access the hedge fund sector. Unsurprisingly, there have been renewed calls in the wake of the global financial crisis to subject the hedge fund sector to greater regulatory scrutiny, but this has not undermined the role played by FoHFs in intermediating between investors and hedge funds.

A FoHF is, in essence, a 'feeder' structure that aggregates the contributions of the investors in FoHFs and allocates that capital across a broad pool of hedge funds. In this manner, an investor can efficiently obtain exposure to a diversified portfolio of hedge fund managers and hedge fund investment styles. While a FoHF can be seen as analogous to a mutual fund that invests in wholesale mutual funds, the former is more commonly structured in the same manner as the hedge funds in which it invests and thus any similarities with the latter are only superficial.

## 29.2. THE PRINCIPLES OF FIDUCIARY INVESTING

The regulatory responses in the major financial markets to the global financial crisis have largely followed the predictable path of focusing on the hedge funds

Reconsidering Funds of Hedge Funds. http://dx.doi.org/10.1016/B978-0-12-401699-6.00029-0

themselves rather than FoHFs, which are often the common interface between investors, particularly institutional investors, and hedge funds. The managers of these hedge funds have been subjected to an increased regulatory burden as to how they conduct their business. Less attention, however, has been paid to the extent to which the FoHFs and the institutional investors in FoHFs might bear some degree of responsibility for the losses suffered by them when allocating funds under management to hedge funds.

This focus on the sell side has obscured the reality of contemporary hedge fund investment where the 'buy side' is characterized not by investors acting as if they were no different to individuals, but by chains of legal relationships arising from the delegation of particular investment-related functions by the ultimate investors to intermediaries. This means that between the ultimate investor (such as the member of a pension fund) and the underlying hedge fund there are multiple intermediaries who invest not for their own account, but on behalf of others, and, because of this, those parties may be described as fiduciary investors. A prime example of a fiduciary investor is the institutional investor who allocates part of its assets under management (AUM) to a FoHF.

When considering investing in a FoHF or making any other investment, a fiduciary investor must act prudently. This legal duty of prudence, which is referred to as the 'prudent investor rule,' requires two things of fiduciary investors. (i) Fiduciary investors must invest the assets entrusted to them by, for example, their fund members. (ii) Fiduciary investors must, when deciding to buy, sell, or hold an investment, have regard to the suitability of the investment and the need to ensure portfolio diversification. The prudent investor rule applies to all fiduciary investors in the United States and in other markets governed by laws based on English common law.

## 29.3. PRUDENT INVESTING

The Uniform Prudent Investor Act of 1994 (UPIA) which applies to US fiduciary investors provides the clearest statement of what constitutes prudent investing in English law-based systems: a fiduciary investor must, in investing and managing fund assets, consider the purposes, terms, distribution requirements, and other material circumstances of the fund (Ali et al., 2003). Decisions made by the fiduciary investor concerning individual assets, like FoHFs investments, must be evaluated in the context of the fiduciary investor's portfolio as a whole and as part of its overall investment strategy. The fiduciary investor must therefore take account of the impact of an allocation to a FoHF on the risk-to-return profile of the fiduciary investor's portfolio as a whole; this means examining the expected returns from the FoHF, the risks associated with an investment in the FoHF, and the impact on the diversification, liquidity, income, and growth requirements of the fiduciary investor's portfolio.

The UPIA has been adopted in the majority of the States in the United States (including New York and California) (Ali et al., 2003). In the remaining States, principles consistent with those contained in the Act have been accepted as part of the unwritten, common law. Equivalent requirements apply to fiduciary investors in Australia, the United Kingdom, and the majority of the Canadian Provinces (Ali *et al.*, 2003). While other common law jurisdictions like, for instance, England and Australia lack the comprehensive statement of investment-related duties articulated by the UPIA, the laws governing fiduciary investments in those jurisdictions are today consistent with the UPIA due to a combination of legislative reform (e.g., the Trustee Act 2000 of the United Kingdom and the 1997 amendments to the Trustee Act 1925 of New South Wales, Australia) and judicial opinion (where, for example, the English and Australian courts have utilized modern portfolio theory to explain the investment duties of fiduciaries).

In addition, under the UPIA, a fiduciary investor is able to delegate the exercise of its investment powers to a third party — thus, a fiduciary investor is free to allocate assets under its management to the manager of a FoHF (where the selection of the underlying hedge funds has effectively delegated to the FoHF manager). It should, however, be noted that there are residual concerns in some common law jurisdictions about a fiduciary investor's ability to delegate the exercise of its investment powers to a third party. In England, these concerns have been laid to rest by the Trustee Delegation Act of 1999. In Australia, while these concerns have been addressed in relation to mutual funds by the Managed Investments Scheme Act 1998 of Australia, the position in relation to pension funds is, arguably, less clear. The market consensus is nonetheless that the Superannuation Industry (Supervision) Act 1999 of Australia has been effective in enabling pension funds to delegate their investment powers to third parties such as managers of FoHFs (Ali *et al.*, 2003).

## 29.4. INVESTING IN FoHFs

The prudent investor rule requires a fiduciary investor that is considering investing in a FoHF to (i) assess the structural advantages and disadvantages of a FoHF, and (ii) assess the risk-to-return profile of the FoHF and impact of investing in the fund on the risk-to-return profile of the fiduciary investor's portfolio.

### 29.4.1. Structural Factors

FoHFs are typically structured in the same manner as their underlying hedge funds (Martin, 2003). The preferred structures are onshore limited partnerships, and offshore corporations and trusts. An investor normally participates in a FoHF by making a cash subscription for interests in the fund, although if there is a secondary market for interests in the FoHF the investor may obtain exposure to the FoHF by purchasing an interest from an exiting investor (Ali *et al.*, 2003).

The key selling point of a FoHF is the access that they offer to the underlying hedge funds (Fothergill and Coke, 2001). Hedge funds typically demand substantial minimum investments from investors and, once a hedge fund reaches what its manager considers to be an optimum size, it will often be closed by the manager to new investors.

Meeting the minimum investment requirement will not normally pose a difficulty for most fiduciary investors, but it may be an amount higher than what the investor wishes to allocate to an individual hedge fund or to a particular strategy. FoHFs thus enable investors to obtain exposure to a range of hedge funds without having to commit a substantial amount to each individual fund. In addition, an investor in a FoHF can obtain exposure to a hedge fund that is no longer accepting new money.

Another selling point is the prospect of increased liquidity. A FoHF can be viewed as a secondary market in the hedge funds in which it has invested (Ali et al., 2003). This provides a mechanism whereby investors can exit their exposure to the underlying hedge funds by having the manager of the FoHF buy back or redeem their interests in the FoHF. This is attractive since hedge funds are often characterized by limited liquidity; hedge funds prescribe minimum holding periods for investments, and permit investor withdrawals only within specified exit windows and only after lengthy advance notice. FoHFs, in contrast, offer enhanced liquidity. They permit more frequent investor exit and do not generally impose lockups. It is also more common for a FoHF to be listed on an official exchange than it is for that fund's underlying hedge funds and this provides a second means of exit for investors who can liquidate their interests on the exchange.

Moreover, FoHFs introduce an independent third party, the manager of the FoHFs, between the investors and the underlying hedge funds. This fund manager is likely to be better placed, due to their expertise and resources or for relationship reasons, than an individual investor to monitor the performance of the underlying hedge funds, particularly in relation to matters such drawdowns, style drift, and leverage (Ali et al., 2003).

A FoHF, however, carries structural disadvantages that fiduciary investors must take into account when considering making an investment therein. The fiduciary investor should be aware that investing in a FoHF means paying two sets of fees (Brown et al., 2004). The investor pays one set of fees to the manager of the FoHF but, in addition, indirectly incurs a second set of fees, namely the fees charged by the managers of the underlying hedge funds to their own investors (among which number is the FoHF).

Furthermore, the liquidity benefits of a FoHF are not without cost. In order for a FoHF to offer greater liquidity than its underlying hedge funds, it will often need to resort to something that is commonly a feature of mutual funds, namely a cash buffer to finance redemptions. This cash buffer may erode the returns from the underlying hedge funds and by so doing detract from the advantages of exposure to those funds (Ali et al., 2003). Alternatively, a FoHF can preclude over-reliance on a cash buffer by selecting for its portfolio hedge funds with less stringent lockups and exit conditions. This, however, may lead to the FoHF's portfolio being biased in favor of hedge funds whose strategies favor trading in liquid assets such as securities as opposed to hedge funds whose portfolios are dominated by illiquid financial instruments. This can have a negative impact on the diversification benefits for the fiduciary investor's portfolio (Ineichen, 2003).

Another disadvantage associated with the structure of a FoHF is the introduction of a second 'layer' between the fiduciary investor and the underlying hedge funds. The interposition of a FoHF between an investor and the hedge funds may adversely impact the ability of the investor to exit their investment in the event of a sharp market downturn, since the investor will, in fact, be seeking to redeem a fractional interest (the interest in the FoHF) in another fractional interest (the interest of the FoHF in the underlying hedge funds collectively) (Ali et al., 2003). Exiting the first interest depends upon the manager of the FoHF being able to exit the second interest; exiting from that second interest, in turn, depends upon compliance with the exit requirements imposed by the underlying hedge funds.

Finally, the fact that a FoHF may be structured as a hedge fund rather than a mutual fund does not wholly address one of the issues commonly associated with mutual funds. FoHFs, like mutual funds, expose their investors to the decisions of their coinvestors. Investors exit FoHFs normally by redeeming their interests in the FoHFs and the redemption of those interests must be financed out of either a cash buffer or by the sale or redemption of interests in the underlying hedge funds. The latter option typically incurs transaction costs and may also lead to the crystallization of a taxable gain, both of which are borne by the remaining investors in the FoHFs and not wholly by the exiting investor.

## 29.4.2. Diversification Factors

Hedge funds, and the FoHFs that invest in them, hold out to investors the promise of diversification benefits. These benefits, however, are difficult to assess and at least one major study has called these benefits into question (Agarwal and Naik, 2004). This study found that the returns of hedge funds that invested predominantly in stocks were, on the whole, unlikely to increase in line with the overall stock market in a bull market, but were likely to follow the stock market down in a bear market. A fiduciary investor therefore needs to be aware of the risk that, if the FoHF invested in does not bring with it diversification benefits, the fiduciary investor may end up reducing the overall returns on its portfolio or increasing the overall riskiness of the portfolio without any compensating increase in returns.

FoHFs also raise other questions in connection with diversification:

■ A FoHF may be overdiversified by being spread across too many hedge funds. This may lead to a dilution of the contribution of each individual hedge fund to the overall return on the FoHF and will, in turn, affect the contribution of the FoHF itself to the fiduciary investor's portfolio (Lhabitant and De Piante Vicin, 2004).

- As pointed out in a major study on FoHF investments (Brown *et al.*, 2012), having too many underlying hedge funds in a FoHF, may increase left tail risk (the risk of less likely but more extreme outcomes). This study found that the optimal number of underlying hedge funds in a FoHF is between 20 and 25 if left tail risk is to be avoided, but a large fraction of FoHFs have more than 25 underlying hedge funds.
- It appears that, rather than the diversification presented by the mix of underlying hedge funds, it was the ability of FoHFs to substitute their (or a third party's) due diligence of the underlying hedge funds for the due diligence that a fiduciary investor would itself have been required to undertake before allocating assets to a hedge fund that was the major selling point of FoHFs, particularly for first-time or other inexperienced fiduciary investors. Due diligence is a costly process and it may cost a FoHF a minimum of US$12 500 per hedge fund where it outsources the due diligence to a third-party service provider (Brown *et al.*, 2012) (on the other hand, were the FoHF or the fiduciary investor to undertake the due diligence itself the cost could rise to US$50 000–100 000 per hedge fund; Brown *et al.*, 2008). Most FoHFs have insufficient AUM to pay for third-party due diligence reports (let alone undertake the due diligence themselves) and it is likely that, in the case of the 22% of FoHFs that failed during the recent global financial crisis (Brown *et al.*, 2012), a material contributing factor was the failure to undertake or pay for proper due diligence of their underlying hedge funds. The 2012 study referred to here showed that only about a quarter of FoHFs had sufficient AUM to pay for an annual due diligence of their underlying hedge funds (Brown *et al.*, 2012).
- There is a risk of duplication of positions across the different hedge funds invested in by FoHFs (Lhabitant, 2002). This may lead the returns of the underlying hedge funds being more strongly correlated with each other, thus undermining the diversification benefits accruing to investors in FoHFs.

## CONCLUSION

FoHFs offer the attraction of exposure to multiple hedge funds. In deciding whether to allocate AUM to a FoHF, a fiduciary investor needs to consider both structural and diversification factors. The investor must take account of the 'fees on fees' structure of FoHFs and consider whether that is an appropriate price for the putative liquidity benefits offered by a FoHF. In addition, the investor must take into account the fact that the diversification benefits of investing in a FoHF can be eroded or rendered illusory by the overdiversification of the fund and the aggregation of positions across the underlying hedge funds.

A fiduciary investor that fails to undertake a rigorous (i.e., legally defensible) assessment of these factors is exposed to the risk that it will personally be required to make good to its own investors, losses or underperformance attributable to the allocation of assets to a FoHF.

## Acknowledgments

The author gratefully acknowledges the comments of Greg N. Gregoriou and Stephen Brown on an earlier draft of this chapter.

## References

Agarwal, V., & Naik, N. K. (2004). Risks and Portfolio Decisions involving Hedge Funds. *Review of Financial Studies, 17*(1), 63–98.

Ali, P., Stapledon, G., & Gold, M. (2003). *Corporate Governance and Investment Fiduciaries*. Sydney: Lawbook.

Brown, S. J., Fraser, T., & Liang, B. (2008). Hedge Fund Due Diligence: A Source of Alpha in a Hedge Fund Portfolio Strategy. *Journal of Investment Management, 6*(4), 23–33.

Brown, S. J., Goetzmann, W. N., & Liang, B. (2004). Fees on Fees in Funds of Funds. *Journal of Investment Management, 2*(4), 1–18.

Brown, S. J., Gregoriou, G. N., & Pascalau, R. (2012). Diversification in Funds of Hedge Funds: Is it Possible to Overdiversify? *Review of Asset Pricing Studies, 2*(1), 89–110.

Fothergill, M., & Coke, C. (2001). Funds of Hedge Funds: An Introduction to Multi-Manager Hedge Funds. *Journal of Alternative Investments, 4*(2), 7–16.

Ineichen, A. M. (2003). *Absolute Returns: Risks and Opportunities of Hedge Fund Investing*. New York: Wiley.

Lhabitant, F. S. (2002). *Hedge Funds: Myths and Limits*. Chichester: Wiley.

Lhabitant, F. S., & De Piante Vicin, M. L. (2004). Finding the Sweet Spot of Hedge Fund Diversification. *Journal of Financial Transformation, 10*(1), 31–39.

Martin, S. (2003). Legal Issues in Structuring and Operating Funds of Hedge Funds. In S. Jaffer (Ed.), *Fund of Hedge Funds for Professional Investors and Managers*. London: Euromoney.

# CHAPTER 30

# Understanding the Regulation Impact: US Funds of Hedge Funds After the Crisis

**David Edmund Allen, Akhmad Kramadibrata, Robert John Powell, and Abhay Kumar Singh**
School of Accounting, Finance and Economics, Edith Cowan University, Joondalup, Western Australia, Australia

## 30.1. INTRODUCTION

One of the age-old great debates among economists, regulators, and industry participants is the extent to which regulation and government intervention in economies, industries, and markets is necessary or desirable. Proponents of free-market enterprise argue that strong regulation stifles competition, innovation, and growth. The counter-argument is that it aids stability, prevents disasters, and protects consumers and investors. For many decades, free enterprise and deregulation has held sway. Orbach (2009, p. 559) contends that the word regulation has for many decades been 'a bogeyman concept evoking images of unproductive and wasteful government bureaucracy' and that the Global Financial Crisis (GFC) has turned this bogeyman concept on its head.

In particular, the financial services industry has been placed under the microscope since the advent of the GFC, being perceived, along with government policies and regulatory failure, as a major cause of the crisis. As happened after the Great Depression, governments and regulators received the blow-torch treatment, with demands for stronger regulation and greater consumer protection.

The US government responded to these calls in spades, enacting the far reaching Dodd–Frank legislation with requirements for regulators to create hundreds of rules, with dozens of studies and reports probing every corner of the financial services industry. Hedge funds and funds of hedge funds (FoHFs), many of which had previously flown under the regulatory radar, were now dragged into the net, with new advisor registration requirements subjecting funds to greater monitoring, reporting, and examination.

Reaction to Dodd–Frank has ranged from dismay to applause. While many see it as a major over-reaction to the crisis, and an affront to the very principles of free enterprise and capitalism, imposing unnecessary regulatory costs and burdens on market participants, others espouse the improved investor protection and market discipline that it brings.

This chapter examines the regulatory debate in a FoHFs context. The chapter moves from broad economic debate on the merits of market regulation, through regulatory lessons from other industries and an examination of regulation trends in the broader financial services sector, to an assessment of the impacts of the new regulation specifically on hedge funds and FoHFs. The US is not alone in its introduction of new regulation which impacts on FoHFs. In Europe, the new Alternative Investment Fund Managers (AIFM) directive has far reaching implications for European and foreign FoHFs investors in Europe, as well as Europeans wanting to invest offshore. Thus, while predominance in our study is given to Dodd–Frank in our assessment of regulation on FoHFs, some consideration is also afforded to the impact of AIFM on US funds.

## 30.2. THE REGULATORY AND INTERVENTION DEBATE: LOOKING TO THE ECONOMISTS

Throughout history, economists have been divided in their opinions on the merits of government intervention and regulation in economies, markets, and industries. Early economists looked to regulation. Jean-Baptiste Colbert issued dozens of edicts to improve manufacturing quality and is credited with helping bring the French economy back from grave financial crisis in the 1600s. Keynesian economics, which advocate a large role for the government in the form of economic stimulation and intervention rather than regulation, ruled the roost in the United States for some 30 years after World War I and through the Great Depression and then lost favor to a self-regulating free-market approach, advocated by economists such as Milton Friedman.

John Maynard Keynes was a great proponent of economic stimulation through government spending. Keynes was a great believer that government spending increases another's earnings and whose subsequent spending then increases the earnings of others, creating a circular spending cycle that leads to a well-functioning economy. These techniques were used to stimulate the US economy after the Great Depression. Skidelsky (2009), who wrote a biography of Keynes, also wrote a book subsequent to the global financial crisis (GFC), *Keynes: The Return of the Master*, which looks at Keynesian economics in the context of the GFC and post-GFC environment. The author looks at both the causes of the GFC and the responses to it. Among the causes are seen to be innovative financial instruments, the behavior of banks and hedge funds, a lack of regulation, and a failure of the credit ratings agencies. Skidelsky draws parallels between Keynesian economics and the responses of the US authorities to the crisis, such as stimulation packages, which seem to be closely aligned with Keynes' thinking. Skidelsky believes that in a post-GFC environment Keynes would be an advocate of balanced growth with intervention by the government to stimulate the economy and avoid economic shocks.

On the other side of the coin is the argument for a free-market economy with minimal government intervention and regulation. This argument generally surrounds the belief that lack of regulation and interference will stimulate competition, leading to benefits such as increased innovation, productivity, and lower prices. The idea of self-regulating economies was promoted by Adam Smith (1776), who maintained that parties pursuing self interest will inadvertently, through an invisible hand, benefit the economy. Nobel laureate Milton Friedman, through his lectures at the University of Chicago and many publications (notably Friedman and Schwartz, 1963), promoted free-market economics and deregulation, seeing regulation as stifling economic growth, investment, and competition. This type of economic approach gained popularity from the 1970s onwards, with strong deregulation, including in the financial services industry. Friedman's approach was echoed by Stigler (1971), also a Nobel laureate, who advocated free enterprise and less regulation, maintaining that one of the disadvantages of regulation is that governments, large firms, and other interested parties will shape regulation to benefit themselves.

In strongly defending capitalism and deregulation, Smith (2012) draws on the work of the economist Joseph Schumpter, a great champion of capitalism. Smith rallies for businessmen to become stronger defenders of markets free of politics. The author sees capitalism as advancing freedom, order, and fairness, and government regulation as imposing costs and stifling innovation and entrepreneurship. Smith holds that US federal government regulatory costs now approach US$2 trillion and that 'vast swaths of the economy are constrained by mandates and bans, government-subsidized competitors and pervasive moral hazards.'

What are the implications of these economic debates? There is no doubt that regulation and intervention can stifle competition, entrepreneurship, and innovation. There is also no doubt that a hands-off approach can lead to instability and risky practices by market participants, which is what many are blaming financial institutions for during the GFC. The pattern seen here has been to follow Keynesian stimulatory approaches, coupled with increased regulation following financial crises, reverting to hands-off approaches and deregulation in between crisis times, which can then lead again to risky practices and the cycle repeating itself. Perhaps the answer lies in a more consistent, balanced approach such as advocated by Joseph Stiglitz (2001). In looking at past financial crises such as the Asian financial crisis of 1997–1999, Stiglitz found many developing countries to be struggling with over-regulation and over-reliance on capital adequacy regulation, which stifled innovation and credit availability. Stiglitz saw the challenge as being to have a more balanced approach that enhances competition and market openness, while at the same time retaining prudential oversight, appropriate incentives, and needed constraints.

## 30.3. LESSONS FROM OTHER INDUSTRIES

Rogoff (2011) draws parallels between the BP oil spill and the GFC. Millions of gallons of oil spewed into the Gulf of Mexico from a deep sea oil gusher after the explosion of an offshore drilling unit, which took 3 months to cap. Rogoff maintains that, like exotic financial instruments, the case for deep sea drilling was very seductive with the promise of great innovation, unfathomable complexity, and lack of transparency. Technologies had outstripped regulators' ability to keep up with them. In the case of the oil spill, governments and regulators were swayed by intense lobbying as well as concern over the stability of Middle East supplies. Rogoff holds that economics shows that where there is great uncertainty and high risk, we cannot rely on the price mechanism to get things right, and need to balance the complexity and technology with resilient regulation.

In 1937, a drug called Elixir Sulfanilamide killed more than 100 people in the United States. This occurred when a pharmacist for S.E. Massengill Company took a popular drug called Sulfanilamide (used for treating streptococcal infections) and changed it from powder and tablet format to liquid format by dissolving it in diethylene glycol, an antifreeze, which unbeknown to the pharmacist was deadly to humans. Raspberry flavor was added to make the drug palatable. At the time there was no regulation regarding safety tests on new drugs. This disaster led to an increase in the US Food and Drug Administration's drug regulation through the 1938 Food, Drug, and Cosmetic Act. Increased regulation was also brought in after the Thalidomide scandal in the late 1950s and early 1960s, when hundreds of deformed babies were born after their pregnant mothers took this anti-morning sickness drug. However, all the increased regulation has negative side-effects, with long clinical trials and high costs of regulatory compliance resulting in only a small percentage of drugs making it to market. The industry has thus long been characterized by debates on what is seen as negative effects of over-regulation (e.g., deMaria, 2010; Di Mario *et al.*, 2011; Freeman and Fuerst, 2012).

What lessons do we learn from the above? Nobody wants another massive oil spill or mass deaths through unsafe drugs. However, neither do we want to prevent access to important energy resources or stop life-saving drugs reaching the market. Perhaps the answer lies in approaches such as that advocated by Miller and Henderson (2007), who argue for a balanced approach to drug regulation. The authors maintain that if access to drugs is promoted at the expense of safety, a dangerous product could cause great harm, whereas over-emphasizing safety can increase costs in bringing drugs to market and deny patients access to life-saving drugs. In the same vein, it is not in the interests of the financial services industry to curtail growth and innovation, but there should certainly be protections in place to avoid another GFC.

## 30.4. THE ROAD TO DODD–FRANK

Following the Great Depression, the Glass–Steagall Act 1933 created a separation between commercial banking and investment banking activities. This was as a result of ardent investment in the stock market by banks being seen as a major contributor to the crash. This prohibited commercial banks from becoming involved in many investment and securities underwriting activities. While the Act was aimed at safety, there were also adverse effects: the income sources of banks were curtailed and many felt that lack of ability to diversify was leading to increased risk. The Gramm–Leach–Biley Act 1999 reformed parts of the Glass–Steagall Act and other existing legislation, thus allowing some of the large US banks to become major players in some of these markets, as well as to take on insurance business. This opened the way for bank involvement in hedge funds which they took to with enthusiasm.

US hedge funds and FoHFs were traditionally largely unregulated. Brouwer (2001) and Bianchi and Drew (2010) show how these funds were structured to avoid five major pieces of regulation including: the requirement for registration under the Securities Act 1933, the requirement for brokers and dealers to become registered members of a registered exchange or association under the Securities Exchange Act 1934, leverage and derivative restrictions under the Investment Company Act 1940, performance-based compensation restrictions under the Investment Advisers Act 1940, and the derivative monitoring requirements of Commodity Exchange Act 1974.

While many prior attempts to regulate hedge funds had not succeeded, the aftermath of the GFC saw renewed calls for hedge fund regulation. The deregulated, market-based, self-regulatory approach to financial services that was so enthusiastically touted pre-GFC was widely considered to have failed spectacularly during the GFC. If the fragilities of banks, which were the most heavily regulated of the participants, could be so badly exposed, what problems could highly unregulated hedge funds cause? Much of this was perception rather than fact, caused by the lack of disclosure and opaque nature of hedge funds, which surrounded them in mystique, with many perceiving them as exotic, highly leveraged financial instruments with high-risk shorting and derivative strategies. If there was concern over hedge funds, how much more so for FoHFs, where the inability to understand the underlying risk was multiplied by the number of funds in the FoHFs? Hedge funds were also strongly criticized for shorting on banks during the GFC. In the aftermath of the Lehman Brothers collapse, the Securities and Exchange Commission (SEC) banned the short selling of certain US financial institution stocks in September 2008 to stabilize financial markets.

As investors fled riskier investments during the GFC, many funds failed and there was great concern over systemic risk. FoHFs are particularly vulnerable to systemic risk, with many sharing some of the same underlying hedge funds. Concern over systemic risk stemmed from the systemic failure of LTCM (Long-Term Capital Management) in 1999 following the Russian crisis, whereby the Russian government defaulted on their bonds. The combination of all the above factors made hedge funds and FoHFs a prime target for increased regulation – and so it came about under Dodd–Frank.

## 30.5. DODD–FRANK

The Dodd–Frank Wall Street Reform and Consumer Protection Act ('Dodd–Frank') is widely regarded as being the most significant and wide-reaching piece of financial services legislation since the Great Depression. The Act was signed into law by Barack Obama in July 2010. The purpose of Dodd–Frank was to promote greater financial stability and to prevent systemic risk. The Act established the Financial Stability Oversight Council (FSOC) to monitor US financial risk. Dodd–Frank has significant implications for the hedge funds and FoHFs industry, which are contained under Title IV of the Act. This section makes amendments to the Advisors Act, requiring many advisors to private funds (who had previously been exempt from registration) to register with the SEC, and directing the SEC to establish reporting and monitoring requirements for these advisors. This means that advisors to hedge funds and FoHFs need to keep information on a variety of aspects, such as leverage, trading policies, valuation practices, and amounts of assets under management (AUM), as well as file reports required by the SEC. These advisors also become subject to examination, whereby the SEC can conduct periodic inspections of the records of advisors. In addition to existing forms required by registered advisors, the SEC introduced a new reporting form, PF, which allows the FSOC to monitor the systemic risk of private funds.

Dodd–Frank also amended the Advisors Act minimum registration requirements so that advisors with AUM of less than US$100 million are required to register with state authorities rather than the SEC. This required a number of existing advisors registered with the SEC to transfer to State registration. SEC registration exemptions were created for advisors solely to Venture Capital funds and for advisors solely to private funds with aggregate AUM in the United States of less than US$150 million. The registration of affected private fund advisors with the SEC was required from July 2011 and subsequently extended for most funds to May 2012.

There are a range of other stipulations under Dodd–Frank that impact on hedge funds and FoHFs. Accredited investor and qualified client standards have been amended and are subject to ongoing review. Regulators have been given greater authority to adopt rules regarding trading strategies such as short selling and derivatives. Some hedge funds will be required to register with the Commodity Futures Trading Commission (CFTC). The Volcker rule is one of the sections of Dodd–Frank causing most consternation. The rule restricts banks in engaging in trading for their own account or acquiring ownership interest in hedge funds and FoHFs. Initially the rule was to prohibit banks investing in hedge funds altogether, but this was subsequently diluted to restrict such investment to a percentage of their capital. The intended benefit of this rule is that it prevents banks from undertaking risky trading, which many see as being a key contributor to the GFC. There are also several potential downsides of the rule: it places restrictions on the ability of banks to make profits from trading, the hedge fund industry suffers from loss of business from banks, and there are also fears of reduced liquidity in US markets and trading activity migrating to offshore investment centers. Kroszner (2012) outlines some potential negative consequences of the Volcker rule being that natural hedging activities of banks could be curtailed, that the role played by banks as market makers in key global markets could be curtailed or eliminated, that liquidity could be reduced and bid–ask spreads increased, and that risk taking activities could just be pushed outside the banking system making the entire system more, instead of less, risky.

## 30.6. US FUNDS AND THE AIFM DIRECTIVE

The AIFM Directive brings alternative investments funds, including hedge funds and FoHFs, under the supervision of an EU regulator. As with Dodd–Frank, the directive places additional compliance requirements on funds, together with associated compliance costs. A US fund marketing to EU investors must comply with all the requirements relating to marketing applicable under the directive, for which there are stringent authorization, passport, disclosure, capital, and valuation requirements.

## 30.7. FoHFs TRENDS DURING AND AFTER THE GFC

Our discussion so far has shown that there are both disadvantages and disadvantages to regulation. We have seen that there are a number of impacts of the Dodd–Frank on FoHFs, including registration, and the associated disclosure, monitoring, and examination requirements. We have also examined potential upsides of the regulation with regard to increased transparency and investor protection. Concerns over the increased compliance regulation include compliance costs that could lead to many smaller FoHFs closing, reduced returns to investors, and an overall significant reduction in the size of the industry. Proponents of the legislation will argue that it allays investor concerns and this renewed confidence should increase investment. With the extensions in the SEC registration date, it will not be possible to gauge the full extent of the impact of the legislation on the funds for some time. Nonetheless, Dodd—Frank was enacted in July 2010, and the upsides and downsides of this news should be reflected in fund performance, and some of the impact on smaller funds having to leave the market due to inability to meet compliance requirements should already be evident. We thus turn to an analysis of fund performance and numbers in the period leading up to, during, and after the GFC. We use the Global HFRI Fund of Funds Composite index ('FoHFs Index') from Datastream (no specific US FoHF index is available via Datastream or Hedge Fund Research, but the US represents approximately half of global FoHFs) and compare this to two benchmark indices — the HFRX North America Hedge Fund Index ('Hedge Fund Index') and the S&P 500 index.

Figure 30.1 shows that, during the GFC, the FoHF index fell substantially further than the Hedge Fund index. This greater fall can largely be attributed to investors flocking out of FoHFs following the Madoff Ponzi scheme. However, neither FoHFs nor hedge funds fell to the S&P 500 level. Post-GFC, FoHFs recovered much quicker than the other indices, providing a higher overall return for the 7 years analyzed than the S&P 500 and a similar return to the hedge fund benchmark.

The acceleration of performance from 2009 onwards shows that dire predictions about the collapse of FoHFs and hedge funds in the wake of Dodd—Frank have not materialized. From mid 2010, which is around the time when Dodd—Frank was enacted, FoHFs returns flatten out. There is no evidence of FoHFs or hedge fund returns having any significant devastation (or improvement) in reaction to the enactment of the regulation, with returns trends being very similar to those of the S&P 500. All the indices had a similar flat performance in 2011 amid concerns over the European debt crisis. We now turn to analysis of fund assets (see Table 30.1).

FoHFs experienced tremendous growth in the early 2000s, outstripping single hedge funds, with FoHFs growing from 17% to 45% of total hedge fund assets. As expected, asset values dropped during the GFC, and 2010 showed good growth in total hedge funds; however, post-GFC, the popularity of FoHFs reduced, dropping to 33% of total hedge fund assets. There is no overly noticeable post-GFC difference in the mix between onshore and offshore assets brought about by pre-regulation implementation concerns. We now look to Table 30.2 for trends in the number of FoHFs. FoHFs are at 22% of total hedge fund numbers compared to 33% by value, indicating the greater size of FoHFs compared to single hedge funds.

Table 30.2 shows how the average FoHF size reduced during the mid 2000s with the launch of a number of smaller FoHFs. There is clear evidence from the figures that, post-GFC, there has been consolidation into larger FoHFs, with the average FoHF size increasing. During the GFC, launches fell well below liquidations — quite the opposite of pre-GFC. Whilst there has been some improvement in this post-GFC, it is still well below the ratio in the early 2000s, although some of this is attributable to the consolidation into larger funds that we have mentioned.

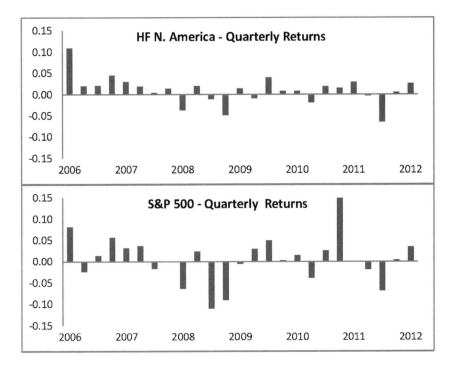

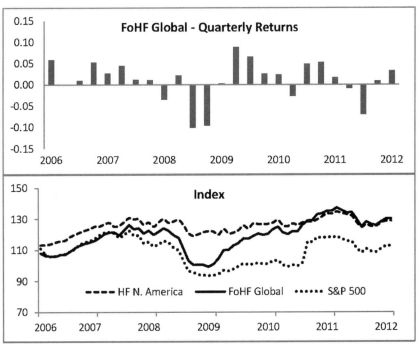

**FIGURE 30.1**
FoHFs performance compared to benchmarks.

| Table 30.1 | FoHFs Asset Growth Compared to Total Hedge Funds |

| | Growth in Assets (%) | | | | FoHFs as % of Total Hedge Funds |
|---|---|---|---|---|---|
| | Total Hedge Funds | Onshore Hedge Funds | Offshore Hedge Funds | FoHFs | |
| 2000 | 7.5 | 14.2 | 4.6 | 9.8 | 17.0 |
| 2001 | 9.9 | 29.3 | 0.7 | 22.8 | 19.0 |
| 2002 | 16.0 | −4.4 | 28.5 | 101.8 | 33.1 |
| 2003 | 31.1 | 21.1 | 35.6 | 41.7 | 35.8 |
| 2004 | 18.6 | 27.5 | 15.0 | 22.3 | 36.9 |
| 2005 | 13.7 | 15.9 | 12.6 | 10.0 | 35.7 |
| 2006 | 32.5 | 33.1 | 32.2 | 66.2 | 44.8 |
| 2007 | 27.6 | 32.6 | 25.3 | 21.8 | 42.7 |
| 2008 | −24.7 | −29.6 | −22.3 | −25.7 | 42.2 |
| 2009 | 13.7 | 17.3 | 12.1 | −3.7 | 35.7 |
| 2010 | 19.8 | 16.9 | 21.2 | 13.1 | 33.7 |
| 2011 | 4.7 | 5.3 | 4.9 | 4.1 | 33.3 |

Derived from Hedge Fund Research, *HFR Global Hedge Fund Industry Report — Year End 2011*, www.HedgeFundResearch.com.

## CONCLUSION

This chapter has shown how, following the Great Depression, intervention and regulation were the order of the day. Over time, this was replaced by free-market economics and deregulation. The GFC brought this back full circle, with calls for stronger protection and regulation resulting in the far-reaching Dodd–Frank Act of 2010. This Act has major impacts on hedge funds and FoHFs in terms of registration, compliance, and disclosure. Our analysis of FoHFs trends has not shown any noticeable regulatory impact on FoHFs performance to date, with FoHFs returns following similar recovery trends to those of equities. Our study does show movement of assets from FoHFs to single funds, although this trend commenced following the Madoff scandal. The high number of fund liquidations and the shift of assets into larger funds tend to support the contention that smaller firms may be scared off by the high compliance and associated costs. Whether Dodd–Frank will have a long-term positive or negative impact on the industry remains to be seen. What is clear is that the Act is wide reaching and is a reaction to a specific crisis. As covered in our chapter, there has long been debate over the merits of intervention and regulation in economies and markets, and whether this stifles or promotes growth and innovation. In line with the conclusions in our sections on economic intervention and lessons from other industries, we maintain that, rather than a stop–start regulation–deregulation–regulation approach, balanced methods that enhance growth and innovation, while at the same time ensuring prudent legislation, are always going to be the best tactic.

**Table 30.2** Number of FoHFs Compared to Total Hedge Funds

| | Growth in Number of Total Hedge Funds (%) | Growth in Number of Single Hedge Funds (%) | Growth in Number of FoHFs (%) | FoHFs as % of Total Hedge Funds | Number of Hedge Funds Launched | Number of Hedge Funds Liquidated | Ratio Launched/ Liquidated | Average FoHFs Size (US$M) |
|------|------|------|------|------|------|------|------|------|
| 2000 | 7.1 | 7.5 | 4.5 | 13.9 | 328 | 71 | 4.6 | 911.9 |
| 2001 | 15.0 | 17.1 | 2.2 | 12.3 | 673 | 92 | 7.3 | 980.1 |
| 2002 | 20.8 | 17.8 | 42.0 | 14.5 | 1087 | 162 | 6.7 | 801.0 |
| 2003 | 17.1 | 10.2 | 57.7 | 19.6 | 1094 | 176 | 6.2 | 665.6 |
| 2004 | 18.1 | 14.2 | 34.3 | 22.2 | 1435 | 296 | 4.8 | 588.0 |
| 2005 | 16.5 | 15.3 | 20.7 | 23.0 | 2073 | 848 | 2.4 | 553.8 |
| 2006 | 9.2 | 8.6 | 11.3 | 23.5 | 1518 | 717 | 2.1 | 659.4 |
| 2007 | 6.7 | 5.4 | 10.9 | 24.4 | 1197 | 563 | 2.1 | 758.9 |
| 2008 | −8.0 | −10.3 | −0.9 | 26.3 | 659 | 1471 | 0.4 | 576.9 |
| 2009 | −2.6 | 0.6 | −11.4 | 23.9 | 784 | 1023 | 0.8 | 740.1 |
| 2010 | 2.1 | 4.6 | −5.8 | 22.1 | 935 | 743 | 1.3 | 941.3 |
| 2011 | 1.3 | 1.4 | 0.7 | 21.9 | 843 | 585 | 1.4 | 984.4 |

Derived from Hedge Fund Research, *HFR Global Hedge Fund Industry Report — Year End 2011*, www.HedgeFundResearch.com.

## Acknowledgments

We thank the Australian Research Council for funding support.

## References

Bianchi, R. J., & Drew, M. E. (2010). Hedge Fund Regulation and Systemic Risk. *Griffith Law Review, 19*(1), 6–29.

Brouwer, D. (2001). *Hedge Funds in Emerging Markets.* Cambridge: Cambridge University Press.

deMaria, N. (2010). Between a Rock and a Hard Place. *Journal of the American College of Cardiology, 56,* 1761–1762.

Di Mario, C., James, S., Dudek, D., Sabate, M., & Degertekin, M. (2011). Commentary: The Risk of Over-Regulation. *British Medical Journal, 342,* d3021.

Freeman, M., & Fuerst, M. (2012). Does the FDA Have Regulatory Authority over Adult Autologous Stem Cell Therapies? 21 CFR 1271 and the Emperor's New Clothes. *Journal of Translational Medicine, 10*(60), 1–5.

Friedman, M., & Schwartz, A. J. (1963). *A Monetary History of the United States, 1867–1960.* Princeton, NJ: Princeton University Press.

Kroszner, R. S. (2012). Stability, Growth and Regulatory Reform. *Banque de France Financial Stability Review, 16*(April), 87–93.

Miller, H. I., & Henderson, D. R. (2007). Governmental Influences on Drug Development: Striking a Better Balance. *Drug Discovery, 6*(7), 532–539.

Orbach, B. (2009). The New Regulatory Era — An Introduction. *Arizona Law Review, 51*(3), 559–573.

Rogoff, K. (2011). *The BP Oil Spill's Lessons for Regulation.* Available at www.project-syndicate.org.

Skidelsky, R. (2009). *Keynes: The Return of the Master.* London: Allen Lane.

Smith, A. (1776). *The Wealth of Nations.* Republished 2007. Petersfield: Harriman House.

Smith, F. L. J. (2012). *Countering the Assault on Capitalism.* Oxford: Blackwell.

Stigler, G. (1971). The Theory of Economic Regulation. *Bell Journal of Economics and Management Science, 2*(Spring), 3–21.

Stiglitz, J. E. (2001). Principles of Financial Regulation: A Dynamic Portfolio Approach. *The World Bank Research Observer, 16*(1), 1–18.

# CHAPTER 31

# Canada and Australia: Do They Provide a Regulatory Model for Funds of Hedge Funds?

**David Edmund Allen, Raymond Robert Boffey, and Robert John Powell**
School of Accounting, Finance and Economics, Edith Cowan University,
Joondalup, Western Australia, Australia

## 31.1. INTRODUCTION

Australia and Canada have many similarities, such as their land size, population density, and economic output (Australian Bureau of Statistics, www.abs.gov.au; Statistics Canada, www.statcan.gc.ca). In addition, the similar resilience of their economies and financial sectors during and after the Global Financial Crisis (GFC) has received a great deal of comparison and commentary (Allen *et al.*, 2011a, 2011b; Dickinson, 2010; Stevens, 2009). A core theme emerging from articles that focus on financial services in these countries is their strong regulatory framework. This study provides a further comparison between these two countries: funds of hedge funds (FoHFs), with particular regard to regulatory similarities and differences. We commence by examining FoHFs asset size and growth, and then go on to show how FoHFs in both countries (prior to, during, and in the aftermath of the GFC) outperform global funds. We then examine and compare their regulatory framework to see if any lessons could be learned which might benefit other FoHFs regulators, followed by conclusions.

Reconsidering Funds of Hedge Funds. http://dx.doi.org/10.1016/B978-0-12-401699-6.00031-9

## 31.2. FoHFs STATISTICAL COMPARISONS BETWEEN AUSTRALIA AND CANADA

### 31.2.1. FoHFs Asset Size and Growth

According to Austrade (Australian Trade Commission, 2011) the hedge fund industry in Australia has AU$35 billion assets under management (AUM) (AU$ being at parity with US$), second only to Hong Kong in the Asia—Pacific Region. The FoHFs sector is $14 billion, which is split into $5 billion in local FoHFs (of which $4.5 billion is managed by nine fund managers), $6 billion invested by Australian retail investors in offshore FoHFs, and $3 billion invested in offshore FoHFs by Australian institutional investors.

The Alternative Investment Management Association (AIMA) (McGovern and Ostoich, 2005; Ostoich, 2010) estimates the Canadian hedge fund industry has AUM of CA$30 billion (CA$ being at parity with US$). Approximately 55% of this is estimated to be in single manager funds placing FoHFs at $14 billion (Table 31.1).

We now examine trends in asset growth for both countries commencing with Australia and then moving on to Canada. It should be noted that there is no single source of FoHFs statistics in either Canada or Australia that comprehensively covers the pre-GFC, GFC, and post-GFC periods. The statistics we present are constructed from the combination of a number reports and statistics on the websites of AIMA Canada, AIMA Australia, Austrade, and Investor Economics.

Australian FoHFs growth, as seen in Figure 31.1, showed a very similar pattern to Canada, starting off small and growing rapidly pre-GFC (with, like Canada, FoHFs increasing proportionally higher than single funds), then reducing during the GFC at a proportionally higher rate than single funds. At 2002, Australian FoHFs were 27% of the less than $2 billion total hedge fund assets, growing to around half ($20 billion) of the $40 billion total hedge fund assets by 2007. Like Canada, FoHFs were somewhat decimated over the GFC, dropping to around 40% ($11 billion) of a much lower $28 billion hedge fund total in 2008, climbing back up to the $14 billion total shown in Table 31.1. Key investors in Australian hedge funds and FoHFs, as provided by Austrade, are Australian retail and high-net-worth investors (64%), Australian institutional investors (19%), and offshore institutional investors (17%). One of the key classes of institutional investors are superannuation (pension) funds, who invest about 3% of their funds in hedge funds, of which around half are FoHFs.

| Table 31.1 | Australia—Canada Comparison 1: FoHFs and Total Hedge Fund Assets ($ billion) | |
| --- | --- | --- |
| **Portfolio Type** | **Australia** | **Canada** |
| FoHFs | 14 | 14 |
| Total hedge funds | 35 | 30 |

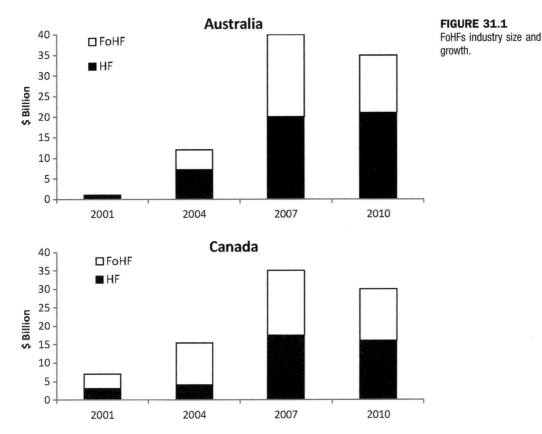

**FIGURE 31.1**
FoHFs industry size and growth.

In Canada, in 1999, FoHFs were 47% of the Canadian hedge fund industry of only $2.5 billion, which grew to $15.4 billion by 2004 with FoHFs having grown proportionally much higher than single funds to 74% of the total. Investors were showing a preference for guaranteed FoHF-linked notes backed by highly rated banks. AIMA (Alternative Investment Management Association, 2011) also attributes some of the popularity of FoHFs to the complexity of strategies and underlying financial instruments of hedge funds, which made it difficult for investors to undertake their own due diligence on a basket of funds. Moreover, many investors could not meet the combined minimum investment requirements of all the funds invested in. As investors, particularly large institutions, became more familiar with hedge funds, there was a swing away from FoHFs to single funds, which held the attraction of not having the higher fees associated with FoHFs structures. Hedge fund assets peaked at $35 billion just before the GFC in 2007, with FoHFs around half of this total, thereafter reducing (in line with the global industry) as a result of the GFC turbulence to the levels shown in Table 31.1. AIMA (Alternative Investment Management Association, 2011) shows this to be a mixture of investor redemptions, fund closures and investment losses, mainly during 2008.

The trends discussed above are reflected in Figure 31.1 which shows assets at 3-year intervals.

### 31.2.2. FoHFs Performance

We compare FoHFs performance between Canada and Australia over the 7 years from 2005 to end 2011, which includes pre-GFC, GFC, and post-GFC periods (Figure 31.2). This is benchmarked against global FoHFs and the S&P 500. For Australia we use the Fund Monitors FoHF index. For Canada we construct our own index using performance data for the 12 largest Canadian FoHFs, obtained from a combination of BarclayHedge and from FoHFs performance reports on individual fund websites whose names were obtained from Bloomberg. We use the global HFRI (Hedge Funds Research Index) Fund of Funds Composite index obtained from Datastream.

We see that Australian FoHFs run at a higher level pre-GFC than the other indices, with Canada highest post-GFC. None of the FoHF indices dips to the same extent as the S&P 500, and Canada and Australia reach a similar level at the low point in 2008/2009. We note too that the S&P 500 follows a sharper upward

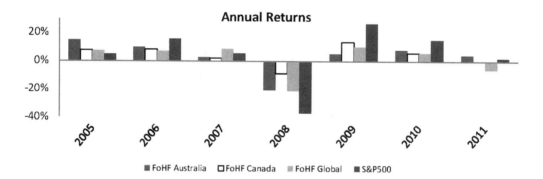

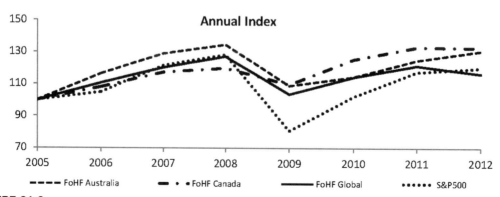

**FIGURE 31.2**
FoHFs annual returns.
*Data from BarclayHedge, Datastream, and www.fundmonitors.com.*

trend after the GFC than the FoHFs as it recovers from the higher fall. Both Australian and Canadian FoHFs run at higher levels than the other indices post-GFC. The Australian and (especially) Canadian FoHFs offer a higher return over the total 7-year period than the global FoHFs and the S&P 500. These figures are summarized in Table 31.2. Although both countries experienced hedge fund closures during the GFC, this was not to the same extent as that seen in the United States.

Whilst, globally, there are a great number of academic research articles on hedge fund returns, there is very little on Canada and Australia. We summarize examples of key studies here, which do not generally distinguish between single hedge funds and FoHFs.

In Australia (Do *et al.*, 2005, 2009) it has been found that Australian hedge fund returns significantly outperform the market and that while Australian hedge fund managers do possess some stock selection skills, they do not show significant market timing abilities. Hutson (2006) found the apparent under-performance of FoHFs relative to hedge funds reported in other studies to be exaggerated, because FoHFs returns more closely reflect reality than the reported returns of hedge funds. He also showed that FoHFs have some important benefits over hedge funds in that they are not as negatively skewed as hedge funds and have lower correlations with the equity market, leading him to conclude that FoHFs are not poor cousins to hedge funds as other academic research had led many to believe.

A study of hedge funds in Canada by Gregoriou (2004) proposed a modified Sharpe ratio to address non-normal returns. Klein *et al.* (2009) found the range of risk and return for individual Canadian hedge funds varies widely, with significant gains to diversification by taking a portfolio approach to hedge fund investing. A separate study involving some of the same authors (Klein *et al.*, 2012) finds that Canadian hedge funds have higher returns and different distributional characteristics relative to global hedge fund indices, and while hedge funds do not time the stock markets, they do time commodities markets, consistent with Canada's high resource industry focus.

Our findings of higher FoHFs returns in Australia and Canada compared to global FoHFs are consistent with the findings mentioned in the above studies.

| Table 31.2 | Australia–Canada Comparison 2: FoHFs Performance Statistics (%) | | | |
|---|---|---|---|---|
| **Fund Index** | **Total 7-Year Return** | **Average Annual Return** | **Best Annual Return** | **Worst Annual Return** |
| FoHFs Australia | 30.5 | 3.8 | 14.6 | −20.6 |
| FoHFs Canada | 32.6 | 4.0 | 15.5 | −14.9 |
| FoHFs Global | 16.3 | 2.2 | 10.1 | −21.1 |
| S&P 500 | 19.9 | 2.6 | 26.4 | −37.0 |

Data from BarclayHedge, Datastream, and www.fundmonitors.com.

## 31.3. FoHFs REGULATION

### 31.3.1. Australian FoHFs Regulation

To date, Australia has had no regulation specific to hedge funds. Regulation falls under the Corporations Act of 2001 and the Financial Services Reform Act 2001 (FSRA, which applies only to retail investors). Under the Corporations Act, hedge funds, as with all other entities dealing in financial services and products, whether retail or wholesale, are required to hold an Australian Financial Services License (AFSL), and are subject to strict compliance, reporting, and audit requirements. Bianchi and Drew (2010) found that (at the time of their 2010 article) the key difference between the hedge fund legislative framework in Australia and the United States is that whereas all hedge funds were regulated via the AFSL in Australia, the same fund operating in the United States could avoid almost all US regulation, as the US regulatory environment provided enough exemptions for US hedge funds to circumvent many established regulations governing financial markets. The FSRA requires entities providing services or products to retail investors to follow certain disclosure requirements and standards of conduct. Disclosure requirements include the provision of a Product Disclosure Statement (PDS), a Financial Services Guide (FSG), and a Statement of Advice where advice is given. If funds investments are offered to wholesale clients (investment exceeds a specified level, or high-net-worth investors or institutional investors) then the FSRA disclosure requirements do not apply.

However, the lack of regulation specific to hedge funds is likely to change. ASIC (Australian Securities and Investments Commission, 2012) has released a consultation document setting out new disclosure requirements specifically for hedge funds and FoHFs. This is due to ASIC's view that hedge funds pose more complex risks than traditional funds due to their complex investment strategies and structures, and use of techniques such as leverage, short selling, and derivatives. In addition, ASIC believes that, as a result, potential investors do not always understand the risks involved, and ASIC wishes to ensure that investors are confident and informed before making their investment. ASIC's document includes two 'benchmarks' and nine disclosure 'principles.'

The two benchmarks include: (i) the specific valuation and custody requirements for a fund, which includes whether valuations are provided by independent third parties and whether custodians are unrelated to the investment manager, and (ii) the periodic reporting requirements and whether periodic disclosure will be provided on the underlying funds of the FoHFs.

The nine disclosure principles relate to features and risks that must be disclosed in a PDS. FoHFs have a specific definition under the new requirements: a FoHF is a fund that has invested 25% or more of its assets in an underlying hedge fund or structured product. These disclosure requirements also apply to those underlying funds. The disclosure principles include: (i) the investment strategy including the type of strategy, how it works, and how risks are managed; (ii) the investment manager, including qualifications, experience, and time devoted to managing the fund; (iii) fund structure, including jurisdiction, relationships between funds in a FoHF, and due diligence performed on the underlying funds in the FoHF; (iv) valuation, location, and custody of assets, including the types of assets, their location, how they are valued, and custodial arrangements; (v) the liquidity of the fund, which is designed to ensure that investors are made aware of the nature and risks involved if at least 20% of assets cannot be sold at market value within 10 days; (vi) proposed leverage must be disclosed, including leverage embedded in the assets of the funds; (vii) use of derivatives and structured products and the associated risks; (viii) how short selling is used as part of the investment strategy, and the associated risks and costs; and (ix) withdrawals, and the circumstances under which these are permitted and how this might change. It is intended that these new requirements will apply from 1 March 2013.

## 31.3.2. Canadian FoHFs Regulation

There is also no specific hedge fund regulation in Canada. Rather, hedge funds fall under securities legislation of the various provinces and territories, which may differ from each other. This is typical of the Canadian legislative system, where a great deal of legislative power rests in provincial hands. Securities law across the provinces (which was revised in 2009) generally requires that investment fund managers and advisors (including hedge funds and FoHFs) must be registered as advisors (or be able to rely on registration exemption), and are subject to various compliance and capital requirements. A prospectus must be issued unless funds are trading in the exempt market, which is largely the same across the regions and typically the market in which FoHFs trade. Funds are typically exempt from issuing a prospectus, as well as from certain other regulations applying to the non-exempt market, if certain conditions are met such as the minimum investment exceeding a specified level or if the investor is an accredited investor (institutions or high net worth individuals). Reports of all trades made under prospectus exemption must be made to the relevant securities legislators within prescribed timeframes and most funds provide an offering memorandum to the client. Most regions also require funds to either file financial statements with the registration authorities or, if trading in the exempt market, to provide them to the investor.

Although each province has its own provincial regulator, certain responsibilities are delegated to two national self regulatory organizations: the Investment Industry Regulatory Organization of Canada (IIROC) and the Mutual Fund Dealers Association (MFDA). The IIROC oversees the activities of all regulated investment dealers and debt and equity trading. This includes setting rules and regulations making sure sufficient capital is held, setting minimum education standards for advisors, and monitoring the financial health of regulated firms. The MFDA regulates sales of mutual funds, but not the funds themselves, which is the responsibility of the provincial regulators. Leverage or short selling is prohibited for mutual funds sold to retail investors (although this can be avoided if funds are structured as closed-end funds where redemptions only take place at a maximum of once per year). Although the two self regulatory Canadian organizations ensure a good deal of coordination between the provincial regulators, the Canadian Government is nonetheless working towards the establishment of a Canadian Securities Regulatory Authority (CSRA) which will be a single central regulator for securities.

### 31.3.3. Comparisons Between Australian and Canadian FoHFs Regulation

In comparing the regulatory frameworks of Australia and Canada, we find both similarities and differences, summarized in Table 31.3. Neither currently has regulations applying specifically to hedge funds, but both have strong regulation applying generally to securities investments which requires licensing/registration of hedge fund managers/advisors, bringing with it compliance, capital, and reporting requirements. A further key similarity is a more stringent set of regulations applying to dealings with smaller and individual investors (who are the primary market the regulations are seeking to protect), with relaxation of regulation for the more sophisticated market comprising larger investors and corporations. A key difference is the centralized regulatory framework of Australia versus the decentralized Canadian framework (the latter nonetheless having some important coordinating mechanisms such as the delegation of responsibilities to the two self-regulatory centralized bodies). Both countries are likely to be experiencing some regulatory changes in the near term as we have previously outlined, Australia's relating to greater disclosure requirements for hedge funds and Canada's to greater regulatory centralization.

In addition to the individual country regulations already discussed, two other key aspects of legislation that impact on FoHFs, and where the two countries

| **Table 31.3** | Australia–Canada Comparison 3: Regulations | |
| --- | --- | --- |
| **Legislative Aspect** | **Australia** | **Canada** |
| Primary industry regulator | ASIC | Province-dependent with delegation of some key responsibilities to IIROC and MFDA |
| Legislation specific to hedge funds or FoHFs | No, but specific disclosure legislation has been proposed | No |
| Major legislation affecting FoHFs | Corporations Act 2001; Financial Services Reform Act 2001 | Provincial Securities Legislation |
| Licensing and registration | Licensing with ASIC | Registration of managers and advisors with the relevant regulator |
| Potential regulation changes | Greater disclosure requirements | Greater centralization |

have very similar requirements, are (i) privacy, and (ii) money laundering and terrorist financing. FoHFs must comply with privacy legislation that addresses the collection, use, disclosure, and disposal of personal information. FoHFs must also comply with all the record-keeping, reporting, and client identification requirements of the anti-money laundering and terrorist financing legislation. FoHFs must report suspicious or large transactions, in the case of Canada to the Financial Transactions and Reports Analysis Centre of Canada (FINTRAC) and in the case of Australia to the Australian Transaction Reports and Analysis Centre (AUSTRAC).

## CONCLUSION

Australian and Canadian FoHFs outperformed global FoHFs in the period leading up to, during, and after the GFC. We examined their regulatory frameworks to see if there were any key similarities that may have influenced this outcome. Regulation can, of course, be a two-edged sword, proving greater safety but potentially restricting growth. During a crisis, however, safety becomes of paramount importance. We found both similarities and differences in the regulatory framework. The key difference lies in the centralized process of Australia as compared to the provincially decentralized Canadian system. Despite this, there is a core similarity in that both countries to a large extent incorporated their hedge funds and FoHFs into the strong regulatory framework that applies to all securities or investment funds — the same framework that assisted in serving their financial markets and services systems so well during the GFC. Whilst both countries have some regulatory exclusions for corporates and high-value individuals, especially regarding disclosure, nonetheless their regulatory systems provide a robust registration, compliance, and reporting framework for FoHFs, which can serve as useful models for other regulators to learn from. Indeed, the United States has now moved in a similar direction with the registration and reporting requirements that have been introduced under the Dodd—Frank Act.

## Acknowledgments

We thank the Australian Research Council for funding support.

## References

Allen, D. E., Boffey, R. R., & Powell, R. J. (2011a). Peas in a Pod: Canadian and Australian Banks Before and During a Global Financial Crisis. *Modelling and Simulation Society MODSIM 2011 Conference*, Perth 1444—1450.

Allen, D. E., Boffey, R. R., & Powell, R. J. (2011b). Survival of the Fittest: Contagion as a Determinant of Canadian and Australian Bank Risk. *World Business, Economics and Finance Conference*, Bangkok 1—9.

Alternative Investment Management Association (2011). *AIMA Canada Hedge Fund Primer*. Available at www.aima-canada.org.

Australian Securities and Investments Commission (2012). *Consultation Paper 174, Hedge Funds: Improving disclosure — Further Consultation*. Available at www.asic.gov.au.

Australian Trade Commission (2011). *Australian Hedge Funds*. Available at www.austrade.gov.au.

Bianchi, R. J., & Drew, M. E. (2010). Hedge Fund Regulation and Systemic Risk. *Griffith Law Review, 19*(1), 6–29.

Dickinson, A. (2010). *Canadian Economy and Major Banks: A Comparison with Australia (KPMG Study)*. Available at http://www.kpmg.com.

Do, V., Faff, R., & Veeraraghavan, M. (2009). Do Australian Hedge Fund Managers Possess Timing Abilities? *Journal of Financial Economics, 19*(1), 27–38.

Do, V., Faff, R., & Wickramanayake, J. (2005). An Empirical Analysis of Hedge Fund Performance: The Case of Australian Hedge Funds Industry. *Journal of Multinational Financial Management, 15*(4–5), 377–393.

Gregoriou, G. N. (2004). Performance of Canadian Hedge Funds Using a Modified Sharpe Ratio. *Derivatives Use, Trading and Regulation, 10*(2), 149–155.

Hutson, E. (2006). Funds of Hedge Funds: Not the Poor Cousins of the Hedge Fund Industry. *JASSA, 4*(Summer), 22–26.

Klein, P., Purdy, D., & Schweigert, I. (2009). *Risk and Return in the Canadian Hedge Fund Industry*. Available at www.aima-canada.org.

Klein, P., Purdy, D., Schweigert, I., & Vedrashko, P. (2012). *The Canadian Hedge Fund Industry: Performance and Market Timing*. Available at http://ssrn.com/abstract=2002649.

McGovern, J., & Ostoich, G. (2005). *The Hedge Funds Industry in Canada*. AIMA. Available at www.aima-canada.org.

Ostoich, G. (2010). AIMA Canada Interview. *AIMA Journal, Q4*(85), 8.

Stevens, G. (2009). Australia and Canada — Comparing Notes on Recent Experiences. Speech Delivered at *Canadian Australian Chamber of Commerce Canada–Australia Breakfast*. Sydney.

# CHAPTER 32

# South African Regulatory Reforms of Funds of Hedge Funds

**David Edmund Allen, Akhmad Kramadibrata, Robert John Powell, and Abhay Kumar Singh**

School of Accounting, Finance and Economics, Edith Cowan University, Joondalup, Western Australia, Australia

## 32.1. INTRODUCTION

Historically, Africa was often bypassed by overseas investors, with a perception of being a crime- and conflict-ridden third-world continent with high exchange controls and little investment opportunity. This is rapidly changing, particularly in South Africa, whose economic performance over the Global Financial Crisis

(GFC) showed far greater stability than that of many leading global nations. Whilst part of this success can be attributed to factors such as investment incentives (Tuomi, 2012) and strong demand for resources (Ouma, 2012), it also partly lies in the strong financial services regulatory framework in South Africa (Alao and Raini, 2011; Botha and Makina, 2011). We examine the regulations as they apply to FoHFs before, during, and after the GFC. We find that the many regulatory changes that have been made over the past few years have opened up investment opportunities, while at the same time retaining strong investor protection. The study commences with an overview of the general investment climate in South Africa and then provides information on the FoHFs industry. This leads into a discussion on the regulations surrounding FoHFs, followed by conclusions.

## 32.2. THE INVESTMENT CLIMATE IN SOUTH AFRICA

During the GFC, South Africa fared far better than many leading economies. Banks remained profitable and well capitalized, and while share markets fell sharply in response to global events, recovery was stronger and swifter. Over the 12 years to 2012, South African equity markets had an average 14.2% annual return and FoHFs had a 5-year 9% annual return to 2011, compared to negligible returns in US markets over the same period. Much of this has been attributed to the sound financial services and markets regulatory framework in South Africa, which we deal with later in this chapter. Indeed, the International Monetary Fund (2008, p. 6), finds that 'South Africa's sophisticated financial system is fundamentally sound. The system is diversified and spans a broad range of activities that are supported by an elaborate legal and financial infrastructure and a generally effective regulatory framework.' South Africa has the highest S&P Sovereign credit rating in Africa ('A'), followed by Botswana ('A−'). All of this provides a sound climate for investment in South African FoHFs.

## 32.3. FoHFs IN SOUTH AFRICA

This section examines various aspects of South African FoHFs, including the size of the industry by assets managed, asset growth, and FoHFs performance. We also examine the performance of various strategies and construct an optimal South African FoHFs portfolio.

### 32.3.1. South African FoHFs Assets

A timeline analysis by AIMA (Alternative Investment Management Association, 2010) shows that the first South African hedge funds made their appearance in 1995, with FoHFs gaining in popularity from 1999 onwards. In 2005, assets under management (AUM) for South African hedge funds first exceeded R10 billion (US$1.2 billion). This grew to R25 billion by 2007 with FoHFs being 63% (compared to 40−50% globally) of this total and the most popular category for new entrants. AIMA estimates there are approximately 128 licensed managers for hedge funds and FoHFs. The FoHFs industry has been characterized by a high level of self-regulation and AIMA sees FoHFs as being the key

| Table 32.1 | South African FoHFs Assets | |
|---|---|---|
| Year | FoHFs Assets (R billion) | FoHFs Asset Growth (%) |
| 2005 | 3.3 | |
| 2006 | 10.4 | 215.2 |
| 2007 | 18.4 | 76.9 |
| 2008 | 21.5 | 16.8 |
| 2009 | 22.8 | 6.0 |
| 2010 | 23.4 | 2.6 |
| 2011 | 21.1 | -9.8 |

Asset figures obtained from HedgeNews Africa (www.hedgenewsafrica.com).

driving force behind operational and compliance standards for South African hedge funds, given that they are the predominant vehicle of choice for South African hedge fund investors. Hedge funds AUM at 2011 was approximately R30 billion, with FoHFs at R21 billion. Growth in FoHFs is shown in Table 32.1.

Strong growth is seen in the mid 2000s. This tapers off during the GFC, but is nonetheless positive. Pension funds are one of the primary investors in South African hedge funds and FoHFs. Investment limits for different classes of assets are specified by the Pension Funds Act of 1958. Regulation 28 regarding pension funds (discussed further in Section 32.5.4) has brought private equity and onshore and offshore hedge funds into the same category, and HedgeNews Africa (www.hedgenewsafrica.com) attributes the 2011 reduction in asset growth to capital withdrawals as the result of pension funds recalibrating their portfolios due to the new regulation. Although the overall growth of AUM decreased in 2011, HedgeNews Africa shows the number of funds is increasing. There were 31 FoHFs launches in 2010 and 28 closures, with 23 FoHFs launches in 2011 and 16 closures. Among the new launches were some funds creating strategy-specific mandates. A Novare Investments (2011) survey shows that FoHFs contributed the bulk of capital to new startups during 2011, holding 32.5% of capital invested in these funds (followed by seed investors and then high-net-worth individuals investing directly).

## 32.3.2. South African FoHFs Performance

The indices in Figure 32.1 compare South African and global FoHFs during the periods leading up to, during, and after the GFC. We see that during the overall 5-year period, South African FoHFs significantly outperformed global FoHFs, maintaining a far more stable growth trend and superior cumulative performance. Table 32.2 shows the difference in returns between South African, all-African (including South Africa) and global FoHFs. All-African figures are close to the South African figures, given that South Africa comprises the majority of FoHFs in the all-Africa index. The South African 5-year average and cumulative return figures are substantially above global figures. Indeed, in every single year during the 5-year period, South African returns exceed the global figures.

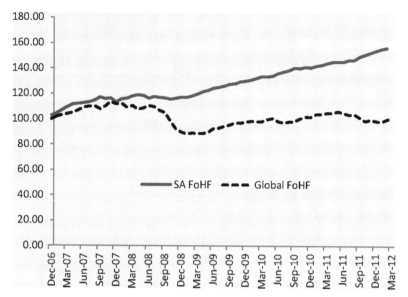

**FIGURE 32.1**
Comparison of South African and global FoHF indices. Data from HedgeNews Africa South African Fund of Funds Composite index; HFRI global Fund of Funds Composite index obtained from Datastream.

| Table 32.2 | FoHFs Returns | | |
| --- | --- | --- | --- |
| | **South African FoHFs (%)** | **All-African FoHFs (%)** | **Global FoHFs (%)** |
| Year end | | | |
| 2007 | 16.48 | 17.08 | 11.90 |
| 2008 | −0.09 | −0.52 | −10.28 |
| 2009 | 11.29 | 10.94 | −2.22 |
| 2010 | 9.00 | 9.11 | 1.89 |
| 2011 | 8.04 | 7.38 | −1.28 |
| 5-Year average | 8.94 | 8.80 | 0.00 |
| Cumulative | 52.52 | 51.39 | −1.28 |
| Monthly $\sigma$ | 0.57 | 0.61 | 2.00 |
| Monthly VaR | 0.94 | 1.00 | 3.28 |

South African and all-African figures supplied by HedgeNews Africa (www.hedgenewsafrica.com); global returns are derived from HFRI global Fund of Funds Composite index obtained from Datastream.

We have calculated the standard deviation ($\sigma$) and value at risk (VaR) figures from the monthly returns. These South African risk indicators are substantially lower than the global figures and show how South Africa had significantly lower FoHFs volatility during this period than did global FoHFs.

### 32.3.3. South African FoHFs Strategies and the Optimal FoHFs Portfolio

Of all the major South African FoHFs categories (Long/Short Equities, Market Neutral, Fixed Income, and Multistrategy), HedgeNews Africa (2012) FoHFs tables

| Table 32.3 | Fund Strategies | | |
|---|---|---|---|
| **Strategy** | **5-Year Annual Return (%)** | **Annual Standard Deviation (%)** | **Annual VaR (%)** |
| Long/Short Equities | 10.05 | 6.50 | 10.69 |
| Market Neutral | 9.55 | 2.10 | 3.45 |
| Fixed Income | 15.70 | 3.10 | 5.10 |
| Multi Strategy | 8.25 | 6.70 | 11.02 |

Data from Symmetry (2012).

show that Fixed Income tended to give the best returns over the 12 months to April 2012, as well as for a 5-year average. The Novare Investments (2011) survey reports that the Fixed Income components consist predominantly of negotiable certificates of deposit at 71.0% of assets, with other popular instruments including government bonds, floating rate notes, forward rate agreements, and over-the-counter options, with lesser used instruments observed in these portfolios including contracts for difference, equity default notes, and futures and options on currencies and equity.

What would the optimal South African mix of strategies in a FoHFs portfolio be? To answer this, we use returns and standard deviations ($\sigma$) obtained from the Symmetry (2012) South African survey of underlying hedge funds as shown in Table 32.3 for the 5 years to end 2011, to optimize a FoHFs portfolio. It should be noted that the VaR figures shown in Table 32.3 are not provided by Symmetry and are not used in the optimization process, but are calculated by us for information purposes only, given that VaR is one of the most widely used risk measures among South African hedge funds (Novare Investments, 2011). VaR shows maximum expected losses over a defined period for a selected confidence level. We use the RiskMetrics (JP Morgan and Reuters) parametric methodology to calculate monthly VaR at the 95% confidence level, whereby $\sigma$ is multiplied by the normal distribution factor applying to the specified level of confidence (95% confidence level $= 1.645\sigma$).

To obtain the optimal portfolio, we first calculate correlations between these South African fund strategies using AfricaHedge monthly time series returns and use these to construct a variance–covariance matrix. The portfolio is then optimized to achieve the combination of asset strategies yielding the minimum risk for each selected return level:

$$\min_x \sum_{i=1}^{n} \sum_{k=1}^{n} \sigma_{ik} x_i x_k, \tag{32.1}$$

subject to:

$$\sum_{i=1}^{n} x_i = 1 \tag{32.2}$$

$$\sum_{i=1}^{n} \mathbb{E}[r_i] x_i = r_p \tag{32.3}$$

$$0 \leq x_i \leq v_i, \tag{32.4}$$

| Table 32.4 | Optimal FoHFs Portfolios | | | | | | | |
|---|---|---|---|---|---|---|---|---|
| | No Investment Constraints | | | | Minimum 10% for Each Strategy | | | |
| Return (%) | 15.7 | 14.3 | 12.9 | 11.5 | 14.7 | 13.8 | 12.8 | 11.9 |
| $\sigma$ (%) | 3.1 | 2.4 | 1.9 | 1.7 | 2.4 | 2.4 | 2.2 | 2.1 |
| Optimal FoHFs mix (%) for each return level | | | | | | | | |
| Long/Short Equity | 0.0 | 5.8 | 0.1 | 0.0 | 10.0 | 10.0 | 10.0 | 10.0 |
| Market Neutral | 0.0 | 17.3 | 45.1 | 67.8 | 10.0 | 10.1 | 25.2 | 40.3 |
| Fixed Income | 100.0 | 76.9 | 54.8 | 32.2 | 70.0 | 69.9 | 54.8 | 39.7 |
| Multistrategy | 0.0 | 0.0 | 0.0 | 0.0 | 10.0 | 10.0 | 10.0 | 10.0 |
| | 100.0% | 100.0% | 100.0% | 100.0% | 100.0% | 100.0% | 100.0% | 100.0% |

where $x_i$ are portfolio weights, $r_i$ is the rate of return of strategies $i$ and $k$, $r_p$ is the expected return on the portfolio, and $\sigma_{ik}$ is the covariance between returns of different strategies $i$ and $k$ (and similarly for all other strategies). Weighting for any portfolio cannot be negative and can also be constrained to exceed (or not to exceed) a specific weighting $v$ (in order to ensure the portfolio is diversified). Table 32.4 shows, firstly, a portfolio with no constraints on investment strategy and then where a minimum of 10% in each strategy is required.

Our maximum return point is the highest return that can be generated by any strategy. The minimum return point is the return associated with the lowest possible $\sigma$. We select two equidistant points between minimum and maximum returns (giving a total of four return points) and calculate the minimum portfolio $\sigma$ associated with each point. These $\sigma$–return combinations make up the efficient investment frontier. We see that the best returns can be generated investing all the funds in fixed income. Risk is minimized with a combination of Fixed Income and Market Neutral strategies. The low returns and relatively high volatility of the other two strategies means they do not feature as favored portfolio assets and fail to rise above the 10% minimum constraint.

## 32.4. KEY CONSIDERATIONS FOR INVESTORS IN SOUTH AFRICAN FoHFs

Taking into consideration the unique characteristics of the South African Market, AIMA (Alternative Investment Management Association, 2010) provides a number of key considerations for investors in FoHFs:

- The *fund investment philosophy*, with diversification benefits and low correlation between underlying fund strategies being a major attraction of FoHFs. AfricaHedge provides regular FoHFs comparisons showing the strategies and performance of individual South African FoHFs.

- *Risk management experience* of funds managers. Around half of AUM is managed by a quarter of fund managers in South Africa, who have long-term track records.
- *Due diligence.* Here AIMA provide a list of more than 20 aspects to consider in the due diligence process encompassing a wide range of considerations such as management experience, strategies, environmental conditions, performance, and fees.
- *Manager diversification.* Whereas multistrategy funds can provide investment diversification, a FoHF also provides fund manager diversification.
- *Transparency.* Globally, this has become a very hot topic since the GFC with global FoHFs and hedge funds historically having escaped many of the compliance and reporting requirements applying to other investments. In South Africa, there has always been high transparency, with underlying hedge funds providing daily reports to FoHFs, allowing FoHFs to undertake daily compliance checks and regular quantitative analysis. The Novare (2010) survey shows that a large percentage of this administration and reporting by hedge funds to FoHFs and other investors is outsourced, with 89% of funds outsourcing the annual audit, 69% outsourcing their client accounting responsibilities, 50% outsourcing their client reporting, and 90% outsourcing their valuation responsibilities (wholly or partly). As these outsourced providers are highly specialized, this generally ensures a high standard of reporting up to the FoHFs investors.
- *Leverage*, whereby funds must have the ability to monitor accounting and risk based leverage.
- *Regulation*, which is a major topic and is covered in the remaining sections of this chapter.

## 32.5. REGULATION IMPACTING ON SOUTH AFRICAN FoHFs

### 32.5.1. Regulatory Overview

FoHFs in South Africa are impacted by a number of regulatory aspects which we explore in the following subsections:

- We examine the role of the Financial Services Board (FSB) in relation to FoHFs, given this is the key financial services regulator.
- We discuss exchange control regulations and how they impact on overseas investment in South African FoHFs as well as South African investment overseas.
- We examine regulation surrounding restriction on pension fund FoHFs investments, given that they are a key FoHFs investor.
- As short selling is an important strategy of hedge funds, we discuss regulation affecting this.
- This is followed by a section on the impact of overseas legislation on South African FoHFs, including the Dodd—Frank Act and the European Alternative Investment Fund Managers (AIFM) Directive.

The impact on FoHFs of the five regulatory items is summarized in Figure 32.2.

**FIGURE 32.2**
Summary of the regulation framework as it impacts South African FoHFs.

## 32.5.2. Regulatory Framework impacting on FoHFs: The FSB and the South African Reserve Bank

The FSB is a government agency that oversees all non-bank financial services in South Africa and has been regulating these industries for 20 years. Their mandate is to maintain a sound climate for financial investment with mechanisms for consumer protection. Industries and activities regulated include collective investment schemes, financial services providers, friendly societies, insurers, market abuse, nominee companies, and pension funds. Hedge fund products are not specifically regulated by the FSB, but hedge fund managers are. All investment managers and advisers, including hedge fund managers, are required to be licensed with the FSB under the Financial Advisers and Intermediary Services Act (FAIS), with this registration process having commenced in 2007. This registration allows close monitoring of funds by the FSB, who have access to all the fund information regarding clients, managers, and products. Fund managers have generally been accepting of this process (Pengelly, 2010). Hedge fund managers and advisors are required to meet certain education, disclosure, and reporting requirements, and the FSB undertakes regular audits. The license requirements for hedge funds fall under Category IIA — a special category introduced in 2007 for hedge funds, which is more stringent than for other fund managers falling under Category II. A recent policy document released by the South African Treasury announced reforms to the regulatory environment, whereby prudential supervision and market conduct will be separated. This changes the roles of the South African Reserve Bank (SARB) and the FSB regarding investment regulation. The SARB will be the lead prudential supervisor and the FSB the lead market conduct regulator, with the FSB's role now including retail banks.

## 32.5.3. Exchange Control Regulation Impacts on FoHFs

The SARB controls the flow of all money in and out of South Africa. Limitations on funds flowing out the country impact on overseas investments. While there is no limitation on funds flowing into the country, all inflows must be declared and overseas investors in South Africa need to provide evidence that funds originated from offshore when withdrawing funds previously introduced.

While South Africa has had some form of exchange controls dating back to the 1930s, the regulations really accelerated in 1976 following the Soweto uprising, in order to prevent the mass exodus of funds from the country. This led eventually to the introduction of regulation such as blocked funds, which restricted the withdrawal of sale proceeds of assets by non-residents, and to the introduction of the financial rand, tradable at a discount (lower value) to the South African rand to discourage outflow of funds. This effectively led to a two-tier exchange rate. After the 1994 democratic elections in South Africa, which led to a new government and the removal of economic sanctions that had previously been imposed by many countries, it was recognized that the exchange controls were causing many distortions and restricting investment, and a process of relaxing the controls commenced. The financial rand was abolished, overseas investors were permitted to make greater investments in South African companies, and restrictions on the amounts transferred out of the country were reduced. Importantly for FoHFs, prior restrictions on the movement of funds by foreign investors have been removed, creating a climate for increased global investment. At present, investments into South African hedge funds from investors abroad are only a nominal part of industry assets at 1.9% (Novare Investments, 2011).

According the SARB (Stals, 1999), the relaxation of controls in the 1990s led to institutional investors increasing their business in the areas of conventional short-term trade financing, short-term inter-bank financing facilities, loans to South African borrowers, investment in equities, bonds, and investment subsidiaries, branches, and joint ventures with South African businesses. Since then, exchange controls have been progressively further relaxed. Recent changes in 2010 increased the amounts that institutional investors can invest overseas. This affects hedge funds and FoHFs, with the percentage that Collective Investment Schemes can invest offshore increasing from 30% to 35%.

### 32.5.4. Impact of Regulation 28 on FoHFs

The impact on FoHFs of amendments to Regulation 28 of the Pension Funds Act of 1958 (known commonly as simply 'Regulation 28') is potentially far reaching, allowing hedge funds and FoHFs to compete on a more equal footing with other investments for the pension fund dollar. Pension funds are one of the primary investors in South African hedge funds and FoHFs. 'The main source of capital for hedge funds is from the retirement fund industry and pension funds (Hamilton, 2010, p. 6). Regulation 28 specifies investment limits by pension funds for different classes of assets. Up to now, investments by pension funds in hedge funds or FoHFs were limited to 2.5%. This was generally viewed by the hedge fund industry as being extremely restrictive to hedge fund growth. However, the FSB recently amended the Act to increase this to 10%, with a limit of 2.5% per hedge fund and 5% per FoHFs. This could be a dual benefit for FoHFs and pension funds. The new regulation should facilitate FoHFs growth, and investments in FoHFs and hedge funds could also potentially provide pension funds with more balanced portfolios with better returns and lower volatility (Vawda, 2011).

### 32.5.5. FoHFs and Short Selling Regulations during the GFC

Consistent short selling regulations in South Africa were a key contributor to the relatively sound and stable performance of FoHFs in South Africa. During the GFC, many countries experienced changes to their short selling rules, causing reduced liquidity and increased volatility for FoHFs. South African rules effectively prohibit naked short selling and short selling rules stayed consistent throughout the GFC period. Allen *et al.* (2011) provide a comprehensive overview of short selling rules in South Africa and show how this consistency allowed the markets to avoid negative consequences (such as reduced liquidity and increased volatility) that can be associated with changing short selling rules. 'As a result local hedge funds were able to continue operating as usual during this turbulent period' (Alternative Investment Management Association, 2010, p.15). The approach to short selling in South Africa is in line with many calls (e.g., see Avgouleas, 2010; Masciandaro, 2010) for global markets to maintain a consistent approach to short selling rather than having to introduce disruptive emergency measures during times of crisis.

### 32.5.6. The Impact of Overseas Regulation on South African FoHFs

The AIFM Directive in Europe introduces regulations for AIFM, including hedge fund and FoHFs managers. In a similar vein, the Dodd–Frank Act has increased regulatory requirements for advisors and managers in the United States, requiring a great deal more transparency. These overseas regulations can have three potential key implications for South African funds. (i) They need to ensure they meet the regulatory requirements when doing business in these areas. (ii) There could be an impact on investments in South Africa. For example,

Section 102 of the AIFM Directive requires that European funds can only market third-country (non-EU) funds if the third country complies fully with the AIFM Directive. This curtails the ability of European investors to invest in funds outside the European Union. This could directly affect alternative investment fund centers such as South Africa (Kaal, 2011). (iii) The strong focus on regulation and transparency in these leading nations could cause a domino effect with more hedge fund regulation being called for in other nations such as South Africa. Parallels can be drawn with the resources industry, where increased transparency being called for in the United States and Europe regarding resource payments has led to consternation in Africa that these regulations are leading to calls for greater transparency in other G20 nations such as South Africa, Australia, and Canada, where this sector is already highly regulated, thus potentially leading to over-regulation (Whitehead, 2012).

## CONCLUSION

The South African FoHFs industry has seen significant changes in regulation, stemming from the free elections and government change in the 1990s. The industry has sound regulation with licensing and compliance requirements for fund managers. The progressive changes to exchange controls have considerably opened up the South African market for overseas investors as well as permitted increased offshore investment by South African funds. The regulatory framework has served the industry well, with South African FoHFs outperforming those of leading global nations during and after the GFC.

## Acknowledgments

We thank the Australian Research Council for funding support and HedgeNews Africa for data.

## References

Alao, O., & Raini, L. (2011). Global Economic Melt-Down and the Role of Financial Institutions: Lessons from South Africa for Policymakers in Nigeria. *Humanomics, 27*(3), 201–211.

Allen, D. E., Powell, R. J., & Singh, A. K. (2011). Short Selling Consistency in South Africa. In G. N. Gregoriou (Ed.), *Handbook of Short Selling* (pp. 381–386). Amsterdam: Elsevier.

Alternative Investment Management Association (2010). *South African Hedge Funds: A Guide for Investors.* Available at www.aima.co.za.

Avgouleas, E. (2010). A New Framework for the Global Regulation of Short Sales: Why Prohibition is Inefficient and Disclosure Insufficient. *Journal of Law, Business and Finance, 15*(2), 376–425.

Botha, E., & Makina, D. (2011). Financial Regulation and Supervision: Theory and Practice in South Africa. *International Business & Economics Research Journal, 10*(11), 27–36.

Hamilton, I. (2010). Africa — The New Frontier. *Hedgeweek Special Report: South Africa Hedge Funds 2010,* October, 2010.

HedgeNews Africa. (2012). Retrieved 30 June, 2012. Available at www.hedgenewsafrica.com.

International Monetary Fund (2008). *South Africa Country Report 08/349.* Washington, DC: IMF.

Kaal, W. A. (2011). Hedge Fund Regulation via Basel III. *Vanderbilt Journal of Transnational Law, 44*(2), 389.

Masciandaro, D. (2010). Reforming Regulation and Supervision in Europe: Five Missing Lessons from the Financial Crisis. *Intereconomics, 45*(5), 293–296.

Novare Investments (2010). *South African Hedge Fund Survey*. Available at http://www.ohpisnevets. com/assets//ResearchDocuments/Novare_HFSurvey_2010.pdf.

Novare Investments (2011). *South African Hedge Fund Survey*. Available at www.novare.com/uploads/ files/hedge-fund-survey-oct-2011.

Ouma, S. (2012). The New Scramble for Africa. *Regional Studies, 46*(6), 836–838.

Pengelly, M. (2010). Regulation Consternation. *Risk, 23*(3), 70–72.

Stals, C. (1999). Governor of the Reserve Bank, The Changing Face of Exchange Control and its Impact on Cross-Border Investment Opportunities in South Africa. *Annual Australia/Southern Africa Business Council Meeting*. Sydney.

Symmetry (2012). *South African Hedge Fund Survey*. Available at www.symmetry.co.za/media/66664/ hedge-fund-survey-2012-03.pdf.

Tuomi, K. (2012). The Role of the Investment Climate and Tax Incentives in the Foreign Direct Investment Decision: Evidence from South Africa. *Journal of African Business, 12*(1), 133–147.

Vawda, F. (2011). Pension Funds Need to Do Some Comparative Shopping. *HedgeNews Africa Special Report: Allocating to Alternative Assets*. Third Quarter.

Whitehead, E. (2012). Africa: The Dodd–Frank Effect. *AllAfrica*, 5 March.

# Index

Note: Page numbers with "*f*" denote figures; "*t*" tables; and "*b*" boxes.